Intercultural Communication

A Layered Approach

John G. Oetzel

University of New Mexico

vango books | Read it.
Get it.

New York   San Francisco   Boston   Upper Saddle River
London   Toronto   Sydney   Tokyo   Singapore   Madrid
Mexico City   Munich   Paris   Cape Town   Hong Kong   Montreal

Library of Congress Cataloging-in-Publication Data

Oetzel, John G.
  Intercultural communication: a layered approach / John G. Oetzel.
    p. cm.
  ISBN 978-0-13-243284-9 (alk. paper)
  1. Intercultural communication.   2. Intercultural communication—Problems, exercises, etc.   I. Title.
  HM1211.O38 2009
  303.48'2—dc22   2008036375

Acquisitions Editor: Jeanne Zalesky
Editorial Assistant: Megan Lentz
Marketing Manager: Suzan Czajkowski
Production Supervisor: Roberta Sherman
Editorial Production Service: Elm Street Publishing Services
Manufacturing Buyer: JoAnne Sweeney
Electronic Composition: Elm Street Publishing Services
Photo Researcher: Annie Pickert
Cover Administrator: Joel Gendron

Credits and acknowledgments borrowed from other sources and reproduced, with permission, in this textbook include: **Page 1:** Brian Luna Lucero; **page 5:** Lorenda Belone; **page 28:** Alex Brandon/AP Images; **page 40:** Lawrence Migdale; **page 55 (top):** AP images; **page 55 (bottom):** Steve Pope/EPA/Corbis; **page 88:** Dorling Kindersley Media Library; **page 97 (left):** Dave Martin/AP Images; **page 97 (right):** Chris Graythen/Getty Images; **page 119:** John Oetzel; **page 122:** Chen Chao/Dorling Kindersley Media Library; **page 139:** Pearson Education/PH College; **page 149:** Trish Gant/Dorling Kindersley Media Library; **page 166:** John Oetzel; **page 179:** Susan Kugelman; **page 208:** Dorling Kindersley Media Library; **page 228:** Dorling Kindersley Media Library; **page 240:** Michal Heron/Pearson Education/PH College; **page 273:** Rene Macura/LA County Dept. of Public Health/AP Images; **page 277:** Christophe Ena/AP Images; **page 306:** Bjarne Fostervold. Used with permission; **page 310:** Uwe Lein/AP Images; **page 323 (left):** ABC-TV/Picture Desk/ Kobal Collection; **page 323 (right):** Danny Field/ABC-TV/Picture Desk/Kobal Collection; **page 327:** Damian Dovarganes/AP Images; **page 337:** Palace of the Governors/The New Mexico History Museum; **photo 350:** Phola Mabizela.

VangoBooks™ is an imprint of Pearson Education
Pearson® is a registered trademark of Pearson plc

Pearson Education Ltd., London
Pearson Education Singapore, Pte. Ltd
Pearson Education Canada, Ltd
Pearson Education-Japan
Pearson Education Australia PTY, Limited

Pearson Education North Asia, Ltd
Pearson Educación Mexico, S.A. de C.V.
Pearson Education Malaysia, Pte. Ltd
Pearson Education Upper Saddle River, New Jersey

10 9 8 7 6 5 4 3 2 1

ISBN 13: 978-0-13-243284-9
ISBN 10:   0-13-243284-6

DEDICATION

To my family:
Spencer, Ethan, and Keri

CONTENTS

SECTION ONE Introduction to Intercultural Communication

1 Defining Intercultural Communication 1

Introduction 2

Defining Intercultural Communication 4

Culture and Cultural Diversity 4

Communication 11

Intercultural Communication 15

Why Study Intercultural Communication? 16

Global Demographics 16

(In)effective Outcomes 17

Peace and Conflict 18

Ethical Considerations 19

How Can We Study Intercultural Communication? 22

Different Perspectives 22

Pedagogical Approaches in This Book 24

Summary 25

Review Questions 27

Exercises 27

2 A Layered Approach to Intercultural Communication 28

Introduction 29

A Layered Approach: The Social Ecological Framework 30

Layered Model 31

Benefits and Challenges of a Layered Perspective 33

Four Layers of Intercultural Communication 35

Individual Layer 35

Interpersonal Layer 37

Organizational Layer 38

Cultural Layer 41

Connecting the Layers 51

Summary 52

Review Questions 54

Exercises 54

SECTION TWO The Individual

3 Identity 55

Introduction 56

Characteristics of Identity 57

Multifaceted 57

Social and Personal 58

Salience and Strength 59

Fluid and Stable 61

Avowed and Ascribed 62

Passing and Outing 62

Performance and Expression 63

Concept Check 66

Explaining Cultural Identities: Development, Differentiation, Negotiation, and Deconstruction 66

Development of Cultural Identities 67

Differentiation of Cultural Identities 69

Negotiation of Cultural Identities 71

Deconstruction of Cultural Identities 74

Concept Check 77

Layers of Identity 78

Bottom-Up Effects 78

Top-Down Effects 79

Challenges and Skills 80

Summary 84

Review Questions 86

Exercises 87

4 Attributions and Attitudes 88

Introduction 89
Attributions 90
Nature of Attributions 90
Cultural Differences in Attributions 93
Attribution Errors 95
Concept Check 98
Attitudes 98
Intercultural Sensitivity 98
Prejudice 101
Communicating Prejudice 105
Layers of Attributions and Attitudes 112
Bottom-Up Effects 112
Top-Down Effects 113
Challenges and Skills 115
Summary 116
Review Questions 118
Exercises 118

SECTION THREE   Interpersonal Relationships

5 Initial Intercultural Interactions 119

Introduction 120
Types of Initial Intercultural Interactions 121
Travel 121
Sojourners 123
Migrants: Refugees and Immigrants 124
Explaining Initial Intercultural Interactions: Cultural Adaptation Perspectives 125
Culture Shock 126
Cultural Adaptation 129
Concept Check 134
Explaining Initial Intercultural Interactions: Communication Strategy Perspectives 134
Anxiety and Uncertainty Management (AUM) Theory 134

Communication Accommodation Theory 137
Concept Check 141
Layers of Initial Intercultural Interactions 141
Bottom-Up Effects 141
Top-Down Effects: Initial Interactions and Individual Effects 142
Top-Down Effects: Culture, Media and Initial Interactions 143
Challenges and Skills 145
Summary 146
Review Questions 147
Exercises 148

6 Intercultural Friendships and Relationships 149

Introduction 150
Friendships 152
Factors for Intercultural Friendship Formation 152
Challenges to Intercultural Friendship 153
Building Intercultural Alliances 157
Concept Check 159
Romantic Relationships 159
Managing Relationships: Negotiating Dialectics 160
Managing Conflict and Differences 165
Concept Check 173
Layers of Intercultural Friendships and Relationships 173
Bottom-Up Effects 173
Top-Down Effects: An Intercultural Relationship's Impact on Attitudes 174
Top-Down Effects: Society's Impact on Relationships 175
Challenges and Skills 176
Summary 177
Review Questions 178
Exercises 178

SECTION FOUR Organizational Contexts

7 Higher Educational Contexts   **179**

Introduction   **180**

Disparities in Educational Outcomes   **182**

Instructional Communication   **185**

Classroom Management   185

Learning Styles   190

Peer-to-Peer Communication   195

Concept Check   197

Layered Perspective of Educational Contexts   **197**

Bottom-Up Effects   197

Top-Down Effects: Educational Institutions' Impact on Individuals   198

Top-Down Effects: Society's Impact on Educational Institutions   200

Challenges and Skills   204

Summary   **205**

Review Questions   **206**

Exercises   **207**

8 The Workplace   **208**

Introduction   **209**

Workplace as a Context for Cultural Diversity   **211**

Benefits and Challenges of Cultural Diversity   **214**

Value Added Perspective on Diversity   214

Potential Barrier Perspective on Diversity   216

Poor Analysis of Diversity Issues   217

Concept Check   219

Intercultural Communication in the Workplace   **220**

Organizational Culture   220

Work Group Processes   222

Managing People   225

Individuals' Reactions to the Organization   229

Concept Check   231

Layers of Intercultural Communication in the Workplace   **231**

Bottom-Up Effects   231

Top-Down Effects: The Workplace's Impact on Attitudes and Individual Behavior   232

Top-Down Effects: Society's Impact on the Workplace   233

Challenges and Skills   235

Summary   **237**

Review Questions   **238**

Exercises   **239**

9 Health Care Contexts   **240**

Introduction   **241**

Health Disparities   **243**

Factors Related to Health Disparities   **248**

Socioeconomic Status   248

Health Care System Problems   250

Cultural Health Beliefs and Behaviors   252

Service Utilization Obstacles   255

Culturally Competent Communication   258

Concept Check   262

Layers of Health Care Contexts   **263**

Bottom-Up   264

Top-Down: Influence of Health Care Contexts on Individuals   264

Top-Down: Influence of Society on Health Care Contexts   265

Challenges and Skills   269

Summary   **274**

Review Questions   **276**

Exercises   **276**

SECTION FIVE Community and Societal Contexts

10 Intercultural Communities   277

Introduction   **278**

Community and Culture   **279**

Challenges to Intercultural Communities: Community Conflict   **284**

Scarce Resources and Disenfranchisement   285

Cultural and Value Differences   286

Institutionalized and Internalized Racism   293

Concept Check   296

Layers of Intercultural Communities   **297**

Bottom-Up Effects   297

Top-Down Effects   299

Challenges and Skills   299

Summary   **306**

Review Questions   **308**

Exercises   **309**

11 Media and Popular Culture   310

Introduction   **311**

Media Production   **313**

Agenda Setting   313

Cultural Studies   314

Cultural Industries and Media Ownership   316

Homogeneous Sources and Cultural Imperialism   317

Concept Check   318

Media Messages   **318**

Homogenization of Content   319

Patterns of Coverage   319

Concept Check   323

Media Reception   **324**

Uses and Gratification   325

Cultivation   325

Hybridity   327

Concept Check   328

Layered Perspective of Media   **329**

Bottom-Up Effects   329

Top-Down Effects   330

Challenges and Skills   331

Summary   **333**

Review Questions   **335**

Exercises   **335**

12 History(ies) and Future(s) Shaping Intercultural Communication   337

Introduction   **338**

Why Does History Matter?   **339**

Memory and Identity   340

Historical Trauma   344

Consequences of History for Today   347

Concept Check   350

Future of Intercultural Communication   **351**

Globalization   351

Intercultural Relations   355

Concept Check   359

Layered Perspective of History(ies) and the Future(s)   **359**

Bottom-Up Effects   359

Top-Down Effects   360

Challenges and Skills   360

Summary   **362**

Review Questions   **363**

Exercises   **364**

Glossary   365

References   372

Index   390

PREFACE

I wrote this book because I feel that intercultural communication has not been adequately taught from a contextual approach. Intercultural communication takes place in a variety of communication contexts including the workplace, health care settings, mass media, and history. Therefore, I wanted to develop a text that emphasizes context and, more importantly, the interrelationship of contexts.

To this end, my approach is to develop a new way to teach the course, which helps integrate and restate previous research in a unique way. Specifically, I use a layered approach in which individual behavior is nested within specific contexts and intercultural communication takes place at each layer (e.g., intercultural communication takes place in organizations, but the organizational context also influences and is influenced by individuals' communicative behavior).

I accomplish this layering using the *social ecological framework*. The social ecological model frames individual communication behavior in a series of layered contexts: individual, interpersonal, organizational, and community/societal. Each of these contexts emphasizes an important part of intercultural communication with a different set of communication skills for readers. The individual layer emphasizes identity and attitudes. The interpersonal layer includes interaction with family, friends, partners, and strangers. The organizational layer examines the coordinated activities of people working toward common goals. The community/societal layer focuses on the historical, political, economic, and media factors in constructing cultural institutions. Communication at each layer has unique characteristics; for example, what it takes to increase intercultural sensitivity is not the same as what it takes to be an activist working toward culturally inclusive communities. These relevant communication challenges are emphasized at each layer in order to understand the complexity of intercultural communication, but in a practical manner.

In addition to each layer framing the layer before it (called top-down effects), the framework also emphasizes that individual behavior can change and shape the higher layers (called bottom-up effects). In this manner, individual responsibility and empowerment are emphasized, but the model also recognizes that there are a variety of societal and cultural factors shaping our behavior. Thus, the model attempts to strike a balance between individual and contextual influences in understanding intercultural communication. Each chapter discusses communication challenges and principles at the relevant layer, but also with the understanding that each layer impacts those above and below it.

This framework serves as an organizing tool to help synthesize a wide variety of theoretical perspectives and concepts. The field of intercultural communication has a variety of meta-theoretical perspectives including interpretive, social scientific, and critical. Research from each of these areas is integrated throughout the textbook so that readers understand each, but also see how they connect. For example, the interpretive approach often describes culture and cultural acts and is the foundational understanding about cultural behavior. The social scientific approach helps to understand how different concepts fit together and how culture impacts behavior and outcomes. The critical approach helps us to understand the role of power, privilege, and politics to challenge the status quo and encourage growth in intercultural understanding.

The pedagogical approach of this book includes several facets. First, I do not come from any particular theoretical perspective. Rather, **I want to integrate perspectives for readers to appreciate how each perspective can help us to see certain aspects of intercultural communication** (and I think these perspectives complement each other). In this manner, I see this book as blending perspectives and operating in the "middle." I prefer to focus on particular "problems" of intercultural communication (e.g., social justice, health disparities, conflicts, ethics, and effective interactions) and examine what perspectives may help us address these problems. Second, **I believe in examining intercultural communication in a holistic manner.** For me, the layered perspective allows students to consider multiple influences on intercultural behavior such as the media, history, and family interactions. Third, I think the book should have a strong theoretical foundation. To this end, **I integrate intercultural communication theories (or theoretical models) in each chapter** and do my best to organize around these theories. I place a premium on digesting these theories for students and offer instructional aids/exercises to assist in this effort. Finally, **I think an experiential approach is critical for teaching intercultural communication.** To this end, I integrate stories of students (and others) within the text (as boxes) as well as refer to current events.

In sum, my purpose in writing this text is to provide readers with the following perspectives: a) understanding the complexity of intercultural communication; b) understanding the relationship among different contexts of intercultural communication; c) developing an appreciation for various meta-theoretical perspectives (appreciate cultural patterns and relationships, but also the importance of power and privilege in societies); d) striking a balance between individual and structural influences for communication behavior; and e) developing a reflexive attitude for addressing communication challenges at various layers. My goal is to have readers engage with the material so that they have some sort of organization framework, but also the opportunity to experience and feel facets of intercultural communication. In this manner, I want to increase the reflexivity of readers and improve awareness of intercultural communication challenges (and their ability to address such challenges).

I have tried to write the book in a personal, easy to read style. The research and theories of intercultural communication can be complex, and I try to help readers digest this complexity in a concrete manner. I attempt to strike the balance of making the theories/concepts easy to understand without watering down the function and importance of the topic.

Each chapter includes multiple and concrete examples to illustrate concepts and theories. These examples include a variety of cultural and ethnic groups in the United States and around the world. The examples center on events occurring in other countries as well as everyday interactions in culturally diverse environments. I make every attempt to make all cultural and ethnic groups visible in the text.

Each chapter includes several features to help organize and illustrate points. First, each chapter opens with a chapter outline and set of learning objectives. The text begins with an Opening Vignette (a current event or hypothetical scenario) to capture attention and asks readers to use chapter concepts to analyze and make sense of the situation. Second, the concluding materials include brief answers to this opening scenario, a Summary of the chapter organized around Learning Objectives, Review/Reflection Questions, and Exercises. Third, each chapter (after the opening two) has a final section preceding the Conclusion that emphasizes layered effects. In addition to presenting top-down and bottom-up perspectives, the chapter describes communication challenges from a layered perspective. These are practical recommendations and ideas that readers can use to enhance reflexivity and skills, at that layer, but which also influence lower and higher layers. Fourth, the chapters have visual elements to help break up text and to present information in a different way (and meet different learning styles). The visual elements include photographs of events and interactions as well visual models to organize and illustrate theories and concepts.

Fifth, the chapters include "boxes" to call out critical concepts and theories. There are five types of boxes: **Voices, Talking about Ethics, What Went Right/Wrong, Layered Effects,** and **Globalization.** The **Voices** boxes include stories from students, faculty, workers, and community members that illustrate concepts and theories. The **Talking about Ethics** boxes describes current events and individual struggles that present potential ethical dilemmas for consideration and discussion. The **What Went Right/Wrong** boxes present a situation or interaction that had a positive or negative outcome and asks readers to analyze the situation. The **Layered Effects** boxes present research that illustrates the layered perspective. These often are specific studies that emphasize top-down and bottom-up effects. The **Globalization** boxes present stories, research, and examples that illustrate the "shrinking" of the world and the frequency with which technology, ideas, and people cross boundaries.

Chapter Summaries

The text is organized in five main sections, each with two to three chapters.

Section One: Introduction to Intercultural Communication

This section serves as an overview of the text and to organize the remaining chapters. The first chapter provides an introduction to intercultural communication. Specifically, I define the concept and introduce the key elements of intercultural communication (messages, culture, and context). I also explain why it is important to study intercultural communication in this day and age. The reasons include the fact that the world is diverse and technology/travel makes it easy to interact with culturally different people, but also that there are ethical and social justice implications. Finally, I discuss the approaches (meta-theoretical and pedagogical) taken in the text.

The second chapter introduces the primary model for organizing the text. Specifically, I introduce the social ecological model, which frames individual communication behavior in a layered approach. I use a model of concentric circles to introduce this approach with the individual at the core and interpersonal, organizational, and community/societal circles surrounding the individual. I discuss how each subsequent layer frames the previous one (top-down effects), but also how the inner circles affect the outer ones (bottom-up effects). This approach shows that our behavior is shaped by other contexts, but that we also have the power to change and shape these contexts (balancing the responsibility of individual and society). Finally, I discuss how culture fits into this model and why this model is an appropriate framework for studying intercultural communication. Basically, I discuss the four layers of intercultural communication and different approaches to defining/viewing culture.

Section Two: The Individual

This section explores characteristics of the individual. The third chapter centers on identity—one of the core concepts of intercultural communication. This chapter explores individual and cultural identities. It includes various perspectives that examine identity, including theories about the role of communication in general and language in particular, for developing, differentiating, negotiating, and deconstructing cultural identities. As with every chapter, the conclusion considers communication skills/challenges from this layered perspective for students to apply in their own lives; in this chapter, it focuses on how other layers shape identity and how individuals' identities can collectively construct culture.

The fourth chapter describes attributions and attitudes. Attributions center on how people interpret and misinterpret others' behavior when using cultural knowledge. Attitudes range from ethnocentrism to ethnorelativism. The chapter includes a discussion of prejudice and communicating prejudice and concludes by presenting communication challenges to help readers become more relative within the layered perspective.

Section Three: Interpersonal Relationships

The third section focuses on interpersonal relationships. The fifth chapter discusses initial interactions between people from different cultures. There are two main sections. The first examines cultural adaptation perspectives including cultural shock and long-term adaptation. The second section examines theories of communication strategies in initial interactions including anxiety and uncertainty management theory and communication accommodation theory. The conclusion examines the individual skills that enhance cultural adaptation and communication strategies, but also the larger cultural institutions that shape the adaptation process.

The sixth chapter focuses on friendships and romantic relationships. The first section explores interethnic/intercultural friendships. It considers challenges to developing such friendships and how to develop intercultural alliances. The second section discusses intercultural romantic relationships at two levels. First, general dialectics and specific intercultural dialectics are presented as challenges to manage in these relationships. Second, managing conflict is discussed through the use of a contextual model. The conclusion discusses the layered aspect and some communication skills for managing the challenges presented in the chapter.

Section Four: Organizational Contexts

The fourth section turns to a variety of organizational contexts and the importance of intercultural communication. The seventh chapter examines educational contexts. It begins with a focus on educational disparities (or differences in educational outcomes by ethnic/cultural background or gender). Then, the contribution of intercultural communication to these disparities is noted by examining classroom management, learning styles, and peer-to-peer communication. The layered perspective emphasizes individual and larger societal factors that shape the problem of educational disparities.

The eighth chapter emphasizes cultural diversity in the workplace. It begins with a focus on the benefits and challenges to diversity. There is a special emphasis on why organizations have difficulty addressing diversity problems. The next section examines communication at several layers including organizational culture, work groups, superior/subordinate relationships, and individual communication choices. The impact of these layers on benefits and challenges is noted. The layered perspective emphasizes the larger legal context and individual choices for addressing challenges.

The ninth chapter discusses the health care context. The main focus of this chapter is on health disparities or that people from different cultural backgrounds have different health statuses. This chapter explores why disparities occur and the role that intercultural communication (among other factors) has to play in creating and alleviating the disparities. The layered perspective emphasizes communication challenges from an individual and media perspective.

Section Five: Community and Societal Contexts

The final section examines the larger societal context for intercultural communication. The tenth chapter explores notions of community and how people who are physically or psychologically co-located live. It discusses the importance of community and the challenges of creating intercultural communities. These challenges include scarce resources and disenfranchisement, conflict, and racism. The layered perspective considers transcendent communication and community-based participatory approaches as communication approaches do address challenges to creating intercultural communities.

The eleventh chapter introduces the media and popular culture. The chapter considers three aspects of media: production, messages, and reception. The chapter considers the role of media organizations (and who owns those organizations) in the production of culturally (in)appropriate messages. Additionally, the impact of those messages is considered. Finally, the audience role in accepted, and altering sent messages is discussed. The layered perspective reemphasizes the impact of individuals on this process and how the media impacts intercultural relations.

The final chapter discusses history(ies) and the future of intercultural communication. The first section examines why history matters. These reasons include memory/identity, historical trauma, and the consequences of history today. The second section considers the future of intercultural communication. Discussion centers on globalization, technology, conflict, and peace. The layered perspective considers individuals' role in constructing a future.

Acknowledgments

Writing any book is a huge undertaking and would not be possible without the support of many people. I start with my family—my wife, Keri, who provided love, encouragement and support throughout this process. To my sons, Spencer and Ethan, who were born during the time I wrote this book. All three of them give my life meaning and purpose.

To the folks at or affiliated with Allyn & Bacon: My editor, Jeanne Zalesky. Thanks for your focus and commitment to bring this book to fruition. You provided a lot of resources and support to make this possible. To Karon Bowers, Editor-in-Chief of Communication at Allyn & Bacon for convincing me that A & B was the right publisher to go with. To my developmental editors at Ohlinger—Erin Curtis and Joanne Vickers: you provided great vision about the content, feel, and look of the chapters. You took what I had in my head and put it on paper and made it even better than I intended. To the production team at Elm Street Publishing Services, thanks for the careful copyediting and moving the book through production.

To people at UNM: Jessica Crespo and Chie Torigoe for writing the instructor's manual. You provided excellence exercises and insights on how to teach the material. Your insights also helped me strengthen the chapters. To Courtney Fletcher, Sachi Sekimoto, and Chie Torigoe: Thank you for trying out the book and giving me feedback about what works and what did not. To my students in Spring 2008: Thank you for participating in my first class using this book and thanks for sharing with me your thoughts. To my colleagues and students: Thanks for providing a stimulating work environment to help me develop my ideas. Your feedback, camaraderie, and intellectual stimulation have made my work so much better over the years. We have a special department and I am grateful for all that you have done for me.

To the reviewers of the book in its earlier versions: Daren C. Brabham, University of Utah; Annick Conis, James Madison University; Leda Cooks, University of Massachusetts, Amherst; Sheila A. Cuffy, IPFW; Karen F. Dajani, Chatham College; Leonard M. Edmonds, Arizona State University; Laura K. Hahn, Humboldt State University; Janie M. Harden Fritz, Duquesne University; Joyce L. Harris, University of Texas at Austin; K. B. Hom, University of Utah; Dr. Jacqueline Irwin, California State University-Sacramento; Danette Ifert Johnson, Ithaca College; Charlton McIlwain, New York University; Mary M. Meares, Washington State University; Thomas P. Morra, Northern Virginia Community College; Jillian Pierson, Annenberg School of Communication; Rachel Reynolds, Drexel University; Dr. Arvind Singhal, Ohio University; Rachel A. Smith, University of Texas at Austin; Denise Sperruzza, St. Louis Community College at Meramec; Dr. Robert N. St. Clair, University of Louisville; Jeffrey Tyus, Sinclair Community College; Alan Yabui, Bellevue Community College; Mark Zampino, University of Hartford; Alan Zemel, Drexel University: Thank you for your careful read and critical feedback of the chapters. I received many useful tips and recommendations for sources, examples, and topics to include. The final version is much better because of this process.

John G. Oetzel (Ph.D., University of Iowa, 1995) is a Professor and Chair in the Department of Communication and Journalism at the University of New Mexico. The University of New Mexico has one of the top ranked programs in intercultural communication. He teaches courses in intercultural, health, and organizational communication, as well as research methods. His research interests focus on culture and conflict communication in work groups, organizations, and health settings. His work has appeared in journals such as *Human Communication Research, Communication Monographs, Communication Research,* and the *International Journal of Intercultural Relations.* He is co-author of *Managing Intercultural Communication Effectively* and *The Sage Handbook of Conflict Communication.*

CHAPTER 1

Defining Intercultural Communication

CHAPTER OUTLINE

I. Introduction

II. Defining Intercultural Communication
    a. Culture and Cultural Diversity
    b. Communication
    c. Intercultural Communication

III. Why Study Intercultural Communication?
    a. Global Demographics
    b. (In)effective Outcomes
    c. Peace and Conflict
    d. Ethical Considerations

IV. How Can We Study Intercultural Communication?
    a. Different Perspectives
    b. Pedagogical Approaches in This Book

V. Summary

VI. Review Questions

VII. Exercises

CHAPTER OBJECTIVES

After reading this chapter, students should be able to

- define culture, communication, and intercultural communication.
- list five reasons why it is important to study intercultural communication.

| How does cultural diversity enrich our lives? How does it challenge us?

- describe three meta-theoretical perspectives for studying intercultural communication.

- explain the pedagogical approach taken in this text.

Introduction

Gillian Gibbons is a British woman who was working in a Sudanese school as a teacher of young children. As part of the mandated government curriculum to learn about animals, Gibbons asked one of her students to bring a teddy bear to class. She asked the predominantly Muslim students to identify some names for the bear and then to vote on their favorite name. The voting was a way to introduce the students to democracy. The students, all around 7 years of age, identified Abdullah, Hassan, and Muhammad as possible names. Ultimately, the vast majority chose Muhammad. The students took turns taking the teddy bear home and writing in a diary, which was labeled "My name is Muhammad."

Gibbons was arrested in November 2007 and charged with inciting religious hatred—a crime that is punishable by 40 lashes and 6 months imprisonment. The Prophet Muhammad is the most sacred symbol in Islam and to name an animal Muhammad is insulting to many Muslims. Gibbons said that she had not intended to insult anyone and was very sorry. However, she was tried and found guilty of a lesser crime: insulting the faith of Muslims in Sudan (Article 125 of the Sudanese Criminal Code). She was sentenced to 15 days in prison and deportation (Associated Press, 2007).

Reactions in Sudan were mixed. Officials in Sudan's Foreign Ministry tried to play down the case, calling it an isolated incident and initially predicting Gibbons would be released without charges. However, the day after her sentencing, several thousand protesters took to the streets to argue that the sentencing was too light. One protester said, "What she did requires her life be taken." Protesters chanted "Kill her by firing squad" and "No tolerance: execution" (Osman, 2007). Mariam al-Mahdi, a leader in Sudan's main opposition party (Umma), said the government had deliberately escalated the case.

The case set up an escalating diplomatic dispute with Britain, Sudan's former colonial ruler. In London, Foreign Secretary David Miliband said, "There is an innocent misunderstanding at the heart of this, not a criminal offense." Many British and American Muslim groups also criticized the decision to arrest Gibbons and were mystified by it (Osman, 2007). In the end, President al-Bahir pardoned Gibbons after she served about half of her sentence.

A number of journalists and analysts in the West have suggested that the case can be understood in the ideology that President Omar al-Bashir's Islamic regime has instituted in Sudan: anti-colonialism, a sense that the West is laying harm to Islam, and religious fundamentalism (Osman, 2007). In 2006, al-Bashir vowed to lead a jihad, or holy war, against U.N. peacekeepers if they deployed in the Darfur region of western Sudan. Although he later relented and allowed a U.N.-African Union force there, U.N. officials say his government has thrown numerous obstacles to its deployment, and there continue to be clashes and incidents. In June 2008, the Sudanese government continued to have incidents with the U.N. and the International Criminal Court as it begins prosecution of Darfur war criminals. The Sudanese government says it supports the investigation, but also has objected to the lead prosecutor and accused him of terrorism.

After returning home, Gibbons did not condemn the decision to jail her. In fact, she encouraged others to visit Sudan and said that she loved her time there. She found the Sudanese to be extremely kind and generous. In January 2008, she went to China to continue teaching young children.

> Question: What intercultural communication concepts can explain what happened in the Gillian Gibbons case?

With rapid changes in global economy, technology, transportation, and immigration policies, the world is becoming a small, intersecting community. We find ourselves in increased contact with people who are culturally different. In a global work force, people bring different work habits and cultural practices. They may approach teamwork and problem-solving tasks differently. They may develop friendships and romantic relationships differently. They may also have different needs, wants, and expectations. In some instances, these differences do indeed divide us, pitting "us" against "them." This book, in part, examines why this division occurs, but also presents new possibilities for embracing cultural diversity through effective intercultural communication.

Direct contacts with culturally different people in our neighborhoods, schools, and workplaces are an inescapable part of life. You have all heard about the increasing cultural diversity in the world. People are moving across and within national boundaries at a rapid pace. Thus, the places in which we live and work are more culturally diverse now than at any point in our history. Let me give you some examples. I live in a country, the United States, that has a culturally diverse population with 69% of the population non-Hispanic White, 12.5% Hispanic or Latino, 12.3% African American or Black, 4% Asian American or Pacific Islander, and 1% American Indian or Alaska Native (U.S. Census, 2006). Within the United States, I live in New Mexico—one of only four U.S. states considered an ethnic plurality (Hawaii, Texas, and California are the others). An ethnic plurality exists when there is no one racial or ethnic group that by itself is a majority of the population. In New Mexico, approximately 45% of the people are non-Hispanic White, 42% are Hispanic, 10% are American Indian, and 3% are African American, Asian American, or other groups (U.S. Census, 2006). In the past few years, I have worked with people from a variety of countries including Germany, Japan, China, Senegal, South Africa, Chile, Colombia, Nigeria, France, Malaysia, Peru, Kuwait, and Israel. My work with these individuals has included face-to-face interactions and interactions via the Internet. Although demographic percentages and national cultural differences are one way to see cultural diversity, we will explore other ways throughout this book as well.

For many people, intercultural interactions are very rewarding. They teach us about our culture and help us to understand and grow. That does not mean there are never any misunderstandings or conflicts, but these too are part of growth. The purpose of this opening chapter is to introduce the topic of intercultural communication. It begins with definitions to clarify what we mean by culture and cultural diversity, communication, and intercultural communication. Then, it presents reasons why it is important to study intercultural communication. Finally, the chapter outlines the approach used in this book to studying and understanding intercultural communication.

Defining Intercultural Communication

Before continuing with the key principles and theories about intercultural communication, it is first important to define a few key terms. I have been using the terms *culture, communication*, and *intercultural communication*. These terms have numerous definitions; while each definition has some overlap, there are also unique points. Therefore, defining these terms, and discussing key features about them, will help us to understand what we are focusing on.

Culture and Cultural Diversity

"Culture" is a difficult term to define even though we use it in our everyday language. When we refer to other people as belonging to different cultures from our own, we often use concrete markers such as clothes, language, food, art, and ceremonies. However, we recognize that underlying values, norms, and other abstract components also make up the culture of a group of people. Following is a working definition for this book.

Culture is "a learned system of meanings that fosters a particular sense of shared identity-hood and community-hood among its group members. It is a complex frame of reference that consists of a pattern of traditions, beliefs, values, norms, symbols, and meanings that are shared to varying degrees by interacting members of an identity group" (Ting-Toomey & Takai, 2006, p. 691). Chapter 2 will introduce variations of this definition of culture depending on particular perspectives; in this chapter, we will focus only on this general definition as an introduction. In the section that follows, we break down this definition, examine its parts, and also discuss cultural diversity by providing examples of different cultural reference points.

PATTERNS OF TRADITIONS, BELIEFS, VALUES, NORMS, SYMBOLS, AND MEANINGS   Some key markers of culture are traditions, beliefs, values, norms, symbols, and meanings. These markers are repeated and create a pattern that enables members of a culture, as well as outsiders, to identify a cultural group. Traditions are rituals and ceremonies that mark important times in the year, developmental points in life, and relationships. For example, feast days are an important part of pueblo Indian culture in New Mexico. They are celebrated with various dances, such as the Corn Dance and the Buffalo-Deer Dance, and are often associated with religious figures. Additionally, the feast day might be associated with the growing season or hunting season and provide an opportunity for the community to come together, dance, pray, and celebrate. In Hispanic cultures, the quinceañera is a coming-of-age ceremony that celebrates a girl's 15th birthday. In mainstream United States, Thanksgiving is a traditional day for families to give thanks for all that they have. In Canada, Great Britain, Australia, and New Zealand, Boxing Day, celebrated on December 26th, is a time for people to recognize the contributions of people from lower social classes by giving gifts, especially to the poor and needy.

Beliefs, values, and norms are underlying facets of behavior. Beliefs focus on the cognitive assumptions that members of a culture hold on to, often without questioning. Beliefs may focus on the origin of people, the nature of time, the existence of a Supreme Being, and life after death. Religion provides a foundation for many of these beliefs, but a country's history and constitution are part of the foundation as well. These bases also provide the foundation for values, which

In many Navajo families, shearing sheep is a family tradition and marks the beginning of the summer. This grandmother is passing down the tradition to her granddaughter. What traditions are celebrated in your culture?

are the judgments about right and wrong and good or bad. Values provide a framework for what is desirable or undesirable and serve as a motivational basis for behavior. Norms are the implicit rules about what behaviors are appropriate or inappropriate in a given situation. For example, a norm indicates how we should greet someone or what is the best way to give someone bad news. Beliefs, values, and norms are the deeply held foundations for the observable behavior in a culture. Collectively, they provide a pattern of thoughts, rules, and emotions for members of a culture.

Symbols are signs, artifacts, or words that stand for something other than themselves and which represent something meaningful for members of a culture. Meanings are the objective and subjective interpretations that members of a culture hold about the symbols. For example, in 2006, there was a controversy about some cartoons that appeared in a Danish newspaper about the Prophet Muhammad. One of the cartoons showed the prophet with a bomb in his turban. These symbols were clearly identified as representing the Prophet and Muslims (objective meaning), but the subjective meanings were quite varied. Most Muslims were outraged by these acts, as their religion forbids the symbolic portrayal of the Prophet in the first place. Adding to the outrage was that the prophet was portrayed in such a violent and ugly light. In the West, some individuals were offended while some found the portrayal accurate. Most newspaper editorialists, however, supported the freedom of speech to publish such cartoons. This example also illustrates an ethical dilemma, which we discuss later in this chapter.

SYSTEM OF MEANINGS/COMPLEX FRAME OF REFERENCE   Culture serves as a frame of reference for its members—that is, culture becomes a point of reference for making sense of the world. When interpreting someone's behavior, we use our cultural values, beliefs, and norms to identify what a behavior or message means and to label whether it is good or bad. The frame of reference is created through a system of meanings that cultural members generally agree upon. For example, greeting rituals provide a way of recognizing and respecting other people. In many developed nations, a traditional greeting ritual is a hello and/or handshake. If you see the same person throughout the day, it is not necessary to greet him or her again. However, other cultures find it important to say hello (or something to this effect) every time you see the person. It is a way of acknowledging the existence and, therefore, the importance of another person. If another person does not say the greeting every time, cultural members interpret that the person is rude or something is wrong. Imagine if a member from this group ended up working in an office in a large Western city. He or she would be "lucky" to get a single greeting each day, which would not be a sign of rudeness, but rather a different cultural frame. See Box 1.1 for an example of a cultural frame of reference.

This frame of reference is complex as the set of interrelated rules and meanings are dynamic. We often treat cultures as static, unchanging entities. The truth of the matter is that cultures do change, although slowly. However, with frequent interaction with people of other cultures, cultural members have a greater opportunity to

Box 1.1 Voices: Creating New Cultural Frames of Reference

There are 19 pueblos in New Mexico ranging from 750 to 10,000 people. All of these communities are concerned with how to improve the educational opportunities for younger tribal members, increase the economic opportunities for tribal members, and strengthen cultural traditions. In one sense, these goals are counter to one another in that more economic opportunity and education may mean adopting more of the values of mainstream U.S. culture. Many mainstream cultural values are in conflict with many of the traditional values of the tribe. Some of the tribal administrators, government officials, and community members embrace and lament the change and attempt to strike a balance between change and tradition. Others try to hold on to culture at all costs; still others embrace change completely. The result is new frames of reference for interpreting the behavior of outsiders and pueblo members.

1. Is it important to you to participate in the traditions of your culture?
2. In what ways do you balance traditional culture and mainstream culture?

learn and change their culture (for good and bad). In this manner, cultures interact, collide, conflict, and thus adapt.

SHARED IDENTITY, BUT TO VARYING DEGREES   Members of a cultural group recognize the culture as a key part of their identity, which they share with other members of that group. It may not be the most important part of who they see themselves to be, but it is a key part of who they are (see Chapter 3 for more on identity). Culture creates a sense of identity that often is hidden from even the cultural members until that identity is called into question or challenged or the members interact with people from a different culture. This identity is shared through rituals, ceremonies, and language.

However, the level of shared identity varies for cultural members. Not everyone has the same interpretation about all aspects of his or her culture. **Subjective culture** is an individual's interpretation of the beliefs, values, and norms associated with a culture (Triandis, 1972; also see Box 1.2). A subjective cultural approach allows for exploration of the within-group variation that characterizes a culture.

Have you ever met someone who was offended by your characterization of his or her culture? For example, you might have said, "I'm surprised you went away to college as I understand that _____ tend to be very family-oriented." The person may have reacted negatively to this statement or simply felt the need to correct you by saying "I am family-oriented, but going away to school was important to me and my family." As we will discuss in Chapter 4, we have a tendency to stereotype members of a culture. Understanding that individuals of a culture have different interpretations of shared values (for example, behaviors that indicate a family orientation) can help you avoid stereotyping cultural behavior.

INTERACTING MEMBERS   Members of a culture interact with one another to create patterns of culture and a shared frame of reference. Cultures are formed by the repetition and sharing of social practices such as traditions and rituals. Through daily

Box 1.2 Voices: Subjective Culture for One International Student

Yuko was an international student from Japan. She had wanted to come to the United States to study ever since she was little. When she arrived, she was excited to meet U.S. Americans and learn more about their culture (she had studied English and about the United States for many years). She fit in well and was able to adapt to the communication norms easily. Several other international students from Japan used to say to her that she should act more Japanese, telling others that Yuko was not a good example of Japanese culture. Yuko was hurt by these statements and wondered why she was not considered a "good Japanese" person. She ended up marrying someone from the United States and living there. However, she still considers herself very much Japanese, speaks the language, and is teaching her children to speak Japanese and about Japan (as well as teaching them English and about the United States).

1. Does Yuko's behavior make her less of a Japanese person (in other words, is she inauthentic in her cultural practices)?
2. Who gets to determine the "right" way to behave culturally?

communication, cultural members create beliefs, meanings, and traditions that are then recognized as integral to the shared/collective identity and to the survival of the group of people. In this manner, culture is socially constructed. It does not exist outside of the interactions of its members; we create and reinforce culture through our interaction. The repetition of these patterns and reinforcement of central values and beliefs is how a group of seemingly different people can create a common core of what we call culture. For example, many cultural groups have a strong emphasis on family. This emphasis is reinforced through various interactions, such as when group members talk about how the family is doing and as the family gets together for traditions (such as a Sunday dinner or shearing sheep together). These interactions are simply the social practices of a single family unless or until a larger group of people accepts these practices, at which time they become part of a collective culture—"we all emphasize family and that is a core element of what it means to be X." The creation of a culture around a core value of family is not created quickly, but rather in the passing of meaning from generation to generation. Over time, family might still be important, but the traditions used to enact family as a cultural meaning change.

Traditionally, we think about people of the same culture interacting in close proximity (often face-to-face) in order to learn about and create culture (passed down from one generation to another). However, in today's technologically enhanced world, it is possible to interact through the Internet, text messaging, and other new communication mediums. In these settings, new cultural groups can be formed. For example, one study examined how members of different cultural groups came together in an online, mediated course for intercultural learners at a Canadian university (Chase, Macfadyen, Reeder, & Roche, 2002). The authors found that cyberspace itself has a culture(s). The cultural gaps between individuals who identified with the dominant cyberculture and those who did not increased the chances of miscommunication. For example, people who did not understand shorthand messages or emoticons had trouble

Box 1.3 Globalization: Creating Culture through Electronic Media

Around the world, a religious culture of people follow the teachings of Mata Amritanandamayi, a woman based in India. Most of her followers have never met or seen her, however. Instead, they learn about her teachings through the Internet and meet with other cultural members electronically. Although traditional face-to-face interaction continues to be a way for people to create cultural values, beliefs, and symbols, this example illustrates a new way for members of a culture to interact.

1. How has digital and electronic media changed the way we connect to people?
2. Is it possible to be more connected culturally to people you have never met and who have different nationalities than to people from your own nationality?

communicating with others in the course. Additionally, people's identification with a specific cultural group (for example, Canadian or Middle Eastern) also problematized intercultural communication because the online communication limited the opportunities to display emotion and to infer meaning from nonverbal cues. Thus, multiple cultural identities played a role in this online course and made intercultural communication complex and challenging (also see Box 1.3).

CULTURAL DIVERSITY   The concept of cultural diversity is critical for intercultural communication and can help us better understand examples of culture. **Cultural diversity** is "the representation, in one social system, of people with distinctly different group affiliations of cultural significance" (Cox, 1993, p. 6). Group affiliations of cultural significance can include such characteristics as national culture, race, ethnicity, gender, job position, social class, job/educational training (such as engineering, marketing, law, social science), age, sexual orientation, and disability. When most people think about culture, they tend to focus on national culture (nationality) or race and ethnicity. These are the easy references that are commonplace in the media. However, as the above definition notes and as research and the popular press supports, other characteristics can also serve as a group's cultural reference points (Chase et al., 2002; Clare, 2001; Engen, 2004; Koinage, 2006; Mulvaney, 1994). Simply stated, members of a variety of groups create collective identities with shared patterns of interactions that create a culture. Specific cultural groups may include men, women, homosexuals, heterosexuals, transgendered people, the lower social class, the upper social class, older and younger generations, people with disabilities, and people without disabilities (see Box 1.4).

More importantly, these cultural groups have intersections and overlaps for individual members. We are simultaneously members of multiple cultural groups, such as a national culture, ethnic culture, religious culture, and gender culture, which overlap to varying degrees. Some argue that national culture is the primary orientation and that other cultures are subsumed within nationality (that is, the rest are sub-cultures). The fall of Yugoslavia and the difficulties in creating a

Box 1.4 Talking about Ethics: Labels for Cultural Groups

Whenever you talk about a group of people, you need to choose a label to reference that group. The terms can have positive and negative meanings for people. Call one person an "American" and he or she is proud, while another might be offended. The use of particular terms has a history for individuals and it can be difficult to know all of these histories. For example, when referring to non-Whites in the United States, some choose the label "people of color," while others choose "minority." Each has a particular frame and perspective. The label non-White is accurate, but references groups of people to the majority culture (as if all should be compared to it). The concept of "minority," which refers to people who have less wealth, less political power, and who generally are numerically in the minority, is seen as derogatory by some (more about these concepts in Chapter 3). Throughout this book, I use

the concepts of "minority" and "people of color" interchangeably; I refer to "_____ American" to refer to specific ethnic groups in the United States (except American Indian, which is preferred over Native Americans by scholars in this area); I use the term "U.S. Americans" when referring to residents of the United States (because "American" refers to all people from North and South America); and I use other labels that I believe are preferred by most members of the groups. If I refer to a specific study or report by the government, I use the label provided by the authors.

1. Why is it important to consider the history of labels?
2. Do you agree with my choice of labels and my taking the time to discuss this issue? Am I making too big a deal out of this? Why or why not?

government in Iraq illustrate that national states are not always the best cultural reference points for people. In Iraq, there are three primary ethnic groups—the Kurds, the Sunni Muslim, and the Shi'a Muslim. They are all Iraqi, but the specific ethnic culture for these three groups is a stronger reference point than nationality. In other situations, cyberculture, disability, social class, or sexual orientation might be a stronger reference point than other cultural identities. The context of interaction is important in making certain cultural identities stronger than others in a particular situation.

CONCEPT CHECK   In summary, culture is a pattern of behaviors, values, and beliefs that serve as a frame of reference and that are shared to varying degrees for a group of people. In essence, culture is a theory or explanation for why people do what they do when they do it (Keesing, 1974; Gudykunst & Lee, 2002). Culture allows people to interpret others' behavior in a relatively consistent manner and to ensure that we are using the same rules when we interact with others.

Visually we can represent culture with the iceberg model. Culture is seen as an iceberg with only a small portion visible to outsiders. This visible portion represents the artifacts, language, appearance, and behavior. Underneath the surface, the core of the iceberg is hidden from others, which represents the values, norms, and beliefs that serve as the core of culture.

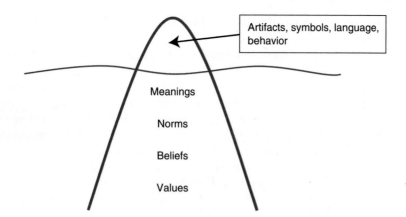

Artifacts, symbols, language, behavior

Meanings

Norms

Beliefs

Values

Figure 1.1
Iceberg Model
of Culture

Communication

Now that we have defined culture, let us look at the next key concept for this book—communication. Communication is the way that we share and create culture and the way that we transmit meaning and information. **Communication** is a process whereby people collectively create and transmit meaning through the exchange of verbal and nonverbal messages in a particular context. In the following section, we will examine each of the parts of this definition.

PROCESS   Communication is something that is ongoing and continual. When we communicate with others, we share numerous messages in a back-and-forth nature. This communication can take place over different time periods (an argument lasting several days or weeks) and in different locations (via phone or the Internet).

Many people tend to think about communication in more finite terms. They believe that communication is time specific and has a concrete beginning or end. Anyone who has an argument over time with a loved one knows that communication is not finite. We might go to bed thinking that the argument is over, but our partner will bring it back up the next day (or sometimes six months later). The issue never was resolved. Additionally, any given exchange or message is influenced by prior interactions. Although messages have beginnings and endings and are critical parts of the communication process, it is important to think about communication overall as a process and not as having a finite beginning or end.

CREATION AND TRANSMISSION OF MEANING   Communication involves the creation and transmission of meaning. Communication is very powerful because we create new possibilities and new perspectives by interacting with others. I remember a time when I was interacting with a group of people about the best way to prevent workplace bullying at a particular organization. All of us had different ideas, but through our interaction, we came up with a policy that no one individual had entered the room with. This illustrates the power to create meaning or what some people call the "social construction of meaning"—that is, we create meaning through our social interaction with others.

The transmission of meaning involves sharing various meanings with others through a variety of channels. We can transmit meaning through face-to-face interaction, over the phone, through electronic mail, or via the mass media. For many people, the goal of communication is mutual understanding. We believe that we have communicated when the other person understands what we feel or mean (and vice versa). While this is a laudable goal, it is not the only time that communication takes place. In many situations, we do not understand the other person. In reality, we can never fully understand another person's perspective as we have not had the same experiences. Even without a full understanding, has communication taken place? The answer is "Yes," although some would call this "miscommunication" or "misunderstandings." However, we have transmitted meaning, just not as effectively as we would have liked. See the example in Box 1.5.

Box 1.5 What Went Wrong?: Creating Intercultural Misunderstandings

Not every interaction goes well. Sometimes, the meaning we create is not the one that was intended. This happens more frequently between people of different cultures (but also within cultures) because the cultural frame of reference causes us to perceive messages differently. Consider the following example between Paul a (U.S. American) and Yizhou (pronounced "ee-joe," an international student from China). Paul and Yizhou have been in engineering classes together for a year and are becoming somewhat friendly. Paul is talking with classmates one day when Yizhou walks up.

Y: What are you doing this weekend?

P: I'm building this outside patio for my parents on Saturday. I know you like construction—you want to help out? They'll pay us.

Y: I really have to study this weekend.

P: It'll be fun and I could really use your help. Rudy here is coming too.

Y: The exam is very important.

P: I know, but you have all weekend.

Y: Well, I'll try to make it.

P: Great. Here is the address.

The weekend comes and Yizhou doesn't show up.

1. What meanings would you construct if you were Paul? Yizhou?
2. What went wrong?
3. What might you do differently?

VERBAL AND NONVERBAL MESSAGES   The transmission of meaning occurs through the messages that we exchange with other people. Verbal messages are the written and spoken language, while nonverbal messages are nonlinguistic features of communication.

Language is one of the most identifiable features of intercultural communication. Most people tend to think that if people share a common language, effective communication is relatively easy. However, understanding a language does not mean that a person understands a culture and can effectively communicate with members of that culture. Understanding the culture is a key part of translating one language to another.

Three perspectives about the relationship between language and culture are universalism, linguistic relativism, and functional relativism (Lim, 2002). The position with the least research support is universalism, which states that language does not differ across culture. From the universalism perspective, languages have different grammars and words, but they can be translated and there is universal meaning. The second perspective, linguistic relativism, is a popular approach in communication textbooks. Linguistic relativism is reflected by the Sapir-Whorf hypothesis, which argues that language affects the way we see the world. Thus, the language we have affects what we can perceive in the world. In this manner, language, in part, explains why cultures differ. A popularly cited myth in support of this hypothesis is that Eskimos have over 20 different words for snow, which allows them to perceive many different varieties of snowfall. In reality, Eskimo languages (there are many) can have more or less words for snow than English. According to the third perspective, functional relativism, the grammatical system of language is closely related to cognitions, values, and beliefs found in a culture. In this sense, it is culture that drives the language (basically the opposite of linguistic relativism). Thus, the reason we have different language systems is because the culture drives the creation of particular words and grammars. For example, in Spanish there are two forms for you: *tu* and *usted*. *Tu* is used for people you are familiar with and close to, or who are lower in status (a child). *Usted* is used for people you do not know well or of higher status. In contrast, English only has one form of you and does not distinguish between formal and familiar terms.

Meaning is also communicated through nonverbal messages. There are eight different nonverbal codes along which cultural differences exist:

- *Chronemics* centers on time and the meanings attached to the various ways we use time.
- *Proxemics* is the use of personal space—the invisible "space bubble" that we maintain around us and the circumstances under which we let others into that bubble.
- *Kinesics* is the use of body movements and gestures.
- *Haptics* focuses on the use of touch.
- *Physical appearance* references the use of clothes and artifacts to adorn our body.
- *Oculesics* is the study of eye gaze.
- *Vocalics* focuses on the way we use our voice to qualify verbal messages and to make vocalizations (sounds apart from speech such as cries and laughter).
- *Olfactics* is the study of odor as a communicative message.

Nonverbal differences lead to some of the most interesting anecdotes about cultural misunderstanding. For example, if you are from North America and you travel to Brazil, you do not want to use the "OK" sign (thumb and forefinger together), as this has roughly the same meaning as raising your middle finger in the United States. Examples of both verbal and nonverbal messages throughout the text illustrate concepts and theories.

Context Communication always takes place in a context. **Context** is the frame of reference for understanding communication behavior. Context includes the features of an interaction such as social relationships, historical relationships, and culture. Specific situations occur within any particular context. Think of context as participants interacting in a scene (Gudykunst, Ting-Toomey, Sudweeks, & Stewart, 1995). The scene includes the physical setting (physical locale and time) and the purpose of the interaction (type of activity). Participants bring to the scene complex backgrounds (for example, culture and individual characteristics) and the relationships with other participants. Context is the overarching term used to describe situations, scenes, and participants. Situation is the overarching term for scenes and participants. So, within a particular context, there can be specific situations and within a particular situation, there are particular scenes and participants.

Concept Check Communication is a process of creating and transmitting meaning through verbal and nonverbal messages in a particular context. These four features are critical to understanding effective intercultural communication. Intercultural communication takes place every day—sometimes effectively, but sometimes ineffectively (in the case of wars and misunderstandings). Figure 1.2 displays the transactional model of communication, which fits this definition. The transactional model demonstrates that communication is a back-and-forth process of exchanging and interpreting messages within a particular frame of reference.

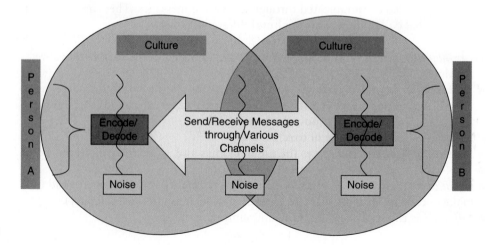

Figure 1.2
Transactional
Model of
Communication

Intercultural Communication

Now that we have defined culture and communication, we are ready to define **intercultural communication.** A simple, yet effective, approach is to define it as communication that occurs between individuals and entities that are culturally unalike (Rogers & Steinfatt, 1999). Using this definition, intercultural communication can take place between two individuals who might be married (one partner from South Africa and the other from Argentina), but also between international entities such as rival governments. The key focus is that the individuals or entities are culturally different. These cultural differences influence communication in the particular interaction. See Box 1.6.

People use other labels to refer to intercultural communication. For instance, many people use the terms **cross-cultural communication** and intercultural communication interchangeably. However, you will see later in this chapter that cross-cultural communication is one particular perspective that focuses on comparing/contrasting two different cultures (such as China and Germany). The purpose of cross-cultural communication is to understand the differences between these cultures without examining what happens when members of these cultures interact with each other (a Chinese with a German). Rather, the focus is on how members of a culture interact with other members of their same culture. In Europe, the study of comparative management is comparing/contrasting cultural approaches to business behavior. The study of cross-cultural communication has provided understanding about cultural behavior, but the focus in this text is more on what happens when we interact with people of different cultures.

Additionally, if you read research about intercultural communication, you will see that certain scholars use other terms to refer to certain types of intercultural communication. For some scholars, intercultural communication is the study of interpersonal communication between individuals of different cultural backgrounds. **International communication** is the study of mass-mediated communication between entities (governmental, private industry, or non-profit agencies) from two or more countries. **Developmental communication** is the study of social change brought about by the application of communication, theory, and technologies from one culture to

---

Box 1.6 Layered Effects: Intercultural Communication Depends on Context

The definition for intercultural communication is purposively broad to allow focus on a variety of relationships that might be considered intercultural. For example, intercultural communication in Iraq focuses on religion and ethnicity (Shi'a, Sunni, & Kurd). For a homeless person, social class distinguishes people of different cultures. For an international business person, nation states might be the particular focus. And for a homosexual who is politically active, sexual orientation might be the emphasis. All of these particular interactions are intercultural communication if the people view themselves as coming from different cultural groups. That perception is largely influenced by the social and historical contexts of the interaction. Thus, it is a combination of our individual perceptions and societal structures.

another (Rogers & Hart, 2002). These definitions show the distinctions some scholars make in the study of intercultural communication. While there are clearly distinctions, it is important to blend these perspectives. For example, mass media influence our interpersonal communication with others. This blended perspective will be discussed in Chapter 2.

Finally, a key concept associated with intercultural communication is globalization. **Globalization** is the increasing interconnectedness of people and places as a result of changes in communication technologies, communication, and migration patterns, which cause political, economic, and cultural convergence (Ladegaard, 2007). Globalization is considered in both positive and negative ways. Positive aspects of globalization include increased cultural contact and opportunities to grow and change. Negative aspects of globalization include the homogenization of cultures; that is, the movement of cultures toward a single common ground that is often considered to be Western and based in the popular media. For example, some lament the "McDonaldization" and "Starbuckization" of the world—where Western-based companies export their products and where U.S. cultural icons pop up on every street corner around the world. Throughout this text, boxes appear to provide examples of how globalization is present in various cultures and types of intercultural communication.

Why Study Intercultural Communication?

The study of intercultural communication is an important topic in today's world for many reasons. First, the demographics of the world are changing so it will be important to understand how these changes impact communication. Second, the way that we communicate with others has an impact on a variety of societal outcomes. Third, intercultural communication is powerful in that it can create both peace and conflict. Fourth, an understanding of intercultural communication may help alleviate some of the issues associated with social injustice. Finally, ethical considerations relating to communication are prevalent in a diverse society.

Global Demographics

While there are many ways to illustrate the increasing diversity in the world, let's look at the global demographic characteristics of four national cultures (Germany, the United States, China, Japan) and one religious culture (the Muslim World). Germany's relative prosperity, its involvement in the European Union, and the unification in 1990 of the former West Germany and East Germany have made the country a prime destination for many immigrants (Federal Statistics Office, 2005). Most notably, Turkey, the countries formerly represented under Yugoslavia, and Greece constituted 43% of the immigrant population residing in Germany in 2004 (Federal Statistics Office, 2005). In the United States, the North American Free Trade Agreement (NAFTA) contributes to immigration from Central and South America. Hispanics (mainly from Mexico) accounted for 50% of the overall U.S. population growth in 2004 and represented 14% of the overall population (U.S. Census, 2005). Further, there are more than 35 million foreign-born people in the United States (U.S. Census, 2005). For China, its accession into the World Trade Organization (WTO) in 2001 has dramatically increased trade, making the country the world's third largest trading nation, second only to the United States and Germany (Allen, 2003). As a result, in 2002 China became the second largest net sender of migrants to other countries—totaling 230,000 people—second only to Mexico (Allen, 2003). Japan, a highly urban society with only 6% of the labor force in agriculture, continues to rely heavily on foreign countries for food, clothing, travel and a wide variety of other goods and services (Number of Japanese Living Abroad). From 2000 to 2004 the total number of Japanese living abroad increased by 16%, to almost one million people (Number of Japanese Living Abroad). Finally, the Muslim world is a complex multinational and multicultural global phenomenon with roots in the Middle East. The Muslim supra-culture, or *ummah*, is global in its cultural diversity, geography, and size (about one fifth of the world population). The largest Muslim cultures are non-Arab and are not located in the Middle East. In fact, less than 20% of Muslims are Arabs. The largest Muslim populations are in Indonesia (171 million), Pakistan (119 million), Bangladesh (100 million), India (100 million), Turkey (56 million), and the Asian countries of the former Soviet Union (50 million) (Shabbas, 1998). These demographic trends help to illustrate the diversity of the world. Coupled with communication technology, all of us are likely interact with people from different cultures on a daily basis.

(In)effective Outcomes

Diversity on the global level represents both opportunities and challenges to individuals, organizations, and communities. Effective intercultural communication will help determine if the results of this increased cultural contact will be positive or negative (or a combination of both).

At a personal level, effective intercultural communication can create stronger personal relationships and ties. For example, conflict with culturally different people provides a testing ground for the resilience of our everyday relationships. It is not the frequency of conflict that determines whether we have a satisfying or dissatisfying relationship. Rather, it is the competencies that we apply in managing our conflicts that will move the relationship along a constructive or destructive path (Cupach & Canary, 1997). When managed well, conflict clarifies misunderstandings and strengthens common interests and goals. It also promotes individual and relationship growth. On the other hand, incompetent conflict management affects physical and mental health. Negative conflict behaviors (for example, verbal criticisms, defensiveness, anger explosion, or suppression) in marital relationships evoke hypertension, raise blood pressure, and produce ulcers (Gottman, 1999).

At an organizational level, individuals must rise to the challenge of serving as global leaders to manage diversity with skill and cultural sensitivity. Three competencies that are critical in the global workplace are communication skills, problem solving, and leadership (Training and Development, 1999). Inattention and poor communication about diversity issues in the workplace can lead to the following costs: a) low morale due to culture clash; b) high absenteeism due to psychic stress; c) costs associated with high employee turnover; and d) time wasted because of miscommunication between diverse employees (Loden & Rosener, 1991). In contrast, the long-term advantages of managing diversity through effective intercultural communication include: a) full utilization of the organization's human capital; b) increased knowledge and enhanced mutual respect among diverse employees; c) increased commitment among diverse employees at all organizational levels and across all functions; d) greater innovation and flexibility as others participate more constructively in problem-solving teams; and e) improved productivity as more employee effort is directed at achieving the system's goals and less energy is expended in dealing with cultural miscommunication issues (Loden & Rosener, 1991).

A variety of potential pitfalls and advantages exist at the community level. With ineffective communication, diverse communities tend to have increased conflict compared to homogeneous communities. Further, immigrant populations that have members with low education and low socioeconomic status place strains on social services and health care resources. For example, uninsured people use emergency health care, which contributes to rising health care costs, and also may require translation services (although immigrants are not the only uninsured population by any means). On the other hand, immigrant populations often take low-paying jobs in service industries that help keep costs down (such as for food) for others in the community. Additionally, immigrants contribute to the resources of federal, state, and local governments through taxes and participate in the local economy.

Peace and Conflict

Intercultural communication has the power to create both peace and conflict. The creation of intercultural conflict is often studied (Oetzel & Ting-Toomey, 2006; Ting-Toomey & Oetzel, 2001) and focuses on many factors. First, with all things being equal, the more cultural diversity in a community or organization, the more likely there is to be conflict (Cox, 1993; Oetzel, 2005). That does not mean that cultural diversity causes conflict but rather is a condition that increases the likelihood of conflict. Some of these conflicts occur simply because of cultural ignorance or misunderstanding. When using our cultural values and norms as we interact with people from different cultures, we may misunderstand others at best or create conflict at worst.

Not all intercultural conflicts are based on miscommunication, but poor intercultural communication exacerbates the conflict. Some intercultural conflicts are based on deep-seated hatred and centuries-old antagonism often arising from long-standing historical grievances (for example as in Northern Ireland and the Middle East). Conflict in culturally diverse communities often is not based on miscommunication, but again miscommunication makes the situation worse. In these communities, conflict is often created when certain conditions are present—such as mistrust of authorities by community members or socioeconomic inequalities (often along cultural lines)—and then a triggering event occurs (for example, the shooting of an ethnic minority by police officers) (Warfield, 2006). Chapter 10 discusses these types of conflict in depth.

However, intercultural communication also has the potential to create peace. A number of communication scholars have examined the conditions and communication techniques needed to bring people together after years of conflict and hatred (Barge, 2006; Broome & Hatay, 2006; Littlejohn, 2006). This type of communication emphasizes transcending differences through respectful and equal dialogue. The key is to understand why the conflict occurred in the first place and then use techniques to bridge these differences. If we can understand how to use communication to create peace (or avoid conflict), we have a powerful tool to benefit societies. See the example in Box 1.7.

Ethical Considerations

Ethics focuses on the principles of right or wrong in human conduct. Codes of ethics are guidelines that designate appropriate behavior in a given situation. Many such codes of ethics are designated by religious teachings. For example, "do unto others as you would have them do unto you" is a Christian ethic called the Golden Rule (and

Box 1.7 What Went Right?: Creating Peace in Cyprus

Cyprus has been divided into Greek-Cypriot and Turkish-Cypriot administered zones for over 40 years. It has been physically divided by war and socially divided by differences in language, cultural heritage, religion, politics, view of the past, and vision of the future. Ethnically, approximately 80% of the population is Greek-speaking, Orthodox Christian, and 18% is Turkish-speaking, Sunni Muslim. There are also small communities of Maronites, Armenians, and Latins (all groups that are today overwhelmingly Greek-speaking), and Roma. The physical division of the island has affected nearly every aspect of peoples' lives, including the psychological condition of residents. Both the Greek-Cypriot and the Turkish-Cypriot communities carry a sense of injustice and victimization. These feelings stem from historical incidents—for the Turkish Cypriots stemming from their experiences as a minority in a Greek Cypriot dominated state in the 1960s, and for the Greek Cypriots from the events of 1974 (where Greek ultra-nationalists tried to unite Cyprus with Greece and Turkey responded by launching a military intervention, seizing control of 37% of the island's territory).

Benjamin Broome, a communication scholar, has participated in a series of planning and design workshops with a group of 30 Greek Cypriots and Turkish Cypriots. Over a 9-month period, Broome facilitated weekly sessions focused on developing a strategy for peacebuilding efforts in Cyprus. During these sessions, the group progressed through three primary stages: (a) analyzing the current situation affecting peacebuilding activities in Cyprus, (b) building a collective vision for the future of peacebuilding efforts, and (c) developing a collaborative action agenda. These efforts (and other similar efforts) provided opportunities to interact and to reduce the psychological burden from past harms, helped to break the cycle of blaming the other, and created an opportunity to create an alternative vision for the future. This doesn't mean the conflict still does not exist, but the situation has improved, especially for those who have participated in the dialogue sessions.

Source: Broome & Hatay (2006)

other religions have a similar creed). Other codes of ethics are developed through political systems (such as democratic principles). In the study of intercultural communication, three sets of ethical guidelines are important to consider: cultural universalism/cultural relativism, inclusion/exclusion, and social justice.

CULTURAL UNIVERSALISM/RELATIVISM   Universalism/relativism focuses on the approach to judging other people's behavior. **Cultural universalism** emphasizes a single set of standards that should be used to judge others' behavior as good or bad (Pedersen, 1997). Thus, one code of ethics is used for all behavior. Unfortunately, the single code usually comes from a dominant group, and it is imposed on other less powerful groups (for example, people who are immigrants, poor, or culturally different). Fundamental religious perspectives are an extreme example of a universal code of ethics, while the Golden Rule is a milder case of cultural universalism (treat everyone the same—like you want to be treated). In contrast, **cultural relativism** is a code of ethics that judges people based on their own cultural standards (that is, different cultures have adopted their own codes of ethics) (Pederson, 1997). In this sense, we use the Platinum Rule, which is to treat people as they wish to be treated (Bennett, 1980). Cultural relativism has certain strengths but also has certain challenges. It is difficult to find discrimination against women or use of torture as ethical just because it is the norm in some cultures. We turn to the next two standards to help us resolve this seeming discrepancy.

MORAL INCLUSION/EXCLUSION   **Moral inclusion/exclusion** focuses on the degree to which we believe that people are within the boundaries of respect, fairness, and moral values. Moral inclusion occurs when we treat all people with dignity and respect, when we treat everyone as human. In contrast, moral exclusion happens when we feel that certain people do not deserve fair treatment, our respect, or to be valued. Moral exclusion can be severe or mild. Severe forms including killing other people who we feel are unethical (for example, the killing of Matthew Shepard, a gay man) and politically repressing those who disagree with us. Milder forms are excluding people from resources (such as not hiring people of a certain background), not talking to those who are different, and not recognizing those who are suffering (poor). The United States often debates different immigration policies. One core issue is whether to give amnesty to people who have come to the United States illegally (mostly from Mexico) or to brand them as criminals and deport them. This debate is not unique in developed countries and provides an excellent example of the difference between moral inclusion (amnesty) and moral exclusion (criminals and deportation).

SOCIAL JUSTICE   **Social justice** is a philosophical stance that emphasizes fair distribution of wealth, power, and income across cultures (see Box 1.8). It is based on democratic principles of equality and the ethic of human rights. Throughout history, when cultural groups come into contact, often one (or more) group gains an advantage at the expense of others—or there is a perceived advantage gain. One of the reasons for this advantage is that the cultural group with the power uses its values, norms, and behaviors to "play the game." When we use one culture's rules, it is not surprising that that culture comes out on top.

The United States has a long history of inequality and mistreatment of cultural groups. We have a legacy of slavery of Blacks, relocation and attempted extermination of American Indians, and internment of Japanese in World War II, to name just a few incidents. Today, we look at those legacies in shame but forget about their impact on people from those groups. These histories provide one explanation of why the educational achievements or health status of American Indians and African Americans lag behind those of White Americans (Williams & Williams-Morris, 2000). The United States is not unique in history, as most developed nations have a history of conquering or attempting the extermination of groups of people (examples include the Holocaust and horrible acts against Koreans and Chinese by the Japanese).

Some argue that these negative histories should not be used today; however, clear disparities exist in health, education, and income for American Indians, African Americans, and Hispanics/Latinos in the United States. Around the world, wealthy nations (for example, the United States, European nations, and East Asian nations) are perceived to have gained their incomes at the expense of poorer and colonized nations (such as India, African nations, and South American nations). The perception is that free trade agreements contribute to the further disparities between rich and poor.

The study of intercultural communication makes an important contribution to the social justice debate. Communication creates the perception about social justice and the image of people and cultures. We need to understand why these perceptions occur, what role history plays in constructing these perceptions and disparities, and how we might be able to reduce disparities within and between nations.

Box 1.8 Talking about Ethics: Social Justice

Some people accept social justice principles as a given, while others think they are principles associated with "political correctness" and are a waste of time. The position in favor of social justice has it roots in notions of human rights and equal opportunity. This position assumes that people are hard working and that their position in society is largely determined by historical and political events rather than individual effort. The position against social justice is that in a capitalistic society (and world), everyone has the opportunity to succeed and benefit if they are willing to work hard enough. If one is not succeeding, it is because one has not tried hard enough or has not mastered key skills. Both of these positions (for and against social justice) are rooted in deeply held ethical principles (equality and fairness versus the Puritan work ethic).

1. What position do you hold and why?
2. Does your cultural background and experience influence the position you hold?
3. What cultural sayings influence or reflect your position (for example, the adage "pull yourself up by your bootstraps" reflects an individual focus and responsibility)?

Box 1.9 Voices: My Perspective about Why I Study Intercultural Communication

As the author of this book, I want to give you a sense of who I am, as this will help you interpret and make sense of what I present. I have a particular perspective that certainly influences what I present and why. I am also an educator who wants to try and teach without preaching so I attempt to be open about discussions and allow you to make up your own mind.

I am a White (mixed European decent—Irish, Italian, German, Polish), heterosexual male; married with two small children. I grew up in Ohio in the late 1960s and through the 1970s—a time when civil rights and advances in race relations were common topics and fresh on people's minds. Despite the popular notions of a "melting pot" and a "color blind society," I noticed that there were inequities in how people were treated based on skin color (in my community that meant Black and White). I also noticed that Blacks and Whites did not interact together very much except in certain schools settings such as sports.

When I was 13, I moved to Albuquerque, New Mexico. It was the first time I had seen (except on TV) Hispanics (the reference for people of Spanish, Mexican, Central American, and Cuban descent in New Mexico) and American Indians. It was also the first time in my life that I was a numerical minority

based on skin color (although my ethnic group still had political and economic majority status). My high school was composed of a majority Hispanic population with smaller Anglo (as Whites or European Americans are referred to in New Mexico), American Indian, and African American populations. I found it exhilarating. I loved interacting and making friends with people from different cultural backgrounds. I recall that culturally different people in New Mexico interacted with each other more than what I experienced in Ohio. There were still "race disputes," but they seemed to be infrequent. I later learned that there are still segregated communities in Albuquerque, that some high schools are largely homogeneous, and that race relations are not ideal (much animosity was below the surface).

These experiences planted the seeds of interest in diversity and culture. My own ethical standards lean toward moral inclusion, social justice, and cultural relativism—although I do think that some cultural practices (such as treating women as second-class citizens and killing dissidents because they speak out) are deplorable. I believe that effective communication can create possibility and improve cultural relations and that is predominantly why I study intercultural communication.

How Can We Study Intercultural Communication?

When people study intercultural communication, they can use a variety of perspectives. The perspective one takes is much like a lens that is used to focus on particular aspects or behaviors related to culture while limiting the view and the understanding of other aspects of culture. In the scholarly study of intercultural communication, three predominant perspectives have been used: interpretive, social science, and critical. This following section briefly explores each of these perspectives and then introduces the approach used in this book.

Different Perspectives

The history of the study of intercultural communication can be traced to the work of Edward T. Hall and the Foreign Service Institute after World War II

(Leeds-Hurwitz, 1990). After World War II, the United States was very interested in broadening its foreign relations and influence. To meet this goal, U.S. diplomats went to different countries to establish economic and political contacts. Hall is a cultural anthropologist who was charged with teaching the diplomats about the different cultures. In addition to language skills, the diplomats were trained in the skills, concepts, and principles of intercultural communication. Hall's approach to the study of intercultural communication was to immerse himself in a different culture in order to understand the values, norms, and behaviors of that culture. He then identified a set of concepts that could explain differences in the types of behavior people within a culture exhibited.

Hall's predominant approach illustrates the **interpretive approach.** This perspective provides detailed descriptions of culture and cultural communication. The goal is to identify a unified culture and the ways of knowing and understanding the culture. From this perspective, it is critical to be able to understand the subtle nuances and meanings of behaviors in order to understand culture. People who follow an interpretive approach tend to use ethnographic research methods. These methods require an individual to spend a great deal of time (months and even years) living and interacting with cultural members. A researcher will ask questions about behavior, take detailed notes, transcribe these notes, spend a great deal of time making sense of the notes, and then check to make sure that his or her understandings make sense to the cultural members. While Hall used this approach to examine national cultures, researchers using this approach today tend to study "small" communities as cultures since it would be impossible to provide a detailed understanding of a large nation (Hall, 1959).

While the foundations of intercultural communication can be found in the interpretive perspective, many scholars took this detailed information about culture and sought to identify patterns in communication. This approach is called the **social scientific perspective** (although some call it the normative or functional perspective). Early researchers (including Hall) who used this perspective attempted to compare and contrast cultures. Their goal was to develop a set of dimensions on which cultures could be compared. The purpose was to help individuals improve their communication with members from a different culture and to get a better understanding of how their own culture influenced their behavior. Hall stated that culture is to humans as water is to fish. We do not really see and understand the importance of culture until we are out of it—hence, the need to make cross-cultural comparisons.

Later, social scientific research questioned whether cross-cultural research would really help intercultural interaction. Does knowing how a Mexican communicates with another Mexican, for example, help a Canadian communicate with a Mexican? Would the Mexican behave differently with a Canadian versus another Mexican? These social scientists then began to study intercultural communication. Social scientists who study cross-cultural communication and social scientists who study intercultural communication share perspectives and methods. The purpose of the social scientific perspective is to identify patterns of communication and attribute behavior to cultural values. They tend to use quantitative methods such as surveying individuals and asking them to complete a questionnaire that quantifies their communication behavior. These scholars then use statistical analysis to make the comparisons and identify patterns of behavior.

Other scholars take a different approach toward intercultural communication: the **critical approach/perspective.** These scholars emphasize power differences between different cultures and study the domination of one group by another. They examine ways that certain communication patterns privilege certain individuals over others and try to point out this privilege to improve social relations and social order. For example, a critical scholar might argue that corporate communication is based on Western male norms (or White male norms) and that this bias is one reason a disproportionate number of White men are executives of companies. Or, a critical scholar might question the work of the Foreign Service Institute by arguing that the notion of improving foreign relations was a false front and the real purpose was a political one—so that the United States could protect its economic interests in other countries. Or a critical scholar might study diasporas and the social, political, and economic forces they have created. A **diaspora** is a massive migration of people caused by wars, colonization, slavery, persecution, and famine; this migration results in a cultural group being geographically dispersed. The African diaspora and the Jewish diaspora are two examples. Such movement is forced on the culture. Critical scholars tend to use ethnographic methods and open interviews to collect detailed information. While their techniques are similar to those of interpretive scholars, the critical scholar will move beyond simple description to comment on issues of power, domination, and privilege in a culture or between cultures. Thus, the analysis of the data is very different from that of interpretive scholars.

Each of these perspectives contributes important information about intercultural communication. The interpretive perspective is vital because it provides detailed understanding of a culture. In order to improve intercultural interaction, we need to understand other cultures' norms, beliefs, and values. The social scientific perspective is critical as it helps to identify patterns of communication behavior across and between cultures. It provides a framework for the vast array of cultural differences around the world. Finally, the critical perspective helps to recognize that the world is not a "level playing field." Clearly some groups and cultures have more power than others. In the interest of fairness and justice, it is important to identify issues of power, privilege, and domination. As you read these brief descriptions (or perhaps after you read more about them and understand the differences in the perspectives), you might have found yourself with a preference for one over another. We tend to have a learning and personal philosophy that leans toward one of these. However, each is important and used throughout the text to help illustrate intercultural communication.

Pedagogical Approaches in this Book

In addition to presenting research from each of these perspectives, this book uses specific pedagogical, or instructional, approaches to help you learn the material. My overarching method used in this book is called a **layered approach.** While this approach is explained in Chapter 2, a brief definition is that it emphasizes that individuals around the world are organized in various interconnected layers. Specifically, we are individuals within family units, who work in particular organizations, that are situated in particular communities, within specific cultures.

Many scholars study intercultural communication within only one or two of these layers. Studying all of the layers together is a holistic approach. We tend to think of ourselves as individuals (and perhaps part of a family), but events and behavior impact people in direct and indirect ways—we are all connected together in some fashion. So, racism in a society may directly impact people of a certain skin color, but it impacts even those who do not directly experience racism. It lowers trust among cultural groups and has economic impacts for everyone. For instance, racism has negative health effects for those who experience it (Williams & Williams-Morris, 2000). These effects increase the need for and the use of health care, which leads to a rise in the cost of health insurance premiums for everyone. This example is unique to the United States because it does not have universal health care. In other nations as in the United States, racism can have other indirect effects such as turnover in the workplace or racial violence in communities.

One of the best ways to learn about intercultural communication and culture is to experience it directly. Living with people of different cultural backgrounds and interacting with culturally diverse people is the best way to learn and understand intercultural communication principles. While no book can help you experience anything directly, this book does share stories about individuals from various cultures. This book is not about any particular culture—thus you cannot learn a lot about any particular culture in detail by reading it—but you can read stories that help to illustrate concepts. These stories, or anecdotes, make this book experiential. In addition, at the end of each chapter (beginning with Chapter 3), there is a section called "Challenges and Skills." This section demonstrates particular intercultural communication challenges and communication skills that are relevant for the topic of the chapter. These ideas focus on improving your intercultural experiences.

While experiencing culture is important for learning, we also need some sort of organizing framework to put all the information together. Imagine trying to remember thousands of bits of information for each culture. That would be a difficult task. Instead, this book takes a theoretical approach to organize this information. A theory is a coherent set of principles that explains phenomena—that is, a theory explains what is going on using specific concepts and ideas to provide a general understanding about something (in our case intercultural communication). Usually, a theory focuses on a particular type of communication behavior (for example, conflict within work groups). A theory can be applied to a number of related interactions. In this manner, a theory is a tool that helps us understand, organize, and explain a lot of information rather than a single anecdote.

SUMMARY

Returning to the opening story: The case of Gillian Gibbons illustrates many facets of intercultural communication. First, it demonstrates the importance of key symbols (the Prophet Muhammad) for members of cultures. Cultural symbols have great significance and to misuse these symbols can be quite insulting to members of a culture. Second, the case demonstrates that members of the same cultural group view their culture in different ways. Some Sudanese Muslims were extremely offended by Gibbons' actions and called for her death. Other Sudanese Muslims thought that the government was using this case as a political ploy and thought the situation was blown out of proportion. British and American Muslims were mystified by the decision in the case. Third, the case demonstrates that even misunderstandings have significant impact on the effectiveness of intercultural encounters. This seemingly innocent misunderstanding by Gibbons was viewed as a threat to culture and identity by some Sudanese Muslims. Such a situation creates conflict. Fourth, the case raises key ethical considerations. By what standards do we judge a person's behavior? In evaluating a person's behavior, should we consider the historical and political condition when considering (social) justice? Finally, the case demonstrates the importance of understanding intercultural communication from a layered perspective. This case involved a president who offered a particular ideology and might have used the case to rally support for his position on peacekeepers in Darfur. Additionally, Sudan was a British colony and there is resentment toward Britain. Thus, a British teacher who comes to Sudan and violates cultural practices (intentionally or not) is seen as someone who is trying to change Muslim children, who is forcing the children to adopt Western values and customs. Such practices insult members of a culture and need to be defended against.

Here is the chapter summary based on the opening learning objectives:

- **Culture, communication, and intercultural communication.** Culture is "a learned system of meanings that fosters a particular sense of shared identity-hood and community-hood among its group members. It is a complex frame of reference that consists of a pattern of traditions, beliefs, values, norms, symbols, and meanings that are shared to varying degrees by interacting members of an identity group" (Ting-Toomey & Takai, 2006, p. 691). Communication is a process whereby people collectively create and transmit meaning through the exchange of verbal and nonverbal messages in a particular context. From these definitions, we see that intercultural communication takes place between people and entities that are culturally unalike.

- **Importance of studying intercultural communication.** We should study intercultural communication for many reasons. Global demographic trends (both shifts in people and ease of interaction created by travel and technology) provide a primary reason for studying intercultural communication. The increase in intercultural interaction creates opportunities for productive (and destructive) outcomes and peace (and conflict). These disparate results of intercultural communication create an ethical imperative to understand, and apply fairly, principles of intercultural communication. An understanding of effective intercultural communication is thus critical for success in business, politics, negotiation, and travel.

- **Three perspectives for studying intercultural communication.** Three perspectives for studying intercultural communication are the interpretative, social science, and critical perspectives. The interpretive approach emphasizes the importance of studying culture and communication in depth and providing a detailed description of what is going on. The social scientific perspective emphasizes patterns of communication and attributing those patterns to cultural values. The critical approach emphasizes the study of power differences and how certain groups are privileged at the expense of others.

- **Pedagogical approaches.** The primary approach of this book is to emphasize the layers of intercultural communication in a holistic manner. Additionally, this text emphasizes the importance of experiencing culture and using theories to explain intercultural communication.

REVIEW QUESTIONS

1. Define culture, communication, and intercultural communication.
2. What are the components of culture? Provide an example of each.
3. What are the components of communication? Provide an example of each.
4. What are similar terms used to describe intercultural communication? How are these terms similar to and different from intercultural communication?
5. What are the primary reasons to study intercultural communication?
6. How can intercultural communication have both productive and destructive aspects? Give an example of each.
7. What are three ethical considerations when studying intercultural communication? Make an argument in support of or against these ethical considerations.
8. Describe the three theoretical perspectives for studying intercultural communication.
9. What is the pedagogical approach taken in this book?

EXERCISES

1. Visit the Web site, Diversitydata.org at http://diversitydata.sph.harvard.edu/index.jsp. It describes diversity trends in the United States. How do certain outcomes vary across population groups? What might account for the variations?
2. Watch the movie *Hotel Rwanda* for an account of the ethnic war between the Hutus and Tutsis. How was communication used to create war and peace in this situation?
3. Consider the following quote from documentary filmmaker Bill Brummel: "Imagine we are all the same. Imagine we agree about politics, religion, and morality. Imagine we like the same types of music, art, food, and coffee. Imagine we all look alike. Sound boring? Differences need not divide us. Embrace diversity." What is your reaction to this quote? Is it cliché or meaningful? In what ways to we allow diversity to divide us? In what ways do we embrace diversity?

CHAPTER 2

A Layered Approach to Intercultural Communication

About 20,000 people attended a rally in Jena, Louisiana, to protest what many felt was the unfair and racially biased treatment of six African American youth by the judicial system. This case was affected by many layers of intercultural communication including the legal system, school system, interpersonal relationships, and individual attitudes. What are the various factors that shape our intercultural communication?

CHAPTER OUTLINE

I. Introduction

II. A Layered Approach: The Social Ecological Framework
   a. Layered Model
   b. Benefits and Challenges of a Layered Perspective

III. Four Layers of Intercultural Communication
   a. Individual Layer
   b. Interpersonal Layer
   c. Organizational Layer
   d. Cultural Layer
   e. Connecting the Layers

IV. Summary

V. Review Questions

VI. Exercises

CHAPTER OBJECTIVES

After reading this chapter, students should be able to

- describe what it means to say that intercultural communication and culture is layered.

- explain the four layers of intercultural communication.

- describe culture from an interpretive, social science, and critical perspective.

- identify the ways that the four layers influence each other.

Introduction

On December 4, 2006, six African American teens allegedly attacked and severely beat a White American teen (Justin Barker) at Jena High School in Jena, Louisiana. The beating was a culmination of a series of events at the school, which is composed of approximately 80% White Americans and 15% African Americans. The events appear to have begun on September 1, 2006, when three nooses were hung from a tree in the school courtyard by three White American teens; several African American students had sat under the tree the day before during a school assembly. The noose is often seen as a reference to the past history of the lynching of African Americans, and using the noose to intimidate or cause fear may be viewed as a hate crime. (A federal prosecutor concluded that the act was a hate crime, but could not prosecute because the offenders were juveniles.) The White students were going to be expelled by the principal, but the expulsion was overturned by the school board, and the students instead served in-school suspensions. On September 10, 2006, African American students wanted to address the school board about the issue but were not allowed to do so as the school board felt the issue had been adequately resolved. African American residents said that the school board's decision stoked racial tensions in the community. The U.S. attorney's office agreed that the incident was symptomatic of racial tensions, but that there was not evidence that the event was directly linked to the beating.

A fight that occurred on December 1, 2006 appears to be more directly related to the beating. On that day there was a private party, attended mostly by Whites but with some Blacks, at the Jena Fair Barn. Six Black youths, including Robert Bailey, Jr. (one of the Jena 6), attempted to enter the party at about 11 p.m. They were told by a woman that no one was allowed inside without an invitation. A White male, who was not a student, then jumped in front of the woman and a fight ensued. After the fight broke up, the woman told both the White male and six Black students to leave the party. Once outside, the Black students were involved in another fight with a group of White males, who were not students. How this fight involved Barker or the entire Jena 6 has not been explained.

That the teens severely beat up Barker has not been in question. Barker spent three hours in the emergency room and had severe wounds. However, the means of punishing the teens has been in question. Five of the six teens were originally charged with attempted second-degree murder. In June 2007, one of the teens, Mychal Bell, faced trial; he was charged as an adult and was found guilty of aggravated assault and battery by an all-White jury of six (no African Americans showed up for the jury pool) and faced a potential sentence of 22 years. The day Bell was to be sentenced, on September 20, 2007, at least 20,000 people went to Jena to protest his trial (arguing that Bell should not have been tried as an adult and that his fate should not have been decided by an all-White jury). Bell's sentence was thrown out by a judge who said that he should not have been tried as an adult. In December 2007, Bell eventually pleaded guilty to second-degree battery in return for an 18-month sentence, with credit for 10 months that he already has served. The remaining five defendants were awaiting trail as of July 2008. Their lawyers field a motion to remove Judge J. P. Mauffray arguing that his bias against the youth made it impossible for the youths to get a fair trial (Mauffray had presided in the original trial against Bell). A decision on this motion was to be made in late July 2008. Additionally, the family of Justin Barker filed a civil suit against the six youths—the adult teens directly and the other teen's parents—and the local school board. As of July 2008 this suit had yet to go to trial.

> Question: What layers of intercultural communication can you identify in this story? What caused the problems?

Like all human behavior, intercultural communication takes place in many interrelated contexts or layers. We tend to think that any given interaction, even with people from a different cultural background than our own, is just between two people. Our tendency is to focus on our goals, relationships, and what we are trying to accomplish at that point in time. However, a wide variety of factors shape that interaction, including past histories between the cultural groups; stereotypes in the media about other cultural groups; the cultural values of our own groups; our personal thoughts, biases, and emotions; and the current political contexts. We do not walk into an interaction as a blank slate, and the goal of this chapter is to better understand the factors that influence and shape intercultural interactions.

This chapter provides an organizational framework for this text and introduces the layered perspective of intercultural communication. It begins by describing what a layered approach is and the benefits and challenges of such an approach. Then it explains how culture fits within this layered perspective by introducing four specific layers: individual, interpersonal, organizational, and cultural.

A Layered Approach: The Social Ecological Framework

Many scholars argue that most issues, including intercultural communication, are too complex to be adequately explained by only individual behavior (Stokols, 1996). For this reason, many scholars began to rethink their approach to provide more integrated and complex models. One of these models is the **social ecological framework.** Social ecology refers to the study of relationships between organisms and their environment (Hawley, 1950). It emphasizes that organisms are connected to their physical surroundings. Human beings are also organisms, and we are connected to the physical and social environments in which we live. For example, we are dependent on the physical resources of the earth for our survival. Additionally, we are connected to the people whom we live among. The nature of these connections (for example, competitive or collaborative) is where the focus of social ecology lies. In the following section, I describe the layered approach used in this text and the benefits and challenges of using such an approach.

Layered Model

Social ecology was developed by scholars in many different fields of study to better address the influences of social and cultural contexts or environments on human behavior (Brofenbrenner, 1977, 1979; McLeroy, Bibeau, Steckler, & Glanz, 1988; Stokols, 1996). "An ecological perspective implies reciprocal causation between the individual and the environment" (McLeroy et al., 1988, p. 354). The social ecological framework refers to the key principles and the specific contextual or environmental layers. This book uses the concepts of context and environments interchangeably to refer to the specific layers of the model. Reminiscent of the Taoist philosophy of dialectical balance through the "yin-yang" complementary approach, this framework involves *simultaneous,* not separate, examination of behavior at two or more layers (Klein, Tosi, & Cannella, 1999; Rousseau & House, 1994; Stokols, 1996).

The social ecological perspective is rooted in four core principles. First, individual communication and behavior is influenced by the cumulative effect of multiple physical, social, and cultural factors. For example, our communication style is influenced by the physical locations we are in (for example, we might be more aggressive in a crowded room), the social relationships we maintain (for example, our family relationships affect how we choose to handle conflict), *and* the culture we are socialized in (for example, Saudi Arabians handle conflict differently than do Russians because of value differences in the cultures). Second, individual communication is also affected by individual attributes. Our communication style is a product of our personality; thus, if you are assertive, you might be labeled as having an "aggressive" personality.

Third, individuals are interdependent, or interconnected, in a variety of contexts. In this manner, our behavioral choices impact, and are impacted by, other people, relationships, organizations, and societies. Thus, our communication style impacts other people and our relationships (see Box 2.1 for an illustration). Fourth, the social ecological perspective is interdisciplinary and incorporates different methods for understanding how the pieces of the puzzle fit together.

Box 2.1 Voices: Illustrating the Layered Perspective

I never really thought about how my behavior impacted others. Sure, I can think about times when I was short with my parents and they got mad at me. However, I had this class where one of the students was obnoxious. She knew every answer and never gave anyone else a chance to speak. She was also argumentative with the instructor. It created such a tense atmosphere in the class, and I could tell by the instructor's expression that she did not like it. I did not realize how it impacted my life until my boyfriend asked me why I always picked a fight with him after this class. It dawned on me that I was so upset at my classmate that I took it out on my boyfriend.

1. Does another person's behavior absolve us of responsibility for our own behavior? In what situations might this be the case?
2. How does our individual behavior impact those around us and society in general?

Similar to the notion that different perspectives for understanding intercultural communication exist, understanding the layers of intercultural communication requires knowledge of history, economics, social science, anthropology, politics, and communication.

The social ecological framework can be visually displayed by thinking about a series of concentric circles to represent the layers (Figure 2.1). In the inner circle is the individual. The next circle represents the interpersonal relationships we create with others. The third circle symbolizes the organizations in which we work, play, get educated, and receive health care. The outer circle illustrates the culture and societal institutions that we live in. In this way, each circle is nested within other circles just like individuals are in relationships within organizations that are within particular cultures.

In examining the relationship between the individual and the environment, we focus on two specific types of relationships between and among layers of intercultural communication: top-down effects, and bottom-up effects (Klein et al., 1999; Rousseau & House, 1994). Figure 2.1 also illustrates both of these effects. The arrow going toward the individual illustrates how cultural and societal layers (such as mass media and cultural values) shape individual communication behavior. These are called **top-down effects.** Specifically, the cultural layer affects the organizational layer, which, in turn, shapes the interpersonal layer, and then influences the individual.

Bottom-up effects focus on how lower layers (such as individuals and interpersonal relationships) affect higher layers (such as culture). The arrow going from the individual to the cultural layers illustrates the bottom-up effect and the power of the individual to impact culture. Civil rights leaders like Dr. Martin Luther King, Jr.,

Figure 2.1
Layered Model
of Intercultural
Communication

and Gandhi had a great deal of power and changed the world. While these might be unique examples, it is important for us to realize that individuals reinforce and re-create culture through individual behaviors. If you accept cultural norms, you will follow them and sanction others when they do not follow them. If you think the cultural norms are wrong or oppressive, you will resist them and encourage others to resist (subtly or directly). In each remaining chapter of this text, we discuss specific top-down and bottom-up relationships for each topic.

Benefits and Challenges of a Layered Perspective

The layered perspective is relatively new to the study of intercultural communication, but it has been used in other fields, such as family systems (Brofenbrenner, 1979, 1989), organizational behavior (Klein, Tosi, & Cannella, 1999; Rousseau & House, 1994), and public health (Oetzel & Duran, 2004; Stokols, 1996). In the next section, I describe the benefits and challenges of using a layered approach for the study of intercultural communication. See Box 2.2.

A layered perspective offers a number of benefits. Only focusing on a single layer, such as individual choices, presents the problem of underestimating the effects of other contexts (Klein et al., 1999; Rousseau & House, 1994). The tendency in intercultural communication is to focus on the individual in order to understand why we communicate differently than people from other cultural backgrounds. In this way, we tend to miss the influence of such factors as historical incidents and economic systems on our communication behavior. By using a layered perspective, we get a sense of how individual choices and historical incidents impact intercultural communication. In this manner, we can create a rich, complex picture of intercultural communication. A layered perspective fosters synthesis and synergy, creates links and loops where there were none before, and also illuminates reciprocal contextual influences (Klein et al., 1999). Thus, we might get a sense of how our history shapes our individual behavior, but also how we as individuals can change history.

Additionally, the social ecological approach helps to avoid blaming the victim for all of his behavioral choices, but at the same time recognizes the importance of individual responsibility for behavior choices. When an adolescent makes a choice to use aggressive communication to resolve conflicts (for example, yelling or physical violence), the tendency is to label that child as "bad." However, the child's choices may be influenced by numerous factors such as media violence, a culture that is accepting of violence, an abusive upbringing, and an aggressive personality. The layered approach considers all of these factors and places behavior in context rather than simply viewing behavior as a series of individual choices. Now, the limitation might be to "excuse" poor behavior by not considering individual responsibility at all, but this is not the focus of the layered approach—it does not remove individual responsibility but rather highlights other explanatory factors as well. In this manner, the layered approach brings up ethical considerations for explaining behavior.

Box 2.2 Talking about Ethics: Layered Perspective versus Individual Responsibility

The layered perspective argues that people's behavior is not entirely their own responsibility. It contends that our communication with others is influenced by other factors including history, economics, politics, culture, families, and organizations as well as individual choices, thoughts, and feelings.

1. What do you think about this perspective?
2. Does it give people excuses to explain away their bad behavior? Does it provide a good balance between individual choices and societal influences? Does it not put enough emphasis on the role of society?

A final benefit of the layered approach is that it helps identify how certain contexts support or inhibit behavioral change. For example, let us assume that a school wants to reduce prejudice and discrimination at a high school because a number of racial conflicts have occurred. The school officials hire intercultural communication experts to design a state-of-the-art program that has proven to be effective in similar institutions. The experts then train the individual students, and the program shows initial success at reducing prejudice. However, will these changes last? A lot will depend on the teachers, parents, and friends that the students interact with. If your parent expresses prejudice against certain racial groups, you are likely to have similar prejudice. At the very least, it will be harder for you to reduce your prejudice than it would be for a student whose parents do not express the same prejudices.

The layered perspective does pose simultaneous challenges and burdens for the study and understanding of intercultural communication. First, a layered perspective is quite complex. Rather than focusing on a single issue, the layered perspective requires the consideration of a number of concepts and issues. Second, given that the layered approach includes multiple issues, it can be easy to conclude that "everything matters." However, in any given situation, certain factors matter more, and these need to be emphasized. Thus, the layered approach requires students to be critical thinkers and sort through a lot of information to make reasonable conclusions. Third, it can be difficult to organize and read layered research books. Since it is not a linear perspective, it is hard to figure out where to start and where to stop. In this book, I have made a choice (an arbitrary one) to start with the individual and work my way out. I could also have started from the outer layer and worked my way in. Thus, the challenge is keeping all of the information straight. However, the complexity of the layered approach represents social reality and provides rich theoretical and practical insight into layered human cognition, affect, and behavior. While this approach is complex, the key is to think that there are many different factors nested together than influence our communication behavior. These different layers affect us in different ways and in different situations. The focus of this book is to uncover these layers to better understand intercultural communication and thus provide skills and solutions that will address intercultural communication problems.

Four Layers of Intercultural Communication

Earlier in this chapter, we identified four specific layers of intercultural communication: individual, interpersonal, organizational, and cultural. In this section, I describe each layer and then discuss the intersections among them (that is, the mix of cultural and individual layers). We proceed from a bottom-up perspective, beginning with the individual layer and moving toward the cultural layer. This ordering is consistent with the chapters presented in the book.

Individual Layer

The individual layer of intercultural communication focuses on an individual's interpretations of the beliefs, values, and norms about a culture as well as the socialization that one receives from family and organizations (Triandis, 1972). This layer includes several factors that mediate the influence of culture on specific individual behavior (Gudykunst et al., 1996). What this means is that communication behavior is learned within the primary socialization process of one's cultural group. Individuals learn the norms and scripts for appropriate and effective conflict conduct in their immediate cultural environment (for example, in the family and in organizations). Additionally, these tendencies, in turn, also influence individual-level factors such as the way individuals conceive of themselves. However, just because a person lives in a particular type of culture does not mean that she will be just like others in the dominant culture. This is the **ecological fallacy** or the assumption that what is true of the collective is true of all the individuals of that collective. In fact, individuals can vary from the predominant culture (for example, a person can have a collectivistic orientation in an individualistic culture). In the following section, I discuss two individual conceptions related to the cultural values of individualism-collectivism and power distance: self-construal and horizontal and vertical selves. The cultural values will be discussed in a later section.

SELF-CONSTRUAL   Self-construal is a key individual factor that relates to cultural individualism and collectivism (Markus & Kitayama, 1991). **Self-construal** is one's self-image and is composed of an independent and an interdependent self. Our self-construal within our culture profoundly influences our communication with others. Individuals with a strongly **independent self-construal** tend to see themselves as autonomous, self-reliant, unencumbered, and rational choice-makers. In contrast, individuals with a strongly **interdependent self-construal** tend to see themselves as ingroup-bound, obligatory agents and relational harmony seekers.

Independent-self individuals tend to make sense of their environment through their own viewpoints while interdependent-self individuals tend to make sense of their surroundings through a viewpoint of their cultural or interpersonal groups. When communicating with others, high independents believe in voicing their personal opinions, striving for personal goals, and expressing their conflict needs assertively. On the other hand, high interdependents prefer self-restraint and self-monitoring strategies in order not to bring relational chaos or disharmony to the group. They tend to practice other-centered communication in anticipating the thoughts and feelings of the other person in situations (Ting-Toomey & Oetzel, 2001).

Both types of self-construal exist within a culture. Overall, however, independent self-construals are more common in individualistic cultures, and interdependent self-construals are more common in collectivistic cultures. Individuals also have both construals that are constrained by particular situations (Gudykunst et al., 1996). For example, we might be focused on our independent self when at work, but our interdependent self when interacting with family members. What type of self-conception do you have? Fill out the Self-Assessment 2.1 for an indication.

HORIZONTAL AND VERTICAL SELVES   Power distance also has an individual-level component. Similar to the arguments with self-construal, cultures are categorized as large- or small-power distance, but individuals do not necessarily follow all cultural values. Thus, some individuals in large-power distance cultures believe that power should be distributed evenly while some individuals in small-power distance cultures believe that power should be distributed unevenly.

Individuals and their behaviors can be conceptualized as either moving toward the "horizontal self" spectrum or the "vertical self" spectrum. Individuals who endorse **horizontal selves** prefer informal-symmetrical interactions (equal treatment) regardless

Self-Assessment 2.1

SELF-CONSTRUALS

For each of the following statements, place a number in the blank that best corresponds with your belief: 1 = strongly disagree, 2 = disagree, 3 = neutral, 4 = agree, 5 = strongly agree.

1. My personal identity is very important to me. _____
2. I maintain the harmony in the groups of which I am a member. _____
3. I am a unique person separate from others. _____
4. I sacrifice my self-interest for the benefit of my group. _____
5. I try not to depend on others. _____
6. My relationships with others are more important than my accomplishments. _____
7. I enjoy being unique and different from others. _____
8. My happiness depends on the happiness of those around me. _____

Scoring: The independent items are the following: 1, 3, 5, 7. Add up these items for your independent self-construal score. The maximum is 20 and the minimum is 5. The closer you are to the maximum, the more independent you are. The closer you are to the minimum, the less independent you are.

The interdependent items are the following: 2, 4, 6, 8. Add up these items for your interdependent self-construal score. The maximum is 20 and the minimum is 5. The closer you are to the maximum, the more interdependent you are. The closer you are to the minimum, the less interdependent you are.

Source: Gudykunst et al. (1996)

of people's position, status, rank, or age. In comparison, individuals who emphasize **vertical selves** prefer formal-asymmetrical interactions (differential treatment) with due respect to people's position, titles, and age. As Triandis (1995) observed, "This [conceptualization] means that people will seek different kinds of relationships and when possible 'convert' a relationship to the kind that they are most comfortable with. Thus, a professor from a horizontal-based self may convert a professor-student relationship to a friend-friend relationship, which may well confuse a student from a vertical-based self" (p. 164). While horizontal selves tend to predominate in small-power distance cultures, vertical selves tend to predominate in large-power distance cultures. Do you lean toward a vertical or horizontal self? Fill out Self-Assessment 2.2 below for an indication.

Interpersonal Layer

The interpersonal layer, the third layer of intercultural communication, focuses on the primary relationships that we have with others. These relationships include friendships, intimate relationships, and family relationships. The family layer is the primary place where people are socialized about their culture (Gudykunst et al., 1996).

Self-Assessment 2.2

HORIZONTAL AND VERTICAL SELVES

For each of the following statements, place a number in the blank that best corresponds with your belief: 1 = strongly disagree, 2 = disagree, 3 = neutral, 4 = agree, 5 = strongly agree.

1. In most situations, people in authority should make decisions without consulting their subordinates. _____
2. In work-related matters, people in high status positions have a right to expect obedience from lower-status people. _____
3. Employees who often question authority sometimes keep their managers from being effective. _____
4. Once a person in authority makes a decision, people under him or her should not question it. _____
5. Low-status people should not express direct disagreement with high-status individuals. _____
6. People in authority should be able to make the proper decisions without consulting others. _____
7. People in authority who consistently consult others in decisions are indecisive. _____
8. In most situations, leaders should tell subordinates what to do rather than consult with them. _____

Scoring: Add up the scores of the 8 statements. The maximum score is 40 and indicates a vertical self. The minimum score is 8 and indicates a horizontal self.

Source: Earley and Erez (1997)

We learn about our culture from our parents and siblings who teach us the dos and don'ts about how to interact with others and what to value. For example, one recent study explained that young adults and children learn their communication styles from family socialization (Koerner & Fitzpatrick, 2006). The nature of this socialization depends, in part, on the family communication patterns.

There are two predominant family communication patterns: conversation orientation and conformity orientation (Koerner & Fitzpatrick, 2006). **Conversation orientation** is "the degree to which families value and create a climate of open flow of communication and exchanges of ideas about attitudes, beliefs, and values" (Koerner & Fitzpatrick, 2006, p. 168). Families high in this orientation tend to interact about a lot of topics, have a tolerance toward different attitudes, and use direct conflict strategies. In socializing children about culture, parents high in this orientation will teach children about the culture, but will also be open to other cultural groups and ideas. Children will be encouraged to make choices for themselves about how they want to belong to a culture, but also who they want to date (whether it is someone from the same or different cultural or racial group). In contrast, **conformity orientation** is "the degree to which families create a climate that stresses homogeneity of attitudes, values, and beliefs" (Koerner & Fitzpatrick, 2006, p. 168). Families high in this orientation tend to hold similar attitudes, focus on harmony and obedience to the parents, and avoid conflict in order to emphasize harmony. In terms of cultural socialization, parents will expect children to adopt the traditional cultural practices and to date/marry within the cultural group. It is important to note that these two orientations are extreme orientations and that "in-between" points exist as well (such as a family who is open to dating outside one's culture, but wants the child to retain his or her own cultural values). (See Box 2.3 for an illustration of how these two orientations differ.)

The interpersonal layer includes several other factors besides family communication pattern. First, increasingly more and more families include parents from different cultural backgrounds (for example, Turk and German, Hispanic and African American, Japanese and Chinese, Francophone and Anglophone). These different backgrounds and the parents' attitudes toward their backgrounds influence whether a child is raised in a family that blends two traditions, in a family with two separate cultural traditions, or some other type of family environment that is neither of the original cultural backgrounds. Second, friends also shape and affect a person's attitudes toward his or her own culture, as well as attitudes toward members of different cultural groups. If your friends are accepting of different cultural groups, then you likely will have friends from different cultural groups. Thus, the interpersonal layer has a key influence on our individual perspectives about culture.

Organizational Layer

The second layer of intercultural communication, the organizational layer, focuses on culture in the places in which we work and go to school. Organizations provide us with an opportunity to interact with people from other cultures that we normally might not have contact with. In many parts of the world, neighborhoods are segregated by ethnic or cultural groups—Chinese tend to live near Chinese; Mexicans near Mexicans, and so on. We explore one reason for this in Chapter 3 on identity,

Box 2.3 What Went Right? Conversation Orientation and Confirmatory Orientation

An example can help illustrate the differences in conversation and confirmatory orientation in families. Consider a daughter, Isabella, who is talking to her parents about her cultural identity and how she is teased by "friends" from other cultures. (M = Mother, F = Father)

Conversation Orientation

I: My friends say that our culture is weird.

M: Honey, it may be weird to other people because they do not know about it. What do you think about it?

I: I like it and what we do, but sometimes it is hard. I don't like to be teased.

F: I know that is hard. What do you do?

I: I tease them back sometimes, when I know we are joking. Other times, I just avoid them.

M: How do you feel about it?

I: I want to tell them that they are mean and I don't want to be their friend.

F: I know what you mean. That is how I felt when I was growing up too.

M: But you need to understand that our culture is very important to your father and I and we are going to continue to practice it with you. You'll have to decide whether you want to do that at school—it might be easier just to do it at home. As you get older, you'll have to decide whether you want to carry on the cultural traditions and how you want to do that.

F: Of course, we are always here to talk to you about it.

I: Thanks mami and papi. I do like being who I am—I'm just going to ignore those stupid kids.

Conformity Orientation

I: My friends say that our culture is weird.

M: Honey, it may be weird to other people because they do not know about it. Our culture is very important to us, you, and our people.

I: It makes sense to me, but sometimes it is hard. I don't like to be teased.

F: Yes, that is hard. But our people have been teased and worse for a long time. You will gain strength in the culture and facing adversity. You know what you should do: you can teach them about who we are or simply ignore them.

I: But what if they don't stop?

M: They might not stop and that means they probably aren't your real friends. You need to understand that our culture is very important to all of us. It is important that you carry on the traditions of our family for your children to keep our culture alive. Our elders depend on our children to carry on the culture. Do you understand?

I: Yes. Thanks mami and papi. I do like being who I am—I'm just going to ignore those stupid kids.

1. This example illustrates that the outcome of both conversation works for the respective families. Which orientation best reflects your own upbringing?

2. What would happen in each orientation if you wanted something different than what your parents wanted (such as dating someone from another race or culture or not wanting to practice the culture the way your parents do)? What strategies might you use from each orientation to be effective in convincing your parents that your choice was right?

Many families are intercultural. What are the benefits and challenges of having an intercultural family? In what ways do differences in cultural values impact families?

but for many people the only time they come into contact with people from different national or ethnic groups is when they go to school or work. In these settings, we are socialized on how to communicate with other members.

The socialization of interacting with others can be positive or negative depending on the organizational culture. Much like a nation or community constructs a culture, schools and workplaces also develop a culture—the organizational culture (Eisenberg & Riley, 2001). Through the interactions among participants (such as students or employees) and the media distributed by the organization, members of the organization are socialized into a culture. They are taught what to value, how to interact with others, and what is important. Some organizations encourage diversity and respect for differences, while others encourage conformity (see Box 2.4).

It is also important to think about diversity beyond simply cultural and ethnic differences. Diversity includes other factors such as worldviews and cognitive flexibility. A colleague once commented to me that people trained in business schools in the United States, regardless of ethnic and national cultural differences, are more alike than they are different. Her perspective was that U.S. business schools socialize their members in very similar ways and that this socialization becomes a very important guideline for behavior whether a person is from India or Japan or is an African

Box 2.4 Globalization: Diversity in the Workplace?

With the globalization of the world, the notion of cultural diversity has changed. It is no longer simply whether the workplace has a balance of the ethnic groups in a nation (although this is still a concern). Large companies that compete around the world need to attract the best talent, individuals who can work with people of different cultures and serve and sell to people from different backgrounds. They also want people to work around the clock and take advantage of communication technology and time. Thus, intercultural communication might take place through electronic means (e-mail and teleconferencing) among people from many different nations as well as traditional face-to-face communication. Their training might be from a variety of university and technical colleges so that they have different perspectives in experiencing work. Employees come from different cultural backgrounds and social classes. We might find, however, that we have more similarity with someone from a different ethnic group or national culture because of our socialization or training than someone from our own cultural group. The end result is that diversity is the norm in this type of workplace and not the exception. It is not a simple focus on demographics, but a conglomeration of factors that sometimes matter a great deal and other times matter only a little. Complexity is the norm and a focus on intercultural communication can help us understand how the various factors come together.

An example of such diversity and globalization comes from Melissa. She worked on a marketing team for a large multinational firm. Her office was her home in Albuquerque (she was the only employee in Albuquerque), while corporate headquarters were in New York. Her teammates lived in New York, Europe, and Asia. Almost all of their communication was via e-mail with limited telephone and annual face-to-face meetings. They shared projects by contributing to a document during their own work hours and then passing it on to one of their teammates to continue in the same day (she usually received it last, which meant she was responsible for making final corrections and submissions). Cultural differences sometimes created conflict as she didn't always understand their messages or work styles. In general, however, the team worked very well together, and she considered her teammates to be good co-workers and friends.

American or American Indian. Her point is that many workplaces want to have a culturally diverse workforce, but if the company only hires business school graduates, it is not going to get a diverse workforce. Do you think that training in business schools erases cultural diversity? Or do people still retain their own cultural identity?

Cultural Layer

In Chapter 1, we emphasized the different approaches to the study of culture: interpretive, social scientific, and critical. From each of these perspectives, culture is defined in a different manner that emphasizes certain aspects over others. This section details how each of these perspectives describes culture.

INTERPRETIVE: CULTURE AS A SPEECH CODE   The most popular interpretive perspective on culture is speech codes theory, which describes culture as people who share culturally distinct ways of speaking. It is a theory that attempts to interpret or explain observed communication conduct by referencing situated speech codes. A **speech code** "is a system of socially-constructed symbols and meaning, premises, and rules, pertaining to communication conduct" (Philipsen, Coutu, & Covarrubias, 2005, p. 57). These codes are used by cultural members to situate specific communication actions in a localized context. The codes help members make sense of their world, describe it for others, help them figure out what to pay attention to and what to ignore, and provide social norms for approach behavior.

Speech codes theory has six specific propositions or statements about the relationships among concepts (Philipsen et al., 2005). First, a distinct cultural community has a distinct speech code. In this manner, a culture is not a distinct nationality or geographic area, but rather a community of people who share similar ways of speaking (that is, speech codes). For example, members of the Blackfeet American Indian tribe in the United States use the speech codes of "listen" and "sit down and listen" to express a complex system of meanings (Carbaugh, 1999). What makes the Blackfeet a cultural community is not that they share ancestry or physical geography, but rather that they share speech codes. Second, any given cultural community has multiple speech codes. These codes are often used to juxtapose one community with another. For example, in a classic study of a working-class neighborhood in Chicago labeled "Teamsterville," Philipsen (1992) identified a speech code that cultural members used to describe themselves, but also found codes used to contrast their ways of speaking with other cultural communities. Third, speech codes reference specific psychological, sociological, and rhetorical content. Thus, the speech codes go beyond simply describing communication conduct; in fact, they relate to human nature (psychology), social relations (sociology), and strategic behavior (rhetoric).

Fourth, speech codes constitute the meanings of communicative acts. For example, in one culture, the concept "speaking like a man" might have certain frames such as not showing emotions and not letting people know you are hurt or upset. In another culture, "speaking like a man" might mean being sensitive to others, expressing feelings of sorrow, and taking the other's perspective. Fifth, the rules and underlying premises of a speech code are found within the speaking itself. Many words and expressions contain metacommunication (or words/expressions about how to communicate). For example, if you tell someone "don't talk to me that way," you are telling them how you expect them to communicate with you. Finally, the artful use of speech codes provides a guide for ethical communication conduct. Speech codes dictate to people how we should interact with others and why (see Box 2.5).

In summary, speech code theory provides a strong example of the interpretive perspective of culture; that is, it focuses on observing and describing the cultural community as indicated by the speech codes. In this sense, culture is locally determined by speech codes rather than by nationality, race, or geography. From this perspective, the citizens of Iran only form a culture to the extent that they share a speech code. More likely, Iran (or any other nation for that matter) includes many cultural communities.

SOCIAL SCIENTIFIC: CULTURE AS COMPARABLE PATTERNS   Whereas the interpretive perspective focuses on local communities, the social scientific perspective tends to emphasize patterns of values and communication behaviors that can be compared across larger national,

Box 2.5 Voices: Speech Codes in a Working-Class Community

Gerry Philipsen (1992) is a communication scholar who studied the speech codes of a working-class community for nearly 30 months in the early 1970s. This neighborhood, which he called Teamsterville, was located in south Chicago. Through his ethnographic study, he identified a number of speech codes for this community. I highlight a few of the speech codes for men and boys—what Philipsen called "speaking like a man." These codes are the prominent ones in the community, but it does not mean everyone followed them exactly.

First, when the men or boys hung out with people who were like them (same ethnicity, age, social status), there was supposed to be a lot of banter, a sharing of put-downs and teasing. However, when the men or boys hung out with people who were not like them (women, people of different ethnicity or different social status), it was inappropriate to speak a lot. Second, men and boys needed to be careful to sound like everyone else in the community. Using big words or proper grammar would make a man stand out and not be accepted in the community. It would show he thought he was better than everyone else.

Third, situations in which a man or boy was in power called for action and not speaking. Philipsen described a director of a youth program for boys who wasn't from Teamsterville. The boys were being rude and undisciplined. The director used his own speech codes to address the disruptions, which consisted of talking with the boys to identify the problems and involve them in the decision making for the solutions. An adult male from the community who saw this felt that the director's behavior was inappropriate and that he should "beat the hell out of the kids." He even told the director that he could get the parents' permission to beat them.

Another code that called for action was the honor code. It was particularly important for the men and boys in Teamsterville to defend themselves and the people linked to them. For example, if a female linked to the boy or man (such as a mother or girlfriend) was insulted, the male was bound by honor to defend her. Such defense usually called for fighting, not words. If a man was not willing to fight to defend his honor or those around him, the other men and boys viewed him as homosexual, weak, or a "wuss." This code only applied to outsiders; for insiders, verbal insults could be responded to by verbal put-downs that humiliated or defeated the person making the insult.

1. How do these speech codes compare to the codes from where you are from?
2. Do speech codes vary across communities of different socioeconomic classes?

racial, and geographic lines. Much of the research has focused on identifying patterns in national cultures, but some scholars have investigated specific patterns among racial and ethnic groups as well. From the social science point of view, culture provides an overarching perspective about a group of people that can best be understood by comparing one culture to another. Culture is not meant to pigeonhole or stereotype people; it simply describes general patterns that influence, to a certain degree, the members of the culture, whether the influence is positive (that is, reinforces the culture) or negative.

The most popular social scientific perspective on culture is a model offered by Geert Hofstede. Hofstede (1991, 2001) conducted a study of over 100,000 employees of IBM in over 50 nations around the world. Exploring the responses on a series of questions, he identified broad patterns that he found distinguished the cultures. These patterns are often called dimensions of cultural variability because they describe how cultures vary on a set of common conceptions. These patterns are not meant to describe everything about cultures, but rather are the most critical concepts in terms of comparing and contrasting cultures. The dimensions are individualism-collectivism, power distance, uncertainty avoidance, masculinity-femininity, and short-term versus long-term orientation.

Individualism and Collectivism   Individualism refers to the broad value tendencies of people in a culture to emphasize the individual identity over group identity and individual rights over group obligations. The predominant communication style is low-context orientation (Hostede, 1991; Triandis, 1995). **Low-context communication** focuses on the transmission of explicit, precise, and direct messages relying on verbal communication. Meaning resides in the message (Hall, 1976). Individualism is a cultural pattern that is found in most northern and western regions of Europe and in North America. In comparison, **collectivism** refers to the broad value tendencies of people in a culture to emphasize the group identity over the individual identity as well as group-oriented concerns over individual wants and desires. The communication style is a high-context approach. **High-context communication** focuses on the transmission of implicit, ambiguous, and indirect messages often relying on nonverbal communication. Most information in the message is either in the physical context or internalized in the person (Hall, 1976). The cultural pattern of collectivism is common in Asia, Africa, the Middle East, Central and South America, and the Pacific Islands. One-third of the world population resides in cultures with high individualistic value tendencies, and two-thirds of the people are in cultures with high group-oriented value tendencies (Triandis, 1995). A summary of the differences between collectivistic and individualistic cultures is displayed in Table 2.1.

Table 2.1

DIFFERENCES BETWEEN COLLECTIVISTIC AND INDIVIDUALISTIC CULTURES

Collectivistic	Individualistic
Identity is based on the group membership ("We" identity)	Identity is based in the individual ("I" identity)
Group rights prevail over individual rights	Individual rights prevail over group rights
Values harmony, face-saving, filial piety (duty toward parents), modesty, moderation, thrift, equality in the distribution of rewards among peers, and fulfillment of others' needs	Values freedom, honesty, social recognition, comfort, hedonism, and equity (to each according to his or her contributions to group performance)
Relationship prevails over task	Task prevails over relationship
Opinions are predetermined by group membership	Everyone is expected to have a private opinion
High-context communication	Low-context communication

Sources: Adapted from Hofstede (1991); Ting-Toomey & Kurogi (1998)

Power Distance   Power distance is the second dimension. **Power distance** is "the extent to which the less powerful members of institutions and organizations within a country expect and accept that power is distributed unequally" (Hofstede, 1991, p. 28). Small power distance refers to broad value tendencies of people in a culture to emphasize individual credibility and expertise, a democratic decision-making process, equal rights and relations, and equitable rewards and punishments based on performance. Children can contradict their parents and speak their own minds. They are expected to learn verbal articulateness to defend their own viewpoints and positions. Parents and children attempt to work toward achieving a democratic family decision-making system. Likewise, power is distributed evenly in small power distance work situations. Subordinates expect to be consulted, and the ideal boss is a resourceful democrat. Small power distance index values are found, for example, in Denmark, Norway, Sweden, Israel, and New Zealand. Large power distance refers to broad value tendencies of people in a culture to emphasize status-based credibility and experience, a benevolent autocratic decision-making process, asymmetrical role-based relations, and rewards and punishments based on age, rank, status, title, and seniority. Children are expected to obey their parents. The value of "respect" between unequal status members (for example, young siblings respecting and obeying their older siblings) in the family is taught at a young age. Parents and grand-parents assume the authority roles in the family decision-making process. Similarly, in large power distance work situations, the power of an organization is centralized at the upper management level. Subordinates expect to be told what to do, and the ideal boss plays the benevolent autocratic role. Large power distance index values are found, for example, in Japan, Malaysia, Mexico, Venezuela, and many Arab countries (Hofstede, 1991). Table 2.2 displays difference between small and larger power distance cultures.

Table 2.2

DIFFERENCES BETWEEN SMALL AND LARGE POWER DISTANCE CULTURES

Small Power Distance	Large Power Distance
Inequalities among people should be minimized	Inequalities among people are both expected and desired
Privileges and status symbols are frowned upon	Privileges and status symbols for managers are both expected and popular
Narrow salary range between top and bottom of organization	Wide salary range between top and bottom of organization
Students are expected to demonstrate their knowledge and command of the subject matter, participate in discussions with the teacher, and even challenge the teacher	Students are expected to be modest, polite, and respectful by allowing the teacher to lead the class
All should have equal rights	The powerful have privileges
Certain distrust for authority is shared	Respect for authority and authority viewed as desirable and beneficial

Source: Adapted from Hofstede (1991)

Uncertainty Avoidance   The third dimension is **uncertainty avoidance, which** is "the extent to which the members of a culture feel threatened by uncertain or unknown situations" (Hofstede, 1991, p. 113). People in low uncertainty avoidance cultures are open to change, believe that the fewer rules the better, and are tolerant of diversity and innovation. In family situations, children are taught broad rules about dangers and taboos, but are encouraged to be open to new experiences and people. At school, teachers are leaders, but do not have to know all the answers and encourage students to explore new ideas. Low uncertainty avoidant cultures include Denmark, Sweden, Great Britain, the United States, Hong Kong, and Singapore. In contrast, people in high uncertainty avoidance cultures are conservative, have formal rules, and are less tolerant of deviant ideas or innovation. In the family, children are taught to avoid new people, and truth tends to be much more certain than in low uncertainty avoidance cultures. At school, teachers are all knowing, and the classroom environment is highly structured for students to learn. High uncertainty avoidant cultures include Greece, Belguim, France, Japan, Spain, Guatemala, and Turkey. A summary of the differences between low and high power distance cultures is displayed in Table 2.3. A key way to think about uncertainty avoidance is whether difference is seen as dangerous (high uncertainty avoidance) or curious (low uncertainty avoidance).

Table 2.3

DIFFERENCES BETWEEN LOW AND HIGH UNCERTAINTY AVOIDANCE CULTURES

Low Uncertainty Avoidance	High Uncertainty Avoidance
Comfort in ambiguous situations and with unfamiliar risks	Acceptance of familiar risks; fear of ambiguous situations and of unfamiliar risks
What is different is curious	What is different is dangerous
Few and general laws and rules	Many and precise laws and rules
Students comfortable with open-ended learning situations and concerned with good discussions	Students comfortable in structured leaning situations and concerned with right answers
Teachers do not have to know all the answers	Teachers are supposed to have all of the answers
Low stress and subjective feeling of well-being	High stress and subjective feeling of anxiety
Lenient rules for children on what is dirty and taboo	Tight rules for children on what is dirty and taboo
No more rules than absolutely necessary	Emotional need for rules even if they will never work

Source: Adapted from Hofstede (1991)

Masculinity-Femininity   The fourth dimension is **masculinity-femininity.** This dimension focuses on the extent to which a society stresses achievement or nurture (Hofstede, 1991). This dimension was labeled masculinity-femininity to reflect gender role differences in Hofstede's study of employees at IBM. The labels themselves reflect gender bias in what it means to be masculine or feminine. Masculinity "pertains to societies in which social gender roles are clearly distinct…; femininity pertains to societies in which social gender roles overlap" (Hofstede, 1991, p. 82). Masculine cultures focus on achievement and material success; men are seen as assertive and tough while women are seen as nurturing and modest. At work and school, competition is encouraged and brilliance appreciated. In families, men deal with facts and women deal with feelings. Conflict is resolved by "fighting things out." Masculine cultures include Mexico, Japan, Austria, Italy, Great Britain, the United States, and the Philippines. Feminine cultures emphasize caring and nurturing behaviors, sexuality equality, relationships, and equal gender roles. Both men and women are supposed to be assertive and nurturing in family, work, and school settings. Conflicts are resolved through compromise and negotiation. In feminine cultures, gender roles overlap so that men and women have similar jobs and communication styles. Feminine cultures include the Scandinavian nations (for example, Denmark and Norway), Costa Rica, Chile, and Thailand. Table 2.4 summarizes some differences between feminine and masculine cultures.

Short-Term/Long-Term Orientation   The last dimension is **short-term versus long-term orientation.** "Long Term Orientation stands for the fostering of virtues oriented towards future rewards, in particular perseverance and thrift. Its opposite

Table 2.4

DIFFERENCES BETWEEN FEMININE AND MASCULINE CULTURES

Feminine	Masculine
Focus on sexual equality, nurturance, quality of life, supportiveness, and affection	Focus on achievement, competitiveness, assertiveness, strength, and material success
Both boys and girls are allowed to cry but neither should fight	Girls cry, boys don't; boys should fight back when attacked, girls shouldn't fight
Dominant values in society are caring for others and preservation	Dominant values in society are material success and progress
Everybody is supposed to be modest	Men are supposed to be assertive, ambitious, and tough; women are supposed to be tender and to take care of relationships
Average student is the norm	Best student is the norm
Managers use intuition and strive for consensus	Managers are expected to be decisive and assertive

Source: Adapted from Hofstede (2001)

pole, Short Term Orientation, stands for the fostering of virtues related to the past and present, in particular, respect for tradition, preservation of 'face' and fulfilling social obligations" (Hofstede, 2001, p. 359). With a short-term orientation, there is a great focus on going after what you want now. The focus is on the bottom line and communicating in a strategic manner to meet those goals. With a long-term orientation, there is a focus on the long-term future and possibly on short-term goals. Communication is centered on relationship building. Countries that tend to have a short-term focus include Pakistan, Canada, the United States, Great Britain, and the Philippines. Countries that tend to have a long-term focus include China, Japan, South Korea, Brazil, and India. Table 2.5 contrasts these two orientations.

In summary, the social scientific perspective views culture as a set of broad patterns that can compare and contrast people who belong to national, racial, and geographic groups. Hofstede's (2001) study of IBM employees provides a key exemplar of how social scientists approach culture, although other approaches exist as well. Among social scientists in general, individualism-collectivism and power distance are the concepts used most frequently in the intercultural communication literature, and thus these concepts will be used more frequently than uncertainty avoidance, masculinity-femininity, and short-term/long-term orientation throughout this book.

CRITICAL: CULTURE AS SITES OF STRUGGLES   From the critical perspective, culture is a site of power struggle that involves competing interests and a multitude of meanings; therefore, culture also reflects the structural and material disparities that shape our everyday engagement with members of different cultural groups. The focus of critical scholars is to identify how culture is used to privilege and reinforce the power of certain groups at the expense of other groups. There is no single critical theory, but different scholars working within this broad perspective are united by some similar

Table 2.5

DIFFERENCES BETWEEN SHORT-TERM AND LONG-TERM ORIENTATIONS

Short-Term	Long-Term
Emphasis on quick results	Emphasis on persistence
Status not a major issue in relationships	Relationships ordered by status
Personal steadfastness and stability important	Personal adaptability important
Face-saving is important	Face-saving is common but seen as a weakness
Spend	Save, be thrifty
Bottom line important	Relationships and market position important
Belief in absolutes about good and evil	Good or evil depends on circumstances

Source: Adapted from Hofstede (2001)

philosophical assumptions, goals, principles, and concepts. In the next section, I briefly introduce the critical commonalities as they relate to intercultural communication.

A major source of theoretical and methodological influence is Western Marxism (Martin & Nakayama, 1999). Early interests focused on understanding the complexity of power relations in society and criticism of domination of some people by others through various practices. Much of this work takes the form of an ideology critique in which the focus has been on identifying problems (scholars call this problematizing) in cultural relations and lived experiences from both macro and micro perspectives of ideology. **Ideology** is the worldview of a group of people. Macro perspectives emphasize political ideologies and their oppressive function as they manifest in different cultures and co-cultures. The micro perspective focuses on ideology as distorted communication. In this manner, those with the dominant worldview (that is, the people who have most power) distort communication to get those who have less power to accept the dominant worldview as their own (Habermas, 1987). Immigration issues are examples of ideological critique in intercultural communication. Many people in power want (and try to create laws to enforce) immigrants to assimilate to a society (for example, learn the language and accept the cultural practices as their own). From a critical perspective, the strategic communication represented by the dominant worldview is distorted because assimilation benefits those in power more than those not in power. Those not in power give up their culture and try to compete in a culture with rules that are strange to them. Those who do assimilate tend to be better at competing for jobs than those who do not assimilate, but also experience a loss of culture. Those in power benefit because without having to do any work, they gain access to many of the material benefits that an immigrant workforce brings (such as low-cost goods and services). See the story in Box 2.6.

Given the interest in critical studies to unmask all forms of domination as they occur in everyday social relations, critical researchers invest in the notion of their knowledge as having the potential to reform the investigated social/cultural conditions (Moon, 1996). Therefore, the researchers have much power over the researched, especially in the ability to incorporate the voices and experiences of the researched in the already privileged vocabulary of the researchers. From this perspective, the critical scholar emphasizes who is (not) studied and for what purpose. A number of understudied groups exist in intercultural communication. In North America, American Indians, Alaska Natives, and First Nations (Canada) are understudied groups. In terms of nations, very little research has been conducted about African nations, South and Central American nations, and Middle Eastern nations (for example, Iran, Jordan). The critical scholar views this lack of scholarship as indicative of the "worth" that mainstream researchers place on them because of their economic and political power (notice that most of the groups are developing nations or impoverished communities). The result is to further marginalize these groups and reinforce the perception of worth.

A third principle is that critical scholars want to recognize diversity of experiences and acknowledge the existence of paradoxes, contradictions, ironies, and ambivalence rather than simply focus on consistent patterns, as the social science perspective does

Box 2.6 Voices: A Story of Assimilation

Carlos immigrated to the United States from Mexico when he was very young. His parents wanted him to have the best opportunity to succeed in life, and they felt that meant having him grow up in the United States, even if they were illegal immigrants. They worked at several low-paying jobs to make sure that Carlos was taken care of. They encouraged him to learn English, and he became fluent quickly. They encouraged him to study hard and get good grades, which he did. He was very successful in school and was often the best in his class. He grew up in East Los Angeles among working-class families, many recent immigrants from Mexico. He endured taunts and teasing from his Mexican American peers who said that he was an oreo (a derogatory term to say he was dark on the outside and white on the inside) and simply wanted to show everyone up. He was also teased by African American and White American students who made fun of his accent. When he talked to his parents, they told him that he should be proud of being Mexican and American and that doing well in school was not showing people up, but helping to support his culture and family. Further, people from other cultures would accept him so long as he was

successful. He persevered without having a lot of friends and ended up being the first in his family to graduate from a university—in fact, he received an advanced degree in business. He became quite successful in his career in marketing, especially focusing on Hispanic, Mexican, and Latin American populations. He took care of his parents, buying them a house and making sure they could finance and took care of all of their expenses. He married a White woman and had several children. Carlos and his wife decided to teach their children a little about Mexican culture, but not necessarily to be bilingual—they could make their own choice when they were older.

1. What would you have done if you were in Carlos' position? His parents' position?
2. How did the following parties in this story benefit (or not) from what happened: a) Carlos' parents, b) Carlos, c) the Mexican immigrant population in East Los Angeles, d) the business that Carlos works for, e) Mexican American culture, and f) U.S. culture?
3. What cultural ideologies can you see expressed in this story?

(Deetz, 2001; Martin & Nakayama, 1999). Some critical researchers seek to construct spaces for alternate voices and perspectives, as well as alternate vocabularies, to capture the complexity of everyday human experiences. For example, certain groups may wish to be identified by a particular label that group members have created rather than one that is provided to them by the mainstream culture (for example, Black vs. Negro in the 1960s civil rights movements in the United States). The purpose of these alternative voices and vocabularies is to provide a source of power for marginalized groups, for the power to control language and the messages that are sent is a great one. If you control the vocabulary, you control how the game is played. Additionally, the power to have one's voice heard (rather than being muted or silenced) is important as well (Clair, 1998).

CONCEPT CHECK   Each of the three approaches to the study of culture provides different insights about the cultural layer of intercultural communication. The interpretive perspective emphasizes shared ways of speaking as the critical component of culture. The social scientific perspective emphasizes the comparison and contrast of values and communication behavior among people who belong to particular cultural groups (usually national cultures, but also racial and ethnic groups). The critical perspective emphasizes societal structures and histories (for example, who has political power and wealth) among people and seeks to unmask the domination of one group by another. Thus, culture is a site of contest and struggle between groups. As mentioned in Chapter 1, none of these perspectives is wholly right; each offers certain insights. The interpretive perspective is localized and provides detailed knowledge about a particular group. The social science perspective helps to compare cultures. The critical perspective reminds us that we do not live in an equal world and that negative acts such as discrimination and prejudice have key impacts on people. The commonality among these perspectives is that they describe a "larger group of people" that shares the culture to a certain degree (as noted in the definition in Chapter 1). This layer frames the remaining layers of intercultural communication.

Connecting the Layers

The possible connections among the layers are great. We have already discussed the possibility of both top-down and bottom-up effects. The result of the top-down or bottom-up influence, however, is not uniform. Figures 2.2a and 2.2b show two possible results. In Figure 2.2a, the circles representing the four layers overlap greatly. In this manner, the individual being represented has a subjective culture that is consistent with the larger culture (for example, interdependent and vertical self in a collectivistic, large power distance culture). Additionally, the family and organizational socialization reinforces the cultural values. Notice that the overlap is not perfect as no individual is the perfect exemplar of a culture. Figure 2.2b demonstrates a different outcome in which the individual's subjective culture is different than the larger culture (independent and horizontal self in a collectivistic, large power distance culture). The family and organizational socialization also is distinct from the cultural values. Notice that the circles

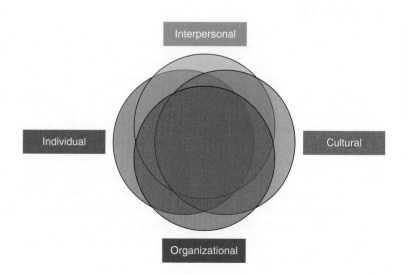

Figure 2.2
Venn
Diagrams of
Connection
among Layers

a. Overlapping
   Layers

Figure 2.2
(*continued*)
b. Divergent
Layers

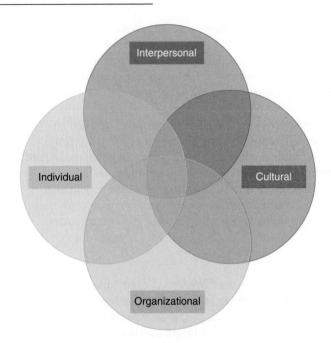

still overlap, as we cannot help but be impacted by the larger culture to a certain degree. Additionally, we negotiate the degree of cultural fit and identity (Chapter 3) within a cultural framework. Thus, we might be different from the larger culture, but we still receive cultural socialization and define ourselves within this larger culture. If you were to map out the four layers for yourself, what would it look like?

SUMMARY

Returning to the opening story: There are examples of all four layers of intercultural communication in this case. At the cultural layer, historical racial relations have often been negative in the Southeastern United States. The larger historical context includes negative relations stemming from slavery, segregation, and the civil rights movement in the 1950s and 1960s. That the legal system tried an African American teen as an adult with an all-White jury is evidence of inequities in the legal system. At the organizational level, Jena High School is mostly White. The leadership of the school (at least the school board members) minimized the effects of a hate crime and did little to punish the offenders. Thus, the organizational culture toward minority groups was negative. At the interpersonal layer, there were some media reports that there was not a lot of integration of White Americans and African Americans prior to the incident. Further, racial tensions were high before the beating took place. At the individual layer, there is evidence that some individuals' attitudes were quite negative toward other cultural groups (as demonstrated in the hanging of the nooses and the beating of someone from a different cultural group).

The critical perspective is emphasized in the analysis of this case, as we see the culture as a site of struggle over power and domination, as evidenced in both prior historical relations and in the context of legal battles. The interpretive perspective is illustrated in that the speech codes of White Americans and African Americans in Jena appear to be different. For some African Americans, social justice and defending oneself in the face of oppression are emphasized; for many of the community members, the fact that the students who hung the nooses were not punished created the climate for the beating. Additionally, many felt that the legal system cannot be trusted since it is stacked against African Americans. For some White Americans, the prevalent feeling was that the punishment should fit the crime and that the legal system should do the judging. For these individuals, the beating was much more severe than hanging nooses, and so a severe punishment was warranted. Furthermore, many believed that the legal system should be used to determine justice. It is important to note that not all African Americans or all White Americans shared these perspectives. The social scientific perspective focuses on differences related to power distance. The school board expected the teens to accept their ruling (large power distance) while African American teens wanted a voice before the board to argue their case (small power distance).

Here is the summary of the chapter based on the learning objectives:

- **Intercultural communication as layered.** This chapter introduced the layered approach to intercultural communication. The layered model is based on the social ecological framework, which focuses on how people relate to their contexts or environments. The benefits of such an approach are that it provides a realistic understanding of intercultural communication and does not place the burden solely on individual choices, although it recognizes the importance of individual choices. The challenge is that the model is complex, but then so is intercultural communication.

- **Four layers of intercultural communication.** The model introduces four specific layers: cultural, organizational, interpersonal, and individual. The cultural layer includes definitions and descriptions of culture from three different perspectives (see next bullet). The organizational and interpersonal layers describe the processes by which members are socialized into the culture or away from the culture. The individual layer looks at how subjective interpretations of cultures are illustrated through different types of selves (independent/interdependent and horizontal/vertical).

- **Culture from interpretive, social scientific, and critical perspectives.** The interpretive perspective focuses on culture as a community that shares a code for how to communicate (or speech codes). The social science perspective focuses on culture as comparable patterns of values and behaviors and uses four dimensions to describe these patterns: individualism-collectivism, power distance (large and small), uncertainty avoidance (high and low), and masculinity-femininity. The critical perspective focuses on culture as sites of contested space where one group usually has power at the expense of others. The emphasis of the critical scholar is to identify communication that privileges one group of people at the expense of others and to overcome these discrepancies.

■ **Four layers influence each other.** Bottom-up effects focus on how lower layers influence higher layers. For example, we can consider how individuals can change their relationships, organizations, and societies. Top-down effects emphasize the impact of culture on organizations, interpersonal relationships, and individuals. These bottom-up and top-down effects are not uniform for all people of a culture, as illustrated by Figure 2.2. Specifically, the four layers may form a close fit or be relatively discrepant.

REVIEW QUESTIONS

1. What is the social ecological framework, and why does it reflect a layered perspective of intercultural communication?
2. What are two benefits and two challenges of the layered perspective?
3. Make an argument in favor of or against the following statement: The layered approach provides an ethical orientation toward intercultural communication.
4. What is a top-down effect? A bottom-up effect? Why are both important to understanding intercultural communication?
5. What are the four layers of intercultural communication?
6. Compare/contrast how culture is defined from the interpretive, social science, and critical perspectives.
7. How does the organizational layer relate to culture?
8. Compare/contrast monolithic, plural, and multicultural organizations.
9. Describe the conformity and conversation orientations and how they influence socialization about culture.
10. What is the ecological framework, and how does the individual layer help to avoid it?

EXERCISES

1. Watch the film *Mi Familia* and reflect on how family socialization of culture is not the same for every child in the family. How does this film illustrate the layered perspective?
2. Watch the film *Bend it Like Beckham* for two different examples of conformity orientation families. How does the culture of each family demonstrate differences in how confirmatory orientation is expressed? What are the strategies of the two main characters in "getting their way"?
3. Complete a Venn diagram of your cultural, organizational, interpersonal, and individual layers. Think about the experiences and socialization you have experienced that lead you to draw the figure as you have. How different is this figure from the one you might have drawn five years ago?

CHAPTER 3

Identity

CHAPTER OUTLINE

I. Introduction

II. Characteristics of Identity
   a. Multifaceted
   b. Social and Personal
   c. Salience and Strength
   d. Fluid and Stable
   e. Avowed and Ascribed
   f. Passing and Outing
   g. Performance and Expression
   h. Concept Check

III. Explaining Cultural Identities:
Development, Differentiation,
Negotiation, and Deconstruction
   a. Development of Cultural Identities
   b. Differentiation of Cultural Identities
   c. Negotiation of Cultural Identities
   d. Deconstruction of Cultural Identities
   e. Concept Check

IV. Layers of Identity
   a. Bottom-Up Effects
   b. Top-Down Effects
   c. Challenges and Skills

V. Summary

VI. Review Questions

VII. Exercises

CHAPTER OBJECTIVES

After reading this chapter,
students should be able to

- describe six characteristics of
  identity.

- explain models of identity
  development for minority and
  majority group members.

Identity is complex and includes many
facets. Tiger Woods and Barack Obama have
biracial identities, among other identities.
How do you identify yourself?

- identify the ways that people differentiate their identity from others.
- describe how identity is negotiated
  and the motivations behind identity
  negotiation.

- discuss the role of political and historical factors that shape identity
  development and negotiation.
- explain the bottom up and top-down
  effects of identity.

Introduction

Al is a biracial child—the son of an African American father and an Irish American mother. He had a stable home life and lived in a predominantly White suburb of a large city. His parents loved him very much and raised him to be an American first but also to have strong respect for both his African American and Irish roots. He had a number of friends and was very happy. He had little trouble understanding his identity—he knew he was both Black and White, but really saw himself as racially neutral. His senior year in high school changed that. Early in the year, one of his friends (Jamal), who happened to be African American, was beat up by some new kids at his school. Al and some other kids showed up just as the new kids were leaving, and one of the kids yelled at Al directly "You _____ better watch out." His White friends told him to forget about those "assholes." Unfortunately, he couldn't. Even though he never saw those kids again, he was deeply affected by that moment. He didn't identify with his White friends (even though they remained friends). He tried to connect to his African American friends, but they told him he could pass as White and he really didn't know what it was like being a Black man in this neighborhood. He went away to college and joined the Black Student Union and majored in Africana studies. He studied the history of African Americans and Africans to get a better sense of who he was. His parents encouraged these studies, but also reminded him that he was Irish and American too. He fought with them, telling them they didn't understand (they said they knew very well, being an interracial couple). After several years of this struggle, he began to forge a new identity that recognized all of his roots. He came to this realization by interacting with people from different backgrounds and being open to different perspectives. His coursework also helped; he learned about the history of both African Americans and Irish Americans (he took classes on European history at his parents' urging). He realized that he had some very good friends who were from all cultural backgrounds and that he didn't want to take that for granted. He also decided that he needed to be more direct with all these friends about power in society. He didn't want to force his agenda down people's throats, but he also did not want to avoid situations because they were difficult. So, he took the opportunity to educate his friends about his identity and struggles and to learn from his other friends about their struggles.

Questions: What concepts and models about identity help to explain Al's experiences? What struggles have you faced in understanding your identity?

Who am I? Who are you? The answer to these questions is central to our identity. Answering these questions, however, is difficult because we have multiple identities, depending on particular contexts. Identity is "a person's conception of self within a particular social, geographical, cultural, and political context" (Yep, 1998, p. 79). In other words, identity is a sense of self or who we are in a specific situation.

Identity is socially constructed (Collier & Thomas, 1988; Nance & Foeman, 1998; Spellers, 1998; Yep, 1998). A social construction is created over time and is subjective rather than fixed and objective. A social construction is given meaning through interaction with others. It is not assigned or concrete; rather it is created, reflected, and maintained through interactions among people (Yep, 1998). "We create our identities with those individuals with whom we interact and in the context of specific communication episodes and encounters" (Yep, 1998, p. 81). For example, for a person with a disability, identity does not have a fixed meaning. Rather, what it means to be a person with a disability is created through interactions with others—both those with and without disabilities. Once this identity is created, it does not stay fixed; it is re-created, changed, and maintained via everyday interactions.

This chapter explores the concept of identity and how it is developed and negotiated. The first section of this chapter describes seven characteristics of identity. The second section focuses on explaining how identity is developed, differentiated, negotiated, and deconstructed. Finally, the chapter concludes by describing the layers of identity within the context of the social ecological framework.

Characteristics of Identity

Identity has a number of characteristics. Scholars research these characteristics to understand how people create, negotiate, challenge, and renegotiate identities with other people. Some of their conclusions about identity include the following: a) identity is multifaceted; b) identity consists of social and personal identities; c) identity is salient and can be strong or weak; d) identity is fluid but stable; e) identity can be avowed and ascribed; f) identity includes aspects of passing and outing; and g) identity is expressed and performed in various modes. Let's look at each of these characteristics in more detail.

Multifaceted

When we say that identity is **multifaceted,** it means that people have multiple identities rather than a single identity. In other words, an individual's identity is composed of multiple dimensions, and it is this constellation of identities that makes us who we are.

A quick way to think about the range of your identities is to construct a pie chart of who you are. Simply answer the question "who am I" as many times as necessary. Most students have about 8 to 15 prominent answers to this question. Once you

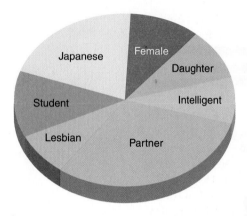

have this completed, examine the pie chart to see if it is an accurate reflection of who you see yourself as. Do the slices represent your strongest identities? Have you positioned similar identities near one another? Have the slices changed recently? Figure 3.1 illustrates a pie chart for a hypothetical student to give you an idea of what this might look like. There are other key characteristics not shown on this pie chart, but it clearly shows the multifaceted nature of the student's identity. See the example of multifaceted multicultural identities in Box 3.1.

Social and Personal

The multiple identities that we have are composed of social (or cultural) and personal aspects (Collier & Thomas, 1988; Imahori & Cupach, 2005). **Personal identities** are unique qualities of ourselves such as personality and personal relationships, whereas **social identities** are aspects we share with other individuals who belong to the same perceived group.

Personal identities might refer to individual personality characteristics, hobbies that you might have, or relationships that you have created. You might see yourself as an athlete, a computer "geek," a stamp collector, or a dancer. You might also consider yourself to be smart, outgoing, shy, or demure. Additionally, the individual relationships that you have created have an identity to them. Some call this a relational identity, but I have chosen to link it to the personal identity because all relationships are unique to you and a very small group of people.

Figure 3.1
Pie Chart of
Identity

Box 3.1 Globalization: Virtually Multicultural

A recent study examined a Web site dedicated to Kimura Takuya, a male Japanese singer and actor. He is very famous in Japan and around Asia. The Web site uses a Bulletin Board System (BBS) for members to post messages, not in real time. The site calls itself "the Official English Kimura Takuya site." Many aspects of globalization and multifaceted identities are present in this site. The members come from 14 different countries and four continents. The language of the postings is English even though not all of the members feel they can express themselves well in English. The members appreciate the international flavor of the site and the openness to other cultures, even though the main reference is to Japanese popular culture. The members recognize the site as being gendered—its members are primarily female and they perceive the discussions as female focused. Finally, the members emphasize the importance of belonging to this community and being part of the identity of Kimura Takuya international fans. When the Web site server went down for some time, members commented about how nice it was to be back and posting messages and catching up with their friends once the site was running again. The site was not simply about getting information about the star, but forming friendships and connections to others who were fans.

Source: Darling-Wolf, 2004

When my brother was younger, he and his friends created a rock band they called "Bonher". For years, the three of them referred to themselves as Bonher and wrote down their band image and name everywhere. This personal identity was a key part of who they were.

Social identities are shared with a larger group of people than just a few friends. As we pointed out in Chapter 1, identities are shared to varying degrees. There are many important social identities including nationality, ethnicity, gender, social class, sexual orientation, religion, and disability. In essence, social identities reflect a sense of belonging to one or more particular group, such as gay, women, Bosnian-Turk, Xhosa, Black, or a member of the deaf community. For example, people with a disability share a common culture and shared social identity from their experiences in interacting with people without disabilities and by navigating a world created for and by people without disabilities (Braithwaite & Thompson, 2000; Coopman, 2003; Moser, 2006). This culture is reinforced by technology that enables and enhances interactions between people with and without disabilities. Such technology includes electric wheelchairs to facilitate movement and communication devices that encode movements (such as typing) into sounds and language. Moser (2006) argued that these devices help to compensate disabilities and facilitate interaction, but also reinforce boundaries between those with disabilities and those without since they mark disabled as less than and in need of compensation. These experiences and technology contribute to the social identity of having a disability.

Salience and Strength

If we have multiple identities, does that mean all of them are equally important and operate at the same time? Or do some identities have more intensity than others? And, do certain identities operate only in certain situations? The concepts of salience and strength provide answers to these questions. Identity *salience* refers to the degree to which an identity is prominent or stands out to us in a given situation (see Box 3.2). While everyone has some sense of social identities, we are not always thinking about each of them (although they still impact who we are). Typically, our identity is salient when it becomes challenged, called into question, or is relevant for the discussion. This might happen when you travel to a different country; have a conversation about gender, sexual orientation, or ethnicity during class; or when you watch a TV program that does not have any people from your cultural group in it.

Identity *strength* or intensity refers to the degree of importance of a particular identity (Collier & Thomas, 1988). Identity intensity varies on a continuum from strong to weak (Phinney, 1991). Individuals with a strong social identity evaluate their group positively, enjoy their membership in the group, and are involved in social practices. Individuals with a weak ethnic identity have little identity interest, tend to identify with another social group (or personal identities), and have little involvement in social practices (Phinney, 1991). Ting-Toomey and her colleagues surveyed nearly 700 college students from four different

Box 3.2 Voices: Salience of Ethnic Identity

Finally, I touched down in Champaign, Illinois. As soon as the doors to the small prop aircraft opened, the Illinois chill that I have heard so much about became a reality. During the drive to Chanute Air Force Base (AFB), I was taken aback by the vast nothingness of the landscape—it was the corn-belt and I had never seen anything like it before in my life....I arrived at my room and unpacked my belongings. I emptied all of my personal belongings out of the duffel bags onto the bed and I noticed that my hair-care products were missing. My hair was a very important aspect of my life at that time (I was a teenager). I thought to myself, "This is a perfect opportunity for me to acquaint myself with Chanute AFB and find the main exchange." I went to the Chanute AFB main exchange to buy some toiletries and African American hair-care products. I arrived at the main exchange and I immediately felt uneasiness—I felt different. There were no familiar faces around me—everything was different, or was it just me? I tried to shake my feeling of uneasiness and proceeded to find my hair-care products. However, aisle after aisle produced no products specifically tailored for African Americans. My dismay was compounded by the apparent lack of African American workers at the main exchange who would have been able to help me. The only items that had a tinge of African American culture were the token *Jet* and *Ebony* magazines that are ubiquitous in all convenience

stores. At that particular moment, I realized I was different.

Being reared in New York City, there was always a wide array of persons from different ethnic groups. In addition, the exposure I had to the divergent views and cultures that exist in New York had a profound impact on my identity. I rarely thought of myself in the context of being different; I was just one of the kids on the block who was African American....This is not to say that I know nothing of African American history. The civil-rights movement and the struggles of the past were common knowledge in my household. My parents were from the South (North Carolina). Although they did not have stories about lynchings and segregation, they always stressed that "everyone knew their place" in the South, and very rarely did anyone venture outside of it. Furthermore, my parents told me, "There will be a time in your life when you are all alone; there will be a time when there are no other 'Black people' around you. When that time comes, be 'cognizant of your actions,' for everything you do will be scrutinized." From that peculiar day in the main exchange, all those things my parents stressed became a reality, and I have been since very cognizant of my actions. The feeling of constant scrutiny can be an unnerving experience for anyone to endure.

Source: Bailey & Oetzel (2004, pp 218–219)

ethnic groups in the United States to determine which groups had the strongest ethnic and cultural identities. They asked the students to answer over 50 questions about their degree of identification toward the larger U.S. culture and their particular ethnic culture. For example, they asked them if they agreed with statements such as "Most of my friends are from my own ethnic group" and "I see myself as a member of the larger U.S. culture." They found that African Americans have a stronger ethnic identity than Asian Americans, European Americans, and Latin Americans, but also that European Americans have a lower ethnic identity than Asian Americans and Latin Americans (Ting-Toomey et al., 2000). Further, African Americans have a weaker national cultural identity than any of the other three groups. Researchers have found that European Americans often practice "symbolic ethnicity" because of their ability to choose ethnic identity or not. European Americans can select a few symbolic elements of ethnicity (such as celebrations) because ethnicity is peripheral to their lives (Alba, 1990; Waters, 1990). It is taken for granted and hidden in ways that are not possible for members of other ethnic minorities (Waters, 1990), who can experience oppression and power struggles in society.

The salience and strength of identity can also be illustrated visually. Figures 3.2a and 3.2b present two pie charts for a single person, illustrating that one of the slices is more salient than the other. In Figure 3.2b, the African American identity is moved outside the pie to illustrate its salience. This might represent the story told by the student in Box 3.2. However, 3.2a represents identity in a different situation. Notice that the father identity is more salient in this situation and that the size of the slices has changed because the strength of the identity has changed in that particular situation. The figures help to illustrate the fluid nature of identity as well, which is discussed next.

Fluid and Stable

One question about identity that intrigues scholars is whether identity is stable and enduring or whether is it fluid and changing. The answer is that it is both. Over time, social identities change and endure due to a variety of historical, political, and social influences. For example, one recent study (Rao, Singhal, Ren, & Zhang, 2001) found that the self-conception of the Chinese appears to be in transition. The researchers in China (half in urban areas and half in rural areas) and interviewed 20 additional Chinese international students. They asked them to fill out a self-construal assessment (like that in Chapter 2) and answer questions about their notions of self and what factors influence those notions. Traditionally, Chinese people were considered collectivistic with an interdependent self-construal and a high respect for authority based on Confucian values (Rao et al., 2001). However, the participants in this study reported stronger independence on the self assessment than expected, and interviewees reported a willingness to ignore voices of authority if they conflicted with personal and career goals. These interviewees still reported a desire for harmony and collective goals in most situations. Three factors explain this transition. First, the Cultural Revolution in China (1966–1976) encouraged people to not accept authority for authority sake. Second, many young Chinese are moving from small villages to the urban business centers for career development. They are forgoing some of their cultural traditions for independence and

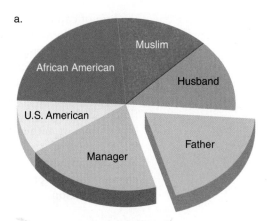

a.

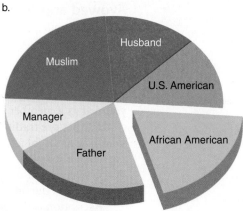

b.

Figure 3.2a and 3.2b. **Salience of Identity**

the lure of capital success. Finally, since China is opening its markets to compete in a global economy, new information and images have filtered into the country that are slowly impacting many Chinese.

Additionally, social identities are fluid in interactions because they are socially constructed; that is, social identities in a particular situation take shape according to whom we are talking with and what we are talking about. However, despite the fluid and changing nature of identity, most of us tend to think that we have some sort of core or authentic identity; that is, what it means to be a member of a particular culture is relatively stable for us and serves as a reference point for our interactions with others. Finding a balance between these two seemingly opposite identity characteristics represents a dialectical tension that is prevalent in much intercultural communication.

Avowed and Ascribed

Identity can be avowed and ascribed. **Avowal** is the process of telling others what identity(ies) you wish to present or how you see yourself. We avow identities through various modes of expression (see next section) as well as by directly stating what these identities are (for example, "I am Russian" or "I am Filipino American"). This process can be both conscious and unconscious. For example, you might identify yourself as a member of a particular ethnic or cultural group and choose to wear clothes that are traditionally associated with that group. On the other hand, you may take your cultural identity for granted and not think about it at all and assume that everyone else operates as you do. This type of unconscious avowal is typical for people who are in the dominant group in a particular culture because their group perspective is the one that is most prominent in the society.

Ascription is the process of assigning in another person what you think his or her identity should be (see Box 3.3). Ascription can occur with the best of intentions through unconscious stereotyping or with malicious intent. The U.S. government used to ascribe identities to people when they classified racial and ethnic groups through the U.S. Census. The Census now allows people to avow certain identities, particularly bicultural and multicultural identities. For example, Jamie is a college student of both Hispanic and White descent. He identifies himself primarily as U.S. American and is proud of both heritages. However, some Hispanic friends think he acts "too White" and call him "oreo" (a derogatory term as noted in Chapter 2). This form of ascription comes from within the culture, and Jamie understands that it is a way for some to show pride in their culture. He tends to laugh it off, but it upsets him because he feels he is Brown enough. People outside one's culture also ascribe identity. A teacher in a classroom might stereotype an Asian American student as a good student and expect him or her to study hard.

Passing and Outing

In all societies, some social identities have more power and prestige than others. As result, some individuals who share physical and linguistic characteristics with the

Box 3.3 Talking about Ethics: Ascribing Identity

In 1955, Rosa Parks rejected the ascription assigned to her when she refused to give up her seat to a White man on a bus in Montgomery, Alabama. She was arrested and tried, which led to one of the largest boycotts in history (the Montgomery Bus Boycott). This boycott helped to launch Martin Luther King, Jr., as a leader in the civil rights movement as he organized the Montgomery Bus Boycott.

Rosa Parks fought against racism as a Black woman whose identity in a public space was ascribed by Whites; that is, she was ascribed a lower or subjugated place than that of Whites. Her actions subverted her ascribed gender and racial identity and renegotiated her identity to what she avowed (that is, she was a person worthy of respect). Her actions are cited as a critical example of standing up for oneself in the face of adversity in order to negotiate one's avowed identity. While most of us do not have to face quite that level of adversity, our social and personal identities are often ascribed to us. Consider the following questions:

1. In what ways have people ascribed an identity to you? How did you feel about this?
2. Why do you suppose that people ascribe identities to others? Does this have a positive function?
3. Do you think it is unethical to ascribe identities and that we should simply let people be who they want to be?
4. What happens if someone is not displaying what we think is an authentic identity? What does it mean to have an authentic identity?

dominant social group try to "pass" as a member of the group (see Box 3.4 on p. 64). Their goal often is to be associated with prestige and power or to avoid marginalization and discrimination (Land & Kitzinger, 2005; Shugart, 2003). For example, some homosexuals hide their sexual identity at work in order to avoid workplace discrimination (Catalyst, 2004). Others do so for strategic reasons in order to gain acceptance and enhance performance, such as Ellen DeGeneres—a comedian who is a lesbian but who passed for a number of years as heterosexual before "coming out" (Shugart, 2003). Coming out is a very difficult decision and process to negotiate for many gays and lesbians (Land & Kitzinger, 2005).

Outing refers to expressing one's "true" identity such as "coming out of the closet" for homosexuals or having one's "true" identity exposed to others ("being outed"). Being outed usually results from ill will from another person who wants to expose the person as a fraud and remove any privilege gained. Coming out is usually a choice to express pride in one's identity and to accept oneself (Land & Kitinger, 2005).

Performance and Expression

Identity is expressed through a variety of nonverbal and verbal messages. Our appearance (dress, hairstyle, jewelry, piercings, and tattoos) and communication style reflect who we see ourselves as and are constitutive of (that is, help to create) cultural identity; that is, if a group of people consistently use particular messages of identity, these messages create cultural identity and are performances of identity. Communication scholars often focus on core symbols, labels, rituals, and language as key aspects that constitute and perform identity.

Box 3.4 Layered Effects: *Zainichi* Koreans Passing and Outing

Zainichi Koreans are individuals, and their descendants, who voluntarily and involuntarily relocated from the Korean Peninsula to Japan during the colonial period (1910–1945). More than a million Koreans were forcefully brought to Japan in the late 1930s due to the labor shortage caused by the war, and many of them remained in Japan as permanent residents when the war ended in 1945. *Zainichi* Koreans, the largest non-Japanese ethnic group in Japan, have struggled with discrimination and marginalization in society and have experienced constant tension between assimilation and separation. To deal with these issues, many *Zainichi* Koreans choose to "pass" as Japanese. Most younger and second-generation *Zainichi* Koreans were born in Japan, speak fluent Japanese, and look Japanese; it is difficult to distinguish *Zainichi* Koreans from Japanese as long as they use a Japanese alias (Fukuoka & Kim, 1997). On the other hand, those who have a strong Korean ethnic identity are more likely to choose "coming out" to confront the issue of discrimination and marginalization by using their true Korean name in public, speaking Korean, and not hiding their *Zainichi* Korean status in society (Matsunaga, 2007; Matsunaga & Torigoe, in press).

That *Zainichi* Koreans have to choose to pass or to come out in their interactions with mainstream Japanese demonstrates the layered effects of history and politics on identity. Historically, *Zainichi* Koreans have held a lower social status in Japanese society. They were not allowed to be Japanese citizens but rather only permanent residents—a clear political move to not "lower the quality of a homogeneous society" even though they were forced to reside in Japan. Thus, passing and outing have a basis in power. Those of us who are part of dominant social groups do not have to worry about passing or outing. Our identity is accepted as is.

Core symbols are messages that signify the central issues of identity (Hecht, Ribeau, & Collier, 1993). For example, five core symbols have been identified for African American identity: sharing, uniqueness, positivity, realism, and assertiveness (Hecht et al., 1993). Sharing reflects collectivism or the valuing of the group whereas uniqueness reflects individualism or the valuing of individual difference. African American identity is a process of managing the dialectic of paying homage to the group (family) and the individual person. Further, African American identity stresses a positive and emotional outlook on life (positivity) juxtaposed with a strong grounding in reality (realism). Finally, assertiveness means standing up for oneself in the face of oppression.

Labels are the terms that we used to describe our identities. Labels can express relationships within a culture. For example, in the South African ethnic group Xhosa, parents' labels change from their name to a title associated with their children. When a child is born, a father becomes "tata-ka-Phola," which, literally translated, means father of Phola. In Xhosa, the label reflects the importance of relationships in defining oneself. With particular cultural and ethnic groups, different labels express different viewpoints about cultural identities. For example, "Hispanic" is the designation the U.S. government uses (ascription) for people whose origins are in Spain or the Spanish-speaking countries of Latin America and the Caribbean, or persons who identify themselves as Spanish, Spanish American, Hispanic, Hispana(o), or

Latina(o). It is also chosen (avowal) by people who wish to emphasize their Spanish roots, such as families in northern New Mexico who trace their roots to Spain more than 400 years ago. Latina(o) is chosen by people who want to emphasize their roots in Latin American. Other people in this ethnic group emphasize their country/commonwealth of origin such as Mexican, Cuban, or Puerto Rican. Certain others emphasize both country of origin for their family and also their ties to the United States by choosing labels such as Mexican American or Cuban American. Finally, others select Chicana(o), emphasizing a political activism perspective about their Mexican American heritage.

Rituals are communal activities that perform and reflect cultural identity. Rituals are a structured sequence of actions that honor something sacred such as a person, relationship, religious icon, or culture (Philipsen, 1987). Rituals are organized in a particular sequenced manner that is recognizable to members of the same culture. Rituals can be formal ceremonies such as religious ceremonies or weddings, but also informal conversations (see Box 3.5).

Language is another critical mode for expressing cultural identity. For many people, a key sign of cultural identity and personal comfort is speaking their native language. People who are bilingual or multilingual often reflect on how good it feels to return home and speak their native tongue. The sounds and lilt of one's native language provides a sense of place and comfort because it is a reflection of cultural identity. In fact, for bilingual individuals, speaking in the native language tends to reflect values associated with their culture. For example, one study has shown that bilingual students in Hong Kong who speak both English and Cantonese expressed more traditional Chinese values when taking a test in Cantonese than when taking the same test in English (Yang & Bond, 1980).

The corollary, the loss of one's language, is also a factor in cultural identity. Parents who see themselves from a traditional culture often lament the fact that their children grow up to speak only the mainstream language and turn their back on their culture. To be fair, many people in the United States feel they identify with their

Box 3.5 Voices: A Conversational Ritual in Filipino Culture

Many Filipinos thrive on throwing and attending parties. In these venues, a particular practice related to eating food may be observed, although it is never articulated openly. Food is always plentiful at these parties, and Filipinos are usually not shy about eating their share. However, a dilemma presents itself when it is time to empty the plate. Filipinos normally do not take heed/notice who eats what and how much until only one piece or a small portion remains on the plate. When this time comes, a discussion arises about who should eat the last piece. No one will offer to take the last piece because each individual at the party feels it is inappropriate to do so; the point is that one piece or a small portion should be left for somebody else. Consequently, the argument or the discussion as to who should eat the last portion almost always remains unresolved. As a result, one may observe that, for every plate or serving placed on the table, one last piece of chicken or a small serving of noodles is left untouched.

traditional culture even though they only speak English. However, many feel they are missing a key part of culture. In New Mexico, tribal leaders of the American Indian pueblos and reservations place a great deal of emphasis on preserving language and culture for their communities. Many tribal languages are only oral languages and thus the preservation of the language is contingent on having the members of the tribe pass it on from generation to generation. Even those whose language is written (for example, Navajo) are concerned with passing their language to the next generation. They feel the language is key to preserving culture, and thus it is a vital characteristic. American Indians are not unique in their concern about preserving language, as it is a factor in many parts of the world including (but not limited to) Lituanian Americans (Kelly & Nagel, 2002), Tetouans in Morocco (Sayahi, 2005), Anglo-Nigerian Pidgin (Mann, 2000), and Wolof, Pulaar, Seereer, Mandinka, Joola, and Soninke in Senegal (Ngom, 2004). In the following pages, this chapter will revisit many other factors about language and identity including ethnolinguistic vitality, media, and language policies.

Concept Check

This section reviewed seven characteristics or properties about identity: a) multifaceted, b) social and personal, c) salience and strength, d) fluid, but stable, e) avowed and ascribed, f) passing and outing, and g) performance and expression. These seven properties provide a general description about identity and serve as concepts for explaining what happens as we interact with others who share our cultural identity or some form of it or who come from a different set of cultural identities. The next section examines theories and models that explain how identities are developed, how we differentiate our identities from others, how we negotiate our identities, and how we can deconstruct identities to understand how power and privilege play a role in these processes.

Explaining Cultural Identities: Development, Differentiation, Negotiation, and Deconstruction

We do not create our identity in a vacuum. Many interesting factors are associated with the development and negotiation of identity. From the layered perspective, we can consider historical, societal, psychological, and communication factors in the creation, maintenance, and reflection of identity. This section examines four processes associated with identity using particular theories and models. First, the text describes several models that explain how particular cultural identities are developed. Second, it illustrates how we differentiate our cultural identities from others, particularly in the sense of creating an "us versus them" perspective. Third, we look at several ways in which we negotiate our cultural identities, particularly with people from different cultural groups. Finally, we deconstruct various processes of identity to illuminate some of the historical and contextual factors that reinforce power and privilege around identity.

Development of Cultural Identities

Models of identity development describe the various stages or phases that people go through in the process of developing cultural identity. As with any model, these models describe the experiences that many people go through, but they may not be accurate for everyone. Additionally, some people spend a great deal of time in a particular stage while others might go through that stage rather quickly. Further, some people may not reach the final stage and instead remain in an earlier place. Finally, some people might cycle back to earlier stages or skip a stage altogether. Thus, you should keep in mind that these models provide a general description of how cultural identity develops, but do not necessarily show how they should progress. This section describes three models of cultural or social identity. The first is a general model for all people. The second is a model for minority identity development. The third is a model for majority identity development. By minority, I am referring to a group of people who have less economic and political power than the majority group. Many times this includes being in a numerical minority as well. For example, African Americans, Asian Americans, Hispanic Americans, American Indians, homosexuals, and people with disabilities are minorities both in numbers and in power in the United States, compared to White Americans, heterosexuals, and people without disabilities. However, it is not always the case that the people with less power are in the numerical minority. For example, Sunni Muslims in Iraq under Saddam Hussein were the numerical minority, but the majority group in terms of power, while Blacks in South Africa are the majority in terms of numbers, but minority in terms of power (especially under apartheid).

GENERAL MODEL OF CULTURAL IDENTITY   A general model of cultural identity identifies three stages of development: unexamined cultural identity, cultural identity search, and cultural identity achievement (Phinney, 1993). During the **unexamined cultural identity** phase, young children (or perhaps young adults in a culturally homogeneous environment) do not question their cultural identity. They learn about their culture from their parents, but take it for granted and are not aware of cultural differences. During the **cultural identity search,** individuals become aware of cultural differences and begin a continuous process of looking for information and explanation about their culture and other cultures in order to define their identity. Their awareness may be triggered by a conflict, an act of discrimination, a mediated image that makes difference salient, or an interaction with someone from a different culture. In this search process, they reflect on what they learn and evaluate how they fit within their various groups. This evaluation may lead to an identity crisis in which their perceived notion of their cultural identity does not fit with how others see them, particularly in terms of physical characteristics and behaviors. The final phase, called **cultural identity achievement,** occurs when individuals feel they have a good grasp of their cultural identity; that is, they have reached a sense of clarity and confidence about their identity. Adults continue to reflect and evaluate, but, when encountered with negative messages about their cultural identity, they are strong enough to deflect such comments and not internalize them.

MINORITY GROUP MODEL OF CULTURAL IDENTITY   The general model of cultural identity provides a good description of the basic processes, but it does not reflect the fact that societies have groups in power. Cultural identity development for minority group members is different from that of majority group members because of that power. One model of minority cultural identity development includes four phases: pre-encounter, encounter, immersion-emersion, and internalization-commitment (Helms, 1993). The pre-encounter phase is when the minority group member is unaware of the cultural differences or his or her cultural identity, or is simply not interested. This person may have grown up separate from the majority group or simply was raised with the values of the majority culture in order to fit in and blend. These individuals tend to identify themselves as a member of the larger culture (such as Canadian, Chinese, American, or straight) or by their personal identities. Essentially, the person conforms to the majority culture. The encounter stage is a marginal identity phase when a new cultural identity is awakened because of a shattering event such as experiencing racism or being labeled as different. Often, this is a negative event directed at the person, who comes to realize that he or she cannot pass or be fully accepted in the majority world. The immersion-emersion stage often reflects a strong minority cultural identity accompanied by a rejection of the majority culture. The person withdraws to the safe confines of the minority culture and emphasizes all cultural elements (dress, food, friends, and so on). The person will learn more about her culture and the history of its people. Finally, the internalization-commitment phase occurs when the person develops a clear and confident sense of her cultural identity, but also is able to develop genuine contacts with members of the majority culture. The person develops a strong sense of cultural identity, but also a respect for other cultural groups. Experiences of racism (and other "isms" such as sexism, ageism, heterosexism) and discrimination are dealt with in reconstructive ways rather than rejecting all members of other cultural groups.

MAJORITY GROUP MODEL OF CULTURAL IDENTITY   The majority identity model has both similarities and differences with respect to the minority identity model. Its five phases include: unexamined identity, acceptance, resistance, redefinition, and integration (Hardiman, 1994). The unexamined cultural identity phase is similar to the phase in the general model; majority individuals are either not aware of differences or, if they are, they do not create a hierarchy among the differences (that is, no fear or racism). During the acceptance phase, majority members internalize a racist ideology either consciously or unconsciously. They view their own group as superior and believe that minority group members need help to assimilate to the majority culture. At a minimum, they avoid contact with minority group members or take a patronizing stance toward minorities. In some extreme cases, they might actively express sexist or racist attitudes or engage in activities against minority group members. In the third stage, resistance, majority group members shift from blaming minority group members for their problems and place the blame on the majority group. They begin to disassociate with members of their own group and seek out minority group members. The fourth stage begins a period of redefinition, during which majority group members are aware of the dominant ideology of the majority group, but begin to redefine their group in nonracist terms. They see positive aspects about their own culture and feel comfortable being a member of their group. In the final stage, integration, majority group members integrate their cultural identity into all facets of their identity. They recognize their majority group identity, but also appreciate other cultural group identities.

Differentiation of Cultural Identities

As we develop our cultural identities, we learn to differentiate ourselves from others in different cultural groups. During our interactions with members of our own groups and those of others, we learn to distinguish the **ingroup** from the **outgroup** ("us vs. them" or members of our own cultural groups versus those of others). These distinctions are not necessarily positive or negative; however, in many cases, a sense of superiority or ingroup bias or favoritism results. This section describes two related theories that describe the process of differentiation and the reasons we favor the ingroup. The first theory is social identity theory (Tajfel & Turner, 1986), and the second is ethnolinguistic identity theory (Giles & Johnson, 1981).

SOCIAL IDENTITY THEORY   Social identity theory (SIT) focuses on how the social categorization of people into groupings affects interactions between people of different social identities (for example, national or ethnic culture) (Tajfel, 1978). In particular, it emphasizes that people have a desire to enhance their self-image and to differentiate themselves from other groups. Awareness of membership in a social group is the most important factor influencing intergroup behaviors and results in a process of comparing oneself and one's group to others for the purpose of establishing a positive social identity. The desire to achieve a positive social identity results in a positive bias favoring the ingroup (Tajfel & Turner, 1986). Group members achieve this positive identity in several ways including preference and intergroup competition.

SIT explains that individuals with a strong ingroup bias or identification have a preference for, or discriminate in favor of, the ingroup as a result of striving for positive social identity. They view members of the ingroup as more similar to themselves than outgroup members and have loyalty toward the ingroup. To test SIT, researchers frequently use the minimal group technique; this involves allocating resources to two arbitrary social groups, anonymous members of both the ingroup and outgroup. In a minimal group technique, individuals are placed in a hypothetical work group composed of ingroup and outgroup members and assigned an ingroup identity. For example, they might be told that there are two members of their group and three members from another group working together. Then, the individuals allocate rewards to each of the hypothetical group members. The studies demonstrate that the greater individuals' ingroup identification is, the more likely they are to discriminate in favor of the ingroup (Gagnon & Bourhis, 1996; Perreault & Bourhis, 1999); that is, we give more rewards to our ingroup members than the outgroup members for the same level of work.

In addition to ingroup preference, individuals tend to engage in social competition to preserve a positive social identity when interacting with members of outgroups (Turner, 1975). The amount of competition that people engage in is contingent on several factors including competition for resources, unequal status, and imbalance between ingroup and outgroup members. Competition for resources focuses on whether a particular resource is prevalent or not. If resources are scarce, then competition is higher. For example, competition among social groups is down in times of economic prosperity and up in economic recessions. Unequal status refers to the image that a cultural identity has in a society. In general and overall (that is, not any individual's opinion, but rather the society as a whole), the majority group has a high status identity relative to that of the minority group (see Box 3.6). Finally, imbalance between ingroups and outgroups focuses on the actual number of people in a particular interaction ("Am I the only one from my group when there are three people from the other group?").

ETHNOLINGUISTIC IDENTITY THEORY   Related to SIT, ethnolinguistic identity theory (ELIT) focuses on the conditions upon which identity differentiation occurs, particularly around language and identity (Giles & Johnson, 1981). A key concept associated with ELIT is **ethnolinguistic vitality,** which is the extent to which a language is desirable and viable in a society. The conditions that lead toward differentiation of cultural or ethnic identity include the following: a) identifying with an ingroup that considers its language to be important, b) perceiving the groups'

Box 3.6 Layered Effects: Factors Affecting Differentiation

Several researchers have found that minority group members compete with majority group members when they are a numerical minority in a group, but cooperate when they are equal in number or the numerical majority. In contrast, majority group members are not affected by the ingroup/outgroup balance (Espinoza & Garza, 1985; Garza & Santos, 1991). The reason for the difference in competitive behavior from a SIT perspective is that majority groups already have a number of socially valued dimensions along which they can positively differentiate themselves from others such as education and occupation. As a result, they do not have to consider the ethnic minority group members as a relevant group for social comparison and do not feel the need to compete with them. The majority group members do not have to rely explicitly on their ethnic/cultural background, not necessarily because race or ethnic group composition is not important to them, but because the structure, rules, and ideology of the work are set up according to the majority ideology. In contrast, minority group members lack a preexisting positive social identity, and therefore perceive the majority group as a relevant social comparison. Consequently, minority group members feel the need to compete when they are in a numerical minority in a group to achieve a positive social identity. These findings illustrate the importance of the layered perspective of identity—we all do not practice ingroup bias and social competition in the same way. The structures in society encourage competition in different ways for minority and majority group members.

ethnolinguistic vitality as high, c) perceiving boundaries between ingroups and outgroups as closed and hard, d) not identifying with other social categories, and e) perceiving the status of the cultural or ethnic identity as higher than with other social category memberships. The presence of these conditions results in greater differentiation between an ingroup identity and the cultural identity of other groups. However, this differentiation does not necessarily mean a sense of superiority. In fact, some scholars have argued that the more secure individuals' ethnolinguistic identity is, the more tolerant and receptive they are toward members of other groups (Gudykunst, 1988). In contrast, people who perceive low ethnolinguistic identity and vitality experience a threatened identity and thus engage in processes to improve cultural identity, including preference and intergroup competition (Abrams, O'Connor & Giles, 2002).

Some of the factors that impact ethnolinguistic vitality include status, demography, and institutional support. Status refers to the degree to which a language is valued and is spoken in a society. We get indicators of the status of a language if it is an official language (such as French, Dutch, and German in Belguim) and if individuals can conduct business and day-to-day life in the language. Demography emphasizes the number or proportion of people and concentration of people who speak the language in a particular culture, community, or country (see Box 3.7). The vast majority of people in the United States speak English, but Spanish also has a large number of speakers. Further, Spanish is concentrated in certain areas (such as Los Angeles and Miami) but not in others (such as Minneapolis). Finally, institutional support is the degree to which the economic, political, and media institutions support the language. Some indicators of support include whether policies support the language, whether the language is represented in media, and whether people can conduct business in the language.

Negotiation of Cultural Identities

During the processes of differentiation and identity development, we essentially are negotiating our identities with others through our communication. Our interactions with others provide us with the opportunity to reflect our identities to others and create and re-create our desired identities. In the next section, we examine the basic motivations of identity negotiation and some of the challenges we face as we negotiate our identities.

MOTIVATIONS FOR IDENTITY NEGOTIATION   People in all cultures appear to have the same basic set of motivations when they negotiate identities (Ting-Toomey, 2005). Specifically, we all have the need for an identity(ies) that is secure, included, predictable, connected to others, and consistent. These five motivations have some overlap with one another. Security refers to a sense of emotional safeness with others; that is, we feel emotionally stable when we interact with others. Inclusion occurs when others accept us for who we are and when they view our identities as positive. Predictability relates to the certainty we have about our identities during interactions with others. We view this predictability as an indicator of the acceptance we have with others; if our interactions with people from different cultures are predictable,

Box 3.7 Voices: Ethnolinguistic Vitality for American Indians

State Senator Leonard Tsosie, Navajo, from Crownpoint, New Mexico, wrote the following editorial in the *Albuquerque Journal* on June 9, 2006. His letter is in response to a proposed immigration bill in the United States as well as another editorial written by John Dendahl. Dendahl was the leader of the Republican Party in New Mexico at the time.

Native Americans across the country and the state of New Mexico are outraged by the amendment in the Immigration Bill identifying English as the national language. Even as a symbolic message, this is an insult to Native Americans—many of whom remember the abuse they received for speaking their own language—whose languages are indigenous to this country and to the state of New Mexico....

Long before English was first spoken in New Mexico, members of the 19 pueblos and Navajo and Apache tribes spoke their own languages and still do....

The English language itself was developed from different languages. The term "lingua franca," used by John Dendahl in a recent column, refers to a language created from other languages for the purpose of bartering, international commerce, and diplomacy. English serves this purpose well, but New Mexico's indigenous languages have the same value as the English language. And if John Dendahl doesn't like this cultural fact, maybe he could go live someplace else.

Tragically, at this point in time, all Native American languages are endangered. Numerous efforts are taking place to maintain and revitalize our indigenous languages.

In 1990, the U.S. Congress passed the Native American Language Act stating that the status of the cultures and languages of Native Americans is unique and the United

States has the responsibility to act together with Native Americans to ensure the survival of these unique cultures and languages.... (That is the purpose of the New Mexico Indian Education Act, which I sponsored. It went into effect as a state law in 2004. The act reinforces state bilingual laws and the teaching of native languages at the same level and time as the instruction of English to ensure the maintenance of tribal languages.)

To implement the spirit of the law, resources are needed for research, academia, curriculum, and professional development materials. Funding for these resources will be jeopardized if English is established as the national language....

Consider the value of native languages. The loss of linguistic diversity represents a loss of intellectual diversity. Each language is a unique tool for analyzing and synthesizing the world, incorporating the knowledge and values of a speech community. Ignoring the linguistic history of New Mexico is ignoring our rooted identity both as a people and a state...

The federal Native American Languages Act declares that it is the policy of the United States to preserve, protect, and promote the rights and freedom of Native Americans to use, practice, and develop Native American language and supports the use of Native American languages as a medium of instruction for Native American language survival.

This law demonstrates a value for the preservation of indigenous languages because this is our history and this is who we are: a diverse people with diverse languages.

Senator Tsosie's words illustrate how languages that are spoken only by a small number of people still have ethnolinguistic vitality, but they also face challenges. Notice the layered factors that Tsosie calls on to describe the vitality of American Indian languages (such as history, acts, and school practices). Consider these questions:

1. How do you feel about the English-only debate?
2. Should we force people to speak a dominant language even if they have been in the country longer than any other group?
3. What aspects of ethnolinguistic identity and identity differentiation are illustrated in the English-only debate?

Source: Tsosie (2006). Reprinted by permission of Leonard Tsosie, Crownpoint, NM

then we can build trust with them. Connection refers to the quality of relationships we have with others. We want to be able to have meaningful, close relationships with others; the ability to establish such relationships is an indicator of acceptance and trust for our identities. Finally, consistency focuses on the number of cultural routines we experience. Routines allow us to feel safe and connected to others.

While these five motivations are important, they may have some drawbacks. Ting-Toomey (2005) explains that too much security, inclusion, predictability, connection, and consistency leads to a rigid, closed identity that views members of different groups as inferior and unworthy (that is, extreme differentiation). The reason for this is that these feelings only happen when we have total support, and this likely does not happen when we interact with people from different cultural groups. When we do interact with members of different cultural groups, our identities are sometimes questioned, challenged, distrusted, and misunderstood. Thus, intercultural communication provides the opportunity for growth and transformation in our identity development and differentiation. In fact, Ting-Toomey argued that there is an optimal range between these five motivations and their five opposites: security-vulnerability, inclusion-differentiation, predictability-unpredictability, connection-autonomy, and consistency-change. Identity negotiation is a process of managing these five dialectics (or tensions between opposites on a continuum) to the optimal range, which will vary from person to person. The bottom line is that effective management of these dialectics results in being understood, respected, and affirmatively valued (see Figure 3.3 for a model of identity dialectics).

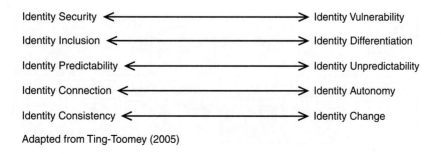

Identity Security ⟷ Identity Vulnerability

Identity Inclusion ⟷ Identity Differentiation

Identity Predictability ⟷ Identity Unpredictability

Identity Connection ⟷ Identity Autonomy

Identity Consistency ⟷ Identity Change

Adapted from Ting-Toomey (2005)

Figure 3.3
Identity
Dialectics

CHALLENGES FOR IDENTITY NEGOTIATION   Being understood, respected, and affirmatively valued makes sense but can present a challenge—both when interacting within our own culture (think about teenagers and parents interacting) and when interacting outside our culture. Differences in cultural values and identities can make the attainment of these three goals difficult. Identity management theory (IMT) (Imahori & Cupach, 2005) describes several challenges that people face during intercultural identity negotiation, particularly when people are meeting for the first time. The first challenge occurs when people from different cultural backgrounds only view their interaction partner as a member of a cultural group and ignore other aspects of his or her identity. This challenge is called **identity freezing** because it limits the other person's opportunity to avow different identities such as personal or relational values. The result is that the person whose identity is frozen feels powerless, trapped, and manipulated. The second challenge is the opposite and occurs when people's cultural identities are ignored and they are treated only as an individual. This challenge is called the **nonsupport problematic** because all people desire to have positive cultural identities, and cultural identities are a key part of who we are. Essentially, these two challenges create a dialectic between supporting others' cultural identities and their personal and relational identities. The third challenge is managing the dialectic between supporting your own cultural identity versus that of the other person (**self-other dialectic**). If you choose to support the other person's cultural identity, you might threaten your own pride and belongingness and vice versa. This challenge is more difficult to manage the more distinct the cultural identities are. Managing these dialectics and challenges is difficult, but necessary to establish positive interpersonal relationships that demonstrate understanding, respect, and affirmation. The final section of the chapter introduces some strategies for managing these challenges.

Deconstruction of Cultural Identities

This final section changes somewhat from the first three. Identity development, differentiation, and negotiation are processes that all people engage in. However, these processes are not equivalent for all people. In the first two sections, we

Figure 3.4
What are some of the ways we freeze other people's identities? What can we do to avoid this challenge to identity? How would you respond to this challenge?
© United Feature Syndicate, Inc.

discussed how minority and majority group members experience development and differentiation differently. This section further deconstructs identity to illustrate that identity is political and that people's cultural identities are not universally accepted and valued. In particular, this section describes some of the historical and societal constraints on identity to illustrate the politics of identity.

Focusing on the politics of identity largely comes from a critical theory perspective. One particular critical theory of cultural identifications (Collier, 2005) demonstrates four key aspects about the politics of identity: a) importance of reflexive dialogue, b) differing levels of agency, c) cultural identities' intersection with historical and societal context, and d) privilege and subjugating ascriptions. First, **reflexive dialogue** focuses on communication with others (and with oneself) to uncover and examine biases, hidden assumptions, and privileges. All of us have biases and stereotypes of other cultural groups. To be effective intercultural communicators and negotiate satisfactory cultural identities, we must be aware of and be honest about these biases. We also have to recognize the privileges that we have in society. Second, **agency** focuses on the freedom to choose action and to enact identity (Collier, 2005). Collier argued that members of different cultural groups have different levels of agency while most people tend to perceive that all people (at least within the United States) have the same level of agency. In particular, Collier noted that members of minority groups in the United States and in other countries (such as Muslims in the United States, Palestinians in Israel, and Blacks in South Africa) take greater risks and experience different and more severe consequences for choosing to speak up and express their preferences and identities. For example, growing up in South Africa during apartheid, Blacks risked their safety by asserting their cultural identities. More subtly, ethnic minorities in Western Europe and the United States can risk promotion and achievement in the workplace if they assert their cultural identities. Many workplaces expect people to suppress their cultural identities for the good of the workplace and employees are viewed as too radical if they assert cultural identity.

Third, cultural identities cannot be separated from the historical and societal context. Who you are is partially derived from current society and how your family was treated in the past. The legacy of slavery in the United States still impacts African Americans today because it framed how society is today. Similarly, the removal of American Indians from their lands to reservations impacts the cultural identities of current American Indians even though they are several generations removed from the events. Further, women not being allowed to vote or have equal rights negatively impacted their status in society and their value in the workplace. Specific events of the past shaped current society, and generations pass on their perspectives about identity. More on this process will be presented in Chapter 12 on historical trauma.

Finally, privilege often results in **subjugated ascriptions,** identities given to others that put them in a lower or inferior position compared to one's own group. Privilege occurs from a particular ideology (or worldview) that is taken as the norm. Typically, this privilege is invisible to insiders of the group. In the United States, Europe, and European colonies (for example, South Africa), this invisible privilege is associated with Whites and is labeled Whiteness:

> Whites as the privileged group take their identity as the norm or standard by which other groups are measured, and this identity is therefore invisible, even to the extent that many Whites do not consciously think about the profound effect being white has on their everyday lives (Martin, Krizek, Nakayama, & Bradford, 1996, p. 125).

Whiteness ideology is expressed in interaction and allows insights into the way that privilege is used to interpret and negatively judge the behavior of others. For example, Collier (2005) provided an example of a White female judge discussing Hispanic women in domestic violence cases:

> I think the Hispanic women are much more passive, and it takes more assistance on the part of the court to bring out the facts of the case. I think that may be due to embarrassment or the acculturation that they're not as important as their male companion assuming the relationship is of that nature (p. 246).

The subjugated ascription is that Hispanic women, because of their culture, are meek and see themselves as less than males in their culture. Additionally, the judge could be saying that she sees these women as less than her because they do not stand up for themselves. The interesting point is that many women of all ethnic groups have trouble going to court and testifying for a number of reasons, including wanting to keep the family together, not wanting their personal business shared with strangers, and stigma from being labeled a "weak woman" (Little & Kantor, 2002; Stephens, 1999).

The notion of Whiteness also impacts members of minority groups, although minority group members appear to recognize the privilege more easily than whites. A Black student from South Africa described Whiteness ideology in his country:

> There are black [sic] people in this country who still worship white [sic] people, still everything white is good. "I want to be like a white person, I want to own a house in a nice suburb and drive a Range Rover."... It's still if you are white, you are good. If you are black, you are probably a thief or rapist or whatever (Collier, 2005, p. 248).

Thus, the student is explaining how Whiteness also affects the viewpoint of minority members who accept it uncritically (also see Box 3.8).

The critical examination of privilege is important for moving beyond Whiteness ideology. Critical examination and reflexive dialogue help to move beyond unfair privilege and work for change, improved intercultural relations, and fairness for all (social justice). Collier (2005) provided an example of self-reflexive dialogue that a White female judge expressed:

> We need to worry about whether we have white [sic] rules or black [sic] rules, not so much in a conscious way.... Sometimes I'll make it personal, it feels very "alright, you go girl!"... but I also feel like my initial gut is, "Good heavens, that's unladylike." And so I think to myself, hmmm, so I expect white women to be ladylike, maybe I think black women shouldn't be so ladylike. You know I've got some categories going here that I need to be pretty aware of to get past that initial gut sense of... is it self-defense? (p. 249).

Box 3.8 Talking about Ethics: Whiteness Ideology

Whiteness can be very controversial. When I bring the notion up in class, students have mixed reactions. Many students of color nod in understanding and validation, while a few suggest that labeling it Whiteness gives more power to Whites than needed (They say, "Why not just call it unearned privilege?"). Still others suggest that we need to get over these past feelings and move forward. White students also have mixed reactions. Some think this is more "political correctness" and think every group has some unearned privilege (especially if they came from a low socioeconomic class). Others realize their privilege and agree with the notion and commit to trying to be more self-reflexive. Still others get the notion, but dislike the label (they too

want to call it unearned privilege). Regardless, the notion of Whiteness makes many students uncomfortable because it deals with issues of power that are not easy to identify. Consider the following questions:

1. Do you feel there is unearned privilege in society?
2. If so, does it make sense to call it Whiteness?
3. What strategies and emotions do you have in response to Whiteness (avoidance, confrontation, feelings of guilt, feelings of hopelessness)?
4. What strategies are most effective in addressing Whiteness?

This judge is at least aware of the privilege and responsibility she has in making a ruling. She recognizes that she has different rules and needs to struggle to be fair in her application of these rules. An obvious next step is to create a larger dialogue so that judges and attorneys can discuss these issues of privilege in order to improve the quality of their rulings and the fairness of the trials. This type of dialogue can be applied to other contexts as well. Can you provide another example of your own that follows Collier's?

Concept Check

This section examined various facets of identity including how it is developed, differentiated, negotiated, and deconstructed. Identity development focuses on the phases that majority and minority groups go through in the development of stable and positive cultural identities. Differentiation occurs in striving for a positive cultural identity and often results in ingroup preference and intergroup competition. Language, through ethnolinguistic vitality, is a critical part in the creation of a positive cultural identity. Identity negotiation centers on the desire to be understood, respected, and affirmed. However, several challenges to identity negotiation such as identity freezing and the nonsupport problematic make the achievement of these desires difficult. Finally, deconstruction of identity examines the politics of identity. This focus describes the invisible privilege that majority groups have compared to minority groups. Majority group members have more agency and the invisible privilege (for example, Whiteness ideology) that creates an unfair playing field and results in minority group members having to take more risks, and facing more severe consequences when they do, than majority group members. This invisible privilege can be very difficult for majority group members to see. Further, this type of privilege is not the same that comes with economic or political privileges directly; it is simply associated with cultural identity. There are poor and rich people in all cultural groups, but when we examine people from the same socioeconomic class, majority group members have more privilege than minority group members.

Layers of Identity

This chapter has presented many layered aspects about identity. A key point is that identity itself has four layers: personal (individual layer), relational (interpersonal layer), organizational (organizational layer), and cultural/social (community/cultural layer) (Hecht, Warren, Jung, & Krieger, 2005). Collectively, these layers make up our identities. In certain situations, the four layers of identity may be consistent with one another. In a different situation, they may be contradictory or inconsistent. This section examines the layers of identity by focusing on bottom-up and top-down effects. Since this chapter focuses on identity as a component of the individual layer, I discuss how identity shapes the other three layers and vice versa. This section concludes with a discussion of the challenges and skills for constructing and supporting cultural identities.

Bottom-Up Effects

Individual identity is directly associated with the various layered identities. Recall the definition of culture in Chapter 1. A key component of this definition is that culture involves a shared identity to varying degrees. Thus, culture is created, in part, by individuals who communicate a shared cultural identity. This is not the only component of culture, however. In like manner, the creation of relational and organizational identities occurs with a collection of people who share an identity to varying degrees.

Individual identities can also have a very different effect on the shared social identities. In some situations, individuals avow an identity that is not consistent with the collectives' perspective. Consider, for example, a second-generation son who expresses a cultural identity that blends traditional culture with that of his adopted homeland. Specifically, in his traditional culture, parents choose whom their children should marry. However, this individual wants to marry someone of his own choice, but from his same cultural background. In this case, his cultural identity and communication about this identity challenges that of his parents. Eventually, the child and parents will negotiate the cultural identity, and change will follow. Similarly, culture changes because individuals challenge traditions with a unique identity, and when a critical mass occurs (that is, a significant number of people share the same perspective), the culture will change. Of course, the culture and the family may try to ascribe the traditional cultural identity to the individual (for example, by insisting that the parents choose the spouse or pointing to the embarrassment the child will cause the family)—to various degrees of success. Thus, the negotiation of identity can take place at various layers of the social ecological framework depending on the context and issue under consideration.

Top-Down Effects

Individuals' identities are shaped by interpersonal, organizational, and cultural/community layers. As the specific models and theories described in this chapter point out, identity is not constructed in a vacuum. We create, negotiate, and reflect our identities through interaction with other people—with both members of our culture and different cultures. Identities are most clearly researched at the interpersonal and cultural/community layers.

At the interpersonal layer, communication and relationships with others—particularly members from different cultural groups—are critical to identity development, differentiation, negotiation, and deconstruction. Interpersonal interactions are critical for identity development models in that they often are the impetus for moving from one phase to another in identity construction. For example, moving from an unaware phase to a cultural search phase is precipitated by some interaction with members from a different cultural group. The differentiation process is often heightened when we interact with members of different cultural groups because of ingroup bias. During identity negotiation, we face certain challenges to achieve identity respect, understanding, and affirmation when we interact with members of different cultural groups. Finally, deconstruction helps to illustrate how privilege and agency are distributed unevenly and how members of majority groups benefit compared to member of minority groups.

At the community/cultural layer, the focus has been on historical context and the media in impacting culture. The critical theory of cultural identifications emphasizes the importance of prior history and social structures as shaping individuals' identities. Essentially, it argues that identities cannot be separated from these experiences. ELIT also emphasizes the importance of institutions, including the media, for supporting languages. For both of these theories, laws are critical to framing privileged identity. For example, in the United States, most states have laws banning homosexuals from marrying. These laws privilege a heterosexual identity. Box 3.9 discusses another such case related to religious culture.

Other research also helps to illustrate how the media can shape cultural identities. This research is critical because the media is a primary form of interaction that many people have with members of different cultural groups. Consistent with SIT, one study examined the news coverage of nonofficial actors (such as businesses, sports teams and celebrities) engaged in international activities from three national newspapers (*La Prensa*—Argentina, *The New York Times*—United States, and *Berlingske Tidende*—Denmark). They had independent coders categorize two years of stories from each newspaper. The study found that the newspapers presented stories about the actors in a manner that reflects favorably on the national self to promote a positive cultural identity (Rivenburgh, 2000). Also consistent with SIT, another study found that White students who are exposed to stereotypical media

Box 3.9 Talking about Ethics: Religious Rituals vs. Federal Laws

Mamie Manneh emigrated from Liberia in Western Africa to the United States in the early 1980s, bringing her religious rituals with her. The rituals were a multifaceted blending of Christianity and tribal customs including eating monkey meat for religious rituals (such as a baptism ceremony). In 2006, Manneh was accused by U.S. customs officials of smuggling monkey meat from Africa's green monkey population into the United States. Federal prosecutors have accused Manneh of threatening conservation efforts designed to protect the monkey population, and also threatening U.S. citizens by risking exposure to heath risks associated with diseases such as Lassa fever, Ebola, SARS, HIV, and monkeypox. Her defense attorneys argue that the demand for monkey meat is too small to have any significant impact. One member of her congregation, Leona Artis, said that the appetite for monkey meat is misunderstood by most in the United States: "Where some people have turkey, we'll have monkey meat. I've been eating it all my life. It's delicious. Baptisms, Easter, Christmas, weddings—all are occasions for eating monkey."

1. Should Manneh be found guilty or are her practices simply freedom of religion and protected by constitutional rights?
2. Does Manneh have a privileged identity in the United States? Explain your answer.

Source: Hays (2007)

representations of Latinos committing criminal acts will engage in greater differentiation in favor of the ingroup (Mastro, 2003). Essentially, these studies help to illustrate that the media reinforce notions of ingroup bias and the desire for a positive cultural identity.

Challenges and Skills

One key to improved intercultural communication is the development and support of cultural identities. However, there are many challenges to developing a positive cultural identity as well as supporting others' cultural identities. The key point to remember in striving for positive identities is that all of us want to be understood, respected, and affirmed. The means to achieve these goals differs from culture to culture. Identifying the challenges and certain strategies to address these challenges is the goal of this section.

One of the first challenges is becoming aware of our culture and the privileges within our culture and those of other cultures around us (see Box 3.10 on p. 85). Developing a positive cultural identity means learning about the history and struggles of your culture. You can talk to your family about your cultural history and research about significant people from your culture. You can learn about the struggles that members of your culture faced within their homeland (if they have a homeland) or when they have moved around the world (whether by choice or by force). Learning about these struggles creates an appreciation and sense of pride about your culture. What if your culture did not face a lot of struggles? This may be an indicator of invisible privilege. You want to become aware of how privilege benefits your group at the expense of others. A key strategy to meet these challenges is to be self-reflexive.

Being self-reflexive is engaging in self-examination and creating awareness about your culture. This strategy can help you through identity development and prepare you to better understand, respect, and appreciate members of different cultural groups.

As you are engaging in the work of self-reflexivity, you will likely have opportunities to interact with members of different cultural groups. These opportunities will provide challenges as we negotiate our cultural identities with others including managing identity freezing, managing the identity-freezing and nonsupportive problematic, and the self-other dialectic. Tables 3.1 to 3.3 provide several strategies to consider in addressing these challenges. No one strategy addresses every situation, so it is best to have a variety ready to use. Which of these make most sense for your experiences?

Table 3.1

STRATEGIES FOR COPING WITH IDENTITY FREEZING

Strategy	Definition	Example
Education	Educating other about the freezing	"Let me tell you about the experiences of my parents...."
Disregard	Discounting the validity of the freezing	"Man, that's just not true."
Simple request	Asking other to stop the freezing	"I'd appreciate if you wouldn't stereotype people like that."
Request empathy	Asking other to empathize what it is like to be frozen	"How would you feel if everyone lumped you into a category?"
Request confirmation	Asking other if he or she meant to freeze	"Were you trying to say that was true about all Chinese?"
Laughter	Laughing off the freezing	"That's too funny."
Humor	Joking back to the other about the freezing	"Yeah, if we are all so smart, how come I'm driving this beat up old car?"
Acceptance	Accepting the stereotype as a compliment or true	"Thanks. There are a lot of talented African Americans."
Apology	Apologize for being true to the stereotype	"I'm sorry, but you know that White men can't jump."
Avoidance	Avoiding interaction about the freezing	"Let's talk about something else."

Adapted from Imahori & Cupach (2005)

Table 3.2

STRATEGIES FOR COPING WITH THE IDENTITY FREEZING–NONSUPPORT PROBLEMATIC DIALECTIC

Strategy	Definition	Example
Bouncing past	Supporting the other's cultural identity within his/her comfort zone that was learned from past interactions	"Last week, you said that your parents will arrange your wedding for you. How do you feel about that?"
Bounding explicit	Supporting the other's cultural identity until she or he says explicitly to stop	"I think it is really cool that you choose to dress in traditional ways. It is great that you want to express your culture."
Bouncing sign	Supporting the other's cultural identity until she or he shows signs of discomfort	"I think it is really cool that you choose to dress in traditional ways. Oh, I'm sorry—I think I said something to make you uncomfortable."
Focus shift	Avoiding imposition on the other by shifting focus away from his/her cultural identity	Suggesting that you go play basketball together because that is a shared interest rather than talking about culture
Self support	Allowing time and space for the other to support his/her own cultural identity	Not giving your friend a hard time when he or she has to leave for family gathering
Subtle nonverbal support	Engaging in nonverbal acts that support the other's identity	Nodding in approval when asked if you like the traditional dress your friend is wearing
Avoidance	Avoiding interaction that causes the tension	"Before we go there again, let's just change the subject."
Apology	Apologizing for imposing other's cultural identity	"I'm sorry for asking so many questions, but I really want to learn about your culture."

(continued)

Table 3.2 (continued)

Strategy	Definition	Example
Justification	Justify why one imposed on other's cultural identity	"I'd really like to take pictures of your sister's *quinceañera* because I need to make sure my photo collage represents all cultures."

Adapted from Imahori & Cupach (2005)

Table 3.3

STRATEGIES FOR COPING WITH THE SELF-OTHER DIALECTIC

Strategy	Definition	Example
Other orientation	Supporting the other's cultural identity while sacrificing one's own cultural identity	"Instead of celebrating Passover this year, let's just go to your family's house for Easter."
Reciprocity expectation	Supporting the other's cultural identity with an expectation that the other will reciprocate	"We'll celebrate Hannukah with your family (said to self—'but you sure better come to Christmas dinner with my family')."
Advice acceptance	Accepting the other's comment about how one should enact cultural identity	"OK, I'll try to be less assertive about my cultural beliefs next time we are with your co-workers."
Assertion	Asserting one's own cultural identity over the other's cultural identity	"We need to teach our children about racism, even though I know you never really experienced it."

(continued)

Table 3.3 (continued)		
Strategy	**Definition**	**Example**
Justification	Justifying the support of one's own cultural identity	"I think it is more important to raise our children as Catholic since your religion isn't as important to you."
Mutual support	Supporting both one's own and the other's cultural identities in alternative areas or alternative occasions	"We'll celebrate Hannukah with your family, but I want to celebrate Kwanzaa with mine."
Mutual adaptation	Adapting to each other's cultural ways of doing things	A family raising their children with both Peruvian and Chinese traditions
Adaptation facilitation	Not changing one's cultural ways, but helping the other to adapt to one's culture	"Since we are going to live in Japan, I think it is important for you to learn some important customs. Let me show you."
Adaptation facilitation request	Asking the other to help you to adapt toward the partner's culture	"Since we are going to live in Japan, can you teach me about some of the customs?"
Avoidance	Avoiding interaction that causes tension	Never discussing religion because it causes fights about how to raise the children
Difference recognition	Recognize the differences in identities and in some cases choosing to behave in separate ways	"We'll go ahead and raise the children both as Jews and Christians and let them choose when they are old enough."

Adapted from Imahori & Cupach (2005)

SUMMARY

Returning to the opening story: There are several concepts and models about identity that can explain Al's story. First, his struggle to understand his identity followed the four phases of the minority identity development model: a) pre-encounter (being content with his identity and identifying with mainstream cultural values—American

Box 3.10 What Went Wrong? Challenges to Identities

Chris and Paul are classmates working on a class paper to identify an intercultural problem and to propose solutions to the problem. Chris is Hispanic and Paul is African American, and they are trying to decide on a topic.

C: I want to select something about cultural diversity in the workplace. What do you think?

P: Sounds good to me.

C: I think we make too much out of diversity in the workplace. There is too much stereotyping about groups and we need to focus on individuals.

P: There might be some truth in that. What do you think it takes to be successful?

C: I think that the key is hard work, education, and perseverance. Everything else is superficial and unimportant.

P: I think we need to research this more.

C: I agree, but this is where I'm coming from. For example, look at you—you get great grades, you work hard, and you are going to be successful regardless of what you do. You're not an African American man who is going places—you're just a man going places.

P: Thanks, but I'm more than just a man going places—I am African American and that matters to me. And, you are going to be successful because of your hard work, education, and your culture.

C: You are making too big a deal about culture. My culture isn't doing the work for me.

1. What challenges to identity are expressed in this situation?
2. What strategies do you think are most effective in this situation?

identity), b) encounter (having the incident with the racists that awoke his identity struggles), c) immersion-emersion (identifying more strongly with his minority identity and seeking out information about his group), and d) internalization-commitment (developing a confident sense of self and ability to interact with members of other groups). Second, the story illustrates many of the characteristics about identity (the most salient are included here): a) personal and social identities (unique family identity and a conception of being Irish American and African American), b) salience of identity (becoming aware of who he was in a particular situation), c) avowal and ascription (he had his identity ascribed to him by the racists, but also his parents ascribed his identity; in contrast, he avowed his own identity), and d) fluid, but stable (experiencing changes and some sense of a core identity). Finally, the story illustrates aspects of differentiation (becoming aware of us versus them), negotiation (figuring out who he was and what it meant to him), and deconstruction (becoming aware of the power issues in society that made it easy for his White friends to minimize the event when he could not).

Here is a summary of the chapter based on the opening learning objectives:

■ **Seven characteristics of identity.** Cultural identities are socially constructed through our interactions with others and have several characteristics: a) identity is multifaceted, b) identity consists of personal and social components (including racial, ethnic, and cultural identities), c) identities become salient in particular situations and vary from weak to strong, d) identities are relatively stable at any given point in time, but also are fluid and change over time, e) identities can be avowed by individuals or ascribed by others, f) identities include passing and outing, and g) identities are performed and expressed through various modes including core symbols, labels, rituals, and language.

- **Models of identity development.** Identity is developed over time in three general phases: unexamined cultural identity, cultural identity search, and cultural identity achievement. This basic model varies for minority or majority group members because of social power. The resulting models include phases of individuals negotiating identity through racism, blame, and acceptance.

- **Differentiating identities.** As part of the identity development, we engage in a process of differentiating our cultural identities from that of others. Two theories, social identity theory and ethnolinguistic identity theory, describe the various conditions that encourage us to engage in ingroup favoritism or social competition to create positive cultural identities.

- **Negotiating identities.** We negotiate cultural identities through interactions with others in such a manner as to be understood, respected, and affirmed. However, there are challenges to these interactions, including identity freezing, the nonsupport problematic, and the self-other dialectic.

- **Deconstructing identities—political and historical factors.** A final challenge is understanding the politics of identity. These politics include realizing that history and social structures create privilege for the majority group. These privileges (Whiteness) result in subjugated ascriptions about cultural identity and limitations on agency for the minority group.

- **Bottom-up and top-down effects.** This chapter concluded by describing how identity is layered. First, negotiating our own identities impacts those around us and especially those who are closest to us (families and friends). Historical and societal factors share our identity development. For example, media images can influence the construction of positive social identities and the degree to which we engage in ingroup favoritism and social competition. Further, laws influence what identities are considered privileged.

REVIEW QUESTIONS

1. What does it mean to say that identity is socially constructed?
2. What are the seven characteristics of identity?
3. What is the difference between avowal and ascription? Do these concepts have an ethical component? If so, what is it?
4. Describe the four modes of expression of identity presented in this chapter.
5. Compare and contrast the models of identity development for minority and majority group members.
6. What are the factors that lead to differentiation of identity?

7. What are the five motivations for identity negotiation? Describe and provide an example of the three challenges during identity negotiation.
8. What does it mean to say that identity is political?
9. What is Whiteness ideology, and how does it affect identity development and negotiation?
10. How is identity layered?

EXERCISES

1. Read Senator Barack Obama's autobiography, *Dreams from My Father: A Story of Race and Inheritance* (New York: Three Rivers Press). Identify different aspects of identity development, differentiation, negotiation, and deconstruction in his story.
2. Compare and contrast the language of two indigenous languages in your area with that of English. You'll need to identify two languages and look for information on the Internet or at your local university. Are the languages written or oral? How do you say different phrases in those languages? What efforts are done to maintain the language?
3. Visit the Web site, "First People's Language Resources" at http://www.yvwiiusdinvnohii.net/language.html. Examine what resources are available. Do you think these languages have ethnolinguistic vitality? Why or why not?

CHAPTER 4

Attributions and Attitudes

How are our attitudes about others expressed? What meaning do we give to others' behavior?

CHAPTER OUTLINE

I. Introduction

II. Attributions
    a. Nature of Attributions
    b. Cultural Differences in Attribution
    c. Attribution Errors
    d. Concept Check

III. Attitudes
    a. Intercultural Sensitivity
    b. Prejudice
    c. Communicating Prejudice

IV. Layers of Attributions
and Attitudes
    a. Bottom-Up Effects
    b. Top-Down Effects
    c. Challenges and Skills

V. Summary

VI. Review Questions

VII. Exercises

CHAPTER OBJECTIVES

After reading this chapter, students should be able to

- identify the characteristics of attributions.

- describe and provide an example of seven attribution errors.

- explain the model of intercultural sensitivity.

- describe the causes and functions of prejudice.
- discuss how prejudice is expressed.
- identify bottom-up and top-down effects of attitudes and attributions.

Introduction

In the summer of 2006, the actor Mel Gibson was pulled over by a police officer who "clocked" Gibson driving 40 miles above the speed limit in Malibu, California. As Gibson was booked for drunk driving and speeding, he became belligerent and obnoxious with the officer. The officer, who is Jewish, reported that Gibson said "[explicative] Jews" and "The Jews are responsible for all the wars in the world." Gibson argued that his capacity was diminished because he had been drinking and was impacted by the "horrible disease of alcoholism." He apologized twice, through his publicist, to the Jewish community.

The incident touched off debates about Gibson's sincerity and whether he is anti-Semitic. Fellow actors (some of whom are Jewish) came to Gibson's defense and said that he is not anti-Semitic, but that he is a different person when he drinks. Some Rabbis were reported as saying that Judaism emphasizes forgiveness and that his apology meant a lot. Others, however did not buy Gibson's excuse; one columnist, in particular, disputed that a "little tequila, or even a lot of tequila, can somehow turn an unbiased person into a raging anti-Semite—or a racist, or a homophobe, or a bigot of any kind for that matter" (Robinson, 2006, p. A7). This incident occurred at the same time that Israel strongly retaliated against Hezbollah in Southern Lebanon for the capture of several of its soldiers, an event that also sparked debates of anti-Semitism and anti-Arabian sentiments by different social groups.

> Questions: What concepts associated with social cognition (attributions and attitudes) are illustrated in this story? What is your opinion about Gibson's behavior? How would you respond to someone making such remarks if you were in a similar situation?

This story illustrates the role of social cognition in intercultural communication. Social cognition focuses on our thought processes about human interaction; in other words, it is how we acquire and process knowledge about other people (Gudykunst, Ting-Toomey, Sudweeks, & Stewart, 1995). Two key components of social cognition are attitudes and attributions. Our attitudes toward other people are often reflected through our verbal and nonverbal communication with them. These attitudes, and the way in which we make sense of the world (attributions), impact our interactions with others. Our cultural backgrounds and social identities also influence the ways we process information and form attitudes. This chapter examines the process by which we explain another's behavior (attributions), the dispositions we have toward others (attitudes), and the behaviors that reflect these dispositions.

Attributions

Attributions are our explanations of others'—or our own—behavior. When we observe or engage in behavior, we attempt to make sense of that behavior and to explain its cause. The process is important in intercultural communication, as our choices are often based on our views of the other person and on our own needs and wants. This section examines the nature of attributions, cultural differences in attributions, and errors in making attributions.

Nature of Attributions

The process of making attributions is based on collecting information and then making sense of it. In this process, we act as intuitive scientists as we try to move beyond what we directly observe and hear in an attempt to figure out its meaning. This interpretation of behavior is what constitutes reality rather than our actual experiences. (Figure 4.1 displays an example of this difference.) The figure displays a character whose prejudice frames his reality. The attribution process has many characteristics including the following: a) factors that we attribute behavior to, b) differences between attributions of self

Figure 4.1
Actual Experience versus Attribution/ Reality

Actual Experience

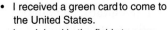

- I received a green card to come to the United States.
- I work hard in the fields to earn money for my family.
- I am a good provider, father, and husband for my family.
- I obey all of the laws of this country.
- I'm sending my children to school and having them learn English.
- I am proud of my Mexican heritage and listen to Spanish music and television.
- I obtained food stamps so my family can eat healthy.

Attribution/Reality

They're here illegally and just stealing our jobs and living off welfare.

versus others, c) incomplete information in making attributions, d) confidence and accuracy of attributions, and e) individual versus social attributions.

In making sense of behaviors, we focus on three factors: individual characteristics, group characteristics, and the physical characteristics of the situation. Individual characteristics focus on the unique aspects of people apart from their group memberships. Such information includes personality, dispositions, and individual experiences. Attributions based on individual characteristics are called **person-based attributions.** Group characteristics are the factors associated with our social memberships or identities. Attributions based on group characteristics are called **category or group-based attributions.** Finally, we look at the physical characteristics (people, place, things) of a given interaction, information that forms the basis for **situation-based attributions.** When we attribute the cause of behavior to person-based or category-based factors, we hold individuals responsible for their behavior; that is, we say that negative behavior is their fault or part of their disposition. When we attribute the cause of behavior to situation-based factors, we do not hold people responsible for their actions. What we are saying is that external factors account for why people behave as they do. See Box 4.1.

We use these three factors differently when we explain our own behavior versus another's behavior. In general, we attribute our own behavior to situational characteristics. We tend to see ourselves as stable and consistent people in regard to attitudes and values; we attribute differences in our behavior to changing situational factors. However, we tend to attribute the behavior of others to person- and category-based factors. We typically observe another's behavior in limited situations (except for close friends and family), and thus the factors that are most salient to us are the individual and cultural characteristics.

When making attributions about others, we tend to have incomplete information. In general, the person engaging in a behavior has more knowledge and experience about his or her own behavior than the observer. For example, say you are interacting with some co-workers whose socioeconomic status is different from yours. There are two people you know well—one you like and one you do not like because she always

---

Box 4.1 Voices: Person-Based, Category-Based, and Situation-Based Attributions

In the early 1990s, there was a movie called *Waiting to Exhale* about four African American women and the friendships and relationships they developed. I remember a conversation I had with several friends. One of my friends complained about the attributions that members of the media who were White made about the movie. She said they were calling it a great "Black film" and saying it was an excellent example of "Black culture." My friend was upset because she felt that calling it a "Black film" limited its impact. She said that the relationships could have occurred in any culture and, in fact, the movie was about women and friendships as much as it was about Black women and friendships. Her attributions focused on person-based and situation-based factors rather than category-based factors. This example also illustrates facets of identity such as ascription and salience (see Chapter 3).

"pushes your buttons." She is always talking about how poor people need to "pick themselves up by their own bootstraps." You grew up with not a lot of money, but you saw your parents working very hard to provide for their family and clearly saw that they "picked themselves up by their own bootstraps." If you are hostile toward your co-worker when she makes her comments, she may attribute your behavior to your hostile personality or simply to how poor people act. However, you feel that you are rarely hostile toward others, and it is simply this person who brings out the worst in you (a situation-based attribution). Your co-worker does not have a complete picture of you but makes the attribution based on repeated observations of your behavior toward her. Incomplete information is the general rule, particularly when we interact with people of different cultural backgrounds.

Even when we do not have complete information about another person's culture we still make attributions about that person's behavior and become confident in those attributions. This confidence is due to two factors. First, when interacting in new situations or with new people, we tend to perceive ourselves as tentative in making attributions; that is, we know we are in a new situation and thus we believe that we take "our time" to figure out why others are behaving as they are. In reality, however, we still make relatively quick attributions given the amount of information to process (even if we wait an hour to make an attribution, we are still ignoring many types of behaviors). Second, there are limited explanations for why most people believe someone behaves in a particular way (such as being hostile), and we tend to believe those explanations that are most consistent with our own beliefs (such as, "it is his personality," "she was provoked," or "people of that culture are just like that"). These limited explanations and the fact that we think the person involved is similar to us gives us confidence in our attributions once we have made them. However, research shows that there is no relationship between our level of confidence and the accuracy of our attributions relative to actual experiences (Gudykunst et al., 1995). Figure 4.1 displays someone who is very confident in his attributions but who is not very accurate.

The final characteristic about attributions is that they can be individually or socially based. An individually based attribution is one that we hold on our own and that is unique from members of our social groups. In contrast, social attributions are those explanations that members of a particular social group make about their own or other groups' behavior. Many groups make attributions that are biased toward the ingroup. For example, people from a higher socioeconomic status might explain the poor school performance of children from a lower socioeconomic status on the lack of involved parents. This social attribution enhances social identities and is a part of the ingroup favoring the process of social identity theory. Someone from the same social group with an individual-based attribution might say, "I know some people who are poor and they care deeply about their children. The poor performance is a product of many factors, but parental involvement is not one of them." Individual-based attributions are difficult to make in situations where there is strong ingroup bias or peer pressure to conform to the group.

These five characteristics help to illustrate the nature of attributions. They illustrate general tendencies about attributions and provide information about some difficulty in intercultural communication. Misattributions are a contributing part of poor intercultural communication, and, in the following two sections, we explore several different sources of misattributions.

Cultural Differences in Attributions

Cultural misattributions occur when people use their own attribution tendencies in assigning meaning to someone from a different culture. In Chapter 2, we discussed several dimensions along which cultures vary. Individualism-collectivism (I-C) is one dimension that has been found to contribute to cultural misattributions (Judd, Park, Yzerbyt, Gordijn, & Muller, 2005; Lien, Chu, Jen, & Wu, 2006). This section will focus on I-C, but other dimensions also play a role in cultural misattributions (Albert & Ha, 2004).

The types of attributions people make in individualistic and collectivistic cultures differ. Compared to collectivistic cultures, members of individualistic cultures make more attributions about behavior based on person-based characteristics (Anthony, Rosselli, & Caparyan, 2003). In contrast, compared to individualistic cultures, members of collectivistic cultures make more attributions about behavior based on situation-based characteristics. These attribution tendencies are based on cultural differences, including the fact that members of collectivistic cultures have a tendency to use more high-context communication patterns while members of individualistic cultures tend to use more low-context communication.

Not understanding cultural differences in communication style can create misattributions about communication behavior. If you are from an individualistic and lower-power distance culture and do not understand how a collectivistic or person from a high-power distance culture communicates, you can easily misunderstand the meaning of that person's behavior. For example, a member of a collectivistic culture may use the pronoun "we" to offer a personal opinion ("We feel it is inappropriate to use first names during an initial interaction") because of a strong group identity. A person from an individualistic culture may not attribute this behavior to a personal opinion, but rather see it as a description about the culture in general ("Interesting— what is your own opinion about it?"). Also see the example in Box 4.2 on page 94.

Attempting to resolve misunderstandings that are caused by misattributions can be difficult because we typically use the same styles that created the misunderstanding in the first place (Tannen, 1994). For example, people from individualistic cultures have a greater tendency to use direct communication and a lesser tendency to use indirect communication styles compared to people from collectivistic cultures. People who have an indirect communication style often use questions to imply opinions (for example, "Do you want to eat pizza tonight?"). As a result, they answer questions as if they were statements of preference and not a request for an opinion ("Sure, that sounds good to me" even when he or she wanted something else). These style differences initially create a misunderstanding, while their continued use actually exacerbates the misunderstanding. Many times people agree initially, but do not realize it because of style differences. As is illustrated in the example of Jim and Toshi, clashes of direct and indirect styles can create—and continue—a conflict.

Box 4.2 What Went Wrong? Culture and Misattributions

Jim and Toshi are roommates. Jim is White American, and Toshi is an international student from Japan. They are discussing where they are going to eat tonight.

	Message	Attribution
Jim:	So, what do you wanna eat tonight?	He may have some idea, and I don't want to force my tastes on him.
Toshi:	I don't know. Whatever you like.	I should listen to his opinion first.
Jim:	How about sushi? Do you remember the restaurant we went to last time? You said you liked it.	Sushi is OK, but I'd rather eat somewhere else. I know he likes sushi, and I'm willing to go with his wishes.
Toshi:	Well, yeah…that was nice…	Actually, I do not like sushi, but I could not tell him because he paid for me that night. I hope he can sense it.
Jim:	So, do you wanna go there?	He is always ambiguous.
Toshi:	Umm…well…you pick wherever you want to go.	It is bad to say no to his suggestion, but I hope he picks something else.
Jim:	Come on, you should tell me what you want. You know, I always tell you that you should speak up. You should be more open and direct to your friends.	I tell him this because I am his friend. He is too timid. I just want to know his opinion.
Toshi:	All right, let's see…	He cannot sense my feeling at all.
Jim:	Mexican? Pizza? Greek? Chinese? Italian? Oh, how about the new sushi bar around the corner?	He is indecisive. I am giving some suggestions for him.
Toshi:	Ok, let's go there.	I do not want to argue with him anymore, and he just doesn't get it.

In this case, Jim attributes Toshi's indirectness to indecisiveness. However, Toshi is using his cultural values to be considerate of Jim and chooses an indirect style to hint at what he does *not* want. Toshi attributes Jim's approach to insensitivity. However, Jim is simply being polite and expects Toshi to state his opinion if he has one. It is important to remember that this is an illustrative example and is not meant to stereotype all White Americans or Japanese as following these patterns exactly. Some Japanese are very direct, and some U.S. Americans utilize high-context communication. How might you handle this situation differently in order to avoid some of these attribution errors?

According to Tannen (1995), differences in direct and indirect communication styles also contribute to misunderstandings and misattributions in conversations between men and women in the United States. Tannen argued that men and women represent different "cultures" with different communication rules. Some of the differences include the following: rapport-talk versus report-talk (women use talk to convey information and emotions whereas men only use talk for information); competitive versus cooperative styles (men see conversations as having a winner and loser, while women use conversations as a way to negotiate and get closer), and affiliation and control (men use conversation devices such as interruptions to control the floor, while women use the same devices to share the floor and support the other person). As a result of these conversational differences, men and women misattribute each others' intentions. Men sometimes feel that women are too weak and simply talk too much about their feelings and never get to the point. Women often feel that men are too domineering and never listen to them. Some researchers feel that Tannen relies too much on stereotypes about men and women without supporting evidence (Goldsmith & Fulfs, 1999), but her approach remains popular with mainstream audiences. Do you think that men and women come from different cultural groups and have different communication styles?

Hofstede's (1991) research on culture strongly suggests that the misattributions between men and women occur most often in moderately to highly masculine cultures. The reason is that men and women in these cultures have relatively rigid roles and expectations for communication. In contrast, feminine cultures (such as the Scandinavian nations) do not generally have these types of problems because men and women's communication style is not as distinct as in masculine cultures.

Attribution Errors

People tend to follow certain patterns when making attributions. Sometimes, these tendencies result in accurate interpretations. However, in the majority of cases, the tendencies result in misattributions and misunderstandings because we rely on certain factors at the expense of others. For example, if your partner is late arriving home from work and you simply conclude that she is inconsiderate you may have a misattribution because it is possible that an accident happened on the freeway and that is why she is late. There are seven types of attribution errors: egocentric bias, egoprotective bias, fundamental attribution error, self-effacement bias, premature closure, principle of negativity, and ultimate attribution error.

The **egocentric bias** results when we tend to view our own behavior as normal and appropriate and the standard by which to judge others' behavior (Caruso, Epley, & Bazerman, 2006; Kelley, 1967). When other people behave differently than we expect, we attribute their behavior to their personal characteristics. For example, if you think it is appropriate to say "hi" to a stranger on the street and you meet someone who does not do this, you will likely interpret this behavior as rude and attribute it to that person's personality (she is a rude person). In general, this error results because we use our own standards for judging others' behavior.

Relatedly, the **egoprotective bias** focuses on the desire to maintain a positive self-image (Caruso et al., 2006; Kelley, 1967). To protect this self-image, we attribute our own positive behavior to person-based factors, but we attribute our negative behavior to situation-based factors. So, if you are kind to a co-worker, it is because you are a good colleague with a nice disposition. If you are rude to a co-worker, it is because you were provoked or are having a bad day. It is not because you are a bad colleague. This attribution tendency results in errors, since we certainly are not always good because of our disposition and not always bad because of the specific situation. Some of us have mean streaks and impulse control problems and other negative characteristics; they are what makes us human, even though we would much rather think positively about ourselves.

The third error focuses on explaining other people's behavior. The **fundamental attribution error** (Lien et al., 2006; Ross, 1977) is the tendency to overestimate the influence of personal characteristics and underestimate the influence of situational factors when we explain others' negative behavior—particularly people from different cultures or who are unknown to us. We think that a person who was rude to a co-worker is a jerk rather than thinking that he or she was provoked. When the behavior is positive, we overestimate the situational characteristics and underestimate the personal characteristics. Thus, a pleasant co-worker is simply trying to "suck up" to the boss rather than being a genuinely nice person.

The egoprotective bias and fundamental attribution error are more applicable in individualistic than collectivistic cultures. Conversely, because of the focus on context and situation in collectivistic cultures, there is a tendency for people in these cultures to overestimate situational factors and underemphasize personal factors for positive behaviors (the opposite is true for negative behaviors). In some collectivistic cultures, it is important not to "stick out" from the group, and thus individuals downplay some positive characteristics, which leads to the fourth type of attribution error: the **self-effacement bias** (Kashima & Triandis, 1986; Wakimoto, 2006). For example, a co-worker who does a great job may attribute her accomplishment to a supportive boss and a great team rather than to her own work ethic and abilities. In contrast, failure is often attributed to a lack of ability and causes great shame—when in fact the failure may be due to limitations of informational technology or not enough resources to complete a job.

The fifth error is **premature closure.** This error occurs when we stop looking for explanations for behavior (our own and others') once we have found a plausible or reasonable explanation (Borrell-Corrio & Epstein, 2004; Taylor & Fiske, 1978). Essentially, we tend to be lazy in trying to make sense of people's behavior unless we are quite aware of what we are doing. It is easier to come to a quick solution even if it is not critically thought through. This is one reason why confidence in attributions does not relate to accuracy. For example, you meet someone from a perceived lower socioeconomic class and see that the person is buying beer and wearing grimy clothes. Using a premature closure bias, you might simply conclude that the person is an alcoholic. In reality, however, this individual has just got off work and has decided to join some friends who are watching a game. The beer is for his friends; this individual doesn't drink alcohol at all.

The sixth error is the **principle of negativity.** We have a tendency to overemphasize negative information when making attributions about behavior

(Kanouse & Hanson, 1972). Most teachers are guilty of this when grading students' papers—we comment on what is wrong rather than pointing out what is correct. In part, this is because it is easier, but also because we tend to focus on what is wrong. During intercultural interactions, this error results in us thinking that people who are culturally different engage in more negative behavior than they really do.

The final attribution error is the **ultimate attribution error** (Pettigrew, 1979). This error is shaped in part by prejudice and stereotypes. Specifically, we have a tendency to overemphasize category-based factors and underemphasize situation-based factors to explain negative behavior from people who are culturally different from us. When we observe negative behavior in an individual, such as rudeness, hostility, or violence, we often attribute the behavior to the larger, cultural group (thinking for example, "they are violent people"). The same negative behavior from a member of our own cultural group is downplayed and attributed to situation-based factors. An example of this is seen in the aftermath of Hurricane Katrina, which hit New Orleans in 2005 (see Box 4.3).

Box 4.3 Layered Effects: Ultimate Attribution Error in the Media

The media are not immune from attribution biases. Media biases have an impact on viewers by creating and reinforcing stereotypes and prejudice. Two photos and captions in Yahoo news immediately after Hurricane Katrina illustrate this layered effect. In the days after Hurricane Katrina, individuals took items from grocery stores to survive. Two White individuals are captured in one picture and are framed as finding supplies. Another picture captured a Black man—who is framed as a looter. Yahoo news removed the stories and photos within hours of posting it, recognizing the inherent bias of the reporters. Regardless, it demonstrates that individual attribution biases are a part of the media and not just individuals.

As a corollary to the ultimate attribution error, positive behavior from culturally different people is attributed to different factors. We tend to see this behavior as an "exception to the rule"; that is, rather than viewing this positive behavior as a positive characteristic of the cultural group, we attribute the positive behavior to situational characteristics (for example, "Who couldn't do the right thing in that situation?"). Occasionally, we will attribute the behavior to the exceptional qualities of the individual and wish more of that group could be like him or her.

Concept Check

In this section, we examined the nature of attributions, cultural differences in making attributions, and common errors that occur in the attribution process. This review illustrates that our explanations of others' behavior, particularly people from different cultural backgrounds, tends to be inaccurate and incomplete. A simple conclusion is that we are probably better off assuming we do not know why people from different cultures behave as they do rather than trusting our own attributions. At the very least, we need to be aware of the challenges that are created in making sense of intercultural interaction.

Attitudes

The attributions we make and the behaviors in which we engage are related to the attitudes we have about people from different cultural groups. **Attitudes** are our predisposition toward an object or person. They include our likes and dislikes, and they are a key cognitive component for communication. In this section, several attitudes and how they relate to intercultural communication are discussed. In particular, intercultural sensitivity and its components—ethnocentrism and ethnorelativism—are introduced. Finally, prejudice and how prejudice is communicated is described with a focus on stereotypes and discrimination.

Intercultural Sensitivity

With increasing diversity in the world and within the United States, teachers, scholars, and community practitioners have become increasingly interested in attitudes that people have toward each other. One particular attitude is **intercultural sensitivity,** which is the progressive capacity to accept and accommodate cultural difference (Chen & Starosta, 2000). The more we are able to accept different cultures and integrate different cultures into our world views, the more interculturally sensitive we become. Bennet (1993) offered a developmental model of intercultural sensitivity to explain this progression. The model consists of six stages, displayed in Figure 4.2.

The first three stages are ethnocentric stages. **Ethnocentrism** is the inherent belief in the superiority of our own culture versus others. All of us are ethnocentric to varying degrees because it is a defensive attitudinal tendency to view our norms, values, and beliefs as important and as the most reasonable and proper ways to live. It is a way to rationalize and justify why we do what we do, and it is also a way to

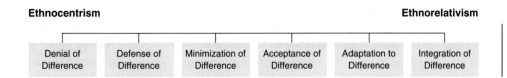

Ethnocentrism   Ethnorelativism

| Denial of Difference | Defense of Difference | Minimization of Difference | Acceptance of Difference | Adaptation to Difference | Integration of Difference |

Figure 4.2
Model of Intercultural Sensitivity

support our cultural identities (ingroup favoritism). High and rigid levels of ethnocentrism foster attitudes that "we" are superior and more civilized than "them," and we expect others to adapt to our way of life. The comic strip shown in Figure 4.3 addresses ethnocentrism.

The three specific stages of ethnocentrism are a) denial of difference, b) defense of difference, and c) minimization of difference. In the first stage, we completely deny that people are different. At this stage, people are not aware of cultural difference and simply view culturally different behavior as inferior or inappropriate, thinking of others, for example, that "They simply have not been taught how to act appropriately." The second stage is defense of difference. This stage is developmentally

Figure 4.3
Opus
© Berkeley Breathed, dist. By *The Washington Post* Writers Group.

advanced from the first because it recognizes cultural differences. People at this stage can identify cultural difference, but defend difference with the belief that their culture is better than others, and others are to be avoided and disparaged. For example, some in the United States view the behavior of fundamentalist Muslims as unethical, violent, and backwards compared to people's behavior in their own country. These viewpoints stereotype the behavior of fundamentalist Muslims, but also the viewpoints are evaluations based on U.S. cultural norms. The evaluations defend the differences by explaining, "We are better than they are." The final stage is minimization of difference. Cultural differences are recognized, but only thought of at the surface level. People recognize basic differences in food or appearance, but do not process these differences in values and norms; that is, they continue to think that people are basically the same.

The second three stages move the person from ethnocentrism to ethnorelativism. **Ethnorelativism** is the belief that all cultures are appropriate and normal and recognizes the value in evaluating and interpreting people's behavior from their cultural background (such as using Japanese culture to interpret and evaluate Japanese behavior). Ethnorelativism does not view difference as threatening; rather it attempts to create new categories and interpretations and does not force people to fit into existing categories. The specific ethnorelative stages are a) acceptance of difference, b) adaptation of difference, and c) integration of difference. In the acceptance of difference stage, people begin to appreciate cultural value differences and accept them as the norm. They believe that people have different worldviews and respect these different views as important and appropriate. They exhibit an increasing curiosity about cultural differences; thus, people in this stage begin to ask more questions about others' cultures and to read more about other cultures. For example, instead of putting down fundamentalist Muslim culture, a person tries to better understand the values and history. In the adaptation of difference stage, people are able to change their communication patterns to better interact with people from different cultural groups. They develop cultural communication competence or the ability to communicate effectively and appropriately with people from a different cultural group than their own. Thus, this stage is marked by an increase in intercultural communication skills, not just attitudes. For example, a person without a disability works to practice appropriate communication skills when interacting with people who have a disability (such as making eye contact with a person who is deaf rather than making eye contact with the sign language interpreter). The final stage represents the willingness to integrate people's cultural difference as a normal part of our lives and others. We accept that everyone is a member of one ore more cultures and that these cultures are normal, important, and simply different—not better or worse. We have a deep understanding and appreciation for the impact that culture has in our interaction with others and work to achieve fairness in our interaction.

These six stages are not necessarily fluid or fixed. Individuals can progress through the stages in order, go through three or four stages and get stuck, cycle back through stages, and spend more time in one stage than another. These stages describe a general pattern of intercultural sensitivity. While the model is not meant to be an evaluative one, it implies that there is a best place to be—that is, it seems it is better to be in the integration of difference stage. Box 4.4 opens this up as an ethical debate. Also, an assessment tool is included to identify your level of intercultural sensitivity.

Box 4.4 Talking about Ethics: Is Intercultural Sensitivity the Ideal?

The model of intercultural sensitivity implies that each stage is a progression in which people develop and grow. Thus, people who are in the integration of difference stage are better than those who are in the defense of difference stage. Do you think that the stages imply developmental growth in our attitudes? Is intercultural sensitivity a desirable trait? Why or why not? Using the ethical standards from Chapter 1 (cultural universalism/relativism, moral inclusion/exclusion, and social justice), explain whether supporting intercultural sensitivity is an ethical stance to take.

Once you have answered these questions, think about cultural behavior that is very different from your own and that you may not accept. For example, how do you feel about female circumcision?

Suppression of free speech? Subordination of women? Getting plastic surgery? Using artificial insemination to have a baby? Eating genetically modified food? The depiction of sex and violence in the media? All of these behaviors are culturally accepted in certain groups, although they might be labeled differently. For example, what one culture might negatively view as the subordination of women might be labeled and viewed positively as distinct gender roles for men and women in another culture. Most people from the United States likely have a problem accepting the first three behaviors, while people from other parts of the world might reject the last four behaviors. Can you reconcile an attitude of intercultural sensitivity and acceptance of behaviors you find reprehensible?

Prejudice

Prejudice is an attitude that relates closely to intercultural sensitivity. It is more commonly held and expressed by people in ethnocentric stages of the sensitivity model compared to people in the ethnorelative stages. **Prejudice** is an attitude that combines both belief (cognitive) and affect (emotion) toward a group of people (Hecht, 1998). It is seen as having three components: prejudgment, prejudgment with evaluation, and prejudgment with a negative evaluation (Hecht, 1998). First, we simply prejudge someone based on his or her cultural group membership without really knowing who the person is or what he or she will do. Second, we begin to evaluate the prejudgment as a factor that is good or bad. Prejudice often refers to negative evaluations, but, in fact, we can be positively prejudiced toward others. For example, we might view people of our own ethnic group as better than those of other ethnic groups. At the final level, we negatively evaluate the other group to create distance between them and us. Several closely related concepts to prejudice are stereotypes, racism, and discrimination, which are discussed in the section on communicating prejudice. This section examines the causes of prejudice and the functions that it serves.

CAUSES OF PREJUDICE   Scholars often attempt to explain why prejudice occurs. In so doing, they have developed a variety of theories that focus on authoritarian personality, scapegoating market economy, social competition, social dominance, and intergroup contact (Esses & Hodson, 2006; Hecht, 1998).

The most straightforward explanation follows the authoritarian personality. Those with an authoritarian personality have a desire for power, an unquestioning acceptance of authority, and a rigid adherence to norms. This combination results in

Self-Assessment 4.1

INTERCULTURAL SENSITIVITY

Complete the following statements to obtain an indication of your level of intercultural sensitivity. First, complete the statements honestly, and then review the scoring. Use a scale of 5 = strongly agree, 4 = agree, 3 = neutral, 2 = disagree, 1 = strongly disagree.

Statement	Score
1. I have a feeling of enjoyment toward differences between culturally different people and me.	
2. I often give positive responses to my culturally different counterpart during our interaction.	
3. I am open-minded to people from different cultures.	
4. I respect the ways people from different cultures behave.	
5. I respect the values of people from different cultures.	
6. I can tell when I have upset my culturally distinct counterpart during an interaction.	
7. I always know what to say when interacting with people from different cultures.	
8. I can be as sociable as I want to be when interacting with people from different cultures.	
9. I am sensitive to my culturally different counterpart's subtle meanings during our interaction.	

Scoring: Add up the score for each of the items. The maximum score is 45 and the minimum score is 9. The greater the score, the more interculturally sensitive you are. A score of 9–18 demonstrates little to no sensitivity; 18–27 minimal sensitivity; 28–36 moderate sensitivity; 37–45 high sensitivity. Does your score surprise you?

Adapted from Chen & Starosta (2000).

an inclination toward prejudice and discriminatory behavior to ensure that people follow authority in an appropriate manner. This explanation is limited because it ignores contextual and interactional explanations.

Scapegoating approaches argue that people with high levels of prejudice see themselves as victims of society. Rather than accepting responsibility for their own failure, they typically shift the focus of responsibility to some vulnerable group. History provides numerous examples of scapegoating, including the Nazis attempt to blame Jews for the economic woes of Germany, which led to the Holocaust in World War II.

Critical theorists often trace expressions of prejudice to the economic or market climate in a particular culture or country. The market economy creates a structural climate where competition and inequality is the norm; another way of putting it is that the climate develops a situation of the have-nots versus the haves. For example, if you perceive that immigrants are taking jobs from you and others like you, you are likely to adopt prejudiced attitudes toward these immigrants. People are forced to fight for resources, and the fear of job exodus to other countries drives people to consider members of other cultural groups as the enemy. Prejudice against others is one way to succeed in competition and to reduce the number of people with whom one has to compete (see the example of free trade agreements in Box 4.5). Such prejudice has obvious negative consequences for immigrants (for example, facing discrimination in job searches), but also for non-immigrants and organizations such as limiting the pool of human resources. For example, the immigrant population tends to be younger than mainstream populations and contributes significantly to the economy (such as social security taxes).

While the market economy creates competition over scarce resources, competition itself is not the sole factor for creating prejudice. Social identity theory (see Chapter 3) argues that the categorization of people into two groups—"us" versus "them"—is also a factor for fostering prejudice and intergroup discrimination. Recall that this categorization results in ingroup bias and social competition with other cultural groups.

Extending the notion of social competition is the social dominance theory. This theory explains that prejudice against other cultural groups arises from a universally held desire to form and preserve social hierarchies. The basic instinct is not only to create "us" and "them," but also a situation where members of the "us" group have more power and resources than "them." This ideology is maintained by legitimizing myths, which may be described as prejudice about people in different social strata and from different cultural groups. People in majority power groups (for example, White Americans, heterosexuals, rich) hold a stronger social dominance orientation

Box 4.5 Globalization: Free Trade Agreements and Prejudice

Free trade agreements (FTA), such as the European Union and North American Free Trade Agreement, open up borders to facilitate commerce. The general idea is to strengthen and clarify rules and procedures governing trade and investment between nations. These trade agreements enable companies to import and export goods and services easily, and advocates argue that it provides economic benefits to all nations and parties. FTAs bring out advocates, such as the "Office of U.S. Trade Representative" [http://www.ustr.gov/Trade_Agreements/Regional/NAFTA/Section_Index.html] as well as critics, such as the group "Global Issues" [http://www.globalissues.org/TradeRelated/FreeTrade/Criticisms.asp.]

Regardless of your position on FTAs, some workers view these agreements very negatively. Union workers are one particular group that views FTAs as taking jobs from the United States and moving them to other nations because of cheaper labor costs. This economic situation can create and facilitate prejudice, as some workers might argue, for example, that Mexican workers are stealing their jobs. Some of these workers utilize the ultimate attribution error to develop prejudice against individuals who appear to be Mexican, even if these individuals were born in the United States and are not of Mexican decent. Such prejudice increases tension and creates conflict within communities. The interesting aspect is that the decision makers who move jobs overseas are executives within the company and not the overseas workers. This situation provides an example of how borders are opening up, but globalization is not seen as a positive by everyone. In fact, it can hurt interpersonal interactions between people of different cultures. The perception of competition from other groups can result in negative attitudes toward all individuals in those groups regardless of situation.

than members of minority power groups (for example, African Americans, homosexuals, poor) (Hecht, 1998).

Finally, intergroup contact focuses on the amount of interaction that we have with members of different cultural groups. Some of us grow up in areas where we meet people from different cultural groups on a regular basis, while others of us grow up in areas where it is rare to meet someone from a different cultural background. For people with low intercultural contact, prejudice is based on negative stereotypes of other cultures and the perception that members of the other groups are threats. For people with high intercultural contact, prejudice is based on the quality of interaction we have had with members of a cultural group. Thus, quality interaction functions to reduce prejudice while lack of intergroup interaction can result in prejudice if we have constructed perceived threats or negative stereotypes of other groups' members (either through the media or through information from people close to us—such as having a prejudice parent).

FUNCTIONS OF PREJUDICE   Closely related to the causes of prejudice are the functions of prejudice, which provide explanations as to why prejudice exists. If you ask most people if prejudice is bad, they will say yes. If you ask most people if they are prejudiced, most will say no. Thus, most people agree that being prejudiced is wrong and we should take action to stop it. However, that is easier said than done because prejudice has particular functions for us. In fact, all of us are prejudiced; what varies is how much prejudice we have.

To say that prejudice serves certain functions for us means that it helps us in certain ways that may be described as ego-defensive, value-expressive, utilitarian, economic, and vulnerability-protection (Hecht, 1998; Jost & Hamilton, 2005). The ego-defensive function is similar to the attribution bias (ego-protective) noted above. Prejudice helps to protect our identity at the personal and cultural levels. If we can demonstrate that others are bad, we look better. This function is often invoked when talking about the need to limit immigration—"we are losing our culture." The value-expressive function focuses on the consistency in how values and beliefs are expressed; prejudice functions to support our own values and to diminish those values from other groups. Thus, prejudice helps to justify the importance of one's own culture. For example, many Western nations have an emphasis toward a youth culture. The mainstream culture encourages new technology and young faces in the media and relegates older people to behind-the-scenes roles. In this manner, we demonstrate a value of youth and novelty in the culture and not a reverence for older people. The utilitarian function focuses on the simplicity of processing information. We often experience information overload in our lives, and prejudice, along with stereotyping, is often simpler for us to rely on than actually expending the time and effort to get to know someone else; that is, we use our pre-existing biases to organize information about people rather than creating and learning new categories. The economic function focuses on the use of prejudice to maintain economic power. Prejudice is used to rationalize why certain groups should have power (for example, "we work harder," or "we are better prepared").

Finally, the vulnerability-protection function uses prejudice to allay one's fears and provide safety for self and family. Prejudice is used to keep us away from people who might be potentially harmful.

In sum, prejudice has many causes including limited interaction, economic disadvantages, and hierarchy among groups. In addition, prejudice has certain functions including positive group identity, protection against feeling vulnerable, and making information processing simpler. While prejudice is functional for members of a group in certain ways, it also hurts the group by limiting exposure to new ways of thinking and by reducing the effectiveness of interacting and succeeding in a global economy.

Communicating Prejudice

One way to identify the functions that prejudice serves is by looking at the stories or narratives that they tell about other groups. These narratives provide rationalizations of why people are prejudiced (Hall, 1998). Hall identified five types of narratives from his study of 120 university students who wrote 123 stories of prejudice. He labeled these narratives as "morally better," "personally afflicted," "social pressure," "their turf," and "system abuse." "Morally better" narratives come from people who find fault in other groups of people (also see Box 4.6 on p.106). These stories describe other groups as inferior or short-sighted (for example, "they are uncivilized" or "they are barbarians—look how they treat women"). People assume that individuals from these groups could make better choices, but they refuse to. "Personally afflicted" narratives come from people who perceive that they have experienced negative behavior from another group. These past experiences cause them to fear and hate all members of the other group. For example, if you were called names or "beat up" by a member of a particular group, you might not trust any members from that group. Therefore, the individual expressing this story feels that he or she has the right to hate "those people." "Social pressure" narratives express conformity of attitudes within a culture group about members of a different group. Individuals within their group might think that the other cultural group is okay, but they receive too much pressure from their peers discouraging positive attitudes and interaction with members of the cultural group. They want to maintain their friendships with members of their own cultural group at all costs. "Their turf" narratives express prejudice by saying that the neighborhoods in which members of "that culture" live are unsafe and violent and therefore it is best to avoid them. Perceptions of the other group are often created by the media, not through direct contact with the group. The primary concern is safety, and feelings of vulnerability influence these narratives. Finally, "system abuse" narratives focus on members of a different cultural group getting unfair advantages. The perception is that "I work hard for a living and I can't stand that those people get extra rewards like welfare or food stamps just because they are from their cultural group, not because they work hard." People expressing these stories fear losing their rewards and resent "freeloaders."

Box 4.6 Talking about Ethics: Prejudice and Moral Exclusion

People who are prejudiced clearly have reasons for being so. The moral inclusion/exclusion dimension is an ethical rationale often given to justify our prejudice. We often feel that certain people are not morally worthy and therefore we create negative attitudes about them. In the five types of narrative about prejudice, Hall (1998) has identified five "others" about whom we are prejudiced. The morally better other is someone who chooses wrong. The personally afflicted other is someone who is a mean trouble starter. The social pressure other is someone who is nice, but different. The turf other is a dangerous criminal. Finally, the system abuse other is a freeloader. Do you think it is acceptable to be prejudiced toward certain people such as those in these five narratives? Can you justify prejudice against certain of these people more than others? Or is prejudice wrong no matter what? Is a morally inclusive stance the appropriate one?

Other scholars have attempted to "unpack" the way that we express prejudice about other cultural groups. Smith (1994) presented a basic form that shows how prejudice develops:

Negative stereotype:	Those people are rude.
Leads to	
Prejudice attitude:	I don't like those people.
Leads to	
Discrimination:	I won't talk to those people or hire them.

Thus, it is important to examine stereotypes since they lead to prejudice.

STEREOTYPES   **Stereotypes** are overgeneralized cognitions about a group of people with no attempt to identify within-group variation. Stereotypes are often based on learned and widely shared beliefs about another group that reinforce or justify prejudice. Stereotypes often reduce uncertainty and ambiguity about a group of people, but do so in an inaccurate way. This subsection examines characteristics about stereotypes and distinguishes between mindful and mindless stereotyping.

Stereotypes have a number of characteristics. First, we can create stereotypes about our own group (autostereotypes) or other groups (heterostereotypes). Second, stereotypes can be personal or normative. Personal stereotypes are based on our own limited personal experiences with other groups. They tend to be inaccurate because our experiences represent a limited and skewed sample. Normative stereotypes are based on information from other sources, such as media or books. Normative stereotypes have accurate and inaccurate parts. If the normative stereotype is based on strong research, such as what you read in most textbooks and journal articles, the stereotypes may have accurate characteristics. For example, describing U.S. culture as individualistic is largely accurate, but, of course, some U.S. Americans are more collectivistic than individualistic. Normative stereotypes are inaccurate when they are based on limited information or reflect individual biases. For example, the pictures presented of White Americans and African Americans during Hurricane Katrina's aftermath would lead us to believe that African Americans loot stores, which is highly inaccurate. Finally, stereotypes can be both positive (Chinese are good at math) and negative (Chinese are bad drivers). However, even positive stereotypes are quite limiting to individuals who perceive themselves as unique within their group. Positive stereotypes ascribe an identity to an individual that he or she may not want.

Since most people acknowledge the limitations of stereotypes, why do you suppose they persist? The primary reason is that they serve a cognitive function. Stereotypes help us organize and make sense of the world. Imagine trying to explain to someone from a different culture what your culture is like using only individualized information. You would find this difficult because you have to use generalizations to describe a culture. All of us stereotype; however, we can distinguish between mindless (and often inaccurate) stereotypes and mindful (and more accurate) stereotypes.

Mindless stereotyping occurs when we do not think about how we are processing information. Think about a task that you do often, such as driving a car. Can you think of a time when you could not remember what you were doing during five minutes of driving? For example, have you ever missed a turn when you were driving because you were used to driving home and instead you were going to the store? This is an example of mindlessness during a task. Mindlessness can also occur when we interact with others because we expect the conversation to go in a similar manner (as it has in the past). This is one reason we often drift away when listening to others. In contrast, mindful stereotyping occurs when we think carefully about the information we are receiving and remain open to the possibility that we are wrong about a group or individual (see Box 4.7 on p.109). Table 4.1 compares and contrasts mindful and mindless stereotyping.

In sum, while stereotypes are a key element of prejudice and discrimination, they can also be used more effectively when we are mindful about stereotypes. The willingness to seek and consider new information and to alter categories to make them more accurate are signs of mindful stereotyping. When we are mindless about stereotyping, the result is often racism and discrimination.

RACISM AND DISCRIMINATION   Racism and discrimination are concepts closely related to prejudice. **Racism** includes both attitudes and behaviors. It is an irrationally based negative attitude toward a racial or ethnic group, coupled with actions that discriminate against that group. Race is a social construction about people with similar physical characteristics. That is, race exists because we view a social group as being distinct from others. Biologically, a racial group has more differences within that group than when compared to other racial groups. Thus, racial groups are not "real." However, from a social standpoint, we have constructed racial groups to be real and meaningful, and we re-create these groups through questions on the census about race and by labeling people as having a race. **Discrimination** is action that

Table 4.1

MINDLESS VERSUS MINDFUL STEREOTYPES

Mindless Stereotypes	Mindful Stereotypes
Holding on to categories about other groups rigidly	Recognizing that we are using a stereotype about a group of people
Holding on to old stereotypes and ignoring new information	Realizing that the stereotype is the first best guess rather than the definitive answer
Using emotional evaluations (often negative) to guide how we are processing information	Using categories that interpret behavior rather than evaluate behavior
Limiting information about contextual cues to behaviors and only focusing on cultural explanations	Using contextual information to explain behavior in addition to cultural and individual attributions
Distorting contradictory information so that it fits our preconceived stereotypes	Being open to new information and contradictory evidence and being willing to redefine the categories
Assuming that one person's behavior reflects all of the members of a cultural group	Seeking a variety of sources of information about a group and individuals before forming categories
Maximizing the distance between your group and the other group through exaggerated categories	Minimizing difference between your group and the other group by recognizing meaningful similarities and differences

Source: Ting-Toomey (1999)

maintains the dominance of one group of people over another. The power to enact the behavior is a key component to racism and discrimination. That power can be from a held position (being a boss) or social power (being part of a group that has political power). Racism and discrimination can be overt or covert. Overt racism and discrimination is explicit and direct. For example, Mel Gibson's attitudes in the opening story were overt. Covert racism and discrimination is hidden and subtle. People experiencing covert discrimination often cannot "put their finger on the discrimination," but rather have just a feeling. Thus, racism and discrimination can be "in your face" and obvious, but more often are simply hidden from most people's view (see the example in Box 4.8).

While we could consider a variety of discriminatory actions, such as not hiring or renting to a person from a particular cultural group, the remainder of this section focuses on racism and discrimination as the communication of prejudice. Through the study of elite discourse around the world (the communication of people in power from a variety of circles including education, politics, and

Box 4.7 What Went Right? Mindful Stereotypes

We return to the example of Jim and Toshi from earlier in the chapter (roommates discussing where they are going to eat tonight). This time they use mindful stereotyping in making attributions.

	Message	Attribution/Mindful Stereotyping
Jim:	So, what do you wanna eat tonight?	He may have some idea, and I don't want to force my tastes on him.
Toshi:	I don't know. Whatever you like.	I should listen to his opinion first.
Jim:	How about sushi? Do you remember the restaurant we went last time? You said you liked it. Otherwise, we can eat pizza, burgers, or Mexican food or whatever.	I assume that he likes sushi since we went before and he said he liked it. And, I think sushi is very popular in Japanese culture. I will give him other options just in case. I'd rather eat Mexican, but the others are fine.
Toshi:	Well, sushi was fine. I like those other options. Do you prefer pizza?	Actually, I do not like sushi, but I could not tell him because he paid for me that night. I think probably likes pizza the best because it is American. I love Mexican food.
Jim:	I really am flexible, but have a slight preference for Mexican.	He is not usually direct so I'll let him know my preference. I got the sense through the way he said it that he was offering pizza just to make me happy.
Toshi:	I love Mexican food.	I'm surprised that he likes it, but happy we agree.
Jim:	Are you sure? I think sometimes that you simply go along with what I say.	I learned in class that Japanese tend to be less direct than Americans and focus on harmony. I'll check my perceptions with him.
Toshi:	You are perceptive, but in this case I really love Mexican. Know what—not all Japanese like sushi. I can't stand it.	I like that he understands my culture somewhat, but I want to correct his stereotype about sushi.
Jim:	Really? I don't like it either. How about going to eat at Abuelitas?	That's good to know—I really don't want to be closed-minded about my friend.
Toshi:	Sounds good.	

business), van Dijk (1993) identified several ways that people express prejudiced attitudes. He argued that these strategies serve to reinforce elite power and hierarchical relations in society. He identified a variety of strategies, but we focus on four here: a) face saving, b) negative other presentation, c) blame the victim, and d) paternalistic rhetoric.

First, face saving is a strategy to present a positive self-image before expressing a racist/sexist/homophobic attitude. It often follows the form, "I'm not X, but Y." For example, "I'm not prejudiced, but there are too many illegal immigrants from Mexico taking our jobs," or "Some of my best friends are White, but they do not

Box 4.8 Voices: Covert Racism/Discrimination

I am an African American woman with over 25 years experience in corporate America. I am a senior manager at a large semiconductor manufacturing plant and have heard stories about racism in corporate America. I have been fortunate to largely avoid these problems and feel supported by my supervisors. Of course, I have felt that there have been decisions made in my company based in racist motives, but I never have had any direct evidence. As a result, I have been largely optimistic about fairness and positive race relations. However, a recent event has changed my perspective somewhat.

I decided that I wanted to obtain a Ph.D. for my own edification. I have been taking classes part-time and have had a wonderful experience. The courses were challenging, the professors supportive, and classmates have provided a wealth of knowledge. In a recent class, I was teamed up with four other students (all White Americans) on a group project. We did well as a group, but individually I received a B on the project (and my teammates received As or A+s). I didn't begrudge them their grades, as they worked hard and were smart people. The feedback on my paper was dead on, too. I was disappointed to have my writing critiqued, but every point was accurate and I appreciated the care the professor gave in editing my paper. At the end, he said that my conclusions lacked depth and recommended that I consult with my teammates as they had done a great job. I took him up on that and I was shocked by what I found out. The paper was a combination of team and individual effort. The individual effort was only 2–3 pages at the end of a 15-page paper. Their individual sections were similar in content and format to mine, but more importantly, their group sections had not been edited in the same manner as mine (and the group section was exactly the same). Rather, they all received comments about what great writers they were.

I pointed this out to my teammates and they were shocked and agreed that the grades were a problem. I decided to talk with the professor, not to try to get my grade changed (I think I deserved the B), but to point out his biases. To his credit he owned it and said, "Wow, you can see my southern biases coming out here." I suggested that he could really make a strong point about diversity and racism by sharing this with the class or at least with my group. He said that was a good idea, but never did bring it up. These conversations lasted several weeks (as I persisted in my challenge) and over this time, three of my teammates ended up saying that I must have "pissed off" the professor to get the low grade and that I was making too big a deal of it. I think they simply didn't want to lose their As, but I was disappointed they were unwilling to stand up to blatant racism. One teammate was very supportive and stood by me. The result of this experience is that I am much more suspicious than I used to be. I also wondered whether Whites received benefits because of their skin color and now I have direct evidence that in certain cases they do. I am still optimistic, but realize that race relations still have a way to go.

work hard enough" or "I'm not homophobic, but gays shouldn't be able to get married." The negative attitude is obvious, and it is clear that the function of the strategy is to preemptively save face and not get labeled as racist or prejudiced. Politicians use this strategy when dealing with immigrant or minority groups: "We are tolerant and give them X, but they abuse our tolerance and do Y." It is a stereotype to justify racism.

Second, negative other presentation is another face-saving strategy that presents the other group members in a negative way in order to justify the racism.

Specific tactics to accomplish this strategy include scapegoating, name calling, and dehumanizing. Box 4.9 from the book *The Kite Runner* illustrates this type of racism.

Third, the blame-the-victim strategy is invoked to explain why a racist attitude is appropriate. The victim might experience a negative racial act, such as not being hired even though he or she was the most qualified. A person invoking the blame-the-victim strategy might use some aspect of the victim's behavior as the cause of the unfair hiring practice, saying, for example, that the victim did not get the job because he or she did not wear the proper clothes. Box 4.8 on covert racism also demonstrates this strategy, as some of the students blamed the unfair grade on the victim, saying "She must have done something to upset the professor."

Fourth, paternalistic rhetoric is often used by well meaning but misguided individuals who want to solve the problems of a group of people. These individuals want to help the other group, but imbedded in their language is the belief that the group cannot help themselves. An example of this comes from a colleague of mine. She works with American Indian communities on health issues. She was working with a group of students, and one of them, a White middle-class woman, said, "I want to work with American Indians so I can give them a voice." My colleague responded by saying, "What makes you think they want you to do that for them or that they do not have their own voice?" This student wanted to help, but her racial and socioeconomic biases, left unchecked, could have caused more harm than good.

CONCEPT CHECK   In summary, this section examined the ways that prejudice is communicated and why. First, we explored the narratives that rationalize why prejudice is acceptable to some people in some situations. Second, we examined

---

Box 4.9 Voices: Negative Other Presentation and Racism

"For years, that was all I knew about the Hazaras, that they were Mogul descendants and that they looked a little like Chinese people. School textbooks barely mentioned them and referred to their ancestry only in passing. Then one day, I was in Baba's study, looking through his stuff, when I found one of my mother's old history books. It was written by an Iranian named Khorami. I blew the dust off it, sneaked it into bed with me that night, and was stunned to find an entire chapter on Hazara history. An entire chapter dedicated to Hassan's people! In it, I read that my people, the Pashtuns, had persecuted and oppressed the Hazaras. It said the Hazaras had tried to rise against the Pashtuns in the nineteenth century, but the Pashtuns had "quelled them with unspeakable violence." The book said that my people had killed the Hazaras, driven them from their lands, burned their homes, and sold their women. The book said part of the reason Pashtuns had oppressed the Hazaras was that Pashtuns were Sunni Muslims, while Hazaras were Shi'a. The book said a lot of things I didn't know, things my teachers hadn't mentioned. Things Baba hadn't mentioned either. It also said some things I did know, like that people called Hazaras mice-eating, flat-nosed, load-carrying donkeys. I had heard some of the kids in the neighborhood yell those names to Hassan."

—Amir in *The Kite Runner*, Hosseini, 2003, p. 9

a model of communicating prejudice that includes stereotypes and discrimination. The distinction between mindful and mindless stereotypes was emphasized. This section concluded by exploring four communication strategies used to express discrimination and racism in subtle and covert ways.

Layers of Attributions and Attitudes

Attributions and attitudes are often treated as solely individual phenomena; that is, most people and scholars treat these aspects of social cognition as the responsibility and domain of individual people. From this perspective, the way to reduce prejudice and improve the quality of attributions is for individuals to increase their cognitive effort and recognize the flaws in their thinking. While this perspective has some validity in that all individuals can make improvements by being more mindful, this perspective is quite limited in identifying what causes prejudice, stereotyping, and faulty attributions (Hecht, 1998). Thus, the layered perspective can be quite illuminating about these aspects in social cognition. This section examines these layers, starting with bottom-up effects and then focusing on top-down effects.

Bottom-Up Effects

The ways in which individual bias impacts relationships, organizations, and communities are well documented. Any individual with prejudice can make people from other cultural groups uncomfortable and even fearful. I suspect that anyone reading this book can picture a neighbor, co-worker, or family member who expresses prejudice regularly. I have extended family members who do this, and it makes me uncomfortable, and I get frustrated and angry, especially when I have asked them not to do this. However, it is relatively easy for me to avoid these people so that I do not have to experience this discomfort. But what happens if we cannot avoid people like this?

The key influence on whether individuals have a lasting and deep impact on others appears to depend on the power of the individual. Power is relationally created in that people only have power if others choose to give it to them. However, sometimes we have limited choice for giving others power such as in cases where the person is in a hierarchy above us. These individuals include bosses, government officials, and parents. If your boss is prejudiced against people from your cultural group, he or she has the ability to make your life difficult. If you need this job and have poor options for another job, you may feel (or even be) stuck in a miserable situation. A stranger may have incredible power if he is violent and engages in a hate crime. If you are in the wrong place at the wrong time, this individual has a deep impact on you individually, but also on society. For example, think about the individuals who killed Matthew Shepard simply because he was gay.

The Matthew Shepard case is a sensational one and relatively rare. I think the more important cases we need to examine are those involving people with the power to control what others see and do. The editor of a newspaper or newscast, for example, has incredible power to shape what people see and how they think. Their individual biases determine which pictures and stories are shown and told. The pictures of the survivors of Hurricane Katrina in this chapter demonstrate how cultural prejudice can frame the way stories are told. Additionally, owners of companies, chief executive officers, and managers have a great deal of power in determining who gets raises and promotions. Their individual biases have a strong impact on those choices and whether a company is culturally inclusive or fraught with discrimination. Finally, our governmental officials make policies that impact intercultural relationships in our society. The members of Congress in the United States are predominantly upper class, White heterosexual, able bodied, older men—yet they are expected to represent all cultural groups. Recognizing and addressing individual biases, especially for those in power, is important to improving intercultural relations.

Top-Down Effects

While the previous section examined how individual biases impact organizations and society, in this section we examine the reverse effect; that is, how do societal and organizational institutions impact an individual's attributions and attitudes? The primary focus on top-down effects is **institutionalized racism,** which is "differential access to goods, services, and opportunities of society by race" (Jones, 2000, p. 1212). In essence, these are organizational or community prescribed actions that maintain the dominance of one group over another. Institutionalized racism can be direct, such as restricted membership lists of country clubs that keep out certain groups, or indirect, such as a company moving its headquarters out of an inner city area to a suburb. Indirect institutionalized racism is not motivated by prejudice, but the impacts of the actions serve to harm members of a particular cultural group (Kitano, 1991). In the following section, we examine two types of institutions that show how racism impacts individuals' attributions and attitudes: the media and public policy.

The media are often our first, and sometimes only, introduction to people of different cultural groups. However, the presentation of information is often biased in a particular direction because of the function of the media. Individual executives impact the way that certain cultural groups are presented (as was noted in the bottom-up section). With a few exceptions, the basic function of most of the media is entertainment. The media are big business, and their goal is to have strong ratings so that they can charge "top dollar" for advertising on their television shows, in their papers, and on their Web sites. Therefore, they present images of what they think people want to see. Their primary concern is not whether people are portrayed in complex or accurate ways. Simple descriptions are often easier to sell. Although the media have an ethical responsibility to present people in more complex ways, the focus of attention in media changes so fast that simple stereotypes are easiest to present.

The result of this focus on quick entertainment is a simple representation of cultural groups. However, these images often create and reinforce stereotypes about cultural groups for many viewers/readers. For example, the picture of the African American "looters" on YahooNews likely reinforced a stereotype of African American as criminals for viewers who held this stereotype. The picture of the White "finders" likely created sympathy for people in a difficult situation; notice the

Box 4.10 Talking about Ethics: Reverse Racism and Discrimination

In the past few decades, members of majority groups (often White males in the United States) have claimed that laws and policies have created reverse discrimination; that is, they claim that affirmative action, targeted scholarships, and set aside contracts (where the government sets aside contracts for minority-owned business) are discriminatory for White men. Their perspective is that open competition should be allowed and the best person should win.

The opposing argument is that these policies are necessary to stem discriminatory practices that have harmed ethnic minorities for years. The policies are necessary to help equate society after years of discrimination and are still necessary because of continuing inequality. They argue that reverse discrimination is not possible at this junction because ethnic minorities cannot do to White males what was done to them because of a stratified society. Stratification is inequality in social status, power, and economics among ethnic groups. Figure 4.4 below illustrates that, while some individuals in Group One have less power than those in Group Two, overall Group One has more power than Group Two.

Which of these positions do you agree with? What cultural or ethical values guide your decision?

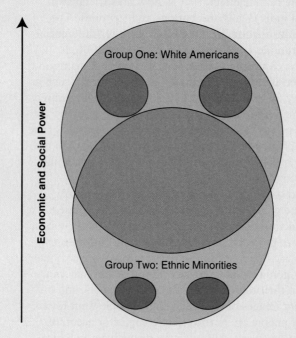

Figure 4.4
Social
Stratification

attribution biases and focus on situational versus cultural explanations for the same act. Those that did not hold this stereotype likely were outraged by this presentation of both sets of individuals. The media do not work in a direct manner; rather they work with other societal institutions and individual relationships to affect individuals' social cognition. The media do, however, have an important functional role on the attributions and attitudes that people have.

Public policy also shapes individual attitudes and attributions. The vast majority of people in a society follow the laws set forth for them. They believe that most laws are important to create a cohesive and organized society. However, many laws negatively impact intercultural relations and members of particular cultural groups. I want to share two examples. First, for many years in the United States, it was illegal to have an interracial marriage (more discussion on this topic in Chapter 6). These laws dictated what for many U.S. Americans is a personal choice and, as a result, helped to restrict interaction among cultural groups. Of course, prejudiced attitudes helped to create these laws in the first place so laws and individual action/attitudes reinforce each other. The second example is immigration policies. Immigration policies are sensitive, hot topics around the world. While immigrants are recognized as critical to the economic success in a country and a positive way to increase diversity of perspective and lifestyle, people may also have concerns about safety and security and fear losing their culture (notice these are the rationalizations for prejudice noted above). In the United States, the focus is on restricting the number of illegal immigrants, particularly from Latin America and especially Mexico. These policies, which the columnist Ruben Navarrette (2006) labels as racially motivated, target a particular group of people. Navarrette argued that securing the Mexican border for national security appears racist when the Canadian border is unguarded and when Canada was the choice for two caught terrorists groups. In fact, the immigration laws help to reinforce xenophobia (fear of foreigners) and thus limit intercultural interaction. We will explore the impact of public policy and the media in more depth in later chapters in this book.

Challenges and Skills

Trying to change attitudes and attributions about other cultural groups presents many challenges. Certainly, one key challenge is, "How do you change institutions that have deeply imbedded practices and policies?" If societal and organizational institutions have an impact on individuals, we have to be able to change these institutions to make a lasting impact. Unfortunately, change is slow and difficult, but it does appear to be happening. Today, it is clearly inappropriate to be a bigot and express prejudiced ideas toward most groups (gays and immigrants might be exceptions), and thus progress is happening. Challenging public policy and media representations is a skill that individuals can develop and is a topic we will discuss in more depth in Chapters 9 and 11. At the very least, we as individuals need to make sure to use our agency. We can educate friends and classmates about our culture. We can be nonverbally expressive to people from other cultures (such as through smiles and nods of hello). We can ask those who tell racist/sexist/homophobic jokes to stop or at least communicate to them that we do not like it. We can write letters to the editors of newspaper and to other media outlets to criticize stereotypical portrayals of cultural groups. To effectively address racism, we need to recognize that all of us express—or at least think—prejudiced ideas at some point in time; we can try to address the context-specific reasons for the prejudice rather than labeling ourselves or others as prejudiced or racist. Thus, it would be better to say "John said something I would call bigoted" rather than "John is a bigot."

A second challenge is, "How do individuals change their attributions and attitudes about other cultures?" Since individuals impact others' attitudes, some effort needs to be placed on the individual level. Being aware of attribution biases and mindful stereotyping are good first steps to improve the accuracy of perceptions about other cultural groups. Additionally, we should think about ways to improve the quality of intercultural interaction since this is one component of reducing prejudice (Stephan & Stephan, 1996). Researchers have identified several factors that help to improve the quality of intercultural interaction: voluntary contact, equal status, personal contact, and cooperative opportunities (Gaertner, Dovidio, & Bachman, 1996; Stephan & Stephan, 1996). Intercultural interaction needs to be voluntary rather than forced in order to avoid resentment. Equal status refers to ensuring that people working together are at the same hierarchical level in order to avoid one cultural group dominating another. Personal contact is the opportunity to get to know members of another group rather than having impersonal contact. Finally, the focus of the interactions should be on cooperative opportunities rather than encouraging competition. A challenge is figuring out how to foster each of these characteristics.

Finally, we as individuals can learn to be allies for members of different cultural groups. The key focus is not to try to solve *for*, but rather work *with*; that is, we must avoid a paternalistic stance. Some strategies for becoming an ally include the following:

1. Own your own biases, and recognize how you contribute to a stratified society, particularly if you are a member of a dominant group.
2. Talk about your own feelings using "I" statements (rather than saying "*you shouldn't feel this way*").
3. Listen and believe the members of other cultures when they tell stories of racism and discrimination.
4. Give members of other groups the opportunity to talk (do not "hog" the conversation).
5. If you are a member of a dominant group, limit the sharing of your stories about how you have been victimized, too. During initial conversations, these victimization stories can be viewed as a rationalization for prejudice. If you become trusted and respected among members of another culture, then these stories can be about healing and conflict resolution.
6. Do not expect to get a "pat on the back." Members of ethnic minorities have to combat racism on a daily basis and never get thanked.

SUMMARY

Returning to the opening story: Gibson's remarks reflect the ultimate attribution error in blaming Jews for all the wars. Additionally, his comments were prejudicial and racist. He has the power to impact the perceptions of others because of his status in society. Gibson's apology reflects the egoprotective bias and the fundamental attribution error (over attributing the effect of alcohol on his behavior). He and the actors who came to his defense were making primarily situation-based attributions of his behavior, while Robinson was making a person-based attribution. The debates that were sparked help to illustrate the layered effect of media on attributions and intercultural communication.

Here is the chapter summary based on the learning objectives:

- **Characteristics of attributions**. Attributions are our explanations of behaviors that focus on situational, category, and personal factors. Attribution characteristics include the following: a) we attribute our own behavior to different factors than we do behavior the of others; b) we tend to have incomplete information when we make attributions of others; c) we tend to be confident in the accuracy of our attribution despite having limited information; and d) our attributions are shaped by cultural values.

- **Seven attribution errors**. There are seven types of attribution errors: egocentric, egoprotective, fundamental, self-effacing, premature closure, negativity, and ultimate. These errors tend to encourage us to look at ourselves and members of our cultural group in the best possible way while they encourage us to look at members of other groups in neutral or negative ways.

- **Model of intercultural sensitivity**. Attitudes are the predispositions we have about other objects and people. Intercultural sensitivity is a key attitude about members of other cultural groups and ranges from ethnocentric to ethnorelative. When we are ethnocentric, we tend to express prejudice toward other cultural groups.

- **Causes and functions of prejudice**. Prejudice is caused by several factors including authoritarian personalities, scapegoating, market economy, social competition, and the amount of interaction we have with other cultural groups. Prejudice serves five functions for people who express it: ego-defensive, value-expressive, utilitarian, economic, and vulnerability-protection.

- **Expression of prejudice**. Prejudice is expressed through stories that we tell and often reflects negative stereotypes about other cultural groups. Racism and discrimination are the primary expressions of prejudice. Racism includes irrationally negative attitudes, discrimination, or action to maintain dominance of one group over others, and the power to enact actions. Four strategies for expressing prejudice include face saving; negative other presentation; blame the victim; and paternalistic rhetoric.

- **Bottom-up and top-down effects**. The layered approach illustrates that societal and organizational institutions shape individuals' attributions and attitudes. Two examples include the media and public policy. The biases we have and the deeply ingrained institutional structures and discrimination present challenges on how to improve intercultural attitudes and interaction. As individuals, we can become aware of our biases, create positive situations for interaction, and use the skills of an ally. However, we also need to challenge individuals and institutional structures to create lasting change. Each of us has agency.

REVIEW QUESTIONS

1. Describe the five characteristics of attributions.
2. Explain how culture influences attributions, and provide an example from your own experience.
3. What are the seven attribution errors? Provide an example of each and discuss how they have impacted the intercultural interactions that you have had.
4. Describe the model of intercultural sensitivity and characteristics of individuals at various stages in the model.
5. How do narratives of prejudice reflect causes and functions of prejudice; that is, what causes and functions are involved in each narrative?
6. Explain how stereotypes and discrimination are related to prejudice. Provide an example from the news to illustrate this relationship.
7. Compare and contrast mindful and mindless stereotyping and provide an example of each.
8. Provide an example of each of the five strategies for expressing prejudice.
9. Make an argument in favor of or against whether reverse discrimination exists. Use concepts and evidence from this chapter to support your argument.

EXERCISES

1. Keep a diary of the attributions you make when you interact with people from different cultural groups. Identify the attribution biases and attitudes (ethnocentric, ethnorelative, mindful vs. mindless stereotyping). Are there ways you can improve your attributions of others' behavior? How will this improve your intercultural interaction?
2. Read the book *Radical Hope: Ethics in the Face of Cultural Devastation* by Jonathon Lear (Harvard University Press). It discusses the ways that the Crow (an American Indian tribe in the western United States) responded to being forced to a reservation. It describes how they have responded to the loss of their culture and to racism.
3. Analyze the content of news stories on your favorite Web site or TV news (choose about 30 minutes a day for a week—or one "section" of a Web-based paper a day). Use the attribution biases or various attitudes presented in this chapter to systematically categorize the stories presented about members of particular cultural groups. Do you find that certain groups are portrayed better than others? How so?

CHAPTER 5

Initial Intercultural Interactions

CHAPTER OUTLINE

I. Introduction

II. Types of Initial Intercultural Interactions
  a. Travel
  b. Sojourners
  c. Migrants: Refugees and Immigrants

III. Explaining Initial Intercultural Interactions: Cultural Adaptation Perspectives
  a. Culture Shock
  b. Cultural Adaptation
  c. Concept Check

IV. Explaining Initial Intercultural Interactions: Communication Strategy Perspectives
  a. Anxiety and Uncertainty Management (AUM) Theory
  b. Communication Accommodation Theory
  c. Concept Check

V. Layers of Initial Intercultural Interaction
  a. Bottom-Up Effects
  b. Top-Down Effects: Initial Interactions and Individual Effects
  c. Top-Down Effects: Culture, Media and Initial Interactions
  d. Challenges and Skills

VI. Summary

VII. Review Questions

VIII. Exercises

Greeting

Misunderstandings can result from simple differences in cultural practices such as during initial greetings. What other difficulties occur with people from other cultures during initial interactions?

CHAPTER OBJECTIVES

After reading this chapter, students should be able to

- describe several types of initial interactions with people from different cultural backgrounds.

- describe the model of culture shock and the different responses that people "choose" during cultural adaptation.

- explain how anxiety and uncertainty management impact effective communication with people from different cultures.

- explicate the reasons why we use accommodation and nonaccommodation during our communication with people from different cultures and the effects of such behavior.

- discuss the bottom-up and top-down effects of intercultural communication during initial interactions.

Introduction

Khadi was an international student from Senegal who came to the United States for her graduate degree. She was very excited about the opportunity to study in the United States because of its overall high-quality education. She was looking forward to taking home what she learned so that she could help her people. During her first few weeks in the United States, however, she had a rude awakening. She couldn't find food she liked; moreover, she felt that most of her classmates, while generally polite, were distant and unwilling to interact with her on any sustained level. She could not figure out whether it was her lack of understanding of the culture or her language skills. She tried to ask people for help, but found them not very forthcoming. It made her upset because she knew how much Americans wanted people to learn their culture; here she was trying to learn, but not getting any help. She tried to mirror the way the other students asked questions in class and talked to one another, but it didn't seem to help her. She missed home, but was determined to get her degree, so she decided to stay.

During her first year, she began to make some friends—both other international students from Africa and some U.S. students. The international students who had been here awhile started explaining situations to her, and she began making sense of what was going on by careful observation. She also liked having the support network of African friends—they came from different cultures, but they shared some similarity in language (French) and in lived experiences.

During her second year of studies, Khadi became much more confident in her interactions with Americans, and her peers began to think she was from the East Coast, but American. She became a mentor to new graduate students, helping them learn about American culture. She was able to tell new students when to try and mirror the communication of U.S. Americans and when to communicate based on their own cultural norms. When it was time to leave the U.S., she had mixed emotions—happy to go home but also sad to leave. She knew that she had made some great friends and would be back.

Question: What concepts and theories of initial intercultural interactions explain this student's experience?

As individuals, we have different perspectives about meeting people who are new to us. Some of us like the excitement of meeting a person who is new. We enjoy learning about that person and about his or her distinctive characteristics and background. We may know other people from that culture or we may have learned a bit about it from a class or through the media. For others, meeting new people, especially a person from a different culture, is difficult and uncomfortable. Some of us get anxious, and our first response is fear, not excitement. Regardless of our personalities, meeting someone from a different culture for the first time tends to escalate our emotions (Duronto, Nishida, & Nakayama, 2005; Furnham & Bochner, 1986).

As we initially develop these relationships with people from different cultures, we tend to engage in intergroup communication. **Intergroup communication** is when our messages and identity tend to focus on the cultural and group identities (for example, I see myself as Hispanic, and you see yourself as White, or I see myself as Sunni, and you see yourself as Shi'a) (Gudykunst, 2005.) Our motivations, norms, and rules for communication are based on cultural knowledge and expectations. If we develop the relationship, we have a greater tendency to engage in interpersonal communication. **Interpersonal communication** occurs when the motivations, messages, and rules focus on the unique aspects of our relationships (Gudykunst, 2005). Both interpersonal and intergroup communication occur in any given relationship, but it is the predominance of one type over the other that describes the nature of the relationship at a particular stage.

This chapter focuses on the relationships we create with people from other cultures when our communication is based mostly on intergroup communication. (Chapter 6 focuses on more developed relationships that include interpersonal communication.) Further, this chapter discusses the different types of initial interactions that we have with others and describes four theories for these interactions. Two of these theories focus on adapting to different cultures, and two of these theories describe communication strategies during initial interactions. The final section of this chapter describes layers of initial interactions and examines skills and challenges for initial interactions with people from different cultures.

Types of Initial Intercultural Interactions

During our lifetimes, we have the opportunity to meet a great number of people from different cultures. We might meet others during our travels, during a study abroad or work abroad experience, or during our everyday lives when we meet immigrants (both recent and not so recent).

Travel

The ease and frequency of foreign travel have made intercultural interactions a common occurrence as well as a big business. "According to the World Tourism Organization, 698 million people traveled to a foreign country in 2000, spending more than US$ 478 billion. International tourism receipts combined with passenger transport currently total more than US$ 575 billion—making tourism the world's number one export earner, ahead of automotive products, chemicals, petroleum and food" (UNEP, 2007).

Foreign and "exotic" travel provides many of us with the opportunity to meet people from different cultures, individuals that we normally would not meet in our everyday lives. Foreign travel generally provides us with safe and superficial interactions that create positive and romantic impressions of other cultures. However, travel rarely leads to deep and sustained interpersonal relations (unlike the romantic images created in books and movies, such as *How Stella Got Her Groove Back*). Travel does have important functions (and certainly is fun), but keep in mind some of the potential negatives as well.

First, travel often creates goodwill and positive feelings for the traveler. Places that depend on tourism tend to have very inviting climates and people. Tourism in many countries is big business, and the local economy depends on tourists coming

Souvenirs are often seen as a link to other cultures. However, they often "exocticize" and stereotype indigenous cultures—that is, they lead us to value the other cultures because they are so unique and different from our own, but in the process encourage us to ignore the human and "real" elements of other cultures. In what way does travel help enhance intercultural interactions? In what way does it hurt intercultural interactions?

back. Thus, we often do not see the "real" culture as the people we meet are trying to adapt to our needs. We might see some cultural performances (for example, a hula dance or a powwow), but not a detailed glimpse of the culture. That is not to say that our hosts do not like us, but the experience really involves a business relationship, and a reduction of cultural distance (for example, developing interpersonal relationships) will not happen quickly (Lawson & Jaworski, 2007). For example, in a study of British tourists in Gambia, Lawson and Jaworski examined 194 tourist/host interactions as described in 20 communication diaries (2007). The authors found that tourist/host relationships are transactional in that tourism workers treat guests as potential sources of income. The tourism workers did engage in small talk with their visitors, but the purpose of the interactions was purely business.

Second, travelers can do more harm than good on a vacation. The stereotypical "Ugly American" (Lederer & Burdick, 1958) who is brash and arrogant during his or her travels is often what comes to mind when we think of this term. For example, a colleague told me a story that dramatically brought home to her the meaning of "the Ugly American.' She and her husband were staying at a bed and breakfast hotel. One morning at breakfast, a U.S. American couple came into the hotel and asked for a room—in loud English. The concierge replied in French that no rooms were available. The Americans asked for a room several times, again in increasingly louder English, and the concierge, whose face was getting red, kept shaking his head no. Ten minutes later, a Dutch couple came in the door and asked for a room in halting, badly accented French. The concierge smiled at them and told them he would have a room immediately prepared for them.

Third, when thinking about traveling as an intercultural experience, it is always important to keep power in mind. Power is always functioning and is a key aspect of tourism (Buzinde, Santos, & Smith, 2006; Cuillier & Ross, 2007; King, 2006). As travelers, we have power (the buyer generally has power over the seller in a negotiation). The locals who depend on tourists' money know this and adapt to the travelers' needs. Tourist/host interactions are made more complicated by media outlets that market their stories to tourists by presenting stereotypical and exotic images of ethnic minorities in order to attract tourists (Cullier & Ross, 2007; King, 2006; Lindenfeld, 2007). Nothing is wrong with this transactional arrangement in principle; we just need to keep these facts in mind, not expect our traveling experience to be more than a vacation, and work to break down these stereotypical images (see Box 5.1 on p.124).

Sojourners

Millions of people cross cultural and national boundaries to live for a short or long period of time in another country. Business people take overseas assignments, and students study abroad to learn about new cultures and languages. For example, the number of international students enrolling in U.S. American universities has increased significantly in recent years; specifically, the number of international students has grown 17 times since 1954 with 586,323 international students studying at U.S.

Box 5.1 Voices: Pitfalls of Initial Interactions While Traveling

I love to travel to new countries and meet new people. My parents took me to many countries for a month at a time as I was growing up, and I got to see so many different places and people. I loved the cultural performances that we would experience during the various shows, as well as the local art and food. I thought I was learning a lot about the culture and making connections with local people. I remember many times meeting people my own age and talking with them for days; when it was time to leave, we'd exchange addresses. Although I would write to them, I would never hear back. As I got older, I learned why. On one visit, I was conversing with locals (who happened to work at the resort we were staying at); I told them how much fun I was having, how much I learned about their culture,

and what great friends we had become. One of their friends overheard this (he didn't work at the resort) and started telling me off. He said that I didn't know anything about his culture and that this resort was an illusion. He said that people were nice to me because they needed tourist dollars, but that I wasn't getting to know the real Mexico. He said that if I wanted to see the real Mexico, I'd have to learn the language, spend a long time here, recognize that I had money and the people here didn't, and not be stuck up. I was offended and left thinking I never wanted to come back here. After reflecting on my experience, however, I realized he was right—I had simply been traveling and having fun, but had not made real connections. I decided to follow his advice and be an exchange student the following year.

American campuses in 2002 and 2003—a 13% increase from 1999 (Chin, 2003). Many universities want to enroll international students to broaden and strengthen the educational experience of all students (Axelsson, 2005).

People who go to another country to stay for a certain period of time and then return home are called **sojourners** (Gudykunst, 2005). Although no fixed length defines a sojourner, most criteria use six months to five years (Ward, Bochner, & Furnham, 2001). If you stay for less than six months, you tend to be classified as a tourist/traveler; if you stay for more than five years, you tend to be an expatriate or immigrant. Sojourns provide individuals with significant opportunities to meet people from different cultures; the experience is beneficial for both the sojourners and the individuals in the host countries.

Migrants: Refugees and Immigrants

Migrants are people who move to a new permanent cultural context that is different from the one in which they were raised. Immigrants and refugees are two types of migrants. Immigration is the movement of non-residents from one country to another. An expatriate is someone who gives up his citizenship in one country to live in another. Immigration can be legal or illegal depending on whether the government has sanctioned the choice to move to the country. (We will discuss more about immigration policies in the layered section of this chapter.) A refugee is a person seeking asylum in a foreign country in order to escape persecution, war, terrorism, extreme poverty, famines, or national disaster. In 2005, the United States had 1,122,373 new legal immigrants and

53,738 refugees (Department of Homeland Security, 2006). The history of the United States is one that consists of immigration from a variety of countries and ethnic groups. Figure 5.1 provides a graphic of the immigration diversity of the United States from the 2000 Census. See Box 5.2 on page 126 for another reason why people might seek refuge.

Explaining Initial Intercultural Interactions: Cultural Adaptation Perspectives

The two theories discussed next primarily consider what it is like for people of one culture to meet individuals from another culture. What is it like for the "stranger" coming to a new culture? What are the difficulties, challenges, and processes that

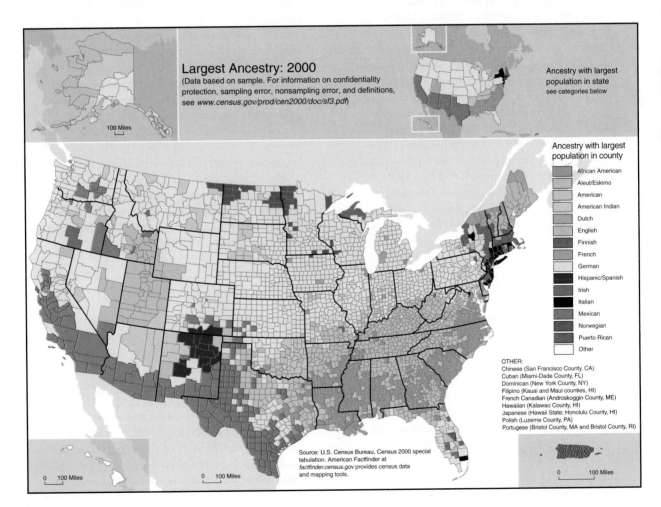

Figure 5.1
2000 U.S. Census Ancestry Map

Box 5.2 Globalization: HIV Refugees

Not all refugees seek asylum because of their ethnic or racial background—some seek it for health related reasons. In September, 2006, "more than 130 HIV positive South African women sought asylum in Canada after a U.N. Aids conference. The women were part of a larger group that included conference participants from El Salvador, Eritrea, Uganda, and Zimbabwe who refused to return home and decided to take their chances with Canada, which rejects at least half of all asylum applications. The South Africans blamed their decision on the President Mbeki government's ambiguity on the causes and treatment regimes for the killer disease with most arguing that they could not be guaranteed access to anti-retroviral medicine which could prolong their lives. Other asylum seekers said they were fed up with the stigma attached to their sero-positive status, while some feared discrimination and physical abuse because of their sexual orientation.... But they were lucky because many are probably educated and could either afford tickets to Toronto, or were able to sweet-talk someone with deep pockets and a big heart in flying them out. There are millions of South Africans who're not so lucky. The South African Medical Research Council estimates that there are around 5.5 million South Africans who are infected, the world's second highest total after India's. Two recent council reports also estimated that 947 South Africans die from AIDS-related illnesses daily, 1,443 become newly infected every day, and put the death toll over the last 12 months at 330,000. Meanwhile, only 200,000 of the 5.5 million infected are on anti-retroviral drugs. Who can blame someone from fleeing such purgatory?" (*The Nation*, 2006)

These refugees are an example of the diversity of reasons that people seek asylum elsewhere. In this case, it is to receive better health care. In other situations, it is to escape violence and persecution. The choice to leave is a difficult one—it is not easy to leave the place you call home for a chance at a better life because these individuals risk marginalization in the new country. The migration of refugees results in a new tapestry of cultures that creates both problems and opportunities. One of the key problems is that cultures can become a diaspora or a group of individuals widely dispersed as a result of social, political, economic, and health problems (Albizu, 2007).

individuals face when they interact with a larger culture? The first perspective describes culture shock for sojourners; the second perspective introduces models of cultural adaptation for immigrants and refugees.

Culture Shock

The frequency with which people travel around the world on temporary assignments has led to a great deal of study about sojourners and their experiences. Most researchers use the term *culture shock* to describe the feelings of sojourners interacting with a new culture for the first time. **Culture shock** is the psychological and emotional reaction people experience when they encounter a culture that is very different from their own (Furnham & Bochner, 1986). The anthropologist Kalvero Oberg is one of the first to use the term *culture shock*. He stated that the anxiety "results from losing all our familiar signs and symbols of social intercourse" (Oberg, 1960, p.177). Further, culture shock involves threats to our identity. Most people, when first faced with an unfamiliar culture, experience an identity disequilibrium phase that includes identity strain, identity loss, identity confusion, and/or identity rejection (Furnam & Bochner, 1986). Our sense of "stable" identity is called into question as we experience new events and new people and as our practices are questioned; that is, we begin to realize changes in how we see our self and in how we view our cultural identity.

Culture shock is loaded with negative connotations such as stress, shock to the system, fear, exhaustion, and hazards (Ward, Bochner, & Furnam, 2001). The idea of having our identities called into question is disconcerting for many. Additionally, psychosomatic difficulties, such as headaches, and social difficulties, such as loneliness, can occur. However, culture shock does not have to be negative; rather, it can be a stimulating, exciting, and learning experience (Ward, Bochner, & Furnam, 2001). We can meet new friends, learn new ways of thinking, and experience growth in our identity (the fluid aspect of identity). The key is how we manage culture shock (see Box 5.3).

Box 5.3 Voices: Disability and Culture Shock

Manique Gunaratne is a Sri Lankan professional with a visual impairment. She had worked for two private companies before she experienced the culture shock of becoming disabled, going blind in 2000 because of a genetic disorder for which there is no cure. She experienced difficulties in finding employment after going blind. She was marginalized by employers and had to adjust to her lost vision. She chose to become an advocate for people with disabilities and fight her marginalization in order to address her culture shock. She now works as a Junior Executive for the Employer's Federation of Ceylon (EFC), where she has been for six years. Gunaratne has also won numerous international and local awards, including the award for the world winner of Hand for Light Study Tour, Diriya Kantha 2007. At present she is the South Asian representative for the Asian Blind Union Women's Forum and President of the Colombo district Sri Lanka federation of the visually handicapped, among many other posts.

Adjusting to culture shock is not simply the responsibility of individuals, but also that of organizations. In order to address the culture shock, all Gunaratne asks for is an attitude change from the people. "The message I would like to give to the society is that attitudes should change from sympathy to empathy, dependence to independence." Other organizations assist with the culture shock of becoming disabled in Sri Lanka (or for those who were born with a disability). The Employers' Network on Disability seeks to improve the standards for the disabled in Sri Lanka by encouraging employers to hire them in a variety of positions. "We are looking to create equal opportunities and stop the marginalization of the disabled," says Meghamali Aluwihare, the Coordinator of the Employers' Network on Disability. And there are a growing number of organizations moving rapidly to support, encourage, and get the disabled employed. "We do not have to take overpowering measures to employ them," says the CEO of Standard Chartered Bank, Clive Haswell. Leading firms in Sri Lanka have begun giving employment to disabled people as a conscious policy to support an otherwise marginalized group and invite more such people to join them. New government regulations on improving accessibility for the disabled were passed in March 2007 making it compulsory for all public buildings to have accessibility means for the disabled within three years. Also, the regulations make it mandatory for all new public buildings to have accessibility for the disabled.

Source: Bandara (2007)

In order to better manage culture shock, many researchers have attempted to describe the stages of cultural shock to create a model of the sojourner's expected experience (Oberg, 1960; Ward et al., 2001; Zapf, 1991). The rationale is that if we know what is going to happen, we can train people to better manage the stress, so they experience more of the positives. Many different names are given to these stages (see Zapf, 1991 who compares 19 different models), but, predominantly, researchers focus on four stages that occur in a U-shaped model: honeymoon, crisis (culture shock), recovery, and adjustment (Lysggard, 1955; Oberg, 1960). Gullahorn and Gullahorn (1963) added two stages to describe what happens to sojourners as they adapt to their culture when they return home: reentry culture shock and resocialization. This revised model is called the W-shaped model (adding an extra curve to the U-shaped model).

In the **honeymoon stage,** sojourners are enthusiastic about being in a new place. We feel fascination and excitement and have positive expectations about the new culture and its people. This stage happens before and upon arrival in the new environment. We experience some "strange" aspects, but it is our curiosity about an exotic place (much like traveling) that is appealing. Any anxiety and stress we experience tends to be interpreted positively as part of an adventure.

The second stage, **crisis,** begins after the initial excitement wears off. The differences between sojourners and the host culture create problems. Events start to go wrong, minor issues become major problems, and cultural differences become irritating. Rather than just being able to go to class and learn, we get dirty looks from classmates, and we do not know what we have done wrong. We feel disappointment because experiences are not going as well as we thought. Our language skills are not as good as we thought, and people tease us about our pronunciation. In addition, we might complain about the host culture and its people, blame them for their problems and mistakes, and feel that our home and culture are a better and more wonderful place than this new culture. This is the stage at which people experience the actual shock of the new culture. Moreover, it is during this phase that many sojourners get homesick, decide to cut their stay short, and return home.

During the third stage, **recovery,** sojourners can see some positive aspects about the host culture and its people again. We start to laugh at our cultural faux pas with our new peers. We learn how to better function in the new culture and realize that the host culture is just different, not better or worse. We start to improve our work performance, interpret some cultural clues (e.g., now we know why we got the dirty looks), and feel less isolated and more familiar with the host culture. We stop feeling inadequate and have the ability to see some events from the perspective of the host culture.

In the fourth stage, **adjustment,** sojourners have gained a level of competence in the new culture. We begin to feel truly comfortable and function well in the host culture although we may still experience periodic difficulties and strains. We make some friends and can easily "pass" (at least behaviorally if not physically) for a member of the host culture. Overall, sojourners enjoy life in the host culture.

In the fifth stage, **reentry culture shock,** sojourners are reacting to the return to their home culture. We were excited about going home a few weeks ago to see old friends and eat some of our favorite foods, but, now that we are here, we see some flaws. People in our home culture seem so pedestrian and uncultured. Now that we have this new experience, we realize how narrow-minded some of our friends are, and they, in turn, think we are "stuck up." We long for our old life and miss our new culture.

In the sixth stage, **resocialization,** sojourners begin the adjustment back to their home culture. We remember all of the positives about being home and realize we were being too harsh on our friends. We come to understand that we have a new experience that has changed our lives forever, but people in different cultures just function differently. We might look forward to another overseas experience, but also enjoy our lives where we are.

The U-shaped and W-shaped models present typical descriptions of sojourner life. However, how accurate and useful are these models? The models have come under criticism since the evidence in support of them is "weak, inconclusive and overgeneralized" (Church, 1982, p. 542). For example, Kealey's (1989) longitudinal research on 277 Canadian technical advisors posted to 20 developing countries found that only 10% of the sample provides data that supports the traditional U-shape curve (the first four stages). Other studies have found that, in contrast to entry euphoria as proposed by some researchers, sojourners suffer more severe adjustment problems at the initial stage of transition. For example, Ward, Okura, Kennedy, and Kojima (1998) tested students within 24 hours of their arrival to New Zealand and then again at four-, six-, and twelve-month periods to identify the entry euphoria and U-shaped curve hypothesis. They found that the level of depression was highest during the entry period with a significant drop thereafter, which is in contrast to the U-shaped curve hypothesis. Along a similar line, Ward and Kennedy (1996) found that the overall level of depression was significantly greater at one month and at one year of stay than at the intermediate six-month time period.

If the evidence supporting the culture shock model is questionable, then why am I including it in this book? The answer is that it provides a general model that is quite useful in training people for a sojourning experience. While not every person will go through every stage at the same pace (and some will not go through some of the stages at all), the model provides some expectations for what may happen. If a sojourner knows what might happen and is given skills and strategies to address these changes, he or she is better able to manage culture shock if it does happen. For example, if we know that loneliness and isolation might happen, we can learn strategies for making friends in the new culture. In fact, sojourner training might help us avoid loneliness in the first place. The order of the stages is not the key; rather, it is that the different stages exist at some level for many people (see Box 5.4 on p.130).

Cultural Adaptation

In contrast to the sojourner, the refugee or immigrant is moving to a new culture on a permanent basis. Refugees and immigrants do not have the desire and/or choice to return to their home culture. Therefore, they engage in a more permanent process of cultural adaptation. **Cultural adaptation** is "the entirety of the phenomenon of

Box 5.4 Layered Effects: Factors that Affect Individuals' Culture Shock

The W-shaped model is useful in general, but we should consider why some variation in the model might happen. These differences will change our actual curves. First, the level of cultural differences between your home and host culture has an impact on the degree of culture shock. If you are from England and go to New Zealand or the United States, you likely will not experience as much culture shock as you would if you went to Chile or Iran because of similarity in language and cultural values. Second, the degree to which the host culture accepts sojourners impacts culture shock. If the host culture accommodates individuals and welcomes individuals from other cultures, the culture shock can be minimal. Third, individuals experience culture shock in a different manner. Anderson (1994)

identified four types of experiences in relation to culture shock: a) early returnees who exit the sojourn before its scheduled completion, b) time servers who stay the entire time, but do so with resentment and cannot wait to go home, c) adjusters who are able to do a moderately effective job interacting with host members, and d) participators who are performing optimally in their jobs and are emotionally and behaviorally integrated with the local culture. Figure 5.2 displays the W-shaped model with several of these individual variations to reflect that not all people experience culture shock in the same manner. Thus, factors at many layers impact the way you might experience culture shock and hence the pattern of the W-shaped model.

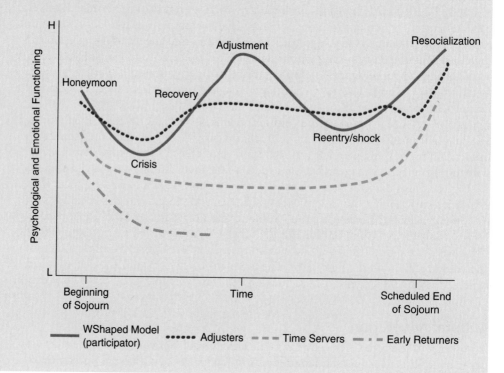

Figure 5.2 Models of Culture Shock

individuals who, upon relocating to an unfamiliar sociocultural environment, strive to establish and maintain a relatively stable, reciprocal, and functional relationship with the environment" (Kim, 2005, p. 380). Cultural adaptation is a process of compromise for people in finding a fit between themselves and their environment.

Cultural adaptation involves both **deculturation** (unlearning a part of old cultural values and practices) and **acculturation** (learning some, but not all, of the host culture values and practices) to varying degrees. As a result of the choices and environmental factors that people make, Berry (2007) described four types of adaptation: marginalized, traditional, assimilated, and bicultural. Table 5.1 displays these four types in relation to the level of identification with the home culture (deculturation) and host culture (acculturation). People who do not identify with either the home or the host culture feel marginalized. Marginalization can occur as the result of the host culture's actions. For example, the economic system in the United States has forced some American Indians to live in urban areas away from their reservation. Some of these individuals do not feel a part of mainstream society, and they also feel like an outsider when they visit their reservation (Walters, 1999). People who identify highly with their home cultures but not the host culture are traditional. They prefer to speak their home language and live in ethnic enclaves (for example, Chinatown or Little Vietnam) so that they can be around people who are like them. People who identify highly with the host culture but not the home culture choose to assimilate to the mainstream culture. They learn the new language quickly and try to adopt the values and practices of their new culture. Finally, people who identify highly with both host and home culture are bicultural. These individuals are comfortable in both cultures and are able to "code switch" (that is, change communication patterns) to communicate in culturally appropriate ways (see Box 5.5 on p.132).

Kim (2005) developed an integrated theory to describe cultural adaptation that includes several organizing principles. First, adaptation is natural and universal. Everyone experiences it when they move to a new culture, and it is neither positive nor negative (it can be both). Second, adaptation is an all-encompassing phenomenon. It is not simply a process that a person experiences in a vacuum, but rather represents the dynamic interplay of people and the environment. Third, adaptation is

Table 5.1

TYPES OF CULTURAL ADAPTATION

		Identification with the host culture (level of acculturation)	
		Low	High
Identification with the home cultures (level of deculturation)	Low	Marginalized	Assimilated
	High	Traditional	Bicultural

Box 5.5 Talking about Ethics: The Choice of Assimilation

Immigration often sparks controversy and debate. Members of the host culture have varying perceptions about the benefits of immigration and the ideal response from immigrants. Many believe that assimilation to the new culture is very important for both the culture and the new immigrants; that is, immigrants will be happier and more successful if they learn the language, adopt the cultural values, and try to fit in. Immigrants who do not assimilate may be judged harshly by members of the host culture for not making the proper choice. The choice to assimilate is an interesting and ethical position. Consider the following questions around this ethical debate:

1. To what degree do individuals have a choice to assimilate or not?

2. In what ways do members of the host culture affect immigrants' choice to assimilate?

3. In what ways do the system/structures of the host culture affect immigrants' choice to assimilate?

4. Should immigrants have the right to choose whatever identification (traditional, bicultural, etc.) that they want?

5. What are the ethical standards that guide your answers to these questions?

a communication-based phenomenon. It is through interaction with others and the larger culture (for example, through cultural institutions such as the mass media) that people adapt to a new culture.

For Kim, adaptation is a process that is closely related to stress and growth. In fact, she calls this the stress-adaptation-growth dynamic. The adaptive process results from an identity conflict—the desire to maintain a stable identity that retains home culture customs, but also to change behavior to seek harmony with the new culture (Kim, 2005). This identity conflict creates stress in the individual who thus partakes in acts of adaptation to attempt to find equilibrium between new and old. The result of the stress-adaptation is growth. The growth might be learning a new way to interact with strangers or understanding how to get ahead at work. This stress-adaptation-growth dynamic is a cyclical and continual process, as represented in Figure 5.3.

A variety of factors at the individual, interpersonal, and cultural layers explain the rate and extent of the stress-adaptation-growth dynamic in individuals. In this section, we consider the interpersonal factors; individual and cultural layers are discussed in the final section. At the interpersonal level, a migrant's social communication with the host culture and the cultural community are critical factors. Effective interpersonal interaction with members of both of these groups can both speed and slow adaptation. For example, if we are able to make acquaintances from the host culture, we can learn some of the inside rules for behaving. However, if the people we meet from the host culture are rude, distant, or discriminatory, that can encourage us to find solace with members of our own

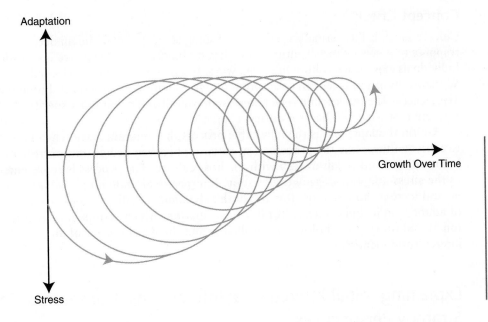

Figure 5.3
Stress-Adaptation-Growth Dynamic (Kim, 2001)

Reproduced with permission of Sage Publications Inc. Books via Copyright Clearance Center

cultural group and slow adaptation. In addition, if we find complete comfort with members of our own cultural group and have limited interaction with the host culture, our cultural adaptation will be truncated. However, members of our own cultural group who have successfully adapted to the host culture can help "show us the ropes." They can teach us how to apply and interview for jobs, help us figure out the rules for interacting with professors, and introduce us to members of the host culture.

The result of interactions that helps us adapt is called intercultural transformation (Kim, 2005). **Intercultural transformation** is the progression of internal change that results in observable behavioral changes representing adaptation to the new culture. The outcome of such transformation includes functional fitness, psychological health, and the development of an intercultural identity. Functional fitness is the ability to perform activities and tasks in an effective manner. For example, functional fitness allows us to complete our studies successfully, get a date with a member of the host culture, and improve our occupational and socioeconomic status (Kim, 2005). Psychological health includes mental well-being and satisfaction with life, which increases with adaptation (Kim, 2005). Finally, people who can culturally adapt develop an intercultural identity. Kim stated that this type of identity emphasizes individualization and universalization. Individualization is the ability to see beyond conventional categories and stereotypes and recognize individual characteristics. Universalization is recognizing the points of consent, harmony, and complementarity between different cultural groups, thus widening identification (that is, being able to identify with multiple cultural groups).

Concept Check

Culture shock is the normal experience of feeling identity threat and anxiety in response to a new culture. Culture shock has both positive and negative implications. Individuals experience culture in varied ways, but researchers have identified a W-shaped model as a general description of what sojourners can expect during their experiences. The model should be taken as an overall guide, but not a specific prediction of what will happen during a sojourn.

Cultural adaptation is the inevitable process that migrants face when moving to a new culture. It is the process of negotiating between deculturation from one's home culture and acculturation with the host culture. The process is represented as the stress-adaptation-growth dynamic. Interpersonal, individual, and environmental factors can speed or slow down this dynamic. Finally, the positive outcome of adaptation includes intercultural transformation, which results in increased functional fitness, psychological well-being, and the development of an intercultural identity.

Explaining Initial Intercultural Interactions: Communication Strategy Perspectives

The communication strategies that we use during initial interactions are critical in developing relationships. For this reason, several scholars have attempted to explain why we communicate as we do with people from different cultures (Gallois, Ogay, & Giles, 2005; Gudykunst, 2005). These theories explain the factors that influence our communication in these settings and the ways we can be effective and develop positive relationships. The first is called anxiety and uncertainty management (AUM) theory, and the second is communication accommodation theory.

Anxiety and Uncertainty Management (AUM) Theory

Gudykunst (2005) developed AUM theory to explain effective communication with strangers. A **stranger** is "an individual who is a member of a system but is not strongly attached to that system" (Rogers, 1999, p. 61). The stranger is someone who is close to us physically (for example, he or she might live near us or go to school with us), but is far away emotionally or culturally. Strangers usually do not know the language (slang), customs, beliefs, and everyday behavior patterns that people from a particular culture know and share. For both strangers and members of a larger culture, the experience of interacting for the first time is new and unique. This "newness" creates uncertainty and thus needs to be managed. To manage unknown or new situations, people use information-seeking behaviors to increase their ability to predict or explain others' behaviors (managing uncertainty), and they use tension-reduction behaviors to reduce the anxiety (managing anxiety) felt when interacting with people from different cultures (Gudykunst, 2005). The following section defines the key concepts of AUM theory and then introduces verbal and nonverbal message strategies for managing uncertainty and anxiety.

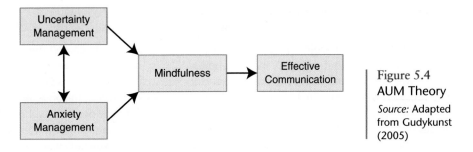

Figure 5.4
AUM Theory

Source: Adapted from Gudykunst (2005)

Figure 5.4 displays a visual model for the AUM theory. The primary purpose of the theory is to explain **effective communication.** "Communication is effective to the extent that we are able to maximize understandings" (Gudykunst, 2005, p. 289); that is, the meaning that we receive from a message is relatively similar (not the same since a perfect match is not possible) to what the person who sent the message intended. A number of factors limit our ability to communicate effectively, and having different cultural backgrounds exacerbates these factors.

To communicate effectively with strangers, we have to manage uncertainty and anxiety. Uncertainty is a cognitive phenomenon while anxiety is an emotional one. Two types of uncertainty affect interactions with strangers: predictive and explanatory (Berger & Calabrese, 1975). Predictive uncertainty is the degree to which an individual can predict strangers' attitudes, feelings, and behaviors. Explanatory uncertainty is the degree to which an individual can explain strangers' attitudes, feelings, and behaviors. Anxiety is an unpleasant, transitory state characterized by tension and apprehension (see Box 5.6 on p.136). When interacting with hosts, people experience anxiety based on the anticipation of negative consequences: negative psychological consequences for the self (such as fear of embarrassment), negative behavioral consequences for the self (such as fear of being yelled at or put down), and negative evaluations by others (such as fear of negative stereotyping) (Stephan & Stephan, 2001).

Gudykunst (2005) argued that people have maximum and minimum thresholds for both uncertainty and anxiety. When cognitive and behavioral uncertainty is between the two thresholds, we have enough confidence to predict others' attitudes, feelings, and thoughts, and we are comfortable enough to interact with that person. If uncertainty is above the maximum threshold, we view the other person as unpredictable: We do not have confidence to predict or explain others' behavior. If anxiety is above the maximum threshold, we feel paralyzed and unable to communicate. The anxiety may be the result of some vague or uneasy feeling that cannot be specified. If either uncertainty or anxiety is above the maximum, people tend to avoid the interaction (Duronto et al., 2005). On the other hand, if our uncertainty is below the minimum thresholds, we become overconfident and likely misinterpret others' messages because we do not consider that our interpretations could be wrong. If anxiety is below the minimum threshold, there is no motivation to interact at all. Thus,

Box 5.6 Voices: Anxiety in Intercultural Communication

I am a Muslim woman from Africa who came to the United States to get my Ph.D. in communication. I was very excited about my program and the prospect of living in the United States. I had heard so many positive stories. My actual experiences were both positive and negative. The experience that surprised me the most is the anxiety I had during my interactions with U.S. students (both students in the class I was teaching and my peers in the classes I was taking). I had multiple examples of this anxiety in the first semester of my studies. I remember not wanting to talk in class because I was afraid I would make a fool of myself (I was self-conscious about my accent, my knowledge, and my appearance). I also remember being afraid of interacting with strangers because I didn't want them to say something negative to me and because I thought they were stereotyping me. I realized that I had become a shy, scared child and that was not who I was. After I adjusted, I started to become more outgoing—more in line with my personality. I still had some anxiety, but I was managing it better so that I would say what I felt. I was still aware of cultural norms since I was new to the country, but I learned a lot more about myself and others from that point on. Not all my experiences were positive. I had some people tell me to "take my Jihad home" and other racist things. I still had to manage my anxiety in those situations, but I learned quickly who to avoid and how to not make the situation worse. My experience is a classic example of the importance of managing anxiety for effective intercultural communication.

communicating effectiveness with strangers requires that anxiety and uncertainty be below the maximum but above the minimum thresholds (Gudykunst, 2005).

In order to manage uncertainty and anxiety effectively, people need to be **mindful** of their thoughts, actions, and messages. People are frequently in a mindless state and communicate with a lack of conscious awareness of what or how they are thinking (Burgoon, Berger, & Waldron, 2000). When they are in a mindless state, they predict and interpret the host's behaviors using their own frames of reference, which cause miscommunication and misunderstanding. When we have a conversation with our partner and we are thinking about our day at work or about what to watch on TV, we are in a mindless state. On the other hand, when people are in a mindful state, they become critical thinkers and recognize factors relevant to the communication situation (Langer, 1989). So, in a conversation with your partner in your mindful state, you realize that he said that he wanted to have your friends over for dinner instead of his usual "I just want to watch TV." Your mindfulness may avoid another fight about this subject.

Mindfulness itself involves three components: "(1) creation of new categories, (2) openness to new information, (3) awareness of more than one perspective" (Langer, 1989, p.62). As part of sense making, we categorize information based on such factors as culture, job category, color, and size. Mindfulness involves learning to see people as belonging to a wide variety of categories. Many times, when people are mindless, they use broad categories such as ethnicity, gender, or nationality. These broad categories can be useful at times, but we will be more accurate if we can think about people as having a variety of categories. For example, it might be more accurate to think about someone in terms of her occupation rather than her gender, especially on the topic of work behavior. This does not mean that her gender does not matter; it just does not always matter in the stereotypical ways.

Mindfulness also involves being open to new information. New information forces people to reconsider what might be outmoded ways of thinking and to see inappropriate beliefs and attitudes. According to Gudykunst (1995), "Being open to new information involves focusing on the process of communication that is taking place, *not* the outcome of our interactions" (pp. 16–17). When people concentrate on the outcome, they miss signs in interactions, and this results in misunderstandings and miscommunication (see Box 5.7 on p.138).

Finally, mindfulness also includes being aware of more than one perspective. We have a tendency to think that only one right way can work in a situation; for example, you have one right way to be respectful to your elders; you have one right way to manage conflict; you have one right way to run a meeting. In reality, you have multiple ways to perform all of these communicative actions. For example, I have students who refer to me as "John," "Dr. Oetzel," "Mr. John," "Professor," and even "Herr Professor Doctor Oetzel" (a German style of address). I could simply use the perspective that I was taught, which is to use the title and last name to address a teacher, to determine whether my students are respectful. However, all of these forms of address convey respect; each was created based on norms of a particular culture. This awareness of new perspectives helps to avoid simple misunderstandings and results in effective communication.

While mindfulness is one effective tool for helping to manage uncertainty and anxiety, additional specific communication strategies can be used as well. Information gathering is one of the primary means for reducing uncertainty (Berger & Calabrese, 1975). Information gathering includes both active and passive approaches. Active approaches include direct questions and requests for information and self-disclosure to elicit conversation. Passive approaches include observing others through the media or without direct interaction (for example, watching what people do). The key factor for reducing uncertainty and anxiety is that we need to gather the right information and be confident in its accuracy. When you have a lot of information about someone, it does not necessarily mean you will not have anxiety or uncertainty interacting with him or her. Having a cultural insider (someone who knows the norms and rules of the culture) to help you make sense of the information is helpful as well (Stephan & Stephan, 2001).

Communication Accommodation Theory

Communication accommodation theory (CAT) (Gallois, Ogay, & Giles, 2005) has been developed over three decades to explain why people accommodate (or not) their verbal and nonverbal messages to others during initial encounters. **Accommodation** includes the use of similar speech patterns and nonverbal behaviors to another person (also called convergence); **nonaccommodation** includes the use of differing verbal and nonverbal patterns (also called divergence). Accommodation is often used to appear similar to the other person and thus more likeable as well as to facilitate understanding.

Box 5.7 Talking about Ethics: Ethical Practices and Effective Communication

Gudykunst (2005) argued that ethical approaches to interacting with others help to reduce anxiety. Specifically, he said that when we treat people with respect, dignity, and moral inclusiveness, we will reduce our anxiety. The reason for this result is twofold. First, an ethical approach toward others creates an expectation in ourselves that others are worthy of dignity and respect. Second, strangers are likely to reciprocate the ethical treatment toward us. Notice that ethical treatment does not directly reduce uncertainty because it does not help us gather new information. Nonetheless, according to anxiety management theory, ethical practices should help us communicate more effectively with people from other cultures.

1. Do you agree with this argument? Why or why not?
2. How would you go about finding evidence to support or deny this claim?

In contrast, nonaccommodation is often used to emphasize distinctiveness (or a positive sense of self) and to remind others of nonshared memberships and thus avoid misunderstandings. Through accommodation and nonaccomodation, we attempt to negotiate our identities and meanings during initial interactions with members from other groups. For example, if we like someone and want to get to know him or her better, we might consciously or unconsciously mirror the person's patterns of interaction.

This theory describes the initial orientations two people bring to an interaction, their motivation during interaction, and then the expectations of future interactions (Gallois et al., 2005). The initial orientation that we might have toward someone else is based on the sociohistorical context and prior interpersonal interactions with that individual. The sociohistorical context includes the history of relationships and the relative social status (equal or unequal) between our cultural group and the group of the other person. We tend to be oriented toward accommodation if our two groups have had positive interactions in the past, if we had a positive interaction with a member from that group (even if the groups themselves had negative interactions), and/or if we have had positive interactions with that particular individual. We tend to have a nonaccommodation orientation if our two groups have had negative interactions in the past (such as the Israelis and Palestinians or the Sunnis and Shi'a) or if we had negative interactions with that particular individual.

During interaction, we are considering the negotiation of our identities (affective motives) and general meanings (cognitive motives) with the other person (Gallois et al., 2005). For affective motives, when we interact with the other person, we have to decide whether we see our identity tied to the other person (that is, developing a relationship with that person) or whether we see ourselves as distinct (that is, maintaining a positive self identity that is different from that of the other person). If we want to develop a shared identity with the person, we tend to use similar verbal and nonverbal strategies. If we want to differentiate ourselves, we use dissimilar verbal and nonverbal strategies. For cognitive motives, we tend to want to enhance comprehension (or at least avoid misunderstandings) and have to decide whether similarity or

Are these people displaying accommodation or nonaccom- modation? Do you think they like each other?

dissimilarity will enhance understanding. In some cases, being dissimilar will help facilitate understanding. For example, suppose that I am from Colombia. I am fluent in English and Spanish but am much more confident of my speaking in Spanish. You are from the United States and are monolingual. I might be afraid that you think that I know everything about your culture. So even though I speak English, I might exaggerate my accent so that if I make a mistake you will know it is due to my "foreignness." In this manner, I want to make sure you do not misattribute my motiva- tions (for example, by thinking I'm rude when I just do not know your customs). My exaggerated accent reminds you that I do not know all of your customs.

The result of accommodation (or nonaccommodation) behaviors during an interaction creates anticipation and expectations for future interaction (Gallois et al., 2005). Accommodating behaviors might include asking questions to check understanding, focusing on the other person's conversational needs (such as by letting them choose the topics), and expressing emotions such as warmth, support, and caring. Nonaccommodating behaviors include being negative/hostile, using stereotypical behavior of the other group to patronize, and maintaining your own behavior (neutral). In general, accommodating behavior is viewed positively and results in a desire for future interaction, while nonaccommodating behavior is viewed negatively and results in not wanting to interact with that person or members of that cultural group (if we perceive that person as a typical member of his or her cultural group) (Gallois et al., 2005; Ota, Giles, & Somera, 2007). There are two caveats about the generalization that accommodation is viewed positively. First, accommodation is not positive if we question an individual's motivation to use accommodation. For example, if we think someone is being nice to us because of an outside motivation, such as wanting a promotion at work, we might not want to have future interactions with the person. Second, attributions, evaluations, and anticipation of future interactions are transactional (reflecting the back and forth nature of communication and the negotiation of meaning) and are not simple judgments. All of us have made snap decisions about someone's character only to find out as we talk further that we were wrong. Thus, we may initially find someone's accommodating behavior positive, but later realize she is a jerk. Also see Box 5.8.

Box 5.8 Voices: Accommodation and Nonaccommodation for International Teachers

As told by a student: It was the first day of class and I was waiting for the teacher when an Asian (she was South Korean, but I didn't know that at the beginning) woman walked in and went to the front of class. You could see the reactions of my classmates—in unison, we all slumped back in our chairs, gave a look of disinterest, and crossed our arms. Here we go again—another Asian teacher who can't speak English. I half-heartedly listened that first day and then went to look for another class. I couldn't find one I needed at that time so I decided to stick it out. I am so glad I did. She was amazing—she gave the most exciting lectures, had great activities, and was always willing to spend time with us to help us learn. Sure, there were times I didn't understand her, but all I had to do was ask and she was more than happy to repeat until we understood. All of my classmates and I talked about our first impressions and how wrong they were. I know we gave her nothing but negative behaviors and I wonder how she overcame such initial negativity. She did nothing but give us supportive and accepting behaviors. We eventually returned her supportive behaviors, and you could tell how engaged everyone was.

As told by the teacher: I was teaching a class on intercultural communication for the third time since I started at my university. However, I had 12 years of training in Korean and a graduate degree from a U.S. university where I taught for four years. I speak with an accent, but I am fluent in English. I know the material very well and I know how to teach. On the first day, I received the typical reactions. No matter how enthusiastic I am or how many "cool" visual aids I use, the students slump in their chairs and disengage from me. It is very frustrating. I know that I have to spend the next two months working extra hard to get them to come around and believe that I can teach well and that I know English. I know they will come around—I have always received excellent ratings by the end, but I know I have to work extra hard to engage the students. It is worth the effort as I really want students to learn, but it also isn't fair that I am the one who has to make all of the efforts initially. The students don't have to do anything (and some even drop the course). I also work much harder than my American colleagues who simply are accepted from the beginning of the class.

Concept Check

Managing uncertainty and anxiety so that it is moderate (not too much and not too little) is the key for having effective communication with people from different cultures. Mindfulness is one cognitive tactic that helps us to manage uncertainty and anxiety. Information gathering and ethical treatment are communication strategies that help to manage anxiety and uncertainty. While AUM is a useful theory for explaining initial interactions with strangers, not everyone is motivated by anxiety and uncertainty management. Thus, the theory works well for some people, but not others.

CAT describes why people are motivated to use similar and dissimilar behavior with members of different cultural groups during initial interactions. The sociohistorical context and previous interactions create a starting point for our motivation. During interaction, we decide our affective and cognitive motivations and make behavioral choices that reflect these motivations. Finally, as a result of interacting with that person, we make attributions of his or her behavior and evaluate that behavior to determine if we want to have future interactions with the person.

Layers of Initial Intercultural Interactions

The process of cultural adaptation and initial interactions with strangers is not isolated to the interpersonal layer. We simply do not interact with someone else in a vacuum. Our interpersonal interactions have impacts on individual attitudes and also the larger culture in which we live. Additionally, environmental, cultural, and media factors shape the speed and nature of cultural adaptation (Khan, 2005). This section examines the layers of initial interactions focusing on bottom-up effects, top-down effects of interpersonal interactions on individual attitudes, and top-down effects of media and cultural factors on initial interactions. We conclude by discussing some challenges and skills for initial interactions.

Bottom-Up Effects

Our own individual skills and attitudes can facilitate cultural adaptation and effective communication with strangers. For example, a migrant's own communication competence and predispositions are critical factors (Khan, 2005; Kim, 2005). Communication competence is the degree to which the individual has knowledge of the host culture, the motivation to interact with the host culture, and the skills to interact effectively with the host culture. The more competence an individual has, the faster and easier it is to adapt to the new culture. Predispositions are the internal conditions of the migrants prior to settling in the host culture and include preparedness, adaptability, and ethnic/cultural distance. The more that migrants are prepared, adaptable, and have a similar cultural background to the host culture (both values and physical markers such as skin color and clothing), the faster and easier the cultural adaptation will be (Kim, 2005).

Similarly, the communicative strategies and motivations we have during initial interactions impact our ability to manage uncertainty and create the potential for future interaction. According to AUM theory, if we are open to new interactions and tolerant of ambiguity, we can increase our likelihood for managing uncertainty and anxiety. According to CAT, if we want to have future interactions with an individual, it will be important for us to choose accommodating behaviors (Gallois et al., 2005). While this oversimplifies whether two people will develop a long-term relationship, accommodating behaviors increase the likelihood (see Box 5.9).

Top-Down Effects: Initial Interactions and Individual Effects

The nature of our initial interactions has an impact on both our own and other people's attitudes toward members of our cultural group. Kim's (2005) theory of cultural adaptation explains that having positive interactions with migrants increases the speed and effectiveness of their cultural adaptation; migrants (both the ones you interact with and others who witness the interaction directly or indirectly) increase their positivity toward the culture and cultural members in these situations. Thus, if you think it is important for migrants to "learn the language and assimilate to our culture," you can help by creating opportunities for them to interact with you and enhance their view of your culture. Similarly, the CAT explains that our initial

Box 5.9 What Went Right? Communication Skills Enhancing Cultural Adaptation

When Marilyn moved from Cuba to the United States, she wanted to adapt quickly to her new culture. She was proud of her Cuban heritage, but she also was proud to be a U.S. American too and wanted to show her pride by being bicultural. She took English classes to learn the language and watched television only in English. While these steps helped, what was most important to her was to learn how to communicate effectively with U.S. Americans. She watched what they did and mirrored their gestures and their sayings. She didn't mirror others in an obvious way but found that when she did this, people were more willing to talk with her in the future. She asked friends about the appropriate times to swear, tease, and joke to reduce her uncertainty about how to effectively communicate. She was willing to take chances and talk to strangers and whenever those interactions went poorly, she'd ask her friends what might have gone wrong. She knew that some people were simply shy or closed minded to immigrants, and she didn't take things too personally. Of course, very rude people hurt her feelings, and she experienced some discrimination from employers. Within a year, she had a number of U.S. American friends and was able to interact effectively with them. Her individual skills enabled her cultural adaptation.

attitudes about interacting with members of a different culture come, in part, from the previous initial interactions members have had with that culture. In summary, initial interaction not only affects our own attitudes about a cultural group, it also affects the attitudes of others from the stories we tell and the direct observation of others (Gallois et al., 2005). For example, if you watch a friend ask the teacher a question and the teacher responds with sarcasm, you likely will not risk talking with the teacher even though you did not experience the negative interaction directly. Additionally, if your boss says he is open to all people and then you hear him telling negative jokes about homosexuals, you might wonder what other groups he makes fun of. Or, you might understand why your gay colleague does not feel supported at work.

Top-Down Effects: Culture, Media, and Initial Interactions

Both the larger host culture and the media influence the speed and effectiveness of cultural adaptation and the effectiveness of initial interaction. At the cultural layer, Kim (2005) has identified three characteristics that affect interactions: host receptivity, host conformity pressures, and ethnic group strength. Host receptivity is the degree to which a culture is structurally and psychologically accessible. Around the world, most large cities are receptive to migrants given that ethnic communities already exist in these cities. Thus, a new migrant can find a social community, materials written in their language, and foods from home. Additionally, the laws and political climate also affect host receptivity. The United States historically has been open to migrants (relative to most nations), but the events of 9–11 and a desire by some to tighten the Southern border have created a negative climate for some migrants (Numbers USA, n.d.). Japan, in contrast, traditionally has been a closed nation to migrants, but is changing its attitudes as its population falls and the need for migrant workers increases (Caryl & Kashawagi, 2006). People's physical markers also relate to host receptivity. Colloquially, this has been referred to as "passing." People who look like the host cultural members tend to get more receptivity than people with a different skin color (see Box 5.10).

Host conformity pressures refer to the degree to which members of the host culture expect migrants to conform to the dominant culture (Kim, 2005). Conformity pressures vary across communities and nations. Large urban areas tend to exhibit fewer conformity pressures than do small towns. Certain states and regions express different conformity pressures. Along the Southern United States border with Mexico, the states have different pressures toward Mexican and Latino immigrants than other U.S. states. Both Arizona (Proposition 203) and California (Proposition 227) have passed English-only instruction in schools to force assimilation. In contrast, New Mexico has not formally considered such propositions.

Ethnic group strength is the level of influence that a migrant culture has on the dominant home culture. A strong ethnic group can limit the conformity pressures of the dominant culture if the ethnic group is large enough and has a positive regard for the culture. One explanation for the difference between Arizona/California and New Mexico is the ethnolinguistic vitality of a community. Ethnolinguistic vitality

Box 5.10 Talking about Ethics: Illegal Canadians in the United States

A great deal of energy in U.S. politics is spent on debating immigration—the costs, benefits, and solutions to any problems associated with it. Illegal immigrants from Mexico are one focus of this energy. Discussions arise about putting up a 2,000 mile fences to secure the border. Why aren't we as concerned about the Northern border as well? A number of Canadians live illegally in the United States but this is rarely discussed. I know a Canadian family who has lived in Arizona for nearly 20 years—completely illegally. They came to the United States for better work opportunities for the father and settled in Northern Arizona. No one asked them any questions since they are White and speak English. The father received citizenship early on, but the mother and children did not. They could not work legally and instead worked odd jobs for cash to make ends meet. None of their friends knew. They eventually all became citizens through marriage.

1. Why do you think certain groups are the focus of immigration debates?
2. Do we base our decisions about the severity of the immigration problem on the color of immigrants' skin?

(from Chapter 3) is the value and strength of a language. New Mexico has a large Spanish-speaking population and a large percentage of Hispanics throughout that state (around 42% of the population compared with 45% Whites). Hispanics have been in the state for around 400 years, and Spanish has been a prominent language since that time. A positive regard for Spanish is clear, and thus any forced conformity measures would not have the majority support of the state.

At the media layer, the migrant culture's access to the media of the dominant host culture plays a role in the stress-adaptation-growth dynamic. Dominant mass media can help a migrant adapt effectively and quickly to his or her new culture. Radio, television, newspaper, and the Internet can help a migrant learn the language and culture of the host culture (Kim, 2005). Media enable migrants to have access to parts of the culture that they would not normally have, especially during the early stages of adaptation. A colleague told me about a Japanese international student she knew. He came to the United States to attend a university, but knew only a handful of English words when he arrived. He spent the month before classes started holed up in an apartment watching television virtually 24/7. By the time classes started, he had a well-developed vocabulary that even demonstrated a familiarity with U.S. idioms and slang. His fluency made it easy for him to assimilate into the culture. However, reliance on host culture media can limit adaptation if migrants rely on the media as the only source of interaction. Similarly, ethnic-specific media can both help and hinder adaptation. It can hinder adaptation if we only use ethnic-specific media, particularly media that is related to our home culture (for example, CNN for a U.S. American living in China or Univision for a Mexican living in the United States). However, ethnic-specific media campaigns have been used to provide educational materials to traditional migrants in order to provide informational, tangible, and social support. Ethnic-specific magazines like *Latina Style* for Latina women interested in professional success, *PLUS Journal of Polish American Affairs* on Polish-American relations and Polish culture, and *Kashrus Magazine* featuring articles on Kosher foods are three examples of many ethnic-specific magazines that are published in the United States.

Challenges and Skills

There are many challenges to communicating effectively in initial interactions. Two of the more salient ones appear to be the challenge of overcoming past negative history and the challenge of overcoming social inequalities (Kim, 2005; Thompson & Collier, 2006). A number of groups have negative social histories; for example, Protestants and Catholics in Northern Ireland, and African Americans and White Americans in the United States. Further, most of us around the world live in societies where one group has economic advantages over another. We did not necessarily create these situations, and it can be frustrating when social constraints limit our ability to develop relationships with other group members. Developing positive relationships with members of the other cultural group can be challenging in these situations; however, it is important to remember that our behaviors can reinforce the existing social structures and power imbalances, or we can challenge these structures and develop new types of relationships.

Several scholars have suggested communication strategies for moving beyond these challenges. These suggestions by no means provide the entire solution, but they do provide some concrete actions that we can consider in creating positive initial interactions (Gallois et al., 2005; Thompson & Collier, 2006). In order to be more mindful and have effective communication, one strategy is to practice the DIE model for understanding others' behavior: Description, Interpretation, and Evaluation (Gudykunst, 2005). Many times when we interact with members of other cultural groups, we have the tendency to evaluate or at least interpret behavior. We judge it as good or bad (evaluation) or try to explain what it means (interpretation) because we assume we know what the behavior means. For example, if a stranger does not make eye contact with you—and you think eye contact is important—you might interpret this to mean the person is shy, devious, or disrespectful. All of these interpretations would be evaluated as negative to varying degrees (we'll be more forgiving if we think the person is shy rather than disrespectful). In contrast, a more mindful approach is simply to describe the behavior and try to figure out what it means. We can say to a friend from that cultural group (or to a teacher), "I noticed that Ian was avoiding eye contact with me when we were talking about X. Do you know what that is about?" We can check our perceptions with the actual person if we have enough trust and goodwill. This strategy helps us to be more accurate with our attributions and avoid misunderstandings based on false attributions.

Additionally, we can adopt conversational strategies that show accommodation and nonaccommodation depending on the motivation we have. Martin, Moore, Hecht, and Larkey (2001) investigated the strategies that African Americans in Phoenix use for interaction with White Americans. They interviewed 10 people and asked them how often they used certain conversational strategies when they had particular conversational goals with White Americans in the workplace. For example, when faced with a lack of acceptance, the African Americans predominantly found that an accommodating behavior strategy was effective; for example, by showing an other orientation (asking about the other person, talking about his or her topics, etc). To achieve work goals, both accommodation (making the conversation go smoothly) and nonaccommodation (avoiding interaction or asserting oneself) worked. To respond to stereotyping, both accommodating (treating the other as an individual) and nonaccommodation (confronting and educating) worked. For example, confronting a co-worker about a stereotype and educating him or her actually can help some African American workers gain respect in the workplace and advance in their career. However, note that the burden is placed on the person who is being stereotyped; it speaks to issues of unearned privilege and power in the workplace. The study illustrates that accommodating communication strategies can achieve multiple goals, but also that nonaccommodation strategies can help improve work relationships with members of other cultural groups.

SUMMARY

Returning to the opening story: Khadi experienced the classic stages of the W-shaped model of culture shock—she had a honeymoon stage, then crisis, followed by recovery, and adjustment. Initially, she had some difficulty because she was not receiving support from host nationals, and her attempts at accommodation were not well received. It may be that she had too much anxiety to effectively manage her uncertainty. Over time, she was able to communicate effectively in her new culture for several reasons. First, she had host students who were willing to help; host support assists in the cultural adaptation process. Second, she found a balance between maintaining ties to her home culture and host culture. Third, she was effective at gathering information to enhance her predictive and explanatory uncertainty. Thus, this story illustrates factors that facilitate and impede cultural adaptation as well as communication strategies that facilitate effective interaction.

Here is a summary of the chapter based on the learning objectives:

- **Types of initial interactions:** This chapter examined cultural adaptation and initial interactions with people from different cultural groups. It discussed three types of initial interactions: travels, sojourners, and migrants. These three types vary in the degree of time spent in the host culture from temporary to permanent.
- **Model of culture shock:** Sojourners and migrants experience different types of cultural adaptation processes. Sojourners go through a temporary adjustment period in a new culture and then the adjustment period of returning to their home culture, a process often described through the W-shaped model. In contrast, migrants are permanently moving to a new culture and have some choice in whether they adopt their new homeland, their original homeland, a combination of both, or neither. A variety of factors impacts

the speed and effectiveness of adaptation, including media, interactions with members of the host and home culture, and individual attitudes and skills.

- **Anxiety and uncertainty management:** The historical and current migration patterns create frequent opportunities to interact with people from different cultural groups than our own. According to anxiety and uncertainty management theory, when we meet new people from different cultural groups, we have to manage uncertainty and anxiety to have effective communication. The key to managing uncertainty and anxiety is to be mindful. Mindfulness involves the creation of new categories, openness to new information, and awareness of more than one perspective.
- **Accommodation and nonaccommodation:** According to communication accommodation theory, accommodation generally helps to reduce intergroup barriers and creates a desire for future interaction and a movement to an interpersonal relationship. Nonaccommodation can demonstrate a limited desire for future interaction or also a desire to emphasize cultural distinctiveness. Our motivation to use accommodating or nonaccommodating behaviors comes from prior historical relationships among cultural groups and our individual desires for identity management and being understood.
- **Bottom-up and top-down effects:** Cultural adaptation and other initial interactions shape attitudes and are shaped by the culture and media. Our interactions with strangers impact our own attitudes, but also other members of the cultural groups we represent. The cultural and media layers emphasize socio-historical relations and social status. Many of these factors relate to the relative power that one group has over another. It is important to consider that social structures and social history generally provide advantages to those in the dominant group relative to the nondominant group (such as migrants or ethnic minorities). These factors create challenges for effective communication if we are to develop interpersonal relationships with people from other cultural groups.

REVIEW QUESTIONS

1. Describe and give an example of interpersonal and intergroup communication.
2. Distinguish between sojourners, refugees, and immigrants. What challenges do each of these groups face in intercultural communication?
3. What are the stages of culture shock?
4. Describe the advantages and disadvantages of the culture shock model.
5. Argue whether you think the culture shock experience is the same for everyone who travels to another culture for a sojourn. What points and evidence support your position?
6. What is cultural adaptation, and what are the four different types of adaptation? Provide an example of each.
7. Give examples of the stress-adaptation-growth dynamic. Think about cultural groups other than nationalities for the examples.

8. Which factors influence the stress-adaptation-growth dynamic? Provide an example of each.
9. Explain in what situations we need to have anxiety and uncertainty in order to develop effective communication and why.
10. Apply the concepts of AUM to a situation where you met someone from a different culture. Does the theory explain whether your interaction was effective or not?
11. Which factors influence whether we will accommodate someone from another culture? Give an example of each.
12. Explain how mass media inhibits and facilitates cultural adaptation.
13. Describe the communication skills that can facilitate cultural adaptation. Develop a hypothetical example that illustrates how the skill can be performed poorly or well.

EXERCISES

1. Interview an international student at your university. Find out his or her difficulties and triumphs in interacting with people of your host culture. Determine what a host culture member could do to help the sojourn be successful. If you are an international student, interview a host culture member to find out his or her approach to interacting with international students.
2. Investigate the immigration policies of two developed nations (for example, the United States and Germany or Japan). Do you consider these policies open or closed to immigrants? Do they establish the correct balance in immigration? Why or why not?
3. Read *The Spirit Catches You and You Fall Down* by Anne Fadiman (Farrar, Straus, & Giroux) to investigate the cultural adaptation processes of one refugee group (the Hmong). Or read Maya Angelou's autobiography, *I Know Why the Caged Bird Sings* (Bantam), to understand the cultural adaptation processes she underwent throughout her lifetime living in the United States and Africa.
4. Examine some of the ethnic-specific media referenced in this chapter. How does this type of media facilitate and inhibit cultural adaptation?

CHAPTER 6

Intercultural Friendships and Relationships

CHAPTER OUTLINE

I. Introduction

II. Friendships
   a. Factors for Intercultural Friendship Formation
   b. Challenges to Intercultural Friendship
   c. Building Intercultural Alliances
   d. Concept Check

III. Romantic Relationships
   a. Managing Relationships: Negotiating Dialectics
   b. Managing Conflict and Differences
   c. Concept Check

IV. Layers of Intercultural Friendships and Relationships
   a. Bottom-Up Effects
   b. Top-Down Effects: An Intercultural Relationship's Impact on Attitudes
   c. Top-Down Effects: Society's Impact on Relationships
   d. Challenges and Skills

V. Summary

VI. Review Questions

VII. Exercises

Relationships come in all different types, and all are important for their partners. Do intercultural relationships face more challenges than intracultural relationships? Or are there simply different types of challenges?

CHAPTER OBJECTIVES

After reading this chapter, students should be able to

- describe what a relational culture is.

- identify five factors for intercultural friendship formation.
- explain three challenges for intercultural friendship formation and ways to overcome these challenges by building an intercultural alliance.
- define dialectics, and specify nine different dialectics (three for relationships in general and six for intercultural relationships specifically).
- describe the culture-based situational conflict model.
- discuss the bottom-up and top-down effects of intercultural friendships and relationships.

Introduction

Soumia is from India, and David is from England. They met in classes while Soumia was an international student in England. They became friends over the first year and then began dating a year later. Soumia decided to stay in England, and they married. While they were dating, Soumia liked how private David was and how he put a lot of focus on their relationship. David liked how open Soumia was and appreciated that she wasn't afraid to show her feelings and express herself. Both liked the qualities in each other that they wished they had themselves. The longer they have been together, however, the more they get annoyed by what they originally liked. David wishes Soumia wouldn't be so forthcoming about all of their news—new jobs, pregnancy, difficulties in the marriage—with friends and especially family. Soumia wishes David wouldn't be so uptight.

While they were courting, they had some difficulty deciding how much and when to tell their family about their relationship. David told his parents right away, and they were neutral—said it was fine, but didn't really show enthusiasm. The couple told Soumia's family after two years, and her family was opposed to him—they wanted her to marry a nice Indian man even though they didn't expect to arrange the marriage. Soumia's family eventually became accepting and even liked David, eventually moving to England to be closer to the couple. Soumia's family members live nearby and constantly visit, many times unannounced. David's family lives out of town and rarely visits. His family likes it that way because, while neutral, they don't really accept Soumia as a member of the family.

During courtship and even now, Soumia feels like an outsider in England. She feels that people stare at them when they are together and holding hands. David says that she is just being paranoid, but Soumia swears that she is not accepted. She tells him that he just doesn't know what it is like to be Asian in England. He says that they just need to worry about their own relationship and not care what anybody else thinks. He thinks that everything in their relationship except family and her feelings about being an outsider is perfect and that those issues are minor; she agrees, but thinks these two factors are causing a lot of problems in their relationship.

Question: Which concepts and principles of intercultural relationships help to explain Soumia's and David's interaction?

Over the past decades, attitudes and behaviors toward intercultural relationships have been changing. Intercultural relationships used to be frowned upon, particularly intercultural marriages. But as more tolerance and appreciation of cultural difference are developing, so is more acceptance of intercultural relationships than in the past. For example, one study examined the dating behavior of 468 university students from various ethnic groups in the United States using a 24-item confidential survey (Reiter, Krause, & Stirlen, 2005). Sixty-six percent of the participants who were in a relationship reported being involved in an intercultural romantic relationship. An intercultural relationship was defined as dating someone from a different race (27.5%), national culture (45.0%), or religious background (27.5%). In another study, 85% of a representative sample of 934 African Americans approve of interracial marriage (Jacobson & Johnson, 2006). Moreover, African American participants in that study who had White American friends were more likely to approve of interracial marriage than those participants who did not have White friends. In contrast to the acceptance of these intercultural relationships, a 2006 Gallup poll found that only 39% of U.S. Americans are in favor of same-sex marriages and 58% are opposed. The attitudes are changing, however, as the same organization's poll in 1996 found that only 27% were in favor with 68% opposed (ReligiousTolerance.org, 2006).

Despite some growing acceptance of intercultural relationships, communication challenges still exist. Some argue that intercultural relationships are more difficult than intracultural relationships (Diggs & Clark, 2002; Orbe & Harris, 2001; Thompson & Collier, 2006) because of societal constraints and because prejudice and discrimination still exist in certain people (from all cultural groups). Cultural differences among the relational partners also provide potential difficulties in establishing a strong relationship. A key to having a successful intercultural relationship is establishing an effective relational culture. A **relational culture** refers to "processes, structures, and practices that create, express, and sustain personal relationships and identities of partners" (Wood, 1995, p. 150). In essence, relational partners develop their own culture—a mix of both of their larger cultural backgrounds and their idiosyncratic behaviors and personalities. Effective relational cultures are based on positive affect toward the partner, perception of positive motives (that is, assuming your partner is supporting you), and a perception of the relationship as a benefit to each other (for example, I'm better off with my partner than without her). In contrast, an ineffective relational culture produces negative affect toward the partner, perception of negative motives, and the perception that the relationship is hurting the individuals (Ting-Toomey, 1999). This chapter examines some of the challenges, opportunities, and suggestions for effective communication in intercultural friendships and romantic relationships.

Friendships

Since the Brown vs. Board of Education U.S. Supreme Court decision in 1954 outlawed segregated public schools, the opportunity to form intercultural friendships in the United States has steadily increased. Additionally, global migration and globalization (such as increased virtual communication) have increased the opportunities for people around the world to form friendships with others from different cultural backgrounds. Research tells us that we become friends with people who live in close proximity to us and with whom we have an opportunity to interact (Kudo & Simkin, 2003). In more recent times, the Internet has given us the opportunity to meet and interact with people from different cultures and to make virtual friendships. However, while we may have wonderful opportunities to make intercultural friends, these opportunities present some challenges as well. In the following section, we examines some of the attitudes and communication behaviors associated with intercultural friendships, the challenges to intercultural friendships, and the ways to build intercultural alliances.

Factors for Intercultural Friendship Formation

Why do we form friendships with people from other cultures? A variety of factors associated with intercultural friendship formation have been demonstrated in studies of a number of cultural groups (Kudo & Simkin, 2003; Lease & Blake, 2005; Ying, 2002). These factors include the opportunity to interact with culturally different people, the personality of the individuals, similarity in characteristics, positive attitudes toward other cultures, and appropriate communication skills.

First, we have to have the opportunity to meet and have frequent contact with people from different cultures. If we live in a homogeneous community, it is difficult to meet and get to know friends from different cultures. One study examined which factors were important for Japanese students studying at an Australian university to make friends with Australians (Kudo & Simkin, 2003). The researchers interviewed the students and identified four key themes that were related to the desire and formation of intercultural friendships. One of the key themes was frequent contact (other themes are presented in the coming paragraphs). Interestingly, the absence of people from our own culture (for example, being an international exchange student) also increases the likelihood of forming intercultural friendships; if we want friends in this situation, we have to seek out members of the host culture (Ying, 2002).

Second, much like friendships within cultures, similarity in personal characteristics and age are important for intercultural friendship formation (Kudo & Simkin, 2003). While we can have an appreciation for cultural difference, friendships are based in the sharing of interests, values, and experiences. For example, a sport such as soccer (or football, as most of the world calls it) might provide the opportunity and impetus to make intercultural friends (see Box 6.1).

Third, certain personality characteristics are associated with intercultural friendship formation. One study examined 155 Taiwanese graduate students at arrival in the United States and then determined which factors were associated with intercultural friendship formation 14 months later (Ying, 2002). The study found that the more extroverted people were, the more likely they were to have intercultural friends.

Box 6.1 Globalization: Forming Relationships in Interesting Places

Zheng is an Indonesian citizen of Chinese descent and Catholic upbringing. Her family owns several restaurants in Java, and Zheng wanted to go into the family business. She decided that she wanted to open an upscale, gourmet restaurant and went to study at a French culinary institute. There she met Heinrich, a Swiss citizen of German descent, who shared her passion for gourmet cooking. As they became friends, they decided to open a restaurant together. Eventually, they became lovers and married. Their story provides an interesting illustration of how national culture boundaries are minimized through common interests.

Another study examined 260 White American and African American students in 4th to 6th grade who were racial majorities in their classrooms; that is, the class was mostly African American or mostly White American (Lease & Blake, 2005). Overall, the study found that racial majority children with a racial minority friend were perceived by others as high status (or popular) and willing to help others.

Fourth, the attitude toward other cultures is predictive of intercultural friendship formation (Kudo & Simkin, 2003; Ying, 2002). In the study of Taiwanese graduate students and the study of Japanese international students, receptivity toward members of the host culture was positively associated with intercultural friendship formation (see Box 6.2 on p.154). In addition, the Taiwanese sample indicated a greater likelihood to have intercultural friends if the participants had a negative attitude toward forming friends with members of their own cultural groups. In contrast, in the study of elementary school children, students were more likely to have an intercultural friend when they were socially satisfied with members of their peer group. This difference might be due to the fact that the children in the elementary school study had frequent opportunities to interact with both majority and minority group members (that is, they have friends within both racial groups) whereas the Taiwanese students were sojourners and had limited opportunity to interact with both Taiwanese and U.S. Americans.

Finally, having certain communication skills is associated with intercultural friendship formation. In the study of Japanese international students, the students perceived that good English skills and an openness to communicate and self-disclose were necessary to form intercultural friendships (Kudo & Simkin, 2003). In the studies of elementary school children and Taiwanese graduate students, the personality characteristics of extroversion and being prosocial (wanting to help others) are related to communication behaviors of openness and willingness to communicate with others. Essentially, we have to be willing to go up and talk with people from different cultural groups in order to form friendships.

Challenges to Intercultural Friendship

Cultural differences and prejudice/discrimination are constraints that make intercultural friendships more challenging than intracultural friendships. Cultural differences lead to misunderstandings and misattributions about behavior that can be potential

Box 6.2 Voices: Forming Intercultural Friendships as an International Student

When I first went to Taiwan as an international student from the United States, I found it very difficult to meet people. I was fluent in Mandarin and had no problem interacting with people or finding my way around. I didn't experience a lot of culture shock; I simply found it hard to get to know people. What I realized is that relationships in Taiwan take longer to form than in the United States. Fortunately, I had Taiwanese friends back home, and they reminded me to be patient. They said

that I should continue to interact with people (I wouldn't make friends if I stayed in my apartment all the time) and be a good student and that friendships would come. I eventually got to know some people, and we shared some interests in politics and shopping. They eventually accepted me as one of their own group, and these people became some of my best friends. I still interact with them almost every week and make sure to visit them at least once a year.

pitfalls to forming a strong intercultural friendship. Additionally, historical relationships among cultural groups and the accompanying racism and prejudice can inhibit the development of trust (Collier, 1998; Orbe & Harris, 2001). This next section examines three specific challenges to intercultural friendship: a) different definitions of friendship, b) communication style differences, and c) prejudice/discrimination.

DIFFERENT DEFINITIONS OF FRIENDSHIP   Researchers have found some similarities about what it means to be a friend, but also some important differences as well. Collier (1991) examined the definitions of friendship among African American, White American, and Mexican American college students. She completed in-depth interviews with 70 students (almost evenly split among men and women in the three groups) in which she asked the students to define a close relationship. Members of all three groups said that close friendships are based on trust and acceptance. African American students also mentioned the importance of problem solving; Mexican American students mentioned support and expression of feelings; White Americans mentioned the importance of freedom of expression. A second study compared the perception of intimacy in relationships by college students in Japan and the United States (Gudykunst & Nishida, 1986). The researchers asked the students to rate how intimate certain types of relationships are on a 9-point scale (1 being very intimate and 9 not at all intimate). The results of this study are seen in Figure 6.1. Essentially, both cultures find that strangers are the least intimate, followed by acquaintances, friends, and best friends. Differences occur between best friends and romantic relationships. In the United States, students rated romantic relationships as more intimate than best friends while in Japan the opposite pattern was found. The authors concluded that these findings are due to the difference in masculine and feminine cultures of the two countries (see Chapter 2). Japan is a more masculine culture and the United States more feminine, relative to each other. Masculine cultures show relatively little informal communication in opposite sex relationships, and these relationships are thus not very intimate. Both of these studies illustrate some subtle differences in what it means to be a close friend. If we are

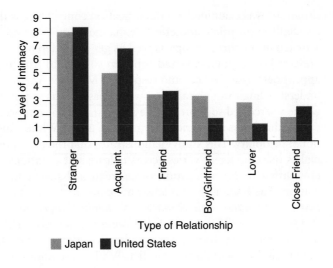

Figure 6.1

Perceptions of Intimacy in Relationships in Japan & the United States.

Source: Gudykunst & Nishida (1986)

Note: Low numbers equal high levels of intimacy

thinking of a close friend from another culture through our own cultural perspective, we may end up misunderstanding the other person.

For example, Courtney, a White woman from the United States, married Jiang from China. After the honeymoon phase wore off, she struggled with how little he told her about his feelings and what was going on in his life. She would tell him everything about her life and thought of him as her best friend. They had many fights about this topic until one day, she asked him who his best friend was and he responded that it was Bodi, one of his male friends. She asked him why she wasn't his best friend and he said, "You are my wife and that is very important, but you can't be my best friend too." It was an "ah ha" moment for her and while she didn't like it, she better understood the differences in their expectations of the relationship. Jiang tried to compromise by sharing some of his feelings and also adjusted his expectations. They were able to manage the difficulty, but it took many fights for them to understand each other better.

DIFFERENCES IN COMMUNICATION STYLE   Cultural differences not only produce differences in definitions of friendship, but also differences in communication style. Communication style is the general pattern of interaction we have when interacting with others. Communication style can vary across situations. In Chapter 2, we discussed some communication style differences related to patterns of cultural variability (for example, individualism-collectivism and high-low context communication). These communication style differences can result in misunderstandings about the other person's intentions and purpose. Chapter 4 explained several examples of misunderstandings due to cultural difference. These misunderstandings can also result from different expectations of communication behavior in a particular situation.

In Collier's (1991) study of 70 African American, Mexican American, and White American college students (Collier, 1991), the perception of competence in conflict situations was examined. Communication competence is the ability to communicate in a socially appropriate and effective manner. Collier found some differing expectations for each of the three groups as well as gender differences: a) African American men preferred clear arguments and problem-solving; b) African American women preferred appropriate assertiveness and respect; c) Mexican American men perceived that mutual understanding through talking over the issues was important; d) Mexican American women perceived support for the relationship was important; e) White American men valued directness and rational argument; and f) White American women valued situational flexibility. This study demonstrates that the perception of the specific skills that makes one competent varies across culture and situations and helps to demonstrate how different communication styles create a challenge to intercultural friendship formation. The findings in this study are consistent with popular books such as at *You Just Don't Understand: Women and Men in Conversation* (Deborah Tannen) and *Men Are from Mars, Women Are from Venus* (John Gray). These books present differences between men and women across cultures in the use of problem solving (men) and relational talk (women) during conflict. While these books oversimplify gender differences, there is a need to be aware of how friends and partners define effective communication during conflict to make relationships go smoothly (see Box 6.3).

PREJUDICE AND DISCRIMINATION Hostility, or at least preference for separation, toward other cultures has been the norm throughout history (Orbe & Harris, 2001). The

Box 6.3 Voices: Subtle Communication Differences

Growing up in Los Angeles, you are bound to have friends from different cultural backgrounds. What I found is that there are subtle communication differences when interacting with Vietnamese, Whites, Blacks, and Mexican Americans. Sure, there are individual differences, too, but these patterns happen more in specific cultural groups. For example, with my Black friends, the most important thing I can do is be straight—no sugar coating, just "tell is like it is." If I don't like that a friend was drinking too much, I can say (and with other friends around), "Man, it wasn't cool that you were drunk the other night. You embarrassed yourself and I'm worried that you might have a problem." With my White friends, I have to be a little more face saving—I have to make sure I don't hurt their feelings. If that friend was drinking too much, I'd have to talk

with him without anyone else around and say, "The other night, you might have had too much to drink. Do you do that often?" and take it from there. With my Vietnamese friends, we talk about issues more indirectly and they get the point. If they ask me to go to a party with them, I'll just say, "no thanks—too much drinking going on" and they'll get the point. With my Mexican American friends, I just need to make sure I put our relationship first. I'll just say, "We've been friends for a while and I'm worried about you. You were way drunk and I don't want anything to happen to you." These are stereotypes, and I do have friends that don't fit this pattern perfectly, but I find this works for my friendships.

1. Are these explanations stereotypes?
2. Do you agree with this person's assessment?

accompanying attitudes of racism, stereotypes, and prejudice often still get in the way of forming intercultural friendships. Even if we are not directly responsible for such attitudes, the historical context has created expectations of mistrust, miscommunication, and hostility for intercultural relations. This does not mean every intercultural friendship will experience such behaviors, but they are likely to come up. For example, I have a friend who is American Indian. She told me about her experience at another university where the dean asked her to come perform a rain dance for him. This was troubling to her for several reasons—first, her tribe does not do rain dances; second, it put her in a subservient position where she had to perform inappropriate acts in the work place. The dean did not ask any of the other faculty members to perform cultural acts for him. This story became part of our friendship. Racism, race hostility, and stereotypes are challenges to intercultural friendship formation.

Building Intercultural Alliances

Two communication scholars described their formation of an intercultural relationship in the article "It's a struggle, but worth it" (Diggs & Clark, 2002). The scholars (one African American and one White American) discussed their experiences in graduate school and identified what they needed to do to maintain their friendship. They relied on spiritual, racial, and personal identities to help them through the difficult discourse. They also described a process of talking through difficulties; specifically, they talk, reflect on the talk, check in with people from other races/cultural groups, and return to talk with each other again. Essentially, they have maintained a dialogue over time to manage their tensions. For example, they found they were both Christian and had some differences in how they conceived their religon. They also had experiences where they were offended by the other. But, they found that they both listened and supported each other even when they did not agree on every point. They worked through differences and built a relationship where they could trust one another, a relationship where they could go to ask about each other's culture to better understand different cultural perspectives. Collier (1998) described this type of relationship as an **intercultural alliance.** The relationship is more than a friendship— it is a relationship where parties can go to each other to better understand cultural misunderstandings and also to stand up and support each other when cultural issues are raised. In her study of intercultural relationships between women, Collier identified three key issues that need to be addressed through dialogue in order to create an alliance: addressing power and unearned privilege, recognizing the influence of history, and having an orientation of affirmation.

Power and unearned privilege refers to unstated power that exists in societal relations (see also Chapter 3). Most of us are able to recognize power that is attributed to wealth, politics, or hierarchy in an organization. For example, we often know who the boss in an organization is. What many people do not realize is that unstated, unearned power operates among cultural groups. In the United States, historically White Americans, men, heterosexuals, and Christians have had power and privilege relative to other groups. As was pointed out in Chapter 4, this does not mean that all White Americans have more power than other ethnic groups (socioeconomic status also comes into play), but that being White (and even light skinned) confers power in the United States and around the world. What Collier found was that White American women were rarely aware of their power until female friends of color informed them of their privileged racial position in society. White American women were aware of the power men had, but tended to equate all women together. A successful alliance was formed if the women could dialogue about and recognize this unearned privilege (see Box 6.4).

Similarly, intercultural alliances occur when the partners involved acknowledge the influence of historical relationships among the cultural groups. For example, it is important to recognize that slavery in the United States still has repercussions today even if it ended more than 150 years ago. Sensitivity to and awareness of how some cultural groups have been oppressed historically helps the partners to understand their friends' point of view. Notice that Collier did not say the privileged friend needs to feel guilty or try to correct the past. Rather, the key factor is acknowledging and dialoging on how not to make the same mistakes of the past.

Finally, intercultural alliances have an orientation in which partners affirm the others' cultural identity. Collier found that women who valued difference, affirmed

---

Box 6.4 Layered Effects: Unearned Privilege and Intercultural Alliances

Unearned privilege is a hard concept to grasp for people from the dominant culture, but often easy for people from minority cultures. McIntosh (2003) described what it is like to have unearned privilege. She describes many factors that White Americans take for granted, such as the following: a) being able to find flesh-colored Band-aids; b) not having people cross the street to avoid passing near you, c) having teachers assume that you are a good student rather than a bad student when they first meet you, and d) not having police officers stop you for driving in the "wrong" neighborhood. Unearned privilege exists for every group to a certain degree, but the dominant group in a society has more advantage than other groups (and at the expense of other groups). For example, the U.S. Department of Justice, Bureau of Justice Statistics, found the following associated with U.S. drivers: a) while White, Black, and Hispanic drivers were stopped by police at similar rates, Blacks and Hispanics were three times more likely than Whites to be searched; b) Blacks and Hispanics were more likely than Whites to have force used against them

by police; c) Blacks were twice as likely as Whites to be arrested; and d) White drivers were more likely than Black or Hispanic drivers to be stopped by police for speeding, but Blacks (78%) and Hispanics (85%) were more likely than Whites (70%) to receive a ticket (Durose, Smith, & Langan, 2007).

Unearned privilege makes intercultural alliances difficult. Many White Americans do not realize that certain actions—such as taking a friend from a different culture to a homogeneous neighborhood—can have some negative repercussions. It doesn't mean that they shouldn't go or that the friend perceives a problem. That is the point about unearned privilege: those in power don't have to worry about their basic, everyday actions. Those without it have to (almost) always be on guard. However, there is a balance because you do not want to make unearned privilege the center of the relationship—there has to be a focus on the uniqueness of the relational culture. But unearned privilege illustrates one way that historical and societal relations impact intercultural communication among friends.

that cultural identity was a key part of who their friends are, and accepted that identity were able to build strong friendships. Friends can learn about each other's culture and learn to appreciate difference through dialogue. This appreciation of cultural identity is not at the expense of individual personalities and interests. It is a both/and situation rather than either/or; that is, I can recognize your individual characteristics and your cultural characteristics together. For example, two students, one a White American Christian and the other an international student, Indonesian and Muslim, met at school in the United States. They had no awareness of the other's culture initially, but became friends because of their interest in art and their value of family and cultural ties. They shared experiences about their culture, especially about art, and visited each other's families. Their friendship recognized individual personalities and interests, but also the importance of each other's cultural history, religion, and background.

Concept Check

A variety of factors predict whether we will form an intercultural friendship. We must have an opportunity to interact with people from different cultures, find similarities in interests and experiences, have positive attitudes toward other cultures, and have certain communication skills. Even with these factors, a number of challenges to friendship formation exist. Specifically, cultural differences and prior historical relationships create misunderstandings and tensions that have to be addressed. Successful intercultural friendships form an alliance that is negotiated through dialogue to address these challenges. The dialogue needs to center on three factors: recognizing power and unearned privilege, acknowledging the history of intercultural relations, and affirming cultural identity. Like any other friendship, intercultural friendships still hold a lot of uniqueness. In fact, friendship rules are individually negotiated so that no two friendships are alike. We create our own relational culture that determines whether we will be successful.

Romantic Relationships

Intercultural friendships are related to the development of intercultural romantic relationships in several ways. Growing up in diverse neighborhoods, having diverse friendship networks, and having family members who had intercultural romantic relationships all increase the likelihood that a person will have intercultural romantic relationships (Jacobson & Johnson, 2006; Martin, Bradford, Drezewiecka, & Chitgopekar, 2003). In addition, people with culturally diverse friends are more likely to approve of intercultural marriage than those participants who did not have such friends (Jacobsen & Johnson, 2006).

Navigating any romantic relationship is challenging and requires a great deal of emotional and communicative energy. As we develop our relationships, we are faced with contradictions, inconsistencies, and conflicts. Intercultural relationships also have some unique challenges that a couple must face (see Box 6.5 on p.160). This section explores two particular challenges in maintaining romantic and family relationships: managing relationship contradictions (or dialectics) and managing conflict.

Box 6.5 Globalization: Maintaining Long-Distance Intercultural Relationships

Chie was an international student from Japan studying in the United States. She met Michael, an international student from Germany. They met through mutual acquaintances and slowly became friends. Neither spoke the other's native language or understood the other's culture well, but they shared the English language and many similar interests. Their friendship grew into an intimate relationship. While they told each other about their respective cultures, their relationship was formed in English and was based in a lot of communication norms that are part of American culture.

Michael completed his studies and returned to Germany while Chie still had two more years left in her program. They decided they still wanted to be together and relied on communication technology—specifically, the Skyped—to maintain their relationship. Skype is a free software program than that enables people to talk directly via computer over the Internet (similar to a voice-over Internet provider). Skype is available in 28 languages and is used in almost every country in the world. They connected cameras so that they could see each other as well as talk. This technology helped them feel connected to each other and maintain their relationship. They continued to talk only in English and visited each other several times a year. The distance was hard, but the technology made it easier than if they only had the phone.

1. In what ways has technology enabled us to form and maintain intercultural relationships?
2. When two people do not speak each other's language and use English only (or some other language), do you think that the individuals will lose some of their own culture? Or will they find a way to blend their three cultures (in this case Germany, Japan, and the United States.)?

Managing Relationships: Negotiating Dialectics

All relationships are fraught with difficult challenges. One key aspect of this challenge is that relationships are filled with contradictions or dialectics (Baxter & Montgomery, 1997; Chen, 2002). A **dialectic** is the contradiction of two opposing forces along the same continuum that appears mutually exclusive (Baxter & Montgomery, 1997). By addressing one end of the continuum, we exclude the other end. Dialectics are inherent contradictions in all relationships; that is, we cannot avoid them, as they are just part of life. Managing the tension between the opposing ends becomes the challenge for those of us in relationships. This section examines general dialects in relationships and then dialectics that are unique to intercultural relationships.

GENERAL DIALECTICS IN RELATIONSHIPS   The dialectical perspective identifies three general dialectics associated with interpersonal relationships: openness-closedeness, autonomy-connection, and prediction-novelty (Baxter & Montgomery, 1997). Each of these presents a challenge to couples to negotiate and manage. No one perfect way exists for couples to manage these dialectics, but rather each couple must figure out what works best for them. In addition, cultural difference also makes managing these dialectics challenging.

Openness-closedness is the self-disclosure dialectic. It involves revealing information about ourselves to the other person in order to develop intimacy (Baxter & Montgomery, 1997). Telling your partner about your interests and your past gives him or her the opportunity to get to know you and also the opportunity for you to build trust (that is, will your partner tell your secrets or use them against you?). However, opening up ourselves to others puts us in a vulnerable place. We are willing to be vulnerable to a certain degree, but remaining closed also protects us. Over the course of our relationship, we manage this tension of being open and closed with our partner. For example, during a fight, we might choose to be closed. Or, if we know that sharing certain feelings makes our partner uncomfortable, we might choose to be closed. Each couple has to figure out the appropriate balance between these two ends; one person in a couple might choose to be completely open about everything while the other might be open about most but not all subjects (for example, the person may not want to talk about past relationships or political differences).

Managing the openness-closedeness dialectic is made more challenging by cultural differences in self-disclosure norms. A classic study of self-disclosure in Japan and the United States helps to illustrate these differences (Barnlund, 1975). Barnlund hypothesized that individualists (U.S. Americans as the example) would reveal more information about themselves than would collectivists (Japanese as the example). He compared six topics of self-disclosure to six targets (people we self-disclose to such as same-sex friend, opposite sex-friend, mother, father, stranger, untrusted acquaintance) among college students. He found that certain topics (tastes and opinions on public issues) were more preferred by both cultures than other topics (personality traits and physical attributes). Additionally, the two cultures had similar preferences in the targets. However, across all targets and topics, college students in the United States self-disclosed more than those from Japan. While this study is over 30 years old, more recent research (e.g., Chen, 1995) has found support for this finding. It is important to note that while individualism and collectivism are related to self-disclosure, we should not stereotype all Japanese and U.S. Americans as following this pattern. For example, a colleague of mine told me a story about a Japanese international student who went on a date with a U.S. American. Having studied about self-disclosure norms in class, this student decided to share a great deal of personal information with her date (for example, her father was an alcoholic) to make a good impression and adjust to the U.S. culture. Her date was quite surprised by the revealing nature of the disclosures and never asked her out again.

The **autonomy-connection** dialectic refers to the degree of interdependence in a relationship (Baxter & Montgomery, 1997). Autonomy is the desire to be different and unique from others. Connection is the desire to be included or interdependent with other people. Throughout relationships, we negotiate with our partner the degree of autonomy and connection we have. During early stages of the relationship, most couples emphasize autonomy. As the relationship becomes more intimate, couples move toward connection. Throughout the course of the relationship, couples might negotiate different levels of autonomy and connection. If the couple is going through a "rocky patch," they might choose autonomy. The couple also figures out how to balance needs for both by using strategies such as having different nights for self and couple (for example, Friday night is "Girls/Boys Night"; Saturday is couple night).

Just as with self-disclosure, individualism and collectivism have an influence on preferences for autonomy and connection. The study described in Figure 6.1 indicates the perception of intimacy in certain types of relationships in Japan and the United States. Romantic relationships are perceived to be more intimate and connected in the United States than in Japan. Again, be careful of stereotyping your partners as "just like all of those...." Your attributions might be creating a problem in the relationship where none exists.

The **prediction-novelty** dialectic refers to the degree to which we prefer routine versus newness (Baxter & Montgomery, 1997). Prediction is the desire to know what is going to happen. Knowing what your partner is going to say or do indicates a great deal of intimacy. We also need routines in life to function in a fast-paced world. Predictability can also be a little boring, however, so some of us like to have novelty. Novelty includes spontaneity and experiencing new challenges and people. Couples have to negotiate the balance between novelty and predictability based on their own needs. Some couples prefer one end of the continuum versus the other while other couples try to balance both. For example, we might have a weekly date night (routine) in which one person has to pick something new to do (novelty). Another couple might plan romantic getaways that involve surprising their partner.

Research about cultural difference and the prediction-novelty dialectic is limited. However, it appears that uncertainty avoidance (see Chapter 2) is the cultural factor associated with this dialectic. Individuals from high uncertainty avoidance cultures likely have a greater preference for predictability and routine and a lower preference for novelty than individuals from low uncertainty avoidance cultures.

SPECIFIC DIALECTICS IN INTERCULTURAL RELATIONSHIPS   The general dialectics are true of all relationships. However, intercultural romantic and family relationships also have unique dialectic challenges. Most of these dialectics are associated with how the couple interacts with the rest of their families and society in general. The six dialectics for intercultural relationships include a) identity vulnerability-security, b) privilege-disadvantage, c) history-present, d) revelation-nonrevelation, e) separation-integration, and f) conventionality-uniqueness.

The **identity vulnerability-security** dialectic is the degree to which we feel valued and supported in terms of our cultural identity (Kim, 2005; Ting-Toomey, 1999). Intercultural couples not only have the challenge of supporting each other individually (that is, ensuring your partner feels loved, wanted, etc.), but also making sure that each other's cultural identity is valued. This might seem like a contradiction in that an intimate relationship should be based on individual aspects. It is important to remember that people in a relationship are individuals and that having a strong sense of self is beneficial for relationships. Research has demonstrated, however, that the strength of cultural identity is also related to relationship quality. Leslie and Letiecq (2004) surveyed 76 interracial couples (African American and White American couples) and found that racial/cultural identity was the strongest predictor of marital quality. Partners who had pride in their race, but were also accepting of others' races and cultures experienced higher marital quality than those who did not. This finding was true for both African American and White American participants, but to a lesser extent for White Americans. In managing the identity vulnerability-security dialectic, intercultural couples need to employ strategies that focus on enhancing cultural identity and social esteem for their partners.

The **privilege-disadvantage** dialectic was discussed under friendship alliances and refers to the degree to which one partner in the relationship has unearned privilege relative to the other (Collier, 1998; Martin & Nakayama, 1999). If both partners come from cultures with generally positive historical relations (for example, United States and England), privilege-disadvantage likely will not be an issue. However, many intercultural relationships have one partner in a privileged position relative to the other. As Collier (1998) pointed out with intercultural alliances, couples have to address and recognize the societal privilege to avoid repeating privilege in their own relationship, although certain relationships are successful because one partner is willing to be in a subordinate position. The study in the previous paragraph about African American/White American interracial couples also provides an example of privilege (Leslie & Letiecq, 2004). That White American identity was less related to marital quality than African American identity illustrates that White Americans have privilege. They do not have to think about their racial identity to the same extent that African Americans do in order to have a successful relationship.

The **history-present** dialectic refers to the degree to which individuals emphasize historical relations among cultures or simply focus on the present or even the future (Martin & Nakayama, 1999). Similarly to the privilege-disadvantage dialectic, prior historical relations among cultures have influenced the ways culture functions today. People who have societal disadvantage often want to recognize the historical events that have helped to create the present (such as the slavery of Africans; the colonization of American Indians, as well as many African, South American, and Asian nations; and the persecution of various religious groups). People with privilege want to concentrate on how status has improved and focus on the future. Intercultural couples have to manage this tension in a way that allows both partners to be supported.

The **revelation-nonrevelation** dialectic focuses on the degree to which a couple shares information about their relationship with other people (Chen, 2002). If an intercultural couple reveals that they are in a relationship, they are making themselves vulnerable. They risk social sanction from others in society (such as nasty stares from others when they hold hands) or their family (such as predictions of the demise of the relationship— "It'll never last" —or being shunned— "You are never bringing that X in my house"). On the other hand, they also have the opportunity to receive the social support necessary for the relationship to thrive. It is always nice to have people who support your relationship and encourage it to develop. Intercultural couples have the unique challenge of deciding who and how much to tell their friends, family, and society—and then dealing with the consequences of their decision. It can be very traumatic to tell your parents about the love of your life only to receive an insult or be shunned. Homosexual couples have to make a choice either to keep their relationship in the closet or to come out when dealing with co-workers and family members. The choice often depends on the degree of acceptance they will receive (Land & Kitzinger, 2005).

The **separation-integration** dialectic is the external management of the interdependence in the relationship (Chen, 2002). Once a couple has revealed their relationship, they have to make a decision as to how to separate or integrate themselves within each other's social networks. For example, if my parents have expressed a dislike for my partner, do I continue to bring her around to family gatherings? How do we choose to celebrate holidays, particularly if we have different religious backgrounds? If our community shows its displeasure toward our relationship, do we move away? These are the type of questions that intercultural couples face. They need to make sure they receive sufficient support (no couple can do it on their own)—both from the outside world, and also from their family and friends. If the family and friend networks are supportive of the relationship, this is less of a challenge for the couple, but each couple must still make important choices.

The **conventionality-uniqueness** dialectic is the external management of predictability-novelty (Chen, 2002). An intercultural couple may present uniqueness in a community that others are not prepared for. To what degree is the couple going to push the social norms and flaunt or display (depending on perspective) their uniqueness, or simply keep a more private relationship and allow the community the feeling that everything is stable? For example, does the couple hold hands and engage in public displays of affection or simply reserve these for home? Relatedly, the couple also has to decide if they are going to try to restart or repair family relationships if the initial reaction from parents was negative. Do they break away from the prediction and stability they have in their current relationship to try to make it work with their parents? See Box 6.6.

Dialectics are challenges for every couple to manage. For intercultural couples, the added difficulties of cultural differences for dialectical preferences and the dialectics that result from the larger society are real (Chen, 2002; Collier, 1998; Martin & Nakayama, 1999). As part of their relational culture, every couple has to make choices to manage

Box 6.6 Layered Effects: Dialectics in Intercultural Relationships

The dialectical tensions specific to intercultural relationships illustrate the layered perspective. Unfortunately, no couple gets to create their relationship in a vacuum. There are always in-laws and social pressures ("so when are you going to have children?") in every relationship. However, intercultural relationships also have to face the scrutiny of society. Many (perhaps most) people are open to intercultural relationships, but some segments of society are still not accepting of these type of relationships. They become one more issue the couple has to deal with. Managing the larger layers is a combination of effective communication between the partners (negotiating the dialectics, so it works for both) and effective communication with the outside world. These outside strategies include boundary setting (to parents: "you are not going to talk to my partner in that way or we won't be in your life"), avoidance (moving out of an area that is not accepting of your relationship), and seeking support (interacting with friends who accept and value your relationship). Thus, communication needs to be within the relationship and across layers.

Box 6.7 What Went Right? Managing Dialectics in Interracial Relationships

Thompson and Collier (2006) interviewed 12 interracial couples who had been married an average of 9.4 years. They were interested in understanding the couples' negotiation of the intersecting cultural identities in their relationships. They found that the couples reported contradiction and change throughout their relationship in addressing the challenges. One common strategy in the relationship was to disassociate from the label "interracial." The couples reported emphasizing the unique relational culture rather than the interracial identities. Another strategy included protecting the relationship and the other partner from racism/discrimination. However, the individual partners would approach the same problem differently. One partner might explain that he or she "just puts blinders on and ignores it" while the other partner is always looking and watching to protect the family. A final strategy was to minimize the interracial aspect by using jokes. One couple reported teasing about race to support each other. This study illustrates a variety of strategies for addressing dialectic tensions. What other approaches can you think of to manage intercultural dialectics?

the dialectic. The success in managing dialectics goes a long way in determining whether a relationship will last. Box 6.7 discusses findings from a study involving strategies for managing dialectical tensions in intercultural/interracial relationships.

Managing Conflict and Differences

Conflict is inevitable in any relationship. Intercultural relationships simply provide different types of topics for conflict, but not necessarily an increased amount of conflict. **Conflict** is "the perceived and/or actual incompatibility of values, expectations, processes, or outcomes between two or more parties over substantive and/or relational issues" (Ting-Toomey, 1994, p. 360). Examples of conflict might include disagreeing about whether to tell your parents about your intercultural relationship, how much time to spend together, or how to raise your children.

Conflict has both positive and negative aspects for a relationship (Ting-Toomey & Oetzel, 2001; Wilmot & Hocker, 2007). On a positive level, conflict provides an opportunity for personal and relational growth. The negatives include the potential to damage a relationship. What determines whether conflict is positive or negative is the manner in which we communicate about and manage it. Managing conflict is complex as it involves a great many factors. The Culture-Based Situational Conflict Model (CBSCM) (Ting-Toomey & Oetzel, 2001) provides a framework for understanding the multitude of factors involved during relationship conflict.

The CBSCM is a contextual model to describe intercultural conflict and can be used as a guide for individuals in everyday relationships. To be competent in situations of intercultural conflict means communicating in such a way that is inclusive, yet aware of our own ethnocentric lenses. This model includes cultural, personal, and situational factors that shape face-to-face intercultural conflict. Specifically, Ting-Toomey and

Conflict is an evitable part of relationships. What factors affect how conflict is managed?

Oetzel (2001) identified four clusters of factors in this model: a) primary orientation factors; b) situational and relationship boundary features; c) conflict communication process factors; and d) conflict competence features (see Figure 6.2 for a picture of this model).

PRIMARY ORIENTATION FACTORS   In conflict episodes that include two polarized intercultural parties, the participants often carry with them different cultural values, personality orientations, and face concerns. These different cultural values and patterns often affect the fundamental expectations and attitudes indicating how an intercultural conflict should be approached, managed, and resolved (Ting-Toomey & Oetzel, 2001). The primary cultural value examined in the research is individualism-collectivism. Personal attributes include the notion of independent and interdependent self-construal. Recall that individuals with a strongly independent sense of self tend to see themselves as autonomous, self-reliant, unencumbered, and rational choice-makers; individuals with a strongly interdependent sense of self tend to see themselves as ingroup-bound, obligatory agents, and relational harmony seekers. Independence is related to cultural individualism, and interdependence is closely related to cultural collectivism

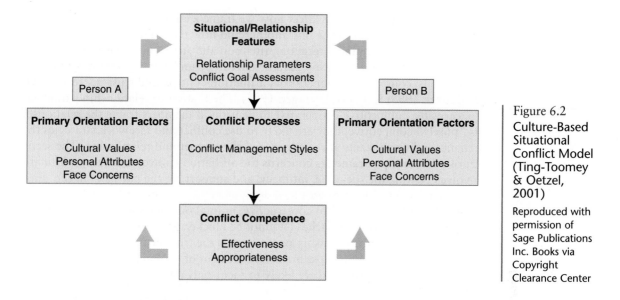

Figure 6.2
Culture-Based
Situational
Conflict Model
(Ting-Toomey
& Oetzel,
2001)

Reproduced with
permission of
Sage Publications
Inc. Books via
Copyright
Clearance Center

(Markus & Kitayama, 1991; Ting-Toomey & Oetzel, 2001; also see Chapter 2 for a more detailed explanation).

Face is the claimed sense of favorable social self-worth and/or projected other-worth in a public situation (Ting-Toomey & Kurogi, 1998). It is a vulnerable resource especially in conflict situations because this resource can be threatened, enhanced, maintained, and bargained over. Since face is vulnerable, recovering it becomes a primary goal and can supersede any other concern in conflict. Face is associated with respect, honor, status, reputation, credibility, competence, network connection, and relational obligation issues. Face concerns determine the direction of the subsequent conflict messages. Self-face concern is the protective concern for one's own image when one's own face is threatened in the conflict situation. Other-face concern, on the other hand, is the concern for accommodating the other conflict party's image in the conflict crisis situation. Mutual-face concern is the concern for both parties' images and/or the "image" of the relationship (Ting-Toomey & Kurogi, 1998).

SITUATIONAL AND RELATIONSHIP BOUNDARY FEATURES   **Situational and relationship boundary features** refer to the setting and nature of the relationship that we have with the other party. In order to manage intercultural conflict effectively, we have to understand the features that mediate between the primary orientation factors on one hand and the conflict communication process factors on the other. Even though numerous situational and relational features are possible, how intercultural couples perceive the nature of their relationship (relationship parameters) and how they evaluate the different goal types of the conflict will have a profound influence on how they manage the conflict.

Relationship parameters affect how we frame a conflict. Framing is critical to how two conflict parties view one another and how they view their relationship and the conflict task. Framing directs our attention and steers our focus to what is at stake in a conflict. Relationship parameters can be understood in terms of three dimensions: competition-cooperation, affiliation-control, and trust-distrust (Lewicki & Bunker, 1995; Rubin & Levinger, 1995). The first set of relationship parameters concerns the competitive-cooperative dimension. If members frame the relationship as "purely" competitive, they are likely to use conflict and facework strategies that enhance individual gains at the expense of the partner and relationship. The second set of relationship parameters concerns the affiliation-control dimension. Affiliation involves viewing the social tie, intimacy, and support for the partner. On the other hand, control focuses on social dominance/submission within the relationships. A focus on affiliation leads to constructive, mutual outcomes while a focus on control leads to win-loss approaches (Wilmot & Hocker, 2007; Ting-Toomey & Oetzel, 2001). A third set of relationship parameters is the trust-distrust dimension. Trust is often viewed as the single most important element of a good relationship. If we view our partner with distrust, we are likely to focus only on our own goals at the expense of our partner.

The second situational/relationship feature is **conflict goal assessments.** How we perceive the conflict, whether we choose to engage in or disengage from it, and how we attribute different weights to the different goals in a conflict episode can vary greatly across cultural lines. The perceived or actual conflict differences often rotate around the following interrelated goal issues: content, relational, and identity (Wilmot & Hocker, 2007). Content conflict goals are the substantive issues that are external to the individual involved. For example, partners who are engaged in a discussion about where to spend a holiday are involved in the content of "where to spend the holiday." Relational conflict goals refer to how individuals define, or would like to define, the particular relationship (such as nonintimate vs. intimate, formal vs. informal). For example, in deciding where to spend the holiday, one partner might view the conflict in terms of what is best for the family while the other sees the conflict in terms of "what I want." Identity-based goals revolve around issues of validation-rejection, approval-disapproval, respect-disrespect, and valuing-disconfirming of the individuals in the conflict episode; they are directly linked to face concerns and the general sense of personal and cultural identity (Ting-Toomey & Oetzel, 2001). For example, determining where we spend the holiday might be about my cultural identity because your family does not support who I am, and I am not comfortable with them. In fact, any given conflict can be about content, relational, and identity goals, but relational and identity goals tend to drive conflict management decisions. Further, content conflict issues that tend to repeat at least three times are generally about relational and identity conflict goals rather than content (Wilmot & Hocker, 2007).

CONFLICT PROCESSES   Conflict communication processes are the manner in which we manage conflict. The most common way to describe conflict processes is to focus on conflict management styles. **Conflict management style** refers to patterned responses to conflict in a variety of dissenting situations (Ting-Toomey, 1994). Findings in many past studies indicate that people display consistent styles across a variety of conflict situations in different cultures (Breshnahan, Shearman, Lee, Ohari, & Mosher, 2002; Chiu & Kosinski, 1994; D'Silva & Whyte, 1998; Earley, 1997; Ohbuchi, Fukushima, & Tedeshi, 1999). Conflict style is learned within the primary socialization process of one's cultural or ethnic group.

Conflict styles can be conceptualized along two dimensions. For example, Rahim (2001) based his classification of conflict styles on the two conceptual dimensions of concern for self and concern for others. The first dimension illustrates the degree (high or low) to which a person seeks to satisfy her or his own interest or face need. The second dimension represents the degree (high or low) to which a person desires to incorporate the other's conflict interest. The two dimensions are combined, resulting in five styles of handling interpersonal conflict: integrating, compromising, dominating, obliging, and avoiding. Briefly, the integrating style reflects a need for solution closure in conflict and involves high concern for self and high concern for others in conflict negotiation. The compromising style involves a give-and-take concession approach in order to reach a mid-point agreement concerning the conflict issue. The dominating style emphasizes conflict tactics that push for one's own position or goal above and beyond the other person's conflict interest. The obliging style is characterized by a high concern for the other person's conflict interest above and beyond one's own conflict interest. Finally, the avoiding style involves eluding the conflict topic, the conflict party, or the conflict situation altogether. In the U.S. conflict management literature, obliging and avoiding styles often take on a Western slant of being negatively disengaged (i.e., "placating" or "flight" from the conflict scene). However, collectivists do not perceive obliging and avoiding conflict styles as negative. These two styles are typically employed to maintain mutual-face interests and relational network interests (Kim, 2002; Ting-Toomey & Oetzel, 2001). For example, rather than confronting a friend about why he did not call you last night, it might be better to avoid the issue so as not to negatively impact the friendship. If the problem persists, discussion of this issue might be necessary. See Figure 6.3 for a comparison of Western and Intercultural Models.

CONFLICT COMPETENCE   Conflict processes affect the rating of intercultural conflict competence. Intercultural conflict competence refers to communicating in a culturally appropriate and effective manner (Ting-Toomey & Oetzel, 2001). Appropriateness refers to the degree to which the exchanged conflict behaviors are regarded as proper and match the expectations generated by the insiders of the culture. Effectiveness refers to the degree to which conflict partners achieve mutually shared meaning and integrative goal-related outcomes. Perceived appropriateness and effectiveness are inferred through the exchange of messages between persons of different cultures and the outcome that is generated as a result of such exchange. Competent exchange of messages means that both intercultural communicators perceive that they and their messages are being understood in the proper context and with the desirable effects. When interested conflict parties experience communication appropriateness and effectiveness, the experience can impact satisfaction in the relationship and help the partners to develop a quality

Figure 6.3
Western and Intercultural Conflict Models (Ting-Toomey & Oetzel, 2001)

Reproduced with permission of Sage Publications Inc. Books via Copyright Clearance Center

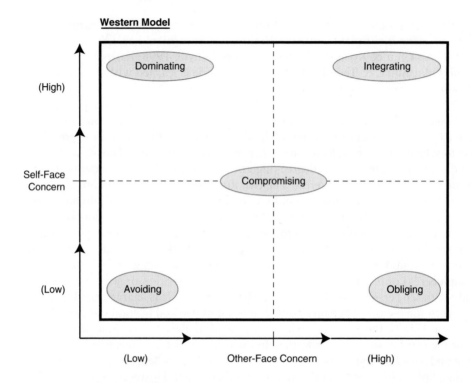

Western Model

Dominating

Integrating

Compromising

Avoiding

Obliging

(High)

Self-Face Concern

(Low)

(Low)   Other-Face Concern   (High)

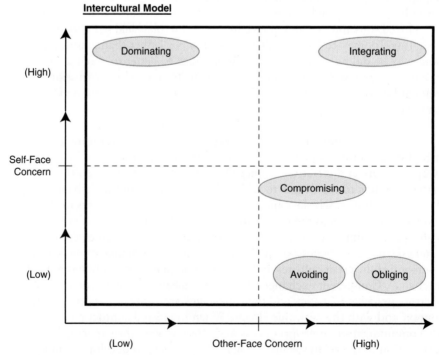

Intercultural Model

Dominating

Integrating

Compromising

Avoiding

Obliging

(High)

Self-Face Concern

(Low)

(Low)   Other-Face Concern   (High)

relational culture (Canary, 2003). For example, the study by Diggs and Clark (2002) illustrates competent conflict management. The participants were able to talk about issues that bothered them and make sure they felt supported on a variety of racial, spiritual, and content issues. Additionally, they were able to address their problems in an appropriate manner. Thus, they developed a unique relational culture and a satisfying relationship.

PUTTING THE PIECES TOGETHER   The starting place for the model is the primary orientation factors. Differences in cultural values often give rise to different ideals of how conflicts should be managed. In particular, the cultural values lead to differences in face concerns. The majority of research investigations indicate that individualistic cultures and independent types have more self-face concern and less other-and mutual-face concerns than collectivistic cultures and interdependent types (Chiu & Kosinski, 1994; Earley, 1997; Gao & Ting-Toomey, 1998; Oetzel et al., 2001).

Face concerns affect conflict styles. Self-face orientation is associated with dominating and integrating styles while other-face concern is associated with avoiding, compromising, integrating, and obliging styles (Oetzel, Myers, Meares, & Lara, 2003). Research across many cultures and ethnic groups (for example, in Germany, China, Hong Kong, Japan, Korea, Taiwan, Mexico, and the United States) clearly indicates that individualists and independents tend to use more dominating styles in managing conflict than do collectivists and interdependents (Oetzel & Ting-Toomey, 2003; Ohbuchi et al., 1999). In comparison, collectivists tend to use more integrative and avoiding styles in dealing with conflict than do individualists (Oetzel & Ting-Toomey, 2003; Ohbuchi et al., 1999; Trubisky, Ting-Toomey, & Lin, 1991). In general, however, both individualists (and independent self-construal) and collectivists (and interdependent self-construal) prefer to use constructive means to manage conflict. The secondary strategy that individualists employ is dominating while collectivists use avoiding as a secondary strategy (Oetzel & Ting-Toomey, 2003; Ohbuchi et al., 1999).

Situational/relationship boundary factors also impact conflict processes. Content, relational, and identity goals shape the nature of the conflict processes, but appear only to impact conflict processes to the extent that partners see the goals as cooperative (versus competitive), affiliative (versus control), and trust based (versus distrust). Relational partners who perceive relational parameters as cooperative, affiliative, and trusting are likely to have other- and mutual-face concerns and therefore use integrating, compromising, and avoiding conflict strategies (Ting-Toomey & Oetzel, 2001).

Finally, the perception of the competence of conflict behaviors shapes future conflict interaction for the couple (Canary, 2003). If we perceive our partner's behavior as competent, our primary orientation toward our partner moves to a stronger level of collectivism, which reinforces our concern for our partner. Additionally, we tend to view the relationship as cooperative and trusting. In contrast, if we think our partner was incompetent, we become more individualistic, self-face oriented, and competitive toward our partner. See Box 6.8 on page 172.

Box 6.8 What Went Wrong? Conflict in Intercultural Relationships

Jurgen from Germany and Rosa from Colombia met as international students in the United States. They dated for four years and then decided to marry. Neither spoke the other's native language (English was their common language). They decided to move wherever the first good job offer came. It was in Colombia, and so they married and moved to Bogota. The first year was very difficult on them, and they had lots of conflicts about family, privacy, and culture. Jurgen was frustrated as he had difficulty interacting with her family because of language barriers (he was learning Spanish and doing well, but still wasn't proficient). He also felt they spent way too much time with her family. On top of that, he felt Rosa was working too much and they didn't have enough time together. Rosa was happy to be home and felt for Jurgen being in a new culture. She thought he was doing great learning Spanish; her family really liked him, and that made her happy. She did wish that he was more open with her family and more expressive in general. She wished he could find a good job, but knew that would come. The following conversation is one example of the conflict they faced.

R: Where are we going to spend the holidays this year?

J: Well, we live here, so I think we should go visit my parents in Germany.

R: I think that is a great idea, but we really don't have the money, and I'm going to have trouble getting time off from work. Let's think about how we can make it work.

J: Great—throw that in my face again. I'm trying to find a job. And, I'm tired of being around your family all of the time. They always want to be with us, and I want to have some time with just you and me.

R: I'm sorry—I know you'll find a job, and I'm not upset about it at all. My family really likes you, and they like being around us. They haven't seen me for nearly four years, and they miss me. It means a lot to me that they love you as one of their own. They love that you have wanted to learn the language and culture and that you make me so happy.

J: I know and I like them, too, but it's too much. And, I'd like to see home.

R: Well, let's think about how we can make it work. We love to travel, and we can figure something out.

J: Sure—that's your way of saying "it can't be done."

1. Using the CBSCM, explain what you think is going on in their conflict. Consider all of the elements of the model.
2. Which relational dialectics are present? How is this couple managing the relational dialectics?
3. How might they communicate differently (and perhaps more effectively)?

Concept Check

Intercultural relationships are filled with contradictions, challenges, and difficulties. This chapter introduced nine different dialectics—three general to all relationships (openness-closedness, autonomy-connection, prediction-novelty) and six specific to intercultural relationships (identity vulnerability-security, privilege-disadvantage, history-present, revelation-nonrevelation, separation-integration, and conventionality-uniqueness). Managing the dialectic tensions means being aware of typical relational patterns for all couples, but also unique differences due to cultural values. Further, intercultural couples have to manage unique dialectical tensions in regards to how the couple relates to family, friends, and society in general.

Managing these dialectical tensions ultimately means managing conflict. As we negotiate our preferences, we will have differences. If we can manage these conflicts in a productive manner (that is, meeting both partners' goals), we are likely to have strong satisfaction and a quality relational culture. Productive management of conflict means being aware of a variety of factors of the CBSCM including primary orientation factors (cultural values, personal attributes, face concerns), situational and relationship boundary factors (relationship parameters and conflict goal assessments), and conflict processes, including management styles and conflict competence.

Layers of Intercultural Friendships and Relationships

Our relationships with our friends and romantic partners are unique, and therefore we have the tendency to think about them as isolated from other people and society (except other friends and family members). However, the relationships we form with others affect society and are also shaped by societal forces. We truly are not isolated individuals even though we might like to frame our relationships in that manner (Thompson & Collier, 2006). This section examines the layered effects of interpersonal relationships starting with the bottom-up effects and then moving toward the top-down effects.

Bottom-Up Effects

Until 1967, anti-miscegenation laws outlawed interracial marriage in many states. In fact, 41 states had anti-miscegenation laws at some point in their history (Lopez, 1997). In 1958, Richard (White American) and Mildred (African American) Loving married in Washington, D.C., where interracial marriage was legal. They lived in Virginia, where it was illegal for them to be married. The Lovings were arrested in 1959 and sentenced to one year in prison; they received a suspended sentence that required them not to return to the state for 25 years. A few years later, the Lovings were approached by and retained an American Civil Liberties lawyer to fight the unconstitutionality of their extradition from Virginia. In 1967, the Lovings won a legal victory (*Loving v. Virginia Supreme Court*) that changed the marital laws in the United States. The U.S. Supreme Court ruled unanimously to remove anti-miscegenation laws, forcing Virginia and 15 other states to revoke their laws. This case demonstrates that an intercultural couple can make significant changes in the laws and norms of a society.

Top-Down Effects: An Intercultural Relationship's Impact on Attitudes

Intercultural friendships and romantic relationships provide us with the opportunity to learn about other cultures, confront our own stereotypes, and learn new skills. These types of relationships also help those in our family and friendship networks do the same. I am not saying that we should form friendships with people from other cultures simply to help us and people closest to us grow and learn. In fact, if that is the only reason to have the friendship, we are using the other person, and the relationship likely will not last (see Box 6.9 for a potential ethical dilemma). However, these changes in attitudes and individual behaviors are extra reasons for us to be open to relationships with people from other cultures.

When we form an intercultural relationship, we end up learning new patterns and values. While reading about and studying intercultural communication can be enlightening, an actual relationship brings concepts such as culture, collectivism, and high-context communication to life. For example, I have learned what it means to be privileged from countless colleagues. The story I mentioned early in this chapter about a colleague whose dean asked her to do a rain dance is one such example. I have never had someone at work patronize or minimize my culture in such a manner. Additionally, intercultural relationships help us break down stereotypes and face our own prejudices. For example, one of my students from Japan confessed that, when she came to the United States to study, she had hoped she would have limited interaction with Hispanics (most Japanese students do not have this concern at all). They were people she felt were criminals and thus scary (mainly because of the focus on illegal immigration in the media). Being in New Mexico, she interacted widely with Hispanic students and colleagues and came to realize how diverse and wonderful most of these students were. She was embarrassed to admit her own limitations of having false and negative stereotypes about Hispanics, especially as a student of intercultural communication.

Box 6.9 Talking about Ethics: Reasons for Forming Intercultural Relationships

Jill (Chinese American) spoke of one of the reasons why she started dating Tom (African American). "I really wanted to teach my parents a lesson. They were so prejudiced against Blacks, and I knew they needed to change. Don't get me wrong. Tom was a great guy. He was funny and good looking, but there wasn't that immediate spark. Tom really liked me a lot, too, and that was nice. I thought what the heck, I'll give it a chance, and my parents can learn a thing or two." They dated for almost a year and half, and Jill really grew fond of Tom; her parents, who were absolutely appalled at first, grew to love him, too. In the end, Jill realized that she didn't truly love Tom and admitted this to him, even telling him that she had initially entered into the relationship because she wanted to teach her parents a lesson. Tom was very hurt (more so about not being loved), but also knew in his heart how Jill felt. He hoped that he could change her mind over time. Jill and Tom remain friends to this day, and Tom is still good friends with Jill's parents.

Do you think Jill's choices were ethical, especially since the relationships ended up being genuine and important to all involved?

Top-Down Effects: Society's Impact on Relationships

The societal layer has a great impact on intercultural relationships. Laws and the historical context shape whether we form relationships in the first place. Integration of schools, neighborhoods, and social networks provides an opportunity (or not) to interact with people.

Historical relations among cultural groups provide a context for current intercultural relationship formation (Kim, 2005). Much of the history of the world has focused on the struggle for power and domination of one group over another. The dominated group was often seen as less than the dominating group and therefore was oppressed, contained, or even faced attempts of extermination (examples include the Holocaust, U.S. policies toward American Indians, and Japanese rule over Koreans) (Kim, 2005). In this context, intercultural contact was minimized, and people were encouraged to interact "with their own kind." Laws, such as anti-miscegenation laws, were enacted to prohibit people from marrying and to preserve "racial purity" (see Box 6.10 on the debate about laws prohibiting same-sex marriage). Other laws such as the "One Drop Rule," which stated that if you had one drop of Black blood, you were Black, were enacted to discourage racial mixing (Orbe & Harris, 2001). Such racial purity laws clearly reflect racist attitudes held by those who created them, and these attitudes are a key reason why such laws have been stricken down. The absence of these laws is one reason why attitudes toward intercultural relationships are more positive now than in previous decades. However, some people continue to discourage intercultural relationships despite their absence.

The Loving case went a long way to change the attitudes and behaviors associated with intercultural marriage. However, the social history created by these laws still

---

Box 6.10 Talking about Ethics: Defense of Marriage Laws

Around the world, in the past decade, many gay-rights advocates have encouraged the enactment of legislation to protect the rights of gays and lesbians. As of early 2007, in the United States only 17 states have laws that prohibit discrimination against sexual orientation or gender identity, and only 9 states have laws that prohibit discrimination against transsexuals and transgendered individuals (Crary, 2007). Further, the United States is still firmly entrenched in prohibiting homosexuals from marrying or even having civil unions (with only a handful of states permitting it). Some see the Defense of Marriage law (banning homosexuals for marrying) as discriminatory. It forbids people who love each other from solidifying their bonds and also from having the economic benefits that marriage allows (Social Security spousal benefits, automatic inheritance rights, and health benefits). Other people, whose definition of marriage is based on religious principles, believe that marriage can only take place between a man and a woman.

1. What position do you take on the Defense of Marriage law? How about anti-discrimination laws for sexual orientation and gender identity?
2. Why is it acceptable to have different laws and standards for different cultural groups? That is, most now think anti-miscegenation laws are outlandish, but some feel laws banning homosexuals from marrying is appropriate. How do you explain this discrepancy?

influences current norms today to the extent that it continues to discourage intercultural marriage. Although more young adults are dating and cohabiting with someone of a different race, one study of a U.S. sample of participants (Joyner & Kao, 2005) found that interracial relationships are considerably less likely than same-race relationships to lead to marriage (and only 2.9% of all marriages in the United States are interracial). Further, differences among other ethnic groups include these: Hispanics had the highest rate of interracial relationships: 45% of 18- to 19-year-olds and 33% of 24- to 25-year-olds were in interracial relationships in the early 2000s compared with African Americans (20% and 14%, respectively) and White Americans (16% and 12%, respectively) (Joyner & Kao, 2005). Asian Americans appeared to be comparable to Hispanics in terms of rates of interracial involvement, but they were not formally included in the study because so few were within some of the age groups in the surveys. While society is becoming more accepting of intercultural marriage in general, the idea of intermixing some groups still meets with resistance (Joyner & Kao, 2005).

Another key aspect for the formation of intercultural relationship formation is the integration of social networks. As was discussed in the friendship section, we have to have the opportunity to interact with people from other cultural backgrounds in order to form friendships and date. Many neighborhoods and schools around the United States are relatively homogeneous. Homogeneity in contact during childhood results in a greater likelihood of homogeneous contact as an adult (Jacobson & Johnson, 2006). Globalization, and the accompanying movement of people, has created increased opportunities to develop broader social networks and create intercultural friendships and romantic relationships.

Challenges and Skills

Historical relations and laws have created some constraints for forming intercultural relationships. Despite growing acceptance, intercultural romantic relationships in particular are still seen as somewhat taboo. In addition, a variety of challenges need to be overcome. This chapter examined these challenges in both friendships and romantic relationships; these challenges include limited opportunity, unearned privilege, cultural differences, and dialectical tensions. This chapter also included some strategies for building alliances and for managing dialectics. We now conclude with a few additional, general suggestions for communication skills to enhance relationship building.

Houston and Wood (1995) offered several communication strategies to overcome the challenges of intercultural relationships. First, we have to realize that we may not completely understand the other person. Most people perceive that communication is about understanding; however, in intercultural relationships, we have to recognize that differences exist, and this relationship provides an opportunity to learn about others and their culture (and our own culture). Second, we must avoid imposing our standards on our relationship partners. We have many "right" ways to behave in a relationship, and the one we are familiar with simply works for us. We can tell our partners what we prefer and negotiate the appropriate communication style, but we have to have a true give-and-take style of interacting. Third, we have to be willing to respect others' experiences and interpretation of those experiences. For example, our partner might share a story about racism that she experienced. We should not minimize and deny that experience, but rather listen and believe our partner. Our partner has no reason to lie and simply has lived a different life than we have.

SUMMARY

Returning to the opening story: Dialectical tensions help to explain Soumia and David's relationship. First, Soumia prefers to be more open than David (openness-closedness). Second, several intercultural dialectics are involved: a) revelation-nonrevelation—Soumia chose not to reveal their relationship to her family for several years, and David chose to reveal right away; b) separation-integration—they have chosen to separate from his family because she is not accepted and integrate with hers, although the unannounced visits may be difficult for David if he is individualistic; c) privilege-disadvantage—Soumia is not a privileged member of English society, but David is; they disagree about how relevant this is; d) conventionality-uniqueness—she has a desire to be conventional while he is satisfied having a unique relationship (who cares what others think?). Because they disagree about the impact of family and society on their relationship, conflict is also important. Not much detail is provided on the specifics, so it is difficult to know how much cultural values, face, and conflict management styles play a role. However, the conflict goals are somewhat clear—while both address the issues or content, she has a concern for identity issues (how she belongs and is viewed by society), and both have relationship issues (their relationship with their respective families).

Here is a summary of the chapter based on the learning objectives.

- **Relational culture.** Processes, structures, and practices create, express, and sustain personal relationships and identities of partners. In other words, it is the unique culture that partners create in their relationship that is a key component to having a successful relationship.
- **Five factors for intercultural friendship formation.** We are more likely to have intercultural friendships with the following conditions: a) frequent contact with other cultures, b) similarity in personal characteristics and age, c) being extroverted, d) having a positive attitude about other cultures, and e) having prosocial skills (wanting to help others) and being willing to communicate.
- **Three challenges to intercultural friendship.** Cultural differences in the definition of friendship, cultural differences in communication style, and prejudice/discrimination are three challenges to intercultural friendship. Intercultural alliances have overcome these challenges in part by having dialogue about three factors: unearned privilege, historical relations among cultural groups, and affirming cultural identity.
- **Dialectics.** A dialectic is the contradiction of two opposing forces along the same continuum that appear mutually exclusive. Successful relationship partners manage three general dialectics to all relationships (openness-closedness, autonomy-connection, prediction-novelty) and six specific to intercultural relationships (identity vulnerability-security, privilege-disadvantage, history-present, revelation-nonrevelation, separation-integration, and conventionality-uniqueness).

- **Culture-based situational conflict model.** This conflict model explains that a number of factors illuminate the conflict between people from different cultural backgrounds. The key components of the model are primary orientation factors, situational/relationship boundary factors, conflict communication processes, and conflict competence. The model helps to explain why various conflict patterns exist, but also why our communication sometimes exacerbates intercultural conflict.
- **Bottom-up and top-down effects.** The historical context of a society (such as anti-miscegenation laws in the United States) often creates an environment that is discouraging to intercultural relationship formation. While attitudes toward intercultural relationships are changing and intercultural dating is increasing, there are still relatively few intercultural marriages in the United States. Our communication behavior toward intercultural couples and the communication behavior of those couples impact the degree of acceptance of these relationships. Changing demographics and increased acceptance likely will result in greater numbers of intercultural relationships in the future.

REVIEW QUESTIONS

1. What is a relational culture, and how can I get one?
2. Identify five factors that influence intercultural friendship formation. Describe how the factors apply to where you live. Are there a lot of intercultural friendships?
3. Provide an example of the three challenges to intercultural friendship.
4. What is an intercultural alliance? How might you build an alliance to address the challenges to intercultural friendship?
5. Define dialectic, and describe the three general relationship dialectics.
6. Which dialectics are particularly relevant to intercultural relationships and why? Provide examples of how to effectively manage these dialectics.
7. Describe the CBCSM, and provide an example to illustrate the model.
8. Which factors influence the manner in which we manage conflict according to the CBCSM?
9. How do historical aspects of a society shape the formation of intercultural relationships? How can we change such aspects?
10. Which communication skills can be useful to overcome challenges to intercultural relationship formation? How do these apply to your life?

EXERCISES

1. Investigate the number of intercultural relationships in two countries. Can you explain the differences in the numbers? What are the attitudinal, cultural, and historical contexts of these countries?
2. Read Peggy McIntosh's (2003) article "White privilege: Unpacking the invisible knapsack." What reactions do you have to this article? Reflect on the ways that you and others have privilege in your culture.
3. Interview a couple in a long-term intercultural relationship. What is difficult for them? What strategies do they use to make their relationship successful? If you are in an intercultural relationship, answer these questions with your partner.

CHAPTER 7

Higher Educational Contexts

CHAPTER OUTLINE

I. Introduction

II. Disparities in Educational Outcomes

III. Instructional Communication
   a. Classroom Management
   b. Learning Styles
   c. Peer-to-Peer Communication
   d. Concept Check

IV. Layered Perspective of Educational Contexts
   a. Bottom-Up Effects
   b. Top-Down Effects: Educational Institutions' Impact on Individuals
   c. Top-Down Effects: Society's Impact on Educational Institutions
   d. Challenges and Skills

V. Summary

VI. Review Questions

VII. Exercises

CHAPTER OBJECTIVES

After reading this chapter, students should be able to

- identify some disparities in educational outcomes.

- define classroom management and provide examples of the various types of classroom management behaviors.

Classroom
Classrooms around the world are becoming more and more culturally diverse. How does this impact your educational experience? How does this impact your educational success?

- describe two approaches to understanding learning styles.
- identify two types of peer-to-peer communication behaviors that are associated with disparities in educational outcomes.

- explain how instructional communication contributes to disparities in educational outcomes.
- discuss the bottom-up and top-down effects of educational outcomes.

Introduction

Andres is a second-generation Mexican American. His parents came to the United States as documented workers and were working class. They made decent money and achieved middle-class status. When they had Andres, they wanted to make sure he was well educated. They were quite involved in his schooling, even though they did not speak English fluently. Growing up, Andres lived in a Mexican American community with a strong cultural identity. His family and community emphasized a passion for both the United States and Mexico. He graduated in the top 10 of his high school class and decided to go to the local university to stay close to home and be a part of his community. His parents encouraged him to live in the dorms to make sure school was a priority.

Andres did well overall. He struggled in some courses, especially when he had trouble seeing the connection between his education and his community. Initially, he was not sure how math and science were going to help him make a difference in his community. Most of his teachers were fine—very knowledgeable, but somewhat distant. He found difficulty connecting with the teaching styles and felt it was simply him against the world (or at least the rest of the class). He also did not have a lot of friends at college. Most of his high school classmates did not go to college and when he went home on the weekends, his friends teased him about being book smart and simply trying to be better than they were. His parents were very proud and did not ask him about school much. They wanted to make sure he was doing well and that he was going to get his degree, but they did not understand completely what he was studying.

During his sophomore year, he had Dr. Martinez in a biology class, and she was able to connect with him and help him see how science mattered. She related material to his life and also showed interest in him. She gave him a job in her lab where he worked with a group of students. These students became good friends and they supported each other and helped each other learn. He decided to major in biology and get a degree in medicine. His friends from back home still shunned him, but he decided to persevere. He eventually received his medical doctorate. He became a family practice doctor and returned to his home community. He is now a revered member of the community.

Questions: What instructional and intercultural communication concepts can explain Andres' story? How would you feel if you were in Andres' position?

Andres' story illustrates some of the challenges facing students and higher educational institutions both in the United States and in other developed nations with large multicultural populations. The context of education in the United States has changed dramatically in recent decades, and more change is imminent. A strong influence of instructional technology is present in all classrooms, and distance and online learning are becoming more available. Most importantly, given the context of this book, cultural diversity at all levels of education is increasing. The students who are graduating from high school now are more diverse than at any point in history, and this diversity is projected to increase in the future. The U.S. Census (2008) estimates that in 2050 the population will include the following: less than 53% will be White Americans, 16% will be Black Americans, 23% will be of Hispanic origin, 10% will be Asian and Pacific Islander; and about 1% will be American Indian, Eskimo, and Aleut. Even more diversity occurs in higher education because of the presence of international students. Figure 7.1 displays the percentage of the total undergraduate and graduate student population for each racial/ethnic group, as well as for men and women (also see Box 7.1 on p.182).

The significant levels of cultural diversity in schools provide interesting challenges and opportunities for teachers, students, and administrators. One of the key challenges is the disparity of educational outcomes, such as enrollment in colleges and universities, progress toward obtaining a degree, and graduation rates. An **educational disparity** exists when one cultural group has an educational outcome that is worse than that of another cultural group. The first goal of this chapter is to identify some of these disparities at the university/college level. When we understand this challenge, we can begin to examine what role intercultural communication plays in these disparities. Then, we can examine the larger context of education from the layered perspective and discuss some of the opportunities that effective intercultural communication provides to address disparities in educational

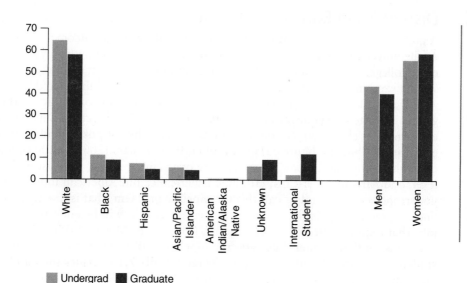

Figure 7.1

Percentage of Undergraduate and Graduate Students at Four-Year Institutions in the United States by Race/Ethnicity and Sex, Fall 2004

Source: National Center for Education Statistics (2006)

Box 7.1 Globalization: International Students Abound

One of the factors associated with globalization is the number of students who study abroad. For example, the total enrollment of international students in Australian universities increased to 203,890 in semester 1, 2006 (IDP, 2007). This was an annual increase of 2.9% from semester 1, 2005. International students represent approximately 16.8% of the total population of Australian university students. The top five countries for international students in Australia were China (34,985), India (16,969), Malaysia (12,037), Hong Kong (9,208), and Indonesia (7,552). In 2006, UNESCO estimated that over 2.5 million higher education students were being educated in countries other than their homes, up from an estimated 1.7 million in 2000. A report from IDP Education Australia predicted that, by 2025, almost 8 million students will be educated transnationally (Institute of International Education, 2007).

International students are not only prevalent, but they have a significant impact on the economy of a nation. In 2002 and 2003, International students contributed almost $12.9 billion to the U.S. economy through tuition and cost-of-living expenses, and, in some cases, through expenses associated with their spouses and dependents who came to the United States with them (Chin, 2003). As examples of international students' contribution to local economies, California gained $1,7790,287,737, New York gained $ 1,517,701,997, and Massachusetts gained $889,694,728 in state income.

outcomes. There are no simple solutions to addressing educational disparities, as the problem is quite complex. The layered approach helps to illuminate this complexity while also considering the importance of effective intercultural communication.

Disparities in Educational Outcomes

A great deal of focus has always been placed on educational outcomes of students. At the university level, we tend to focus on the following: a) how many students enter college, b) how many get their degree, and c) how long it takes them. This section examines these key outcomes for particular groups in the United States.

The first key indicator of disparities is whether students of all racial/ethnic groups are attending college at the same rate. Figure 7.2 directly compares the enrollment in elementary/secondary education and that of postsecondary or higher education. While the figure compares two different years (2002 to 2004), it appears that White and Asian Americans are overrepresented at the postsecondary level, and African Americans, Hispanic Americans, and American Indians are underrepresented. Scholars call this the **pipeline problem;** that is, the result of this underrepresentation is that members of certain groups will be underrepresented in jobs that require college degrees (Cooper, Chavira, & Mena, 2005).

An issue that further illustrates the pipeline problem is the number of students who actually obtain college degrees. Table 7.1 provides the number and percentage of degrees received by members of these five ethnic groups along with international students in the United States. Comparing this table to Figure 7.1, we can see that, for bachelor's and master's degrees, White Americans, Asian

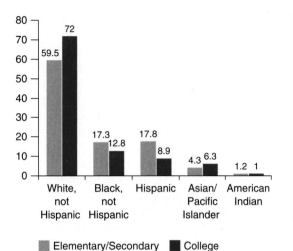

Figure 7.2
Percentage of Enrollment in Elementary/ Secondary (2002) vs. Postsecondary by Race/ Ethnicity (2004)

Source: National Center for Education Statistics (2004, 2006)

Americans, and international students are overrepresented—and other groups are underrepresented—based on the numbers of students who enroll in college. For doctoral degrees, international students are overrepresented, and other groups are underrepresented. Even if we factor out the number of international

Table 7.1

PERCENT OF TOTAL DEGREES CONFERRED BY U.S. INSTITUTIONS OF HIGHER EDUCATION BY DEGREE, SEX, AND ETHNICITY, 2002–2003

Sex and Ethnicity	Percent of Total			
	Total Population	Bachelor's	Master's	Doctor's
Sex				
Men	49.2	42.5	41.2	52.9
Women	50.8	57.5	58.8	47.1
Ethnicity				
White	73.9	70.0	60.3	56.2
African American	12.4	8.7	7.8	5.1
Hispanic	14.8	6.3	4.4	3.2
Asian/Pacific Islander	4.4	6.2	4.8	4.9
American Indian	0.8	0.7	0.5	0.4
Ethnicity unknown or other	8.4	5.0	8.3	4.9
International	—	3.2	14.0	25.3

Source: National Center for Education Statistic (2005b) and U.S. Census (2006)

Note: Ethnicity does not add up to 100% because Hispanics are also classified in other groups.

students and the number of students whose ethnicity is classified as "unknown or other," White Americans and Asian Americans are still overrepresented, and the other three groups are underrepresented. Additionally, men are overrepresented at the doctoral level and underrepresented at other levels.

Part of what explains the disparity in the number of students in these groups receiving degrees is the 6-year graduation rate. Six years is the standard timeframe for measuring degree completion (even though many students have to work and therefore may take longer to complete their degree). Figure 7.3 compares the graduation rates of the five ethnic groups and men/women for bachelor's degrees only. This figure illustrates that men, African Americans, Hispanic Americans, and American Indians have a lower 6-year graduation rate than other groups.

Overall, the statistics demonstrate important disparities in higher education, disparities that can have a long-term impact on overall achievement. As the Figure shows, some disparities relate to the number of students from each ethnic group grad-uating with a college degree. Additionally, men have lower rates of success in college than women (except for the granting of doctoral degrees). The reasons for these dis-parities are complex and include such factors as the diversity climate and the match of the university culture to home culture, socioeconomic status, community/family sup-port, and the educational level of the parents (Castillo, Conoley, & Brossart, 2004; Suárez-Orozco & Suárez-Orozco, 2001; Villegas & Lucas, 2002; Hale, 2004). It is important, however, to remember not to stereotype individuals based on these general statistics or to put the blame solely on the individuals. The disparity problem in education requires a complex, layered approach that examines factors affecting individual students, school administrators, instructors, and policies. We now focus on the role of intercultural communication in the classroom in explaining educational disparities. The section on layered effects will explore other factors that illustrate the complexity of education disparities.

Figure 7.3

Percentage of Students Completing Bachelor's Degree in Six Years

Source: National Center for Education Statistics (2005a)

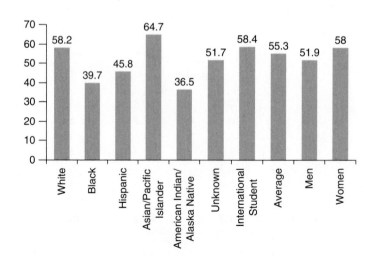

Instructional Communication

Instructional communication focuses on the wide range of communication behavior related to teaching and learning (Civikly, 1992). Much instructional communication occurs in the classroom and consists of teacher-student interaction and peer-to-peer interaction. However, instructional communication also occurs in out-of-class settings such as teacher-student interaction during office hours. In this section, we examine several facets of instructional communication to help us understand the role that intercultural communication plays in disparities in educational outcomes. In general, intercultural communication can contribute to disparities when it helps to construct a mismatch between the school culture (which is often based on mainstream White American cultural values) and the home culture of students of color (non-whites, for example African Americans, American Indians, Hispanic or Latin Americans, and Asian Americans) (Castillo et al., 2004; Castillo, Conoley, Brossart, & Quiros, 2007; Suárez-Orozco & Suárez-Orozco, 2001). Three categories of instructional communication are relevant: classroom management, learning styles, and peer-to-peer communication.

Classroom Management

Classroom management is "a broad set of teaching behaviors through which the teacher shapes and maintains learning conditions that facilitate effective and efficient instruction resulting in a learning community. Effective classroom management is an ongoing, maintenance-oriented process. It involves motivating students to learn, providing appropriate instruction and feedback, and managing student work" (Colville-Hall, n.d.). Thus, the focus is on how the teacher creates an effective learning climate and how he interacts with students on a day-to-day basis. This section examines three different classroom management behaviors: immediacy, communicating expectations, and engaging and culturally appropriate content. For each behavior, the implications for intercultural communication and educational disparities are considered.

IMMEDIACY   **Immediacy** is the extent to which communication behaviors enhance closeness and reduce physical and/or psychological distance between teacher and student (Mehrabian, 1969). It refers to how close we feel toward a teacher and how approachable we find the teacher to be. Immediacy includes verbal and nonverbal behaviors such as sharing personal examples, using humor, addressing students by name, having conversations with students before and after class, smiling at students, gesturing while talking, and moving around the class (Gorham, 1988). Additionally, teacher immediacy focuses on three primary roles: instructional, relational, and personal (Zhang & Oetzel, 2006). **Instructional immediacy** focuses on communication behaviors associated with classroom instruction and direct learning. **Relational immediacy** focuses on communication behaviors that enhance the psychological closeness between teacher and student. **Personal immediacy** focuses on communication behaviors related to the moral and ethical behavior of the teacher. Self-Assessment 7.1 provides a tool to rate the immediacy of your own teachers.

Teacher immediacy is a critical component in the learning process for most cultures. Immediacy has not been studied in every culture, but it has been found to be important in every culture in which it has been examined. Teachers who display immediacy with students encourage students' perceptions for affective and cognitive learning. Affective learning emphasizes the learner's attitude and feelings toward the subject and/or the teacher (do you like the subject and teacher?) while cognitive learning focuses on the comprehension, retention, recall, and application

Self-Assessment 7.1

TEACHER IMMEDIACY

Rate the immediacy of your teacher according to the following assessment. Use the following scale for each item: Strongly agree = 5; Agree = 4; Neutral = 3; Disagree = 2; Strongly Disagree = 1.

Item	Score
1. My teacher is committed to teaching.	
2. My teacher is well-prepared in teaching.	
3. My teacher is passionate about teaching.	
4. My teacher answers questions earnestly.	
5. My teacher is patient in teaching.	
6. My teacher understands students.	
7. My teacher treats students fairly and equally.	
8. My teacher respects students.	
9. My teacher does not hurt students' self-respect.	
10. My teacher encourages students.	
11. My teacher provides timely responses to students' concerns.	
12. My teacher has good morality.	
13. My teacher sets a good example for others.	
14. My teacher is approachable.	
15. My teacher conducts him/herself well.	

Instructions for Scoring: Add up the scores of 1–5 and divide by 5; add up 6–11 and divide by 6; add up 12–15 and divide by 4. This will provide an average score for instructional (1–5), relational (6–11), and personal immediacy (12–15). The higher the score, the higher the rating of immediacy.

of knowledge and information (did you actually learn something?) (Bloom, 1976; Zhang & Oetzel, 2006). Studies consistently demonstrate that teacher immediacy is positively related to students' perception of affective and/or cognitive learning in cultures such as China, Japan, Germany, Australia, Finland, the United States, and France (Allen, Witt, & Wheeless, 2006; McCroskey, Fayer, Richmond, Sallinen, & Barraclough, 1996; Myers, Zhong, & Guan, 1998; Neuliep, 1997; Roach, Cornett-DeVito, & DeVito, 2005; Rodríguez, Plax, & Kearney, 1996; Witt, Wheeless, & Allen, 2006; Zhang, Oetzel, Gao, Wilcox, & Takai, 2007).

The means to which immediacy is related to affective and cognitive learning was tested in a cross-cultural study of 695 college students in Japan, Germany, China, and the United States (Zhang et al., 2007). The researchers asked students to fill out a questionnaire about teacher immediacy, motivation, affective learning, and cognitive learning. They found that teacher immediacy first increases students' affect (positive feelings) for the course and the teacher; affect then motivates students to take actions to learn; and finally, the motivation leads to increased cognitive learning. Thus, engaging teachers increase the affect a student has for the course, which results in students being motivated to learn and an increase in cognitive learning.

Given the strong support of this model, how can an understanding of immediacy help to explain educational disparities? Three systematic cultural differences are involved in what it means to be an immediate teacher. First, differences exist in the immediacy received by students of color compared to White American students, with students of color often experiencing less immediacy. Research has shown that, in general, both in the classroom and in out-of-class contexts, students of color receive less positive interaction from teachers than do White American students (Bradford, Cooper, Allen, Stanley, & Grimes, 2006).

Second, there are cultural differences in what is considered appropriate immediacy, differences reflected primarily through power distance. For example, in the United States, it is often appropriate to engage in small talk, self-disclosure, and addressing students by their first names in order to establish immediacy; in other, large power distance countries, such as China, these behaviors are considered inappropriate (Myers et al., 1998; Zhang, 2005a, 2005b). Teachers are treated as the authority, and obedience and conformity are expected from students. Chinese teachers usually address students by their full names, including surnames and first names, and students address teachers by their surnames with their professional titles (Zhang & Oetzel, 2006).

Third, it is important to consider differences in the expectations of instructional, relational, and personal roles. In the mainstream United States, more focus is generally put on instructional immediacy with less focus on relational and personal immediacy. However, in many cultural groups, including many minority groups in the United States, relational and personal immediacy are highly emphasized (Hofstede, 2001, Zhang et al., 2007). Thus, a teacher who only emphasizes the subject matter and puts no focus on the relationship with the students may have difficulty connecting with some students of color.

These cultural differences in immediacy can help to explain some of the educational disparities in the United States. A disproportional majority of teachers in the

Box 7.2 Voices: Differences in Immediacy for International and U.S. Students

As a professor, I have had the opportunity to supervise nearly 50 graduate students from all over the world. About one-third of these students are international students. They exhibit many cultural differences from U.S. students, but one that stands out the most is the expectations of what a good advisor is supposed to be. All of my students expect me to provide timely and concrete feedback, help them improve their writing and thinking, make sure they complete their dissertation or thesis, and be a sympathetic and supportive person. However, many international students have an expectation that I will also be a mentor to them about their personal lives.

I have had students ask me what they should do about their children, tell me about difficulties they are having with their family and ask for advice, and look for advice about where they should go in their life (beyond basic career advice). Certainly, not every international student has these expectations, and some mainstream U.S. students share these expectations as well, but, on balance, this is a clear trend in my experience. In order for me to be immediate, I have to adapt my communicative behaviors to the needs and expectations of all the students. In class, I can adopt a predominant style, but outside class I need to tailor my behavior to each individual.

United States are White Americans (National Center for Education Statistics, 2006; Villegas & Lucas, 2002). If these teachers enact immediacy behaviors from a mainstream cultural perspective, they will likely focus on the instructional work in the classroom and do so from a small power distance perspective. However, their students come from a large power distance perspective and look for immediacy outside the class, a mismatch in immediacy expectations will occur. These students may feel distant from their teachers and thus have lower affective learning, motivation, and cognitive learning. Unfortunately, no systematic research supports this hypothesis on a large scale, but this is a plausible explanation for one factor contributing to educational disparities. Also see Box 7.2.

COMMUNICATING EXPECTATIONS   The expectations teachers have of students shape a variety of classroom behaviors, but especially student performance. A study of 1,572 college students in the United States found that students' motivation to work was strongly influenced by whether students perceived that their instructors were concerned about them personally (Wilson, 2006). Since motivation is related to learning, teachers' attitudes are critical for student success.

A significant critique of teachers is that they set low expectations for certain students and high expectations of others. Specifically, teachers use their own biases and stereotypes to determine who they perceive as low performers and spend less time and energy in educating such students (Betances, 2004; Suárez-Orozco & Suárez-Orozco, 2001). Unfortunately, many times these targeted students are cultural minorities (Betances, 2004) and women/girls on math tests (Huguet & Regner, 2007). For example, I was in a meeting of a scholarship committee that was determining scholarships for minority students. We were trying to determine how many scholarships to assign to first-year graduate students. One of my colleagues mentioned that the success rate of first-year students in his program was about 30% and for minorities it was even less than that. His conclusion was that we should be conservative in providing scholarship money to first-year minority students until they have proven themselves. I was flabbergasted, perhaps more so because this faculty member was from an underrepresented group. I challenged him and said that when you admit a student (or give a scholarship), your expectation is that they will succeed, not that they will fail.

Teachers create low expectations for students in a variety of ways. For example, a teacher might not call on a student who speaks English as a second language because the teacher fears that the student will be embarrassed. A teacher might grade a student's paper more easily or simply pass him so the student is not left behind (called social promotion). A teacher can dismiss points made by a student in class rather than use the points to further discussion. The key is for teachers to examine their instructional practices to make sure they are not setting low standards for any student's work.

Additionally, students themselves contribute to low expectations. Several studies have found that women and girls are influenced by gender-stereotyped expectations on standardized math tests (Huguet & Regner, 2007; Rosenthal, Crisp, & Suen, 2007; Smith, 2006). In one study, women reminded of gender stereotypes about math performance had low expectations of their performance on a standardized math test (Smith, 2006). Another study found that middle school girls exhibit lower performance when they are led to believe a task measures math skills (Huguet & Regner, 2007). However, this stereotyped effect is reversed under certain conditions. Providing girls with access to positive role models (other girls who are high math achievers) reduces the effect of the stereotype and leads to girls performing at levels equal to boys (Huguet & Regner, 2007). In contrast, girls who work alone or who work with boys only have low performance (and low expectations about performance) (Huguet & Regner, 2007).

ENGAGING AND CULTURALLY APPROPRIATE CONTENT   A third critical aspect of classroom management is for teachers to engage all students with culturally appropriate content. A common critique of education is that the content is divorced from many communities of color and other underrepresented groups such as those with low socioeconomic status (Gaitin, 2006; Suárez-Orozco & Suárez-Orozco, 2001; Villegas & Lucas, 2002). Essentially, the way the classroom works and what is studied is a mismatch to the home culture of many students of color (Gaitin, 2006). If reading assignments only focus on works written by White, European scholars, most minority students will not feel engaged with the material. Certain subject matters are certainly easier to engage students with than others. For example, a class on intercultural communication is easy to connect to all students because all of us have a culture and all of us interact with people from other cultures. However, what about engineering, math, or science? Engaging teachers find ways to show how these subjects matter to their students' lives. An understanding of engineering and construction principles along with culture might help show students how to build culturally appropriate structures.

In attempting to engage with students of color in the classroom, teachers need to be careful to do so in a culturally appropriate manner. Direct discussion about racism and cultural disparities is necessary, but also takes some cultural skill. In one study, researchers identified several barriers to discussing race and culture in the classroom by interviewing college students and hosting five focus groups (Simpson, Causey, & Williams, 2007). Students in this study reported several barriers to participating in discussions about cultural disparities: a) teachers who do not truly value participation; b) teachers who display discomfort in talking about racism; c) teachers who are threatened by students' knowledge; d) gaps in experiences and knowledge among students of color and White students; and e) tension and disagreements. The same study identified several strategies for addressing racism in the classroom: a) teachers laying out clear parameters in advance of the discussion; b) teachers modeling diversity through the structure and content of the class; c) teachers being aware of their own cultural biases, d) students being motivated to learn; and e) students feeling safe and challenged. Thus, effective classroom management skills can establish a climate of engagement, learning, and appreciation of culture.

Some teachers are good motivators but have poor cultural skills when engaging discussion. A teacher might want to discuss racism and culture; she knows it is important. However, the teacher might rely on stereotypes and go too far. The comic strip in Figure 7.4 illustrates one such teacher while Box 7.3 about ethics illustrates another. These teachers should be applauded for wanting to talk about racism and cultural bias—too many teachers simply ignore the topic. However, these teachers also have a responsibility to learn more about culture and enhance their skills before trying out exercises in the classroom.

Learning Styles

While effective classroom management helps to bridge chasms between school and home culture, the individual learning styles of students also contributes to the chasm. **Learning style** is the preferred manner in which people learn (Kolb, 1984). Learning styles affect the ways that students interact with teachers and their peers; learning styles affect how students engage with the material and with other people. People learn differently, and these differences in learning preference contribute to educational outcome disparities. The next section explores two types of

Figure 7.4
F Minus Comic Strip

Sometimes good intentions go awry. What is wrong with this attempt at "racial tolerance"?

© United Feature Syndicate, Inc.

Box 7.3 Talking about Ethics: Experiments in Racism

A teacher, principal, and superintendent in Truth or Consequences, New Mexico, wanted to teach students about racism in schools. The teacher chose an experiment approved by the principal and superintendent to show students what it was like during the Civil Rights era for African Americans. She had students put up signs at a water fountain that said "Whites only." The family of one African American teenager complained, and the state's Public Education Department reviewed the case. Despite accepting that the experiment was well intentioned to teach students about racial sensitivity, the department decided to require racial sensitivity training for the parties involved and issued a formal reprimand as discipline.

The story demonstrates the importance of understanding and applying research ethics. The U.S. Department of Health and Human Services (USHHS) and the Food and Drug Administration

have crafted a code of ethics for engaging in research on human subjects. Additionally, each university has an Institutional Review Board (IRB) that is responsible for reviewing proposed studies to ensure that they meet several criteria: a) risk of participation in the study is minimal; b) the risks are reasonable to its benefits; c) selection of samples to participate are equitable (everyone has a chance to be included); d) participants are informed of the risks and benefits, and the research documents this consent (signing an informed consent form); e) researchers must monitor and protect the data collected in the study; and f) researchers must protect the privacy of the participants (USHHS, 2007).

1. Consider the example above and identify the problems in research ethics the teacher engaged in with her "experiment."
2. Do you think the discipline was warranted?

learning style differences and explains how they contribute to educational outcome disparities: individual vs. cooperation and the experiential learning model.

INDIVIDUAL VS. COOPERATION   One of the fundamental differences in learning styles can be broadly described as individual vs. cooperative learning (also called separate vs. connected learning) (Enns 1993; Gaitin, 2006). **Individual (or separate) learning** focuses on critical thinking, objective observation, abstract analysis, and individual performance. In contrast, **cooperative (connected) learning** focuses on personal reflection, subjective reactions, consciousness-raising, and cooperative performance. Table 7.2 summarizes some of the differences. Most individuals display a preference for one style over the other, but still exhibit behaviors associated with both styles of learning. Also see Box 7.4 on page 192.

Cultural differences in cooperative and individual learning are prevalent and are closely connected to cultural individualism and collectivism (see Chapter 2). One study examined learning preferences in nearly 200 students in Australia (Ramburuth & McCormick, 2001). The authors found that Asian international students (collectivistic) preferred collaborative and group learning opportunities more than Australian (individualistic) students. Similar differences in racial and ethnic groups within the United States have been demonstrated. Specifically, students of color often have strong preferences for collaborative learning, as this is how their family socialization has progressed (Gaitin, 2006). This preference for collaborative learning may

Table 7.2

COMPARISON OF INDIVIDUAL AND COOPERATIVE LEARNING

Cooperative Learning	Individual Learning
Subjective responses	Objective observation
Personal application	Abstract analysis
Awareness and consciousness-raising	Distinguishing fact from opinion
Empathizing	Evaluating and critiquing
Active listening	Debating
Collaborative learning	Competitive learning
Mutual goals	Individual goals
Sensitivity to individual differences	Fair application of principles
Teacher as role model	Teacher as knowledge source

Source: Enns (1993); Gaitin (2006)

explain some of the underachievement in certain minority groups, as their learning preferences do not always match those of mainstream classrooms. Also see Box 7.5.

Cooperative and individual learners also differ in the extent to which they use the communicative processes of "talking" versus "silence." Talking to learn is often used by individual learners; they focus on expressing themselves and using talk to debate and critique ideas. Silence is seen as an indicator of not knowing the answer

Box 7.4 Talking about Ethics: Is Sharing Answers Cheating?

You have just completed an important exam in math and feel very good about your performance. You studied hard and feel as if you answered every question correctly, and you are certain you will receive a high grade. A friend who will take the exam in another section later in the week comes to you and asks whether you will tell him what was on the test and whether you will help him out. What would you do?

Your answer to this question provides some insight into whether you prefer individual or cooperative learning. If you think this is cheating and your friend needs to study hard on his own you have a preference for individual learning (or have been socialized in an individualistic learning environment). If you think you should share your performance to help your friend get ahead because you know that is what your friend would do for you, you likely have a preference for cooperative learning (or have been socialized in a cooperative learning environment). Consider the following questions:

1. In what situations (if any) is cooperative learning unethical?
2. By what ethical standards (culturally relative or culturally universal) do you judge such behavior?
3. If the academic environment you are in has a preference for either individual or cooperative learning, how do we make sure to support people who have a preference for the other style of learning?

or not being well educated. In contrast, active listening and silence are often used by cooperative learners; they focus on digesting and reflecting on what others are saying. Talking is seen as an indicator of selfishness and insecurity. "Talkers" and "listeners" both engage in the other activity, but the difference is the preference and manner in which each activity is done. Talkers tend to listen to critique while listeners listen to understand and engage. A study of American Indian college students identified uses of silence in the classroom (Covarrubias, 2007). The purpose of the study was to examine some of the mismatches between the communication style of American Indian students and the predominant style of mainstream university education. The author identified a preference for using silence in strategic and culturally supportive ways. The American Indian students reported that silence is preferred to talking for learning, but that the strategy did not serve them well in the university classroom. It was one of the reasons the students felt disconnected from the university.

EXPERIENTIAL LEARNING MODEL   One of the most popular ways to examine learning styles is Kolb's (1984) experiential learning model. Kolb conceptualized learning as a cycle of four elements, all of which need to be present for comprehensive learning to occur. The four elements are constructed from two dimensions: a) abstract-concrete (the degree of involvement or analytic detachment from the subject matter); and b) action-reflection (the degree of doing versus reflecting/observing). The first position is **concrete experience,** which provides first-hand experience of the subject matter. As you study intercultural communication, you might directly interact with someone from another culture. The second position is **reflective observation,** which provides the learner with an opportunity to observe and think about the meaning of the observation. As you study intercultural communication, you might watch a

Box 7.5 Voices: Competition/Cooperation and School Performance

An historical example of learning style differences comes to light in the federal government's establishment of Indian Schools at the end of the nineteenth century and early twentieth century in various parts of the country. Children from various American Indian tribes were removed from their reservations and sent to these schools, which were intended to stamp out their native cultures and to inculcate them into the White culture. Part of this process was to adapt to the Western tradition of education, which relied on individual performance and competition to become successful. This was a tradition largely unfamiliar to the Indians who worked cooperatively.

Syd Byrd, a Lakota child who was six years old in 1925 when he was sent to the Genoa Indian School in Nebraska, captures the difficulty the children faced: "In the Lakota way, you are responsible not to yourself, but always to the...group whereas in the school...you have to be your own person. You have to acquire an education...by yourself. You could not be responsible to the group...you take care of number one, and you get to the top at the expense of others."

Source: *In the White Man's Image* (1991), from the anthology series, *The American Experience*

movie about a particular culture and think about the meanings in the culture and how they impact you. The third position is **abstract conceptualization,** which provides the learner with the opportunity to weigh the strengths and limitations of perspectives. As you study intercultural communication, you might read about cultural value differences, such as individualism/collectivism, and think about how these differences impact communication and the strengths/weaknesses of such approaches; that is, how they affect certain outcomes. The final position is **active experimentation,** which provides the learner with the opportunity to directly test what has been learned in the previous three stages. As you study intercultural communication, you might consider applying your understanding of individualism/collectivism to see if you can improve the quality of an interaction with someone from another culture. This active experimentation sets the stage for a new concrete experience.

Although the ideal learning cycle integrates all four elements, Kolb (1984) noted that individuals develop learning style preferences based on the two dimensions. **Accommodators** combine concrete experience and active experimentation. Accommodators solve problems through trial and error and enjoy teaching others. They excel at situations in which it is necessary to adapt to the immediate circumstances. **Convergers** combine active experimentation and abstract conceptualization. Convergers like practical application of ideas and learn by doing and thinking in an unemotional manner. They use deductive reasoning to focus their knowledge on specific problems. **Divergers** combine concrete experience and reflective observation. Divergers excel at viewing an event from many perspectives and organizing many relationships into a meaningful whole. They work well with groups and are imaginative and emotional individuals. **Assimilators** combine reflective observation and abstract conceptualization. Assimilators like to create theoretical models and learn by watching and thinking. They value order, expert opinion, detailed information, and certainty. See Figure 7.5 for Kolb's experiential model.

Figure 7.5
Kolb's (1984)
Experiential
Learning
Model

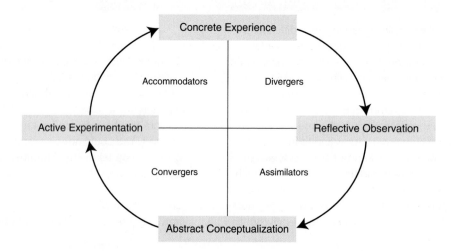

Cultural differences contribute to educational outcome disparities because of the mismatch between preferred learning and the nature of instruction in mainstream education. Studies have demonstrated that differences in learning styles across cultures contribute to disparities in learning outcomes (Bradford et al., 2006; Park, 2001; Yamazaki, 2005). Mainstream education in the United States has a tendency to emphasize convergence (abstract conceptualization and active experimentation), which is based in individualism, low context communication, and clear rules and boundaries (Yamazaki, 2005). This style is focused on the individual and is divorced from the subject matter; that is, the style is unemotional and objective. Students who display a different type of learning style (group orientation, divergence, and emphasis on collaborative learning and connecting to the whole) will be at a disadvantage unless instructional changes are made or if the students can adapt. Students can think about ways to expand learning to include all four elements of the learning cycle. Teachers need to think about ways of engaging all students by using instructional techniques that adapt to all learning styles.

Peer-to-Peer Communication

Interaction with peers is also an important element of the learning process. Students often ask peers questions about instruction and homework assignments and seek out peers for support. Peer-to-peer communication can be negative when tensions between cultural groups escalate. These elements of instructional communication and how they link to educational outcomes disparities are discussed next.

Social support from peers is an important element of the learning process. **Social support** is a part of relationships in which individuals provide aid, assistance, and comfort to others (Albrecht, Burleson, & Goldsmith, 1994; Heaney & Israel, 2002). For example, when our friends have an exam to study for, we can tell them how well we think they will do and also help them to study for the exam. Social support helps students to cope with the stress of learning and is associated with perceived learning (Holmes, 2005; Mortenson, 2006). Social support is also important for helping some international students and students of color to cope in multicultural environments. Holmes (2005) interviewed 13 Chinese international students in New Zealand to understand how these students enlisted and used supportive communication. Holmes found that these international students relied primarily on fellow Chinese students to learn how to interact effectively in the classroom, to better understand the culture, and to enhance their learning. These students desired support from New Zealanders, but found relationships to be challenging because of cultural differences.

Conflict at schools is a critical focus of the U.S. Department of Education because violence and conflict create an unsafe learning environment and are detrimental to learning (Jones, 2006). While many types of school conflicts exist, such as bullying and gang violence, one prevalent type is intercultural conflict. Tensions among cultural groups may build for several reasons: a) cultural differences create misunderstandings among the groups; b) historical treatment of one group tends to be more negative than of another group (or at least it is perceived to be more negative); and c) an incident occurs that escalates tensions into violence (Jones, 2006; Warfield, 2006) (This third type of conflict is discussed in more detail in Chapter 10, in the section on community conflict). Tensions may fester for some time before erupting; however, even tensions that don't crypt inhibit a positive learning environment and negatively impact educational achievement.

Peer-to-peer communication can benefit educational attainment when students receive positive emotional support and when the interaction with peers supports learning. Peer-to-peer communication can hurt educational attainment when students receive negative support, including experiencing intercultural conflict, being discouraged from studying hard, or receiving wrong information from peers. The educational outcome disparities can be explained by at least two research findings a) peer support for students of color is more likely to be negative than for White American students (see the Box 7.6 for a study of these factors), and b) intercultural conflict in schools occurs with greater frequency and has a greater impact on students of color than White American students (Jones, 2006).

Box 7.6 Layered Effects: Popularity and Academic Achievement

A recent study examined the impact of a school's composition (mixed ethnicities or predominantly one ethnicity in the school) on the relationship between popularity and academic achievement in adolescents. While this study focused on secondary education, the success of high school students is critical for educational achievement at the university level. This study used the National Longitudinal Study of Adolescent Health. The authors discovered two significant findings. First, ethnic differences are apparent in the relationship between popularity and achievement. For White Americans, the higher the GPA, the higher a student's popularity is (exhibiting a linear relationship). For African Americans and Hispanic Americans, a curvilinear relationship exists between popularity and achievement. The most popular students are the ones who have middle of the road grades. For African Americans, there was an increase in popularity up to a 3.5 GPA; students who had higher grades than that had sharply fewer friends, such that a student with a 4.0 had the same number of friends as someone with a 2.9. Hispanic American students showed a slight increase

in popularity until they achieved a 2.5 GPA; students who had higher grades had fewer friends, such that a student with a 4.0 had fewer friends than a student with a 1.0. In essence, being "smart" cost students friends. The authors calculated that an African American with a 4.0 GPA had on average 1.5 fewer friends, and a Hispanic American with a 4.0 GPA had on average three fewer friends than a White American with a 4.0 GPA. Second, the ethnic composition of a school affected this relationship for African Americans. The authors found that African Americans in schools with predominantly African American students simply had a linear relationship—the higher the GPA, the higher a student's popularity. (Note: this effect did not happen in private schools.) This finding indicates a layered effect—a school's composition impacts how a student is perceived. It also has implications for academic achievement; in ethnically mixed schools, the potential for academic achievement in African American students is jeopardized because achievement costs them friends.

Source: Fryer & Torelli (2006)

Concept Check

In this section, three types of instructional communication were introduced: classroom management, learning styles, and peer-to-peer communication. Classroom management behaviors are used by teachers to manage the interaction and learning in the classroom. Learning styles relate to students' preferred method for learning and affect the way each student engages the material and interacts with others (for example, teachers and peers). Peer-to-peer communication focuses primarily on social support and intercultural conflict. These communicative elements impact educational outcome disparities in two ways: a) the predominant climate in the classroom does not always match the home culture of students; and b) more negative conflict and more support negative situations exist for students of color than for White American students.

Layered Perspective of Educational Contexts

Educational contexts are layered in many ways. A given educational institution includes numerous layers, such as the students, teachers, administration, school board members, and policy members (such as federal or state legislature). Each of these factors has an impact on the educational achievement of students and the interaction among the various parties. Consistent with earlier chapters, we introduce the bottom-up effects of both the impact of educational institutions on individuals and how society impacts educational institutions. Then, we note some potential skills for addressing challenges presented in this chapter.

Bottom-Up Effects

Bottom-up effects center on individuals as agents of change and on the impact of interpersonal relationships (family and friends) on educational outcomes. Both teachers and students can be agents of change in the classroom. The primary premise in this chapter is that a mismatch of cultures is a key factor hindering academic performance for many students (Castillo et al., 2004; Suárez-Orozco & Suárez-Orozco, 2001). Individual teachers can strive to make their classrooms inclusive of many cultures and perspectives. They can make sure that assignments address many learning styles; they can hold high standards for all students; and they can learn about the cultures of all students. Teachers can make sure to provide positive emotional support to all of their students and to help students to interact with each other in a positive manner. Individual students can also be agents of change for positive intercultural relations. They can challenge a friend who tells racist jokes. They can strive to learn about other cultures and understand ways in which individual biases impact others. They can seek out people from other cultures to help provide emotional support and to grow personally. They can challenge instructors to enhance the cultural relevance of their material and adapt to different learning style. They can study hard, keep up with readings, and seek out help when needed to ensure that they graduate.

Social networks also play a strong role in education success (or lack thereof). Family members and peers can encourage the success or failure of students and thus contribute to education disparities). Some students of color (particularly first generation college students) do not receive support from their networks of family and friends (Suárez-Orozco & Suárez-Orozco, 2001). This lack of support creates a feeling of alienation from their cultures and produces challenges for these students (see Box 7.7 for a story about this alienation). Additionally, some students of color must often manage two different social networks: their home community and their school community. Castillo et al. (2004) surveyed 250 Mexican American women about their level of comfort with mainstream/White educational values and their connection with their cultural communities. The authors found that discomfort with White values and perceived disconnect with their own cultural values were barriers to success for these women. The authors argued that these feelings related to the low number of Mexican American women who graduate from college.

Top-Down Effects: Educational Institutions' Impact on Individuals

If change is necessary and many individuals want to change, why are we not changing? Individual instructors and students do not teach and learn in a vacuum. They are impacted by a variety of organizational constraints (Suárez-Orozco & Suárez-Orozco, 2001). Villegas and Lucas (2002) presented four such barriers to being agents of change: a) institutional barriers, b) resistance from some privileged colleagues, c) lack of personal understanding, and d) despair. Institutional barriers include such factors as the hierarchical and bureaucratic nature of educational institutions. Instructors have a great number of responsibilities (and paperwork), and it is difficult to find sufficient time to try out new ideas. Resistance is another barrier to change. Colleagues from privileged positions who challenge and question

---

Box 7.7 Voices: College Brings Alienation

"My decision to chase a dream, return to college at age 24, and take the liberal arts courses that will help me become a journalist has forced me to be two people. One face is for the family and longtime friends, another is for my classes and college friends. My homeboys have not read Marx, Nietzche, or Freud…For them, intellectual theories are elaborate, unnecessary attempts to explain the inexplicable. Ideas do not feed their families and only seem to highlight the fact that I have begun to change. 'That's enough. Don't read any more. I don't understand a word you're saying,' Fidel, my *compadre*, said after I responded to his request to read him a paragraph from one of my textbooks….

I painfully realize the downside to education; a subtle alienation from friends and loved ones. I understand more clearly why Latinos approach higher learning with trepidation. For beyond the barriers of low income and racism lies another fight; the struggle to blend old and new identities. It is not that education is discouraged; my family is proud of me and would be crushed if I were to quit. But disproportionately few Latinos acquire higher learning and those that do often must balance an incompatible past and future."

Excerpts from Gonzales (1996)

a teacher's educational approach can be stifling (especially in university settings where colleagues vote on whether a faculty member will get tenure or not). Lack of personal understanding is a further barrier. It is difficult to make change if you do not understand and empathize with what a student is experiencing. It is one of the reasons why having role models is critical. Unfortunately, Table 7.3 displays employment statistics in universities to illustrate that there simply are not enough faculty or administrators of color. For example, only 15% of faculty members and 17% of administrators are people of color from the United States. Thus, there are not enough role models in U.S. higher education institutions. Finally, feeling that meaningful change is not possible drives some teachers to despair. They must have hope, and hope starts with a strong diversity climate.

The diversity climate of a classroom and institution has a large impact on whether cultural differences are appreciated or discouraged (Hale, 2004). **Diversity**

Table 7.3

EMPLOYEES IN HIGHER EDUCATION INSTITUTIONS BY RACE/ETHNICITY AND OCCUPATION, 2003

Primary Occupation	Total	White, non-Hispanic	Black, non-Hispanic	Hispanic	Asian/ Pacific Islander	American Indian/ Alaska Native	Other
Total, all institutions	3,194,169	72.0%	9.8%	5.2%	4.9%	0.6%	7.6%
Professional staff	2,272,583	74.2%	6.7%	3.7%	5.4%	0.5%	9.5%
Executive/ administrative/ managerial	186,505	81.8%	9.4%	3.9%	2.7%	0.6%	1.6%
Faculty (instruction and research)	1,174,831	78.5%	5.6%	3.4%	5.1%	0.5%	6.9%
Instruction and research assistants	293,047	51.3%	3.5%	2.9%	7.0%	0.4%	34.9%
Other professional	618,200	74.6%	9.5%	4.5%	5.9%	0.6%	4.9%
Nonprofessional staff	921,586	66.4%	17.4%	8.9%	3.8%	0.8%	2.7%

Note: "Other Professional" includes international students, non-residents, and students whose race/ethnicity is unknown.

Source: National Center for Education Statistics (2006)

climate is the prevailing attitude toward diversity in an organization. The diversity climate shapes the level of hope in faculty and whether they feel empowered to make changes in the classroom. It also affects the ability of an institution to attract and retain faculty and students of color. Diversity climate also shapes the degree to which students learn about diversity and whether they respect difference. Most importantly, a positive diversity climate reduces barriers to student learning and helps to eliminate disparities in educational outcomes (Hale, 2004).

Top-Down Effects: Society's Impact on Educational Institutions

Societal impacts generally focus on the impact of communities and laws/policies for educational institutions. Community factors refer to degree of segregation and integration as well as the level of community cohesion and supervision (Portes, Fernandez-Kelly, & Haller, 2005; Suárez-Orozco & Suárez-Orozco, 2001). Recent immigrants who had formal education in their home country and/or have reached middle-class status are generally able to move into integrated neighborhoods in the United States. Their children have higher educational attainment than those children of immigrants from lower socioeconomic status, who live in segregated neighborhoods (Portes et al., 2005; Suárez-Orozco & Suárez-Orozco, 2001). Box 7.8 presents more details about this finding, introducing a concept called "segmented assimilation." Children of immigrants who live in segregated neighborhoods also achieve educational success if they live in cohesive communities with strong cultural identities. Such cohesion serves to protect children from delinquency (such as gang involvement) and the children focus on academic pursuits (Portes et al., 2005; Suárez-Orozco & Suárez-Orozco, 2001). Specifically, community members supervise each other's children and encourage connection to the cultural community in order to steer children from delinquency.

One of most prominent (and controversial) laws/policies is affirmative action. **Affirmative action** refers to positive steps to increase the representation of groups (women and minorities) in education, employment, government, and business in which they have been historically excluded—hence the term *underrepresented groups*. Affirmative action policies are located around the world and generally involve preferences or quotas in hiring or admissions (Sowell, 2005). The origin of affirmative action in the United States is the Civil Rights Act of 1964. This act had an element called "affirmative action," which was a remedy that federal courts could impose on violators of the Act (Stanford Encyclopedia of Philosophy [SEP], 2005). President Johnson issued Executive Order 11246 in 1965 requiring federal contractors to take "affirmative action" to ensure contractors were not discriminating in hiring. This order was implemented fully by the Secretary of Labor's Order No. 4 (1970) and Revised Order No. 4 (1972). Affirmative action has seen two spikes of debate and controversy: 1972–1980 when the initial gender and racial preferences were debated, and 1990–2003 when the controversy was revisited, particularly on university campuses (SEP, 2005). In this section, I try to provide an objective description of affirmative action as applied to universities. However, I also want to be

Box 7.8 Layered Effects: Segmented Assimilation and Educational Outcomes

Studies examining the children of immigrants in the United States illustrate a diverse set of educational outcomes depending on several layered factors. In general, these studies find that second-generation youths are moving ahead educationally and occupationally, but that a significant minority is being left behind. The authors characterize this phenomenon as "segmented assimilation." Segmented assimilation refers to the fact that almost all second-generation youths have learned English and have adopted educational and occupational goals consistent with U.S. American values, but that their assimilation experiences are quite distinct (some moving ahead and some being left behind).

The reason that some move ahead and some are left behind corresponds to discrimination, social constraints, strength of immigrant community identity, and family income status. Teens in the lower socioeconomic group experience racism and discrimination, which lowers their expectations of educational success. They experience being hassled by police and store owners, being turned down for jobs, and being attacked on the street if they venture into White neighborhoods. These teens also experience social constraints in that schools and the neighborhoods in which they live promote a set of undesirable outcomes counter to success including gangs, dropping out, and selling drugs. Finally, these teens experience weak ethnic identity in the community in combination with a working-class background. The result is low educational attainment and living in marginalized working class communities—an effect the authors call downward assimilation.

In contrast, teens that succeed have one of two combinations of family type and social structures. In one situation, their parents achieved middle-class status on their own, and the teens have high educational and economic attainment and assimilate fully into U.S. society. In the second situation, their parents were of working-class status, but they lived in a community with a strong ethnic identity. The teens tend to attain middle-class status through education. Their children become fully acculturated and have high educational success.

The studies of immigrant children illustrate that youths' educational outcomes are not simply determined by their own efforts; societal layers of discrimination, ethnic identity in the community, and social constraints have a strong impact on children's educational success. These experiences coupled with those of students in the classroom have a strong impact on educational disparities.

Source: Portes et al. (2005)

honest that I am in favor of affirmative action in most cases, and you should keep that in mind as you read this section. I describe the justification for affirmative action, the pros and cons of affirmative action, and some of the historical decisions reached regarding university admissions. Moreover, Chapter 8 discusses affirmative action in the workplace.

The primary justification for affirmative action was to address discrimination practices inherent in society. Before the passage of the Civil Rights Act in 1964, minorities groups in the United States, particularly African Americans, were treated as second-class citizens and faced overt discrimination in education. They went to segregated schools that were typically of lesser quality than White schools and thus received limited opportunities to excel in higher education. The assumption was that access to higher education was not going to improve because the measures of merit were biased against minority groups and the people making decisions on admissions were generally White and often biased toward people of their own background (see social identity theory in Chapter 3). Affirmative action was deemed necessary by President Johnson to change the system. The comic strip in Figure 7.6 illustrates the attitudes of the proponents of affirmative action.

Today, these justifications are still offered by proponents of affirmative action. They argue that the goal for universities is to educate a student body that is representative of society as a whole. If the student body does not reflect the diversity of the society, the reasons must be a combination of biased admissions process, institutional discrimination, and a less than favorable diversity climate. One means to diversify the process is to consider race and ethnicity (gender is no longer needed in most admissions decisions because women have reached parity) as one criterion for the admissions decision. They argue that only qualified people should be admitted, countering the argument than unqualified people can get admitted just because they are an ethnic minority, but that race and ethnicity should be a plus factor; that is, if

Figure 7.6
Affirmative Action Comic Strip

Some believe that, historically, members of privileged groups (such as White American males) have "gotten ahead" because of their race and gender. Do you agree that this is true? If so, is affirmative action necessary to correct past discrimination? Has it outlived its usefulness? Have you been harmed by or have you benefited from an affirmative action policy?

Reprinted with permission of Clay Bennett, North America Syndicate two candidates are equally qualified and one is from an underrepresented group and one is from the majority group, the person from the underrepresented group should get preference.

Opponents of affirmative action offer a variety of counterarguments. Some say that affirmative action was needed in the 1960s, but it has largely achieved its goals and is no longer needed. Others will offer that affirmative action perpetuates new wrongs such as increasing racial tensions. Further, some argue that affirmative action benefits the most privileged people of a minority group (those in the middle and upper-middle class) at the expense of the disenfranchised within the majority group (such as lower-class Whites). Finally, opponents say that affirmative action hurts those it intends to help by admitting minority students who are less qualified than their peers into more rigorous programs where they either cannot keep up or graduate in the bottom of the class.

In the early 1970s, universities were faced with a choice: keep their existing admissions criteria and have few African American and Hispanic students on campus, or change their criteria to get a more substantial representation. Most chose the second path, such as the University of California at Davis Medical School, which reserved 16 of 100 slots for ethnic minorities. In 1973 and 1974, Allan Bakke, a White applicant, was denied admission even though he had better test scores and grades than most of those admitted under the quota program. He sued, and his case, *Regents of the University of California v. Bakke,* went to the Supreme Court. The justices ruled in favor of Bakke, but their opinion left open the use of race and ethnicity in admission decisions. Specifically, they ruled that race could be a plus in a particular applicant's file, but that she or he would still have to be compared to all other candidates for the available seats; that is, it stopped the set aside quota approach, but allowed race to be a contributing factor.

In the 1990s and early 2000s, at admission policies that allowed race to be a factor in admission decisions were struck down at a number of universities, including law schools at the University of Texas, University of Georgia, and University of Michigan. However, Justice Sandra Day O'Connor's lead opinion in the Michigan Law School case (*Grutter v. Bollinger*) ruled that student body diversity is a compelling state interest that justifies the use of race in admissions policies. Many selective universities (those admitting only top-ranked students compared to open universities who admit students with qualifying records) continue some race-based considerations in order to diversify their student bodies.

The fate of affirmative action in the future is an open question. In the past, it has clearly diversified student bodies and faculties. It is also a great example of how laws/policies shape our educational and interpersonal interactions. Other policies, such as vouchers (payment to students in order to attend private schools) and bussing (sending certain groups to a school in order to have a more culturally diverse school), which have also diversified educational institutions, are controversial as well. All of these policies have intriguing ethical implications, such as the question of how much the government should intervene in order to desegregate schools.

Challenges and Skills

This chapter has introduced a number of challenges for creating a positive diversity climate in educational institutions and for reducing disparities in educational outcomes. This final section explores some of the communicative approaches that might address some of these challenges.

The first skill to consider is becoming more self-reflexive. **Self reflexivity** is the ability to understand yourself and your own cultural biases. As we discussed in Chapter 4, our cultural biases impact the attributions we make of our own and others' behavior as well as our attitudes toward other cultural groups. If you are a teacher in a multicultural classroom, you have an ethical responsibility to understand how your culture impacts the way that you teach and the expectations you have of your students. You need to investigate the ways that students from other cultural groups—and your own—learn and how you can create an inclusive diversity climate in your classroom.

The second set of skills is to enhance abilities in dialoging about race and culture. In order to improve the diversity climate, we have to be able to talk about what diversity is, how it impacts us, and ways to remedy the negative aspects of diversity, such as racism. The college students in the study by Simpson et al. (2007) identified three factors that would help them dialogue about race and diversity. First, instructors need to be aware of what diversity means to them; that is, instructors need to be self-reflexive. Second, instructors should model diversity in how they organize the class. If they want all cultural groups to feel included, instructors should include readings and examples from authors from a variety of cultural groups and different perspectives. Additionally, instructors should model positive support for students; that is, they need to validate and listen to the students' perspectives, guide discussion, show what appropriate comments are, and be willing to allow disagreement in a respectful manner. Finally, the instructor should establish parameters for content and discussion. Students should be aware of what is (and what is not) going to be discussed, the manner in which the topic will be discussed (for example, a lecture, open discussion, etc.), and the ground rules for student discussion. Some important ground rules are listening to others, not interrupting, disagreeing with ideas (not people), and not expecting individuals to be "spokespersons" for their cultural group.

Finally, since higher layers shape what happens to individuals, we need to be effective at changing organizations and social structures. These skills include being agents of change in the workplace—findings ways to persuade administrators to allow innovative educational programs and to adopt diversity friendly practices. As students, you can use your voice to challenge instruction and educational climates that are close-minded or that do not fit all cultures. There are some instructors you can directly confront. You can explain to them why the material or approach is not working for you and suggest a different alternative. Of course, you know that some instructors are not open to such a challenge. In that case, you might talk to an advisor or administrator to express your concerns (or wait until after the semester). You can also talk with your peers and collectively address your concerns. The point is that students can make change and it takes courage to stand up for what you believe in.

One way to create change in institutions is to create a community of practice. Communities of practice are "groups of people who share a concern, a set of problems, or a passion about a topic, and who deepen their knowledge and expertise in this area by interacting on an ongoing basis" (Wenger, McDermott, & Snyder, 2002, p. 1). Connecting with others who share a passion is a key way to create change. Peers help to motivate us when we get down and also provide strength in numbers. If you stand by yourself, it is easy for a supervisor to refuse change. If you stand collectively with other students, it is harder for the supervisor to refuse you. Communities of practice can be created by meeting regularly, sharing ideas and research, and creating a network of like-minded individuals. We might do this with people at our institution or through virtual means, such as listserves and blogs.

SUMMARY

Returning to the opening story, Andres' story is an example of the many facets that affect educational achievement. The struggles he faced include the difference between individual and cooperative learning approaches, lack of immediacy from teachers, lack of relevance of his studies to his experiences, and lack of social support from his peer groups. On the latter point, he was alienated from his high school peer group because of his desire to receive an education. His success can be attributed to a number of factors. First, he worked hard and persevered. Second, he had a mentor with whom he connected and a group of peers who provided social support to him and helped him engage in collective learning. His family and community provided some benefit as well. His parents and community instilled a strong cultural identity, and his parents were able to have some economic success in the United States. Thus, Andres has a strong likelihood of education success.

Here is a summary of the chapter based on the learning objectives:

- **Disparities in educational outcomes.** Disparities occur when cultural, ethnic, or racial groups score lower or have lower educational outcomes than other groups. In the United States, White and Asian American students tend to have higher graduation rates and university enrollment than do African Americans, Hispanic Americans, and American Indians. The factors associated with disparities include socioeconomic status, ethnic identity in communities, discrimination, and social constraints (such as alienation from peer groups). Additionally, the mismatch between home culture and school culture is a key element—and is the focus of this chapter.
- **Classroom management and examples of the various types.** Classroom management refers to the behaviors that teachers use to manage the interaction and learning in the classroom. This chapter included three types of classroom management behaviors: a) providing immediacy: the reduction of psychology distance between teacher and students through verbal and nonverbal behaviors; b) communicating expectations: teachers communicate whether they have low or high expectations of students; and c) engaging and culturally appropriate

content: teachers should try to use materials and styles that fit all of the cultural backgrounds of students in their classes.

- **Two approaches to understanding learning styles.** Learning styles relate to the preferred method that students use to learn and affect the way the student engages the material and interacts with teachers and peers. Two approaches to learning style are individual vs. cooperative learning and the experiential learning model. Individual learning focuses on critical thinking, objective observation, abstract analysis, and individual performance, while cooperative learning focuses on personal reflection, subjective reactions, consciousness-raising, and cooperative performance. The experiential learning model has four styles—divergers, assimilators, accommodaters, and convergers—that are a combination of the four stages in experiential learning: concrete experience, reflective observation, abstract conceptualization, and active experimentation.

- **Two types of peer-to-peer communication behaviors.** Peer-to-peer communication includes social support and intercultural conflict. Social support occurs when individuals provide aid, assistance, and comfort to others. This support might include encouragement from classmates or clarification about assignments. Intercultural conflict occurs when students from one cultural group have a dispute with those of another cultural group.

- **Instructional communication and disparities in educational outcomes.** These communicative elements impact educational outcome disparities in two ways: a) the predominant climate in the classroom does not match the home culture of students; and b) often, there are both more negative conflicts and more support negative situations for students of color than for White American students. Instructional communication is not the only factor in disparities in educational outcomes, but it is an important component.

- **Bottom-up and top-down effects.** Bottom-up effects consider how teachers and students can be agents of change—creating a more inclusive and culturally appropriate learning environment and also working hard to achieve success. Further, the social networks of students can encourage or discourage education achievement. Top-down effects impact educational outcomes in three main ways. First, educational institutions both facilitate and inhibit agents of change. Second, communities also both facilitate and constrain educational success. Third, laws and policies such as affirmative action shape the diversity climate of educational institutions.

REVIEW QUESTIONS

1. Describe disparities in educational outcomes at the university level. What factors relate to these disparities?
2. What is classroom management, and what are some types of classroom management behaviors?
3. How does immediacy result in cognitive learning?

4. Compare and contrast individual and cooperative learning styles.
5. Explain the experiential learning model.
6. How does peer-to-peer communication both facilitate and inhibit learning?
7. Explain the role that instructional communication has in disparities in educational outcomes.
8. What is an agent of change, and how do educational institutions inhibit change?
9. How do social networks and communities contribute to educational disparities?
10. Take a stance on whether or not affirmative action is beneficial legislation (be sure to define what you mean by beneficial).
11. Describe several communication skills that are necessary to address the challenges of disparities in educational outcomes.
12. What is a community of practice and how does this help to create change in educational institutions?

EXERCISES

1. Investigate the newspaper stories in your area over the past five years for incidents of intercultural conflict at a school. What happened? What were the identified causes of the conflict? How might you apply some of your learning about intercultural communication to create an intervention to address this conflict?
2. Visit the Web site for the Anti-Defamation League at www.adl.org. Review the stories about racial and religious hatred around the world. What patterns do you notice about the stories? How do they differ from what goes on in your culture? Review the "Combating Hate" under the search box on the left column. What strategies do you think are most effective for combating hate in an educational setting?
3. Interview two or three students from other cultures to determine potential mismatches between their culture and the existing classroom culture. Also, consider ways that your culture is a match and mismatch for the predominant classroom culture at your college or university.
4. Research an educational policy that affects diversity climate and the educational outcomes of this policy. For example, consider school vouchers, bussing, and "No Child Left Behind," and summarize the impact such policies have had on diversity climate and educational outcomes.

CHAPTER 8

The Workplace

The workplace has become increasingly diverse. What are the benefits of having a culturally diverse workplace? What are the challenges?

CHAPTER OUTLINE

I. Introduction

II. Workplace as a Context for Cultural Diversity

III. Benefits and Challenges of Cultural Diversity
- a. Value Added Perspective on Diversity
- b. Potential Barrier Perspective on Diversity
- c. Poor Analysis of Diversity Issues
- d. Concept Check

IV. Intercultural Communication in the Workplace
- a. Organizational Culture
- b. Work Group Process
- c. Managing People
- d. Individuals' Reactions to the Organization
- e. Concept Check

V. Layers of Intercultural Communication in the Workplace
- a. Bottom-Up Effects
- b. Top-Down Effects: The Workplace's Impact on Attitudes and Individual Behavior
- c. Top-Down Effects: Society's Impact on the Workplace
- d. Challenges and Skills

VI. Summary

VII. Review Questions

VIII. Exercises

CHAPTER OBJECTIVES

After reading this chapter, students should be able to

- describe the unique characteristics of the workplace as a context for intercultural communication.

- explain the benefits and challenges of cultural diversity in the workplace and the reasons why organizations have difficulty analyzing diversity problems.

- list four different layers of intercultural communication in the workplace and provide an example of each.

- discuss the bottom-up and top-down effects of intercultural communication in the workplace.

- explain one approach to establishing and implementing a vision that values and embraces cultural diversity.

Introduction

The executive team at ABC Electronics was dumbfounded. Five years ago, ABC made a commitment to recruit and retain a workforce that mirrored the culturally diverse community in which the company was based. ABC spent millions of dollars in public relations efforts and in attending recruiting fairs at universities around the country. The executive team also had all employees attend a cultural sensitivity workshop. During the first two years, ABC had some success recruiting cultural minorities to the company, but it had limited success in retaining those individuals—who left, but not necessarily for better jobs, it seems. After five years, ABC has very few gains to show for its efforts. The members of the executive team are at the point where they wonder if it will not be possible to change the composition of their organization until society changes. The executive team is considering forgoing all of their diversity recruitment efforts since it has cost them a lot of money and time without making any significant change.

> Question: Why has ABC not been successful in creating and sustaining a more culturally diverse workforce?

The experiences at ABC are not uncommon in U.S. organizations and those around the world. Most organizations are relatively homogeneous and are led by people from the dominant culture. For example, in Division I college football, approximately 50% of the athletes are African American, yet only 25% of assistant coaches and 3% of head coaches are African American (Bowden, 2005). In Division I college men's basketball, 25% of the head coaches are African American, but 58% of the players are African American (Majors, 2006). The trend in men's college sports is also apparent across the workforce in general (see Box 8.1 on p. 210). Table 8.1 illustrates that, in general, women and people of color in the United States have a greater representation in the general workforce than they do at the higher levels of management. This is a trend that is largely repeated around the world. People who are not from the majority group have a greater tendency to have jobs at the lower levels in

Box 8.1 What Went Right & Wrong? History in Professional Football

In February 2007, a historical event occurred when Tony Dungy and Lovie Smith coached their teams, the Indianapolis Colts and the Chicago Bears, respectively, in the National Football League's Super Bowl. The 41st Super Bowl featured African American coaches for the first time. Leading up to the event, much was made about the fact that these were the first African American coaches in the big game. Their stories were told repeatedly—both were nice guys who led by example and were proud to represent African Americans but who also wanted to focus on the task at hand. Dungy was also portrayed as a leader, with Smith as one of his protégées. At the end of the game (the Colts won), Dungy met his friend at midfield and said that Smith would get his turn. Both men were held up as wonderful role models.

However, the story was not all positive—many articles were also published about the continuing inequities in professional and college sports. Specifically, many writers noted with amazement that it had taken over 40 years of playing the Super Bowl for an African American coach to reach the big game. The writers also revealed that the majority of athletes are African American, but the vast majority of coaches have been, and continue to be, White. The systematic discrimination in professional football was indicted as the problem, although the Rooney Rule—which requires that all teams interview one minority candidate at the finalist stage—has made strides to improve the number of minority coaches in professional football. The Rooney Rule is one way to address systematic discrimination. Tony Dungy served as an assistant coach for many years because many owners didn't think he was head coach material. How wrong he proved them on this day.

the organization—and thus the lowest paying jobs. The disparity in management positions and income is even stronger for women of color.

Other cultural groups also face challenges in the workplace. According to Catalyst (2004b), 39% of lesbians, gays, bisexuals, and transgendered (LGBT) report facing some form of hostility or harassment on the job. Nearly 20% of LGBT employees report barriers to their promotion because of their sexual orientation/identity. LGBT individuals also face challenges to receiving domestic partnership benefits, with only 51% of Fortune 500 companies providing them. On a positive note, 86% of Fortune 500 companies include sexual orientation in their non-discrimination policies with 98% of Fortune 50 companies providing such policies.

I have yet to meet or hear a government official, manager, administrator, or corporate leader who does not say that she wants a more culturally diverse and representative workforce. This desire for diversity is often framed as a need to compete in a global marketplace. If an executive makes a negative point about diversity, he generally is quickly fired or replaced. If everyone wants more diversity, why do we have such difficulties recruiting and maintaining a culturally diverse workforce? This challenge is one for all organizations, and it is the focus of this chapter.

Table 8.1

WORKPLACE STATISTICS ABOUT WOMEN AND PEOPLE OF COLOR IN THE UNITED STATES

Group	% of workforce	% of management/ professional occupations	% of Fortune 500 corporate officers	% income > $50,000 working full-time
African American	11.4	8.4	3.7	19.7
Asian American	4.4	6.1	1.9	40.5
Hispanic American	13.3	6.6	2.1	15.6
American Indian	3.6	1[1]	0.0	27.9
White American	67.3	71.5	92.3	44.6
Women	46.3	50.5	16.4	16.7
Women of Color[2]	17.2	11.5	1.7	varies[3]

[1] The exact number could not be located.

[2] Women of color include Latinas, Asian American, and African American women.

[3] Asian American women (31.7%), African American women (16.2%), and Latinas (11.5%).

Note: The table should be read across for comparison. The numbers in columns do not add up to 100 because there are overlapping categories (for example, "women of color" are included in "women").

Sources: U.S. Census Bureau (2005), Catalyst.org (2006)

Trends in technology and demographics project a future of increasing intercultural and global interaction. Thus, understanding the impacts of cultural diversity and intercultural communication on the workplace is important for everyone. This chapter examines the distinctive aspects of work organizations and then illustrates the benefits and challenges of having a diverse workforce. Further, we examine the intercultural communication issues in the workplace at several layers, including the organizational culture, the work group, the manager-employee relationship, and individuals' work communication. We conclude by examining the top-down and bottom-up effects of intercultural communication in the workplace and consider, in particular, the globalization of work, including outsourcing and offshoring and the impact of both on intercultural communication.

Workplace as a Context for Cultural Diversity

The workplace means different types of employment and situations for different people. For most of us, it is the place where we get our paycheck. However, the workplace is quite diverse, with some people working in large multinational and global companies and others working in small businesses, non-profits, and governmental entities. Unless we are a sole proprietor with no employees, the likelihood is strong that our workplace includes people from different ethnic, cultural, and national culture backgrounds. Thus, we work in culturally diverse organizations.

The workplace also presents a distinct context for intercultural communication and has special features. The workplace is where people organize their efforts to achieve common goals. An **organization** is composed of a social collectivity (that is, a group of people) that coordinates the actions of individuals to achieve common goals. The coordinated activities are structured, usually by dividing tasks and creating a reporting system; such tasks are our job duties. These duties generally are completed under the supervision of a manager who provides us with feedback and evaluation of our work, which provides the structure for the reporting system. The supervision is provided to help us work with others in order to achieve larger goals (for example, producing a car at an automobile company when our job is to do the accounting). Our work is also located within a larger organizational environment (Miller, 2006). The larger environment includes organizations that affect the work, such as the government, competitors, customers, and concerned publics (for example, environmentalists and consumer watchdog groups). With its transactional and symbolic properties, communication is instrumental in the process of organizing people. Thus, the organization can be thought of both as a physical location where communication takes place to help us achieve our goals, and also as a means to help us create an organizational structure and meaning for our work. For example, we use communication to help us understand what we need to do. We also communicate with co-workers and family members about our work and decide what meaning it has for us (Do we like our work? Do we think what we do is valued? Important?). Organized work can be difficult to conceptualize without a physical building or location, but a workspace still exists. For example, the political organization "MoveOn" does not have a bricks-and-mortar headquarters. Leaders of "MoveOn" coordinate their actions through electronic communication and interact with their constituents via e-mail. Thus, MoveOn does have a workplace—even though the place is cyberspace.

Organizations are often described as systems with interlocking layers of people and functions. A **system** is a set of component parts that have interdependent relationships (Homans, 1950). An organization is a system with inputs, processes, and outcomes where the inputs influence the processes and the processes influence the outcomes (see Figure 8.1). The input of the organization includes the human

Figure 8.1
System model (Ting-Toomey & Oetzel, 2001)

Reproduced with permission of Sage Publications Inc. Books via Copyright Clearance Center

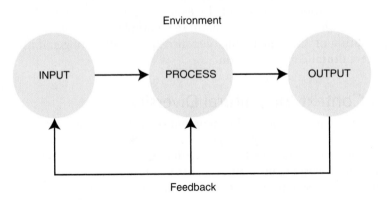

resources and the accompanying cultural diversity, along with capital, infrastructure, and natural resources. Inputs are the people, money, telephones, computer systems, and other components that we need to do our jobs. The process refers to the interaction that occurs among organizational members in performing the work. It is how we talk to one another in order to do our work. The output includes the product produced or service provided along with other influences on the larger organizational environment, such as being a benchmark for other organizations and changing practices and laws by influencing governmental officials. Both the process and output provide feedback to the organizational members. As we talk to one another, we change each other and get a better understanding of needs. As we produce outputs, we get a sense of what people want and refocus our work to give the customer more of what she wants.

Additionally, the system is characterized by various layers of hierarchy. This hierarchy within the organization includes such layers as individual members,

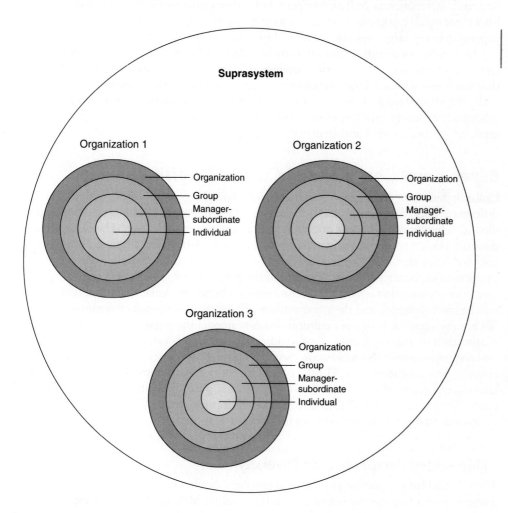

Figure 8.2
Hierarchy in a System

manager-employee relationships, work groups, and organizational or system-wide processes. The organization itself is nested within a hierarchy of other systems and thus external communication, such as advertising, public relations, and political communication, is an important function. For example, consider a public university. Within the university are individuals such as students, faculty, staff, and administrators. These individuals have particular hierarchical relationships, such as professor-student or department chair–professor. Groups of people, task forces and committees, for example, perform the work of the university. University-wide policies cover a variety of issues, including behavioral conduct, employment practices, class registration, and the process of obtaining parking passes. Finally, this university is not a stand-alone entity. It has to create an image as a strong and desirable place to get an education. It has to advertise in order to get the best students. It has to interact with state legislators since it depends on funding from the state government. It also has to coordinate and complement its curriculum with those of other state and national universities as well as compete with other universities. Figure 8.2 displays how three similar organizations, each with its particular layers, exist within a suprasystem (or larger system composed of subsystems).

In review, organizations function by having coordinated activities, division of labor, and structure. Coordination, division of labor, and structure result in a system that functions within a larger organizational environment. The systems level aspects make the workplace a unique context for intercultural communication. While the workplace certainly includes interpersonal relations, the focus of this chapter will be more on its coordinated and structured activities.

Benefits and Challenges of Cultural Diversity

Cultural diversity—or the representation in one social system of people with distinctly different group affiliations of cultural significance—in the workplace is often studied to identify whether it is a benefit and/or a challenge to the organization. The research on diversity takes a predominantly management focus in that the emphasis is on the bottom line (making money) and what is best for the organization. Better employment opportunities, better work conditions, and the potential for growth benefit the individuals. The organization assumes that if it creates a better workplace, then individuals will be more satisfied, and the organization will benefit from productive employees. Within this context, how does cultural diversity impact the organization? Three overall perspectives on this topic exist. First, cultural diversity adds value to an organization and creates a competitive advantage. Second, cultural diversity is a potential barrier to effective process and output. Third, cultural diversity can do both, but generally problems occur because the analysis of diversity issues is poor. While these perspectives are contradictory, each is possible in a specific organization, depending on how diversity is addressed. Each of these perspectives is discussed in turn.

Value Added Perspective on Diversity

The value added perspective assumes that diversity should provide a net benefit and thus a competitive advantage for organizations (Cox, 2001; McLeod, Label, & Cox, 1996).

The assumption is that different ideas, perspectives, and communication patterns will provide the organization with a larger talent pool, one that can create and market products and services to diverse audiences. These advantages are seen in three areas: problem solving, creativity, and marketing (Cox, 2001).

Cultural diversity enriches problem-solving capabilities. No single individual possesses the breadth and depth of knowledge to resolve an entangled issue in the workplace. Our ability to value different approaches to problem solving and mindfully move away from traditional "either/or" thinking can create and expand diverse options in managing difficult problems. Research demonstrates that group members who are exposed to a wide range of opinions and perspectives, including beliefs that differ from those of the majority, are able to make better decisions and resolve problems more effectively than individuals not exposed to these minority opinions (Nemeth, 1992). The rationale is that people exposed to different ideas are more likely to be vigilant in making decisions and thus will carefully consider the consequences of a decision (Hirokawa & Rost, 1992). "Minority opinion" is not necessarily the view of a person of color, but rather is simply an opinion that the majority does not hold. Cultural diversity increases the likelihood that multiple opinions and perspectives are included.

Creativity involves a process of taking in new ideas and being thrown into uncertainty. All types of industries thrive on creativity and innovation. The next great idea can mean the difference between being a market leader or going bankrupt. Certainly, some individuals are more creative than others. However, cultural diversity can benefit the overall level of creativity in an organization. According to creativity research, we learn more from people who are different from us than from those who are similar to us (Goleman, Kaufman, & Ray, 1992). In addition, the quality of ideas produced by culturally diverse teams has been rated an average of 11% higher than those of culturally homogenous teams (McLeod, Lobel, & Cox, 1996). Further, highly innovative companies take "deliberate steps to create heterogeneous work teams with the objective of bringing different points of view to bear on problems" (Cox & Beale, 1997, p. 38). Cultural diversity results in creativity and innovation because a greater variety of viewpoints are brought to bear on the issues, a higher level of critical analysis of alternatives is presented, and a lower probability of group-think (everyone accepting the majority opinion without critical evaluation) is present.

Marketing products and services are critical to organizational survival. Many companies now market products around the world and need to know the buying patterns of people in other cultures, since cultural identities impact consumer spending. Additionally, the buying power of cultural minority groups in various countries is increasing. For example, in 2010, it is estimated that the buying power of African Americans and Hispanics will exceed $1 trillion, that of Asian Americans will exceed $575 billion, and that of American Indians will be about $70 million (Humphreys, 2005). Over the past 20 years, this increase in buying power ranges from 250% (American Indians) to 412% (Hispanics) and is well over the growth rate for White Americans (164%) (Catalyst, 2004a, 2004b, 2006).

Cultural diversity can help organizations enhance marketing in at least three ways (Cox, 2001). First, being a strong proponent of cultural diversity is a public relations advantage. A company that can express how friendly it is to various cultural groups has an advantage both in attracting diverse employees, and also in being able to market to various cultural communities. Second, marketing to a diverse audience requires people who understand and can create messages that relate to various cultures. People from these cultures are an excellent source for organizations. Third, culturally diverse organizations provide the opportunity to enhance customer relations because the organization mirrors the diversity of the society. Thus, the organization can match the customers with employees who know their culture. For example, Goya, a food company, has been very successful in marketing to Latino consumers because of the cultural diversity of their employees and their culturally appropriate marketing strategies (Lowry, Ulanov, & Weinrich, 2003). In general, Goya emphasizes the importance of mealtime and family—this is part of their generic strategy. However, Goya's popularity, with Latinos and with other cultural groups as well, is attributed to its ability to sell different meal products to different cultures—it offers 1,000 products, including 23 rice products and 30 types of peas and beans. Goya segments its market by degree of acculturation as well as by the unique cultures within the broader Latino grouping (creating messages that fit the specific cultural groups). So, while Goya emphasizes family and meals, it does this in a unique way for each cultural group. The company benefits from being a Latino-owned company (public relations advantage) and having a diverse workforce that matches the community to which it markets (mirroring the diversity of the society).

Potential Barrier Perspective on Diversity

While cultural diversity is a benefit to organizations, it does include potential pitfalls to be aware of. A consistent finding about process and performance is that the more culturally diverse an organization is, the more likely it is to have less effective interaction processes and process difficulty (Oetzel, Burtis, Chew-Sanchez, & Perez, 2001; Watson, Kumar, & Michaelsen, 1993). **Process difficulty** refers to communication processes that potentially interfere with performance and include high levels of conflict and tension, power struggles, lack of cooperation, lack of respect for group members, inconsistent norms/rules, and inequality in turn taking (Oetzel et al., 2001). Essentially, the more diverse groups or organizations are, the more difficulty they will have interacting in an effective manner. If the group members have difficulty interacting, they will also have difficulty in coordinating their work and performing well.

While the research overall illustrates that cultural diversity is a potential barrier to effective process and performance, some specific studies help to temper this generalization. I have conducted several studies of culturally diverse work groups in Los Angeles, California, and Albuquerque, New Mexico—cities that have culturally diverse populations (Oetzel, 2001; Oetzel, Torres, & Sanchez, 2004). In Los Angeles (with the city's large populations of Latinos, Asian Americans, White Americans, and its smaller population of African Americans), I studied 36 student work groups composed of 3–6 members and varying levels of diversity (a few groups had members from all the same ethnic/cultural background; some had members from 2–3 different cultures; and others had members from completely different cultures). In New Mexico

Box 8.2 Layered Effects: Group Composition's Effect on Individuals

Interestingly, in my New Mexico study, I found that the cultural diversity of the work group impacted individuals differently. The more culturally diverse a group was, the worse White Americans rated the quality of the interaction. Additionally, the more culturally diverse a group was, the worse Hispanic Americans rated the quality of the interaction. Individuals from other cultural groups perceived better interaction in groups that had higher levels of diversity. The reason for this effect is that White and Hispanic Americans in New Mexico are the largest populations (about 45% and 42% of the total state population respectively). Their interaction patterns are the norm, and thus it is to their advantage for groups to be generally homogeneous (that is, all Hispanic American or all White American). In contrast, other cultural groups are minorities, and thus it is to their advantage that diversity reigns in a work group. These effects are subtle differences, but important nonetheless. It demonstrates that the diversity climate in a work group affects people differently. This is a clear layered effect of diversity on individuals.

(with its large population of Hispanic Americans and White Americans and smaller groups of Asian Americans, American Indians, and African Americans), I studied 41 work groups from a manufacturing plant, and all had varying levels of diversity. In both situations, I calculated the level of diversity and asked participants to describe their process and performance using a set of close-ended statements. In both cases, I did not find that diverse groups had any worse—or better for that matter—process or performance than homogeneous groups. Why is my set of findings different from that of other research on diversity? The reason is that my study settings—Los Angeles and Albuquerque—are both culturally diverse; no majority population exists in either location. Group members are used to interacting with people from different cultures and have learned to do so with relative effectiveness. In contrast, much of the prior research took place in areas with relatively homogeneous cultures, such as Michigan and rural Texas. Thus, the group members in those situations were not used to diversity and still had to learn to interact effectively and hence had process difficulty. See Box 8.2.

Poor Analysis of Diversity Issues

Most organizations do not need to be sold on the benefits of diversity for their organization. Nor do these organizations need to be told about the potential problems. Organizational leaders are generally aware of both, although some think diversity is simply political correctness that will not go away. I like to think that most organizations and people really want to have an integrated and inclusive society and workplace. Why then do we have so many inequities in the workplace, and why do companies like ABC Electronics (in the opening story) have trouble recruiting and retaining diverse workforces? Taylor Cox, a diversity expert at the University of Michigan, has identified three problems that organizations face when analyzing diversity issues: misdiagnosing problems, arriving at the wrong solution, and failing to understand the learning curve of individuals (Cox, 2001). Also see Box 8.3.

Box 8.3 Talking about Ethics: Political Correctness or Cultural Diversity

Some people in the United States are sick of talking about cultural diversity in organizations. They feel that cultural diversity is code for political correctness and that diversity proponents are way too sensitive. These individuals appreciate that historical cases of racism have occurred and that racism still exists, but they believe that it is relatively rare today and that continued efforts to enhanced diversity are not needed. They maintain that safeguards are in place for discrimination cases, such as law and grievance policy, and that the market can take care of the need for diversity; that is, the best qualified individuals will be hired and thrive. Likewise, they believe that competition will push out individuals who discriminate and who are bigots.

1. Do you agree or disagree with this opinion? Why or why not?
2. Do diversity proponents spend too much energy pushing diversity on people? Not enough energy?
3. Have you ever been offended by a comment in the workplace and then were told you were simply being politically correct? How did that feel?

Most organizations misdiagnose the diversity problem as the result of one of two issues: the organization does not include enough people from particular cultural groups, and/or it has too many insensitive people who are not aware of other cultures. However, diversity issues are more complex than this. In fact, the usual problem is that the organizational culture is not supportive of a culturally diverse workforce. Most organizations recruit a diverse workforce to come in and work in a conforming environment. The organization spends a great deal of time and money to socialize new employees to behave and act in ways that meet the organization's needs. For example, if the organization's goal is to produce computer chips, then it trains people about their roles and responsibilities in producing and selling chips. However, there might be many ways to be successful in creating and selling chips. The problem is that most organizations teach people just one way to do it and think that those who do not do it "our way" are doing it the "wrong way." The result is that most organizational cultures strip away real diversity—people come in diverse but then, in order to survive, conform to the mainstream organizational culture. Thus, either people leave the organization or lose the real diversity they originally brought to the organization.

Following this misdiagnosis, the approach most organizations take is simply to add more diverse inputs; that is, hire people from different cultural backgrounds, and train current employees. Organizations that take this approach see the need to recruit more people from other cultures, paying them above market rate if necessary. These organizations also try to train their existing employees about other cultures. Neither diagnosis or effort is wrong in and of itself. Both are necessary, but they are not sufficient efforts. Changing the inputs to the system can be beneficial. If both a critical mass of people from cultural minority groups and leadership that is open to change exist, this mass can start to create a new type of organization. However, this type of change takes a great deal of time. Additionally, changing only inputs ignores other aspects of the system such as performance appraisal processes, hiring criteria (potentially hiring more people not tolerant of other cultural groups), and the structure of the work. Being open to cultural diversity requires changing inputs, but also the other components of the system. For example, Coca-Cola North America set goals to increase spending with women and minority-owned supplier organizations; specifically, $800 million over five years. More than simply having a diverse workforce, their goal was to have the suppliers look like their customer base as well. Thus, Coca-Cola changed how the company invested money in the community and in other organizations and trained managers who were making decisions about this type of spending. They also invested in mentoring their suppliers so the suppliers could be successful. More than simply diversifying the workforce, Coca-Cola changed the organizational culture and the resources that were invested (Diversity/Careers, 2005). These steps represent a major improvement at Coca-Cola, which settled a class-action racial discrimination lawsuit in 2001 for $192.5 million because of the company's discriminatory promotion practices (particularly for African Americans) (King, 2001). Specifically, it had a corporate culture that hired African Americans but kept them at lower levels in the corporate hierarchy rather than at the senior level (and higher paying) jobs.

Finally, most organizations perceive the wrong learning curve about diversity. Like many problems, organizational leaders assume the learning curve about culture and diversity is steep. If they put a lot of time, money, and effort into it initially, they believe that they will be able to improve the organization quickly. In reality, learning about culture and diversity takes a great deal of time. Change will not happen quickly, but rather requires long-term commitment. Organizations also exist within societies, and thus they are limited by what society offers. For example, if you want to increase the number of African American researchers in chemistry, in addition to hiring more qualified individuals now, it will also be important to increase the number of African American students getting bachelor's, master's, and doctoral degrees in chemistry. Obtaining a Ph.D. in chemistry takes a minimum of eight years beyond a high school diploma—so increasing the number of African American researchers in chemistry requires a long-term commitment.

Concept Check

Cultural diversity has both potentially positive and negative results for organizations. The degree to which it is positive or negative depends on several factors, including the amount of prior interaction with members from a particular group and the organizational culture. Essentially, organizational leaders and participants need to develop cultural diversity appropriately. Simply adding more diversity in the form of hiring people from underrepresented groups to the organization is not going to create benefits. People need to learn and be trained how to interact and work effectively with other people. Without appropriate training, increased diversity in and of itself will simply result in more problems for the organization—at least in the short term. In the long term, individual members might be able to learn through trial and error how to communicate effectively. The next section examines in more detail some of the system-wide factors associated with positive and negative diversity.

Intercultural Communication in the Workplace

In thinking about the system-wide factors of diversity, we need to consider various layers of organizations. We cannot simply consider just adding inputs, improving how we recruit new employees, or addressing cultural differences in communication behavior. Changing cultural diversity requires changing the system. To illustrate this point, intercultural communication in the workplace is discussed at four different layers: organizational culture, workgroup processes, managing people, and individuals' reaction to the organization.

Organizational Culture

Organizational culture is very similar to culture as defined earlier in this book; an organization has a culture in that it tends to socialize people to have certain values, norms, and communication patterns that are shared to varying degrees and which create a common identity. For-profit organizations spend a lot of resources creating and communicating a particular culture that organizational leaders think will help them compete in the marketplace. Non-profit organizations tend to develop a culture from the predominant interactions and personalities of the members and the mission of the organization. The organizational culture in regard to diversity is a critical component of whether an organization can be successful at recruiting and retaining a diverse workforce.

Certain types of organizations have a tendency to value and appreciate diversity because of the nature of the larger environment in which they operate. Some organizations operate only in a single country, and their focus on other cultures might simply relate to their exporting business or to adjusting to diversity within their own country. For example, Tillamook Cheese is a farmer-owned cooperative in Tillamook, Oregon. It sells cheese and other dairy products regionally and nationally. So, their focus is on marketing within the United States and employing a workforce from the region. In contrast, other organizations are global in nature and focus on the entire world. A range of organizations exists in the world from domestic to multinational, international, and global (Stohl, 2001). Table 8.2 summarizes the differences among these types of organizations as a result of the larger environment in which they operate. Because of the environmental context, multinational, international, and global organizations have to pay attention more to international cultures than do domestic organizations in order to survive and thrive in business. For example, Coca-Cola operates in 200 countries worldwide. It has to be concerned not only with employing people from all of the countries, but also to marketing to consumers in these countries.

Despite the influence of the larger environment, organizations can still have a wide range of acceptance and appreciation of diversity. A domestic company can strongly emphasize and include diversity while a global company can view other cultures as hurdles to overcome and not truly value them. In regard to cultural diversity, three types of organizations can be distinguished: monolithic, plural, and multicultural (Cox, 1991). The **monolithic organization** is predominantly composed of members from the majority group. If members of ethnic or cultural minorities are represented in the organization,

Table 8.2

TYPES OF ORGANIZATIONS

Orientations	Domestic	Multinational	International	Global
Predominant national orientation	Identification with one country and dominant culture	Identification with one country while doing business in several countries	Identification with two or more countries, each with distinct cultures	Identification with the global system; transcends national borders
Perceived importance of international orientation	None	Important	Extremely important	Dominant
Orientation toward other cultural units	Parochial. The dominant culture is the authority.	Polycentric. Authority is vested in local nationals holding key positions. Managed from the headquarters.	Regiocentric. Regional geographic basis for authority. Interdependence across regions.	Geocentric. Dispersed, interdependent networks, each with different, but integrated contributions.
Management models	Monocultural. Cultural differences are minimized; focus on assimilation.	Cultural compromise. Recognition and acceptance of cultural differences, but dominant culture is final authority.	Cultural synergy. Multiple cultures work together to build a third culture.	Cultural integration. Recognition of diverse cultures and business conditions; cultural adaptation and cultural integrity are key.

Adapted from Stohl (2001)

they are generally restricted to the lower levels of the hierarchy. The organizational culture of monolithic organizations has an unfavorable attitude toward diversity. Employees are expected to assimilate into the workplace, and the organization has little tolerance for differences in procedures and behaviors. As a result, prejudice and discrimination are commonplace. The **plural organization** has a population of employees that is representative of the larger society. However, most ethnic minorities are still located at the lower levels. Those employees from ethnic and cultural minority groups who have made it to the managerial ranks tend not to be informally integrated; that is, they do not have a lot of personal connections to people in power. The organizational culture has a

Box 8.4 Globalization: Brazilians in Japan

Japan is largely closed to immigration. By Japanese law, guest workers have to be of Japanese descent to be admitted into the country. These closed practices have had a negative effect as recently, Japan became the first industrial economy to suffer a decline in population. The population is getting older, and the younger generations are not having as many children to keep up with the retiring labor force.

Given the need to have guest workers be of Japanese descent, Japanese organizations recruited many Brazilians, whose ancestors emigrated to Brazil earlier in the 20th century. This interaction of Brazilians and Japanese has created some difficulties. In some ways, the two countries are alike in that both are collectivistic and have high power distance. However, Brazilian culture tends to be more emotionally expressive and animated than Japanese culture. Additionally, Japanese complain that the Brazilians do not want to assimilate or speak Japanese. For example, Oizumi Major Hiroshi

Hasegawa stated, "We want people to study Japanese and learn our rules before coming here. However, until the national government decides on an immigration system, it's going to be really tough." The Brazilians like Japan because of the high salaries and opportunities, but many dislike the culture and long for home. Carlos Watanabe, a guest worker, said, "I want to go back to Brazil every day, but I don't go because I don't have the money. Sometimes I think I should go home, sometimes stay here, sometimes just go to another country." Some have adjusted to Japanese culture and have assimilated.

Many other industrial nations are facing a rapidly aging labor force and will have to "import" workers from the younger nations of Latin America and Africa to maintain their economic development—a situation likely to create interesting and difficult culture clashes for the future.

Source: Coleman (2007)

neutral attitude toward diversity. Employees of the plural organization are expected to assimilate, but the environment offers some tolerance for deviations if the employees increase productivity. Prejudice and discrimination are still frequent, although there is some willingness to talk about and address problems. The **multicultural organization** has a representative population, and majority and minority members are distributed throughout the levels of the organization. Ethnic minority managers are integrated informally as well. Diversity is viewed as a strength for the multicultural organization, and employees are encouraged to behave in culturally appropriate ways. Prejudice and discrimination are rare, but, when they do happen, an openness to confront problems and find solutions exists. What type of organization do you work in (and go to school in)? Is there a lot of cultural diversity? When you look at your bosses (or teachers), do you see people who look like and are from different cultures? Are people open to diverse perspectives? What type of organization is described in Box 8.4? Box 8.5 discusses attitudes toward family leave and disability to provide a different take on openness to diversity.

Work Group Processes

Much work is organized in teams. No single individual can perform the multitude of tasks needed in most organizations. This is one reason why a division of labor

Box 8.5 Voices: Family Leave Policies and Disability Policies as Openness to Diversity

While most discussions about diversity focus on the inclusion of racial and ethnic diversity, gender and people with disabilities represent other cultural groups to be considered in the diversity discussion. The emphasis on gender diversity covers many topics, but also should include a focus on family leave policies. Family leave policies indicate the degree of flexibility for people with families (for example, caring for a small child or an elderly parent) and is a strong factor associated with the inclusion of women in higher levels of management. Federal law states that women and men who have or adopt a child can have up to 13 weeks of unpaid leave without consequences to their employment. Workplace leave policies can go beyond this basic coverage, however. Will the employer grant paid time off? Will the employer allow someone to work part-time or have a flexible schedule? Family leave is something that affects all families, particularly women. A company with a family friendly culture provides opportunities for those who are caring for family members to still contribute to the organization and advance their careers.

Similarly, an organization's diversity culture can be scrutinized for its inclusion of people with disabilities. The Americans with Disabilities Acts (ADA) prohibits the discrimination of people with disabilities in the workplace. However, as noted in Box 5.3 in Chapter 5, not all nations have laws protecting people with disabilities from discrimination. Additionally, not all organizations are inclusive of people with disabilities. Subtle practices can discourage people with disabilities in the workplace. For example, when speaking with someone who is deaf, it is important to talk to him and not to the translator.

A multicultural organization needs to consider all facets of diversity in the workplace. It is not enough just to consider ethnic or national culture, but gender, disability, age, and LGBT (lesbian, gay, bisexual, and transgendered) issues (among others) should be a focus of diversity as well.

exists—we divide the work, so we can give it to those who do it best. Thus, organizations put a great deal of emphasis on teamwork and on effective work group communication. However, working together as a team is not easy. Functional differences occur (for example, salespeople working with engineers), and cultural differences, communication concerns, and technology needs (such as with virtual teams) need to be considered. This section examines each of these factors briefly.

Often, we think of cultural diversity only in terms of the physical or historical characteristics of cultural groups. However, in work groups and organizations in general, the job training we receive and the type of job we have are critical aspects of diversity (Cox & Finley, 1995). In some situations, differences in job function and training are more important and difficult to deal with than ethnic or cultural differences. Each job function has its own set of norms and rules attached to that position, and these rules are well understood by those who perform that job. In contrast, those norms and rules might be quite "foreign" to someone with a different job. We might be more like someone from a different cultural background who is also a custodian than someone who is from the same cultural background but who is a corporate executive. For example, in a sales meeting, the salespeople are concerned about the client and the desire to promise an amazing product by a certain date—a goal that from their perspective is easily doable. However, the engineers point out the need to test the product adequately to ensure quality and safety, and thus they think that the sales deadline is unreasonable. Both of these perspectives are needed to create and sell a good product (not to mention all other types of functions such as human resources, administrative, public relations, and others). The key is to balance and integrate all of these perspectives. Additionally, diversity of thought (often called intellectual diversity) is important. To create an effective diversity climate, we need people who can describe culture (interpretive thinking), explain a culture's relationship to communication and other behavior (social science thinking), and critique historical cultural relations (critical theory thinking). As you might remember from Chapter 2, these three types of thinking represent the three predominant theoretical approaches in intercultural communication.

In addition to functional and intellectual diversity, we need to be aware of how cultural diversity affects work group communication and subsequently how that communication impacts outcomes. Oetzel's (2005) effective intercultural work group communication theory explores these relationships. This theory defines effective communication in terms of the types of outcomes a group seeks to achieve. Most research on cultural diversity emphasizes work outcomes over relational outcomes. However, two important, interrelated dimensions to work groups include a) a task dimension and b) a social or relational dimension (Bales, 1950). The task dimension refers to the productivity of the group, for example, the quality of the decision or the productivity of the group, while the relational dimension refers to the cohesiveness of the group members, for example, the quality of the relationships. Some individuals (particularly collectivists) emphasize the relational dimension over the task dimension while others (individualists) emphasize the opposite (Oetzel & Bolton-Oetzel, 1997). Thus, effective communication helps groups do good work, but also establish strong relationships. Such communication includes shared participation (everyone does their fair share and shares information), consensus decision-making (all agree with the decision-making process), cooperative conflict (finding win-win solutions), and respectful communication (demonstrating value for others). Most importantly, group members can be taught to employ effective communication, and organizations need to emphasize communication training to shape effective intercultural work groups. Such training can include how to solicit and encourage participation, how to manage conflicts in a cooperative manner (win-win), and how to be assertive with viewpoints without being aggressive.

Finally, given the nature of global organizations, work groups need to be skilled at communicating in virtual environments (see Box 8.6). Many organizations now put individuals in global teams where no one is co-located. Much of this work is coordinated and carried out through e-mail and other forms of computer-mediated communication (CMC), since time and differences limit face-to-face communication (FTF). Occasionally, a team will be able to meet in the same location to finalize its product. Most of the time, e-mail is great, as it is quick and efficient. However, conflict is more prevalent in CMC than in FTF situations. Virtual communication is less personal and lacks many nonverbal cues compared to FTF. Conflict often results from two factors. First, in CMC versus FTF, we have reduced understanding of others (Bordia, 1997; DeSanctis & Monge, 1999; Straus & McGrath, 1994). For example, how often have

Box 8.6 Globalization: Global Virtual Teams

To take advantage of skilled labor around the world, the ability to work around the clock, and advanced communication technologies, most large organizations use global virtual teams. The teams involve members of a global corporation or an international joint venture (where two or more companies work on a project together). The team might include Phola from South Africa, Hans from Germany, Anchalee from Thailand, and Yumiko from Japan. All of a sudden, an employee no longer needs to report to work; she simply rolls out of bed and goes to her computer and starts her day. It is a different work experience and one that some enjoy and others can't stand. Regardless, businesses love global virtual teams because of the competitive advantage they provide. Now, the challenge is simply to put the best suited people on the team regardless of where they live.

1. Do you have any experiences working virtually?
2. What do you think are the challenges and benefits of working virtually?
3. What communication strategies would you use in a virtual team?
4. Have you ever miscommunicated with someone from another culture when using virtual communication? What happened? Why do you think the problem occurred?

you received an e-mail message from someone and assumed he or she was mad at you? Or did you wish the person gave more information, so you could understand what was said? You may then respond based on this assumption and offend or confuse the other person. In FTF situations, we can ask for quick clarification and use nonverbal cues to interpret what is meant. Second, in CMC versus FTF, there is an increase of uninhibited/rude behavior (Bordia, 1997; Straus & McGrath, 1994). People communicating via CMC are distracted from the social context and thus are less concerned with what others think. We do not have the other person sitting in front of us, and so we are not as worried about how this person reacts. Both of these factors lead to decreased cohesion or relational effectiveness in CMC, and that means we have to work harder to work effectively. On the positive side, CMC results in increased critical contributions, which is a positive form of conflict for work groups; that is, we get more honest and constructive feedback about our ideas in CMC (Postmes & Lea, 2000).

Managing People

A third important approach is to understand how culture influences the management of people. Managers around the world employ different interaction styles with their employees. Ting-Toomey and Oetzel (2001) offer a model that includes two of the basic cultural value patterns introduced in Chapter 2: individualism-collectivism and power distance. The overlay of these two dimensions results in four predominant approaches to management: personal, status-achievement, benevolent, and communal. The personal approach consists of an individualistic and small power distance orientation; the status-achievement approach consists of an individualistic and large power distance orientation; the benevolent approach consists of a collectivistic and large power distance orientation; the communal approach consists of a collectivistic and small power distance orientation. Figure 8.3 displays this model. The personal and benevolent approaches are the two most common approaches observed around the world (Hofstede, 2001).

In the following section I offer examples of these approaches in national cultures. Please remember, however, that these examples are generalizations and do not mean that every person in every national culture uses this style; there certainly are differences in managerial styles in each national culture.

Managers using the **personal approach** tend to see themselves as independent and at the same level as others (Triandis, 1995); that is, they think of themselves as a unique person separate from others and as similar to other people in terms of status. Two values that pervade this approach are freedom (to be a unique individual) and equality. Countries that predominantly reflect the personal approach include Australia, Canada, the Northern European nations (Scandinavian and Germanic nations), Israel, the United States, and Great Britain. The United States and Great Britain also have tendencies reflective of the status-achievement approach, especially in business settings. Managers from small power distance and individualistic cultures are expected to have a personally developed style based on their own experiences, but also to treat everyone the same (Brislin, 1993; Smith, Dugan, Peterson, & Leung, 1998). Personal approach managers often use impartial rules and guidelines. These type of managers do not give preference to any employees and expect people to follow established rules. They do tolerate differences in individual styles for getting the job done.

The **status-achievement approach** reflects the desire for a status position, but with everyone having the opportunity to achieve such status. Individuals using the status-achievement approach tend to see themselves as independent and at a different level than others (Triandis, 1995). Two values that pervade this approach are freedom and earned inequality (for examples, money and status that comes from work

Figure 8.3
Cultural Approach to Managerial Styles

Source: Adapted from Ting-Toomey & Oetzel (2001)

Individualism

Personal		Status Achievement	
High Individualism		High Individualism	
Small Power Distance		Large Power Distance	
Personally Developed Style		Earned Inequality	
Impartial Rules		Maintenance of Status	
Toleration for Individual Differences			

Small Power — *Large Power*

Communal		Benevolent	
High Collectivism		High Collectivism	
Small Power Distance		Large Power Distance	
Holistic Decision Making		Obligation	
Connected to Others		High Context Communication	
Mutually Acceptable Decisions		Particularism	

Collectivism

achievements). Countries that predominantly reflect the status-achievement approach include the Latin European nations (for example, France and Italy) and the United States and Great Britain in business. The United States and Great Britain are classified as being between the personal and the status-achievement approach because they display characteristics of each. During personal interactions, managers are expected to communicate verbally in ways that reflect the same status. However, middle- and upper-class U.S. Americans and Britons want to "stick out" from others by, for example, driving expensive cars and having the corner office. They emphasize the position that one can earn through hard work and that status should be displayed. The status-achievement manager is concerned with maintaining and recognizing status in addition to developing a unique way of dealing with individuals. The status-achievement manager communicates differently with a co-worker (for example, another manager) than with an employee. Aggression is a hallmark of the status-achievement approach compared to the assertiveness of the personal approach.

Managers using the **benevolent approach** tend to see themselves as interdependent and at a different level than others (Triandis, 1995); that is, as a person with connections to others and as a member of a hierarchical network. Two values that pervade this approach are inequality and obligation to others. Countries that predominantly reflect the benevolent approach include most Latin and South American nations (for example, Mexico, Venezuela, Brazil, and Chile), most Asian nations (for example, India, Japan, China, and South Korea), Arabic nations (for example, Egypt, Saudi Arabia, and Jordan) and most African nations (for example, Nigeria, and Uganda). Managers from a large power distance and collectivistic culture are expected to use a style that is nurturing and demonstrates concern for relationships. Employees who desire a benevolent leader want a manager to treat them like a member of the family (Brislin, 1993). In contrast to the personal manager, the benevolent manager practices particularism by treating members of ingroups better than members of outgroups (Hofstede, 2001). Further, messages are not directly expressed; rather they are displayed through subtle nonverbal cues in a high-context manner. For example, a benevolent manager will spend more time with favored workers and show a lot of interest in their family and general well being. He might also offer advice for these workers on personal matters. Both superiors and subordinates need to be able to effectively read into another's behavior in order to interpret messages accurately. However, subordinates have more responsibility than do superiors for accurately interpreting messages. Finally, subordinates expect managers to direct the work of the employee rather than "be open" to employees' suggestions. The authority of a manager is respected because he or she is believed to have knowledge in a variety of situations.

Managers using the **communal approach** tend to see themselves as interdependent and at the same level as others (Triandis, 1995); that is, as a person closely connected to others and as similar to other people in terms of status. The values that encompass this approach are close connection to others and equality. Costa Rica is the only country found to fit this approach (Hofstede, 2001), but this approaches fits closely with feminist principles. Feminist principles include integrative, holistic decision-making, connectedness of individuals to their emotions, and cooperative

Differences in communication styles can create difficulties between managers and subordinates. What type of manager do you prefer? Is this type of manager prevalent in your culture?

talk and behavior (Buzzanell, 1994). Managers and employees are considered equals who are expected to be open and expressive and work together to develop mutually acceptable decisions. The manager has authority, but only uses that authority to achieve the organization's goals. Those goals include those of the employees and the organization collectively. A communal manager is unlikely to accept special perks for the job and instead suggest that rewards be shared with the entire team.

An example will help to illustrate the differences among these four approaches. Two employees are having a conflict about their responsibilities on a project. They are unable to resolve the conflict. From the personal approach, the employees need to bring the conflict to the attention of the boss. The manager likely confronts the issue directly and brings the disputants together. The manager encourages the disputants to "open up" and share individual feelings and perceptions of the issues. Generally, the manager plays the role of mediator and tries to be objective and encourage the disputants to find their own solution.

Using the status-achievement approach, the manager likely confronts the issue directly and expects the individuals to express their opinions and ideas clearly. Rather than objectively weighing the facts, the manager may look to see which employee has more status from the perspectives of longer tenure or more responsibilities and rule in favor of this employee or place more weight on what this person says. Alternatively, the manager may simply resolve the problem for the employees rather than encouraging them to develop a solution on their own. The effectiveness of the status-achievement approach lies in the ability of the manager to deal with issues in an open and decisive manner.

The benevolent manager does not bring the disputants together to "air out" the issues. Instead, she talks with each of the disputants separately, being careful not to directly challenge the face of either party. The goal is to smooth over the issues to preserve relational harmony. The manager does not encourage direct discussion of the issue and does not ask the parties to solve the problem. Rather, the manager is supposed to make a decision on how to resolve the issues. The manager takes into consideration relational issues as well as the objective facts of the case and makes a decision that is in the best interest of relational harmony.

Finally, using the communal approach, the manager could schedule an open meeting for all concerned parties including other co-workers who may be affected by the conflict. The purpose of the meeting is to air out feelings and to understand how each party's communicative behavior affects the others. Finding a solution is secondary to the issue of understanding how everyone is feeling; the solution often comes naturally from this discussion. The communal approach also involves a great deal of emphasis on trying to find the root of the problem so that the key issues can be addressed. The manager is a subjective participant who also expresses his feelings and viewpoints. A solution is sought that maintains the relationships and addresses core issues.

Individuals' Reactions to the Organization

One part of the system is the individual employees. Organizations socialize new employees to the organization's rules, culture, and ways of performing; that is, organizational leaders teach us how to be good members of the organization. How individuals react to this socialization and others in the organization is an important component of whether cultural diversity will be fostered. Orbe (1998) developed a co-culture theory to understand the ways in which people who are traditionally marginalized in mainstream society and organizations communicate with others (Orbe, 1998, Orbe & Spellers, 2005). Orbe prefers the term *co-culture* rather than ethnic minority because he believes that co-culture better equates different cultural and ethnic groups while minority implies a less than or subsuming role.

Co-cultural theory explains that people have nine different communicative reactions and choices to make based on two factors: preferred outcomes and communication approach. The preferred outcome is based on three choices: assimilation, accommodation, and separation. These choices are similar to those presented in Chapter 5 regarding choices toward home and host cultures. Assimilation attempts to eliminate cultural differences in order to fit in with the dominant society or organization. Accommodation attempts to retain some cultural uniqueness and to transform the existing dominant structures so that there is less hierarchy. Separation rejects dominant society and organizations, and individuals attempt to join similar co-cultural group members to form organizations that are reflective of their own values and norms. The communication approach consists of being nonassertive, assertive, or aggressive. Nonassertion includes inhibited behavior that is nonconfrontational and puts others' needs above one's own. Assertion includes expressive behavior that takes into account one's own needs as well as those of the other. Aggression puts one's needs above others and includes behaviors that hurt and belittle the other. These two factors—preferred outcomes and communication approach—combine into nine communication orientations, displayed in Table 8.3.

The choice of which communication orientation to select is also based on four contextual factors: field of experience; abilities to use nonassertive, assertive, and aggressive tactics; situational context; and costs and rewards of a particular behavior. The field of experience is an individual's lived experience and is continually evolving. For example, if you have lived a life filled with oppression and discrimination, you will likely be unwilling to assimilate into a dominant organization. One's abilities to use nonassertive, assertive, and aggressive tactics also influence the communication orientation. For example, if you are not comfortable using personal attacks, you likely will not choose aggressive tactics even if they might be most effective in a given situation. The situational context is the third factor and is focused on the particular goals, individuals, and setting. For example, if you are interacting with an aggressive co-worker who does not listen to others unless you yell at him or her, you might choose an aggressive line. Finally, individuals need to consider the costs and rewards of a particular behavior. For example, if you know that criticizing your boss about diversity practices in your team will be met with an open attitude and the possibility of change, you likely will choose an assertive accommodating orientation. Orbe's theory does not advocate any one orientation as better than others, but does maintain that an

Table 8.3

CO-CULTURAL COMMUNICATION ORIENTATIONS (ORBE, 1998)

| Communication Approach | Preferred Outcome | | |
	Separation	Accommodation	Assimilation
Nonassertive	Nonassertive Separation Orientation	Nonassertive Accommodation Orientation	Nonassertive Assimilation Orientation
Assertive	Assertive Separation Orientation	Assertive Accommodation Orientation	Assertive Assimilation Orientation
Aggressive	Aggressive Separation Orientation	Aggressive Accommodation Orientation	Aggressive Assimilation Orientation

Reproduced with permission of Sage Publications Inc. Journal via Copyright Clearance Center

individual must do an evaluation of the best orientation while considering all four contextual factors. What orientation do you think is best? How might this change depending on the four contextual factors?

Concept Check

Cultural diversity and intercultural communication are relevant at many layers in an organization. One of the most critical aspects is the organizational culture toward diversity. Organizational culture can focus on the degree of international or intercultural focus in the larger environment ranging from domestic to global, but also the climate within an organization, which Cox and Blake (1991) classify as monolithic, plural, or multicultural. At the work group layer, work specialization, cultural diversity, and electronic media influence intercultural communication in various ways. At the managerial layer, we can expect managers and employees to have various preferences for management styles. Recognizing differences in these styles and being aware of their origin can help both managers and employees adapt their behaviors to others and thus communicate more effectively. At the individual reaction layer, co-cultural theory tries to understand why individuals communicate as they do in society and organizations. The theory specifically focuses on members from traditionally underrepresented or marginalized groups, but also can apply to people from dominant or mainstream cultures. Co-cultural theory simply emphasizes the historical power differences between different co-cultural groups—important to consider when focusing on how to enhance cultural diversity in an organization. If prior relations and organizational practices have created an oppressive or unwelcoming organizational environment, we can expect a limited number of people from underrepresented groups being included. The majority group members likely choose an assimilation attitude that discourages diversity, and the minority group members likely choose to keep separate from that particular organization.

Layers of Intercultural Communication in the Workplace

The organizational context has multiple layers within its inner workings, as the previous section displayed. In addition to the inner layers, the larger environment has layers that the organization operates in and affects (and is affected by). Consistent with prior chapters, we consider the bottom-up effects and the effect of the organization on individual behavior as well as on society's impact on the workplace.

Bottom-Up Effects

Research examining the impact of the workplace on society as a whole is limited. However, the workplace does have a significant impact on society in that work is a prominent fixture of society. In a market economy, those organizations that innovate and are successful get copied. These successful organizations are seen as benchmarks for others to compare with and try to emulate. *Fortune* magazine has an annual list of the "50 best companies for Asian, Blacks, and Hispanics" (notice the absence of American Indians in this article, which speaks to the invisibility of this group in corporate America). These companies receive a public relations boost from this survey, but they also demonstrate to societal institutions and governmental agencies potential ways to embrace diversity and be successful. However, while much discussion exists about the influence of such performance and lists, the extent to which this performance impacts other companies and society in general is not well known.

Top-Down Effects: The Workplace's Impact on Attitudes and Individual Behavior

Organizational culture has a strong impact on individual behavior (Cox, 2001). If the prevailing culture encourages valuing and embracing diversity, the vast majority of individuals will perpetuate this attitude. In contrast, if the organization discourages diversity, individuals tend to do the same. These effects are generally subtle and not overt. For example, institutional racism occurs when the system and practices become so imbedded in organizational culture that they are accepted and treated as unquestioned assumptions. These systems and practices are usually presented with comments such as "that's how we do things around here" and "that is our tradition." Tradition and history are important, but they also must be questioned and understood. For example, if the tradition is only to promote engineers to be managers, then we are excluding people with different work specializations and possibly even members of underrepresented groups (because, at this time, fewer people from underrepresented groups are in the engineering ranks than in other specializations). This exclusion may not be pertinent to the work skills needed to be a manager, which involves administration and leadership skills that are not limited to engineers. However, this attitude is based on the U.S. view of management. In some national cultures, management is based in being a technical expert in the product area and being a leader. Thus, a manager in these cultures might need to come from the engineering ranks. This comparison illustrates the importance of questioning traditions, but not simply assuming something is wrong with a practice either.

Research also helps to illustrate the impact of organizational culture on how issues associated with cultural diversity are treated. Specifically, Meares, Oetzel, Torres, Derkacs, and Ginossar (2004) interviewed nearly 70 employees from various levels at a large culturally diverse research organization about their experiences of mistreatment. Mistreatment is the verbal and systematic abuse of employees on the basis of cultural diversity (also called bullying). The researchers found that some employees (who tended to be White Americans and people in the upper portions of the hierarchy) felt that, if they were mistreated, they would have a voice and be able to redress the abuse. On the other hand, other employees, who tended to be women, ethnic minorities, or people in the lower portions of the hierarchy, felt muted by the organization; that is, the organizational culture encouraged their silence, and the employees felt that they would not be able to address their abuse in any reasonable way. The reasons they were muted was because their stories were repeatedly silenced over time (for example, bosses did not believe them) or through ambiguous policies that did not allow for redress. In both types of muting, individual behavior is being shaped by an organizational culture that encourages certain employees to express a voice while discouraging others from the same voice.

Top-Down Effects: Society's Impact on the Workplace

Societal and cultural impacts consist of two key factors. First, laws within a society provide a framework for understanding behaviors that are permitted in the workplace. Workplace laws in the United States are provided as an example. Second, a key aspect is the globalization of work as represented by outsourcing and offshoring and some of the impacts on intercultural communication in the workplace.

The workplace is probably the most regulated setting when it comes to prohibiting discrimination. The U.S. Equal Employment Opportunity Commission (EEOC) specifies the following laws (U.S. EEOC, 2007):

- Title VII of the Civil Rights Act of 1964, which prohibits employment discrimination based on race, color, religion, sex, or national origin;
- Equal Pay Act of 1963, which protects men and women who perform substantially equal work in the same establishment from sex-based wage discrimination;
- Age Discrimination in Employment Act of 1967, which protects individuals who are 40 years of age or older;
- Title I and Title V of the Americans with Disabilities Act of 1990, which prohibits employment discrimination against qualified individuals with disabilities in the private sector and in state and local governments;
- Civil Rights Act of 1991, which provides monetary damages in cases of intentional employment discrimination.

The EEOC enforces each of these laws. These laws, and the strict set of regulations created by the EEOC, help to regulate fair employment for all cultural groups in the United States.

Of these laws, Title VII and the accompanying affirmative action policies described in Chapter 7 are probably the best known and most controversial. Almost everyone feels that all people should be protected from discrimination, but the use of affirmative action in hiring is debated. In several countries (such as the United Kingdom and Slovakia), affirmative action (or positive discrimination) is illegal. Most countries, including Brunei, China, Germany, India, Indonesia, Norway, South African, Turkey, and the United States, have some hiring preferences in the private and government sectors (Sowell, 2005). In the United States, affirmative action was established because many companies had "facially discriminatory" policies (Stanford Encyclopedia of Philosophy, 2007). For example, such policies might have forbidden African Americans from being hired in a managerial position. In response to Title VII, companies began instigating "facially neutral" policies. For example, a company might suggest that workers give up their seniority before becoming a manager. Thus, a person of color who worked for 25 years in a company would have to give up the benefits of that seniority to become a manager and realistically no one would give up the benefits of seniority to be promoted—the costs would be too high. The courts struck down such "facially neutral" policies and required organizations to comply with the nondiscriminatory aspects of the Civil Rights Acts. As a result, most organizations monitored their practices and policies to create a fair employment environment; in certain cases, the Courts have required organizations to have quotas to address past exclusionary policies. Thus, for most organizations, affirmative action simply means making sure that organizational practices are in line with non-discrimination laws rather than allowing preferential treatment for particular groups.

At a broader level, the global marketplace has created opportunities for organizations to utilize offshoring and outsourcing. **Offshoring** occurs when an organization relocates one or more business functions from its home base to another country (Padmanabhan, 2007). Offshoring can occur when an organization relocates within its own company or to another company. **Outsourcing** occurs when an organization contracts with another organization to perform a job function (Padmanabhan, 2007). Outsourcing can be within the same country or another country. For example, a U.S. company may contract with a company in India to handle its technical support team; this is an example of both outsourcing and offshoring. When a U.S. customer calls the U.S. company's helpline, she is connected with "Sally," who happens to speak British English and with an Indian accent. A primary reason for outsourcing and offshoring is cost saving, particularly related to labor costs, but technical skills may also be more prevalent and available in nations such as China and India (Wareham, Mahnke, Peters, & Bjorn-Andersen, 2007).

Such trends have significant impacts on intercultural communication in the workplace. One such impact is simply communication difficulty resulting from cultural differences present in the primary and offshoring/outsourcing organizations. Wareham et al. (2007) described difficulties between Danish (low power distance) and Indian (high power distance) cultures in a case study analysis they completed. Providing an example of a Danish company offshoring and outsourcing technical function to an Indian company, they explain that Scandinavian bosses expect direct communication and for subordinates to disagree directly with them. In contrast, Indian subordinates do not directly say no to a superior even when they disagree. In some cases, "yes" simply means I acknowledge what you are saying even if I don't agree. Additionally, lower-level Scandinavian managers might have difficulty gaining adherence from Indian subordinates since they are not high enough in the hierarchy. In this case study, the researchers found that 10% of all project expenditures were allocated to cultural liaisons to help manage the conflict that occurred. Despite these difficulties, the project was a success and has continued.

Another possible impact is the development of hybrid management styles or a blending of home culture management style and that of the employing organization. Shimoni and Bergmann (2006) interviewed 24 senior level managers from Israel, Thailand, and Mexico who worked in one of two urban hi-tech global companies employing at least 80,000 (one from Sweden and one from the United States). The authors had the managers tell their stories about their work experiences and found that managers tend to use both the values and practices of the global corporation and their local culture. For example, an Israeli manager working for the Swedish company said that he accepted the importance of planning, but that he also sees the need to improvise, which is critical in his culture. A Mexican manager working for the Swedish company sees the benefit of using global and local values sequentially. When possible, she tries to build consensus, which is reflected in the Swedish company's desire for equality. If that does not work, she relies on the hierarchy that is built into her local culture to make a decision. Similarly, a Thai manager working for the U.S. company sees the value in emphasizing teamwork and communicating in a collaborative way. However, he also recognizes the need to be a leader, particularly at crisis times, and to be authoritarian. He stated, "I still believe, even [with] the team work, we must have a leader" (p. 84). These examples illustrate that local managers learn from their global corporations, but also blend their local experiences.

Challenges and Skills

Creating an inclusive organizational culture that values and embraces cultural diversity of all forms (global, national, ethnic, gender, and so on) involves many challenges. Requiring people to participate in sensitivity training often creates a backlash as some individuals (particularly members of the dominant group) feel that they are being unfairly targeted for past ills. In addition, a lot of intercultural communication sensitivity training uses stereotypes that can exacerbate and perpetuate problems. Both of these efforts are often instituted by well-meaning organizational leaders who want to create a vision of inclusion, but are not completely sure about how to do so. The predominant advice in the literature is that organizations need to manage diversity effectively. However, the metaphor of diversity "management" is potentially harmful to employees if people from diverse backgrounds are treated like commodities (Kirby & Harter, 2001). That is, if you manage people, you control them and can easily replace them if they do not work out. Further, controlling people results in a lack of agency or the feeling of being able to take action. In contrast, a better approach to managing diversity (or forcing diversity) is an integration-and-learning

---

Box 8.7 What Went Right: Building *Puentes* in Wisconsin

An example of the integration-and-learning perspective can be seen in a rural Wisconsin dairy farm. The town of Waumandee, WI (population 14,000; 25,000 cows) found itself in need of a workforce. Many native Wisconsinites shun dairy farm work, and certain farmers began hiring immigrants from Mexico because they worked long hours and many days in a row. Seeing this as a permanent need, an innovative program called *Puentes* (bridges) was created by a small, community-based business (http://www. hispanic-services.org/g5-bin/client.cgi?G5button=7346). The program teaches U.S. farmers Spanish and Mexican workers English and teaches both groups about their respective cultures. The farmers also visit the workers' homes in Mexico to better understand their needs and to improve employee relations. The program works because the cultural adaptations are two-sided—both Mexicans and U.S. Americans are learning about each other's culture and, from this mutual knowledge and understanding, making strides to work together for mutual benefit.

Source: Pabst (2006)

perspective (Ely & Thomas, 2001). The integration-and-learning perspective is characterized by a collective valuing of the cultural backgrounds of employees and a framing of their experiences and perspectives as valuable to the organization (see Box 8.7 on p. 235). It places emphasis on creating vision together rather than excluding certain people or forcing diversity. The justification is on improved business and social relations, not on avoiding lawsuits or problems, so it offers a positive focus of diversity, not a negative one. This approach seems to help avoid employee backlash from those who feel they are being unfairly targeted. Additionally, such an approach can help a global corporation and a local culture blend the best aspects of both cultures.

In addition to having a positive attitude toward diversity, organizations need to have a system for creating, implementing, and evaluating the vision of diversity. The system needs to describe a process of how to address diversity issues, but also ensure that the process is not a one-shot approach. One such sustainable model is called the change model for work on diversity, which is displayed in Figure 8.4 (Cox, 2001).

Figure 8.4
**Change Model
for Work on
Diversity**
Source: Adapted
from Cox, 2001

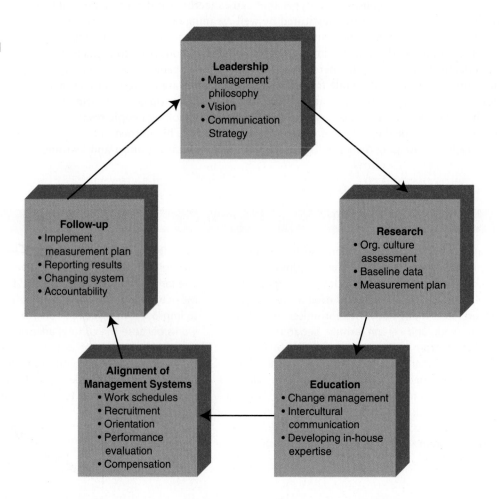

The model emphasizes five key components: leadership, research, education, alignment of management systems, and follow-up. Leadership focuses on developing individuals who are champions of diversity. These leaders have a vision of what to implement and how to communicate that to the organization. Ideally, leadership includes some individuals in upper management, but also representatives from all facets of the organization. Once a vision has been created, we have to measure where the organization is currently; that is, the research should include a comprehensive assessment of the current diversity culture and have a plan for what the organization is striving toward. Once it has the baseline data, the organization is ready to implement training of all employees.

In essence, we want to educate the workforce to embrace and value diversity, not simply tolerate it. Along with education, we have to review the management systems to determine if they are supportive of a diverse workforce. Are flexible work structures in place? Do performance appraisal and orientation processes encourage everyone to advance in the company? Finally, we need to follow up the changes in the management system and education to measure whether the changes were successful. If so, we want to institutionalize the changes. If not, we need to reconsider and rethink additional changes. As Figure 8.4 illustrates, this is a continual process that organizations need to devote time and resources to.

SUMMARY

Returning to the opening story of this chapter: ABC Electronics sounds like a company with good intentions and a willingness to invest in cultural diversity. However, the executive team made several classic missteps in diagnosing the diversity issues. First, it assumed that getting more diverse employees would result in a culturally diverse workforce. Not only do we need to recruit diverse employees, we need to create a culture in which they can thrive. Second, ABC "forced" current employees to attend sensitivity workshops. Forcing diversity "down employees' throats" creates resentment and backlash. A better approach is the integrating-and-learning perspective. Finally, ABC did not spend any of its money and effort on analyzing the organizational culture. It had the leadership, but did not consider research, education, and aligning management systems with diversity goals. Without this comprehensive effort, ABC is likely wasting their time. However, with a little change in focus, ABC's commitment can yield a strong return.

- **Workplace as a unique setting:** The workplace consists of many organizations that are composed of collectives with coordinated goals, structure, and division of labor. These organizations, in turn, operate in a larger organizational context; in this sense, organizations are systems within larger systems. The characteristics of these systems place an emphasis on understanding intercultural communication at the level of individuals, relationships, groups, and organizational culture.
- **Benefits, challenges, and difficulty analyzing problems:** Most organizations want to enhance their cultural diversity as diversity has many benefits, including enhanced

problem solving, creativity, flexibility, and marketing. On the other hand, potential problems with losses to process and productivity can occur if organizations do not handle diversity well. Unfortunately, most organizations do not analyze the issues associated with diversity well and forget to examine and focus on organizational culture.

■ **Four layers of intercultural communication in the workplace:** At the organizational culture layer, we can examine the degree of international focus ranging from domestic to global. In addition, organizations still have an internal focus to their organization ranging from monolithic to multicultural. At the work group layer, work specialization, cultural diversity, and electronic media are three factors that influence group communication. At the managerial layer, we consider different preferences for managerial style based on cultural values, including the personal, status-achievement, benevolent, and communal approaches. At the individual layer, individual reactions to the organization's approach to diversity are critical for creating an inclusive environment.

■ **Bottom-up and top-down effects:** Bottom-up effects are seen by leading organizations such as the "Fortune 50 best companies for Asians, Blacks, and Hispanics." These organizations provide leadership to other organizations and models for society to emulate. Top-down effects consider the societal layer and the ways in which employment laws have shaped attitudes and organizational policies toward diversity—particularly in protecting individuals against discriminatory practices. Additionally, we can consider how organizational culture shapes individual attitudes and behaviors. An inclusive organizational culture encourages people to be inclusive in other facets of their social and personal lives.

■ **Approach to embracing cultural diversity:** An integrating and learning perspective is key for implementing an inclusive organization culture. The integration-and-learning perspective is characterized by a collective valuing of the cultural backgrounds of employees and a framing of their experiences and perspectives as valuable to the organization. It places emphasis on creating vision together rather than excluding certain people or forcing diversity. The change model displayed in Figure 8.4 provides one approach for achieving such a vision. It focuses on leadership, research, education, alignment of management systems, and follow-up.

REVIEW QUESTIONS

1. Describe and provide an example of the characteristics of organizations that makes the workplace a unique context for studying diversity.
2. What are three benefits of diversity? What is the potential barrier of diversity?
3. Why are most organizations unable to address their diversity problems?
4. What is organizational culture, and why is it important for cultural diversity?
5. Describe how organizations vary from domestic to global.
6. What three characteristics influence work group communication?
7. Provide an example to illustrate the different preferences in managerial style.

8. Compare/contrast majority and minority members' responses to organizational diversity using co-cultural theory.

9. How has the legal system in the United States influenced organizational practices toward diversity?

10. In what ways has globalization influenced intercultural communication in the workplace?

11. You are charged with creating an organizational vision for valuing and embracing diversity. What steps would you take? Do you think the change model in Figure 8.4 has value?

EXERCISES

1. Visit the Wikipedia discussion on affirmative action: http://en.wikipedia.org/wiki/ Affirmative_action. Review the discussion on affirmative action related to the article to view different opinions about both the article specifically and affirmative action in general. How do you sort fact from fiction? How does a "Wiki" Web site impact opinions? A "Wiki" source is one that individuals can edit and change freely and thus the accuracy of information is in question.

2. Review cases that have violated EEOC laws at a Web site such as LawMemo: http://www.lawmemo.com/eeoc/. What are common factors about these cases? Do you think most organizations follow EEOC laws? Explain your answer.

3. Visit the Web site of one of the Fortune 500 firms (Google "Fortune 500 firms"). Would you want to work there? Why or why not? Do you feel it has a culturally inclusive organizational culture?

4. Research some of the best companies for diversity (simply Google "Best Companies for Diversity"). What makes these organizations strong for diversity? Would you want to work for such a company?

CHAPTER 9

Health Care Contexts

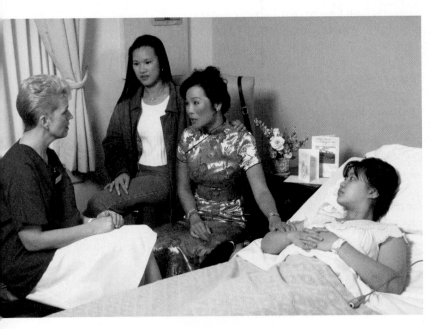

Cultural differences between patient and providers can result in negative health encounters. Has this ever happened to you? What can we do to improve the quality of intercultural health interactions?

CHAPTER OUTLINE

I. Introduction

II. Health Disparities

III. Factors Related to Health Disparities
    a. Socioeconomic Status
    b. Health Care System Problems
    c. Cultural Health Beliefs and Behaviors
    d. Service Utilization Obstacles
    e. Culturally Competent Communication
    f. Concept Check

IV. Layers of Health Care Contexts
    a. Bottom-Up
    b. Top-Down: Influence of Health Care Contexts on Individuals
    c. Top-Down: Influence of Society on Health Care Contexts
    d. Challenges and Skills

V. Summary

VI. Review Questions

VII. Exercises

CHAPTER OBJECTIVES

After reading this chapter, students should be able to

■ define the following concepts: health care contexts, health communication, public health communication, and health.

■ explain what health disparities are and provide examples at a global and national level.

- describe five factors that influence health disparities and explain why they have this impact.

- explain the role of intercultural communication in explaining health disparities.

- distinguish between cultural competence and cultural sensitivity.

- provide examples of cultural competence, cultural sensitivity, and media advocacy.

- discuss the bottom-up and top-down effects of intercultural communication in health care contexts.

Introduction

Siv, a Laotian refugee living in the United States, visited Dr. Jones, a primary care physician at a clinic in Minnesota. Dr. Jones has practiced medicine for 20 years and is relatively familiar with Laotian patients. He has learned to make small talk with his patients and generally is well liked by those in the community. Siv came in complaining of chest pains. Dr. Jones is not fluent in Lao, and his clinic does not have adequate translators. Fortunately, Siv's 16-year-old son Sean came in with his father and translated for him and Dr. Jones. Dr. Jones diagnosed Siv with hypertension and prescribed pills; he also asked to see Siv eight weeks later.

At the follow-up, Sean again came and translated. Siv continued to complain of chest pains, which surprised Dr. Jones because the pills should have shown some effect by that time. Dr. Jones asked Siv, "Have you been taking all of the pills as I prescribed?" Siv said that he had. Dr. Jones repeated the question because he suspected Siv was not taking the pills. Dr. Jones knew that some traditional Laotians tended not to take the medicine because they attributed chest pains to evil spirits and felt medicine was worthless. He asked again, "Did you take a pill every day as I suggested? "Yes," Siv replied. Dr. Jones prescribed more medicine and encouraged him to visit in another four weeks.

Siv came back and continued to complain of chest pains. Dr. Jones was perplexed and sent Siv to see a specialist. Siv decided not to go to the specialist. Some time later, Dr. Jones saw Sean as a patient and asked about his father. Sean said that his dad was complaining of chest pains still, but was not taking the medicine Dr. Jones prescribed. He was going to see a traditional healer instead.

> Question: What intercultural communication concepts can help to explain why this patient-provider exchange was not successful?

This interaction is one example of what can happen when patients from one cultural background see a health care provider from another cultural background. Health care interactions are rife with misunderstandings—even with well meaning providers. In some cases, cultural differences can result in barriers when providers are insensitive or feel that patients should adjust completely to the provider.

The patient-provider interaction is one type of communication exchange that takes place in health care contexts. **Health care contexts** refer to the various situations in which the health of individuals and the population of a community are the focus. In general, two types of contexts exist: clinical and public health. Clinical contexts are locations where patients receive care (usually treatment) from some provider, such as at the doctor's office, hospital, health clinic, or school-based health center, or in a traditional healing ceremony. **Public health** includes efforts toward assuring conditions in which people can be healthy (Institute of Medicine, 1988). Public health differs from clinical medicine in three ways: a) public health focuses on prevention rather than treatment; b) public health measures health outcomes in terms of communities and not individuals; and c) public health involves partnering with the public (Kar, Alcalay, & Alex, 2001). Thus, in a clinical context, you as the patient are the focus and the best outcome is whether you "get better" after visiting. In contrast, public health considers how large groups of people are faring and there is greater emphasis on prevention. Public health is often what we read about in newspapers when we hear, for example, that obesity rates in children are rising.

Health communication is the exchange of symbolic messages related to personal and public health. Health communication includes patient-provider interactions that take place in clinical settings. Health communication also includes organizational aspects. For example, we expect that our health care provider will communicate effectively with those running diagnostic tests (such as blood work) and the specialist or hospital that we might be referred to. In this manner, as noted in Chapter 8, organizational health communication focuses on the coordination of different health care functions in the clinical context. Finally, health communication also focuses on public or mass communication that emphasizes overall public health. Public health communication includes such activities as a public service announcement on the radio or television to stop smoking or a commercial or flier advocating a smoking ban in restaurants.

Let's consider an example of annual flu shots to illustrate the various aspects of health communication. At the patient-provider level, we might talk to our provider about whether we should get a shot and if it will have any side effects. Our provider will talk to us about allergies (if you are allergic to eggs, for example, the basic flu shot is problematic). At the organizational level, the office manager needs to communicate with the public health office and with companies supplying the flu vaccine to ensure that the office has ample supplies. The manager will likely remind providers about who the priority patients are (such as the elderly), especially if the amount of vaccines is limited. The office staff schedules the appointments with patients and bills the insurance companies accordingly. The doctor and nurse talk to ensure that the shot is given, and the patient waits the appropriate amount of time after receiving the shot. Finally, public health agencies will provide news releases to media organizations to announce the availability of the vaccine and whether there will be shortages. These agencies will also encourage the vulnerable (young children, elderly, parents with small children) to get a vaccine. The agencies may release information in multiple languages and provide public service announcements in various media to encourage obtaining the vaccine. This simple health issue—providing annual flu shots—provides examples of the many types of health communication that take place at the patient-provider, organizational, and public layers of health.

When we consider intercultural communication in health care contexts, we are often concerned with the ways that communication promotes and inhibits positive individual and public health. **Health** is a complete state of physical, mental, and social well being, not simply the absence of disease (WHO, 1978). Much of the research on intercultural health communication focuses on health disparities and the ways that communication contributes to these disparities. This chapter defines health disparities and provides appropriate examples of them. Then, it describes intercultural communication factors that contribute to health disparities. These factors include both culturally competent and culturally sensitive communication. Finally, this chapter outlines the layers of health care contexts that emphasize both the challenges and skills required for culturally competent health communication.

Health Disparities

Health disparities are inequalities in health outcomes for different cultural groups (Williams, 2001). A health disparity exists when one cultural group has a health outcome that is worse than that of another cultural group (see Box 9.1). It does not mean that every individual in one cultural group experiences the health problem or that everybody in one culture has a better health outcome than everyone else in a different group. Health disparities focus on general trends in cultural groups, not on individuals. Therefore, health disparities are often presented in statistics about groups. Several types of health disparities are offered in this section, including life expectancy rates across nations, mortality rates by ethnic groups in the United States, patterns of mental health by ethnic groups in the United States, and patterns of breast cancer.

Nations are often compared in terms of such health outcomes as life expectancy, infant mortality, and heart disease. In general, developing nations have worse health statistics than developed nations. Developing versus developed is often defined as the

Box 9.1 Talking about Ethics: Health as a Right or Privilege

A critical ethical issue surrounding health disparities relates to the underlying philosophy and economics of health care. Generally, this discussion focuses on whether health care is a right or a privilege. If health care is a right, we should have coverage for everyone and equal health outcomes for all groups. If health care is a privilege, we have to earn good health and take responsibility for our own health. This underlying philosophy of health care relates to the economics of health care. That is, from a market perspective, we can expect some people to have less health care coverage and worse health outcomes, and thus health disparities might be normal and expected. Correspondingly, competition encourages people to address their own health, and leads many to the belief that individuals should be responsible for their own health. This market competition perspective relates to the philosophy of health care as a privilege.

1. Which position do you take: Is health care a right or a privilege? Are health disparities normal and expected?
2. Does society have a responsibility to care for certain groups such as the elderly? The working poor? The unemployed? Those with mental illness? Those with severe illness?
3. Have you (or someone else you know) ever not dealt with a health issue and ended up having to suffer for it? Did it impact others around you (such as your family members or society in general)?
4. Does your religious, cultural, or moral upbringing have any effect on how you believe society should care for the sick?

degree of industrialization and extent of economic growth. Developed nations have more economic resources to spend on health care and prevention efforts such as sanitation and vaccinations. Developing nations have a greater burden of acute diseases whereas developed nations have a greater burden of chronic diseases. Acute diseases are those that happen quickly, such as infectious diseases (for example, hepatitis or malaria), and are related to unsanitary conditions and a lack of vaccinations. Chronic diseases are those that develop over time and include heart disease, diabetes, and cancer. These diseases often relate to lifestyle choices such as diet and exercise (as well as genetic factors); developed nations have more economic resources to spend on food and entertainment (for example, watching TV instead of exercising).

The results of chronic and acute diseases impact life expectancy: Acute diseases result in shorter life expectancy than chronic diseases. Table 9.1 displays the life expectancy at birth of selected nations included by rank in the world and income

Table 9.1

LIFE EXPECTANCY AT BIRTH AND INCOME LEVEL FOR SELECT NATIONS

World Rank	Country	Life expectancy at birth (years)	Income Level
1	Andorra	83.51	H
4	Singapore	81.71	H
5	Hong Kong	81.59	H
6	Japan	81.25	H
7	Sweden	80.51	H
8	Switzerland	80.51	H
9	Australia	80.50	H
12	Canada	80.22	H
16	France	79.73	H
19	Spain	79.65	H
20	Norway	79.54	H
21	Israel	79.46	H
34	Belgium	78.77	H
37	United Kingdom	78.54	H
38	Finland	78.50	H
40	Jordan	78.40	M
41	Puerto Rico	78.40	M
46	United States	77.85	H
53	Cuba	77.41	M
55	Kuwait	77.20	H
56	Korea, South	77.04	H
57	Costa Rica	77.02	M

(continued)

Table 9.1 (continued)

World Rank	Country	Life expectancy at birth (years)	Income Level
58	Chile	76.77	M
59	Libya	76.69	M
63	Uruguay	76.33	M
65	Argentina	76.12	M
71	Saudi Arabia	75.67	M
72	United Arab Emirates	75.44	H
73	Mexico	75.41	M
74	Panama	75.22	M
83	Venezuela	74.54	M
96	Jamaica	73.24	M
103	China	72.58	M
104	Malaysia	72.50	M
111	Colombia	71.99	M
112	Brazil	71.97	M
116	Korea, North	71.65	M
129	Iran	70.26	M
130	Philippines	70.21	L
141	Iraq	69.01	M
147	Russia	67.08	M
159	Average for the World	64.77	
160	India	64.71	L
161	Uzbekistan	64.58	L
164	Pakistan	63.39	L
176	Senegal	59.25	L
179	Ghana	58.87	L
189	Congo, Republic of the	52.80	L
190	Uganda	52.67	L
196	Ethiopia	49.03	L
198	Kenya	48.93	L
201	Somalia	48.47	L
206	Tanzania	45.64	L
210	Afghanistan	43.34	L
212	South Africa	42.73	M
218	Zimbabwe	39.29	L
222	Swaziland	32.62	L

Sources: Life Expectancy: CIA (2007). *The World Factbook 2007;* Income: World Bank
http://www. worldbank.org/depweb/english/ modules/social/life/datanot.html

Note: H-high; M-moderate; L-low

level (high, medium, or low). The table demonstrates overall that life expectancy in developed countries (Europe, North America, Eastern Asia) is higher than that in developing nations (Africa, South America, Middle/Southeast Asia). The United States has one of the worst life expectancies of developed countries despite spending the largest portion of its gross domestic product (GDP) on health expenditures (over 15%). Other developed countries spend between 7.2% (Ireland) and 11.5% (Switzerland) with an overall average of 9%. In contrast, Mexico only spends 6.5% of GDP on health (OECD, 2006), but only has two years less of life expectancy at birth compared to the United States. The explanations for these patterns have to do with socioeconomic status and the types of health care systems, which are explored in the next section.

Within the United States, a great deal of evidence illustrates health disparities across ethnic groups in terms of mortality rates. In general, African Americans have the highest mortality rates, followed by White Americans, American Indians, Hispanic Americans, and Asian Americans. However, for certain diseases and illnesses, these rates vary significantly. Table 9.2 displays the mortality rates due to specific diseases of these five ethnic groups and graphically shows the disparities for the top five causes of death. These rates are age-adjusted, which means that all groups are equaled statistically to ensure they are the same age. (In reality, Hispanic Americans are on average younger than White Americans.) This adjustment is important because younger people have a lower mortality rate than older people.

Table 9.2

AGE-ADJUSTED MORTALITY RATES & HEALTH STATISTICS FOR ETHNIC GROUPS IN THE UNITED STATES, 2000 (PER 100,000 PEOPLE)

Cause of Death	Ethnic Group				
	White American	African American	American Indian	Asian American	Hispanic American
All Causes	852	1130	697	507	586
Heart Disease	254	327	165	145	165
Cancers	198	250	127	125	121
Stroke	59	82	40	53	39
Injuries	36	38	60	18	31
Suicide	12	6	12	6	6
Cirrhosis of the liver	10	10	29	4	16
Homicide	4	21	8	3	8
HIV	3	24	3	1	7

Source: National Center for Health Statistics, *Health, United States, 2002 With Chartbook on Trends in the Health of Americans* (Hyattsville, MD: NCHS, 2002)

Table 9.2 (continued)

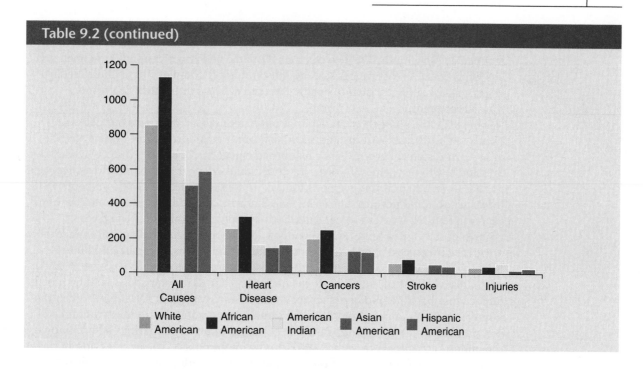

Patterns of illness not necessarily associated with mortality may either vary by ethnic group or be consistent across groups. For example, some patterns of mental health disorders (such as alcohol and drug abuse, depression, anxiety disorders, and bipolar disorder) are consistent across ethnic groups. The National Institute of Mental Health reports that about one in four people suffer from a diagnosable mental disorder in a given year (Kessler, Chiu, Demler, & Walters, 2005; NIMH, 2008). In comparison, the American Indian Service Utilization and Psychiatric Epidemiology Risk and Protective Factors Project, which surveyed American Indians according to a similar procedure that the national study used, found a rate of mental health disorders of 21% to 24% depending on tribe (Beals et al., 2005). The general rates are similar although differences can be seen in specific mental health disorders (e.g., suicide is higher among White Americans and American Indians than other groups) and for specific groups within these five broad categories (e.g., Japanese Americans and Hmong—groups that are both Asian Americans—exhibit different disorder patterns and cultures).

Other diseases indicate complex disparities. For example, the incidence (or presence) of breast cancer is higher for White American women than Hispanic American and American Indian women. However, the five-year survival rate for American Indians is lower than that of Hispanic women, which is lower than that of White women (American Cancer Society, 2001; Frost, Tollestrup, Hunt, Gilliland, Key, & Urbina, 1996). The reason for this difference is that, on average, Hispanic and American Indian women's breast cancer is detected at later stages when the cancer is advanced and spreads because they are less likely to use breast cancer screening techniques (American Cancer Society, 2001; Gilliland, Rosenburg, Hunt, Stauber, & Key, 2000). The reasons that Hispanic and American Indian women are less likely to use breast cancer screening techniques is complex and includes such factors as less access to quality health care and cultural differences in attitudes toward screening.

In summary, all of these statistics about health disparities point out general trends about disease patterns and mortality, but it is important to examine specific diseases and cultural groups—not just broad categories of ethnic groups—when addressing health disparities. In order to understand whether a disparity exists, we need to take several steps. First, we need to look at the same specific health outcome (breast cancer and not just cancer in general; or suicide and not just mental health in general). Second, we need to consider both broader cultural and specific ethnic groups. In the United States, we might consider Hispanic Americans, but in fact there are great differences among Mexicans, Mexican Americans, Cubans, and Puerto Ricans. Third, we need to examine the statistics carefully to see if they have been age-adjusted and if the statistics focus on rates. That is, the statistic should be based on a certain baseline number (such as mortality rate per 100,000 people). When the numbers are age-adjusted and have the same baseline rate, the numbers are directly comparable for a particular group. The existence of health disparities is well known; the important aspect is to try to understand why they exist. The next section in this chapter examines why some of these disparities exist with a strong emphasis on intercultural health communication.

Factors Related to Health Disparities

Healthy People 2010 is a report by the Department of Health and Human Services that establishes goals for health outcomes and specifically sets goals for the elimination of racial/ethnic health disparities in the United States. However, eliminating these disparities is not a simple matter. This section examines factors that are associated to health disparities. Five factors are presented: a) socioeconomic status, b) health care system, c) cultural beliefs and behaviors, d) service utilization obstacles, and e) cultural competence. Not all of these factors are directly related to intercultural communication. However, intercultural communication is a key contributing factor to disparities as will be discussed with the notion of cultural competence, particularly in provider-patient communication (Ashton et al., 2003).

Socioeconomic Status

Socioeconomic status (SES) refers to the financial and educational statuses that mark individuals and cultural groups. SES is often referred to as class or social class and is measured as a comparative element; that is, who has more SES? SES if often measured through educational level, income level, and/or employment status. SES is intermingled with ethnic and national cultural background as some cultural groups have more income and education than others collectively (individuals within groups vary widely). Sometimes it is important to identify SES when focusing on health, while at other times it is more important to focus on cultural differences (Robert & House, 2000; Williams, 2001). In most cases, both factors matter.

The general expectation regarding SES and health outcomes is that the more SES a group or individual has, the better the health (Robert & House, 2000). The rationale is that, if people have more income, they can pay for better health services, buy better food, and live in safer neighborhoods to make sure their family is healthy. However, this rationale does not completely explain the relationship between health and SES. In order to understand this complex relationship, individual and community layers of SES should be considered.

At the individual layer, SES is associated with health in several ways. First, three components of SES are related to poor health: persistent low income, income instability (fluctuating income over time), and low childhood SES (when patterns of behavior such as diet and exercise are established for health problems with long-term causation such as cardiovascular disease) (Robert & House, 2000). Thus, if you grew up in a household where you had little money or the income changed (your parents were in and out of work), your health is likely to be less than that of somebody who grew up in a household with a moderate or high amount of money and the income was consistent. Second, there is a gradient effect in the relationship between health and income; that is the more income, the better health an individual has. However, this effect generally tailors off and creates what is called a ceiling effect of income on health. Specifically, as the level of income rises, so do the health outcomes up to a point. In the United States, that point is the median income. (Based on the U.S. Census, this figure was about $48,000/year for a household in the United States in 2006.) If you make more than the median income, your health is not greatly impacted and thus, income matters most for health for people with low levels of income (Robert & House, 2000).

In addition to an individual's SES, the community in which she lives is also important in two ways. First, the overall SES of a community impacts the individuals living there. Thus, even if you have a middle-class income, your health is negatively affected by living in a poor neighborhood (Robert & House, 2000). This impact of community income on health is smaller than that of individual income, but the effect is important nonetheless. That is, your family income matters more, but the neighborhood income has some impact. Second, for developed nations, the level of income inequality is important. Income inequality is the gap between the rich and poor (Robert & House, 2000). The greater this gap, the worse a nation's health is, but only for countries of significant overall wealth (developed nations). For poorer, developing nations, a simple linear pattern exists between gross domestic product (GDP) and health—the greater the GDP, the better the health. Thus, the ceiling effect comes into play at the community level. Simply having more income does not impact overall health once a nation has substantial overall wealth. When that level is reached, the gap in income is what predicts health. This relationship is one reason for the health disparities in the United States relative to other developed nations. The United States has a large income gap even though it has a lot of wealth. See Box 9.2.

Box 9.2 Layered Effects: Layers of SES and Health

The individual and community components of SES illustrate a key aspect of the layered perspective this book advocates; that is, higher layers actually change how variables are related. Basically, the relationship between health and money is not simply "more money means better health." At the individual layer, a ceiling effect of income on health exists; that is, we need a certain level of income to have good health, but after that certain level is reached, more money does not give you significantly better health.

At the community layer, there is no ceiling effect in developing nations. More income results in better health. However, in developed nations, income inequality is a key factor (see the figures below for an illustration). Once a nation has achieved a certain level of income, what determines health is not more money, but rather whether the differences between rich and poor is large (that is, the income gap). The relationship between SES and health demonstrates the importance of context—we cannot simply assume every culture and every individual works the same way.

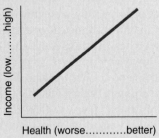

Developing Country

Income (low......high)

Health (worse...........better)

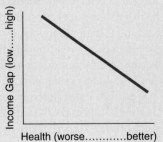

Developed Country

Income Gap (low......high)

Health (worse...........better)

Health Care System Problems

The nature of the health care system also has a role in explaining health disparities. In the United States (other systems will be explored later in the top-down layer section), the health care system includes both public and private aspects (Williams & Torrens, 2002). The public health system includes components of public health care such as the Veterans Association and the Indian Health Service (IHS). These systems of care provide health care services for free in specific facilities (such as an IHS clinic), but are available for only particular populations (veterans of wars, and American Indians, respectively). In addition, public health components such as research and promotion are addressed by the federal and state governments (for example, the National Institutes for Health fund research). The private components are the source of health care for the majority of people. The vast majority of clinics and hospitals are funded by private insurance. Within this system, a number of factors affect the quality of care, including financing and access to services, availability of services, and coordination of services.

The vast majority of U.S. Americans are covered by health insurance, and this private system finances the vast majority of health care. Employers predominantly provide private health insurance. Exceptions to private financing include the public systems, Medicare for people over 65, and Medicaid for people with low income. These latter two represent public financing of health care for particular people, but services are generally received in private clinics. Over 46 million people in 2004 did not have any health insurance, which resulted in limited preventive care, later stage diagnosis for diseases, and poor therapeutic treatment of those diseases (NCHS, 2006). The limited access that the uninsured have is through emergency rooms (which are an extremely expensive source of care). Hospitals must treat all patients regardless of ability to pay and have over $34 billion in uncompensated care (NCHS, 2006). Further, funding for American Indian health care programs (a system that was funded based on a U.S. treaty) falls below the level for every other federal medical program and standard and has been characterized by the U.S. Commission on Civil Rights (2004) as a "revolting disparity" (see Figure 9.1 for an illustration of this funding disparity). The bottom line is that, with poor funding and limited insurance, certain U.S. Americans do not have access to appropriate health care, which negatively impacts their health status.

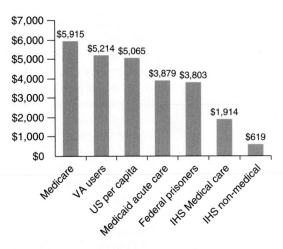

Figure 9.1
Per Capita Health Care Expenditures for Certain Patients

Source: Broken Promises: Evaluating the Native American Health Care System. (2004). Washington DC: US Commission on Civil Rights: Office of the General Counsel

The lack of availability of specialty services and culturally appropriate services is also a factor for health disparities. Specialty services include drug abuse counseling, mental health treatment, psychotherapy, health specialties, gynecological care, alternative therapies, and many other services. Insurance carriers vary in what they will cover, but most cover standard Western-based therapies for physical health. Coverage for mental health and drug abuse is not as consistent although most insurance plans have this coverage. In rural settings, funding may not be available for specialty care, and patients have to travel to more metropolitan areas (Novins, Duclos, Martin, Jewett & Manson, 1999; Williams & Torrens, 2002). In Indian country, many services are not available because of funding shortages. Additionally, the lack of culturally appropriate services and translators is a barrier to effective treatment (Novins et al., 1999; Williams & Torrens, 2002). Most hospitals do not have sufficient services for translators or do not have translators on call for less common languages. The ability to translate addresses language barriers, but also must focus on cultural understanding and respectful communication.

Finally, since the health care system is a loosely connected patchwork quilt of doctors and services, coordination of service is problematic. As a patient, you probably prefer to have your doctor know about all of your care so that she can make sure that treatment from one problem does not counteract or harm another condition. For those who move quite a bit, this coordination is very difficult. The patient bears much of the burden for making sure that records get transferred. Even when records are transferred, nothing guarantees that providers will talk with one another. Lack of coordination contributes to some of the health care disparities for mobile populations such as immigrants.

In summary, the health care system is a complex set of organizations that are not very well coordinated. If this system is hard for you to grasp, you are not alone. Most people do not understand how the health care system operates. They simply know what insurance they have (or don't) and where to get care. Most clinics or hospitals operate as self-contained units with limited interaction among other entities. As patients, we assume that computer systems have made coordination of our care and the resources needed for our care easy. However, there are limitations in the degree to which information can be shared (for example, we often do not want our private information shared and federal law prohibits the sharing of our health information without our consent). Additionally, the funding mechanisms encourage individual health care facilities to operate on their own. One of my colleagues, a public health expert in the state of New Mexico, once told me that we do not really have a health care system. What we have is a great number of organizations that create a maze for patients to navigate. The lack of effective communication among health care organizations creates barriers and obstacles to the prevention and treatment of health.

Cultural Health Beliefs and Behaviors

Health behaviors are influenced by general **health beliefs,** or the attributions we make about health (Janz, Champion, & Strecher, 2002), that is, our explanations about the causes of our health problems and diseases. When you get sick, you often try to figure out what happened and why. For example, if you have a pain in your back, you might decide that you pulled a muscle, slept wrong, or simply have a genetic predisposition to back pain. These attributions are important as they identify what we think is the cause of the disease and hence the solution. Understanding these attributions influences whether we seek care and which type of healer we seek. Two categories of health beliefs are relevant: general beliefs and cultural specific beliefs.

General health beliefs consist of three variables that are associated with most theories of health behavior: perceived threat, perceived efficacy, and barriers (Witte & Morrison, 1995). **Perceived threat** is the degree that a person feels concerned by a particular disease or health problem. For example, "Do I feel like I could get diabetes?" **Perceived efficacy** is the degree to which a person feels he can perform certain behaviors to avoid the threat. For example, "Do I think I can engage in the activities necessary to avoid diabetes like eating more nutritious foods and exercising?" **Barriers** are the perceived psychological, financial, or physical costs that inhibit the behavior. For example, "Do I have the motivation, money, and time to eat better and exercise?"

Cultural health beliefs are culturally based factors that work with threat, efficacy, and barriers to influence health behavior (Witte & Morrison, 1995). There are many such beliefs, including animism, familism, and fatalism. **Animism** is the belief in supernatural beings such as good and evil spirits, spirits of inanimate objects. Animists believe that health conditions are due to such factors as the loss of one's spirits and that such conditions can be prevented by avoiding taboos (for example, avoiding certain locations or talking about a death) and can be repaired by animal sacrifice and by traditional healers such as shamans.

Familism is the influence of family values on health decisions and is closely related to the notions of individualism and collectivism. In individualistic cultures, the family has importance, but most health behavior decisions are up to the individual, who may or may not consult with the family. In collectivistic societies, especially with people who follow traditional cultural beliefs, the family makes the decision and receives the health information. The doctor's diagnosis belongs to the family and should be shared with the family, who will make the key decisions, particularly with influence from the head of the household—male or female, depending on whether the society is a patriarchy or a matriarchy. One of my colleagues shared a story from her own family—one of traditional Italian immigrants. When a medical provider told the wife he suspected she had breast cancer and told her to report to the hospital for a biopsy, the husband refused to let her go. His belief was that when a person goes to the hospital, he or she dies. The daughter in the family had to "kidnap" her mother (when the husband was at work) and take her to the hospital where, ironically, the biopsy showed no malignancy at all. This is not a common practice anymore, but illustrates how health beliefs influence behavior.

Fatalism is the perceived lack of control over one's environment. People who are fatalistic believe that their health is predetermined and that there is not much that can be done about one's health. For example, a person might say, "I'll either get cancer or I won't. There isn't much I can do about it." To understand fatalism, it is helpful to compare two types of health attributions: behavioral-environmental and equity attributions (Murguía et al., 2000). People who are fatalistic tend to make equity attributions. Equity attributions display "beliefs about negative health outcomes due to punishment by an outside force because of a person's violation of community standards, and [...] positive health outcomes due to a person's culturally sanctioned behaviors" (Murguía et al., 2000, p. 271). For example, an equity attribution can be expressed as, "If I am not a good person, I will get cancer." In contrast, people who are not fatalistic tend to make behavior or environmental attributions of illness. Behavioral-environmental attributions include conventional explanations for illness, including an individual's course of action such as exercise or smoking and factors related to the environment such as air pollution. People who use behavioral-environmental attributions tend to see themselves as capable of controlling their health through their own behavior, including such factors as diet, exercise, and being politically active in the support of laws/behaviors related to health.

General and cultural health beliefs influence health-seeking behavior and other types of health behavior. In regards to health-seeking behavior, people who accept behavioral-environmental attributions tend to use mainstream health care services such as visiting a doctor; they avoid traditional cultural practices for healing. In contrast, people who believe in equity attributions often delay seeking health care and use traditional healers such as *curanderas* (traditional healers in Hispanic communities), medicine men (traditional healers in American Indian communities),

Self-Assessment 9.1

EQUITY ATTRIBUTIONS OR BEHAVIORAL-ENVIRONMENTAL ATTRIBUTIONS FOR CANCER

For each of the items listed below, use the following scale: 1 = strongly disagree, 2 = disagree, 3 = neutral, 4 = agree, 5 = strongly agree.

Item	Score
1. Cancer is a punishment from God.	
2. Cancer happens to people who are bad members of the community.	
3. God looks out for people who do not get breast cancer.	
4. There is not a lot I can do to avoid cancer.	
5. People can avoid harmful effects from cancer by maintaining a healthy lifestyle.	
6. People can avoid harmful effects from cancer if they use cancer screening.	
7. My actions have a great deal of impact on whether I will get cancer.	
8. I can avoid the harmful effects from cancer if I eat right and exercise properly.	

Add the scores of items 1–4 and 5–8. Items 1–4 give a score for equity attributions, while 5–8 give a score for behavioral-environmental. The maximum score is 20 while the minimum is 5.

Source: Adapted from Murguía et al., (2000)

shamans (traditional healers in Hmong communities), healing ceremonies, and folk remedies (Murguía et al., 2000). Of course, people can use both types of attributions and both types of healing practices.

Health beliefs also influence everyday choices about health behaviors. As Figure 9.2 displays (and the example of cancer illustrates), the extended parallel process model (Witte & Morrison, 1995) demonstrates how these variables influence how people respond to a message communicating a health threat. **Danger control** is a stance that people take when they feel they can control what happens to them. Some adopting a danger control stance will seek out information on an illness and talk to family members and providers about a problem. They will enact preventive behaviors and also try to help other people control the danger that they face. In contrast, **fear control** is a stance that people take when they do not feel they can control what happens to them. They choose not to talk about the problem and avoid information about it. In this manner, they control the fear they have by ignoring it so it does not affect their everyday life. People who a) accept the threat and perceive that they are able to address it, b) have behavioral-environmental attributions, and c) identify few barriers are likely to control the danger by adopting the behavior suggested (such as exercising more). People who a) accept the threat, but perceive they are incapable of addressing the problem, b) have equity attributions, and c) perceive high barriers

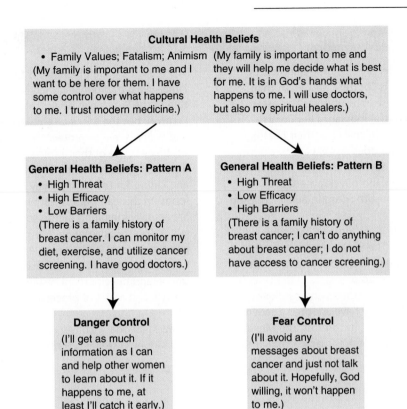

Cultural Health Beliefs

- Family Values; Fatalism; Animism
(My family is important to me and I
want to be here for them. I have
some control over what happens
to me. I trust modern medicine.)

(My family is important to me and
they will help me decide what is best
for me. It is in God's hands what
happens to me. I will use doctors,
but also my spiritual healers.)

General Health Beliefs: Pattern A
- High Threat
- High Efficacy
- Low Barriers
(There is a family history of
breast cancer. I can monitor my
diet, exercise, and utilize cancer
screening. I have good doctors.)

General Health Beliefs: Pattern B
- High Threat
- Low Efficacy
- High Barriers
(There is a family history of
breast cancer; I can't do anything
about breast cancer; I do not
have access to cancer screening.)

Danger Control
(I'll get as much
information as I can
and help other women
to learn about it. If it
happens to me, at
least I'll catch it early.)

Fear Control
(I'll avoid any
messages about breast
cancer and just not talk
about it. Hopefully, God
willing, it won't happen
to me.)

Figure 9.2
Extended
Parallel Process
Model of
General and
Cultural Health
Beliefs

adopt fear control by avoiding messages or denying a problem (such as believing,
"I don't need to exercise—my grandfather lived to 90 and never exercised a day in his
life"). See Box 9.3 on page 256 for an example of the difference between danger and
fear control.

Service Utilization Obstacles

One of the protectors of good health is the utilization of appropriate and effective services. In general, most cultural groups do not use physical and mental health services at
the appropriate level. For example, with regards to mental health services, only about
40% of U.S. Americans (regardless of cultural background) who need mental health
services use them. Some research shows American Indians use mental health services
slightly less than this amount; specifically, only 32% of American Indians with a past-
year mental health disorder sought treatment for mental health problems (Oetzel et al.,
2006). Similar disparities exist in health care use for physical health. For example,
White Americans make 48% more office-based physician visits than African Americans
(3,161 vs. 2,139 visits per 1,000 people) (Bernstein et al., 2003).

Box 9.3 Globalization: Culture, Development, and Health

The extended parallel process model indicates that danger control is "better" for health than fear control. Most research supports this assertion because danger control messages encourage people to take an active stance in their health. However, fear control does not always result in unhealthy behavior. Sometimes other influences such as globalization and development are negative factors for health (despite also increasing income).

A great example is the Pima Indians who live in Arizona and Mexico. The Pimas are one tribe that has two separate bands. The U.S. Pimas are among the most unhealthy group of people in the United States with high rates of diabetes and cardiovascular problems because they have adopted a sedentary and fast-food lifestyle. In contrast, the Mexican Pimas have almost none of these same problems.

The reason for the difference is that the Mexican Pimas live a traditional and active lifestyle. The culture of the Pimas can be described as fatalistic (fear control), but the Mexican Pimas' cultural practices and beliefs serve to protect them from the unhealthy lifestyle of their brothers and sisters to the North. They have active daily lives raising animals and caring for the family. They eat traditional foods. In this case, globalization and development are actually inhibiting factors for health. Traditional cultural lifestyles are generally protective of health and fear control is not a problem. Fear control becomes problematic when accompanying globalization and development results in a sedentary lifestyle and a diet of processed and fast food.

Source: National Institute of Diabetes and Digestive and Kidney Diseases (2002)

Numerous obstacles limit service utilization. One study of obstacles for mental health service use reported by American Indian adults in three communities found four obstacles: a) self-reliance, b) privacy issues, c) quality of care, and d) communication/trust (Oetzel et al., 2006). A vast majority (71%) of participants reported at least one of these obstacles during treatment, and 61% faced two or more obstacles. These four obstacles have been identified in other U.S. cultural groups and physical health services (Bernstein et al., 2003; Williams & Torrens, 2002). Financing and access to care are additional obstacles to health care as noted in the previous section.

Self-reliance obstacles focus on the desire to solve the problem on one's own. People with mental health and substance abuse problems have a tendency to try to solve the problem on their own at first and/or to avoid treatment for disorders (Novins et al., 1999; Pescosolido & Boyer, 1999). The context of self-reliance by cultural minority groups must be considered within the larger context of history and racism. It is well documented that ethnic minority groups have less faith in the U.S. health care system than do White Americans (Aday, 2001; du Pré, 2000; Williams, 2001). For example, African Americans have a greater suspicion than White Americans because of incidents such as the Tuskegee Syphilis study in which male patients of the Public Health Service (PHS) were not treated for their syphilis. The PHS wanted to track the course of the disease to see what happened over time. This decision was made even though there was an effective treatment for syphilis. The PHS decided "in the name of science" that it was important to study the disease, but did not tell the patients and only selected African American men to be followed. American Indians have a large number of incidents (such as the Massacre at Wounded Knee for Lakota, the Trail of Tears for Cherokee, or the Long Walk for Navajos) that have led them to distrust the U.S. government. Much of American Indians' primary care traditionally comes from the Indian Health Service funded by the government. Thus, self-reliance is often a coping strategy for addressing their own health problems.

Privacy obstacles focus on the desire for others not to know that a patient is seeking treatment. This obstacle points to the stigma associated with mental health treatment in particular, but also physical health. We do not like people to know our business or to know that we are somehow vulnerable. For example, treatment for depression and anxiety are seen both some as weaknesses, and thus patients often do not want others to know about the treatment they are engaged in (Givens & Tjia, 2002; Marwaha & Livingston, 2002; Rost, Smith, & Taylor, 1993). Generally, the problem of privacy obstacles occurs because of the stigma associated with health treatment (Richardson & Shiu-Thornton, 2002). Stigma is the negative feelings associated with particular problems. For example, many people are embarrassed to tell their employer or family members that they suffer from depression. Those with depression often prefer to try to deal with the problem on their own rather than suffer inconsiderate attitudes, such as "What do you have to be depressed about?" or minimizations, such as "Just get over it." Also see Box 9.4.

Quality of care obstacles emphasize the available and effectiveness of treatment options. The perceived and actual quality of health services available affects their use. The availability of care focuses on two interrelated aspects. First, treatment sectors need to have culturally appropriate services and clinicians. For example, mainstream psychiatric frameworks and nomenclature are of limited use for understanding American Indian constructions of mental health (Manson, 2000). Additionally, some providers do not have a sufficient understanding of the cultural health beliefs of American Indians and thus are not well suited to provide care for them. Second, the structure and financing of care is undergoing significant changes in both mainstream and tribal sectors. Managed care organizations attempt to reduce use of high-cost

---

Box 9.4 Voices: Privacy in Rural Tribal Communities

When you live on a reservation, there is a danger of everyone knowing your business. There are few towns, but everyone comes to them to buy groceries, socialize, and get medical care. People tend to know everyone and share stories. Most of the time, this deep connection is positive, but it hurt my uncle. He was an alcoholic, but didn't want to seek treatment because everyone would see his car at the clinic and know why he was there (it was a clinic for behavioral health). He knew he needed help, but wanted to keep it private. He also didn't want his employer to find out and stereotype him as a "drunk Indian." The stigma of alcoholism in my community is very strong and actually inhibits people from getting the help they need.

and specialty services and continually search for ways to reduce overall costs. These efforts disproportionately fall on the most vulnerable populations such as the poor, rural, and underserved populations (Kasper, 2000). Overall, what these two aspects mean is that services are often not available, and if they are available, they may not be culturally appropriate.

Communication/trust obstacles focus on interaction with providers and center on trust and understanding. The quality of communication between patients and health care providers is a strong indicator of how well patients tolerate pain, how much stress they experience, whether they follow medical advice, and their overall satisfaction with care (Ashton et al., 2003; Coulter & Fitzpatrick, 2000; Morse & Proctor, 1998). Communication problems occur for several reasons. First, patients' socialization to care regardless of cultural/ethnic background is different than that of doctors (Coulter & Fitzpatrick, 2000; du Pré, 2000). For example, du Pré noted that patients focus on feelings and are diffuse in their explanations whereas doctors are looking for specific evidence for diagnosing illness. Providers tend to use explanation that focus on diagnosing disease or abnormalities in the structure and function of the body. In contrast, many patients suffer illnesses or experience changes in states of overall well being and social function, such as being able to work or play with one's children (Kleinman, Eisenberg, & Good, 1978) (see Box 9.5 for an example of this difference). Second, health care providers often come from different cultural backgrounds than their patients. This second factor is expanded on in the next section, and concrete examples are provided.

Culturally Competent Communication

Health disparities are also related to culturally competent and sensitive communication. In fact, one study found that communication difficulties between providers and patients are the primary factor for health disparities (Ashton et al., 2003). **Cultural competence** is the ability to communicate in a culturally appropriate and effective manner. Culturally appropriate behavior emphasizes the relationships between provider and patient, for example, respect and support for a patient's culture, and using a participatory style; cultural effectiveness emphasizes the goals of the interaction, for example, healing the patient by encouraging the "right" behavior such as taking a particular medicine. Cultural competence also extends into public health communication, but is often called cultural sensitivity in this context. **Cultural sensitivity** is the extent to which ethnic or cultural characteristics, experiences, norms, values, behavior patterns, and beliefs of a target population and relevant historical, environmental, and social forces are incorporated in the design, delivery, and evaluation of targeted health interventions, including behavioral change materials and programs (Resnicow, Braithwaite, Dilorio, & Glanz, 2002, p. 493). Thus, cultural competence focuses on the communication ability of providers and patients while cultural sensitivity focuses on public health communication (Resnicow et al., 2002).

As was noted in the previous section, communication with providers can be an obstacle to seeking health care. If you think the provider does not understand you,

Box 9.5 Voices: How Patient and Provider Explanations Contribute to (Mis)understanding

I am a working class, African American man and I was suffering from chest pains when I was in my late 30s (I am now in my mid 40s). I wasn't overweight, exercised pretty regularly, and ate well. I was quite stressed at work and it was impacting my relationships at home. I was distant when I was with my wife and children and it was causing a strain with my wife.

I went to my doctor, a middle-aged White man who I had seen for several years for basic care. I told him what was wrong and that I thought it was stress. I tried to tell him about how it was affecting my relationships and wanted him to give me a sedative to help me relax and sleep better. I thought this would help me feel better and help me be more present. However, he simply wanted to know when the pains started, where I felt them, and how often I felt them. He reviewed my blood pressure and asked me about my family history of hypertension (high blood pressure). He prescribed blood pressure medication, told me to reduce my salt intake, and get more exercise. I couldn't

understand why he didn't want to treat my stress since I knew this was a factor. And, I didn't see how salt and exercise (which would take me away from my family more and cause me more stress) were factors.

I ignored his advice and three months later the pain was so bad I decided to go to a friend's doctor. She was a middle-aged White woman. She prescribed the exact same thing as the first doctor. However, what she did differently was she listened to what I thought was wrong and didn't discount it. She understood how stress was a factor and how exercise would cause me to have less time with my family. However, she helped me figure out ways to exercise with my family and encouraged me to talk to a nutritionist who helped us prepare healthier, but still good-tasting meals. I felt that she understood my situation and I was willing to listen to her advice. I now have my hypertension under control and my family and I still exercise regularly together. In fact, it helps me relieve my stress, and my relationship with my family is stronger than before.

does not respect your culture, or simply will not take the time to get to know you, you likely will not see that provider as a viable source for your health care needs. Research evidence supports this assertion. For example, a review of research on this subject found that providers contribute to health disparities in three ways (Van Ryn & Fu, 2003). First, providers influence patients' view of themselves and their relation to the world. For example, a provider may communicate (unintentionally through nonverbal behaviors) lower expectations to a disadvantaged patient that discourages this patient from seeking further care. Second, providers use their own cultural frameworks to influence how patients should behave; that is, they "force" their cultural biases on patients. Third, providers are gatekeepers and may influence disparities by providing differential access to care. For example, one study found that African American dialysis patients were less likely than their clinically similar White American counterparts to be told about transplantation, obtain all the medical information about the transplant, and be told about receiving a kidney from a relative (Ayanian, Cleary, Weissman, & Epstein, 1999).

Overall, providers' communication with patients of color is poorer (that is, not as competent) than is communication with White patients and is also reflective of

Box 9.6. What Went Wrong? Patient–Provider Communication Problems

Scenario 1

Bill is a Latino OB-GYN physician who was born and raised in Los Angeles (LA). He does not speak Spanish and is a fourth-generation U.S. American. He grew up in a predominantly middle/upper-class, White suburb of LA. He expects patients to be assertive and ask questions. When they do not, he assumes they do not care much about their health and well being. Julio is a working class, 1st-generation U.S. American who speaks both English and Spanish, but prefers Spanish. His wife, Rosaria, only speaks Spanish. They are traditional Catholics who do not believe in birth control and believe that children are a gift from God. They know good prenatal care is critical to a healthy child so they make all of their doctor's visits together. It is difficult, but worth their time. This is their first time seeing Bill, as they recently moved to the area, but Julio's boss said he was a good provider. They believe that doctors are very smart and are in an authority position. The following conversation took place at their fourth prenatal visit. Bill wanted to talk with them about the ultrasound they performed and to discuss family planning with them.

Bill: Congratulations! Everything looks like it is going wonderfully. The ultrasound looks fabulous. Do you want to know the sex?

Julio: Translates to Rosaria and then says, "We thank you. Children are a blessing. We want to be surprised."

Bill: Yes, they are and I understand. Some patients want to know and others don't. I know you have previous children (checking his chart). Wow! This is your fifth child.

Julio: Yes, and we love them all and we are so happy.

Bill: Thinking about the expense and knowing that Julio is working class says, "Julio, you might think about getting a vasectomy or consider other family planning techniques. I can provide you with a referral if you like."

Julio: Thinking about how his religion would never permit such a travesty but doesn't want to offend Bill says, "Certainly, we will take your referral."

Bill: Of course. Here it is. He is the best urologist in town. Do you have any questions about the referral or about the pregnancy?

Julio: Asks Rosario and says, "Nothing at this time. We'll think about it and come back with questions."

Bill: Excellent. I'll see you next month.

Julio explains what happened to Rosaria and they decide never to return to Bill. They find another physician, a White woman who speaks Spanish, whom Rosario was referred to. Julio never told his boss of the change and Bill wonders what happened to them. He concluded that they simply lost their insurance or really didn't care about their baby. He is sad because they seemed like such a nice and polite couple.

Scenario 2

Richard is a third-generation Japanese American cardiologist who was raised in the United States. He grew up in a predominantly middle/upper-class suburb in the Midwest. He expects patients to be assertive and ask questions. When they do not, he assumes they do not care much about their health and well being. Quentin is an African American man in his 40s with a history of drug use. He has been clean for 5 years. He started seeing his primary care physician (PCP) shortly after getting clean. His PCP, an African American physician, completed a full history on Quentin, including his drug history, and has been a wonderful physician from Quentin's perspective. Quentin trusts him completely.

Quentin is now employed, has a family, and unfortunately has heart trouble that just started. His PCP suggested Richard because he is the best, even though he is a little gruff. Quentin was in shock from the diagnosis and a little scared about his prognosis. He wants to see the cardiologist and will do whatever is necessary to get better. He wants the best treatment possible as he needs to be around for his wife and children. He has the following conversation during his first visit with Richard.

Richard: Welcome. It is nice to meet you. I understand you are having some heart trouble. What seems to be the problem?

Quentin: Yes, thanks and nice to meet you as well. I started having chest pains about six months ago and they became more severe recently. I saw Dr. Brown last week and he suggested that I see you right away. I am quite concerned for me and my family.

Richard: Yes, I understand. I see from your chart that you have a history of drug use.

Quentin: Unfortunately yes, but I'm clean now.

Richard: Yes, drug use may explain some of the reasons for the problems. What about diet and exercise?

Quentin: I eat very well and exercise regularly.

Richard: He notices Quentin's hands shaking and does not believe that he is off drugs. He also notices that Quentin is being very brief in his responses and is not asking many questions. "Well, we have several options, but I think we should start with hypertension medicine. I noticed your blood pressure is high. In three months, if it isn't better, we can try something different." Thinks to himself, "I'm not going to waste my time or resources treating someone who is just going to go out and use drugs. If he really is clean, he'll try this out and come back."

Quentin: OK, thank you doctor.

Quentin returns to his PCP and tells Dr. Brown of his encounter and expresses his concerns. He has now had some time to do some Internet research and found that the complications could be quite serious and in need of intervention beyond a pill for hypertension. He asks Dr. Brown for another referral and Dr. Brown happily complies. This time, Quentin is ready for the appointment and asks lots of questions. The new doctor runs a battery of tests and fortunately finds no serious cardiac problems.

Questions for Both Scenarios:

1. What communication problems do you see in these situations? How did the patient's and provider's communication contribute to these problems?
2. What changes would you suggest for more competent communication?
3. Have you ever had an interaction with a provider where you felt misunderstood, confused, or looked down upon? Why did you feel this way? Did your culture play a role?

racial bias (Ashton et al., 2003; Williams, 2001). The story opening this chapter provides an illustrative example of this poor communication, albeit unintentional. In fact, communication difficulty is more important than racial bias in patient-provider communication in understanding health disparities (Ashton et al., 2003). In general, intercultural health communication between patients and providers is poor when patients and doctors use different explanations to describe illness or disease, patients do not provide a complete narrative to explain their illness experience (and providers do not elicit a complete narrative story), providers do not use a participatory style, and patients and providers use different communication styles resulting from cultural value differences (see Chapter 2 for a discussion of value differences and communication) (Ashton et al., 2003). The examples in Boxes 9.5 and 9.6 on pages 260–261 illustrate many of these problems. However, when communication is done competently, patients are satisfied and tend to comply with their doctors' recommendations (Ashton et al, 2003).

Lack of cultural sensitivity is a factor for health disparities as well. The Institute of Medicine (2002) argues that culture has not been well examined with public health communication interventions. Specifically, culture is often seen only as race, ethnicity, or socioeconomic status or examined only at the surface level. The **surface structure** is the observable characteristics and behaviors of a cultural group such as phyical characteristics, foods, music, and language. In contrast, the **deep structure** of culture focuses on the values, beliefs, history, and social relations of a group that more profoundly impact health behavior (Resnicow et al., 2002). Focusing only on the surface structure is not likely to result in lasting change because it does not address the core of a cultural group's (or individual's) health behavior. Box 9.7 illustrates the differences between surface and deep structure values in a communication campaign and demonstrates why deep structure is more effective at producing behavior change than is surface structure.

Concept Check

This section examined factors related to health disparities: a) socioeconomic status, b) the health care system, c) cultural beliefs and behaviors, d) service utilization obstacles, and e) cultural competence. Several of these factors are not communication factors (SES, health care system, and certain obstacles), but are factors that can be addressed through effective media/communication advocacy (see the next section for details). For example, lack of coordination in the health care system can be addressed by effective organizational communication. Additionally, SES factors can be addressed by advocating for changes in legislation to reduce the income gap. The other factors are directly related to intercultural communication, and negative outcomes are partially related to a lack of cultural competence and sensitivity by providers and public health practitioners. In fact, research demonstrates that lack of cultural competence by providers is the key aspect to explain disparities resulting from patient-provider interaction. Addressing the variety of factors relating to health disparities requires a layered approach that is examined in the following section.

Box 9.7 What Went Wrong and Right: Communication Campaign for the Hmong

The Hmong are an ethnic group based in the mountains of Laos. The Vietnam War forced many thousands of Hmong to the United States as refugees. Dwight Conquergood was a communication scholar who lived among the Hmong in the 1980s at a refugee camp in Thailand called Ban Vinai. He was among many rescue workers who were trying to help the Hmong. He was assigned the project of improving environmental health.

Many of the other rescue workers' efforts had failed. The Hmong avoided the community hospitals, resented the Christian missionaries, and generally resisted the efforts of the rescue workers. Conquergood's first challenge came after an outbreak of rabies in dogs led to a campaign to vaccinate all dogs in the camp. The efforts of others failed to produce a single dog for vaccination by the Hmong. Conquergood came up with a new campaign called the Rabies Parade. It was a procession led by three important symbols in Hmong folktales: a tiger, a chicken, and a *dab* (an evil spirit pronounced da). The parade was made up of all Hmong participants, and the symbols behaved in culturally appropriate ways. The chicken used a bullhorn to explain the cause of rabies. The next morning, the vaccination clinic was so swamped with dogs that they could barely keep up.

What made Conquergood's campaign work when others had failed? First, he involved the community—he worked with them instead of telling them what to do. Second, he lived among the Hmong and liked the Hmong—most of the other rescue workers lived in villages nearby because they were "cleaner." Third, his campaign used culturally appropriate messages and symbols. Fourth, he respected the ways of the Hmong—during his stay, he was treated for ailments using both Hmong and Western treatments. Conquergood was culturally competent and sensitive and saw the Hmong as humans—not as victims, not as inferior—simply humans with needs and important cultural customs.

Source: Conquergood (1988)

Layers of Health Care Contexts

The layered approach to addressing health disparities is advocated by many public health professionals (Little & Kaufman Kantor, 2002; McLeroy, Bibeau, Steckler, & Glanz, 1988; Oetzel & Duran, 2004; Stokols, 1996). The social ecological framework emphasizes a shared responsibility for public health; individuals are responsible for choosing healthy lifestyles; providers are responsible for being culturally competent; health care organizations are responsible for providing effective, appropriate, and coordinated care; and governments are responsible for passing effective health policy. The public's health is broader than just intercultural communication, but intercultural communication has an important role is this big picture.

Bottom-Up

The bottom-up effects include individual cases and individuals organizing for change. We often become aware of the severity of a health problem because of a highly publicized and/or tragic event. For example, when Magic Johnson, a famous basketball player, announced he was HIV positive in 1991, a surge of people got tested for HIV. Additionally, a family that is killed by a drunk driver can bring renewed focus and attention on this critical health issue. Thus, individuals become "poster children" for health issues and help to bring energy and commitment from others to address these problems. They become the basis for policy as well, such as Kendra's Law, which was named for a woman who was pushed in front a subway train in New York by a man with schizophrenia. The law requires individuals with mental health disorders who are deemed a threat to self or others to take medication for their disorders. There is interesting debate about the appropriateness of Kendra's Law. Some mental health advocates that the law further stigmatizes people with mental health disorders because it removes their choice to take medication or not. Further, the law and media coverage about the law stigmatizes people with mental health disorders and it increases the perception that those with certain disorders (such as schizophrenia) are violent. In fact, almost all people with schizophrenia are not violent. Nonetheless, an individual health issue became a public health issue.

In addition to bringing attention to issues, individuals are also critical to organizing people and communities to address health issues. Individuals organize rallies, walks, bake sales, and protests to bring attention, awareness, and change to health issues. A few committed individuals can make a significant difference on a particular issue. This type of organizing is closely related to media advocacy, which will be discussed toward the end of this chapter. Additionally, the next chapter will discuss community organizing in more detail.

Top-Down: Influence of Health Care Contexts on Individuals

The influence of health care contexts on individuals considers factors related to the organization of the health care system. Three specific factors have been noted to illustrate how the health care system can inhibit health-seeking behavior. First, the funding and accessibility of the health care system influences the degree to which individuals use health care (Novins et al., 1999). Second, the lack of culturally appropriate services inhibits certain cultural groups from seeking some health care coverage (Novins et al., 1999; Oetzel et al., 2006). Third, the cultural competence of the providers can be an obstacle to service utilization (Oetzel et al., 2006). As was shown in earlier sections of the chapter, problems in the health care system and lack of cultural competence in providers create a disincentive to seek health care. On the other hand, health care systems that provide timely service, culturally appropriate services and culturally competent care, and a relatively easy system to navigate encourage health-seeking behavior. Most organizations spend a great deal of time and money trying to improve their systems to make them more accessible to patients since a greater number of patients means greater money and improved health outcomes.

Top-Down: Influence of Society on Health Care Contexts

Larger societal, historical, and legal factors have an important role in shaping health care contexts. First, the nature of health care systems has some grounding in the cultures in which the systems operate. Health care systems are generally socialized or privatized. **Socialized medicine** is a system of publicly administered national health care (Williams & Torrens, 2002). Socialized medicine ranges from programs in which the government runs hospitals and health organizations to programs that are part of a national universal health care system; that is, everyone is covered. Socialized medicine can include single payer systems in which the government pays private providers for this care (for example, in Canada) or multi-payer systems in which public and private monies are used (for example, in Germany and Japan). Other socialized systems have the government provide and pay for the services (for example, in Great Britain). **Privatized medicine** is a market-based system in which private providers deliver health services, and private insurance pays for most of these services, although the government may contribute some monies toward these services (for example, in the United States) (Williams & Torrens, 2002). Almost every Western country except the United States has some form of socialized medicine and universal health coverage (see Figure 9.3 for a map of countries with universal health care). The ability to provide universal health coverage is based on the degree to which a country has both the human and financial resources, but also the culture prevalent in the country. For example, the United States has the means to implement universal health coverage, but public opinion has been slow to accept socialized medicine, often on the grounds that the program will be costly and will lower the quality of patient care. To some degree, these arguments are based in individualistic sentiments associated with a strong market economy.

Second, we can consider the effects of globalization on health and health communication. There are several negative and positive effects of globalization. On the negative side, globalization has increased the likelihood of a worldwide pandemic of infectious diseases given the vast migration of people (Gutierrez & Kendall, 2000). Additionally, increasing health disparities are likely given that the economic benefits of globalization are distributed unevenly such that the rich appear to get richer and the poor appear to get poorer (Gutierrez & Kendall, 2000). Finally, the massive migration means that providers and patients will meet in settings in which a match between national culture and ethnic culture is not an option (Koehn, 2006). Thus, communication misunderstandings in health care settings are likely, thus further contributing to health disparities. On the positive side, the enhanced communication technologies make it possible for us to communicate with health specialists and cultural experts regardless of where they are physically located. Thus, coordination of health care systems and enhanced cultural understanding are possible (Gutierrez & Kendall, 2000).

Third, we can consider governmental standards for cultural competence handed down to health care organizations. The U.S. Department of Health and Human Services, Office of Minority Health (DHHS-OMH), issued a set of 14 Culturally and Linguistically Accessible Services (CLAS) standards to enhance cultural competence. The standards are organized into three themes: a) culturally competent care (1–3), b) language access services (4–7), and c) organizational supports for cultural

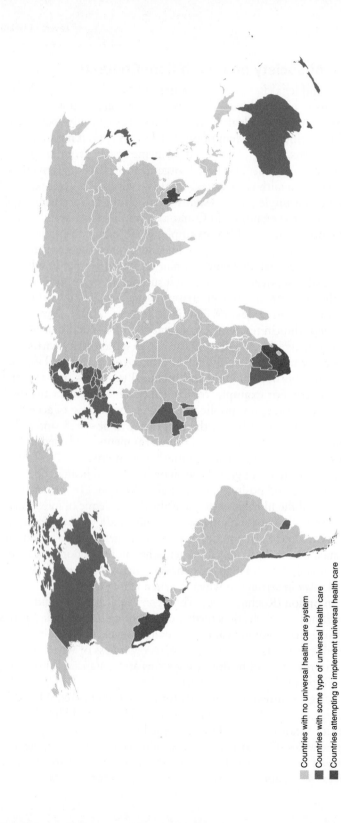

Figure 9.3
Map of Universal Health Care Coverage
Source: Wikipedia. http://en.wikipedia.org/wiki/Image:Health.png

Countries with no universal health care system
Countries with some type of universal health care
Countries attempting to implement universal health care

competence (8–14). They are displayed in Table 9.3. These standards are intended to be inclusive of all cultures and not limited to any particular population group or set of groups; however, they are especially designed to address the needs of racial, ethnic, and linguistic population groups that experience unequal access to health services and disparities in health outcomes. The standards are organized in three levels: mandates, guidelines, and recommendations:

1. Mandates: Standards 4, 5, 6, and 7 are required of all entities that receive federal funds.
2. Guidelines: Standards 1, 2, 3, 8, 9, 10, 11, 12, and 13 are recommended by the Office of Minority Health (OMH) for adoption as mandates by federal, state, and national accrediting agencies.
3. Recommendations: Standard 14 is suggested for voluntary adoption by health care organizations.

These standards provide some framework for encouraging culturally competent care, but health care organizations implement these standards to varying degrees.

Table 9.3

CULTURALLY AND LINGUISTIC ACCESSIBLE SERVICES STANDARDS

Standard 1

Health care organizations should ensure that patients/consumers receive from all staff members effective, understandable, and respectful care that is provided in a manner compatible with their cultural health beliefs and practices and preferred language.

Standard 2

Health care organizations should implement strategies to recruit, retain, and promote at all levels of the organization a diverse staff and leadership that are representative of the demographic characteristics of the service area.

Standard 3

Health care organizations should ensure that staff at all levels and across all disciplines receive ongoing education and training in culturally and linguistically appropriate service delivery.

Standard 4

Health care organizations must offer and provide language assistance services, including bilingual staff and interpreter services, at no cost to each patient/consumer with limited English proficiency at all points of contact, in a timely manner during all hours of operation.

Standard 5

Health care organizations must provide to patients/consumers in their preferred language both verbal offers and written notices informing them of their right to receive language assistance services.

(continued)

Table 9.3 (continued)

Standard 6

Health care organizations must assure the competence of language assistance provided to limited English proficient patients/consumers by interpreters and bilingual staff. Family and friends should not be used to provide interpretation services (except on request by the patient/consumer).

Standard 7

Health care organizations must make available easily understood patient-related materials and post signage in the languages of the commonly encountered groups and/or groups represented in the service area.

Standard 8

Health care organizations should develop, implement, and promote a written strategic plan that outlines clear goals, policies, operational plans, and management accountability/oversight mechanisms to provide culturally and linguistically appropriate services.

Standard 9

Health care organizations should conduct initial and ongoing organizational self-assessments of CLAS-related activities and are encouraged to integrate cultural and linguistic competence-related measures into their internal audits, performance improvement programs, patient satisfaction assessments, and outcomes-based evaluations.

Standard 10

Health care organizations should ensure that data on the individual patient's/consumer's race, ethnicity, and spoken and written language are collected in health records, integrated into the organization's management information systems, and periodically updated.

Standard 11

Health care organizations should maintain a current demographic, cultural, and epidemiological profile of the community as well as a needs assessment to accurately plan for and implement services that respond to the cultural and linguistic characteristics of the service area.

Standard 12

Health care organizations should develop participatory, collaborative partnerships with communities and utilize a variety of formal and informal mechanisms to facilitate community and patient/consumer involvement in designing and implementing CLAS-related activities.

Standard 13

Health care organizations should ensure that conflict and grievance resolution processes are culturally and linguistically sensitive and capable of identifying, preventing, and resolving cross-cultural conflicts or complaints by patients/consumers.

Standard 14

Health care organizations are encouraged to regularly make available to the public information about their progress and successful innovations in implementing the CLAS standards and to provide public notice in their communities about the availability of this information.

Source: Office of Minority Health at http://www.omhrc.gov/templates/browse.aspx?lvl=2&lvlID=15

Challenges and Skills

Addressing health disparities involves many challenges. Improving skills related to effective intercultural communication can do much to help; more specifically, developing cultural competence, cultural sensitivity, and media advocacy skills are important keys (Freimuth & Quinn, 2004).

CULTURAL COMPETENCE   Taking a class in intercultural communication provides some initial development of cultural competence skills. However, many providers have never been trained in cultural competence and simply assume that well-intentioned behavior will be sufficient to meet the needs of all patients. The CLAS standards provide some guidelines for organizations to enhance culturally competent care. Within these standards, we can also consider several examples that help to illustrate culturally competent communication.

One of the challenges of caring for patients from different cultural backgrounds is to meet their expectations of Western and traditional types of medicine. People who identify themselves as traditional may prefer to incorporate both Western and traditional healing (for example, *curanderas*, healing rituals, and medicine men). However, most providers treat patients only with Western medicine—diagnosing and treating the malady without addressing the spiritual needs of the patient. To address this limitation, some advocate an approach called hybrid therapy (Duran et al., 1998). For example, with American Indians, providers are trained in both Western and culturally specific treatment systems. Further, Western-trained American Indian providers work alongside traditional American Indian healers. The bicultural approach is designed to acknowledge historical and spiritual roots of health problems, move the patient toward culturally-appropriate behaviors and effective overall treatment, and allow individuals to redefine themselves in culturally appropriate ways. This therapy is called hybrid because of its blending of approaches and is theoretically and culturally grounded in the historical relationships and experiences of American Indians and other cultural groups. The protocol includes three steps: a) assessment about overall general health functioning, level of acculturation, spiritual functioning, and specific health problem; b) implementation of Western treatment and traditional ceremonies as appropriate to the assessment; and c) evaluation and further recommendation for ongoing therapy and/or participation in traditional ceremonies as warranted (Duran et al., 1998). The assessment is critical because providers should not stereotype and assume all people of a given culture want traditional healing. Some simply want Western-based medicine while others want both (people wanting traditional medicine only likely would not show up in the provider's office). Cultural competence includes not forcing treatment or beliefs on individuals, but rather listening to patients' needs and explanations of their illness.

Another challenge for providers is attempting to change patients' behaviors. Good health often results from behavior change such as eating better, exercising, and stopping substance abuse. Many providers have learned that they simply cannot tell their patients to change and actually expect them to change (although the Western model of medicine trains providers as experts who should be believed). One issue that frustrates providers nonetheless is when patients do not comply with their advice. A culturally competent technique that can actually help providers encourage behavior change in patients is called motivational interviewing. **Motivational interviewing** is a directive, client-centered counseling style for eliciting behavior change by helping clients to explore and resolve ambivalence (Miller & Rollnick, 2002). In essence, it is a way to interact with patients to help them to change in a way that they are comfortable with and want to do. See Box 9.8.

The four basic components to motivational interviewing include a brief structuring statement, reflective listening, affirming, and action planning. Brief structuring statements incorporate open-ended questions (for example, "What has been most difficult for you?") and facilitative statements (for example, "Tell me about..."); these strategies help focus the conversation. The questions should focus on factors of the patient's explanation of the problem such as cause, symptoms, prognosis, and treatment. These questions are designed to elicit information from patients without judgment to find out how they feel, not what the provider thinks is the problem. Reflective listening demonstrates to the patients that the provider is listening (through appropriate nonverbal cues, such as head nods and "mm hmms"), and also that he understands and empathizes with the patient. When providers rephrase what they heard and ask questions such as "Did I get that right?" they are demonstrating reflective listening. Affirming occurs when providers show support and admiration for their patients. For example, a provider might say, "I'm impressed that you got up this morning and walked a mile before work." The opposite of affirming might result in a statement such as "One mile is good, but you really need to be walking for at least

---

Box 9.8 Talking about Ethics: Behavior Change in Other Cultures

Many communication campaigns in developing countries are created by, or include participation by, Western-based non-governmental organizations. These campaigns focus on many laudable goals such as economic development, improving health (for example, stopping the spread of HIV and AIDS), and improving the status of individuals. In all these cases, there is a focus on behavior change—getting people to adopt healthy behaviors such as using a condom for sexual intercourse. Given the background and missions of the organizations (religious missionaries, for example), there is the danger that behavior change is focused on Western culture norms and values rather than the culture of the host nation. For example, encouraging the practice of safe sex may be counter to some cultures, but is critical to stopping the spread of HIV/AIDS. Consider the following questions when reflecting on behavior change in other cultures:

1. Has anyone tried to change your behavior even though it didn't fit with your cultural or moral upbringing? Do you think this was OK?
2. Do you think it is ethical to try to change the behavior of members of other cultures when the proposed change is based on your own culture? If so, under what conditions is it ethical?
3. What good and bad things might happen if we encourage behavior change that is inconsistent with cultural norms? Think about the following examples: a) encouraging condom use in highly religious communities; b) encouraging women to be assertive in highly masculine societies; and c) encouraging the expression of democracy in communist societies.

60 minutes a day." Finally, action planning focuses on small concrete steps that are consistent with what the patient has said. For example, a provider might say, "So it sounds like you are willing to walk a mile each day in the morning because it made you feel so good." If the response is "yes," the provider might follow up with "So what can you do to make that happen?" Each of these steps helps to understand the patient's perceptions and works with him or her at that level rather than trying to force the patient to a place where the provider thinks the person should be.

Finally, patients also need to develop cultural competence with providers. In the United States, patients have a right to ask questions and understand their diagnosis and treatment (including obtaining second and third opinions if desired). In fact, patients can enhance their care and improve the provider's quality of care if they engage in four communication behaviors: provide their explanation of the health problem, ask questions, express concerns, and assert their needs (Ashton et al., 2003). In fact, providers think that patients are more effective communicators when they engage in these four behaviors (Ashton et al., 2003). This responsibility is easier for people with individualistic and low power distance values as those values are more consistent with the Western-based patient-provider interaction that are part of mainstream medical expectations in the United States. Many of us are afraid to confront a provider because we assume the person knows what he is talking about. Or, we do not want to confront a provider and cause that person to lose face. Or, we simply do not feel it is appropriate for us to contradict or challenge someone who has authority over us. However, since these are our lives, we need to assert our own wishes and challenge providers if we are concerned, or find a different provider—one that better understands our needs. Even if asserting our needs is difficult, we can help the provider by offering a detailed narrative of what we think our health problem is, including cause, symptoms, prognosis, and treatment. We can also ask what she thinks is causing the problem so that we provide an opportunity for the provider to share her explanation. These two steps help to start the dialogue.

CULTURAL SENSITIVITY   Developing culturally sensitive communication campaigns to increase awareness and promote behavior change occurs in several steps. First, the medium has to be appropriate. Public health practitioners want to reach the intended audience in a way that they are comfortable with. One of the best examples of culturally sensitive campaigns is entertainment-education delivered through radio and television (Freimuth & Quinn, 2004; Singhal & Rogers, 1999). **Entertainment-education** is a performance that captures the interest of individuals to give them pleasure, but also provides a formal instruction and training designed toward a desired behavior (Singhal & Rogers, 1999). Entertainment-education has been used around the world for social and behavior change, including in such countries as Tanzania, Kenya, Costa Rica, India, Jamaica, and Peru. Entertainment-education works because it involves stories to convey information. Stories are told in all cultures although the development of the story is culture specific. Entertainment-education has enhanced enrollment in adult literacy classes in Peru and other countries of Latin America, family planning in Tanzania, and enhanced attitudes toward equal opportunity for women in India. (Singhal & Rogers, 1999). Freimuth

Box 9.9 What Went Right?: Entertainment Education as Culturally Sensitive

Twende na Wakati (Let's go with the times) was a family planning and HIV prevention radio soap opera broadcast twice weekly in Tanzania from July 1993 to December 1998. The focus of the show was to slow population growth and prevention of spreading HIV/AIDS. Tanzania had experienced rapid growth in its population, and the AIDS epidemic was spreading from other East African nations to Tanzania via long-distance truck drivers. They infected commercial sex workers at truck stops; 28% of truckers and 56% of commercial sex workers were HIV positive. Surveys of the general population demonstrated a high knowledge of HIV and family planning, positive attitudes toward HIV prevention and family planning, but low use of safe sex practices and family planning behavior.

Population Communications International, a non-profit family planning organization, worked with Radio Tanzania to produce an entertainment education soap opera working with experts from the United States and Kenya. Researchers completed 4,800 interviews and 160 focus groups with members of the target audience to develop the script, educational materials, and storyline that

included subtle messages about family planning and HIV prevention. The producers developed three character types: positive, negative, and transitional role models (transitional role models begin with negative behavior and then transition to positive behavior). For example, Mkwaju was a long-distance truck driver who was promiscuous, contracted HIV, and eventually suffered from AIDS. His wife, Tunu, was a compliant, submissive spouse during the early months of broadcasts who eventually became a positive role model for female equality and economic self-sufficiency. She separated from Mkwaju and started a small business. The show was popular (55% of Tanzanians listened to the show) and effective (23% of listeners adopted family planning, and 82% adopted HIV prevention because of listening to the show), based on comparisons between people who listened and those who didn't, as well as comparisons with one city that did not receive the broadcasts. *Twende na Wakati* is hailed as an example of a culturally sensitive and effective communication campaign.

Source: Singhal & Rogers (1999)

and Quinn (2004) reported statistics from the Center for Disease Control that found that, of the people who regularly watch TV, 70% of Hispanic women, 65% of African American women, and 64% of African American men took some actions after hearing about a health issue or disease on a TV show. Thus, entertainment-education has great potential to create behavior change.

Second, public health practitioners need to create an intervention that has culturally sensitive messages. Several steps are usually undertaken in this endeavor (Resnicow et al., 2002). First, the team creating the intervention should be culturally diverse and involve members of the target audience. Second, the intervention team needs to work with the community to assess the problem and the deep structure of the culture of the target audience. This data collection can come from reviews of literature and interviews/focus groups with community members. Third, the team should work with the community to craft or form the messages for the campaign using surface structure characteristics; that is, the message presentation should use people who look like the target audience and who share familiar language, food, and music. Fourth, the team should test out the messages with focus groups to ensure their appropriateness. The focus groups should include a wide range of people from the target audience to ensure the sensitivity. Finally, the team needs to evaluate the effectiveness of the communication campaign to determine its effects and sustainability. These steps have been used in a variety of campaigns and entertainment-education programs to enhance the cultural sensitivity and therefore the effectiveness of the messages. (Box 9.9 presents one such campaign.)

MEDIA ADVOCACY   **Media advocacy** is the "strategic use of mass media and their tools, in combination with community organizing, for the purpose of advancing healthy public policy" (Freimuth & Quinn, 2004, p. 2054). Essentially, media advocacy involves people using the media to promote the health agenda of a particular group. These advocates need to know principles of public relations and how the media works.

Media advocacy is an important component for changing health policy. How many media announcements can you recall that advocate changing health behaviors and/or policies? How effective do you think these are?

Media advocacy has a basis in agenda setting theory (Kosicki, 1993). Agenda setting theory explains that the media are not successful is telling us what to think, but they are very successful at telling us what to think about. If a group of individuals is successful at getting their health agenda in the news (via the Internet, newspaper, or television), they have a greater likelihood of influencing legislative decisions. Ultimately, media advocacy is about changing health policy, such as getting a no smoking law passed or getting tougher drinking and driving laws passed. For example, Freimuth and Quinn report about the Uptown Coalition in Philadelphia, which used media advocacy and community organizing to defeat RJ Reynolds' proposed campaign to market Uptown cigarettes in African American communities.

SUMMARY

Return to the opening story: In this chapter—and throughout the book—we have discussed several components of intercultural communication that can help explain the dynamics of health communication. As in any interaction, these components might not all apply, but all are potential factors. In this particular situation, they are presented in no particular order. First, having Siv's son Sean translate was a mistake. Sean is not a trained medical translator. More importantly, putting Sean in a position of power caused loss of face to both father and son. Lao culture is hierarchical, and fathers have power over sons. In this situation, Siv had to acquiesce to Sean's knowledge. Additionally, the situation might have included some embarrassing questions the son had to ask. Second, from the Lao cultural perspective, the doctor has status in the interaction, and no one would want to cause the doctor to lose face. Even thought Siv had not taken the pills, he could not tell the doctor the truth because that would imply the doctor gave bad advice. So Siv simply responded by saying "yes." Third, relatedly, "yes" does not always mean agreement; some cultures (including Lao) use "yes" to say "I hear you" and not "I agree" or "I did follow your advice." The burden is on the listener to understand the context (high context communication) and interpret the message appropriately. Finally, Dr. Jones only diagnosed the illness and not the overall patient's well being. Western medicine is based on identifying the biological explanation of disease, but many people who favor traditional approaches to health care (and patients in general) center on overall well being. The lack of focus on Siv's spiritual well being contributed to his noncompliance. A better approach might have been to blend Western medicine and traditional practices.

Here is the chapter summary based on the opening learning objectives:

- **Define concepts:** a key aspect about health communication is that we can distinguish between two different types: clinical health communication (for example, patient provider communication) and public health communication (for example, communication campaigns and media advocacy). See the glossary for the specific definitions of all concepts.
- **Health disparities:** Health disparities are inequalities in health outcomes for particular cultural groups. Health disparities happen on a global level with life

expectancy at birth lower in developing nations than in developed nations. They also occur within national cultures where certain cultural groups are disadvantaged over others on general health.

- **Five factors explaining health disparities:** Health disparities can be explained by several factors including socioeconomic status (SES), health care system, cultural health beliefs, service utilization obstacles, and culturally competent communication.

- **Role of intercultural communication for explaining health disparities:** A person's socioeconomic status is not necessarily a communication issue. Additionally, access, financing, and availability of services in the health care system are not communication problems. However, the lack of coordination in access to the health care system can affect some individuals more than others and can be addressed by effective organizational communication (particularly media advocacy). Cultural health beliefs influence what we perceive as risky, what is the cause for disease, and what are appropriate courses of behavior. These beliefs influence which type of communicative messages will be effective for an audience. Service utilization focuses on particular obstacles that inhibit health-seeking behavior. Among these obstacles, lack of culturally competent communication by providers and cultural sensitivity by public health practitioners are key factors for health disparities and areas that intercultural communication scholars are primed to address.

- **Cultural competence versus cultural sensitivity:** These concepts have overlapping meaning in that both focus on effective intercultural communication. Cultural competence focuses on the communication ability of providers and patients to be appropriate and effective (clinical health communication). Cultural sensitivity focuses on culturally appropriate and effective communication campaigns with careful attention to the deep structure of culture (public health communication).

- **Examples of cultural competence, cultural sensitivity, and media advocacy:** Motivational interviewing is one culturally competent communication behavior for health behavior change. Entertainment-education is an example of a culturally sensitive communication campaign. The Truth campaign (the largest U.S. national Youth-focused anti-tobacco education ever in the United States) is an example of media advocacy. These three types of intercultural communication behaviors are appropriate for addressing the layered challenges of health disparities.

- **Bottom-up and top down effects:** The layered approach is key for addressing health disparities because of the wide-ranging causes of disease and illness. Systemic factors, such as universal health care, globalization, and standards for cultural competence, must be considered, but also emphasis should be given to individual and interpersonal communication behaviors. Laws and system coordination impact the quality of care and the communication we receive from health care organizations, but cultural competence skills are the responsibility of individual patients and providers.

REVIEW QUESTIONS

1. Define health, health communication, public health, and health care contexts. Provide an example of each.
2. What is a health disparity? Provide an example at the global and national level.
3. How does each of the following contribute to health disparities: socioeconomic status, health care system, cultural health beliefs, service utilization obstacles, and cultural competence? Consider these concrete questions to help answer the general question just posed: a) How does SES/income relate to health? How does this relationship differ at the individual and community layers? b) What are three health care system factors that limit the quality of care? c) How do general and cultural specific health beliefs relate to danger and fear control? d) What are the four service utilization obstacles? e) How do cultural competence and cultural sensitivity impact health outcomes?
4. Which of the factors in question 3 directly involve intercultural communication? How might the other factors involve intercultural communication as well (or at least communication in general)?
5. Describe the bottom-up and top-down effects from the layered approach to health care contexts.
6. What are the CLAS standards, and how might these influence health communication? Discuss a personal example that followed (or did not follow) the CLAS standards.
7. Provide three examples of cultural competence. Discuss how these might improve a patient-provider encounter.
8. What steps can public health practitioners use to improve the cultural sensitivity of a communication campaign?
9. What is media advocacy? How can it be used to improve health outcomes?

EXERCISES

1. For a detailed account about how cultural perspectives can clash in patient-provider communication, read the book, *The Spirit Catches You and You Fall Down: A Hmong Child, Her American Doctors, and the Collision of Two Cultures* by Anne Fadiman) (Farrar, Straus, & Giroux, 1997). Consider how the interactions described in this book could have been better handled from an intercultural communication perspective.
2. Examine the media advocacy campaign, the Truth (http://www.protectthetruth.org/truthcampaign.htm). What makes this campaign effective? Ineffective?
3. Visit Web sites in favor of or against socialized medicine. For example, see the Web site at http://jmchar.people.wm.edu/Kin493/socmed.html, which has links to sites in favor of and against socialized medicine. As you review these sites, consider whether socialized medicine would help or hurt the level of health disparities currently in the United States.

CHAPTER 10

Intercultural Communities

CHAPTER OUTLINE

I. Introduction

II. Community and Culture

III. Challenges to Intercultural Communities: Community Conflict
   a. Scarce Resources and Disenfranchisement
   b. Cultural and Value Differences
   c. Institutionalized and Internalized Racism
   d. Concept Check

IV. Layers of Intercultural Communities
   a. Bottom-Up Effects
   b. Top-Down Effects
   c. Challenges and Skills

V. Summary

VI. Review Questions

VII. Exercises

CHAPTER OBJECTIVES

After reading this chapter, students should be able to

■ define the following community concepts: social capital, sense of community, neighborhood collective efficacy, community capacity, and community empowerment.

■ describe three sources of community conflict in intercultural communities.

Riot police respond during the Paris Riots in 2005. What are the underlying reasons that such riots occur?

- illustrate the process of scarce resources resulting in intercultural community conflict.

- explain the components of moral conflict.

- provide examples of institutionalized and internalized racism.

- offer examples of top-down and bottom-up effects in building intercultural communities.

Introduction

On October 27, 2005, in Clichy-sous-Bois, a northeast suburb of Paris consisting of mostly dilapidated high-rises and inhabited almost entirely by immigrants and their descendants, Bouna Traore, 15, of Malian origin, and Zyed Benna, 17, whose parents are Tunisian, took refuge with a third teenager in the relay station of a high-voltage transformer. They were electrocuted. Rumors spread throughout the suburbs of Paris that the police had been chasing the boys and caused them to die, although investigations found no police pursuit. Riots ensued for several weeks and were primarily led by French-born and French-raised Muslim youth of Northern African descent and Black and South Asian immigrants. Night after night, thousands of frustrated, unemployed, and angry predominantly young men turned out to torch almost anything in sight (as reported by news media); 27 public buses were burned in Trappes; in Sevran, rioters ambushed a bus, sprinkled gasoline on the passengers, then set it alight, severely burning a disabled woman; roving gangs targeted schools, shopping centers, and businesses as one desolate neighborhood after another joined the mayhem. Riots flared in other French cities as well, such as Dijon, Marseilles, and Rouen. One community leader commented at the time, "We want everyone to stop burning cars, but people have to realize that there was a reason for all of this" (Graff, 2005).

> Question: How does intercultural community conflict escalate, and how can it be addressed and possibly prevented?

The term *community* has been defined in many ways and has been used in many contexts. Community can refer to a psychological sense of community (Parker et al., 2001), an aggregate of individuals who live in or share similar physical spaces (McLeroy, Bibeau, Steckler, & Glanz 1988), or individuals who share a pattern of interaction (Hunter, 1974). Although the common view is that individuals who live in a physical neighborhood constitute a community, some communities of people interact only on the Internet (for example, cancer support groups). In general, a **community** is a collection of people who share interaction, location, and/or a sense of belonging to one another.

Many scholars over the past decades have lamented about the loss of community in the United States (Putnam, 1995), by which they mean the loss of interpersonal relationships among people who live in a similar location. The proliferation of the Internet, increased economic competition, greater focus on individualism, and globalization are all factors associated with this loss in physical communities. The concern with the fall of communities is that a strong sense of community is associated with positive health, social, and economic outcomes (Kawachi, Kennedy, Lochner, &

Prothrow-Stith, 1997; Sampson, Raudenbush, & Earls, 1997). For example, if you have a strong sense of community you are more likely to be physically and mentally healthy, have strong relationships with others, feel socially connected to others, and have a higher socioeconomic status than someone who does not have a strong sense of community.

Another challenge to the development of strong communities is the influx of people from different cultural backgrounds (that is, the globalization or migration of people). As we have discussed previously in this book, all factors being equal, the more diversity in a system, the more conflict and difficulties that occur in the system. However, cultural difference does not have to mean difficulties in a community. This chapter explores challenges to the development of intercultural communities and perspectives for addressing these challenges through a layered approach. We begin by discussing various concepts associated with community.

Community and Culture

The primary focus of community is on the social dynamics among members. These social dynamics have been described using a number of similar but distinct concepts, including social capital, sense of community, neighborhood collective efficacy, community capacity, and community empowerment (Parker et al., 2001). First, we define each of these concepts and discuss the common aspects of community derived from these concepts. Then, we introduce the importance of culture in describing these concepts.

Social capital is likely the most popular concept associated with community. **Social capital** refers to "features of social organization such as networks, norms, and social trust that facilitate coordination and cooperation for mutual benefit" (Putnam, 1995, p. 67). In essence, the focus of social capital is on the quality of the interpersonal relationships among members of a system and the degree to which those relationships can be used for the benefit of the community and individuals. Social capital involves several dimensions, including bonding, bridging, and linking (Baum & Ziersch, 2003). Bonding social capital is the horizontal ties among members of communities; for example, what type of relationship do we have with our neighbors? Bridging social capital are the social networks between the people in one community and those of another; for example, what type of relationship do we have with people in communities around our city or state? Linking social capital refers to the social ties with outside entities that have power relative to the community; for example, what type of relationship do we have with the city council, mayor, and state government?

Sense of community, the second concept related to social dynamics, is the feeling of caring and sharing among people in a community (Parker et al., 2001). Four dimensions of sense of community are relevant: membership, influence, integration, and shared emotional connection (McMillan & Chavis, 1986). Membership refers to the sense of belonging to the community. Influence is the belief that an individual matters and can make a difference in the community. Integration is the feeling that individuals' needs will be met by the resources available in the community. Shared emotional connection is the belief that members share a common history and similar experiences. A sense of community often develops by participating in community activities and by sharing stories about one's community. For example, one study of 184 Asian Pacific American college students found that participating in ethnic clubs and organizations increased ethnic awareness and also deepened the commitment of these students to their ethnic community interests (Inkelas, 2004). By participating in the activities of the club and learning about their cultural group, the students' sense of belonging and shared emotional connection were enhanced.

Neighborhood collective efficacy is the belief that members of a community can act collectively to achieve some goal (Sampson et al., 1997). The important component of collective efficacy is not whether the neighborhood goal has actually been successful, but rather that the members believe they can be successful in addressing issues of importance to the neighborhood. The key word is *can*: Can we do it? Neighborhood collective efficacy has a parallel to individual self-efficacy, which is an individual's belief that she can act to accomplish a task or reach a goal. An example of neighborhood collective efficacy is a neighborhood watch program. Members organize in the belief that "watching" their neighborhood will deter crime and thus make it safer.

Community capacity is "the characteristics of communities that affect their ability to identify, mobilize, and address social and public health problems" (Goodman et al., 1998, p. 259). Community capacity focuses on the assets that communities have—or do not have—to address critical issues and to achieve goals. Capacities might include being able to mobilize people, having organizations to assess community problems and analyze data, and engaging in media advocacy to bring attention to the community. To illustrate capacity, imagine that residents of a neighborhood want to have a community center built. To accomplish that goal, the neighborhood association might need people with political skills who can lobby government officials to fund the project, researchers who can demonstrate the need and value for the neighborhood center, and individuals with marketing/public relations skills who can help strengthen a campaign to encourage voters to pass a sales tax for financing.

Community empowerment is a social action process that promotes the participation of people and organizations toward the goals of community. Empowering individuals focuses on providing them with the skills to achieve their goals. Empowering a community emphasizes the development of personal, interpersonal, and political/advocacy skills (Freeman, 2001; Zimmerman, 2000). Personal empowerment refers to individual feelings about knowledge, power, and self-efficacy. Interpersonal empowerment is the development of skills for influencing others such as problem-solving skills and the education of others. Political empowerment is the ability to advocate for change leading to a sense of collective efficacy and changes in the system. Community empowerment includes perceptions of personal control, a critical understanding of the sociopolitical environment, recognition of the need for group participation, critical consciousness, and willingness to participate in collective action. When developing a neighborhood association, for example,

Box 10.1 What Went Right? Social Capital, Sense of Community, and Communication Empowerment in a Youth Organization

Michael Eichler describes the importance of consensus building in communities (Eichler, 2007). He explains that this process involves identifying the self-interest of community members, having the ideological flexibility to mix and match partners, and working with these partners to maximize mutual self-interest. This approach to community building emphasizes social capital and developing interpersonal networks with a variety of partners (including those that you might not see eye to eye on).

In an earlier work, Eichler (1998) discussed students at El Puente Academy for Peace and Justice in Brooklyn, New York. These students formed their own organization (Youth Organizers, or YO!) and researched and chose their own community issues. During their research in the community, they determined that there were many people interested in becoming street vendors. The students met with the vendors to establish trust and build relationships. Outside the community, they chose a facilitator from Cornell University because she was an immigrant and was willing to deliver her training

in Spanish and English. Additionally, they negotiated with the City of New York to secure a park for the vendors to jointly sell their goods. The students asked the vendors to participate in the creation of the training; by doing so, the vendors had ownership of the project and wanted to ensure its continuation after the students graduated. The project was viewed as a success in building community and promoting economic development but also in terms of enhancing intercultural relationships. The students interacted with people from various ethnic groups, income levels, and educational backgrounds. They found ways to create commonalities among seemingly divergent people.

The project helped to create social capital and a sense of community among the vendors and students. The vendors and students felt value for the project and saw a benefit for all involved. Both the vendors and students had collective self-efficacy, the belief that they could make this project happen. Throughout the process, they developed capacities, which led to feelings of empowerment.

police officers often train members of the community in how to organize people, what signs to look for, and whom to call in case of problems. In this manner, the members of the watch group become empowered to address future problems. Also see Box 10.1.

Collectively, the five community concepts that describe the social dynamics among members of a community emphasize different components, ranging from feelings of belonging to social relationships to action. Combining these concepts helps to illustrate the gamut of what it means to have a community. Social capital provides the overarching framework of this approach and identifies the other key constructs within social capital: collective efficacy, psychological sense of community, and community capacity/empowerment (Lochner, Kawachi, & Kennedy, 1999). In other words, this approach includes all of the key components of community—belonging, social relations, belief in the ability to act, and capacity to act. See Figure 10.1 for a model of these concepts.

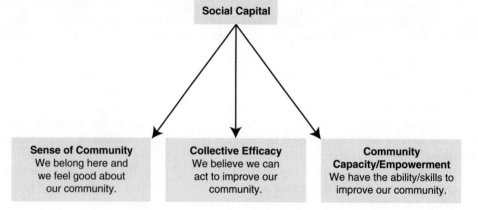

Figure 10.1
Key Concepts:
Community

Overall, these concepts of community are applicable to most cultures. In this sense, these concepts represent etic concepts of community (attributes shared by many cultures). However, specific definitions, beliefs, and behaviors within each of the dimensions may be unique to some cultures. For example, during a five-year period from 2000–2005, I worked with a research team at the University of New Mexico and with members of two American Indian communities to develop a culturally appropriate measure of community capacity that involved five dimensions: youth, elders, sense of community, language/culture, and communication. We held over 40 focus groups with community members as well as discussions with community leaders for three years to identify these components of capacity from these communities' perspective. We created a questionnaire, which community interviewers administered to 500 household members (see Self-Assessment 10.1). We then analyzed and validated the five dimensions of community capacity. These dimensions demonstrate some similarity to community concepts shared by other communities, for example, sense of community and communication, but some uniqueness as well. The culture dimension emphasizes the strong cultural identity and importance of preserving language and cultural traditions and rituals in a tribal community. This dimension is critical and can be considered within a historical framework, such as when the U.S. government marginalized these cultures by forcing them to live on reservations. The youth and elders dimension focuses on two important social groups in these communities: elders, who are the caretakers of culture and who are held in the highest esteem, and youth, who are key for maintaining the strength of the culture. This study helps to illustrate some of the emic characteristics (unique to a particular culture) of perceptions of community and emphasizes the importance of understanding culture when considering aspects of community. Social capital, sense of community, and social action are likewise significant characteristics in all communities, but how we live and reinforce these community aspects have cultural influences. In essence, these cultural influences are important in recognizing the development of intercultural communities.

Self-Assessment 10.1

COMMUNITY CAPACITY FOR AMERICAN INDIAN COMMUNITIES

Rate each of the questions using the following scale: 5 = strongly agree, 4 = agree, 3 = neutral, 2 = disagree, 1 = strongly disagree. For each question, consider a single community that you belong to (for example, a physical neighborhood or a religious or cultural community).

Category	Item	Score
Youth	1. There are enough recreational activities for young people to participate in.	
	2. Youth have opportunity to voice their issues to community leadership.	
	3. Parents and youth communicate effectively with each other.	
	4. Youth have good role models in community leaders/ program staff.	
	5. Children who come home to an empty house can depend on family and neighbors.	
Elders	1. Our elders are strong role models for the younger generations.	
	2. Elders have the opportunity to voice their issues to tribal leadership.	
	3. Family members have enough support to provide appropriate care for their elders in their home.	
	4. Elders and teens communicate effectively about our culture.	
Sense of Community	1. People demonstrate a respect for the beliefs and values of other people's spiritual/religious traditions.	
	2. If a child is misbehaving, other community members will step in.	
	3. Traditional activities bring people together regardless of conflicts in the community.	
	4. I feel accepted in my community.	
Language/Culture	1. It is important for my children and other future generations to speak the_____language.	
	2. I want to learn more about our native language and culture.	
	3. I know where to find knowledge on our native language and culture.	

(continued)

Self-Assessment 10.1 (continued)

Category	Item	Score
Communication	1. Community leaders provide sufficient information about issues affecting the community.	
	2. Community leaders listen to the needs of community members.	
	3. Programs are successful at bringing people together to talk about problems and solutions.	
	4. Programs are effective at informing members about key issues in the community.	
	5. Programs educate members to take responsibility for their own problems.	
	6. Programs are successful at encouraging community members to participate in efforts related to community well-being.	

Scoring: For each dimension, add the items together to create a total score. The higher the score, the more capacity you feel your community has.

Questions: Do these dimensions apply to the communities of which you are a member? Why or why not? Which other dimensions may be important to consider?

Challenges to Intercultural Communities: Community Conflict

The biggest challenge to the development and prosperity of intercultural communities is community conflict. **Community conflicts** are struggles between and among collectives over scarce resources, status, and power in which the aims are to neutralize, injure, or eliminate their rivals (Warfield, 2006). The distinction between community conflict and interpersonal conflict, for example, is the focus on collectives; the conflict involves groups of people rather than individuals. Even though certain individuals may be directly engaging in the conflict, through the media, for example, the conflict itself involves a great number of people and typically is addressed through public forums and media rather than through face-to-face interaction between individuals.

In addition to the focus on collectives, four criteria help to illustrate why community conflict emerges (Coleman, 1957; Warfield 2006). First, the issue must relate to important facets of community members' lives. For example, a large manufacturer decides to stop operations in a small town and move overseas. This issue likely creates a conflict between the manufacturer and members of the community, since jobs have been eliminated (and there is competition for the remaining jobs in the community as the pool of available jobs has shrunk). Second, the issue must have a differential impact on different members of the community. In the aforementioned example, the conflict may result in long-standing citizens in the community being employed differently than recent immigrants in the community. Long-standing citizens may have been employed by the manufacturer, while recent immigrants may have had service jobs (such as in food service or landscaping). Before the company shut down, citizens may not have been concerned about immigrants taking "our jobs," but with the loss of the manufacturer, the issue of employment has been heightened. Third, community members must feel they have sufficient agency to change a condition caused by the issue. Conflict does not usually occur unless people feel action can help. For example, protesting to city council about hiring practices of immigrants might be a viable action to address the concern about who gets the jobs available in the community (or perhaps the community members can petition the city council and state to bring more business to the community). Finally, deep-rooted causal factors may lie outside the local community, but their impact and dynamic is felt locally. For example, even though the manufacturing company may have left because of economic pressures in the global market and cheaper labor overseas, the conflict is felt and debated locally because of the job loss.

While many examples of community conflict abound in intercultural communities, such as friction between law enforcement and minority groups and racial hatred, these types of conflicts can best be understood from the sources or roots of the conflict. This section examines three specific sources: a) scarce resources and disenfranchisement, b) cultural/value differences, and c) racism.

Scarce Resources and Disenfranchisement

The primary source of all conflict is scarce resources. When enough power, enough jobs, enough money, and enough status are available for everyone involved, intercultural community conflict is practically nonexistent. Unfortunately, many material resources are limited, thus creating a zero-sum game, or at least the perception of a zero-sum game. A zero-sum game occurs when the resources are limited such that, if one party gets some, what is available to others is diminished. In some situations, a true zero-sum game exists. If an employer only has 25 jobs, then only 25 people can get them. Many situations are perceived as zero-sum even when they are not. For example, while the one employer might only have 25 jobs, it might be possible to engage in community organizing to convince other employers to come to the area.

Intercultural community conflict that results from scarce resources occurs in two patterns. In the first pattern, the distribution of scarce resources differentially affects certain cultural groups; that is, one group in power has more resources—especially money and political power—than other cultural groups. The disadvantaged group begins to feel **disenfranchised,** or deprived of the rights of citizenship. Disenfranchisement forms the basis of two key roots of community conflict: a) the general perception by disadvantaged people that the system, as shaped by more powerful and dominant culture members, is inherently oppressive and discriminatory; and b) a lack of confidence by disadvantaged people in the interests and capabilities of public and private institutions to provide adequate redress for their grievances (Warfield, 2006). These two key roots generally fester until a triggering event brings the conflict to a boil. Often the triggering event is alleged use of excessive force by police that results in injury or death to a minority member. Members of the disenfranchised group often have rising expectations of hope (that is, members of the group were convinced that "things were getting better") (Oliver, Johnson, & Grant, 1993). The rising expectations create anger and a desire to act in order to improve the situation. The result may be a riot such as those that occurred in Los Angeles (1992), Cincinnati, Ohio (2000), and Paris (2005). Los Angeles was distinctive because the White officers who used excessive force against Rodney King (an African American motorist) were found not guilty by a jury (composed of all Whites), and the rioting began after the verdict was handed down.

In the second pattern, members of the majority culture, particularly those at a lower socioeconomic status, feel that other cultural groups are beginning to take resources that rightfully belong to their cultural group. Similar to the first pattern, this group feels disenfranchised and believes that those in power do not want to address the issues. However, they feel some agency and thus engage in political protests or exclusionary steps to stop the injustice rather than participate in violent acts, although violence does occasionally occur. For example, in 2000 a rancher in Texas shot an illegal immigrant who was on his property; the rancher chased the man for a quarter of a mile in his truck and tried to subdue him for border patrol agents (Gonzales, 2001). To illustrate the second pattern, in the United States during the mid to late 2000s, illegal immigration has been a major topic. Many individuals from the majority culture think the United States is not doing enough to stop illegal immigration, particularly from Mexico, and have advocated tougher laws against immigration. Another example is people who do not hire or rent/sell houses to people from minority cultural groups in order to keep neighborhoods segregated even though this practice is illegal.

Cultural and Value Differences

Throughout this book, examples of cultural differences have been noted in values and communication patterns such as relational communication, communication in education, and workplace communication. These differences can create difficulties in understanding members of other cultures and can also result in seeing other groups and cultural patterns as threats to one's own culture. This section identifies three distinctive types of cultural and value differences that potentially create conflict and interfere with the development of community: differences in autonomy and fellowship, moral conflict, and racial/cultural hatred. The three vary in the degree of perceived threat and emotional involvement from low to high, respectively.

AUTONOMY AND FELLOWSHIP   Cultural differences are often considered challenges to community. Living and interacting with people from different cultures results in different perspectives, beliefs, and rituals, differences that may need to be addressed in order to build community. Difference does not necessarily mean

Box 10.2 What Went Right and Wrong? Hindus and Muslims in India

Hindus and Muslims in India have historically had strained relationships. Their religious differences and socioeconomic statuses—Hindus having higher status than Muslims traditionally—have created community conflicts. This historical context, however, is not a guarantee of what current relations are like. In certain communities, Hindus and Muslims work together and live together in peace. They have created an intercultural community through cooperation and positive interaction. In other communities, Hindus and Muslims are at odds. They do not have similar jobs (Hindus have higher status positions in businesses and government while Muslims run their own small businesses), do not work together on a daily basis, do not live near each other, and thus have limited interaction. Conflict and strife tend to occur in these communities.

What has gone right and wrong in these communities in terms of creating a peaceful intercultural community? Several factors are at work. First, working together and living together creates opportunities for understanding and relationship building. Positive communication is important for creating community. Second, the two ethnic groups have to include people of similar status. In order to avoid disenfranchisement of one group compared to another, members of both groups must benefit from the community, including having good employment and social status and power. Gaertner and his colleagues (1996) said that these conditions are important for creating a common ingroup identity; that is, the creation of an intercultural community results in members seeing themselves as part of a larger collective. They do not give up their own unique cultural identities, but rather add an additional identity associated with the community.

1. Not all scholars agree that a common ingroup identity is necessary for creating an intercultural community. Can we have an intercultural community without having a common ingroup identity; that is, can we co-exist through mutual respect without having a sense of connection to other people?
2. Are other conditions important for creating an intercultural community?
3. Have you ever lived in a multicultural community? What do you think was key for people getting along? If there was conflict, why do you think it happened?

Source: Varshney (2003)

conflict or difficulty; however, difference needs to be identified and addressed. As we discussed in Chapter 3, the construction of a positive social identity encourages people to have an ingroup bias/preference and to compete with other groups (Tajfel & Turner, 1986). Some individuals are able to construct social identities that do not reference cultural differences, but for most people intergroup competition results in conflict (especially under conditions of scarce resources). Recognizing the need for positive social identity, and the differences that are created as a result, is one possible way to prevent intercultural community conflicts. See Box 10.2.

One such difference is the manner in which respect and relationship development are constructed. This difference occurs in the dialectic of autonomy and fellowship face. This dialectic is similar to the relationship dialectic of autonomy-connection discussed in Chapter 6, but it is manifested in different ways at the community level. As described in Chapter 6, face is the concern for one's own image, and facework refers to the communicative strategies we use to construct, maintain, and repair our image. Two of the primary types of facework are fellowship and autonomy (Imahori & Cupach, 2005; Lim & Bowers, 1991). **Fellowship face** emphasizes being approved and included by others while **autonomy face** is the desire to be free of imposition from others (Lim & Bowers, 1991). Fellowship focuses on factors such as respect, appreciation, and value for others; autonomy focuses on factors such as being left alone and having privacy respected. These factors are dialectical in that you cannot achieve fellowship and autonomy at the same time in the same relationship.

Both components of face are important to all individuals and communities. We want to be able to have a private life and not have people "in our business," but at the same time we need to know that members of our community care for us and are available to us when we need them. The balance of fellowship and autonomy appears to be influenced by cultural and contextual factors. At the cultural level, individualism is more closely connected to autonomy while collectivism is more closely connected to fellowship (Triandis, 1995). For this reason, communities composed of both types of people—those emphasizing individualism and those favoring collectivism—may have difficulties striking an appropriate balance of autonomy and fellowship. For example, individualists may perceive the fellowship attempts of collectivistic neighbors as being too imposing while collectivists may perceive the autonomy focus of individualistic neighbors as distant and unapproachable.

For example, consider a fictional suburb outside of a large metropolitan area. Some people have moved there from the city to escape the "rat race" and to slow life down. They are tired of everyone knowing their business and simply want to have a more private existence with their own land. Another group of people have moved to the suburb to enhance their sense of community. In the city, they felt everyone was running so fast and never had time for anyone. They look forward to getting to know their neighbors and have community block parties and garage sales. They like the idea of neighbors looking out for their children and their homes. The first set of families is more individualistic and less collectivistic than the second set. Both have some similar reasons for moving to the suburb, but their face needs and behaviors to meet those face needs are quite different. The first set of families is likely to feel that the second set is imposing on their privacy (autonomy face) while the second set is likely to feel that the first set does not have any sense of community (fellowship face).

The focus on economic development, the building of market economies, and the presence of violence in communities has shifted the focus toward autonomy face, particularly in large urban communities. Economic development and market economies emphasize a focus on individual achievement at the expense of community connection (Triandis, 1995). Fear of violence in the community encourages people to "mind their own business" for fear of reprisal from criminals (Kahn, 2007). As many members of impoverished and violent communities state, "There was a time that when a child was misbehaving you stepped in and scolded the child even if you did not know the family. You simply looked out for one another. Nowadays, you keep your opinion to yourself—you never know when that kid might turn around and shoot you" (Kahn, 2007, p. 84). This fear can be greater when the offender comes from a different cultural background simply because you do not understand the other culture and you are not sure if you are going to offend or be injured by the other party. The safe approach is just to keep to yourself, but the result is that it is difficult to create a sense of community.

One means to address such divides in communities is to use community mediation. Mediation is the assistance to parties in dispute by people who are neutral third parties, but do not have the authority to impose any decisions on the disputants (Barge, 2006). **Community mediation** involves the use of volunteers from differing backgrounds who receive a small amount of training; essentially, they are volunteers who focus on peace-making and fellowship. The United States includes over 550 community mediation programs; over 19,500 volunteers serve as community mediators; over 76,000 citizens have been trained by community mediation programs; over 97,500 cases are referred to community mediation centers on an annual basis; and over 45,500 cases are mediated annually (Barge, 2006). Thus, community mediation provides a great opportunity to repair and build community, but intercultural communities face challenges in mediation; in particular, different cultures have different expectations about such mediation. For people with a mainstream background in U.S. culture, disputants expect mediators to be neutral and not be involved in the decisions; they can be any individual from the community so long as they are well trained. However, recent immigrants from many collectivistic and high power distance cultures expect mediators to be elders and/or trusted leaders of the community; they are supposed to listen to both parties privately and make a decision that the disputants will accept (Barge, 2006). See Box 10.3 on page 290 for an example of unsuccessful mediation.

MORAL CONFLICT   Value differences are the foundation of many conflicts and result in clashes of moral foundations. These types of conflicts are called moral conflicts, or sometimes culture wars (Hunter, 1993). **Moral conflict** "is a clash between opposing parties based on differences in deeply held philosophical assumptions about being, knowledge, and the world" (Littlejohn, 2006, p. 395). Moral conflict is a challenge, but opens rich opportunities for interpersonal learning, improved relationships, and creative collaboration. Moral difference is not surprising or problematic in and of itself, but how we address moral difference when there is a clash can be.

Littlejohn (2006) explained that "personal action is always embedded within a moral order, or set of assumptions about what is real, how we know reality, and what is right" (p. 395). For example, pro-life and pro-choice parties disagree on whether abortion should be legal because their respective positions rely on different moral orders. Arguing about abortion is useless when the two sides share no common way of resolving the issue. This is the essential problem of this moral conflict: The moral orders are incommensurate; that is, the logic and values of the moral orders cannot be directly compared or integrated. In other disputes, moral orders can be compared.

Box 10.3 What Went Wrong? Mediation in a Community Dispute

A dispute over a fence dividing two neighbors occurred in a predominantly South Korean community in Southern California. One of the neighbors (Chung-Ho) was a recent immigrant who identified strongly with the South Korean culture, while the other neighbor (Michelle) was a third-generation Korean American who identified with both the South Korean and the U.S. cultures. Chung-Ho decided that a fence that was on the property line was ugly and knocked it down. Michelle had put up the fence herself before Chung-Ho moved in, and she was very offended by his actions. When the conversation about the fence went nowhere, she decided to take Chung-Ho to small claims court. The judge ordered Chung-Ho and Michelle to attend community mediation. Michelle was happy to attend. She had some respect for Chung-Ho and thought the mediator would help them listen to each other (she had a course in mediation during college and loved it). Chung-Ho was willing to attend as well and thought it might help them resolve the situation. He also had respect for Michelle even if she was "too American" for him. However, he quickly turned against the mediator. The mediator was a young woman, and Chung-Ho thought that she did not have the experience to consider this case

and rule appropriately. Further, he wondered why the mediator kept both of them in the room at the same time and simply encouraged them to talk to each other. He thought this approach was stupid, as that just encouraged them to fight more and simply showed the mediator's immaturity. He stormed out of the room in the middle of the mediation. Michelle was shocked, as she thought it was going well and she had started to learn about Chung-Ho. They returned to court to share their stories with the judge. The judge, an older woman, ruled against Chung-Ho and ordered him to pay for the fence to be repaired. Chung-Ho abided by and respected the judge's decision, while Michelle felt vindicated and empty at the same time. She never could get back the fence she built herself. Chung-Ho and Michelle continue to live next to one another, but they never talk and try to avoid each other.

1. Why was the mediation unsuccessful?
2. Was this a satisfactory solution to the conflict?
3. What might be done differently to alter the outcome of the case?
4. Have you ever participated in mediation? Did you like what happened? Why or why not?

For example, let's examine a dispute in the workplace. You might have a disagreement about whether you or a co-worker should get the highest raise in the department. In making the decision, your boss may consider who works more hours, who is more productive, who is more reliable, and who treats customers better. Although you and your co-worker disagree about who is the better employee, the factors used to resolve the conflict are relatively clear-cut. In contrast, the opposite spectrums for the abortion debate are not directly comparable. (Please recognize there is a broad spectrum of beliefs in this debate and the polar opposites are being used to illustrate moral, conflict.) Pro-life advocates believe that life begins at conception and that society's duty to protect that life is more important than autonomy over one's body, whereas pro-choice advocates believe in the right of a woman to control her own body and to decide for herself whether to have a child or not. You cannot directly compare these fundamental values in order to determine who is right. Both parties are right using their own moral code. The only way in which to resolve the conflict involves consulting an outside or transcendent set of criteria that might provide a means to compare the moral orders (Appiah, 2006). Absent these external criteria, such a conflict is irresolvable—both parties will continue to think they are right. Finding such criteria is difficult because the moral orders are so ingrained in our worldviews; we take these worldviews as normal and appropriate.

Culture and moral orders are directly related to one another. Cultures are "determined in part by underlying belief systems; moral differences among cultures are often salient and can lead to conflict" (Littlejohn, 2006, p. 396). Moral differences can be part of the problem when cultures come into conflict. For example, some individuals' interpretation of Muslim culture often creates clashes with individuals from other cultures because of moral differences (Oetzel, Arcos, Mabizela, Weinman, & Zhang, 2006). Muslim culture places a premium on honor and justice; some Muslims—the minority, but those that are most visibly presented in the media—understand honor as prevailing in physical confrontation despite the fact that Islam encourages harmony through third parties (Oetzel et al., 2006). This belief in physical confrontation creates a moral conflict for those who place value on peace and harmony above confrontation even when honor and justice is threatened. This distinction is found in other religions as well. For example, individuals who bomb abortion clinics in the spirit of Christianity create a moral conflict for those who place peace above other concerns.

Several characteristics of moral conflict are evident when the conflict results in an open clash (Littlejohn, 2006). First the language of both sides may differ, or the parties involved may use concepts differently. For example, pro-life advocates talk about "what God intended," while pro-choice advocates talk about "reproductive rights." In the abortion debate, even the labels—pro-*life* versus pro-*choice*—polarize and oversimplify the view points of both sides. Pro-life advocates do believe in freedom of choice but not when the choice relates to conception; they likely believe in the freedom to choose where to live, what job to accept, whom to vote for, and so on. Conversely, pro-choice advocates believe in the sanctity of life but believe that each individual has the right to decide at what moment life begins and to choose how to manage one's own body without government interference. Additionally, there is a broad spectrum of beliefs with respect to abortion, and research has shown that most people fall in between the two extremes. Second, the parties often seem locked into the dispute and feel they have no choice but to defend their position and fight. Attempts to resolve the conflict may actually end in fueling the conflict. For example, in the abortion debate, the pro-choice faction often fails to see why the other party rejects their case; "surely they understand how important reproductive freedom is." Third, the parties begin to name call, describing others as ignorant, uneducated, evil, or sick. The conflict allows no creativity and no solution other than to eliminate the rival or surrender. Essentially, the conflict becomes intractable—no solution or resolution to the conflict is possible, and it lasts for years. Finally, disputants violate their own moral order as they feel justified in order to preserve their way of life. For example, in the extreme, pro-life advocates who bomb abortion clinics feel justified that they had to kill to preserve the sanctity of life.

In this fourth point, it is important to note that I (and Littlejohn) am suggesting an alternative or transcendent perspective about the conflict. I am labeling the bombing of clinics as violating a moral order particularly based in U.S. law (wrong to kill); in contrast, members who operate from a different moral order may see this act as justified as it preserves life as best as possible. Analyzing moral conflicts is challenging because our moral vocabularies and judgments are based in a particular moral order. Attempting to step outside of them is difficult, and we often present another side as immoral given our perspective. More discussion of transcendent communication is presented later in this chapter.

RACIAL/CULTURAL HATRED   In extreme cases, cultural and value differences result in hate crimes by fringe members of the majority culture. These hate crimes are often founded in irrational fears such as homophobia (fear and contempt of homosexuals) and xenophobia (fear and contempt of foreigners). One of the most visible and memorable cases of a hate crime due to homophobia in recent history was the victimization of Matthew Shepard in 1998. Shepard was a gay college student who was killed by two locals in Laramie, Wyoming. Shepard died of massive head trauma five days after his attack. Examples of xenophobia abound around the world. For example, in Slovakia and Hungary, the Roma (popular press calls them Gypsies) population has been targeted by attacks of skinheads and has been victimized by the police's use of excessive force (Warfield, 2006). In Great Britain, hate group activity has been directed at Asian (Indian and Pakistani primarily) and African immigrants (Warfield, 2006). In the United States, attacks against Arab immigrants and Arab Americans increased post 9/11.

In some cases, xenophobia and homophobia have foundations in economic, religious, and political conditions, but they do not always result in hate crimes. Members of the majority culture may fear another group for a variety of reasons—because they believe the other group will cause loss of the majority culture, because they see the other group as a threat to safety, because they believe the other group is against certain religious values they have, or because scarce resources create competition for jobs. These fears result in political acts such as the Defense of Marriage Act in the United States which developed a constitutional amendment forbidding homosexuals from marrying, or English-only statutes in the Southwestern states of Arizona and Texas. Many individuals consider such legislation part of the usual political process, but historically in the United States such fears have led to political acts that have violated individuals' rights, such as the relocation, confinement, and extermination of American Indians in the nineteenth and early twentieth centuries. See Box 10.4 for a discussion on this point.

Box 10.4 Talking about Ethics: Political Process and Defense of Marriage and English-Only

Almost everyone agrees that hate crimes are deplorable. However, individuals debate about whether political advocacy of such legislation as the Defense of Marriage Act or English-only statutes is the result of hatred. On the one hand, people against such legislation believe that the basis of this legislation is cultural hatred and the desire to preserve the strength of the majority cultural group at the expense of minority cultural groups. On the other hand, people in favor of such legislation feel it is their right to preserve their culture and advocate for their own beliefs. Of course, many positions in between these two extremes exist, but, for the sake of debate, we focus only on these two positions. In the United States, it is the right of all citizens to mobilize and advocate for policies that they believe are in the best interest of their groups and the nation. The question is whether such acts are ethical. Consider the following questions in addressing this ethical dilemma:

1. How would members of each side frame their position as ethical?
2. Do these sides represent different moral orders? If so, can you think of a third perspective by which to resolve the debate? What are some communication techniques that we can use?
3. Are both sides fairly represented in this debate, given that the majority of the members of Congress are White, male, and straight?
4. Can you think of a time when your position was in the minority? How was the situation resolved? Did you think it was fair?

Institutionalized and Internalized Racism

Racism also creates community conflicts—both within the community and between communities. Chapter 4 discussed the basic concept of racism. However, let's now consider another type of racism that affects the development and flourishing of communities. **Internalized racism** is the acceptance by members of the stigmatized race(s) of negative messages about their own abilities and intrinsic worth. Internalized racism is characterized by the stigmatized race not believing in members of their own racial group (for example, others who look like them) and not believing in themselves. "It involves accepting limitation to one's own full humanity, including one's spectrum of dreams, one's right to self-determination, and one's range of allowable self-expression" (Jones, 2000, p. 1213).

In most Western nations, stigmatized races are generally those people with darker skin colors. Jones' research focuses on the United States and especially considers people of color including African Americans, Hispanics, Asian Americans, and American Indians. She explains that internalized racism manifests in several ways: a) embracing "Whiteness" (see Chapter 3) by using hair straighteners, accepting "White" standards of beauty, and stratifying communities by skin tone, that is, lighter skin tones are better; b) engaging in self-devaluation by using racial slurs directed toward members of one's own culture and rejecting one's historical culture; and c) adopting learned helplessness through acts such as dropping out of school, not voting, and not working to help out the community. Box 10.5 on page 294 illustrates the dilemma that internalized racism presents to people who belong to a stigmatized race.

Box 10.5 Voices: Crabs in a Barrel

I can understand the concept of internalized racism as I have experienced that many times in my life. My parents always used to say you have to watch out for Black folks because they are like "Crabs in a Barrel." I used to ask my dad about that, and he said, "If you have ever seen a bunch of crabs in a barrel, you will see one or two try to get out. But the other crabs will always pull them back down in the barrel." He said that is the same way in our community. If one person is trying to succeed, other folks will put him down and say, "why do you have to act better than the rest of us?"—as if it's a sin to try and improve one's position. My parents told me to ignore such talk and try to do my best for myself. They figured that if I succeeded, I could show other young Blacks it could be done and that I could come back to the community and help out more than staying around here waiting for something to happen. I appreciate their support and believe every community benefits when more people make something of themselves. I also understand where the "crabs in a barrel" comes from, though. It is tough growing up and watching your community deteriorate and watch people who have some wealth simply move away. It's scary to think that no one is going to be there to help out or watch out for those who stay in the community. At the same time, it is sad that we have to revert to negative and stereotypical references to each other.

1. Have you ever experienced the "Crabs in a Barrel" phenomenon? How did it make you feel?
2. Have you ever experienced other forms of internalized racism? What happened?
3. What can you do to address this type of racism?

Jones was careful to point out that, while internalized racism is important for intercultural communities and communities of color to address, members of a majority culture and government figures should not interpret any efforts to get rid of this racism as evidence that people of color are to blame for their own situations. She also identified two other relevant types of racism: personally mediated racism (this was described in Chapter 4 as racism and discrimination) and institutionalized racism. **Institutionalized racism** is "differential access to goods, services, and opportunities of society by race" (Jones, 2000, p. 1212). Institutionalized racism has been codified in customs and laws that result in different material conditions, such as better schools and safer neighborhoods, and in differences in access to power, such as holding power positions in government. Jones further explains that institutionalized racism is the key factor to address for long-term change in communities and adds that, ultimately, the government has the power to decide and act. Addressing personally mediated racism and internalized racism can facilitate change in government officials by educating individuals in power and enabling communities to act collectively to address problems in the community. Jones uses an allegory of the gardener to illustrate the three levels of racism that have hurt the development of communities (see Box 10.6).

Internalized and institutionalized racism create conflict within communities in several ways. Internalized racism creates community conflict between those members who buy into self-hate and those who reject it, and thus it impacts the ability

Box 10.6 Voices: A Gardener's Tale of Racism

Let's imagine a gardener who has 2 flower boxes, one that she knows to be filled with rich, fertile soil and another that she knows to be filled with poor, rocky soil. This gardener has 2 packets of seeds for the same type of flower. However, the plants grown from one packet of seeds will bear pink blossoms, while the plants grown from the other packet of seeds will bear red blossoms. The gardener prefers red over pink, so she plants the red seeds in the rich fertile soil and the pink seed in the poor rocky soil. And sure enough...All of the red flowers grow up and flourish, with the fittest growing tall and strong and even the weakest making it to a middling height. But in the box with the poor rocky soil, things look different. The weak among the pink seeds don't even make it, and the strongest among them grow only to a middling height.

In time the flowers in these 2 boxes go to seed, dropping their progeny into the same soil in which they were growing. The next year the same thing happens, with the red flowers in the rich soil growing full and vigorous and strong, while the pink flowers in the poor soil struggle to survive. And these flowers go to seed. Year after year, the same thing happens. Ten years later the gardener comes to survey her garden. Gazing at the 2 boxes, she says, "I was right to prefer red over pink! Look how vibrant and beautiful the red flowers look, and see how pitiful and scrawny the pink ones are."

This part of the story illustrates some important aspects of institutionalized racism. There is the initial historical insult of separating the seed into the 2 different types of soil; the contemporary structural factors of the flower boxes, which keep the soils separate; and the acts of omission in not addressing the differences between the soils over the years. The normative aspects of institutionalized racism are illustrated by the initial preference of the gardener for red over pink. Indeed, her assumption

that red is intrinsically better than pink may contribute to a blindness about the difference between the soils.

Where is personally mediated racism in this gardener's tale? That occurs when the gardener, disdaining the pink flowers because they look so poor and scraggly, plucks the pink blossoms off before they can even go to seed. Or when a seed from a pink flower has been blown into the rich soil, and she plucks it out before it can establish itself.

And where is the internalized racism in this tale? That occurs when a bee comes along to pollinate the pink flowers and the pink flowers say, "Stop! Don't bring me any of that pink pollen—I prefer the red!" The pink flowers have internalized the belief that red is better than pink, because they look across at the other flower box and see the red flowers strong and flourishing.

What are we to do if we want to put things right in this garden? Well, we could start by addressing the internalized racism and telling the pink flowers, "Pink is beautiful!" That might make them feel a bit better, but it will do little to change the conditions in which they live. Or we could address the personally mediated racism by conducting workshops with the gardener to convince her to stop plucking the pink flowers before they have had a chance to go to seed. Maybe she'll stop, or maybe she won't. Yet, even if she is convinced to stop plucking the pink flowers, we have still done nothing to address the poor, rocky condition of the soil in which they live.

What we really have to do to set things right in this garden is address the institutionalized racism. We have to break down the boxes and mix up the soil, or we can leave the 2 boxes separate but fertilize the poor soil until it is as rich as the fertile soil. When we do that, the pink flowers will grow at least as strong and vibrant as the red (and perhaps stronger, for they have been selected for survival). And when they do, the pink flowers will

(continued)

Box 10.6 (continued)

no longer think that red pollen is better than pink, because they will look over at the red flowers and see that they are equally strong and beautiful. And although the original gardener may have to go to her grave preferring red over pink, the gardener's children who grow up seeing that pink and red are

equally beautiful will be unlikely to develop the same preferences.

Source: (Jones, 2000, pp. 1213–1214). Reprinted with permission of the *American Journal of Public Health*

of community members to establish types of social capital, particularly bonding social capital. That is, it is hard to develop relationships with people who do not think you or members of your groups have value, even when it is a member of your own group. Additionally, internalized racism creates conflict between and among members of an intercultural community. Cultural members who reject group self-hate can conflict with majority group members, especially those in power, as they fight against stereotypes of their group and for better resources in their community. In this situation, it is difficult to create linking social capital. That is, a community leader might have a conflict with a politician who points to members of the community who express internalized racism. The politician might say, "You don't even have all of the members of your own community with you." Finally, institutionalized racism primarily creates the sources of disenfranchisement that lead to escalated conflict and violence mentioned in the previous sections. For example, in the book *Dreams from my Father*, Barack Obama talks about his experiences as a community organizer on Chicago's south side. He noticed the conflict among community members who were resigned to life as it was and the organizers who were trying to improve the educational, economic, and sanitary conditions in the community. Additionally, as a community organizer in Chicago, Obama had an uphill battle convincing those in power of the need for change, as the powerful could say, "Most of the people in your community don't care about their situation and aren't willing to work hard to improve their own situation, so why should we help?" Obama also experienced the feelings of disenfranchisement on a daily basis as he struggled to get people involved even though community members were not satisfied with their situation.

Concept Check

The challenges to establishing intercultural community are threefold. First, scarce resources and disenfranchisement create conditions that encourage conflict between cultural groups. Second, cultural and value differences can spark open debate and division and also racial hatred in the worse case scenario. Third, institutionalized and internalized racism create conditions of institutionalized disenfranchisement and also set up difficult interactions both between members of the same cultural group and across cultures.

Layers of Intercultural Communities

Intercultural communities are composed of various layers—individuals with different cultural identities, relationships formed with people of the same and different cultures, and organizations such as schools, churches, and health care clinics. The layered perspective of intercultural communities examines all of these facets to understand the challenges of community conflict from various viewpoints, that is, which facets exacerbate the challenges and which aspects address the challenges. This section examines bottom-up effects of individuals and organizations on communities, top-down effects of communities on organizations and individuals, and then communication skills for developing social capital, sense of community, and community capacity.

Bottom-Up Effects

Individuals and organizations can be both positive and negative factors for the creation of a sense of intercultural community. For example, from a negative perspective, we consider the intentional and unintentional practices of real estate agents and organizations that are discriminatory. Real estate practices are critical to the integration or segregation of communities. Housing discrimination is illegal in the United States but is hard to prove, and subtle practices such as racial steering and redlining often occur. **Racial steering** happens when a real estate agent only shows homes to a family in neighborhoods that are predominantly of the same racial or cultural background. This practice is illegal, but occurs frequently (Baker, 2007). Additionally, it is illegal to refuse to rent or sell to a party because of racial or cultural background. **Redlining** occurs when a bank refuses to lend money to people who live in a certain area—they draw a red line around a neighborhood on a map. This practice was popular in the early twentieth century in the United States and targeted primarily African American neighborhoods. Redlining paralyzed the housing market, lowered property values, and further encouraged landlord abandonment in particular areas. Both racial steering and redlining contribute to segregated communities; another contributing factor is individuals who choose to move when their community becomes more and more multicultural. Obviously, the development of intercultural communities is difficult when culturally different individuals do not get much of a chance to interact.

From a positive perspective, let's consider community organizers and organizations that bring individuals together. Community organizers work with community members to identify issues of importance and seek to bring people together to take collective action. For example, a concern about the quality of drinking water might arise. Community organizers will work with school and church leaders to create forums to identify citizen concerns about the water. They might interview people individually or have a town hall meeting to air concerns. Once the problem is identified, solutions are discussed and might include bringing city leaders to meetings so citizens may share their concerns. The focus on common concerns and collective action helps to bridge cultural differences as it shows common ground and demonstrates what people can do together. See Box 10.7 on page 298.

Box 10.7 What Went Right and Wrong? Community Family Day in La Mesa

At the University of New Mexico, a course in intercultural communication taught by Bhavana Upadhyaya, a doctoral student at the University, partnered student organizations with community organizations in La Mesa, a culturally diverse neighborhood in Albuquerque's Southeast Heights. La Mesa, along with its adjoining neighborhood, Trumbull, has as many as seven different cultural groups including Mexicans, Cubans, Vietnamese, Chinese, American Indians, African Americans, and White Americans. Additionally, these neighborhoods have high rates of crime, drug use and peddling, high school dropouts, and prostitution. Several community organizations work in these neighborhoods to improve community health and enhance opportunities for community members to have a voice.

The initial purpose of the course was to gather data concerning the housing and health-related needs of the community. After several site visits, the students decided that, in addition to collecting data, it was important for the different cultural groups to become visible to each other. They realized that, in spite of the diversity, members of the different cultural groups remained confined to their own groups and did not participate in the larger community-building process. To improve visibility, the students organized a community family day at the community center. To encourage different cultural groups to participate, students of this course along with middle school students in the after-school program at the community center went door-to-door to deliver flyers and invite people personally; they delivered a total of 5,000 flyers. They also connected with important community organizations and leaders of different cultural groups and requested that they encourage their members to attend this event. They invited local restaurants specializing in cultural cuisine to cater the event. Dance and music groups from the elementary school in the neighborhood were invited to perform at this event. Several service and educational organizations were asked to host tables about their organizations at this event.

The family day was a great success on many fronts. About 600 people attended the event. Thus, the class succeeded in providing an opportunity for the different cultural groups to see and interact with each other. Multicultural cuisine was served for free in exchange for filling out a survey form, and hence the students were able to gather requisite data. Many people ate a culturally different food for the first time; for example, Mexican immigrants had an interesting time with the Vietnamese spring rolls; they thought they had to remove the cover of the roll to eat it! However, in spite of the students' efforts, the event did not attract many Vietnamese or African Americans. Unfortunately, the students did not figure out too many details as to why they didn't attract these groups. The class reflected on new strategies to connect with the different communities and bring them together. The refinement and implementation of these strategies are still in process. The project also showed the students the benefits and challenges of community organizing.

Top-Down Effects

Research has shown that community and the concepts related to community, such as social capital and a sense of community, are associated with social and health outcomes in a variety of community settings. For example, Kawachi et al. (1997) examined social capital from a national survey, income inequality from the U.S. Census report, and mortality from the Centers for Disease Control and Prevention in 39 states in the United States. They found that income inequality leads to a reduction in social capital and that reduced social capital leads to increased mortality. The reason that socioeconomic status affects mortality is due, in part, to the reductions in social relationships in a community. Further, neighborhood collective efficacy was associated negatively with violence in 343 communities in Chicago (Sampson et al., 1997); in other words, neighborhoods that had high collective efficacy tended to have low rates of violent crime. Moreover, sense of community was associated negatively with depressive symptoms and self-reported general health in the same study in Chicago; that is, the greater the sense of community, the better the mental and physical health of community members. Thus, health educators, health promoters, and public health professionals advocate community capacity building as critical for improving the conditions in a community. If a community does not have capacity, it cannot sustain new programs and interventions (Goodman et al., 1998). Thus, all the various components of community relate to important social and health outcomes. In general, the more we feel a sense of belonging, the more we have strong social relationships, the more we believe we can act to achieve goals, and the more capacity we have to address problems, the better off we are as individuals and the community collectively. For example, online cancer support groups offer a form of social capital that benefits their members (Lieberman & Goldstein, 2005; Wright, 2002). Cancer survivors, especially in rural areas, may not have a network of people in their physical proximity who can share their experience. These electronic support groups provide sharing of information and social support that helps to improve the health status of the groups' members. These groups are a great example of how communities can be created in unique ways.

Social capital is important for some social and health outcomes, but may not be necessary for economic development (DeFilippis, 2001). DeFilippis argues social capital exists within a system where power and economic benefits are distributed unequally. He points to the fact that wealthy, gated communities do not represent a community filled with social capital, but there is a lot of economic development in them. In contrast, some poor communities have strong interpersonal relationships, but very little economic development. Social capital is not the solution to all of society's problems, but it does have significant positive benefit for some issues.

Challenges and Skills

This chapter has identified many of the challenges to intercultural community building. A number of approaches for community organization and community building, such as social action, community capacity building, and community-based participatory action, are possible (Eichler, 2007; Minkler & Wallerstein, 2003).

Rather than reviewing the history or details of all community building approaches, this section focuses on two approaches. The first, transcendent communication, focuses on building common ground and creating a sense of community. It is an approach for bridging cultural and value differences, particularly those involving moral conflict. The second is community-based participatory approaches. These engage governmental, university, and non-governmental entities and community organizations for collective action.

TRANSCENDENT COMMUNICATION   Most conflict is addressed through communication strategies of advocacy and negotiation. **Advocacy** focuses on asserting and supporting claims and debating positions. For example, "we need to pass Policy X because it benefits our neighborhood." **Negotiation** involves give and take on positions to reach a mutually agreeable solution. For example, "let's discuss the benefits of all of the policies to decide which parties are affected." Unlike transcendent communication strategies, however, neither of these approaches works well for moral conflict and, in fact, they tend to make the conflict more intractable (Littlejohn, 2006). The reason is that advocacy and negotiation aim to achieve first-order change, or movement on the issue of contention (Watzlawick, Weakland, & Fisch 1974). As noted earlier, moral conflict results in positions that are not directly comparable and in which the issues of contention are not clear. By continuing to discuss the issues and trying to clarify the conflict and create understanding, we actually make the conflict worse by creating deeper divisions and providing further evidence of our ineptitude or evilness in the others' eyes. Thus, more communication of this type can actually make the situation worse; counter to the popular assumption that communication is supposed to make situations better, in reality, even the right type of communication does not always work.

Transcendent communication seeks to redefine the conflict in a search for productive dialogue (Littlejohn, 2006). It is a new set of organizing principles that lead participants to think differently about what they are doing as they work through their differences and to help them achieve unimagined outcomes. Successful transcendent communication will achieve second-order change, or change that aims to switch the definition of what we are doing as we work through our differences (Watzlawick et al., 1974). As Littlejohn (2006) noted, it involves a change in the meaning of winning. Where once it meant prevailing on the issue, winning now means communicating in a way that leads to humane outcomes for all. Such discourse may not, perhaps should not, change anybody's position on the issue; but it can profoundly change anybody's ideas about communication and human relationships. When communicators successfully redefine their issues, their points of difference, and their relationship, they are able to *transcend* old patterns that held them in frustrating and negative patterns of interaction (p. 406).

Transcendent communication, which thus helps people move beyond typical patterns found in difficult conflict issues, has three characteristics. First, it creates new frames that help to overcome or redefine differences. Second, transcendent communication transforms relationships by featuring personal stories and working on relationship building. Third, it provides opportunities to explore the strengths and limitations of multiple worldviews. Transcendent communication requires the use of strong facilitation and ground rules; otherwise, people fall back into patterns of advocacy and negotiation. This type of communication allows participants to explore differences, but in a manner that allows cultural group members to learn significant, new ideas, make new distinctions, and realize that every perspective is limited in what it can do. Generally, people do not change their opinions on the issues—although that is possible—but people do change their perceptions of themselves and those who hold opposing views. This allows for the possibility for creative solutions. Table 10.1 compares the communication of advocacy, negotiation, and transcendence. Table 10.2 compares these three techniques on the specific issue of building intercultural community.

Table 10.1

COMPARING ADVOCACY, NEGOTIATION, AND TRANSCENDENCE

Topic	Advocacy	Negotiation	Transcendence
Purpose	Confrontation and winning the conflict	Give and take to manage the conflict (diplomacy)	Moves beyond issues and creates understanding
Type of change	Movement on the issues	Movement on the issues	Redefines the issues and focuses on relationship building
Communication techniques	• Persuades/influences others of the validity of your position • Debates and shows errors in argument of other side • Voting and majority deciding	• Uses compromise to settle disputes • Discusses the issues through give and take • Seeks consensual solutions	• Creates new frames • Changes the context of conversation • Focuses on relationship building • Focuses on listening and learning
Benefits	• Builds identification around an issue • Creates moral order • Fair if equal power and strong ground rules exist	• Reduces tension • Resolves certain conflicts • Stimulates collaborative problem solving	• Builds community • Creates new understanding and learning • Builds respect for other positions
Challenges	• Divides people of different moral orders and identifications • Winners and losers	• Doesn't change issue of contention • Compromise can be perceived as lose/lose	• Requires strong facilitation and ground rules • Doesn't necessarily find solutions

Table 10.2

COMPARING ADVOCACY, NEGOTIATION, AND TRANSCENDENCE ON ISSUES
OF IMMIGRATION IN COMMUNITIES

Topic	Advocacy	Negotiation	Transcendence
Defining the problem	• What is being lost or gained (e.g., jobs, culture)? • Who is benefiting (e.g., social services)? • What are the facts?	• What is being lost or gained (e.g., jobs, culture)? • Who is benefiting (e.g., social services)? • How does the problem affect other cultural groups?	• How can we live together in a productive and peaceful manner?
Resolving the conflict	• Advocacy to government officials to pass laws in your favor: Deny social services to illegal immigrants • Creating propositions to vote on: English-only laws	• Attempt to bring together leaders of cultural communities to discuss solutions: Find ways to create more jobs in the community • Collaborate on ways to integrate the community: having multicultural days	• Engage in dialogue and see what emerges • Don't directly try to resolve the conflict, but rather focus on building relationships: identify ways that illegal immigrants benefit the community
Communication strategies	• Media advocacy: running an ad showing the benefits of immigration • Organizing a protest: bring blue-collar workers together to show they feel jobs are being lost to immigrants	• Discussion of the issues: discuss the pros and cons of illegal immigration • Discussion of the facts and coming to agreement on those facts: realizing that both sides manipulate statistics in their favor	• Reframe the issue from one of racial difference to cultural richness • Focus on open-ended issues: "Learn all you can about community members from different cultures."

(continued)

Table 10.2 (continued)			
Topic	**Advocacy**	**Negotiation**	**Transcendence**
	• Find holes in others' argument: explain that illegal immigration costs the state social service dollars	• Brainstorming to identify solutions to the problems	• Identify multiple viewpoints: compare and contrast your point of view with someone from a different culture. • Tell stories about what has happened to individuals

COMMUNITY-BASED PARTICIPATORY APPROACHES **Community-based participatory approaches** (CBPA) capture the collaborative and democratic processes of the three interconnected goals: research, action, and education (Minkler & Wallerstein, 2003). The thrust of CBPA is to involve researchers, educators, and community members in a collaborative manner to address issues of concern for a community. These approaches have been used primarily to address health and social issues. Rather than having outsiders come in and simply deliver an intervention, the outside entities work closely with the community in defining the problem, investigating the problem, identifying and implementing solutions, and evaluating the interventions. The rationale is that all parties have skills to bring to a particular issue. The outside entities tend to have research and training skills while community members have local cultural knowledge about what works and what does not. In addition, the community has to sustain the project once the outsiders are gone, and thus they need to have the skills to continue to implement and evaluate the project. The core principles of CBPA are as follows:

> It is participatory; it is cooperative, engaging community members and researchers in a long-term joint process to which each contributes equally; it is a co-learning process; it involves systems development and local capacity building; it is an empowering process through which participants can increase control of their lives; and it achieves a balance between research and action (Minkler, 2004, p. 685).

Thus, CBPA is a way to engage in collaboration and research/education for social action.

CBPA focuses on the strengths of a community and collaboration with outside entities. In this manner, it focuses on building strengths or on the community's capacity to make and sustain change. Some of these capacities include member capacity, relational capacity, organizational capacity, and programmatic capacity (Foster-Fishman, Berkowitz, Lounsbury, Jacobson, & Allen, 2001). Member capacity refers to the capacity of participants to perform the tasks and work together. Relational

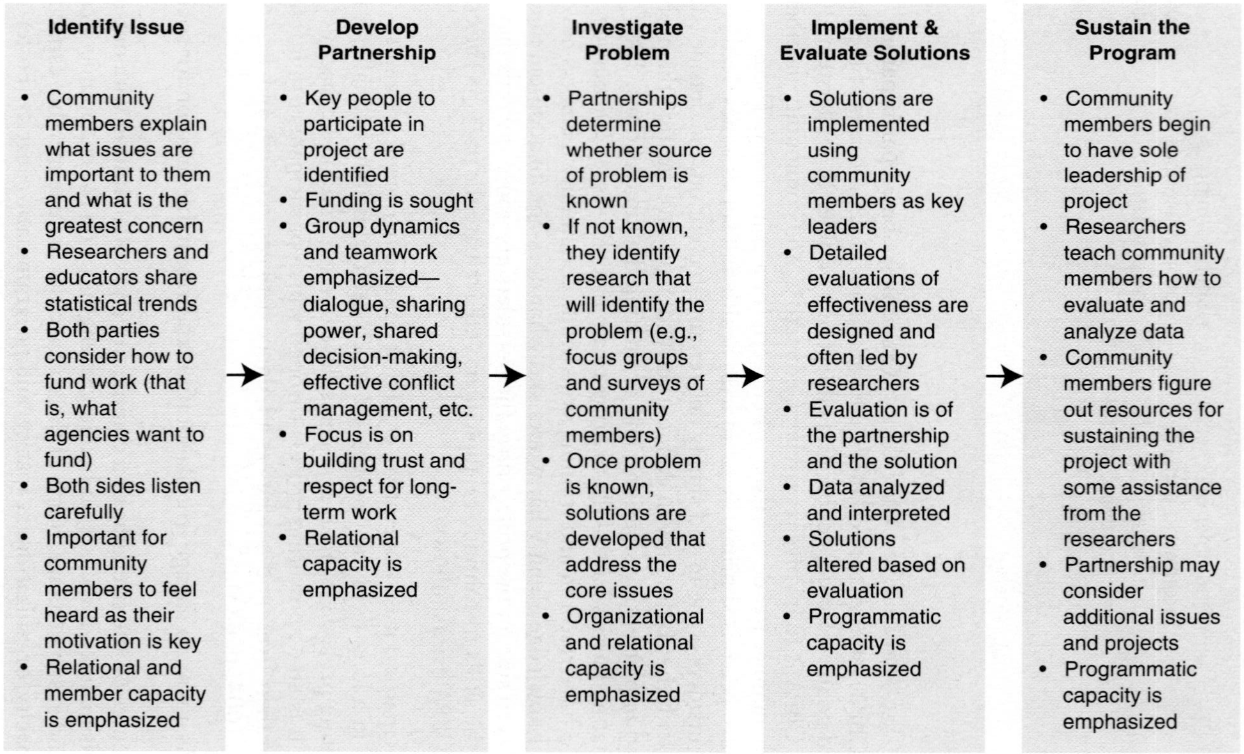

Identify Issue	Develop Partnership	Investigate Problem	Implement & Evaluate Solutions	Sustain the Program
• Community members explain what issues are important to them and what is the greatest concern • Researchers and educators share statistical trends • Both parties consider how to fund work (that is, what agencies want to fund) • Both sides listen carefully • Important for community members to feel heard as their motivation is key • Relational and member capacity is emphasized	• Key people to participate in project are identified • Funding is sought • Group dynamics and teamwork emphasized—dialogue, sharing power, shared decision-making, effective conflict management, etc. • Focus is on building trust and respect for long-term work • Relational capacity is emphasized	• Partnerships determine whether source of problem is known • If not known, they identify research that will identify the problem (e.g., focus groups and surveys of community members) • Once problem is known, solutions are developed that address the core issues • Organizational and relational capacity is emphasized	• Solutions are implemented using community members as key leaders • Detailed evaluations of effectiveness are designed and often led by researchers • Evaluation is of the partnership and the solution • Data analyzed and interpreted • Solutions altered based on evaluation • Programmatic capacity is emphasized	• Community members begin to have sole leadership of project • Researchers teach community members how to evaluate and analyze data • Community members figure out resources for sustaining the project with some assistance from the researchers • Partnership may consider additional issues and projects • Programmatic capacity is emphasized

Figure 10.2
Model of Community-Based Participatory Approaches

capacity recognizes that collaboration is about developing social networks and refers to the capacity to build both internal and external relationships. Beyond relationship development, successful collaborations require organizational capacity, which is the capacity to engage members to achieve goals, including the capacity for decision-making, leadership, and communication. Finally, effective collaborations require programmatic capacity or the capacity to develop and implement changes according to the program's mission. Figure 10.2 displays a descriptive model of some of the basic steps in CBPA.

CBPA can be used to develop intercultural community in a variety of ways. For example, the approach might involve partnering university students and community leaders to develop programs that foster understanding of various cultures in the community. This might involve dialogue groups for young school children. The university might help the community members learn how to use research techniques to monitor the effectiveness of the programs and to help identify funds to sustain the programs. Additionally, CBPA usually involves intercultural teams of community members and members from outside entities, which help to establish organizational networks for the community. Communities with linking social capital have strengths over those that do not. See Box 10.8 for an example of how technology affects CBPA.

Box 10.8 Globalization: Communication Technology Helps Community Organizing

A colleague of mine at the University of New Mexico, Magdalena Hurtado, has worked since 1985 on community organizing projects with the Aché natives of eastern Paraguay. This indigenous tribe wanted to partner with outside organizations on conservation and health goals. They live in a remote part of Paraguay, and daily communication, and therefore organizing, was a challenge. Frequent trips by Hurtado, the research staff, and the Aché were necessary until globalization reached the Aché.

As the photograph on page 306 illustrates, cell phones are now a part of the Aché's daily lives. Phone calls help the participants in the project to organize and meet project goals. Hurtado said that this photo was taken during the first days of a demonstration that the Aché organized to secure a title to land that the Paraguayan government promised to transfer to an Aché community in 1991. Cell phone communication allowed Aché from six different communities to coordinate travel plans, solve logistical problems,

exchange information between demonstration participants and the members of communities who chose not to travel, make calls to key government officials, reporters, and lawyers supporting their cause. Just two years ago this would not have been possible. Currently, a 24-meter tower is being built to bring better cell phone and ham radio communication as well as the Internet to the Aché. The technology has brought increased contact with mainstream Paraguayans and the rest of the world.

1. While this story shares some of the benefits of communication technology, does it bring up any negative consequences that you can think of?
2. In what ways does communication technology simply facilitate communication versus change the nature of relationships?
3. How has communication technology helped you connect with other people? Has this technology hurt your connections in any way?

How has technology changed the way you interact with others?

Photo of the Aché of Paraguay using cell phones.

SUMMARY

Returning to the opening story: The accepted causal factor of the Paris Riots was the disenfranchisement that the youth felt from joblessness and poverty (Graff, 2005), but also from being excluded from French culture (Croucher, 2005). Specifically, many of the Muslims in France explained that they want to be considered French and also maintain aspects of their Muslim heritage; that is, they desire a bicultural existence. However, they lack a sense of community or the social capital or community self-efficacy to enact change. Many youth feel that they are turned away from jobs and housing because of their ethnicity or faith. Unemployment in these neighborhoods is at least double the national average of 9.8% and can surpass 40%. Additionally, some 5 million Muslims live in France, but no Muslim is a member of the National Assembly (Graff, 2005).

This controversy was also inflamed by moral conflict due to cultural differences. The then Interior Minister (and now President) Nicolas Sarkozy encouraged a law-and-order campaign to crack the crime and drug rings in immigrant areas. He said criminal elements should be cleaned out "with an industrial power hose" (Graff, 2005). Graff reported that just days before the mayhem started, when Sarkozy ventured into the troubled *banlieue* of Argenteuil to outline a tough new plan to fight crime, some in the crowd threw stones at him. Sarkozy slammed the troublemakers as "scum," and some protesters took his words personally. The rioting youth who were on the other side of this controversy reverted to violence to protest such tough tactics. Stuck in the middle of this conflict are the vast majority of Paris residents who want both respect and peace. Thousands of people marched silently during the riots as a protest against both the rioters and the French government.

Here is the chapter summary based on the opening learning objectives:

- **Define concepts.** The core concepts of community—social capital, collective efficacy, psychological sense of community, community capacity, and community empowerment— focus on elements such as belonging, social relations, belief in the ability to act, and capacity to act. (See the Glossary for the specific definitions of all related concepts.)
- **Three sources of community conflict.** Building intercultural community is challenging due to three sources of community conflicts: scarce resources and disenfranchisement, cultural and value differences, and institutionalized and internalized racism.
- **Process of scarce resources to intercultural community conflict.** Scarce resources result in competition for jobs and power and often result in the members of certain cultural groups feeling like second-class citizens (disenfranchisement). Two patterns lead to conflict. In the first, the distribution of scarce resources differentially affects certain cultural groups. The feeling of disenfranchisement, along with rising expectations and a triggering event, has created many racial conflicts around the world (such as in the riots in Los Angeles, Cincinnati, and Paris). In the second pattern, members of the majority culture, particularly those at a lower socioeconomic status, feel that other cultural groups are beginning to take resources that rightfully belong to their cultural group. Similar to the first pattern, in this pattern, the group feels disenfranchised and believes that those in power do not want to address the issues. However, they do feel some agency and thus engage in political protests or exclusionary steps to stop the injustice rather than engage in violent acts (although violence can occur as well).
- **Components of moral conflict.** Moral conflicts occur when the worldviews of cultural groups clash. No direct resolution to the conflict can occur because the issues are framed from different moral orders (such as pro-life and pro-choice). Moral conflict includes four characteristics: a) the language of the conflict differs for both sides; b) the parties feel locked into the conflict and, as they fight, they fuel the conflict; c) the parties begin to describe the other group as ignorant, uneducated, evil, or sick, which leads to an intractable conflict; and d) disputants violate their own moral order as they feel justified in order to support their position.
- **Institutionalized and internalized racism.** Institutionalized and internalized racism create inequities within and between cultural/racial groups. These inequities create tensions that are challenges to building a community. Internalized racism occurs when individuals within a cultural or racial group accept the inequities associated with race and culture. These individuals might

equate strength with the majority group or try to squash the efforts of members of their own group who want to improve their situation or that of the community. Institutionalized racism has been codified in customs and laws that result in different material conditions, such as better schools and safer neighborhoods, and in differences in access to power, such as holding power positions in government.

■ **Top-down and bottom-up effects.** The layered perspective of intercultural community building emphasizes bottom-up and top-down effects. From the bottom-up perspective, the action of individuals and organizations can create further challenges and opportunities for building a community. The challenges come from personally mediated and institutionalized racism such as the practices of real estate agents who engage in racial steering or banks that use redlining. These practices segregate communities. On the other hand, the opportunities come from community organizers who identify common ground and bring people together for collective action. The top-down effects focus on the health and social benefits that a community has for its members. Strength of community, social capital, and communication efficacy result in positive effects for community members. Finally, skills in transcendent communication and community-based participatory approaches are useful for building intercultural community. These skills are not the cure-all for all problems, but they provide opportunities and creativity to solve community problems.

REVIEW QUESTIONS

1. Describe and provide an example of the following community concepts: social capital, sense of community, neighborhood collective efficacy, community capacity, and community empowerment. How do these five community concepts fit together (see Figure 10.1)?
2. What are ways the culture and community are related? What are the etic and emic parts of community capacity in American Indian communities (for example)?
3. What are the three sources of community conflicts as challenges to intercultural community building?
4. Explain the process of how scarce resources create intercultural community conflict.
5. Describe three ways that cultural and value differences create community conflict.
6. What is moral conflict? Provide an example and discuss the contrasting moral orders.
7. Discuss how institutionalized and internalized racism create community conflict. Provide an example of each.
8. Provide an example of one bottom-up and one top-down effect of intercultural communities.
9. Compare and contrast advocacy, negotiation, and transcendence for addressing community conflicts. Which of these is best for addressing moral conflict?
10. What are the principles of CBPA?

EXERCISES

1. Transcendent communication has many approaches. Examine several of these approaches, and compare/contrast them. Consider which ones you think are most effective for building intercultural communities. Barge (2006) and Littlejohn (2006) provide excellent references for getting you started.

2. Hold a dialogue about value or cultural differences in your living room. Invite friends, family, and classmates who have different viewpoints on a controversial subject, such as illegal immigration, abortion, gun control, the war in Iraq, or homosexual marriage. Use a dialogue technique such as that produced by the Public Conversations Project (www.publicconversations.org). The focus should be on transcending the controversy, not resolving the issues. Afterward, consider the following questions: What worked and what did not in this dialogue? Why did the techniques work in a positive/negative manner (for example, was it your skill in implementing the techniques, was it that your participants would not follow the rules, etc.)? What did you have trouble implementing? Why and what could you do differently in the future? How did the participants feel about engaging in such a dialogue?

3. Read the book, *Dreams from My Father*, by Barack Obama (particularly the Chicago section). Identify the strengths and pitfalls of community organizing that Obama identifies. What can you learn about community organizing from his story? What does it teach us about intercultural communication in building communities?

CHAPTER 11

Media and Popular Culture

The media are pervasive in our society. How do the media shape our perceptions and beliefs about people from other cultures?

CHAPTER OUTLINE

I. Introduction

II. Media Production
   a. Agenda Setting
   b. Cultural Studies
   c. Cultural Industries and Media Ownership
   d. Homogenization of Sources and Cultural Imperialism
   e. Concept Check

III. Media Messages
   a. Homogenization of Content
   b. Patterns of Coverage
   c. Concept Check

IV. Media Reception
   a. Uses and Gratification
   b. Cultivation
   c. Hybridity

V. Layered Perspective of Media
   a. Bottom-Up Effects
   b. Top-Down Effects
   c. Challenges and Skills

VI. Summary

VII. Review Questions

VIII. Exercises

CHAPTER OBJECTIVES

After reading this chapter, students should be able to

- describe a model of media production, messages, and reception.

- explain two theories of media production.

- discuss the results of having fewer, but large-scale media ownership.
- describe the nature and patterns of messages in the media that represent people of color.

- explain three theories of media reception.
- identify bottom-up and top-down effects of the media.

Introduction

Qin and Zheng, high school students, come from different parts of China. Zheng grew up in Beijing while Qin grew up in a smaller city in western China. Both are large consumers of Western media; in particular, they are heavy viewers of news and entertainment from the United States. Their perceptions of the United States are similar—it is a glamorous, exiting, rich, and violent place. They realize that the nation is multicultural, but assume for the most part that White Americans are rich and glamorous while African Americans and Hispanic Americans tend to be criminals or work in menial jobs; they have no knowledge of American Indians. For Qin, the media are her only exposure to U.S. Americans. Zheng actually had the opportunity to meet some U.S. Americans (several Whites and one African American and one Hispanic American) who were studying abroad, and thus she was able to talk to them about the United States. They told her not to believe all of what she saw in the media. They agreed that glamour and crime were a part of U.S. culture, but not as much as was portrayed. When it came time to apply to universities, their advisors told both of them that they should apply to universities in the United States. Zheng jumped at the chance while Qin decided to apply to universities in Germany and Australia instead.

> Questions: What theories and concepts about the media can explain Zheng's and Qin's different perceptions of the United States?

The study of the media is a critical component of intercultural communication. While most of us have not traveled around the world extensively, we still have some notion about other cultures such as U.S. Americans, French, Japanese, Chinese, Saudi Arabian, South African, Colombian, Mexican, Indian, Sunni Muslims, Shi'a Muslims, Kurds, Palestinians, people with disabilities, and others. Some of us have learned about these cultures by interacting with cultural members or from studying these cultures. However, the majority of us learn much (and at least some) of what we know about other cultures from mediated information; that is, we hear about cultures from broadcast news, see images in television shows and movies, read and view multimedia images on the Internet, and read about them in the newspapers.

Historically, media related to mass capabilities; that is, media were designed to reach mass audiences through such avenues as newspapers, television, music, and movies. The digital age and the Internet, however, have ushered in numerous new media that are both individuated and mass at the same time: cell phones, discussion boards, blogs, YouTube, and MySpace are some examples of media that can be individualized by users, but at the same time can reach a large audience. All of these forms of media convey information about culture and, at the same time, are a part of culture in the sense that the media reflect, create, and reinforce cultural traits and views.

Often, media scholars and audiences describe media as it relates to culture in terms of a hierarchy of high culture and popular culture (Cambell, Martin, & Fabos, 2007). **High culture** refers to products and artifacts associated with "good taste" and the "best elements" of a culture such as fine literature, ballet, operas, art work in museums, and elite mass media such as the *New York Times* (a newspaper that is popular, but considered a sophisticated newspaper by many) and independent films (Campbell et al., 2007). **Popular culture** includes products and artifacts that are shared and understood by most people (Brummett, 2006; Campbell et al., 2007). Popular culture is produced by media conglomerates who are selling a commodity within a capitalist system (Fiske, 1989). Popular culture is often considered "unsophisticated" and includes such venues as soap operas, popular movies, pop music, video games, and radio "shock jocks." Every genre or category of media can be placed in a hierarchy from high culture to popular culture by audiences: newspapers—*New York Times* and *London Times* are high and *USA Today* is popular; magazines—*The Atlantic* is high and *People* is popular; TV news—BBC is high and CBS/ABC/NBC national telecasts are popular; movies—Academy Award–winning movies usually are high and *Spiderman 3* (or anything with a three in the title) is popular. The terms *high culture* and *popular culture* are value judgments offered by elites. They are not absolutes or right answers, but rather one interpretation of what is "good taste." Essentially, high culture is viewed as more sophisticated by people in power and reflects a view that what is popular must not be good because it is so well liked.

You can debate the rankings, but media products in both high and popular cultures are core elements of culture. These products are part of an active process of representing, reflecting, influencing, and creating culture (Fiske, 1989; Hall, 1981). Popular culture, in particular, is very ubiquitous, and the demand for its products is great. For example, in 2006, researchers estimated that the average U.S. American consumed 3,499 hours of media including recorded music, consumer magazines, consumer books, home video/DVD, box office movies, interactive TV and wireless content, television, radio, newspaper, consumer Internet, and video games (Veronis Suhler Stevenson Communications Industry Forecast cited by Campbell et al., 2007). This amounts to 145 days a year, or more than a third of a year.

The way that culture is constructed and reconstructed and how audiences consume or reject these elements in the context of intercultural relations is the focus of this chapter. Media and popular culture shape our intercultural interactions, and thus it is important to understand how they work and how this influence takes place. The chapter is organized around the three key components of the media: production, message, and reception. Figure 11.1 displays a model of how media are produced, encoded into messages, and then received or decoded. Specifically, the producers of media encode a message into a broadcast, magazine, or other product. The receivers then decode this message in a manner consistent with the

Figure 11.1
Model of
Media
Production,
Messages, and
Reception

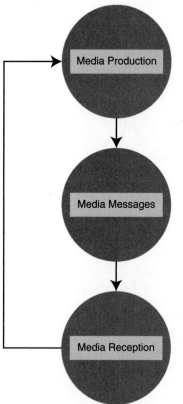

intended message or reject the message and use it in their own way. Finally, the receivers influence the producers of media in two ways. First, producers try to create messages that audiences consume (such as is the case with highly rated shows to enhance advertising sales). Second, audience members can become the producers of media (such as YouTube, MySpace, and blogs). In each main section of this chapter, we discuss relevant media theories, research and examples. In the final section, the layered perspective of media is offered to demonstrate how individuals shape media's presentation of culture and how media shape intercultural communication at an individual and relational level.

Media Production

Media production focuses on who creates and distributes television shows, movies, newspapers, and magazines. The media producers are called **cultural industries.** The products that cultural industries create are highly visible while the producers are generally behind the camera and computer screen and are not as visible. The study of media production seeks to identify who is creating such products and what the dominant ideology is in their products. As was noted in Chapter 2, **ideology** is a set of ideas that structure the worldview of a group of people. In other words, ideology, along with practices, is one way to study culture from a critical perspective. Two theories help to explain the importance of understanding media producers and their ideology: agenda setting and cultural studies. After discussing these theories, this chapter presents some examples of large-scale cultural industries. Finally, two of the potential impacts of such large-scale production—homogenization of sources and cultural imperialism—are discussed.

Agenda Setting

Media scholars have long recognized that media or cultural industries set the agenda for discussion about news on political and societal issues (Dearing & Rogers, 1996; Shaw & McCombs, 1977); that is, as noted in Chapter 9, the media do not tell us what to think, but they do tell us what to think about. The reason for this is that the media have to be selective in what they cover—they simply cannot cover every topic thoroughly. Thus, they serve as gatekeepers who make choices about what to report and how to report it. A gatekeeper is someone who controls information for others. Gatekeepers choose what information to share and what not to share. What the general public largely knows about any given topic is a function of media gatekeeping (Shoemaker, 1996). For example, a crime reporter (and his or her editor) for a daily newspaper selects which crimes committed in a city will receive coverage in the press.

Two levels of agenda setting are relevant (Littlejohn & Foss, 2005). The first level establishes the general issues that are important. The second level establishes the parts or aspects of those issues that are important. For example, when I wrote this chapter (in the summer 2007), immigration reform and policy were a large policy agenda item in the United States. The media covered immigration reform and the potential policy changes debated by the Congress and President Bush extensively. The framing of the immigration debate was whether citizenship should be provided to the 12 million illegal immigrants in the United States. This issue—termed immigration amnesty—was the focus of political and participatory discussion more than any other component of the policy. No changes were made in the policy, setting the stage for the issue to be addressed in the 2008 elections.

The agenda setting function is a three-part process (Dearing & Rogers, 1996). First, the issues to be discussed in the media are set; this is called the media agenda. Second, the media agenda in some way affects what the public seeks; this is called the public agenda. Third, the public agenda has some influence in what policymakers consider important; this is called the policy agenda. The simple view of this process is a linear one in which the media agenda affects the public agenda and the public agenda affects the policy agenda. However, it is possible to have the public influence the media agenda, for example, through protests. Setting the agenda is largely determined by who has the power to determine the agenda. In some situations, governments with a lot of power, especially governments that have a large control of the media such as those in Cuba, China, and Venezuela, determine the media's agenda to start the cycle. In many situations, the media conglomerates have enormous power and control the agenda (Gilboa, 2006). This power is the subject of the next theory.

Cultural Studies

A theory that extends the focus of media ideology beyond simply agenda setting is cultural studies. Cultural studies theory investigates the way the media (and other aspects of culture) are produced and the struggle of ideologies that the productions reflect (Hall, 1981; Hall, 1985; Hall, Hobson, Lowe, Willis, 1981). This production is based on ideology and reflects the power that media have in providing images and practices about culture. Cultural industries are powerful controllers of ideology because what they produce is highly visible and consumed. In this manner, cultural industries can present a dominant ideology to a large number of people while other ideologies are on unequal ground; that is, those that do not have the backing of a powerful cultural industry are underrepresend in the media. Hegemony is one result of such unequal power. **Hegemony** is the process of creating consent and acceptance of one set of ideas or groups as another set of ideas or groups are subverted (Gramsci, 1971).

Cultural studies scholars emphasize several aspects of this struggle of ideologies and the process of hegemony. First, cultural industries are primarily capitalistic endeavors that create products for sale. Thus, the information disseminated is based on what the market is interested in. Second, the control of such information is held within the hands of fewer and fewer industries because of media conglomerates; that is, a few companies have a great deal of power. Cultural studies scholars describe these two points in terms of political economy (Campbell et al., 2007). **Political economy** is the power held by cultural industries in the production of media for capitalistic purposes. Many cultural studies scholars are suspicious of the large media conglomerates because of the power they have in controlling what people see (that is, through limiting the choices of available media) and their concern that this limited perspective reflects only one ideology—a capitalistic one for a small group of elites. See Box 11.1.

Cultural studies scholars recognize the existence of multiple ideologies and alternative voices in the media. However, these alternative voices do not have the same level of power and thus cannot make their message as persuasive or as widespread as the large-scale cultural industries. Additionally, it is easy to identify the alternative voices as "fringe," or outside the mainstream, and thus discount them to a certain degree. Further, many of the alternative voices are in fact owned by a single media conglomerate. Thus, the perception of diversity is false. Finally, large-scale cultural industries are able to present messages that reflect the diversity of opinions and culture, but largely these images are part of the dominant ideology (Carragee, 1993); that is, media try to present people from different cultural groups to show that everyone is included, but, in reality, people are only included if they act in a manner that is consistent with the mainstream ideology (and possibly if they will buy the appropriate products). For example, a study examined the ideology presented in morning television shows (such as *Today* and *Good Morning America*) about mothers and their soldier children and the Iraq War (Cappuccio, 2006). The author found that mothers were presented as justifiers of the war—the mother as supporter/caregiver and the mother as proud mother. There were a few stories offering mothers as dissenters, but these stories were offered as straw man arguments, which were rejected; thus, the stories supported the dominant ideology of mothers as justifiers of the Iraq War.

Box 11.1 Talking about Ethics: Do Those in Power Have a Responsibility to Be Fair? Who Is Really in Charge?

One concern of cultural studies scholars, especially those who emphasize a political economy perspective, is that the power of cultural industries is generally large (not counting small independent companies). Those in power have money and can control the airwaves and print media. In this manner, not all groups have equal access to share their message and set the agenda for society. Ethical questions to this dilemma include the following:

1. Do you think all groups are fairly represented in the media? Is your group(s) fairly represented? What images do you like? Which do you not like?
2. Do cultural industries have a responsibility to be fair to all audiences?
3. How can they be fair? Should they give equal time to groups with different ideologies? Should they simply be more explicit with their ideology?

Some scholars and audience members are not as concerned as cultural studies scholars. These scholars point out that media industries only make money if audiences are happy and thus the audience has the power. Audience members are happy if they receive quality programming, and the media are more than happy to deliver.

4. Who is in power of what is created?
5. As an audience member, do you feel that you can control what is shown or watched in the media?
6. Do all cultural/ethnic groups have equal power to influence what is created? Explain your answer.

Cultural Industries and Media Ownership

Who are these cultural industries, and why are some scholars afraid of them? As defined, cultural industries are any producers of media. They are the newspaper owners, television studio owners, movie studios, video game producers, radio stations, and magazine writers. Media centers are growing around the world including those in Hollywood, Bollywood (India), Mexico, Brazil, Egypt, Taiwan, and Hong Kong (Curran, 2002). Yet, cultural studies scholars lament that these media centers are dominated by just a few large scale conglomerates. In the United States, Bagdikian (2004) identified five corporations that control the majority of newspapers, magazines, books, television stations, and movies: Time Warner, Walt Disney, News Corporation, Viacom, and Bertelsmann. He also noted that a sixth corporation (General Electric, owner of NBC) was very close to these top five.

For example, the largest U.S. media company is Time Warner with $43.7 billion in revenue (Campbell et al., 2007). Time Warner has holdings in television (Turner Broadcasting System [TBS], CNN, CNN Headline News, Home Box Office, and Warner Brothers–CW, a network joint venture with CBS), cable (Time Warner Cable), magazines (for example, *People, Sports Illustrated, Time, Real Simple*), the Internet (AOL), and movies (Warner Brothers and New Line). Other large media companies have holdings as diverse as Time Warner, making their reach broad. Thus, there may be a lot of choices, but the choices we have are still controlled by a handful of companies.

In terms of intercultural communication, a critical focus of media ownership is the staffing of such organizations. In order to have entertainment and news that is culturally appropriate, large organizations need a culturally diverse staff. However, Themba-Nixon (2006) lamented that the large media mergers have negatively impacted diversity in media staffing. For example, the Warner Brothers (WB) television network, which merged with UPN in 2006, used to have 63% of its writers from a minority cultural background. The WB used to market consciously to people of color and provided a variety of programming. The merger with the CW, however, has resulted in less diversity in staffing and in television shows, cutting many of the WB's programming aimed at African Americans (Themba-Nixon, 2006). Additionally, only 4.2% of radio outlets are minority-owned, but those stations employ more than half of all people of color in radio. Further, ethnic minorities are underrepresented in newspapers and especially in sports departments of those newspapers (Hardin & Whiteside, 2006). Thus, those in control of the production of media are not as diverse as the audiences they are producing for. The result is programming that does not present the ideology of people of color and other minority cultural groups, such as people with disabilities and homosexuals.

Another aspect of conglomeration is legal control of the media. The international human rights organization Freedom House identifies the degree to which media have freedom of speech. The map in Figure 11.2 displays their findings. About 73% of the world's people live in countries with less than a free press, with 71 nations having virtually no press freedom. Government control of the media ensures that a political and cultural ideology is reflected in the media. Such ideology still has economic implications, but the focus is more squarely on politics than consumerism. Note that freedom of the press is clearly a cultural ideology that many take for granted and is not universally accepted.

Map of Freedom 2007

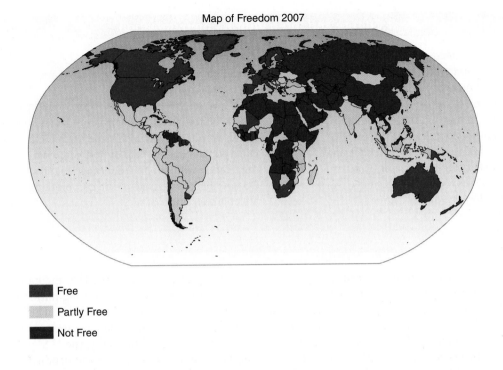

■ Free

▨ Partly Free

■ Not Free

Figure 11.2
Map of Press Freedom 2006
Reprinted with permission of Freedom House

Homogeneous Sources and Cultural Imperialism

The impacts of media conglomeration generally focus on two outcomes: homogeneous sources and cultural imperialism. The first impact examines the degree to which sources of media are shrinking. Homogeneous sources result when fewer and fewer sources produce the media. The result is fewer "real" choices and a similar ideology within those choices. Recall that there are a lot of choices out there, but many of the choices are produced by the same companies. Scholars argue that these limited choices present the ideology of the mainstream culture at the expense of cultural uniqueness (Sanchez, Cramer, & Prieto, 2003). Fu (2006) found support for the homogenization hypothesis. He examined the movie exports of 94 nations, including the United States, France, Italy, the United Kingdom, India, Russia, Germany, Japan, Hong Kong, and others, from 1970–1999. In that time period, he found a sharp decline in the sources of movies that were imported; Hollywood dominated this importing thus illustrating a homogenizing process.

The second impact is cultural imperialism. **Cultural imperialism** is the domination of one culture's ideology by another culture's ideology (Campbell et al., 2007; Curran, 2002). Around the world, cultural imperialism is debated as the influence of U.S. popular culture spreads. U.S. popular culture is widely available around the world, and in some locations it dominates the airwaves. For example, Campbell et al. (2007) stated that 80% of revenue in European movie houses comes from U.S.-made movies. U.S. media are not the only imperialistic entity (for example, Indian films dominate in Asia; Mexican and Brazilian *telenovelas* [soap operas] dominate in Central and South America), but U.S. media are the most pervasive.

Box 11.2 Globalization: Popular Culture and Intercultural Communication

Popular culture is often viewed and understood by people around the world. Some argue that this enables better intercultural communication as it provides some common understanding and perspective of the world. In this way, it does not replace local culture, but rather creates a space where national boundaries can be minimized and connection is possible. Rather than being imperialistic, this perspective emphasizes that we can integrate multiple cultural ideologies. Popular culture is a common global culture that facilitates understanding, but local cultures thrive and endure and create exciting differences.

1. When you see images of people from around the world, do you feel you understand them better?
2. Does popular culture help or hurt your communication with people from other cultures?
3. Do you think large-scale media corporations are culturally imperialistic?

The cultural imperialism argument is that the pervasiveness of the U.S. media influences the cultures, ideologies, and identities of other nations. Developing nations cannot produce enough of their own media, and thus they use U.S. products. The U.S. media have the money to produce exciting and glamorous products, and many nations and cultures cannot compete with these products. Additionally, the U.S. producers recoup their investment in the United States and can distribute the products at a cutthroat rate in other nations. Thus, the U.S. ideals of beauty, justice, politics, and family life are spread around the world and adopted—in part—by these cultures. Further, popular culture creates expectations for people in developing nations that cannot be met because of different standards of living (Campbell et al., 2007); that is, the images in U.S. media include advertisement for products that most people around the world cannot afford—and in some cases do not want. See Box 11.2.

Concept Check

The focus on media production is knowing and understanding who is creating the mediated images. Cultural industries have the power to set agendas for discussion and also present a dominant ideology. These cultural industries are increasingly being held by media conglomerates, which results in homogeneous sources and cultural imperialism. Diverse images and ideologies are not as prevalent as mainstream ideologies, as is discussed in the next section.

Media Messages

The second component of the media is the messages that are produced. The messages are created through a process of encoding the ideology into a series of images and symbols that will connect with an audience (Hall, 1981). Examining these messages allows consumers and scholars of media to understand what ideology is being expressed. The importance of these messages is that many people do not have direct contact with people from other cultural groups on a daily basis or at a deep level (ter Wal, d'Haenens,

& Koeman, 2005). Also, the images are important because they impact the self-perception of members of particular cultural groups (Mastro & Stern, 2003). Thus, the messages are influential in shaping attitudes and behaviors toward people of other cultures. The focus of this section is how cultural diversity and specific cultures are represented in the media. This section considers two aspects of the media messages: homogenization of content and patterns of coverage of different cultures.

Homogenization of Content

Earlier in this chapter, the homogenization of sources was discussed. Homogenization of content refers to the nature of the specific messages and whether they represent diverse voices and perspectives. **Homogenization** is the process of decreasing cultural uniqueness due in large part by the creation of trivialized media products; overall, media products created by large-scale cultural industries are designed for the largest common denominator (Sanchez et al., 2003). The result is fewer choices and a similar ideology within those choices. For example, Sanchez et al. (2003) described the television show *Sábado Gigante (SG)* ["Giant Saturday"], a game/variety show produced by Televisa. Televisa is the largest media conglomerate in Spanish-speaking countries with four televisions channels and 652 television stations in Mexico, 25% ownership of Univision in the United States, and a large percentage of ownership of channels in other Latin American countries. *SG* has been broadcasting for 40 years and has a weekly audience of 100 million across Central and South America. The show follows a format of four musical segments, six grand contests, four smaller contests, four journalism spots, and three to four comic spots.

The themes of the show present Spanish-speaking people as being unified primarily through common language but undifferentiated by cultural or political differences. Social, economic, and political issues as differences are not emphasized and are rarely mentioned. The identity presented is based on capitalist ideas of acquisition and consumerism (Sanchez et al., 2003). For example, one segment that shows travel destinations is geared toward middle-to upper-class people. The segment presents attractive places to travel and briefly shows indigenous and poor people in subservient roles. The segment glosses over any socioeconomic and political issues, but clearly identifies the dominant ideology and intended audience. In sum, *SG* is one example of how mainstream media presents a unified ideology for mass audiences at the expense of culturally diverse lifestyles and perspectives. Homogenization is not unique to Televisa, but rather is prevalent in the broadcasting of all large media conglomerates (Artz & Kamalipour, 2003).

Patterns of Coverage

The representation of different cultural groups has been well researched by media scholars. These scholars seek to identify patterns in news and entertainment media to uncover who is represented, how they are represented, and with what ideology. Such research is often undertaken with one of two research methods. First, scholars often employ content analysis of specific media content. Content analysis is an approach that counts the number of images, shows, articles, and roles that fit a particular category. For example, a researcher might be interested in identifying the number of criminals and their racial/ethnic background presented on the news. In this approach, a researcher randomly samples news broadcasts of a particular type, for example, one 10 p.m. broadcast a week of a particular channel for 12 months. The researcher then has her assistants view the content, count the number of criminals, and identify their racial/ethnic background. This approach enables researchers to provide a fairly objective description of what is in the media and how people are portrayed. In order to identify the detailed and often hidden meanings of a particular ideology, a second method called textual analysis is used. Textual analysis happens when a researcher selects one particular book, television show, or song and closely examines the content. The researcher describes the content and then interprets what ideology is presented. Rather than being satisfied with a superficial examination, he looks closely at the deeper and hidden meanings. For example, a researcher might consider how a particular scene might be played out in real life and compare the mediated presentation to this scene to identify stereotypes and oversimplifications. This subjective approach offers one argument about what is being presented. Collectively, these approaches help to demonstrate the patterns in coverage and the deeper ideology of those patterns.

The predominant patterns of news and entertainment coverage for people of color, people with disabilities, women, members of non-mainstream religious groups, and homosexuals can be characterized as historically absent or underrepresented and negative. Historically, these groups have been underrepresented in most media (Kamalipour & Carilli, 1998; Mastro & Stern, 2003; Media Report to Women, 2006; Thoreau, 2006). For example, in a content analysis of commercials in prime time television of the major networks in the United States, Mastro and Stern (2003) found that, of the 2,315 speaking characters, 83% were White, 12.4% were Black, 2.3% were Asian, 1% were Latino, and 0.4% were American Indians. Additionally, males were more prevalent than females in every ethnic group except Latinos. Only the representations of Black and Whites are at the population levels of these groups in the United States. Klein and Shiffman (2006) used content analysis to examine the presence of people of color in animated cartoons with the target audience being children and found that all groups except Whites were underrepresented—with the representation of people of color actually decreasing in recent years. Further, a report presented in *Media Report to Women* (2006) found that women are underrepresented (only 1 out of 3 characters) in the top grossing general audience movies for young children.

In addition to being underrepresented overall, these cultural groups are often portrayed in negative, stereotypical, or subservient ways. As an example of a negative and stereotypical portrayal, using content analysis, Dixon and Linz (2000) found that African Americans and Latinos were overrepresented as criminals in news broadcasts compared to actual crime reports. In contrast, White Americans were underrepresented as perpetrators of crime while being overrepresented as victims and as officers relative to employment records (see Figure 11.3 for an example of the stereotypes and negative portrays of Latinos). In another examination of negative and stereotypical portrayal, Merskin (2007) used textual analysis to understand the meanings of the character portrayed by Eva Longoria on *Desperate Housewives*. On a positive frame, Merskin noted

Figure 11.3
Stereotypical and Negative Portrayals of Latinos
This cartoon comments on the way the media stereotype Latinos. In what ways do media misrepresent cultural groups?

that it is rare for a Latina to be a lead character on a popular television show. However, Longoria's character—and Longoria herself—is portrayed in a stereotypical manner as the "Hot-Latina" rather than providing an opportunity for a complex character and representation of Hispanic women. Jing (2005) completed a textual analysis of the movie *The Joy Luck Club* to identify stereotypes of Chinese American culture. Using a textual analysis, she illustrated how the movie constructed negative and stereotypical images of a sexist, oppressive, mysterious, and exotic culture. Further, she noted that the movie created a double bind for Chinese Americans and other minority cultures: how to cast off their cultural identities and assimilate into the dominate culture but also retain the exotic otherness of the culture. Morris and Stuckey (1998) used rhetorical analysis (similar to textual analysis) of magazine articles and found that the articles created a romanticized image of American Indians as peaceful and connected to the environment. They argued that this sole image trivializes American Indians and minimizes their relevance for mainstream culture. Specifically, they argued that this romantic image distances American Indians from mainstream culture and keeps the focus on them in the past. See Box 11.3 for another example.

Other cultural groups such as people with disabilities, homosexuals, and members of non-mainstream religions are often represented in marginalized and stereotypical ways as well. For example, Kumari Campbell (2004) examined how people with disabilities are presented, focusing specifically on the case of Clint Hallam (a man who received the first hand–forearm transplant). She found that the medical procedures were reported as factual and uncritically, which communicated that people with disabilities need to be "fixed" and able-bodied to be whole. Additionally, studies of homosexual characters in media have found stereotypical and marginalized representations of gays (Battles & Hilton-Morrow, 2002; Shugart, 2003). For example, Battles and Hilton-Morrow used textual analysis to examine the popular television show *Will & Grace*.

Box 11.3 Voices: The Iran I Know

"My family and I have been visiting Iran ever since I can remember. People often ask if I'm scared to make these trips. I always have to quell my inner sensationalist and admit that I'm not.

When I think of Iran, I don't think of the extremists we see on TV. I think of my family and friends there, trying to live a normal life. In public, they do whatever it takes not to draw attention to themselves. But in the privacy of their homes, they let loose. It's a nation where almost everyone has a satellite dish to watch international programs and where citizens have managed to circumvent censorship to become a country with one of the highest Internet blog rates. I don't envision the anti-America protest when I think of Iran. I think of the kids my age who know more American rap lyrics than my friends back home.

When we hear news about Iran, 'the nuclear nation of Americanhaters,' we must make the distinction between sound bites and reality. This seems like an obvious and easy thing to remember. But from the comfort of a recliner in front of a TV—or behind the desk in the White House—it can be terrifyingly easy to forget."

Source: Moussavi (2006, p. 20)

The show has two main characters who are best friends—a gay man and a heterosexual woman. She argued that while the popular press heralded this show for having positive representations of gay men, in fact, this show trivializes gay men and reinforces attitudes toward heterosexuality as normal. She found that the show equated gayness with lack of masculinity, treated the most subversive character (Jack) as a child, and emphasized the character's interpersonal relationships rather than their connection to the larger social world. Through these techniques, gay identity was minimized and treated as comedy thus making it more acceptable to mainstream audiences. Kerr (2003) completed a content analysis of the coverage of Fundamentalists Christians on network television and found a consistent and negative tone presented, including the use of the following terms: intolerant, racist, violent, and prone to imposing their views on others. The only positive description was "patriotic." Dunsky (2007) reported that coverage of Islam tends to exoticize, oversimplify, and marginalize Muslims. She argued that coverage of the Middle East in the United States tends to present only the U.S. side without providing many details of the historical context of the perspective of Muslims. Further, Muslims are often presented as a homogeneous group.

The representation of minority cultural groups has seen some improvement in some media sectors. Mastro and Stern (2003) found in their study that Blacks and Whites were portrayed in television commercials in complex ways (unfortunately, Latinos, American Indians, and Asian Americans were not). For example, Blacks were found in ads for financial services and food and were presented as attractive, respected adults. Media critiques note that African Americans and Hispanic Americans are better represented than in the past in a variety of roles on television (Albiniak, 2005), and minority reporters were featured in 14% of reports in 2002 (an increase from 12% the previous year) (Media Report, 2004). From 1998 to 2002, there was an increase of 22 gay characters on television (Battles & Hilton-Morrow, 2002), and

These two characters portray different perspectives of Hispanic Americans in television. In what ways do these images represent the diversity of Hispanic American women? In what ways do they simplify or stereotype these women?

advertisements and news coverage in the *New York Times* increased for gays, lesbians, bisexuals, and transgendered (Ragusa, 2005). Despite these improvements, progress still needs to be made.

Media that are tailored toward minority cultural groups offer additional improvements. A number of smaller cultural industries produce media for particular groups or represent the perspectives of certain cultural groups. Knobloch-Westerwick and Coates (2006) examined advertisements in magazines popular with African American, Hispanic American, and Asian American readers as well as ads in mainstream magazines. They found that magazines tailored to these groups had a greater representation of their in-group than mainstream magazines. In fact, African and Hispanic Americans were the most popular models in magazines tailored toward African and Hispanic American readers, respectively. Ogunyemi (2007) studied the *African Voice*, a newspaper directed toward the African diaspora, the community around the world made up of people who have been displaced from Africa. The study found that the newspaper provided greater representation and visibility of the African diaspora than the mainstream press. This newspaper embraces the ideology of providing an alternative viewpoint for this audience. Thoreau (2006) studied the representations of people with disabilities in *Ouch*, an online magazine in Britain; the magazine is owned by the BBC but it is produced by people with disabilities. She found that people with disabilities were presented in diverse perspectives using personal narratives—techniques that differed greatly from mainstream media.

Concept Check

The messages encoded by mainstream cultural industries provide a limited view of cultural diversity and ethnic minorities. The messages tend to be homogenized in order to reach the largest possible audience, thus diminishing cultural diversity.

Further, representations of people of color, women, homosexuals, people from non-mainstream religions, and people with disabilities tend to be negative or absent. Further, these cultural groups are underrepresented in positive roles, overrepresented in negative roles, and often portrayed in simplistic and stereotypical ways. However, improvements in the representations of these cultural groups have occurred, especially in media tailored toward these audiences.

Media Reception

Research on media production and media messages can implicitly assume the audience is a passive receiver of media. For example, one of the earliest explanations of the effect of media on audience was called the hypodermic-needle model. The premise of this model was that the media had a direct effect on the audience; that is, like a hypodermic needle injects vaccines and medicine into patients, the media can shoot their potent effects directly into unsuspecting audiences (Campbell et al., 2007). The model was developed around World War II when scholars were concerned with the effectiveness of Hitler's media propaganda against Jews among the German people. Scholars became worried about the power of media and sought to critique it heavily. However, the hypodermic-needle model has been debunked in numerous studies that show that the audience uses media in individual ways, selecting what they want to expose themselves to. See Box 11.4.

Theories of media reception often seek to explain how each type of media affects the attitudes and behaviors of audience members and how audiences consume media. These theories assume that audience members are active, that they make decisions about

Box 11.4 Layered Effects: Parents' Role in the Effects of Media on Children

One audience that often is considered for direct media effects is children. Scholars sometimes argue that children's brains are not developed enough to adequately interpret and process the media (Campbell et al., 2007). Two common findings are that increased media exposure leads to obesity in children (Buijzen, Bomhof, & Schurrman, 2008) and that watching violence on television leads to children being aggressive and/or developing aggressive mental models of others (Krcmar & Hight, 2007).

Despite the evidence of the effects of media on children, many scholars argue that children are active consumers of media (Campbell et al., 2007). Children still use and reject certain media, and with

their parents' help, children can reduce the effects of media. For example, one study surveyed 451 elementary school children ages 8 to 12 years old to find out to what extent children's exposure to news coverage of a violent news event is related to their feelings of fear, worry, anger, and sadness (Buijzen, van der Molen, & Sondij, 2007). The authors found that parents who actively mediate the news event by helping children understand what they see on the news reduced the impact of the news on emotions for younger children. Restrictive mediation (keeping children from watching the news) had no effect. This study demonstrates a layered effect as children's parental relationship played a role in the impact of media on children's emotions.

what media to consume and how the media will affect them. Audiences decode media messages and choose to use them for their own purposes; audience members might accept the encoded ideology, reject it, or negotiate it and use it in complex ways (Hall, 1981). Overall, these theories help to explain how media can have an effect on individual attitudes and intercultural relations in general. This section presents three theories or notions of media reception: uses and gratifications, cultivation theory, and hybridity.

Uses and Gratification

The uses and gratifications theory proposes an alternative to audience passivity and focuses on the audience as active consumers (Campbell et al., 2007; Katz, Blumer, & Gurevitch, 1974). This theory assumes that audience members function as active and discriminating users of the media and seek out the media to meet emotional or intellectual needs, or **gratifications.** In fact, the media are but one way to meet these gratifications, and a host of media options to gratify needs are available.

With the assumption of an active consumer, the uses and gratifications theory proposes an alternative to the hypodermic-needle theory in explaining how the media affect the audience. Specifically, this theory suggests that the media provide the stimulus, but that the users choose how to attune to the message and how best to make sense of the message. An effect is produced, but the audience use of the media, and not simply the mediated message, is what determines the effect.

Cultivation

Cultivation theory deals with the role of television in distributing and consolidating beliefs about the world (Gerbner, Gross, 1976; Gerbner, Gross, Morgan, signorielli, & Shanahan, 2002). **Cultivation** is the process of homogenizing the beliefs of the audience. The basic notion of cultivation is that the more a person watches television, the more she will adopt the worldview presented. This theory predicts a major difference between heavy and light consumers of television. Specifically, heavy viewers will believe in a reality that is consistent with what is shown on television. From the cultivation perspective, individuals who are heavy users are more likely to believe the stereotypical images of people of color on television than are light viewers. One of the more popular concepts associated with cultivation theory is the **mean-world syndrome.** Heavy exposure to television and its violent images can lead a viewer to conclude that the world is a violent place and people cannot be trusted, especially people of color since they are overrepresented as perpetrators of crime.

Recent developments of cultivation theory help to explain how television viewing affects both individuals' judgments of facts and the attitudes they have (Bilandzic, 2006). Individuals bring with them to a television viewing experience prior attitudes and beliefs about the topics they see. These prior experiences shape whether people are close or distant to the content. People who are close to the content know something about the subject matter and have developed attitudes about it. These attitudes can develop because of **experiential closeness,** or through actual real world experiences, or because of **mediated closeness,** a perceived closeness through viewing of media (Bilandzic, 2006). Mediated closeness occurs because viewers are able to transport themselves into the story. For example, while watching a movie, many of us identify with characters and picture ourselves as part of the story. This is why we cheer heroes and cry during tragedies. Subject matter that is distant from the audience is described as **mediated remoteness.**

Our attitudes and perceptions of facts are shaped by these three conditions. With experiential closeness, mediated images have little effect on our judgments of facts and attitudes unless the images are consistent with our experiences. So, if you are presented with images of people of color as criminals, but your personal experiences do not endorse those stereotypes, you are not likely to believe that those images are typical of the cultural group. If you do endorse the stereotypes, the images reinforce those stereotypes. In conditions of mediated closeness, our perceptions of facts and attitudes about the situation are strongly influenced by mediated images. If you do not have personal experience with a particular cultural group and see portrayals of people of color as criminals, the level of identification or closeness you feel with the victims thus strongly shapes your attitudes about the cultural groups. Finally, if you are in a condition of mediated remoteness, your perception of facts and your attitudes are moderately influenced by the mediated images. The concept of mediated remoteness explains why people's perceptions of other national cultures about which they have no knowledge is influenced by mediated images. In a condition of mediated remoteness, if we know nothing about Iran, the United States, or Nigeria, our beliefs and attitudes are strongly influenced by stories about these countries. Also see Box 11.5.

Box 11.5 Layered Effects: Racial Images of Criminals, Media Use, and Media Effects

A study examined the extent to which television news viewers' opinions on the death penalty and perceptions of crime danger could be influenced by exposure to racial images of criminals. Over 200 college students watched an altered newscast in one of four conditions: a) majority of African American suspects (at least 3 to 1), b) majority of White American suspects, c) suspects not identified by race, and d) a number of non-crime stories. The researcher had the students also complete an assessment of their stereotyping of African Americans and the frequency of their news watching. The researcher found that those who saw the majority of African American suspects or race-unidentified suspects and endorsed African American stereotypes were more likely to support the death penalty than those who did not endorse the stereotypes. Additionally, heavy television news viewers exposed to a majority of

African American suspects were more likely than light news viewers to perceive the world as dangerous. This study demonstrates the cultivation theory in that participants' beliefs (stereotypes) and media usages influenced the effect of media images on attitudes. Participants with light television news viewing and without endorsing a stereotype were not influenced by the media images. Thus, the repeated exposure to mediated images of the African American criminal stereotype alters the cognitive representations of viewers and hence encourages people to view African Americans as criminals. The endorsement of the death penalty results from this repeated exposure as well. Further, layered effects are illustrated because the media does alter the attitudes of certain people.

Source: Dixon (2006)

Hybridity

The cultural imperialism hypothesis assumes that the large cultural industries are presenting a single global culture that benefits the capitalist economy. Other researchers argue that the cultural imperialism hypothesis assumes a passive audience and, in fact, audiences are active. Rather than accepting mediated ideology wholesale, audiences interpret the messages to suit their attitudes and cultures. In this sense, they blend the mediated messages and their own cultures into a new mixture. This process of creating this mixture is called **hybridity** (Kraidy, 2002).

Hybridity considers how local cultures consume and alter global messages. At a basic descriptive level, Tomlinson (1999) described how Coca Cola is used in different national cultures. For example, some cultures believe that it has magical properties, such as smoothing wrinkles (Russia), reviving the dead (Haiti), and turning copper into silver (Barbados). In addition, Coca Cola is indigenized by mixing with local drinks such as rum in the Caribbean, which has been brought to and popularized in the United States. Another example is anime (animation from Japan). Anime has become very popular in other cultures than Japan and is used for narration. See Box 11.6 on page 328.

Beyond the descriptive level of hybridity, Kraidy (2002) explained that hybridity represents a process of political and social negotiation of local and global cultures. He explained that local cultures can make political statements in their choice to mix popular culture with local culture. Hybridity in this sense becomes an occasion or site of struggle and democratic resistance. For example, Iranians have satellite dishes and

Japanese anime has become popular around the world and has been adapted to fit local cultures. What are some products that you use that have come from other cultures? How have these been adapted to fit your culture?

Box 11.6 Talking about Ethics: When Is Hybridity Cultural Appropriation?

Discussions of hybridity often bring up conversations about cultural appropriation. **Cultural appropriation** is the process of taking a symbol from another culture and using it for one's own cultural or individual purposes (Roberts, 2003). For example, in New Mexico, the state seal is a *zia*, symbolic of the sun, which is a symbol from the Zia people, an American Indian tribe in New Mexico. The state never asked permission to use the symbol nor paid for its use. The Zia offer that Southwest Airlines asked for, received permission, and paid to use the symbol on its airplane for New Mexico.

When is hybridity, which is often discussed with the use of popular cultural symbols, cultural appropriation? The discussion often comes back to which cultural group has the power and what is the importance of the symbol. Cultural appropriation is often labeled as occurring when minority and less powerful cultures have their symbols taken and used by people from mainstream and powerful

culture (Roberts, 2003). Some people do not distinguish between cultural appropriation and hybridity and assume that it is the same process (Curran, 2002). This discussion brings up several ethical considerations about using and adapting symbols from other cultural groups:

1. Can you provide an example of hybridity and/or cultural appropriation?
2. When is the use of other cultures' symbols hybridity or cultural appropriation?
3. When is hybridity/cultural appropriation respectful and culturally sensitive? When is it disrespectful and culturally insensitive?
4. How can hybridity/cultural appropriation be negotiated?

Note: You might consult Roberts' (2003) article on White American appropriation of American Indian powwows to stimulate a discussion on appropriation and hybridity.

import Western music as a resistance to censorship of the government (Kraidy, 2002). Further, hybridity is a way for audiences to resist Western-imposed popular culture, as if to say, you can bring your products here, but we get to choose what we want to do with them. Hybridity demonstrates that audiences are active in their use of media in ways that reflect the degree of their acceptance/rejection of the media. In this sense, the dominant ideology of media can be accepted (directly importing or using popular culture), altered (creating a blend of local and global), or rejected.

Concept Check

Theories of media reception assume that the audience is active and not passive. The audience chooses whether and how to consume media and popular culture. This does not mean that media cannot shape beliefs and attitudes of audience members, but rather that its effect is complex. Uses and gratifications theory explains that audiences employ media to meet their own needs. If the media design products that meet people's needs, they can influence the audience. Cultivation theory explains that heavy users of media are more influenced than light users. Additionally, the degree of closeness and remoteness to the topic is important for determining whether media have an influence on beliefs and attitudes. The notion of hybridity explains that an audience can choose to mix local and global cultures in creative ways. However, this creativity is limited in that large cultural industries produce limited choices tailored to the most common or popular tastes.

Layered Perspective of Media

Media are layered in many ways. Mediated messages are created by cultural industries with a certain ideology, but that ideology is produced for an audience. In this sense, all media have a top-down component. Additionally, the bottom-up effects are important to consider. Individuals have a great deal of power in influencing the media, whether through ownership or through the way that they consume media. Consistent with prior chapters, this section considers both the bottom-up and top-down effects. Then, we discuss the challenges and skills of media literacy and media advocacy.

Bottom-Up Effects

The section on media reception considers a key component of bottom-up effects, namely that audiences are active consumers of media. Hall (1981) explained that cultural industries encode mediated messages to be consistent with an ideology in their products. These are provided for audiences, but not blindly consumed. Rather, audiences actively decode the messages and choose how to use these messages.

Audiences have several choices in how they decode these messages (Bilandzic, 2006; Campbell et al., 2007; Hall, 1981). First, they can reject the media products wholesale. They can decide not to consume a product at all and thus completely reject the message. For example, audiences can choose not to watch the news. Second, they can consume the products, but reject the dominant ideology presented. For example, audiences can watch the news and the stereotypes about criminals presented, but reject the presented stereotypes. They can simply say that the messages do not reflect their personal experiences and ignore these components. Third, they can accept the messages and ideology presented. For example, in watching the news, they can accept the stereotypes of people of color as criminals and avoid intercultural interactions as much as possible. Fourth, they can become advocates of ethical and responsible media practice. For example, if they reject the stereotypes presented, they can call or write to the general manager or news director of a station and demand that more representative images of people of color and other minority cultural groups be presented.

Finally, they can choose to create their own media products. Individuals with significant resources can create alternative forms of media that better represent different cultural groups than mainstream media. For example, the editor of the *African Voice* in Britain created a newspaper for the African diaspora (Ogunyemi, 2007). Additionally, Robert Johnson founded Black Entertainment Television in 1980 to provide popular culture tailored toward African Americans. In the early twentieth century, Black directors created "race movies" or "midnight rambles" to Black audiences. These movies were silent films shown after hours during the segregation era of the United States (Bowser, Gaines, & Musser, 2001). Further examples include *Instinct* magazine, which caters to gay men, and *Ouch* magazine, which is produced by and for people with disabilities (Goltz, 2007; Thoreau, 2006). While many of us do not have the resources to produce large-scale products of popular culture, we do have the power to create a message and share it with whomever will view it on the Internet (such as YouTube). The Internet has enabled people to produce their own blogs and videos to share their own opinions.

The individual audience member has some power in interactions with cultural industries. Cultural industries are only powerful to the extent that their products are consumed. If enough people choose not to watch, read, or use their products, advertisers will remove their ads from these sources, and the cultural industries will lose significant revenue. A great example of this power is the firing of Don Imus in Spring 2007. Don Imus was a radio "shock jock" who made offensive statements about the Rutgers' women's basketball team. Individuals complained to the station about his behavior. He was eventually fired because advertisers removed their spots from his show. Imus was hired again about six months later and faced additional controversy over comments Imus made about Cowboy's football player Adam Jones. Imus said he was being sarcastic to make a point that police unfairly target African Americans.

Top-Down Effects

Scholars have long considered the top-down effects of media given the focus of media production for audiences. As has already been established, the media messages and the audience's reception of those messages are both factors that determine the strength of the effect of the message on individuals' beliefs, attitudes, and behaviors. This section examines the nature of these effects at the individual and relational level.

Studies have found that stereotypical presentations of people of color in the news, specifically as criminals, affect the interpretations that White Americans make about people of color. These studies typically manipulate the race of criminals by simply changing a photograph and comparing participants' attitudes in a variety of situations (Dixon & Azocar, 2007; Gorham, 2006). Stereotypical images influence the degree to which White Americans support the death penalty, describe African Americans in abstract terms, and think African Americans face structural barriers in society. Specifically, one study found that people who were exposed to images of overrepresented African American criminals were more likely to support the death penalty and less likely to perceive that African Americans face structural barriers in society (Dixon & Azocar, 2007). Another study (Gorham, 2006) found that participants who observed an African American criminal described the crime in more abstract language than participants who observed a White criminal committing the same act. This distinction in language is important because we tend to use concrete language—such as "he was 6 ft. tall"—when making situational attributions and abstract language—such as "he was large and scary"—when making dispositional attributions. Concrete language reflects specific descriptions of behaviors, while abstract language reflects a value judgment of behaviors. As noted in Chapter 4, the ultimate and fundamental attribution errors overemphasize group or dispositional characteristics for out-group behavior. The use of abstract language encourages this overemphasis, while concrete language brings emphasis to situational characteristics. Thus, certain White Americans, especially heavy television viewers and those who hold stereotypes to begin with, who view stereotypes of people of color are more likely to believe the ideology behind the messages presented.

Media messages also have an impact on relationships. Specifically, prior research has found that the type of media consumption is related to social capital (Beaudoin & Thorson, 2006; Putnam, 2000; Shah, McLeod, & Yoon, 2001). Social capital (from Chapter 10) emphasizes the quality of interpersonal relationships among members of a community and the degree to which those relationships can be used for the benefit of the community. Research on the relationship between social capital and media has found that viewing television news or reading news is positively associated with social capital while viewing entertainment television is negatively associated with social capital; that is, the more we consume news media and the less we watch television entertainment, the more we believe in positive relationships, trust, and a sense of community in our neighborhood. The reason is that news is associated with awareness of what is going on in the community, and entertainment television simply takes us away from the opportunity to interact with other community members (Putnam, 2000). However, further research demonstrates that this relationship is not simple, especially for young adults. Specifically, Shah et al. (2001) found that, for young adults, using the Internet for informational purposes increases civic engagement and social capital more than use of television and print media.

Challenges and Skills

The media shoulders a great deal of responsibility to present accurate, fair, and ethical messages in news and entertainment. Unfortunately, this responsibility is often given second priority as media are businesses and the focus is on gaining audience, selling advertising, and making money. Given that the media impact individual audience members and that audiences can impact the media, the focus of this challenges and skills section is how individuals can have agency over the pervasive media. Specifically, media advocacy and media literacy are considered as ways for individuals to have agency in an increasingly mediated world.

As introduced in Chapter 9, media advocacy is the strategic use of media and community organizing to promote a particular agenda. Media advocates need to know how the media works and also how to organize people. Cultural industries make changes and cover stories when a large number of people are organized around a common cause. Media advocacy can be used for a particular cause (such as seen in Box 11.7 on p. 332 on immigration legislation) or for changing the media. Historically, media advocacy has been used effectively to improve the representation and number of people of color in the media (Wilson & Gutierrez, 1995). For example, in the United States in the 1960s, the United Church of Christ's (UCC) Office of Communication partnered with local communities and used the legal backing of the Civil Rights legislation (1964) to make changes in the Federal Communication Commission's licensing of broadcast stations (Wilson & Gutierrez, 1995).

Box 11.7 What Went Right? Media Advocacy and a Rally on Immigration Legislation

In March 2006, over 500,000 people crammed downtown Los Angeles to protest legislation that would make criminals of illegal immigrants. In Milwaukee, 10,000 protestors showed up while 100,000 showed up in Chicago. Mainstream media outlets were surprised at the size and seemingly spontaneous organization of so many people.

These protests demonstrate how media advocacy and community organizing can be accomplished. Almost all of the protestors learned about the marches through Spanish-language media. Disc jockeys, including some syndicated performers, told

listeners about the marches and the issues and asked listeners to make sure that demonstrations were peaceful. In Los Angeles, 10 prime-time Spanish-language news anchors filmed a promotion of the marches. The media performers requested that protestors bring children (to minimize chances of violence) and to wear white and carry American flags to symbolize peaceful intent and love of the United States. The marches were well covered and brought awareness of the issues to mainstream audiences.

Source: Flaccus (2006)

UCC worked with African American listeners of WLBT radio in Jackson, Michigan, in 1964 to deny licensing because of the station's negative portrayal of African Americans. Additionally, UCC worked with members of the Sioux tribe in Rosebud, South Dakota, to protest the lack of programming for Sioux from KPLO television station. They were able to negotiate program changes and an agreement by KPLO to hire five American Indians to full-time positions. Other media advocacy efforts have resulted in newspapers hiring more people of color and forming professional associations (such as the National Association of Black Journalists, the National Association of Hispanic Journalists, the Asian American Journalists Association, and the Native American Journalism Association) with the goal of improving the employment of people of color and the representation of people of color in the media (Wilson & Gutierrez, 1995).

In order to become an effective media advocate or simply a critical consumer of media, it is necessary to develop media literacy, which involves skills in a variety of areas. **Media literacy** is the ability to access, critically analyze, critically evaluate, and create mediated messages in a variety of forms and contexts (Eagle, 2007; Reichert, LaTour, Lambiase, & Adkins, 2007). Accessing media focuses on being able to find and use different media. If we want to be more informed about intercultural issues in the world, we have to be able to find different types of media that cover particular cultural groups rather than relying on popular culture. Critically analyzing media means being aware of the ideology and purpose of particular media. For example, with advertising, consumers need to be aware that the primary purpose is to persuade consumers to buy certain products and services. Critical evaluation of media focuses on determining whether the underlying ideology is consistent with the direct message being presented, determining the potential positive and negative consequences of the messages, and/or simply identifying the ideology of the creator. When viewing representations of people of color and other cultural groups, we can identify the positive and negative aspects of the messages and how these messages might impact audiences. Finally, creating media focuses on obtaining the skills to produce and edit media (including writing and visual production). These skills involve new technology, but some of the basic steps are accessible to all people who can read and write. Writing letters to the editor is immediately accessible to all of us and provides an avenue to advocate for change in the media.

The challenge is how to enhance media literacy. Evidence suggests that media literacy programs in schools do have benefits although they are not perfect (Eagle, 2007; Reichert et al., 2007). Thus, schools need to be encouraged—perhaps through media advocacy—or required though public policy to develop media literacy programs and to evaluate their effectiveness. As individuals, we can engage in several steps. First, we can investigate how media are created by examining visual and editing techniques. Understanding these techniques will help us understand how ideologies are encoded into particular messages; that is, we can see how the creator uses certain angles, colors, and edits to focus on a particular message. Second, we can work on awareness of how we use media rather than consuming it on autopilot. For example, if we watch/read with others and talk about what we consumed, we are able to get different perspectives that help us get a more complete picture. Third, we can try to directly experience what is being portrayed in the media. If the media are presenting a particular cultural group in a negative light, we can try to talk with someone from that culture for another perspective. These steps help to move us from being passive receivers of media to active and critical consumers.

SUMMARY

Returning to the opening story: As heavy users of Western popular culture, high school students Qin and Zheng were exposed to some of the predominant ideology and patterns in mediated messages as observed in research. They saw the United States as a place with a lot of resources and consumption, but also as a place influenced by violence. Their attitudes and beliefs about people of color were consistent with the predominant images presented to them in the media. At this stage, both women experienced mediated remoteness from the United States, and thus they were strongly susceptible to the mediated messages. Zheng was able to interact with U.S. Americans and gained new experiences. Thus, she had experiential closeness and enhanced skills in media literacy compared to Qin and was better able to decipher the messages from Western popular culture. In both women's cases, it is clear that media producers create messages with an ideology in them that influences audience members. This influence differs for individual audience members based on their media exposure and personal experience, thus illustrating that audiences are active consumers of media.

Here is a summary of the chapter based on the learning objectives:

- **Model of media production, messages, and reception.** The model of media starts with media production. We have to understand who is producing the media and with what purpose, that is, the ideology of the media. The producers of media then create their products with specific messages tailored to the audience. Audiences then receive these messages and choose either to accept those messages as sent, reject those messages, or create new messages. The audiences then provide feedback to the producers about the products and, in some cases, become producers themselves.

- **Two theories of media production.** Two theories of media production include agenda setting and cultural studies. Agenda setting argues that the media determine which issues are discussed in society, but not what people think about those issues. Cultural studies theory investigates the way the media is produced and the struggle of ideologies that the productions reflect. This production is based on ideology and reflects the power that the media have in providing images and practices about culture. Cultural industries can present a dominant ideology to a large number of people.

- **Fewer, but large-scale media ownership.** Media mergers have resulted in fewer, but large-scale media conglomerates. The impacts of media conglomeration generally focus on two outcomes: homogeneous sources and cultural imperialism. The first impact examines the degree to which the number of media sources is shrinking. The second examines the degree to which ideology from one culture is imposed on other cultures through popular culture.

- **Nature and patterns of messages in the media that represent people of color.** One pattern in mediated messages is homogenization; that is, diversity is minimized as cultural industries limit choices in an attempt to reach the largest common denominator. A second pattern of news and entertainment coverage for people of color, homosexuals, women, people from non-mainstream religions, and people with disabilities can be characterized as historically absent/underrepresented, negative, and/or stereotypical.

- **Three theories of media reception.** Three theories of media reception are uses and gratifications, cultivation theory, and hybridity. Uses and gratifications theory assumes that the audience members are active and discriminating users of the media. The audience uses media to meet emotional or intellectual needs or gratifications. The media are but one way to meet these gratifications, and a host of media options exist to gratify needs. Cultivation is the process of homogenizing the beliefs of the audience. The basic notion of cultivation is that the more a person watches television, the more she will adopt the worldview presented. Hybridity considers how local cultures consume and alter global messages. Hybridity is the blending of mediated messages and host cultures into a new mixture.

- **Bottom-up and top-down effects of the media.** Individual audiences are active consumers of media and can choose to decode the mediated messages in ways that are either consistent with the ideology encoded or altered from the encoded message. Audiences can also reject the messages or create their own. Individuals have agency to affect the media through media advocacy and media literacy. Nonetheless, the media still have effects on individuals. Mediated messages influence attitudes and stereotypes about people, particularly about people of color and other cultural minorities, and also affect perceptions of social capital.

REVIEW QUESTIONS

1. Describe the model of media production, mediated messages, and media receptions.
2. Which part of the model emphasizes the active nature of the audience?
3. In what ways are cultural industries powerful? How does this power shape intercultural communication?
4. Compare/contrast agenda setting and cultural studies approaches to media production.
5. Give examples of the homogenization of sources and cultural imperialism.
6. How are people of color, women, homosexuals, people from non-mainstream religions, and people with disabilities represented in the media? Why is it important to identify these patterns?
7. Compare and contrast the three approaches to audience reception presented in this chapter (uses and gratifications, cultivation theory, and hybridity).
8. In which ways do individual audience members have agency regarding mediated messages and media production? What skills can be used in this agency? Provide examples of these skills (bottom-up effects).
9. How do media affect audience beliefs and attitudes (top-down effects)?

EXERCISES

1. Complete a content analysis of the coverage of particular cultural groups in a particular medium (ads in a magazine, news broadcasts, or characters in prime-time entertainment). First, randomly select about 50 ads or 10 segments of a genre (such as 10 sitcoms). Then, identify what it is you want to know about the representations of these groups: Who is present? Are they portrayed in a positive or negative perspective? Are they main or supporting characters? Systematically review the content to determine the answers to these questions. What did you find? Is your information consistent with what is argued in this chapter? How did your findings relate to your expectations after reading this chapter?
2. Complete a textual analysis of media that portrays a particular cultural group. Select one specific media example such as a movie or TV show. Watch/read the example, and describe the action as it relates to the cultural group. Then, try to identify the dominant ideology. What examples can you pull that support this ideology? Then, re-watch the example to see if you can find examples that contradict the dominant ideology. If you can, reconsider whether your initial identification of the ideology is a good fit for the messages presented. Also, consider deeper, more subtle meanings that are present. Do you find examples of cultural group stereotypes? Do you feel this example offers a positive or negative portrayal?

3. Visit the Web site on the Pew Internet Studies. This group examines media and technology use as well as specific topics about the media. Review their studies to understand patterns in media use and to see if you can find cultural/ethnic group differences. http://www. pewinternet.org/topics.asp?c=4

4. Media scholars are divided as to whether the media simply reflect society or whether they strongly influence society—or both. Consider the differences between these positions and make an argument in favor of one of these positions.

5. Hold a discussion group about a particular mediated message (such as a movie). Have everyone consume the message and then consider the following questions as a way to enhance media literacy:

   a. What message did you take from this medium?
   b. How did the style/tone/structure of the medium shape the message?
   c. What did you think of the message this medium presented?
   d. What personal, social, media experiences shape your opinion about this message?
   e. How strongly do you support your opinion of the message?
   f. Do you think exposure to another message on the same topic would be useful for you to consider?
   g. Where might you find additional sources on the same topic to help you consider your interpretation of the message?

CHAPTER 12

History(ies) and Future(s) Shaping Intercultural Communication

CHAPTER OUTLINE

I. Introduction

II. Why Does History Matter?
   a. Memory and Identity
   b. Historical Trauma
   c. Consequences of History for Today
   d. Concept Check

III. Future of Intercultural Communication
   a. Globalization
   b. Intercultural Relations
   c. Concept Check

IV. Layered Perspective of History(ies) and the Future(s)
   a. Bottom-Up Effects
   b. Top-Down Effects
   c. Challenges and Skills

V. Summary

VI. Review Questions

VII. Exercises

CHAPTER OBJECTIVES

After reading this chapter, students should be able to

- define history(ies).

- describe three reasons that history matters for intercultural communication.

Long Walk of the Navajos
Our histories include many events about the harsh treatment of other cultural groups such as is represented in this photo of the Long Walk of the Navajos. What historical events shape the intercultural relations among cultural groups and nations today?

- discuss how history relates to cultural identity.
- describe historical trauma and two ways for addressing it.
- explain three consequences of history today.

- discuss factors to be considered in the future of intercultural communication.
- identify bottom-up and top-down effects of history(ies) and the future(s).

Introduction

In January, 1863, and throughout 1864, the Navajos were forced by the U.S. Army from their homes in eastern Arizona and western New Mexico to make a 300-mile walk to southeastern New Mexico and relocate near what is now known as Ft. Sumner, New Mexico. At least 200 people died along the 300-mile (500 kilometer) trek that took over 18 days to travel by foot. Between 8,000 and 9,000 people were settled on a 40-square mile (104 km²) area, with a peak population of 9,022 by the spring of 1865. The relocation was the first attempt to create a reservation for American Indians in the western United States. The experiment was deemed necessary by the U.S. military after strained relations escalated over previous decades. The reservation at Ft. Sumner had significant problems. First, about 400 Mescalero Apaches were placed there before the Navajos; the Mescalero and the Navajo had a long tradition of raiding each other and had many disputes during their encampment. Second, the initial plan was for the reservation to contain 5,000 people, not 9,000 men, women, and children. Resources were a major concern with limited natural resources and inept management of what supplies were purchased. In 1868, the experiment was deemed a failure, and the Navajos were returned to their homelands with the signing of the Treaty of Bosque Redondo. Today, many elders tell stories of the "Long Walk" and discuss their mistrust of the U.S. government for this event. Many Navajos are still concerned with these events and still think about both the loss of land and the loss of loved ones that occurred. These negative narratives about their history are further enhanced by memories of boarding schools; in the nineteenth and early twentieth centuries, American Indians were forced from their homes to attend boarding schools controlled by the federal government and forced to give up their language and entire culture. Physical, emotional, and sexual violence were rampant in many of these schools (Sharp, n.d.; and Smith, 2007).

> Questions: How does history shape current intercultural relations? What concepts about history and cultural identities help to explain the events in this story?

The history(ies) of a cultural group includes relations with other groups. Every single cultural group has a history that includes stories about ways that they were hated and targeted for violence by other groups. These stories are a critical part of the historical factors that impact intercultural communication. **History** is the retelling of past events and eras that shape cultural identity and social relations and structures (Loewen, 1999). History is often better reflected as *histories* because of the many stories that are told about cultural groups by both members of the culture and by outside cultural groups. When we talk about histories, we recognize that not just one history exists for everyone and also that the same historical event may involve many perspectives.

This concluding chapter considers historical relations among cultural groups and the consequences of those histories. The purpose is to demonstrate why history matters today and how it shapes our intercultural communication, especially future intercultural communication. From the socioecological perspective, history represents the broadest layer and provides a foundation for understanding issues at an individual, interpersonal, organizational, and community level. This chapter is organized in the following manner. First, we undertake a discussion of why history matters. Second, we discuss the future of intercultural communication, including globalization and intercultural relations. Third, we present a layered perspective of history and the future along with challenges and skills that individuals can consider in telling and "rewriting/retelling" our histories for positive future interactions.

Why Does History Matter?

For some of us, the study of history is mundane and seemingly unimportant. If you feel that way, you likely come from a culture that has a present or future orientation, and you have a cultural history that is generally favorable. If you are from a past-oriented culture or a cultural group that has been historically disadvantaged or disenfranchised, the importance of history most likely has been instilled in you by your upbringing.

Regardless of your cultural orientation or past history, the history of intercultural relations is important for numerous reasons. History is a narration about past events that tells us about what was important when the event or era occurred, but also about what we think about the event today (such as when we erect monuments or create museums that center on a historical event) (Loewen, 1999; Roberts, 2007). Loewen (1999) stated that the distinction between what happened in the past and what we remember and retell about the past is critical. The past is the actual events, while history is the stories we share to highlight what we feel is important about the past. These stories, or narratives, identify how we see ourselves, what we value, what we want to be remembered for, and how we see others (Darnton, 2003; Loewen, 1999; Roberts, 2007).

Narratives are fundamental to the human experience (Fisher, 1984). Fisher used the term *Homo narrans* (rather than *Homo sapiens*) because it emphasizes the importance of narratives in human life. Narratives are more than simply recounting what happened; when a narrative becomes repeated and entrenched in a culture, it has the value of reinforcing identity and memory. Narratives that are retold have two characteristics: coherence and fidelity (Fisher, 1984). Coherence describes how well a story flows and the parts are consistent, while fidelity refers to the degree to which a story "rings true" for a group of people. Many histories and perspectives about a single event are possible as the different perspectives ring true for specific cultural groups (Roberts, 2007). Thus, historical narratives present a perception of past events from a particular lens. This section considers three specific aspects of these historical perspectives that impact intercultural relations: a) memory and identity, b) historical trauma, and c) consequences of history for today and the future.

Memory and Identity

Historian Arthur Marwick (1989) stated:

> As memory is to the individual, so history is to the community or society. Without memory, individuals find great difficulty in relating to others, in finding their bearings, in making intelligent decisions—they have lost their sense of identity. A society without history would be in a similar condition. Thus the simplest answer to the question, "What is the use of history?" is: "Try to imagine what it would be like living in a society in which there was absolutely no knowledge of history." The mind boggles. It is only through a sense of history that communities establish their identity, orientate themselves, understand their relationship to the past and to other communities and societies (p. 14).

Thus, history is the collective memory of a group of people that shapes cultural identity (Lerner, 1997). All groups share commonalities in their collective memories, but differences between groups in power and those without power also exist.

For all cultural groups, history represents "the archives of human experiences and of the thoughts of past generations" (Lerner, 1997, p. 52). Previous generations pass on the lessons, important events, interpretations of those events, language, and the cultural norms to future generations to keep the culture alive. Through these experiences and the passage to future generations, our lives as individuals and as cultural beings have meaning. Lerner (1997) argued that modernization and urbanization have isolated people from each other and from important links to nature. As a result, history as identity is even more important as it provides a sense of place and belonging—and thus meaning. In this manner, the way that we represent ourselves, and the way we define ourselves, is firmly rooted in the historical stories that we tell of ourselves. "What we remember, what we stress as significant, and what we omit of our past defines our present" (Lerner, 1997, p. 199). See Box 12.1.

In the process of creating collective memory and cultural identifications, our narratives also tell us about how we view other people. Roberts (2007) argued that as cultural groups tell stories about their own identities, they position the self in relation to the other. Similarly to cultural identity theory in Chapter 3, we define our own group as being differentiated from other cultural groups. Roberts noted that the historical narratives of Western cultures tell us a great deal about these cultures' perceived identities as they relate to other cultural groups. Traditionally, these narratives objectify non-European peoples and put them in a position of inferiority (for example, "the noble savage"). In doing so, narratives allowed cultural groups to define themselves.

While all cultural identities are shaped by histories, the histories of groups in power and those not in power differ as does the ability to place one's history in a prominent position (for example, in the history books). For those in power, history

Box 12.1 Layered Effects: Oral Histories and Culture

There was a time when all cultures told their histories almost exclusively through oral narratives. Collective memory was preserved through the passing of stories from generation to generation. Today, oral cultures (or partial oral cultures) around the world still survive. For example, in New Mexico, a number of American Indian pueblos speak *Keres*, which is solely an oral language. These members also speak English, so they have written electronic histories, but the most significant cultural events are told in *Keres*.

In describing oral culture, Ong (1982) identifies three distinctive characteristics. First, oral cultures have a different sense of time. Stories can only be told in the present, and individuals have no way to go back and check the facts. The past is connected to the present by sharing stories that contain myths and facts. Second, the psychology of oral cultures has a different memory system. Memory is not the repetition of facts; rather, it is thematic and formulaic. The stories capture the basic themes, and while storytellers can remember hundreds of details through transferring the story into formulas, no two storytellers tell the tale in the same way. Third, performance is more important than authorship. Every storyteller reshapes and retells the story. Those with the best memories, as well as the elders, who have great repositories of knowledge, are the most respected members of the culture.

Oral cultures illustrate the layered perspective in that the way that histories are told influences the cultural identity and memories of the individuals. Individuals have a past and present orientation, a respect for elders, and a focus on themes and meaning, not accuracy. Further, oral cultures tend to be homogeneous in terms of cultural values and social norms, which reinforces their ability to create stories.

is a way of celebrating victories and accomplishments of individuals and nations. In most nations, the celebration of independence is a core point of national pride and history. We read about our independence from an oppressive occupier or about how we battled other entities to maintain independence. We have holidays that celebrate independence (such as Independence Day) or other days related to the power of a nation; for example, *Cinco de Mayo* celebrates the victory at the Battle of Puebla on May 5, 1862, when a Mexican army defeated a larger and "superior" French army. National histories are often mythical aggregates of facts and interventions that create a symbolic identity for a sense of pride (Lerner, 1997). These histories legitimize those in power. However, at the same time, ruling classes fear history because they desire to hold on to power (Kaye, 1996). They are fearful that untold histories and past atrocities will be brought up by marginalized groups, and history will be revised. Thus, a dialectic of history functions for those in power—it legitimizes and celebrates power, but also potentially destroys it. See Box 12.2 on page 341.

For cultural groups not in power and those that have been oppressed, history also presents its dilemmas. History provides a chance to celebrate survival and recognize the cultural group as strong and able to stand up to challenges (Lerner, 1997). At the same time, victims of oppression often internalize the guilt for their victimization: Did we commit some act to deserve oppression? Did our ancestors ever fight back (Lerner, 1997)? From this dilemma of guilt and celebration, members of these cultural groups have to choose how to interact

Box 12.2 What Went Wrong? Getting Over Slavery

The following story ran in newspapers through the Associated Press on November 17, 2006.

> Richmond, VA—A state senator said black people "should get over" slavery and questioned whether Jews should apologize "for killing Christ," drawing criticism from stunned colleagues.
>
> Del. Frank D. Hargrove, 79, made his remarks in opposition to a measure that would apologize on the state's behalf to the descendants of slaves. In an interview published Tuesday in the *Daily Progress* of Charlottesville, Hargrove said slavery ended nearly 140 years ago with the Civil War and added that "our black citizens should get over it."

The newspaper also quoted him as saying, "Are we going to force the Jews to apologize for killing Christ?"

Black lawmakers swiftly denounced Hargrove's comments. "When somebody tells me I should just get over slavery, I can only express my emotion by projecting that I am appalled, absolutely appalled," said Del. Dwight C. Jones, head of the Legislative Black Caucus. Del. David L. Englin also criticized Hargrove's remarks, recalling that his grandparents were driven from their homes in Poland "by people who believed that as Jews, we killed Christ."

The story illustrates one of the classic responses to history by those who historically have power—they want people who have been persecuted and oppressed to get over the past because "we don't do that anymore." This state senator simply wants to encourage collective forgetting of the past, which is impossible because history is part of cultural identity and collective memory.

Source: Albuquerque Journal (2006)

with the dominant group in a society or nation. In Chapter 5, we discussed various options that cultural groups and individuals have when interacting with the host culture: We can assimilate, we can stay separate, and we can balance the two. For groups with limited power, the differences between these three choices may be minimal. In discussing Jews' choices after World War II, Lerner (1997) noted that the first choice, assimilation, was a way to minimize difference and to try not to be offensive to the larger cultural group. Their perceived choice was to give up language, dress, and customs. Thus, they had to give up cultural identity and for some this practice involved self-hatred; that is, they chose to assimilate because they did not like their cultural group (Lerner, 1997). The second choice, to remain separate, celebrated cultural identity and also affirmed one's "Otherness" in society. This choice also involved marginalizing oneself from mainstream society. The third choice was to emphasize both characteristics, to try to balance acceptance of history and one's own group and still fit in with the larger groups. Lerner (1997) argued that anti-Semitism marginalized all Jews and did not recognize any difference in the three choices—all individuals were still considered Jews and the choices were only choices in perception. The lack of real choice and the power to enforce anti-Semitism is one distinguishing factor for cultural groups in power and those not in power.

Beyond the dilemmas facing groups not in power, mainstream history also includes a lack of recognition of these groups. Absent or **hidden histories** are those stories of cultural groups that are not often told or are told with inaccuracies or oversimplifications. Lerner (1997) discussed the hidden histories of women. She noted that women have always been at least one half of every cultural group, but the stories of women have rarely been told. For example, until the resurgence of the women's rights movements in the early 1970s, novels written by women, about women, and for women during the eighteenth and nineteenth centuries in the United States were largely unknown and out of print. Now novels like Kate Chopin's *The Awakening* and Charlotte Perkins Gilman's *The Yellow Wallpaper* are common texts in university literature courses. Other groups whose histories have been hidden include homosexuals, people from low socioeconomic classes, and ethnic minorities. As we discussed in Chapter 11, these stories are being told more frequently, although there are oversimplifications in mainstream media. Ethnic and cultural specific media provide a more accurate story of these hidden histories.

Not telling the stories of certain groups marginalizes these groups and minimizes their contributions to societies. Recapturing these hidden stories is a critical part of **revisionist history** (Lerner, 1997). Revisionist history is a critical component for enhancing cultural identity and for improving future intercultural communication. Loewen (1999) provided an example of revisionist history in his book *Lies Across America: What Our Historic Sites Get Wrong*. He presented a review of 95 historical sites (for example, homes, historical markers, and monuments) across the United States in order to identify omitted and mistaken information. He argued that this omitted and mistaken information reflects the identities that people want to be remembered for and not what actually happened. As a result, people are presented in the best possible interpretation and ugly events such as racism are minimized. He identified sites that ignore important negative events such as the Scottsboro case where nine African American men spent 100 collective years in prison for a crime they did not commit. He also demonstrated that women were minimized or omitted, the sexual orientation of gays and lesbians was denied, and people of color were misrepresented (for example, American Indians were presented in romantic terms but also as not very smart, such as the site commemorating the sale of Manhattan to the Dutch). Finally, such sites emphasize the importance of the "great man." The "great man" is the hero character who had no flaws and provided incredible leadership in our country. Loewen noted that sites rarely present blemishes of the great man (especially presidents). Further, and in contrast, the accomplishments of "common men and women" are ignored, such as the individuals who resisted slavery in the United States in the eighteenth and nineteenth centuries.

Historical Trauma

Many cultural groups have experienced traumatic events during their history. These events include forced removal from lands, enslavement, attempts at exterminating the group, and attempts to remove all cultural markers. Traumatic events such as these (and any type of trauma) have direct effects on an individual who experiences them or witnesses them, often in the form of mental health disorders such as post-traumatic stress disorder, alcoholism, anxiety, and depression (Duran & Duran, 1995; Whitbeck, Adams, Hoyt, & Chen, 2004). However, beyond those who directly experience the trauma, does historical trauma affect people in that cultural group today?

The answer is yes for some people. Evidence supports that traumatic events from as long as 400 years ago have mental and physical health impacts on people today. This phenomenon is called historical trauma. **Historical trauma** is "unresolved trauma and grief that continues to adversely affect the lives of survivors of such trauma" (E. Duran, Duran, Woodis, & Woodis, 1998, p. 99). Historical trauma is passed from one generation to the next such that events that happened many years ago still impact people today. In other words, it is intergenerational trauma.

Research on historical trauma has been undertaken with such cultural groups as Holocaust survivors (Steinberg, 1989), African Americans (Apprey, 1999), Japanese Americans who were put into internment camps during World War II (Nagata & Tsuru, 2007), Palestinians and Israelis (McKnight, 2004), and American Indians (Whitbeck et al., 2004). For example, Whitbeck et al. (2004) surveyed 143 American Indian parents of 10–12 year olds about how often they thought about historical losses. They found that one-third of respondents reported thinking about such loss at least daily and some even several times a day. The persistent thought of historical losses has been associated with a number of negative and physical health outcomes such as depression, anxiety, intimate partner violence, and alcoholism (Duran & Duran, 1995; Oetzel & Duran, 2004; Whitbeck et al., 2004).

Since historical trauma has such negative effects, investigating ways to address it becomes important (see the two examples in Box 12.3). Two strategies have proven useful—one at the individual layer and one at the community layer. At the individual layer, engaging in traditional cultural practices helps a person to mitigate the effect of historical trauma. Walters and Simoni (2002) identified cultural buffers as protective factors against the negative health and social outcomes resulting from historical trauma. Cultural practices serve as coping mechanisms to minimize the impact of trauma on negative health outcomes and include having a strong cultural identity and engaging in traditional cultural practices, spiritual coping, and immersion in traditional health practices, such as sweat lodge ceremonies or acupuncture.

At the community layer, the use of healing rituals for addressing historical trauma is beneficial for community members. B. Duran et al. (1998) described an approach used in the Lakota community that they feel has some application to other similarly affected communities. The Lakota intervention model included a memorial for the massacre at Wounded Knee and "catharsis, abreaction, group sharing, testimony, opportunities for expression of traditional culture and

Self-Assessment 12.1

HISTORICAL TRAUMA

The following scale was developed specifically for American Indians, but many of the items can be tailored to other cultural groups as well. For each question, respond how often you think about the item. Put an X in the column that applies.

Item	Never	Yearly or special times	Monthly	Weekly	Daily	Several times a day
Loss of our land.						
Loss of our language.						
Losing our traditional spiritual ways.						
The loss of our family ties because of boarding schools.						
The loss of families from the reservation to government relocation.						
The loss of self respect from poor treatment by government officials.						
The loss of trust in Whites from broken treaties.						
Losing our culture.						
The losses from the effects of alcoholism on our people.						
Loss of respect by our children and grandchildren for elders.						
Loss of our people through early death.						
Loss of respect by our children for traditional ways.						

Scoring: Count the number of items that appear weekly, daily, or several times a day versus the number of items that never appear. The more items noted weekly or more often, the more historical trauma is present.

Source: Whitbeck et al. (2004)

language, ritual, and communal mourning" (p. 72). The purpose of the model was to help the community members facilitate mourning, tolerate effects that accompany the trauma, and validate/normalize the traumatic response. The authors also noted that all participants felt better about themselves after the intervention, with 75 percent expressing high agreement that the intervention helped them reduce feelings of cultural shame.

Box 12.3 Voices: Addressing the Historical Trauma of Comfort Women and the Stolen Generation

Two cultural groups that have experienced histori-cal trauma are the comfort women and the Stolen Generation. Comfort women were nearly 200,000 women, mainly Chinese and Korean, who worked in military brothels during World War II. Many historians have reported that most of these women were recruited by force or deception to serve as "sex slaves" and that the Japanese military was directly or indirectly involved in the kidnapping. Some Japanese historians and politicians have argued that the evidence is not conclusive as to whether the Japanese military was a participant in these activities. Prime Minister Shinzo Abe stated in early 2007 that he would not apologize again. Abe stood by a 1993 apology by the chief cabinet secretary at the time, Yohei Kono, but was vague as to whether the women were coerced. Lee Yong-soo, a Korean who was 15 when she reported being kidnapped from her home, was not satisfied with Abe's lack of apology: "The Japanese government is saying there was no coercion involved, but we didn't do this voluntarily. We were taken forcibly by the Japanese. I want Japan to formally acknowledge what it did. And I want Prime Minister Abe to apologize to my face."

The Stolen Generation is a term used to refer to Aboriginal children in Australia who were removed from their families from 1910 to the 1960s and forced to live with White families and in church-run orphanages. Tens of thousands of children are estimated to have been removed. Poor health and social effects for Aborigines are attributed to these policies, and a 1997 recom-mended report resulted in over $100 million Australian dollars for family support, cultural and language maintenance, and the establishment of a national network to help link lost families. These programs have had positive impacts for Aborigines, but health and social effects still lag behind mainstream Australians. Further, Prime Minister John Howard refuses to apologize, simply expressing deep and sincere regret. Others suggest that this is not sufficient. One journalist reported, "Aboriginal filmmaker and musician, Richard Franklin, whose sister was removed from his family, called for Australians to acknowledge what aborigines have endured. 'We, as a nation, need to mature. And to mature, we must visit the past and recognize it for what is really was. We need to plant seeds in the present for future generations, for our children. Our children need to grow up together, black and white.'"

Sources: de Tarczynski (2007) and McCurry (2007)

Historical trauma also is relevant for the oppressors. Lerner (1997) explained that, for nations to heal, they must face up to what actually happened and make amends. She compared the reactions to the Holocaust by two nations, Germany and Austria. Germany's post-war recovery depended on its confrontation with its guilt for fascism, the Holocaust, and war. It made restitutions to the survivors and some effort at outlawing racism in the direction of healing. In contrast, Austria maintained its fiction in being the first victim of Nazism for many years in an effort to engage in collective forgetting. The result was continued anti-Semitism and the rise of political parties that perpetuated racism. In the 1990s, Lerner argued that Austria finally dealt more honestly with the past and made restitutions to the victims.

Consequences of History for Today

Historical events and eras have consequences for today. Marwick (1989) eloquently stated these effects:

> Other justifications for the study of history are sometimes advanced: that history familiarizes us with customs, thought processes, and standards different from our own, tells us about humanity and its various activities and environments, and then helps us to know and understand our fellow human beings; that knowledge of our past gives us greater freedom in the control of our present; that history is a valuable training of the mind, assisting critical judgment and the orderly presentation of arguments. But these are secondary to, or corollaries of, the central argument: The past determines and pervades the present—we'd better understand it (p. 17).

One of the most often cited consequences of history comes from philosopher and poet George Santayana (n.d.): "Those who cannot learn from history are doomed to repeat it." In this section, several direct consequences of historical events are discussed including disenfranchisement, altered intracultural (within culture) relations, and strained intercultural relations.

One of the consequences of historical relations is that often certain groups become disenfranchised. Cultural groups that have been colonized by another nation are often put in subservient positions that pay poorly and lessen status and pride (Obama, 2004). **Colonization** is the process of a nation extending its control to a foreign territory in order to exploit that territory culturally, economically, and politically. Prior to colonization, the people may have held high status positions, were landowners or occupiers, and had sufficient resources for their families. After independence (or post-colonization), the occupied individuals are often left in poor situations. Some young citizens go to the colonizer nation in hopes of improving their lives. For example, North Africans immigrated to France after World War II in hopes of improving their lives. Although originally France needed a larger workforce to help it catch up with other industrialized nations, these North Africans often were disenfranchised and lived in "immigrant ghettos." In recent years, France has experienced a glut of workers looking for jobs, and unemployment among these immigrants has run between 20 to 40 percent according to different sources; this disenfranchisement finally boiled over into the Paris Riots in 2005, which caused considerable disruption and violence (see Chapter 10) (Paris Riots, 2005). In the United States, African Americans collectively have a lower socioeconomic status than White Americans. This is in part a byproduct of the legacy of slavery. If you imagine socioeconomic status as a race, slavery resulted in African Americans starting the race well behind White Americans because of the legacy of slavery.

In addition, historical relations, especially colonization, alter the ways that members of a cultural group interact with each other. For example, the colonization of American Indians changed the way that American Indian men and women interact with one another, particularly regarding intimate partner violence. Most researchers have found that intimate partner violence was historically rare in American Indian communities, but has escalated in the past 200 years (Hamby, 2000). European colonizers introduced Western patriarchy, rapid transition from hunting/farming to a cash-based economy, removal of children to boarding schools and foster homes at rates 5 to 20 times the national average, and relocations of groups to less desirable areas (Chester, Robin, Koll, Lopez, & Goldman, 1994; McEachern, Van Winkle, & Steiner, 1998). These factors produced cataclysmic changes in the spiritual, social, and economic structure and drastically changed traditional lifestyles. E. Duran et al. (1998) argued that these influences created antagonistic relationships between American Indian and/or Alaska Native men and women. For example, traditionally within Navajo culture, men and women shared equal rights and status. Navajo common law emphasizes reciprocal relationships between a husband and wife (McEachern et al., 1998). But the influences of European colonization robbed most American Indian and/or Alaska Native men of their traditional roles, and they lost status and honor (E. Duran et al., 1998). To regain honor and control of their lives, some American Indian men mirrored the European model of control and power over their intimate partners. Thus, among American Indians, women's subordination or gender inequality is largely a consequence of European contact and colonialism (Chester et al., 1994; E. Duran et al., 1998; Hamby, 2000; McEachern et al., 1998).

Another way that intracultural relations have been altered is through massive migrations caused by wars, colonization, slavery, persecution, and famine; this migration, which results in a group being geographically dispersed, is called a **diaspora.** The African diaspora includes people and their ancestors taken from the continent due to slavery, colonization, and ethnic cleansing. The Jewish diaspora includes people of Eastern European descent who migrated during or after World War II to various countries around the world. For a diaspora, the cultural group may not be a single unified cultural group. Both the Jewish and African diaspora represent people from different cultures and tribes and who speak different languages. However, ancestors may view the groups as more unified than the original members because of fractured identities. Some African Americans, for example, view Africa as a unified and shared culture; in contrast most Africans view their cultures and tribes as very distinct and not necessarily a unified whole.

The diasporic movement results in a fractured cultural group(s) in which individuals feel they have lost a part of their identity. The struggle to construct identity includes fitting in with the new culture, but also a longing for the home culture (Sanchez Gibau, 2005). For example, Cape Verdeans who live in Boston are part of the African diaspora and negotiate identity to include host culture (United States), race, continent (Africa), colonial identity (Portugal), and home culture (Cape Verde) (Sanchez Gibau, 2005). The diasporic community is composed of two distinct sectors: "Cape Verdean Americans" and "Cape Verdean immigrants." This complexity of identity is born of the diaspora and from heated debates about race, culture, and identity.

Historical relations among cultural groups have consequences for intercultural interactions today. Little doubt exists that the legacy of slavery in the United States still impacts intercultural communication between African Americans and White Americans today (see Box 12.4). In fact, Lerner (1997) argued that the inability of the United States to come to terms with its complicity in slavery has made conflict over race a permanent feature of U.S. political and social life. Other examples of negative intercultural relations today based in historical factors abound around the world, including Israeli-Palestinian disputes, apartheid in South Africa, Catholic-Protestant difficulties

Box 12.4 Talking about Ethics: Should the U.S. Government Apologize for Slavery?

A long-term debate in the United States is whether or not the government should apologize for slavery and make reparations to the descendents of those who were enslaved—although these issues are often debated separately. Hatch (2006) analyzed the rhetoric of apology by U.S. Representative Tony Hall, a White American, at the Leadership Conference on Reconciliation and Development in Benin, West Africa. Benin, one of the ports for slaver traders, held the conference as part of reconciliation efforts. Representative Hall had put forward a bill that the United States should apologize for slavery, but the bill never made it out of the House. He went to the conference as an individual, not as a representative of the U.S. Congress, and made a heartfelt apology to African Americans and Africans for White Americans' historic abuses against them. Hatch (2006) analyzed Hall's speech and noted that the apology, which in traditional research is seen as restoring image (such as when politicians apologize for their mistakes), served as a gesture to reconcile history with the purpose of improving intercultural relations. Hatch's analysis, and the general debate about apologizing for slavery, raises several interesting ethical questions:

1. Should the U.S. government apologize to the descendants of those enslaved?
2. Should the U.S. government make reparations to the descendants of those enslaved?
3. Does the purpose of the apology make a difference (that is, restoring image or attempting reconciliation)? What communicative strategies help to insure that the true goal of the apology is met?
4. Would an apology of reconciliation improve intercultural communication between African Americans and White Americans?
5. What ethical standards guide your answers to these questions?

in Northern Ireland, and issues related to Sunni-Shi'a Muslims in many Arab and Asian nations, just to name a few. Each of these situations has a complex history that belies simple solutions to improve relations. How then does a nation move beyond the past to improve intercultural relations?

For Lerner (1997), the process of reconciliation is critical for improving intercultural relations and eliminating disenfranchisement. **Reconciliation** is the process of settling past disputes and abuses for the purpose of establishing close relations. South Africa represents an important case study that may offer insight to other historical conflicts (Oetzel, Arcos, Mabizela, Weinman, & Zhang, 2006). In pre-colonial/pre-apartheid South Africa, conflict resolution among people was guided by *ubuntu*—a way of life that advocated mutual respect, dignity, and humanness. Colonization and apartheid created adversarial relations among many groups and diminished the emphasis of *ubuntu*. At the end of apartheid in 1994, the government instituted the Truth and Reconciliation Commission (TRC), which initiated a process that aimed to make South Africa more governable by facilitating the resolution of conflict ensuing from old wounds of apartheid and colonization. The process initially debated two options: a) to achieve reconciliation through the punishment of past wrongdoing; or b) to find ways to forgive the deeds of the past across the political spectrum. The latter option was chosen, and the TRC became an indicator of a new, reconciliatory national ethos,

South African Group
Reconciliation efforts have enhanced intercultural relations in South Africa. What type of reconciliation efforts would help improve intercultural relations where you live or for cultures of which you are a member?

Photo Credit: Phola Mabizela

one that attempted to recall aspects of *ubuntu* in that it called for compromise and collaboration of all citizens. Public hearings were televised on a daily basis and were vaunted as a therapeutic process for the country. These truth-telling proceedings sought to build a bridge between Blacks, Whites, and other ethnic groups as political conflicts continued to dominate the national landscape (Tutu, 1999). Some efforts at restitution to affected parties followed, such as financial reparation and obtaining answers to questions related to finding out about political activists who either disappeared or were killed and buried in unmarked graves. In addition, the TRC raised the level of social awareness, particularly among White South Africans, about the most awful manifestations of apartheid (Krog, 2000; Tutu, 1999). The effects of 500 years of colonization cannot be removed in less than 20 years, but these efforts have moved intercultural relations in South Africa forward.

Concept Check

History matters because it is a part of collective memory and cultural identity, some historical events are traumatic, and historical relations have consequences for today. From the collective memory aspect, history matters because it is a part of who we are, how we define ourselves, and the meaning we derive from our lives. Historical trauma focuses on how victims and their descendants have been impacted through intergenerational trauma. These effects include negative mental and physical health outcomes. Finally, the consequences of history today include disenfranchisement of certain groups (and resulting violence in communities), altered intracultural relations, and strained intercultural relations. When you hear people ask, "Why don't those people just get over it?" you now have several answers to provide them. We simply cannot get over the past without certain efforts. For example, addressing trauma means honestly confronting the events and individually and collectively forgiving and moving forward. This forgiveness can be done within a group that has been victimized, but reconciliation efforts by the oppressor groups also facilitate the forgiveness and improvement of intercultural relations. Reconciliation is not about romanticizing the past (trying to get back to the ways things were) or blaming groups and feeling guilty for past events (E. Duran et al., 1998). For example, if you are a White American, you did not perpetuate slavery, and thus guilt is not an appropriate acknowledgment. A better approach is empathy and understanding. In general, reconciliation means recognizing and accepting historical events and their consequences today, apologizing for events (to demonstrate understanding and empathy), and forgiving and moving forward to ensure that the past will not be repeated. An apology does not have to signal guilt, but rather can focus on acknowledgment of feelings and empathy for those feelings. These are difficult challenges for cultural groups and nations.

Future of Intercultural Communication

The future of intercultural communication holds a number of interesting possibilities. The narratives of the future are still being written and are certainly shaped by historical narratives of collective memories, cultural identities, historical trauma, colonization, diasporas, and reconciliation. This section examines two broad factors often discussed in the future of intercultural communication: globalization and intercultural relations.

Globalization

As introduced in Chapter 1, globalization is a frequently used concept to describe intercultural communication and the current state of the world. **Globalization** is the increasing interconnectedness of people and places as a result of changes in communication technologies, communication, and migration patterns, which cause political, economic, and cultural convergence (Friedman, 2006; Ladegaard, 2007). That is, the world is becoming smaller and patterns of behavior are becoming similar.

There are several perspectives and arguments about exactly what globalization means. One of these perspectives, the hyperglobal perspective, argues that globalization has led to the end of the nation state (or national culture) or has at least limited its relevance for culture (Friedman, 2006; Ladegaard, 2007). Blasco (2004) argued that "the concept of 'national culture' is fast becoming obsolete" (p. 20) because globalization leads to cultural integration. The central idea is that the process of cultural integration takes place not only on an international level, but that it transcends national boundaries and societies. Kramsch (2002) argued along the same lines, pointing out that "'Culture' has become less and less a national consensus, but a consensus built on common ethnic, generational, regional, ideological, occupation- or gender-related interests, within and across national boundaries" (p. 276). Essentially, from this perspective, national identity is not very important anymore and instead economic factors and communication technologies, such as multinationals, media industries, vast communication networks, and international division of labor, have become more important cultural reference points. Essentially, the influence of this global culture and the media that carry its message is so strong as to "force" the world to converge.

Other scholars dispute this broad impact of globalization on the world. Such scholars agree that there is more migration and communication across cultures, but that the strong effects of the global culture have not occurred (Ladegaard, 2007). Ladegaard (2007) studied a multinational Danish business to see if there was evidence of convergence in work behavior. He had participants in the IT Service Center of the company complete a survey about their communication problems and the extent that culture was involved and then conducted two follow-up focus groups (one in English and one in Danish). He found that participants were quite aware of national culture differences and used national culture to explain communication difficulties. The participants' perceptions of national cultures (or at least stereotypes of national culture) were inconsistent with the hyperglobal perspective, as there was not a convergence of worldview. In fact, there was divergence attributed to national culture.

Friedman (2006) offered a third perspective; one that emphasizes horizontal and vertical aspects of globalization. On the one hand, Friedman noted that there is a stronger emphasis on cultural belonging than on citizenship. In this sense, the nation state is not the key point of identity, but rather there are horizontal (or equal) cultural identities toward other groups. On the other hand, he explained that there is a vertical polarization occurring around the world. Specifically, the elites and upwardly mobile citizens of the world are emphasizing a cultural and cosmopolitan identity. In contrast, the members of lower socioeconomic classes resist globalization efforts and those perceived as supporting a global agenda. There is increasing xenophobia and resistance to global economies as it is perceived to hurt the local economy and cultural identity. Box 12.5 presents the vertical view of globalization.

The future is obviously unknown at this point, and we will not completely understand the effects of globalization for many years. My own perspective is that

---

Box 12.5 Globalization: Protests of the World Trade Organization

The World Trade Organization (WTO) is an international organization designed to supervise and liberalize international trade. It was created in 1995 as the successor of the General Agreement on Tariffs and Trade. The WTO deals with the rules of trade between nations at a near-global level; specifically it negotiates and implements trade agreements and is in charge of policing member countries' adherence to all agreements. The general purpose is to increase free trade around the world. There are 151 member states.

The WTO has a Ministeral Conference that meets every two years. This conference is protested by thousands, primarily from working-class backgrounds. In Seattle in 1999, over 50,000 protested. In Cancun in 2003, a South Korean farmer committed a ritualistic suicide in protest of WTO policies. The farmer, Kun Hai Lee, stood in front of police lines, declared that "the WTO kills farmers," and then slashed himself to death with a blade. His suicide came on South Korea's Day of the Dead (a holiday when family members pray and remember friends and relatives who have died).

Farmers protest strongly against the WTO as they feel that the policies remove subsidies that make it possible for the small farmer's survival in a global economy. The policies facilitate the movement of goods freely, but also can have a negative impact on local economies. These protests fit Friedman's (2006) perspective of vertical polarization as the elites like free trade and people on the lower end of the socioeconomic ladder protest against it vehemently.

globalization has increased the frequency of intercultural interaction and thus increases the need to study and understand intercultural communication. Further, there also will be increasing intercultural conflicts as the globalization of the economy has disparate effects for people around the world. I believe that globalization will make culture a more salient feature in people's lives and that national culture will still matter. Globalization does make the possibility of other cultural reference points more salient as well, such as bicultural identities (connected to two or more national cultures or ethnic groups), professional/workplace cultures, religious cultures (particular those with small numbers), and cultures organized around activities and topic (e.g., the culture of online support groups). Two key features of globalization that lead to the salience of culture are migration and technology.

MIGRATION   Globalization has led to increased movement of people around the world. Two interrelated driving forces are the aging population of industrial nations, and businesses' need for workers. Many industrialized (or developed) nations currently have, or will have in the near future, a shortage of workers despite the fact that the next 50 years is expected to add about 2.5 billion people to the world's population (Mann, 2007). Japan, for example, already has a negative population growth (that is, more deaths than births) and negative population growth is expected in many European nations (Mann, 2007). In the United States, by 2030 it is expected that there will not be enough workers to adequately support social security for the massive influx of the baby boom generation, although the United States is expected to have overall population growth (OASDI, 2004).

The result of such labor shortages is increased immigration. Workers from developing nations with poorer economies than the developed nations migrate and fill labor shortages. Such migrations often result in cultural clashes that can range from uncomfortable or difficult (such as the case of Brazilian workers in Japan referenced in Chapter 8) to violent (such as the case of the Paris Riots references in Chapter 10 and earlier in this chapter). These migration patterns also result in political decisions and affect elections. For example, in Europe from early 2006 to 2007, several national elections (Britain, France, & German) swung more conservatively because of the desire for the curbing of immigration (Robberson, 2006). Nations will have to learn to balance desire for nationalism and national culture with the need for immigration as the economy of these nations is dependent on immigrant workers.

Migration patterns and globalization also increase the need for learning new languages and translation and raise issues about whether English should be the global language (Adejunmobi, 2004; Bielsa, 2005; Kawai, 2007). The increase in migration brings increased contact for people who do not speak the same language. Translation services in hospitals, courts, and businesses become heightened (Bielsa, 2005). Additionally, individuals are faced with the choice of learning new languages or choosing to separate from their new culture. Adejunmobi (2004) argued that Western Africans who migrate should learn new languages, but also retain their distinct and localized cultural identities (that is, establish a bicultural identity). Finally, nations have to decide how to balance the need for participating in the global culture (which generally means speaking English) and retaining cultural traditions and language (Kawai, 2007). Many nations resist adopting English as a national language and instead want to recognize their cultural uniqueness through their language. However, there is little doubt that English is the *lingua franca* especially for business and education. For example, an exchange student from Peru told me that when she searches for research on nutrition and health, much of what she finds is in English. She is glad that she speaks and reads English and can then share with her friends what she learns. However, what does this say about the importance of other languages in generating knowledge? Regardless of your perspective, globalization has resulted in increased intercultural contact and has created dilemmas for individuals and nations to consider.

TECHNOLOGY   Advances in communication technology have increased intercultural contact and have facilitated political, educational, and political ventures (O'Kane & Hargie, 2004). E-mail, teleconferences, videoconferencing, instant messaging, and other communication technologies enable people to communicate frequently (see Chapter 11 for a discussion of media). These technologies allow multinational companies to create global teams where people work together in cyberspace but rarely in the same physical space or at the same time. Thus, globalization has enabled increased contact, but has it made culture more or less relevant?

Evidence suggests that members of different cultures use communication technologies in different ways, ways that are consistent with cultural values (Callahan, 2005; Hermeking, 2006; Teng 2007). For example, Hermeking (2006) found that Internet consumption in a country is positively related to individualism and negatively related to uncertainty avoidance. Thus, the more a country has individualistic values and the less it likes to avoid uncertainty, the greater the number of Internet users (see Figure 12.1). Similarly, another study compared online intercultural work groups

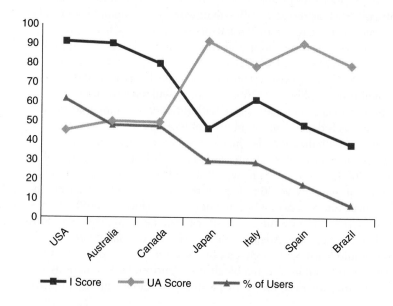

Figure 12.1
Internet Consumption and Cultural Values: Percent of Internet Users, Individualism, and Uncertainty Avoidance

Source: Hermeking (2006)

from Taiwan and the United States (Teng, 2007). The researcher found that U.S. participants enjoyed interacting with group members more, had developed a better sense of community, and were more comfortable with online communication. These findings are also consistent with individualistic cultural values.

In contrast, there are studies that find that technology leads to changes in culture. Another study of communication technology in a Norwegian company and a British company found that usage of technology encouraged Norwegian users to be more individualistic and British users to be more feminine—values opposite of these cultures (O'Kane & Hargie, 2004). This study provides some support for the hyperglobal perspective that communication technologies will lead to convergence. Additionally, there are concerns about the influences of technology on culture as well. For example, Postman (2004) argued that technology has created new problems that lead to convergence of cultures. Technology has enabled the creating and sharing of cultural information, but also has negative consequences. These problems include information glut, information incoherence, and information meaninglessness, which have led to meaningless cultural convergences.

We certainly can expect advances in communication technologies. Exactly what those technologies will be is interesting to ponder. Perhaps someone will develop the technology to provide efficient video with electronic mail to help us to be able to better interpret e-mail messages. Or the introduction of an easy-to-use and effective language translator certainly would help intercultural relations. Despite the evidence and arguments in favor of convergence, the majority of the research evidence suggests that culture influences technology usage more than technology influences culture. The existing technologies facilitate the frequency of intercultural contact, but do not appear to erase cultural values. In contrast, culture seems to influence how we use these technologies and thus misunderstandings and conflict along with increased capacity to work collaboratively are possible. In the future, we will see if this changes and if communication technology leads to greater convergence of cultural values.

Intercultural Relations

The future of the quality of intercultural relations is also important to consider. Globalization, along with migration and technology, has provided increased intercultural interactions. How will these interactions play out? Specifically, will the future be filled with conflict or peace? Which will be more prevalent? Will nations reject migrants and encourage nationalism only? Will nations be able to blend cultural traditions and new cultures of migrants? Will technology enable us to create better understandings and thus peace? Or will this increased contact result in more conflict and war? Will religious values clash and lead to greater conflict? This section considers factors that can lead to conflict and peace. Neither of these possibilities is certain nor exclusive. We can have both in certain circumstances.

CONFLICT   Why will the future be filled with conflict? Three factors suggest that conflict will be a part of our intercultural relations future: social identity, past histories, and resource struggles. First, recall from Chapter 3 that social identity theory (Tajfel, 1978) emphasizes that people have a desire to enhance their self-image and to differentiate themselves from other groups. In this differentiation process, individuals compare themselves to others for the purpose of establishing a positive social identity. The desire to achieve a positive social identity results in a positive bias favoring the ingroup and intergroup competition (Tajfel & Turner, 1986). Thus, a natural tendency of humans is the creation of a positive social identity and to compete and conflict with other cultural groups. One such future conflict might be related to the clash of religious perspectives. Huntington (1996) proposed that religious differences will be the biggest factor for conflicts around identity issues in what he called "The Clash of Civilizations." If you believe that social identity theory is accurate, you can expect the future to include conflict between cultural groups as they struggle to achieve positive social identity.

As discussed in this chapter, past historical relations impact present interactions in significant ways. Overcoming these negative histories involves sharing accurate narratives, apologizing for past harms, and forgiving such harms. Unfortunately, many governments (see Boxes 12.3 and 12.4 on the United States, Japan, and Australia in this chapter) view apology as a weakness and/or admission of guilt and thus refuse to apologize. Such refusals make reconciliation difficult. Cases such as South Africa and Germany, however, demonstrate some positive reconciliation efforts, and it will be interesting to see if more historical conflicts can reach reconciliation.

Finally, scarce resources exacerbate intercultural conflict. In Chapter 10, we discussed how disenfranchisement and scarce resources lead to intercultural community conflicts. Scarce resources make cultural differences more salient and create an increased likelihood that participants will view a conflict as "us vs. them." One of the scarcest resources is water (although there are certainly other scarce physical and human resources). Nations and states struggle over water rights. This leads to a struggle for both people and the environment. In the fall of 2007, Georgia (the U.S. state) was in a severe drought with only three months of water remaining in a lake that provides Atlanta with all of its water. The U.S. Core of Engineers was brought in to release water in order to protect an endangered mussel while state government fought against such acts. The state government wanted to ensure that people received the limited water first. This case exemplified intercultural conflict in that the two parties—entities who support the protection of the environment first and entities who support human use of resources first—represented different positions based on their values. Such types of conflict have played out (and continue to play out) around the world over such bodies of water as the Nile in Sudan, the Rhine and Black Sea in Europe, and the Euphrates and Jordan in the Middle East (Faure & Rubin, 1993). Water has utilitarian purposes, but also is symbolic and tied to cultural histories. For example, in Sudan, some people believe that the Nile is the source of creation and is blessed; others tell of spiritual heroes who were sacrificed to the gods for its continued bounty. Additionally, the river has meanings of danger, safety, and uniting peoples (Deng, 1993). When a resource is limited and it has special cultural meaning, the negotiation of water rights can be very difficult. These types of negotiations often provide an impetus for intercultural conflict. Sharing the resources and respecting cultural uses of the resources are critical elements for managing such intercultural conflicts and creating peace.

PEACE   Although there are many factors working against positive intercultural relations, peace is possible. Peace often relies on our abilities to socially create intercultural situations of collaboration, understanding, and respect. Almost every chapter in this book discussed communication skills that can be used to create peace, such as alliance building (Chapter 6), creating inclusive work cultures (Chapter 8), transcendent communication (Chapter 10), and reconciliation (this chapter). This section discusses two additional ideas for how to create peace in the future: using culture as a bridge and creating third cultures.

Cultural differences become the greatest obstacles to a negotiated agreement when one member fears that the other side will seek to impose its culture or use it to dominate (Salacuse, 1993). The metaphors of culture as a weapon and as a fortress help to illustrate these situations. Culture becomes a weapon when "one party perceives the other side's culture as presenting the risk of forcibly changing the 'shared and enduring meanings, values, and beliefs that characterize' the first party's ethnic group" (Salacuse, 1993, p. 203). When a dominant, powerful nation or culture assumes that a less developed or powerful nation or culture admires or envies its culture, the powerful nation is using culture as a weapon. In response to this ethnocentric attitude, the other party may become defensive and use its own culture as a fortress to protect itself from a cultural onslaught. One method of using one's culture as a fortress is to demonize the other side. Overall, the more one asserts its culture as a weapon, the more the other will retreat within its cultural fortress (Salacuse, 1993) (see Figure 12.2).

Alternatively, culture can also be a bridge between two sides during intercultural negotiations. To build the bridge, members must avoid the weapon or fortress options. Instead, members should try to understand how the other side perceives their culture and avoid statements that the other side might interpret as arrogant or dominant. To build bridges, members should: a) seek common historical elements or personal elements, if they exist, between group members; b) demonstrate interest in and respect for the other's culture by asking about

Figure 12.2
Culture as a Weapon and Fortress

- They want to be like us.

- Our culture is better than theirs.

- If they only knew what they were missing.

- We can bring them a better life.

- We need to protect our culture.

- They are oppressors.

- They are the devil and we need to avoid their influence.

- We must keep them out.

the other's culture; and c) demonstrate tolerance of and respect for cultural differences. Essentially these behaviors allow a group member to give face to the other parties and demonstrate mutual concerns.

Another approach to creating peace is to try and create third cultures (Casmir, 1993). A **third culture** is an inclusive space between two cultures. It includes aspects of both cultures that are shared but is more of a meeting in the middle. It is a harmonious place between two cultures for a set of individuals. Third cultures are open-ended and capable of growth, they can enlarge to create new situations, and they are future-oriented (Casmir, 1993). Lee (2006) explained that a third culture includes three elements: equality, commonality, and transcendence. Equality is a balance of attitudes; commonality is shared goals and similarity between two cultures; transcendence is the creating of something new or beyond the two different cultures. An example of a third culture is an intercultural marriage (such as between a European Christian and an Indonesian Muslim) where both parties celebrate aspects of each other's culture, but also create their own cultural practices unique to their marriage. They might celebrate Muslim and Christian holidays and also celebrate other holidays of their adopted homeland (such as Thanksgiving in the United States). Other family members and friends can be included in their third culture and their marital culture is constantly being added to. Creating third cultures in our relationships is one key way to create peaceful intercultural relationships.

Self-Assessment 12.2

THIRD CULTURE

For each of the following items, consider an intercultural friendship or intimate relationship. Rate the degree to which you agree with the statements using the following scale: (1) strongly disagree, (2) disagree, (3) neutral, (4) agree, and (5) strongly agree.

1. I do not attempt to persuade my cultural values over my friend/ partner.

2. I try to gain my friend's/partner's approval whenever possible.

3. I fully respect the cultural values held by my friend/partner.

4. My friend/partner and I share a lot in common.

5. My friend/partner and I enjoy the similarity between our cultures.

6. My friend/partner and I share some private ways of communicating with each other.

7. My friend/partner and I are trying to resemble each other's culture.

8. My friend/partner and I enjoy something different from our original cultures.

9. My friend/partner and I are willing to negotiate meaning when we misunderstand each other.

10. Cultural differences between my friend/partner and I are no longer a hindrance to our relationship.

Scoring: Items 1–3 measure equality; Items 4–7 measure commonality; Items 8–10 measure transcendence. Add up the score of all 10 items. The higher the scores, the more of a third culture your relationship has. The scores range from 10–50.

Concept Check

The future of intercultural communication includes globalization and intercultural relations. Globalization has already occurred, but the impacts on intercultural communication are still being determined. Migration and technology are two key components of globalization. Both features create increased intercultural contact, but tend to heighten the importance of cultural differences. The heightened importance of culture provides opportunities for both conflict and peace in intercultural relations. Elements that might lead to intercultural conflict include the need for positive social identity, past negative historical interactions, and the struggle over scarce resources. In contrast, peace is possible through effective intercultural communication. Two effective communication strategies include creating situations where culture is a bride and not a weapon or fortress, and creating third cultures.

Layered Perspective of History(ies) and the Future(s)

The layered aspects of history and the future are complex. Most of the time, the layered perspective considers the way that history impacts intercultural communication at the community, organizational, and interpersonal layers (or top-down effects). However, individuals and organizations also have the power to create, re-create, revise, and tell history and shape a new future. Thus, strong bottom-up effects exist. Consistent with the other chapters, we consider the bottom-up effects first and then discuss the top-down effects. Finally, the challenges and skills associated with telling the stories of history and creating the future are addressed.

Bottom-Up Effects

When most of us think about individuals who change the course of history, we consider larger-than-life figures such as presidents and prime ministers, military leaders, and social leaders. However, everyday people also rewrite history and can change future intercultural relations. For example, Chapter 6 noted how Richard and Mildred Loving, an interracial couple, changed history by challenging anti-miscegenation laws. They were able to get the laws banning interracial marriage overturned and paved the way for future couples. Thus, if we want to make history and change the future, we have to be willing to stand up and fight injustices that we perceive and to dialogue with others to understand their histories and create a future that is inclusive for everyone.

Not all of us have to try to make it in the history books—we can write our own history books. Individuals help to capture hidden histories of cultural groups. For example, a number of scholars and writers have written histories of the Buffalo soldiers—Black soldiers who were members of the U.S. cavalry after the Civil War. The Buffalo soldiers worked in the Western United States and territories and are often forgotten in mainstream records of military history. Frank Schubert (2003) wrote a book to recognize this group, called *Voices of the Buffalo Soldier*. Additionally, Gerda Lerner (1997) discussed the hidden histories of women and Jews in her book *Why History Matters*. Numerous examples of how individuals can tell stories about cultural groups are either hidden or not well known.

As individuals, our interpersonal relationships can also include bottom-up effects. We can tell our cultural histories and listen to other individuals as well. Sharing stories and recognizing past wrongs are ways to solidify intercultural friendships, as discussed in Chapter 6. Listening to another's history is a way to demonstrate understanding, consideration, and appreciation for the cultural identity of our friends, co-workers, and classmates. All of us have cultural histories to tell, and we like to have them affirmed.

Top-Down Effects

One of the top-down effects was directly discussed earlier in this chapter; that is, histories are the collective memory of a culture and shape the cultural identity of members of that cultural group. Individuals have their own subjective interpretation of this history and identity, but past events influence that interpretation.

Another important top-down effect is the way that history shapes public policy and its subsequent impact on organizational and individual behavior. Throughout this book, we have noted examples of policies that have both facilitated and limited effective intercultural communication. For example, affirmative action (Chapters 7 and 8) was born of the legacy of slavery, segregation, and discrimination. Affirmative action opened up institutions to ethnic minorities and facilitated greater contact among different cultural groups. Another critical example of public policy that is influenced by history is immigration reform, which is frequently a topic of conversation in the United States and in other developed nations. In President Bush's second term, he made immigration reform a platform issue. Moreover, Congress has considered several immigration measures including criminalization of illegal immigrants (2005), a guest worker program (2006), and a comprehensive policy of tightening borders, providing citizenship to illegal immigrants in the United States, and limiting future immigration to skilled workers (2007). All of these options, however, failed to gain approval. Part of the context of this proposed legislation is the history of the United States as a nation of immigrants. Another factor is the globalization of the economy and need for low-income workers. Thus, both history and the present provide shape to the debate.

Challenges and Skills

As discussed earlier in this chapter, one of the biggest challenges of addressing history is how to move beyond negative historical relations to build a positive future for all involved. Unfortunately, forgiveness and movement are difficult, in part as Hennessey (1993) explained:

> ...the reasons for reading historical sources can be taken to lie in the ideological force which they—or their narration—(continue to) exert on the present....[T]he discourses emerging in a particular social formation continue to exercise ideological pressures on the present (pp. 118–119).

In other words, the past influences the worldviews that we currently hold, and it is difficult to forgive and trust people we feel have persecuted us, treated us poorly, and stolen our lands. No single individual is able to reconcile a negative history, although it is clear that reconciliation efforts, as evidenced by the case of South Africa, are necessary.

What agency do individuals have in reconciling history? Lerner (1997) explained that not only does history matter, but what we do about history matters for the future. First, we have to think small and interact with others in a positive manner. We must become aware of the historical factors shaping intercultural communication and own the responsibilities of our cultural groups for the negative relations. We do not have to feel guilty, but we do need to recognize that our ancestors may have oppressed the ancestors of our friends, co-workers, and classmates. We need to be sure not to minimize the impact of history on people by denying the trauma that may still exist for a cultural group. For example, we should never tell people to "get over it": It is like telling a person who was raped or had a family member murdered to get over it. People who have been victims of trauma or intergenerational trauma need to work through the pain with their own healing rituals. Reconciliation efforts by other cultural groups, especially the oppressor culture, can facilitate this healing, however.

Second, as individuals, we can attempt to create dialogue about historical events with friends, classmates, and co-workers. In many cases, individuals are not aware of the negative history among cultural groups. We know about frequently told stories such as the Holocaust, but we might not know about the struggles that many cultural groups have faced. We can try to create a space to talk about such events and better understand how they impact intercultural communication today and in the future (see Box 12.6). We can also try to understand the ways that forgiveness can be fostered and how we can move forward.

Box 12.6 Voices: Sharing Histories of Discrimination

As the director of cultural diversity programming at my university, I (a White woman) worked with a lot of students of color. I listened to many stories of ancestors' slavery, disenfranchisement of generations of family members in so many political, educational, and social situations, and their own continued difficulties in achieving their goals in a society that they believed still did not recognize and accept them as equals. One day, an older, African American student asked me in a private conversation about why I was so interested and involved in promoting diversity at the university since, to her, I looked like a solid member of the majority culture. I told her the history of my family of Italian immigrants who faced so much discrimination and suspicion in the years after they came here. I told her about how I, a third-generation Italian-American, had experienced discrimination during my educational history. I even told her about how some Italians, like the Japanese, were interred during World War II. She had never heard of any discrimination against Italians in the United States and was shocked to hear about it. Telling my story for the first time to this student was surprisingly liberating, and affirming. Moreover, telling the story allowed both of us a new depth of mutual respect and understanding for each other's histories. Knowing my story—as I knew hers and her peers'—allowed us to work together even more effectively to achieve our diversity goals at the university.

Finally, we have the opportunity to create and re-create our own history. We have a responsibility to revise histories that are unfair and inaccurate and that hide accomplishments and memories of cultural groups. Further, the stories we tell create our own history. As individuals, we have agency to tell stories that foster strong and positive intercultural relations, but also negative and damaging ones. The choices are ours.

SUMMARY

Returning to the chapter's opening story: The Long Walk is a significant part of the culture of the Navajos. It is a part of their collective memory and provides a sense of who they are and how they related to each other in the past. The Long Walk may also present historical trauma for Navajos today even though the event occurred 150 years ago. Retelling this story and acknowledging the lack of reconciliation about the event with the federal government creates wounds. Additionally, the Long Walk—and other limitations placed on Navajos in the reservation system—has disenfranchised many Navajos from the mainstream U.S. culture. This event as well as the broken treaties and boarding school experiences that followed have created many Navajos' mistrust of the government and mainstream Americans. Finally, this story is a hidden one. Very few people know of this event in history. Other American Indians have similar histories, such as the Trail of Tears for the Cherokee and the Battle of Wounded Knee for the Lakota.

Here is a summary of the chapter based on the learning objectives:

- **Define history(ies).** History is the retelling of past events and eras that shape cultural identity and social relations and structures. Telling stories about history is fundamental to the human experience. History is often better reflected as histories for the many stories that are told about cultural groups. It recognizes that not just one history exists for everyone.
- **Three reasons that history matters for intercultural communication.** History matters for intercultural communication for at least three reasons: a) it is part of collective memory and cultural identity; b) past traumatic events are passed down through generations (historical trauma); and c) history has significant consequences for intercultural relations today.
- **How history relates to cultural identity.** History is the collective memory of a group of people that shapes cultural identity. It provides meaning and definition to a cultural group and the individual members of that group. For groups in power, the collective memory is important to recognize the achievements of individuals in that group; there is also the concern of people in power to retain their power and hence histories get retold in ways that support group pride and power. For groups not in power, collective memory recognizes struggle and survivorship, but also the struggle to be recognized by the majority culture. The histories of many cultural groups without power are hidden, thus denying them affirmation of accomplishments and recognition of their contribution to a society. This lack of recognition inhibits the opportunity to succeed.

- **Historical trauma and two ways of addressing it.** Historical trauma is unresolved trauma and grief that are passed from one generation to the next such that events that happened many years ago still impact people today. Historical trauma results in negative physical and mental health outcomes. Cultural groups can address their own historical trauma individually by strengthening cultural identity and practices and collectively by engaging in community healing rituals.

- **Three consequences of history today.** History has three significant consequences on intercultural relations today. First, cultural groups that have been historically oppressed or colonized often are disenfranchised and disadvantaged socioeconomically. Second, colonization and oppression alter intracultural (within culture) relations. They change traditional and positive interaction patterns and introduce negative interaction patterns. Third, negative historical relations usually result in strained modern-day intercultural communication. The conflict persists unless some reconciliation is attempted and established.

- **Factors for the future of intercultural communication.** The future of intercultural communication includes globalization and intercultural relations. Globalization is the increased interconnection of people and movement toward convergences of cultures and focuses on migration and technology. Intercultural relations focus on conflict and peace. Elements that might lead to intercultural conflict include the need for positive social identity, past negative historical interactions, and the struggle over scarce resources. In contrast, peace is possible through effective intercultural communication.

- **Bottom-up and top-down effects of history(ies).** From the bottom-up, individuals make and shape history. We have the ability to tell stories that were once hidden, and we can also revise inaccurate stories. We have agency to create positive histories for the future by listening to our peers and acknowledging their histories and recognizing where our ancestors may have created negative histories. From the top-down, historical events shape cultural identity and also public policy that influences intercultural communication such as affirmative action.

REVIEW QUESTIONS

1. What is history and histories?
2. Distinguish between the past and history.
3. How does history as collective memory shape cultural identity?
4. In what ways does the collective memory differ for cultural groups in power and those without power?
5. What are hidden histories and revisionist history?
6. Provide examples of historical trauma.
7. Compare and contrast individual and community efforts to address historical trauma in particular cultural groups.

8. Can outsiders facilitate healing from historical trauma? Explain your answer.

9. How does colonization lead to disenfranchisement? How does colonization lead to altered intracultural relations?

10. Describe the merits of reconciliation for addressing strained intercultural relations.

11. Discuss the appropriate communicative strategies necessary to achieve reconciliation around slavery.

12. What is globalization and how does it shape the future of intercultural communication?

13. What factors are associated with a future of intercultural conflict? What factors are associated with a future of intercultural peace?

14. Provide an example of a third culture.

15. Discuss the bottom-up and top-down effects of histories and the future.

16. What agency does an individual have in changing a history of negative intercultural relations?

EXERCISES

1. Visit the Web site, "Answers.Com," and look up Sunni-Shi'a relations (http://www.answers.com/topic/sunni-shia-relations). Which historical factors are associated with cultural identity as well as with current intercultural relations between these two groups? Why do the relations vary in different countries?

2. Consider a piece of public policy that influences intercultural communication such as affirmative action and immigration laws. Investigate the historical events and stories of the events that shape this legislation. Was the policy born of positive historical relations or negative historical relations? Why was the legislation enacted at this point in time?

3. Investigate the historical relations of any two cultural groups in conflict such as Israeli-Palestinian, Catholic-Protestant in Northern Ireland, or Hutu and Tutsi in Rwanda. Identify the root factors of this conflict. How has intercultural communication made the conflict better and worse throughout history? Is reconciliation possible? If so, what steps do you think are necessary for reconciliation to occur?

4. View the movie *Matewan* (1987; Director John Sayles, Cinecom Pictures) about events that occurred in Matewan, West Virginia. It tells the histories of Black and White coal miners and the attempts of union organizers to try to get the miners to join a labor union against the Stone Mountain Coal Company in 1920. Consider the intercultural communication concepts that can help explain the events in Matewan. How does this history shape future intercultural relations among Black and White miners?

5. Read the book *Lies Across America: What Our Historic Sites Get Wrong* by James Loewen (1999, The New Press). Are you surprised that so many historic sites omit information or include false information? Does this make you question aspects of history you have learned?

Abstract conceptualization: The third stage of the experiential learning model, which provides the learner with the opportunity to weigh the strengths and limitations of perspectives.

Accommodation: The use of similar speech patterns and nonverbal behaviors to another person.

Accommodators: Learners who combine concrete experience and active experimentation.

Acculturation: The process of learning some, but not all, of the host culture values and practices.

Active experimentation: The final stage of the experiential learning model, which provides the learner with the opportunity to directly test what has been learned in the previous three stages.

Adjustment stage: The fourth stage of the W-shaped model; sojourners have gained a level of competence in the new culture.

Advocacy: Asserting and supporting claims and debating positions.

Affirmative action: Positive steps to increase the representation of groups, such as women and minorities, in education, employment, government, business, and other settings in which they have been historically excluded.

Agency: The freedom to choose action and to enact identity.

Animism: The belief in supernatural beings such as good and evil spirits.

Ascription: The process of assigning in another person what you think his or her identity should be.

Assimilators: Learners who combine reflective observation and abstract conceptualization.

Attitudes: Our predisposition toward an object or person.

Attribution: The process of collecting information and then making sense of it; the meaning we attach to behavior.

Autonomy face: The desire to be free of imposition from others.

Autonomy-connection: A dialectic referring to the strength of a couple's relationship; autonomy is the desire to be unique from others while connection is the desire to be interdependent with another.

Avowal: The process of telling others what identity(ies) you wish to present or how you see yourself.

Barriers: The perceived psychological, financial, or physical costs that inhibit a healthy behavior.

Benevolent approach: Managerial style in which one tends to see oneself as interdependent and at a different level than others.

Bottom-up effects: The effect of lower layers (such as individuals and interpersonal relationships) on higher layers (such as culture).

Category or group-based attributions: Attributions based on group characteristics or social memberships/identities.

Classroom management: A broad set of teaching behaviors through which the teacher shapes and maintains learning conditions that facilitate effective and efficient instruction resulting in a learning community.

Collectivism: Broad value tendencies of people in a culture to emphasize the group identity over the individual identity as well as group-oriented concerns over individual wants and desires.

Colonization: The process of a nation extending its control to a foreign territory in order to exploit that territory and its people culturally, economically, and politically.

Communal approach: Managerial style in which one tends to see oneself as interdependent and at the same level as others.

Communication: Process whereby people collectively create and transmit meaning through the exchange of verbal and nonverbal messages in a particular context.

Community capacity: The characteristics of communities that affect their ability to identify, mobilize, and address social and public health problems.

Community conflicts: Struggles between and among collectives over scarce resources, status, and power in which the aims are to neutralize, injure, or eliminate their rivals.

Community empowerment: A social action process that promotes the participation of people and organizations toward the goals of community.

Community mediation: The assistance to parties in dispute by people who are neutral third parties (specifically volunteers from differing backgrounds who have received a small amount of training), but who do not have the authority to impose any decisions on the disputants.

Community: A collection of people who share interaction, location, and/or a sense of belonging to one another.

Community-based participatory approaches: Involves researchers, educators, and community members in a collaborative manner to address issues of concern for a community.

Concrete experience: The first stage of the experiential learning model, which provides first-hand experience of the subject matter.

Conflict: The perceived and/or actual incompatibility of values, expectations, processes, or outcomes between two or more parties over substantive and/or relational issues.

Conflict goal assessments: The perception of importance of three interrelated issues during conflict: content, relational, and identity goals.

Conflict management style: A predominant patterned response to conflict in a variety of dissenting situations.

Conformity orientation: The degree to which families create a climate that stresses homogeneity of attitudes, values, and beliefs.

Context: Frame of reference for understanding communication behavior; includes the features of an interaction, such as social relationships, historical relationships, and culture, and the specific situation (scene, physical setting, and purpose).

Conventionality-uniqueness: A dialectic referring to the external management of predictability-novelty; that is, a couple needs to decide whether they want to have a conventional life or one in which they are unique.

Convergers: Learners who combine active experimentation and abstract conceptualization.

Conversation orientation: The degree to which families value and create a climate of open flow of communication and exchanges of ideas about attitudes, beliefs, and values.

Cooperative (connected) learning: Learning centered on personal reflection, subjective reactions, consciousness-raising, and cooperative performance; also called connected learning.

Crisis stage: The second stage of the W-shaped model in which the differences between sojourners and the host culture create problems; minor issues become major problems and cultural differences become irritating.

Critical approach/perspective: Perspective that emphasizes power differences between different cultures and studies the domination of one group by another.

Cross-cultural communication: Comparing/contrasting the communication of two different cultures.

Cultivation: The process of homogenizing the beliefs of the audience.

Cultural adaptation: The process faced by individuals who relocate to an unfamiliar sociocultural environment in striving

to establish and maintain a relatively stable, reciprocal, and functional relationship with the environment.

Cultural appropriation: The process of taking a symbol from another culture and using it for one's own cultural or individual purposes.

Cultural competence: The ability to communicate in a culturally appropriate and effective manner.

Cultural diversity: The representation, in one social system, of people with distinctly different group affiliations of cultural significance.

Cultural identity achievement: Third identity phase in which individuals feel they have a good grasp of their cultural identities; they have reached a sense of clarity and confidence about their identities.

Cultural identity search: Second identity phase in which individuals become aware of cultural differences and begin a continuous process of looking for information and explanation about their culture and other cultures in order to define their identities.

Cultural imperialism: The domination of a culture's ideology by another culture's ideology, especially through the use of popular culture.

Cultural industries: Media producers that create and distribute television shows, movies, newspapers, and magazines.

Cultural relativism: A code of ethics that judges people based on their own cultural standards.

Cultural sensitivity: The extent to which ethnic or cultural characteristics, experiences, norms, values, behavior patterns, and beliefs of a target population and relevant historical, environmental, and social forces are incorporated in the design, delivery, and evaluation of targeted health interventions, including behavioral change materials and programs.

Cultural universalism: Emphasizes a single set of standards that should be used to judge others' behavior as good or bad.

Culture: A learned system of meanings that fosters a particular sense of shared identity-hood and community-hood among its group members. It is a complex frame of reference that consists of a pattern of traditions, beliefs, values, norms, symbols, and meanings that are shared to varying degrees by interacting members of an identity group.

Culture shock: The psychological and emotional reaction people experience when they encounter a culture that is very different from their own.

Danger control: Stance that people take when they feel they can control what happens to them. Includes seeking information about the problem, talking with others about the problem, and enacting preventive behaviors.

Deculturation: The process of unlearning some of our old cultural values and practices.

Deep structure: The values, beliefs, history, and social relations of a group that more profoundly impacts health behavior compared to surface structure.

Developmental communication: The study of social change brought about by the application of communication, theory, and technologies from one culture to another.

Dialectic: The contradiction of two opposing forces along the same continuum that appears mutually exclusive.

Diaspora: Massive migration from wars, colonization, slavery, persecution, or famine that results in a culture group being geographically dispersed.

Discrimination: Action that maintains the dominance of one group of people over another.

Disenfranchised: Feeling deprived of the rights of citizenship.

Divergers: Learners who combine concrete experience and reflective observation.

Diversity climate: The prevailing attitude toward diversity in an organization.

Ecological fallacy: The assumption that what is true of the collective is true of all the individuals of that collective.

Educational disparity: When one cultural group has an educational outcome that is worse than that of another cultural group.

Effective communication: Communication that maximizes understanding.

Egocentric bias: Viewing our own behavior as normal and appropriate and the standards by which to judge others' behavior.

Egoprotective bias: The desire to maintain a positive self-image.

Entertainment-education: A performance that captures the interest of individuals to give them pleasure, but also to provide a formal instruction and training toward a desired behavior.

Ethnocentrism: Inherent belief in the superiority of our own culture versus others.

Ethnolinguistic vitality: The extent to which a language is desirable and viable in a society.

Ethnorelativism: The belief that all cultures are appropriate and normal and that recognizes an attempt to evaluate and interpret people's behavior from their cultural background.

Experiential closeness: The perception of closeness to a topic or group through real world experiences.

Face: The claimed sense of favorable social self-worth and/or projected other-worth in a public situation.

Familism: The influence of family values on health decisions.

Fatalism: The perceived lack of control over one's environment.

Fear control: Stance that people take when they do not feel they can control what happens to them. Includes not talking about a problem or seeking information about it.

Fellowship face: Emphasizes being approved and included by others.

Fundamental attribution error: The tendency to overestimate the influence of personal characteristics and underestimate the influence of situational factors when we explain others' negative behavior.

Globalization: The increasing interconnectedness of people and places as a result of changes in communication technologies, communication, and migration patterns, which cause political, economic, and cultural convergence.

Gratifications: Meeting emotional or intellectual needs, especially through use of media.

Health beliefs: The attributions or explanations about the causes of our health problems and diseases.

Health care contexts: The various sites where the health of individuals and the population are the focus. Two types of contexts generally apply: clinical and public health.

Health communication: The exchange of symbolic messages related to personal and public health.

Health disparities: Inequalities in health outcomes for different cultural groups.

Health: A complete state of physical, mental, and social well being, not simply the absence of disease.

Hegemony: The process of domination of one set of ideas or group as it subverts another set of ideas or group.

Hidden histories: Stories of cultural groups that are not often told or are told with inaccuracies or oversimplifications.

High culture: Products and artifacts associated with good taste and the "best" elements of a culture, such as fine literature, ballet, operas, museums (art work), and elite mass media.

High-context communication: The transmission of implicit, ambiguous, and indirect messages, often relying on nonverbal communication.

Historical trauma: Unresolved trauma and grief that continue to adversely affect the lives of survivors of traumatic events. Historical trauma is passed from one generation to the next such that events that happened many years ago still impact people today.

History: The retelling of past events and eras that shape cultural identity and social relations and structures.

History-present: A dialectic referring to the degree to which individuals emphasize historical relations among cultures or simply focus on the present.

Homogenization: The decrease of cultural uniqueness created in large part by the creation of trivialized media products.

Honeymoon stage: The feeling of fascination and excitement about going to a new culture; first stage of the W-shaped model.

Horizontal self: Preference for equal treatment regardless of people's position, status, rank, or age.

Hybridity: The process of blending the mediated messages and host culture messages into a new mixture.

Identity: A person's conception of self within a particular social, geographical, cultural, and political context; sense of self or who we are in a specific situation.

Identity freezing: Viewing a person only in terms of cultural identities.

Identity vulnerability-security: A dialectic that involves the degree to which we feel valued and supported in terms of our cultural identity.

Ideology: The worldview of a group of people, including macro perspectives such as political ideologies and micro perspectives such as distorted communication.

Immediacy: The extent to which communication behaviors enhance closeness and reduce physical and/or psychological distance between communicators.

Independent self-construal: View of self as autonomous, self-reliant, unencumbered, and rational choice-makers; common in individualistic cultures.

Individual (or separate) learning: Learning centered on critical thinking, objective observation, abstract analysis, and individual performance; also called separate learning.

Individualism: Broad value tendencies of people in a culture to emphasize the individual identity over group identity and individual rights over group obligations.

Ingroup: People we identify as members of our own cultural group.

Institutionalized racism: Differential access to goods, services, and opportunities of society by race.

Instructional communication: Communication behavior related to teaching and learning such as teacher-student interaction, peer-to-peer interaction, and out-of-class communication.

Instructional immediacy: Communication behaviors associated with classroom instruction and direct learning.

Intercultural alliance: An intercultural friendship that addresses three key issues through dialogue: addressing power and unearned privilege, recognizing the influence of history, and having an orientation of affirmation.

Intercultural communication: Communication that occurs between individuals and entities that are culturally unalike.

Intercultural sensitivity: Capacity to accept and accommodate cultural difference.

Intercultural transformation: The progression of internal change that results in observable behavioral changes representing adaptation to the new culture; outcomes include functional fitness, psychological health, and the development of an intercultural identity.

Interdependent self-construal: View of self as group-bound, obligatory agents, and relational harmony seekers; common in collectivistic cultures.

Intergroup communication: When our messages and identity tend to focus on the cultural and group identities of the individuals who are interacting.

Internalized racism: The acceptance by members of the stigmatized races of negative messages about their own abilities and intrinsic worth.

International communication: The study of mass-mediated communication between entities (governmental, private industry, or non-profit agencies) from two or more countries.

Interpersonal communication: When the motivations, messages, and rules focus on the unique aspects of our relationship with others, regardless of cultural background.

Interpretive approach: Perspective providing detailed descriptions of culture and cultural communication. The goal is to identify a unified culture and the ways of knowing and understanding the culture.

Layered approach: Approach emphasizing that individuals around the world are organized in various interconnected layers.

Learning style: Preferred manner in which people learn.

Low-context communication: The transmission of explicit, precise, and direct messages relying on verbal communication; meaning resides in the message.

Masculinity-femininity: Dimension focusing on the extent to which a society stresses achievement or nurture; masculinity pertains to societies in which social gender roles are clearly distinct and achievement is emphasized, while femininity pertains to societies in which social gender roles overlap and nurture is emphasized.

Mean-world syndrome: Heavy exposure to television and its violent images leading a viewer to conclude that the world is a violent place and people cannot be trusted.

Media advocacy: The strategic use of mass media and their tools, in combination with community organizing, for the purpose of advancing healthy public policy.

Media literacy: The ability to access, critically analyze, critically evaluate, and create mediated messages in a variety of forms and contexts.

Mediated closeness: The perception of closeness to a topic or group through transporting ourselves into a story.

Mediated remoteness: The perception of distance from a subject matter presented in the media.

Migrants: People who move to a new permanent cultural context that is different from the one in which they were raised. Immigrants and refugees are two types of migrants.

Mindful: A state of awareness of thoughts, actions, and messages of self and others.

Monolithic organization: One that is predominantly composed of members from the majority group; if members of ethnic or cultural minorities are included in the organization, they are generally restricted to the lower levels of the hierarchy.

Moral conflict: Clash between opposing parties based on differences in deeply held philosophical assumptions about being, knowledge, and the world.

Moral inclusion/exclusion: The degree to which we believe that people are within the boundaries of respect, fairness, and moral values. Moral inclusion occurs when we treat all people with dignity and respect, when we treat everyone as human; moral exclusion happens when we feel that certain people do not deserve fair treatment, our respect, or to be valued.

Motivational interviewing: A directive, client-centered counseling style for eliciting behavior change by helping clients to explore and resolve ambivalence.

Multicultural organization: One that has a representative population, and majority and minority members are distributed throughout the levels of the organization; ethnic minority managers are integrated informally as well.

Multifaceted: An individual's identity is composed of multiple dimensions, and it is this constellation of identities that makes us who we are.

Negotiation: Give and take on positions to reach a mutually agreeable solution.

Neighborhood collective efficacy: The belief that members of a community can act collectively to achieve some goal.

Nonaccommodation: Behavior that includes the use of differing verbal and nonverbal patterns.

Nonsupport problematic: Ignoring cultural identities and only focusing on personal characteristics.

Offshoring: When an organization relocates one or more business functions from its home base to another country.

Openness-closedness: A dialectic that involves the amount of information we reveal about ourselves to another person in order to develop intimacy; the more open we are, the less closed we are and vice versa.

Organization: A social collective that coordinates individuals' actions to achieve common goals.

Outgroup: People whom we identify as outside of our cultural group.

Outsourcing: When an organization contracts with another organization to perform a particular business function.

Perceived efficacy: The degree to which a person feels she can perform certain behaviors to avoid a health threat.

Perceived threat: The degree which a person feels concerned by a particular disease or health problem.

Personal approach: Managerial style in which one sees oneself as independent and at the same level as others.

Personal identities: Unique qualities of ourselves such as personality and relationships.

Personal immediacy: Communication behaviors related to the moral and ethical behavior of a teacher.

Person-based attributions: Attributions based on individual characteristics.

Pipeline problem: A situation that occurs when students from certain cultural groups are not well represented at the college ranks, and thus are underrepresented in jobs that require college degrees.

Plural organization: One that has a population of employees that is representative of the larger society. However, most ethnic minorities are still located at the lower levels or are poorly integrated informally if they have made it to the managerial ranks.

Political economy: The power held by cultural industries in the production of media for capitalistic purposes.

Popular culture: Products and artifacts that are shared and understood by most people. Popular culture is often considered "unsophisticated" and "junk."

Power distance: The extent to which the less powerful members of institutions and organizations within a country expect and accept that power is distributed unequally.

Prediction-novelty: A dialectic referring to the degree to which we prefer routine versus newness or spontaneity.

Prejudice: Attitude that combines both belief (cognitive) and affect (emotion) toward a group of people.

Premature closure: An error that occurs when we stop looking for explanations for behavior (our own and others') once we have found a plausible or reasonable explanation.

Principle of negativity: Tendency to overemphasize negative information when making attributions about behavior.

Privatized medicine: A market-based system where private providers deliver health services and private insurance pays for most of these services.

Privilege-disadvantage: A dialectic referring to the degree to which one partner in the relationship has unearned privilege relative to the other.

Process difficulty: Communication processes that potentially interfere with performance and include high levels of conflict and tension, power struggles, lack of cooperation, lack of respect for group members, inconsistent norms/rules, and inequality in turn taking.

Public health: Efforts toward assuring conditions in which people can be healthy.

Racial steering: Occurs when real estate agents only show homes to a family in neighborhoods that are predominantly of the same racial or cultural background.

Racism: An irrationally based negative attitude toward a racial or ethnic group, coupled with actions that discriminate against that group.

Reconciliation: The process of settling past disputes and abuses for the purpose of establishing close relations.

Recovery stage: The third stage of the W-shaped model in which sojourners begin to see some positive aspects about the host culture and its people again (after a crisis).

Redlining: Occurs when a bank refuses to lend money to people who live in a certain area.

Reentry culture shock: The fifth stage of the W-shaped model; sojourners have a negative psychological and emotional reaction upon their return to their home culture.

Reflective observation: The second stage of the experiential learning model, which provides the learner with an opportunity to observe and think about the meaning of the observation.

Reflexive dialogue: Communication with others (and with oneself) to uncover and examine biases, hidden assumptions, and privileges.

Relational culture: Processes, structures, and practices that create, express, and sustain personal relationships and identities of partners; the unique culture that partners create in their relationships.

Relational immediacy: Communication behaviors that enhance the psychological closeness between teacher and student.

Relationship parameters: Factors that affect how we frame a conflict including competition-cooperation, affiliation-control, and trust-distrust.

Resocialization stage: The fifth stage of the W-shaped model; sojourners begin the adjustment back to their home culture.

Revelation-nonrevelation: A dialectic that focuses on the degree to which a couple shares information about their relationship with other people.

Revisionist history: Retelling and recreating history so that it is more accurate and balanced. For example, recapturing hidden histories is a critical part of revisionist history.

Self reflexivity: The ability to understand yourself and your own cultural biases.

Self-construal: One's self-image, composed of an independent and an interdependent self.

Self-effacement bias: Tendency to overestimate situational factors and underemphasize personal factors.

Self-other dialectic: Managing the dialectic between supporting your own cultural identity versus that of the other person.

Sense of community: The feeling of caring and sharing among people in a community.

Separation-integration: A dialectic focusing on the external management of the interdependence in the relationship; in other words, a couple has to decide whether they will integrate their lives with family and friends or separate themselves.

Short-term versus long-term orientation: Long Term Orientation stands for the fostering of virtues oriented toward future rewards, in particular perseverance and thrift, while Short Term Orientation stands for the fostering of virtues related to the past and present, in particular, respect for tradition, preservation of "face" and fulfilling social obligations.

Situational and relationship boundary features: The setting and nature of the relationship that you have with the other party.

Situation-based attributions: Attributions based on the physical characteristics (people, place, things) of a given inter-action.

Social capital: Features of social organization such as networks, norms, and social trust that facilitate coordination and cooperation for mutual benefit.

Social ecological framework: Perspective that examines the relationships between humans and their social, historical, and cultural environment.

Social identities: Aspects we share with other individuals who belong to the same perceived group such as age, class, gender, national culture, religion, and ethnicity.

Socialized medicine: A system of publicly administered national health care; ranges from programs in which the government runs hospitals and health organizations to programs in which there is national universal health care.

Social justice: A philosophical stance that emphasizes fair distribution of wealth, power, and income across cultures.

Social scientific perspective: Perspective that attempts to identify patterns of communication and attribute this behavior to cultural values.

Social support: Part of relationships in which individuals provide aid, assistance, and comfort to others.

Sojourners: People who go to another country to stay for a certain period of time and then return home; generally between six months and five years.

Speech code: System of socially constructed symbols and meaning, premises, and rules, pertaining to communication conduct.

Status-achievement approach: Managerial style reflecting the desire for a status position, but with everyone having the opportunity to achieve such status.

Stereotypes: Overgeneralized cognitions about a group of people with no attempt to identify within-group variation.

Stranger: An individual who is a member of a system but is not strongly attached to that system.

Subjective culture: An individual's interpretation of the beliefs, values, and norms associated with a culture.

Subjugated ascriptions: Identities given to others that put them in a lower or inferior position compared to one's own group.

Surface structure: The observable characteristics and behaviors of a cultural group such as physical characteristics, foods, music, and language.

System: A set of component parts that have interdependent relationships.

Third culture: An inclusive space between two cultures that includes aspects of both cultures that are shared but also a meeting in the middle of those cultures. It is a harmonious place between two cultures for a set of individuals.

Top-down effects: The effects of cultural and societal layers (such as mass media and cultural values) on organizational, interpersonal, and individual communication behavior.

Transcendent communication: A set of organizing principles that lead conflict participants to think differently about what they are doing as they work through their differences and to help them achieve unimagined outcomes through productive dialogue.

Ultimate attribution error: Tendency to overemphasize category-based factors and underemphasize situation-based factors to explain negative behavior from people who are culturally different than us.

Uncertainty avoidance: The extent to which the members of a culture feel threatened by uncertain or unknown situations.

Unexamined cultural identity: First identity phase in which individuals do not question their cultural or ethnic identities.

Vertical self: Preference for differential treatment with due respect to people's position, titles, and age.

Abrams, J., O'Connor, J., & Giles, H. (2002). Identity and inter-group communication. In W. B. Gudykunst & B. Mody (Eds.), *Handbook of international and intercultural communication* (2nd ed, pp. 225–240). Thousand Oaks, CA: Sage.

Aday, L. A. (2001). *At risk in America: The health and health care needs of vulnerable populations in the United States* (2nd ed.). San Francisco: Jossey-Bass.

Adejunmobi, M. (2004). Polygots, vernaculars and global markets: Variable trends in West Africa. *Language & Intercultural Communication, 4*, 159–174.

Alba, R. (1990). *Ethnic identity: Transformation of White America*. New Haven, CT: Yale University Press.

Albert, R. D., & Ha, I. A. (2004). Latino/Anglo-American differences in attributions to situations involving touch and silence. *International Journal of Intercultural Relations, 28*, 253–280.

Albiniak, P. (2005, February 7). The picture isn't perfect, but it is better. *Broadcasting Cable*, 22–23.

Albizu, J. A. (2007). Geolinguistic regions and diasporas in the age of satellite television. *International Communication Gazette, 69*, 239–261.

Albrecht, T. L., Burleson, B. R., & Goldsmith, D. (1994). Supportive communication. In M. L. Knapp & G. R. Miller (Eds.). *Handbook of interpersonal communication* (2nd ed., pp. 419–449). Thousand Oaks, CA: Sage.

Albuquerque Journal (2006, November 17). Legislator says "get over" slavery. *Albuquerque Journal*, A8.

Allen, C. (2003). *China CCG FY 2004—executive summary*. STAT-USA, U.S. Department of State.

Allen, M., Witt, P. L., & Wheeless, L. R. (2006). The role of teacher immediacy as a motivational factor in student learning: Using meta-analysis to test a causal model. *Communication Education, 55*, 21–31.

American Cancer Society (2001). *New Mexico Cancer facts and figures, 2000–2001*. Atlanta: American Cancer Society, Report.

Anderson, L. (1994). A new look at an old construct: Cross-cultural adaptation. International *Journal of Intercultural Relations, 18*, 293–328.

Anthony, K., Rosselli, F., & Caparyan, L. (2003). Truly evil or simply angry: Individualism, collectivism, and attributions for the events of September 11th. *Individual Differences Research, 1*, 147–157.

Appiah, K. A. (2006). *Cosmopolitanism: Ethics in a world of strangers*. New York: W. W. Norton.

Apprey, M. (1999). Reinventing the self in the face of received transgenerational hatred in the African American community.

International Journal of Applied Psychoanalytic Studies, 1, 131–143.

Artz, L., & Kamalipour, Y. R. (Eds.) (2003). *The globalization of corporate media hegemony*. Albany, NY: State University of New York Press.

Ashton, C. M., Haidet, P., Paterniti, D. A., Collins, T. C., Gordon, H. S., O'Malley, K., Peterson, L. A., Sharf, B. F., Suarez-Almazor, M. E., Wray, N. P., & Street, R. L. (2003). *Journal of General Internal Medicine, 18*, 146–152.

Associated Press (2007, November 29). Teacher guilty in "Muhammad" teddy bear case. *MSNBC*. Retrieved December 2, 2007, from http://www.msnbc.msn.com/id/22007049/

Axelsson, J. (2005, March 16). Desire for diversity in U.S. universities, colleges continues to grow. *Mosaic*. Retrieved September 18, 2007, from http://media.www.srumosaic.com/media/storage/paper658/news/2005/03/16/News/Desire.For.Diversity.In.U.s.Universities.Colleges.Continues.To.Grow-894816.shtml

Ayanian, J. Z., Cleary, P. D., Weissman, J. S., & Epstein, A. M. (1999). The effect of patients' preferences on racial differences in access to renal transplantation. *New England Journal of Medicine, 341*, 1661–1669.

Bagdikian, B. H. (2004). *The new media monopoly* (7th ed.). Boston: Beacon Press.

Bailey, C., & Oetzel, J. G. (2004). Tighten me up: Reflecting and maintaining ethnic identity through daily interactions in an African American-owned beauty salon. In M. Fong & R. Chuang (Eds.). *Communicating ethnic and cultural identity* (pp. 217–230). Lanham, MD: Rowman & Littlefield.

Baker, K. C. (2007, April). You can't live here…(unless you're white). *Good Housekeeping*, pp. 174–177, 231–232.

Bandara, S. (2007, July 2) Sri Lankan firms view disabled people in new light. *Lanka Business Online*. Retrieved December 6, 2007, from http://www.lankabusinessonline.com/fullstory. php?newsID=1263702371&no_view=1&SEARCH_TERM=10

Barge, J. K. (2006). Dialogue, conflict and community. In J. G. Oetzel & S. Ting-Toomey (Eds.), *The Sage handbook of conflict communication* (pp. 517–543). Thousand Oaks, CA: Sage.

Barnlund, D. (1975). *Public and private self in Japan and the United States*. Tokyo: Simul Press.

Battles, K., & Hilton-Morrow, W. (2002). Gay characters in conventional spaces: *Will and Grace* and the situational comedy genre. *Critical Studies in Media Communication, 19*, 87–105.

Baum, F. E., & Ziersch, A. M (2003). Social capital. *Journal of Epidemiological Community Health, 57,* 320–323.

Baxter, L. A., & Montgomery, B. M. (1997). Rethinking communication in personal relationships from a dialectical perspective. In S. Duck (Ed.), *Handbook of personal relationships* (pp. 325–349). New York: John Wiley.

Beals J., Manson S. M., Whitesell N. R., Spicer P., Novins D. K., & The AI-SUPERPFP team. (2005). Lifetime and past year prevalence of DSM-IV disorders in two American Indian reservation populations. *Archives of General Psychiatry, 62,* 99–108.

Beaudoin, C. E., & Thorson, E. (2006). The social capital of Black and Whites: Differing effects of the mass media in the United States. *Human Communication Research, 32,* 157–177.

Bennett, M. J. (1980). Overcoming the Golden Rule: Sympathy and empathy. *Communication Yearbook, 3,* 407–421.

Bennett, M. J. (1993). Towards enthnorelativism: A developmental model of intercultural sensitivity. In R.M. Paige (Ed.). *Education for the intercultural experience* (pp. 22–71). Yarmouth, ME: Intercultural Press.

Berger, C. R., & Calabrese, R. (1975). Some explorations in initial interactions and beyond: Toward a developmental theory of interpersonal communication. *Human Communication Research, 1,* 99–112.

Bernstein, A.B., Hing, E., Moss, A. J., Allend, K. F, Siller, A. B., Tiggle, R. B. (2003). Health care in America: Trends in utilization. Hyattsville, MD: National Center for Health Statistics. Available: http://www.cdc.gov/nchs/data/misc/healthcare.pdf

Berry, J. W. (2007). Acculturation strategies and adaptation. In J. E. Lansford (Ed.), *Immigrant families in contemporary society* (pp. 69–82). New York: Guilford Press.

Betances, S. (2004). How to become an outstanding educator of Hispanic and African-American first-generation college students. In F. W. Hale (Ed.), *What makes racial diversity work in higher education: Academic leaders present successful policies and strategies* (pp. 44–59). Sterling, VA: Stylus.

Bielsa, E. (2005). Globalisation and translation: A theoretical approach. *Language & Intercultural Communication, 5,* 131–144.

Bilandzic, H. (2006). The perception of distance in the cultivation process: A theoretical consideration of the relationship between television content, processing experience, and perceived distance. *Communication Theory, 16,* 333–354.

Blasco, M. (2004). Stranger to us than birds in our garden? Reflections on hermeneutics, intercultural understanding and the management of difference. In M. Blasco & J. Gustafsson (Eds.), *Intercultural alternatives: Critical perspectives on intercultural encounters in theory and practice* (pp. 19–48). Copenhagen, Denmark: Copenhagen Business School Press.

Bloom, B. S. (1976). *Human characteristics and school learning.* New York: McGraw-Hill.

Borrell-Carrio, F., & Epstein, R. M. (2004). Preventing errors in clinical practice: A call for self-awareness. *Annals of Family Medicine, 2,* 310–316.

Bowser, P., Gaines, J., & Musser, C. (Eds.) (2001). *Oscar Micheaux and his circle: African-American filmmaking and race cinema of the silent era.* Bloomington, IN: Indiana University Press.

Bradford, L., Cooper, E., Allen, M., Stanley, J., & Grimes, D. (2006). Race and the classroom: Interaction and image. In B. M. Gayle, R. W. Preiss, N. Burrell, & M. Allen (Eds.), *Classroom communication and instructional processes: Advances through meta-analysis* (pp. 169–184). Mahwah, NJ: Lawrence Erlbaum & Associates.

Braithwaite, D., & Thompson, T. (Eds.) 2000. *Handbook of communication & people with disabilities.* Mahwah, NJ: Lawrence Erlbaum Associates.

Bresnahan, M., Shearman, S., Lee, S. Y., Ohari, R., & Mosher, D. (2002). Personal and cultural differences in responding to criticism in three countries. *Asian Journal of Social Psychology, 5,* 93–105.

Brofenbrenner, U. (1977). Toward an experimental ecology of human development. *American Psychologist, 32,* 513–531.

Brofenbrenner, U. (1979). *The ecology of human development.* Cambridge, MA: Harvard University Press.

Brofenbrenner, U. (1989). Ecological systems theory. *Annals of Child Development, 6,* 187–249.

Broome, B. J., & Hatay, A. J. (2006). Building peace in divided societies: The role of intergroup dialogue. In J. G. Oetzel & S. Ting-Toomey (Eds.), *The Sage handbook of conflict communication* (pp. 627–662). Thousand Oaks, CA: Sage.

Brummett, B. S. (2006). *Rhetoric in popular culture* (2nd ed.). Thousand Oaks, CA: Sage.

Buijzen, M., Bomhof, E., & Schurrman, J. (2008). A test of three alternative hypotheses explaining the link between children's television viewing and weigh status. *Journal of Children & Media, 2,* 67–74.

Buijzen, M., van der Molen, J. H. W., & Sondij, P. (2007). Parental mediation of children's emotional responses to a violent news event. *Communication Research, 34,* 212–230.

Burgoon, J. K., Berger, C. R., & Waldron, V. R. (2000). Mindfulness and interpersonal communication. *Journal of Social Issues, 56,* 105–127.

Buzinde, C. N., Santos, C. A., & Smith, S. L. J. (2006). Ethnic representations: Destination imagery. *Annals of Tourism Research, 33,* 707–728.

Callahan, E. (2005). Cultural similarities and differences in the design of university web sites. *Journal of Computer-Mediated Communication, 11,* 239–273.

Campbell, R., Martin, C. R., & Fabos, B. (2007). *Media and culture: An introduction to mass communication* (6th ed.). Boston: Bedford St. Martins.

Canary, D. J. (2003). Managing interpersonal conflict: A model of events related to strategic choices. In J. O. Greene, & B. R. Burleson (Eds.), *Handbook of communication and social interaction skills* (pp. 515–549). Mahwah, NJ: Lawrence Erlbaum Associates.

Cappuccio, S. N. (2006). Mothers of soldiers and the Iraq war: Justification through breakfast shows on ABC, CBS, and NBC. *Women & Language, 29,* 3–9.

Carbaugh, D. (1999). "Just listen": "Listening" and landscape among the Blackfeet. *Western Journal of Communication, 63,* 250–270.

Carl, C., & Kashawagi, A. (2006). This is the new Japan: Immigrants are transforming a once insular society and more of them are on their way. *Newsweek: International Edition,* September 11. Retrieved July 12, 2008, from http://newsweek.com/icl/45527

Carragee, K. M. (1993). A critical evaluation of debates examining the media hegemony thesis. *Western Journal of Communication, 57,* 330–348.

Caruso, E., Epley, N., & Bazerman, M. H. (2006). The costs and benefits of undoing egocentric responsibility assessments in groups. *Journal of Personality and Social Psychology, 91,* 857–871.

Casmir, F. L. (1993). Third-culture building: A paradigm shift for international and intercultural communication. In S. A. Deetz (Ed.), *Communication yearbook 16* (pp. 407–428). Newbury Park, CA: Sage.

Castillo, L. G., Conoley, C. W., & Brossart, D. F. (2004). Acculturation, White marginalization and family support as predictors of perceived distress in Mexican American female college students. *Journal of Counseling Psychology, 51,* 151–157.

Castillo, L. G., Conoley, C. W., Brossart, D. F., & Quiros, D. F. (2007). Construction and validation of the Intragroup Marginalization Inventory. *Cultural Diversity and Ethnic Minority Psychology, 13,* 232–240.

Catalyst (2004). *Quick takes: Lesbians, gays, bisexuals & transgendered workplace issues.* New York: Catalyst. Retrieved October 2, 2007, http://www.catalyst.org/award/files/ 2005/kit/ QT%20Lesbian%20Gay%20Bisexual% 20Transgendered%206-28-04.pdf

Centers for Disease Control (CDC) (2007). United States Cancer Statistics: 2003 Incidence and Mortality. Centers for Disease Control and National Cancer Institute. Retrieved April 5, 2007, from http://www.cdc.gov/CANCER/ healthdisparities/statistics/

Central Intelligence Agency (CIA) (2007). *The World Factbook 2007.* Central Intelligence Agency. Retrieved April 5, 2007, from https://www.cia.gov/cia/publications/factbook/index.html

Chase, M., Macfadyen, L., Reeder, K., & Roche, J. (2002, August). Intercultural challenges in networked learning: Hard technologies meet soft skills. *First Monday, 7,*(8). Retrieved November 15, 2007, from http://firstmonday.org/issues/issue7_8/chase/index.html

Chen, G. (1995). Differences in self-disclosure patterns among Americans versus Chinese. *Journal of Cross-Cultural Psychology, 26,* 84–91.

Chen, G. M., & Starosta, W. J. (2000). The development and validation of the intercultural communication sensitivity scale. *Human Communication, 3,* 1–15.

Chen, L. (2002). Communication in intercultural relationships. In W. B. Gudykunst & B. Mody (Eds.), *Handbook of international and intercultural communication* (2nd ed., pp. 241–257). Thousand Oaks, CA: Sage.

Chester, B., Robin, R. N., Koll, M. P., Lopez, J., & Goldman, D. (1994). Grandmother dishonored: violence against women by male partners in American Aboriginal communities. *Violence and Victims, 9,* 249–258.

Chin, H. K. (2003). *Open doors: report on international educational exchange.* New York: Institute of International Education.

Chiu, R. K., & Kosinski, F. A. (1994). Is Chinese Conflict-handling behavior influenced by Chinese values? *Social Behavior and Personality, 22,* 81–90.

Church, A. T. (1982). Sojourner adjustment. *Psychological Bulletin, 91,* 540–572.

Civikly, J. M. (1992). *Classroom communication: Principles and practice.* Dubuque, IA: Wm. C. Brown.

Clair, R. P. (1998). *Organizing silence: A world of possibilities.* Albany, NY: State University of New York Press.

Clare, E. (2001). Stolen bodies, reclaimed bodies: Disability and queerness. *Public Culture, 13,* 359–365.

Coleman, J. A. (1957). *Community conflict.* New York: Free Press.

Collier, M. J. (1991). Conflict competence within African, Mexican, and Anglo American friendships. In S. Ting-Toomey & F. Korzenny (Eds.). *Cross-cultural interpersonal communication* (pp. 132–154). Newbury Park, CA: Sage.

Collier, M. J. (1998). Intercultural friendships as interpersonal alliances. In J. N. Martin, T. K. Nakayama, & L. A. Flores (Eds.), *Readings in cultural contexts* (pp. 370–378). Mountain View, CA: Mayfield.

Collier, M. J. (2005). Theorizing cultural identifications: Critical updates and continuing evolution. In W. B. Gudykunst (Ed.), *Theorizing about intercultural communication* (pp. 235–256). Thousand Oaks, CA: Sage.

Collier, M. J., & Thomas, M. (1988). Cultural identity: An interpretive perspective. In Y. Y. Kim & W. B. Gudykunst (Eds.), *Theories in intercultural communication* (pp. 99–120). Newbury Park, CA: Sage.

Colville-Hall, S. (n.d.). *Responsible classroom management.* Retrieved June 14, 2007, from http://www3.uakron.edu/education/safeschools/CLASS/class.html

Conquergood, D. (1988). Health theatre in a Hmong refugee camp: Performance, communication, and culture. *The Drama Review, 32,* 174–208.

Cooper, C. R., Chavira, G., & Mena, D. D. (2005). From pipelines to partnerships: A synthesis of research on how diverse families, schools, and communities support children's pathways through school. *Journal of Education for Students Place at Risk, 10,* 407–432.

Coopman, S. J. (2003). Communicating disability: Metaphors of oppression, metaphors of empowerment. *Communication Yearbook, 27,* 337–394.

Coulter, A., & Fitzpatrick, R. (2000). The patient's perspective regarding appropriate health care. In G. L. Albrecht, R. Fitzpatrick, & S. C. Scrimshaw (Eds.). *The handbook of social studies in health and medicine* (pp. 454–464). Thousand Oaks, CA: Sage.

Covarrubias, P. (2007). (Un)Biased in Western theory: Generative silence in American Indian communication. *Communication Monographs, 74,* 265–271.

Cox, T. (2001). *Creating the multicultural organization: A strategy for capturing the power of diversity.* San Francisco: Jossey Bass.

Cox, T. H. (1991). The multicultural organization. *The Executive, 5,* 34–47.

Cox, T. H. (1993). *Cultural diversity in organizations: Theory, research, and practice.* San Francisco: Berrett-Koehler.

Cox, T. H., & Blake, S. (1991). Managing cultural diversity: Implication for organizational competitiveness. *Academy of Management Executive, 5,* 45–56.

Cox, T. H., & Finley, J. (1995). An analysis of work specialization and organizational level as dimensions of workforce diversity. In M. Clemers, S. Oskamp, & M. Costanzo (Eds.), *Diversity in organizations* (pp. 62–90). Newbury Park, CA: Sage.

Crary, D. (2007, February 25). Gay-rights bills likely to pass in '07. *Albuquerque Journal,* A7.

Croucher, S. M. (2005). Cultural adaptation and the situation of French immigrants: A case study analysis of French immigration and cultural adaptation. *International Journal of Communication, 15,* 147–164.

Cuillier, D., & Ross, S. D. (2007). Gambling with identity: Self-representation of American Indians on official tribal websites. *Howard Journal of Communications, 18,* 197–219.

Cupach, W. R., & Canary, D. J. (1997). *Competence in interpersonal conflict.* Prospect Heights, IL: Waveland Press.

Curran, J. (2002). *Media and power.* London: Routledge.

D'Silva, M. U., & Whyte, L. O. (1998). Cultural differences in conflict styles: Vietnamese refugees and established residents. *Howard Journal of Communication, 9,* 57–68.

Darling-Wolf, F. (2004). Virtually multicultural: Trans-Asian identity and gender in an international fan community of a Japanese star. *New Media & Society, 6,* 507–528.

Darnton, R. (2003). *George Washington's false teeth: An unconventional guide to the eighteenth century.* New York: W.W. Norton.

de Tarczynski, S. (2007, June 13). Too little too late for the lost generation aborigines. *Global Policy Forum.* Retrieved August 6, 2007, from http://www.globalpolicy.org/nations/sovereign/sover/emerg/2007/0613aborigines.htm

Dearing, J. W., & Rogers, E. M. (1996). *Agenda setting.* Newbury Park, CA: Sage.

Deetz, S. (2001). Conceptual foundations. In F. M. Jablin & L. Putnam (Eds.) *The new handbook of organizational communication: Advances in theory, research, and methods* (pp. 3–46). Thousand Oaks, CA; Sage.

DeFilippis, J. (2001). The myth of social capital in community development. *Housing Policy Debate, 12,* 781–806.

Deng, F. M. (1993). Northern and southern Sudan: The Nile. In G. Faure & J. Rubin (Eds.), *Culture and negotiation* (pp. 62–96). Newbury Park, CA: Sage.

Department of Homeland Security (2006). *2005 Yearbook on Immigration Statistics.* Retrieved January 18, 2007, from http://www.dhs.gov/xlibrary/assets/statistics/yearbook/2005/OIS_2005_Yearbook.pdf

DeSanctis, G., & Monge, P. (1999). Introduction to the special Issue: Communication processes for virtual organizations. *Organization Science, 10,* 693–703.

Diggs, R. D., & Clark, K. D. (2002). It's a struggle, but worth it: Identifying and managing identities in an interracial friendship. *Communication Quarterly, 50,* 368–390.

Diversity/Careers in Engineering & Information Technology (2005, April/May). *Coca-Cola North America meets and exceeds its diversity goals.* Author. Retrieved October 4, 2007, from http://www.diversitycareers.com/articles/pro/05-aprmay/sd_coke.htm

Dixon, T. L. (2006). Psychological reactions to crime news portrayals of Black criminals: Understanding the moderating roles of prior news viewing and stereotype endorsement. *Communication Monographs, 73,* 162–187.

Dixon, T. L., & Azocar, C. L. (2007). Priming crime and activating Blackness: Understanding the psychological impact of the overrepresentation of Blacks as lawbreakers on television news. *Journal of Communication, 57,* 229–253.

Dixon, T. L., & Linz, D. (2000). Overrepresentation and underrepresentation of African Americans and Latinos as lawbreakers on television news. *Journal of Communication, 50,* 131–154.

du Pré, A. (2000). *Communicating about health: Current issues and perspectives.* Mountain View, CA: Mayfield.

Dunsky, M. (2007) Reporting the Arab and Muslim worlds: It is hard to see "ourselves—our actions and their consequences—in the picture." *Nieman Reports, Summer,* 41–43.

Duran, B., Duran, E., & Brave Heart, M. Y. (1998). American Indian and/or Alaska Natives and the trauma of history. In R. Thornton (Ed.) *Studying Native America: Problems and prospects* (pp. 60–76). Madison, WI: University of Wisconsin Press.

Duran, E., & Duran, B. (1995). *Native American postcolonial psychology.* New York: State University of New York.

Duran, E., Duran, B., Woodis, W., & Woodis, P. (1998). A postcolonial perspective on domestic violence in Indian Country. In R. Carrillo & J. Tello (Eds.) *Family Violence and Men of Color* (pp. 95–113). New York: Springer.

Duronto, P. M., Nishida, T., & Nakayama, S. (2005). Uncertainty, anxiety, and avoidance in communication with strangers. *International Journal of Intercultural Relations, 29,* 549–560.

Durose, M. R., Smith, E. L., & Langan, P. A. (2007). *Contact between police and the public, 2005* (NCJ215243). Washington, DC: Bureau of Justice Statistics.

Eagle, L. (2007). Commercial media literacy: What does it do, to whom—and does it matter? *Journal of Advertising, 36,* 101–110.

Earley, P. C. (1997). *Face, harmony, and social structure: An analysis of organizational behavior across cultures.* New York: Oxford University Press.

Earley, P. C., & Erez, M. (1997). *The transplanted executive.* New York: Oxford University Press.

Eichler, M. (1998). Organizing's past, present, and future: Look to the future, learn from the past. National Housing Institute. Retrieved March 17, 2008, from http://www.nhi.org/online/issues/101/eichler.html

Eichler, M. (2007). *Consensus organizing: Building communities of mutual self-interest.* Thousand Oaks, CA: Sage.

Eisenberg, E. M., & Riley, P. (2001). Organizational culture. In F. M. Jablin & L. L. Putnam (Eds.) *The new handbook of organizational communication: Advances in theory, research, and methods* (pp. 291–322). Thousand Oaks, CA: Sage.

Ely, R. J., & Thomas, D. A. (2001). Cultural diversity at work: The effects of diversity perspectives on work group processes and outcomes. *Administrative Science Quarterly, 46,* 229–273.

Enns, C. Z. (1993). Integrating separate and connected knowing: The experiential learning model. *Teaching of Psychology, 20,* 7–13.

Espinoza, J. A., & Garza, R. T. (1985). Social group salience and intergroup cooperation. *Journal of Experimental Social Psychology, 21,* 380–392.

Esses, V. M., & Hodson, G. (2006). The role of lay perceptions of ethnic prejudice in the maintenance and perpetuation of ethnic bias. *Journal of Social Issues, 62,* 453–468.

Engen, D. (2004). Invisible identities: Notes on class and race. In A. Gonzalez, M. Houston, & V. Chen (Eds.), *Our voices: Essays in culture, ethnicity, and communication* (4th ed., pp. 250–255). Los Angeles: Roxbury.

Faure, G. O., & Rubin, J. Z. (1993). (Eds.), *Culture and negotiation.* Newbury Park, CA: Sage

Federal Statistics Office—Germany. (2005). *Population by sex and citizenship.* Germany.

Fisher, W. R. (1984). Narration as a human communication paradigm: The case of public moral argument. *Communication Monographs, 51,* 1–22.

Fiske, J. (1989). *Understanding popular culture.* New York: Routledge.

Flaccus, G. (2006, March 30). DJs spurred Los Angeles rally. *Albuquerque Journal.* A1.

Foster-Fishman, P. G., Berkowitz, S. L., Lounsbury, D. W., Jacobson, S., & Allen, N. A. (2001). Building collaborative capacity in community coalitions: A review and integrative framework. *American Journal of Community Psychology, 29,* 241–261.

Freedom House (2006). *Map of Press Freedom 2006.* Washington, DC: Freedom House. Retrieved July 5, 2007, from http://www.freedomhouse.org/template.cfm?page=251&year=2006

Freeman, E. M. (2001). *Substance abuse intervention, prevention, rehabilitation, and systems change strategies: Helping individuals, families, and groups to empower themselves.* New York: Columbia University Press.

Freimuth, V. S., & Quinn, S. C. (2004). The contributions of health communication to eliminating health disparities. *American Journal of Public Health, 94,* 2053–2055.

Friedman, J. (2006). Culture and global systems. *Theory, Culture, & Society, 23,* 404–406.

Frost, F., Tollestrup, K., Hunt, W. C., Gilliland, F., Key, C. R., & Urbina, C. E. (1996). Breast cancer survival among New Mexico Hispanic, American Indian, and non-Hispanic white women (1973–1992). *Cancer Epidemiology, Biomarkers, and Prevention, 5,* 861–866.

Fryer, R. G., & Torelli, P. (2006). An empirical analysis of "acting white." *NBER working paper No. 11334.* Retrieved June 19, 2007, from http://www.economics.harvard.edu/faculty/fryer/papers/fryer_torelli.pdf

Fu, W. W. (2006). Concentration and homogenization of international movies sources. *Journal of Communication, 56,* 813–835.

Fukuoka, Y., & Kim, M. S. (1997). *Zainichi kankokujin seinen no seikatsu to ishiki* [The lives and consciousness of young Koreans in Japan]. Tokyo: Tokyo Daigaku Shuppan.

Furnham, A., & Bochner S. (1986). *Culture shock: Psychological reactions to unfamiliar environments.* New York: Methuen.

Gaertner, S. L., Dovidio, J. F., & Bachman, B. A. (1996). Revisiting the contact hypothesis: The induction of a common ingroup identity. *International Journal of Intercultural Relations, 20,* 271–290.

Gagnon, A., & Bourhis, R. (1996). Discrimination in the minimal group paradigm: Social identity or self interest? *Personality and Social Psychology Bulletin, 22,* 1289–1301.

Gaitin, C. D. (2006). *Building culturally responsive classrooms: A guide for K–6 teachers.* Thousand Oaks, CA: Corwin Press.

Gallois, C., Ogay, T., & Giles, H. (2005). Communication accommodation theory. In W. B. Gudykunst (Ed.), *Theorizing about intercultural communication* (pp. 121–148). Thousand Oaks, CA: Sage.

Gao, G., & Ting-Toomey, S. (1998). *Communicating effectively with the Chinese.* Thousand Oaks, CA: Sage.

Garza, R. T., & Santos, S. J. (1991). Ingroup/outgroup balance and interdependent interethnic behavior. *Journal of Experimental Social Psychology, 27,* 124–137.

Gerbner, G., & Gross, L. (1976). Living with television: The violence profile. *Journal of Communication, 26,* 173–199.

Gerbner, G., Gross, L., Morgan, M., Signorielli, N., & Shanahan, J. (2002). Growing up with television: Cultivation processes. In J. Bryant & D. Zillman (Eds.), *Media effects: Advances in theory and research* (pp. 43–68). Mahwah, NJ: Lawrence Erlbaum.

Gilboa, E. (2006). Media and international conflict. In J. G. Oetzel & S. Ting-Toomey (Eds.), *The Sage handbook of conflict communication: Integrating theory, research, and practice* (pp. 595–626). Thousand Oaks, CA: Sage.

Giles, H., & Johnson, P. (1981). The role of language in ethnic group relations. In J. Turner & H. Giles (Eds.), *Intergroup behavior* (pp. 199–243). Oxford, UK: Basil Blackwell.

Gilliland, F. D., Rosenburg, R. D., Hunt, W. C., Stauber, P., & Key, C. R. (2000). Patterns of mammography use among Hispanic, American Indian, and non-Hispanic White women in New Mexico, 1994–1997. *American Journal of Epidemiology, 152,* 432–437.

Givens, J. L., & Tjia, J. (2002). Depressed medical students' use of mental health services and barriers to use. *Academic Medicine, 77,* 918–921.

Goldsmith, D. J., & Fulfs, P. A. (1999). You just don't have the evidence: An analysis of claims and evidence in Deborah Tannen's *You Just Don't Understand. Communication Yearbook, 22,* 1–49.

Goleman, D., Kaufman, P., & Ray, M. (1992). *The creative spirit.* New York: Dutton.

Goltz, D. B. (2007). Laughing at absence: *Instinct* magazine and the hyper-masculine gay future? *Western Journal of Communication, 71,* 93–113.

Gonzales, J. (1996, January 20). College brings alienation from family, friends. *Los Angeles Times,* B7.

Gonzalez, J. (2001, August 25). Rancher convicted in immigrant's death. *Houston Chronicle* (Reuters). Retrieved October 16, 2007, from http://www.commondreams.org/headlines01/0825–01.htm

Goodman R, Speers, M. A., McLeroy, K., Fawcett, S., Kegler, M., Parker, E., Smith, S. R., Sterling, T. D., & Wallerstein, N. (1998). Identifying and defining the dimensions of community capacity to provide a basis for measurement. *Health Education and Behavior, 25,* 258–278.

Gorham, B. W. (2006). New media's relationship with stereotyping: The linguistic intergroup bias in response to crime news. *Journal of Communication, 56,* 289–308.

Gottman, J. (1999). *The marriage clinic: A scientifically-based marital therapy.* New York: W.W. Norton & Company.

Graff, J. (November 6, 2005). Streets of fire. *Time Online.* Retrieved May 10, 2007, from http://www.time.com/time/magazine/article/0,9171,901051114–1126690,00.html

Gramsci, A. (1971). *Selections from the prison notebooks* [Translated by Q. Hoare &G. N. Smith]. New York: International.

Gudykunst, W. B. (1988). Uncertainty and anxiety. In Y. Y. Kim & W. B. Gudykunst (Eds.), *Theories in intercultural communication* (pp. 123–156). Newbury Park, CA: Sage.

Gudykunst, W. B. (2005). An anxiety/uncertainty management (AUM) theory of stranger's intercultural adjustment. In W. B. Gudykunst (Ed.), *Theorizing about intercultural communication* (pp. 419–457). Thousand Oaks, CA: Sage.

Gudykunst, W. B., & Lee, C. M. (2002). Cross-cultural communication theories. In W. B. Gudykunst & B. Mody (Eds.), *Handbook of international and intercultural communication* (2nd ed., pp. 25–50). Thousand Oaks, CA: Sage.

Gudykunst, W. B., & Nishida, T. (1986). The influence of cultural variability on perceptions of communication behavior associated with relationship terms. *Human Communication Research, 13,* 147–166.

Gudykunst, W. B., Matsumoto, Y., Ting-Toomey, S., Nishida, T., Kim, K. S., & Heyman, S. (1996). The influence of cultural individualism-collectivism, self construals, and individual values on communication styles across cultures. *Human Communication Research, 22,* 510–543.

Gudykunst, W. B., Ting-Toomey, S., Sudweeks, S., & Stewart, L. (1995). *Building bridges: Interpersonal skills for a changing world.* Houghton Mifflin: New York.

Gullahorn, J. T., & Gullahorn, J. E. (1963). An extension of the U-curve hypothesis. *Journal of Social Issues, 19,* 33–47.

Gutierrez, E. C. Z., & Kendall, C. (2000). The globalization of health and disease: The health transition and global change. In G. L. Albrecht, R. Fitzpatrick, & S. C. Scrimshaw (Eds.). *The handbook of social studies in health and medicine* (pp. 84–99). Thousand Oaks, CA: Sage.

Habermas, J. (1987). *The theory of communicative action: Lifeworld and system* (Vol. 2; T. McCarthy, Trans.). Boston: Beacon Press.

Hale, F. W. (Ed.). (2004) *What makes racial diversity work in higher education: Academic leaders present successful policies and strategies.* Sterling, VA: Stylus.

Hall, B. J. (1998). Narratives of prejudice. *Howard Journal of Communications, 9,* 137–156.

Hall, E. T. (1959). *The silent language.* Garden City, N.Y: Doubleday.

Hall, E. T. (1976). *Beyond culture.* New York: Doubleday.

Hall, S. (1981). Cultural studies and the centre: Some problematics and problems. In S. Hall, D. Hobson, A. Lowe, & P. Willis (Eds.), *Culture, media, language* (pp. 15–47). London: Hutchinson.

Hall, S. (1985). Signification, representation, ideology: Althusser and the post-structuralist debates. *Critical Studies in Mass Communication, 2,* 91–114.

Hall, S., Hobson, D., Lowe, A. & Willis, P. (1981). (Eds.), *Culture, media, language.* London: Hutchinson.

Hamby, S. L. (2000). The importance of community in a feminist analysis of domestic violence among American Indians. *American Journal of Community Psychology, 28,* 649–669.

Hardiman, R. (1994). White racial identity development in the United State. In E. P. Salett & Dr. R. Koslow (Eds.), *Race, ethnicity and self: Identity in the multicultural perspective* (pp. 117–142). Washington, DC: National Multicultural Institute.

Hardin, M., & Whiteside, E. (2006). Fewer women, minorities work in sports departments. *Newspaper Research Journal, 27,* 38–51.

Hatch, J. B. (2006). Beyond apologia: Racial reconciliation and apologies for slavery. *Western Journal of Communication, 70,* 186–211.

Hawley, A. H. (1950). *Human ecology: A theory of community structure.* New York: Ronald Press.

Hays, T. (2007, November 25). Woman is accused of smuggling monkey meat. *Albuquerque Journal,* A7.

Heaney, C. A., & Israel, B. A. (2002). Social networks and social support. In K. Glanz, B. K. Rimer, & F. M. Lewis (Eds.). *Health behavior and health education: Theory, research, and practice* (3rd ed., pp. 185–209). San Francisco: John Wiley.

Hecht, M. L. (1998). Introduction. In M. L. Hecht (Ed.), *Communicating prejudice* (pp. 3–23). Thousand Oaks, CA: Sage.

Hecht, M. L., Collier, M. J., & Ribeau, S. A. (1993). *African American communication: Ethnic identity and cultural interpretation.* Newbury Park, CA: Sage.

Hecht, M. L., Warren, J. R., Jung, E., & Krieger, J. L. (2005). A communication theory of identity: Development, theoretical perspective, and future directions. In W. B. Gudykunst (Ed.), *Theorizing about intercultural communication* (pp. 235–256). Thousand Oaks, CA: Sage.

Helms, J. (1993). Introduction: Review of racial identity terminology. In J. Helms (Ed.), *Black and white racial identity: Theory, research, and practice.* Westport, CT: Praeger.

Hennessey, R. (1993). *Materialist feminism and the politics of discourse.* New York and London: Routledge.

Hermeking, M. (2006). Culture and internet consumption: Contributions from cross-cultural marketing and advertising research. *Journal of Computer-Mediation Communication, 11,* 192–216.

Hirokawa, R. Y., & Rost, K. M. (1992). Effective group decision-making in organizations: Field test of the vigilant interaction theory. *Management Communication Quarterly, 5,* 267–288.

Hofstede, G. (1991). *Culture and organizations: Software of the mind.* London: McGraw-Hill.

Hofstede, G. (2001). *Culture's consequences: Comparing values, behaviors, institutions, and organizations across nations* (2nd ed.). Thousand Oaks, CA: Sage.

Holmes, P. (2005). Ethnic Chinese students' communication with cultural others in a New Zealand university. *Communication Education, 54,* 289–311.

Homans, G. C. (1950). *The human group.* New York: Harcourt Brace.

Hosseini, K. (2003). *The kite runner.* New York: Simon & Schuster.

Houston, M., & Wood, J. T. (1995). Difficult dialogues, expanded horizons: Communicating across race and class. In J. T. Wood (Ed.), *Gendered relationships* (pp. 39–56). Mountain View, CA: Mayfield.

Huguet, P., & Regner, I. (2007). Stereotype threat among schoolgirls in quasi-ordinary classroom circumstances. *Journal of Educational Psychology, 99,* 545–560.

Humphreys, J. M. (2005). *The multicultural economy 2005: America's minority buying power.* Selig Center for Economic Growth, University of Georgia. Available: http://www. selig.uga.edu/forecast/GBEC/GBEC053Q.pdf

Hunter, A. (1974). *Symbolic communities: The persistence and change of Chicago's local communities.* Chicago: University of Chicago Press.

Hunter, J. D. (1993). Before the shooting begins. *Columbia Journalism Review, 32,* 29–32.

Huntington, S. P. (1996). *The clash of civilizations: Remaking of world order*. New York: Simon & Schuster.

Imahori, T. T., & Cupach, W. R. (2005). Identity management theory: Facework in intercultural relationships. In W. B. Gudykunst (Ed.), *Theorizing about intercultural communication* (pp. 195–210). Thousand Oaks, CA: Sage.

In the White Man's Image (1991). Anthology series, *The American Experience*. PBS Video.

Inkelas, K. K. (2004). Does participation in ethnic cocurricular activities facilitate a sense of ethnic awareness and understanding? A study of Asian Pacific American undergraduates. *Journal of College Student Development, 45*, 285–302.

Institute of International Education (2007). *Atlas of student mobility*. Institute of International Education. Retrieved June 21, 2007, from http://www.atlas.iienetwork.org/?p=46572

Institute of Medicine (1988). *Future of public health*. Washington, DC: National Academy Press.

Institute of Medicine (2002). *Speaking of health: Assessing health communication strategies for diverse populations*. Washington, DC: National Academics Press.

Jacobson, C. K., & Johnson, B. R. (2006). Interracial friendship and African American attitudes about interracial marriage. *Journal of Black Studies, 36*, 570–584.

Janz, N. K., Champion, V. L., & Strecher, V. J. (2002). The health belief model. In K. Glanz, B. K. Rimer, & F. M. Lewis (Eds.), *Health behavior and health education: Theory, research, and practice* (3rd ed., 45–66). San Francisco: Jossey-Bass.

Jing, Y. (2005). Constructing the other: A critical reading of *The Joy Luck Club*. *Howard Journal of Communications, 16*, 149–175.

Jones, C. P. (2000). Levels of racism: A theoretic framework and a gardener's tale. *American Journal of Public Health, 90*, 1212–1215.

Jones, T. S. (2006). Conflict resolution education: Issues, answers and directions. In J. G. Oetzel & S. Ting-Toomey (Eds.), *The Sage handbook of conflict communication: Theory, research, and practice* (pp. 239–265). Thousand Oaks, CA: Sage.

Jost, J. T., & Hamilton, D. L. (2005). Stereotypes in our culture. In J. F. Dovidio, P. Glick, & L. A. Rudman (Eds.), *On the nature of prejudice: Fifty years after Allport* (pp. 208–224). Malden, MA: Blackwell Publishing.

Joyner, K., & Kao, G. (2005). Interracial relationships and the transition to adulthood. *American Sociological Review, 70*, 563–582.

Judd, C. M., Park, B., Yzerbyt, V., Gordijn, E. H. & Muller, D. (2005). Attributions of intergroup bias and outgroup homogeneity to ingroup and outgroup others. *European Journal of Social Psychology, 35*, 677–704.

Kahn, J. (2007). The story of a snitch. *The Atlantic, 299 (3)*, 80–92.

Kamalipour, Y. R., & Carilli, T. (Eds.) (1998). *Cultural diversity and the U.S. media*. Albany, NY: State University of New York Press.

Kanouse, D., & Hanson, L. (1972). Negativity in evaluations. In E. Jones, D. Kanouse, H. Kelley, R. Nisbett, S. Valms, & B. Weiner (Eds.), *Attribution*. Morristown, NJ: General Learning Press.

Kar, S. B., & Alcalay, R. with Alex, S. (2001). Changing health needs: The imperative for a multicultural paradigm. In S. B. Kar & R. Alcalay (Eds.), *Health communication: A multicultural perspective* (pp. 3–19). Thousand Oaks, CA: Sage.

Kashima, Y., & Triandis, H. C. (1986). The self-serving bias in attributions as a coping strategy. *Journal of Cross-Cultural Psychology, 17*, 83–97.

Kasper, J. D. (2000). Health-care utilization and barriers to health care. In G. L. Albrecht, R. Fitzpatrick, & S. C. Scrimshaw (Eds.). *The handbook of social studies in health and medicine* (pp. 321–338). Thousand Oaks, CA: Sage.

Katz, E., Blumer, J., & Gurevitch, M. (1974). Uses of mass communication by the individual. In W. P. Davidson & F. Yu (Eds.), *Mass communication research: Major issues and future directions* (pp. 11–35). New York: Praeger.

Kawachi, I., Kennedy, B. P., Lochner, K., & Prothrow-Stith, D. (1997). Social capital, income inequality, and mortality. *American Journal of Public Health, 87*, 1491–1498.

Kawai, Y. (2007). Japanese nationalism and the global spread of English: An analysis of Japanese governmental and public discourses on English. *Language & Intercultural Communication, 7*, 37–55.

Kaye, H. J. (1996). *Why do ruling classes fear history?* New York: St. Martin's Press.

Kealey, D. L. (1989). A study of cross-cultural effectiveness: Theoretical issues, practical application. *International Journal of Intercultural Relations, 13*, 387–428.

Keesing, R. (1974). Theories of culture. *Annual Review of Anthropology, 3*, 73–97.

Kelley, H. (1967). Attribution theory in social psychology. *Nebraska Symposium on Motivation, 15*, 192–238.

Kelly, M. E., & Nagel, J. (2002). Ethnic re-identification: Lithuanian Americans and Native Americans. *Journal of Ethnic and Migration Studies, 28*, 275–289.

Kerr, P. A. (2003). The framing of Fundamentalist Christians: Network television news, 1980–2000. *Journal of Media and Religion, 2*, 203–235.

Kessler, R. C., Chiu, W. T., Demler, O., & Walters, E. E. (2005). Prevalence, severity, and comorbidity of twelve-month DSM-IV disorders in the National Comorbidity Survey Replication (NCS-R). *Archives of General Psychiatry, 62,* 617–627.

Khan, M. A. (2005). Interpersonal communication and acculturation: A path analysis. *Journal of Development Communication, 16,* 10–19.

Kim, M. S. (2002). *Non-western perspectives on human communication.* Thousand Oaks, CA: Sage.

Kim, Y. Y. (2001). *Becoming intercultural: An Integrative theory of communication and cross-cultural adaptation.* Thousand Oaks, CA: Sage

Kim, Y. Y. (2005). Adapting to a new culture: An integrative communication theory. In W. B. Gudykunst (Ed.) *Theorizing about intercultural communication* (pp. 375–400). Thousand Oaks, CA: Sage.

King, A. G. (2001, February). Coca-Cola takes the high road—race-based employment discrimination suit. *Black Enterprise.* Retrieved October 4, 2007, from http:/findarticles.com/p/articles/mi_m1365/is_7_31/ai_69290709

King, S. A. (2006). Memory, mythmaking, and museums: Constructive authenticity and the primitive blues subject. *Southern Communication Journal, 71,* 235–250.

Kirby, E. L., & Harter, L. M. (2001). Discourses of diversity and the quality of work life: The character and costs of the managerial metaphor. *Management Communication Quarterly, 15,* 121–127.

Kitano, H. H. L. (1991). *Race relations* (4th ed.). Englewood Cliffs, NJ: Prentice Hall.

Klein, H., & Shiffman, K. (2006). Race-related content of animated cartoons. *Howard Journal of Communications, 17,* 163–182.

Klein, K. J., Tosi, H., & Cannella, A. A. (1999). Multilevel theory building: Benefits, barriers, and new developments. *Academy of Management Review, 24,* 243–248.

Kleinman, A.M., Eisenberg, L., & Good, B. (1978). Culture, illness, and care: Clinical lessons from anthropological and cross-cultural research. *Annals of Internal Medicine, 88,* 251–258.

Knobloch-Westerwick, S., & Coates, B. (2006). Minority models in advertisements in magazines popular with minorities. *Journalism & Mass Communication Quarterly, 83,* 596–614.

Koehn, P. H. (2006). Globalization, migration health, and educational preparation for transnational medical encounters. *Globalization & Health, 2.* Retrieved March 16, 2008, from http://www.globalizationandhealth.com/content/2/1/2

Koerner, A. F., & Fitzpatrick, M. A. (2006). Family conflict communication. In J. G. Oetzel & S. Ting-Toomey (Eds.), *The Sage handbook of conflict communication* (pp. 159–183). Thousand Oaks, CA: Sage.

Koinage, J. (2006, August 30). Katrina: When New Orleans went from developed world to Third World. *CNN.com.* Retrieved November 15, 2007, from http://www.cnn.com/2006/US/08/30/btsc.koinange/index.html

Kosicki, G. M. (1993). Problems and opportunities in agenda-setting research. *Journal of Communication, 43,* 100–127.

Kraidy, M. (2002). Hybridity in cultural globalization. *Communication Theory, 12,* 316–339.

Kramsch, C. (2002). In search of the intercultural. *Journal of Sociolinguistics, 6,* 275–285.

Krcmar, M., & Hight, A. (2007). The development of aggressive mental models in young children. *Media Psychology, 10,* 250–269.

Krog, A. (2000). *Country of my skull: Guilt, sorrow, and the limits of forgiveness in the new South Africa.* New York: Random House.

Kudo, K., & Simkin, K. A. (2003). Intercultural friendship formation: The case of Japanese students at an Australian university. *Journal of Intercultural Studies, 24,* 91–114.

Kumari Campbell, F. A. (2004). The case of Clint Hallam's wayward hand: Print media representations of the "uncooperative" disabled patient. *Continuum: Journal of Media & Cultural Studies, 18,* 443–458.

Ladegaard, H. J. (2007). Global culture—myth or reality? Perceptions of "national cultures" in a global corporation. *Journal of Intercultural Communication Research, 36,* 139–163.

Land, V., & Kitzinger, C. (2005). Speaking as a lesbian: Correcting the heterosexist presumption. *Research on Language & Social Interaction, 38,* 371–416.

Langer, E. J. (1989). *Mindfulness.* Reading, MA: Addison-Wesley.

Lawson, S., & Jaworski, A. (2007). Shopping and chatting: Reports of tourist-host interaction in The Gambia. *Multilingua, 26,* 67–93.

Lease, A. M., & Blake, J. J. (2005). A comparison of majority-race children with and without a minority-race friend. *Social Development, 14,* 20–41.

Lederer, W. J., & Burdick, E. (1958). *The ugly American.* New York: W. W. Norton & Co.

Lee, S. (2006). Somewhere in the middle: The measurement of third culture. *Journal of Intercultural Communication Research, 35,* 253–264.

Leeds-Hurwitz, W. (1990). Notes in the history of intercultural communication: The Foreign Service Institute and the mandate for intercultural training. *Quarterly Journal of Speech, 76,* 262–281.

Lerner, G. (1997). *Why history matters.* Oxford: Oxford University Press.

Leslie, L. A., & Letiecq, B. L. (2004). Marital quality of African American and white partners in interracial couples. *Personal Relationships, 11,* 559–574.

Lewicki, R. J., & Bunker, B. B. (1995). Trust in relationships: A model of development and decline. In B. Bunker, J. Rubin, & Associates (Eds.), *Conflict, cooperation and justice* (pp. 39–57). San Francisco: Jossey-Bass.

Lieberman, M. A., & Goldstein, B. A. (2005). Self-help on-line: An outcome evaluation of breast cancer bulletin boards. *Journal of Health Psychology, 10,* 855–862.

Lien, Y-W., Chu, R-L., Jen, C-H., & Wu, C-H. (2006). Do Chinese commit neither fundamental attribution error nor ultimate attribution error? *Chinese Journal of Psychology, 48,* 163–181.

Lim, T. S., & Bowers, J. (1991). Face-work: Solidarity, approbation, and tact. *Human Communication Research, 17,* 415–450.

Lim, T-S. (2002). Language and verbal communication across cultures. In W. B. Gudykunst & B. Mody (Eds.), *Handbook of international and intercultural communication* (2nd ed., pp. 69–88). Thousand Oaks, CA: Sage.

Lindenfeld, L. (2007). Visiting the Mexican American family: Tortilla Soup as culinary tourism. *Communication & Critical/Cultural Studies, 4,* 303–320.

Little, L., & Kaufman Kantor, G. (2002). Using ecological theory to understand intimate partner violence and child maltreatment. *Journal of Community Health Nursing, 19,* 133–145.

Littlejohn, S. W. (2006). Moral conflict. In J. G. Oetzel & S. Ting-Toomey (Eds.), *The Sage handbook of conflict communication* (pp. 395–417). Thousand Oaks, CA: Sage.

Lochner K, Kawachi, I., & Kennedy, B. P. (1999). Social capital: A guide to its measurement. *Health & Place, 5,* 259–270.

Loden, M., & Rosener, J. (1991). *Workforce America! Managing employee diversity as a vital resource.* Homewood, IL: Business One-Irwin.

Loewen, J. W. (1999). *Lies across America: What our historic sites get wrong.* New York: The New Press.

Lopez, I. F. H. (1997). *White by law: The legal construction of race.* New York: New York University.

Lowry, J., Ulanov, A., & Wenrich, T. (2003). Advancing to the next level of Latino marketing: Strike first, strike twice. Boston: Boston Consulting Group. Retrieved October 4, 2007, from http://www.bcg.com/publications/files/ Advancing_Latino_Marketing_OfA_Feb03.pdf

Lysgaard, S. (1955). Adjustment in a foreign society: Norwegian Fulbright grantees visiting the Unites States. *International Social Science Bulletin, 7,* 45–51.

Majors, S. (2006). White men control most NCAA leadership positions. *Associated Press Archive.* Retrieved July 15, 2008, from http://sports.espn.go.com/ncaa/news/story?id=2696678

Mann, C. C. (2000). Reviewing ethnolinguistic vitality: The case of Anglo-Nigerian Pidgin. *Journal of Sociolinguistics, 4,* 458–474.

Mann, D. (2007, March 14). A bi-weekly commentary on population and immigration issues *Negative Population Growth Journal.* Retrieved October 25, 2007, from http://www.npg. org/npgjournal_9.html

Manson, S. M. (2000). Mental health services for American Indians and Alaska Natives: need, use, and barriers to effective care. *Canadian Journal of Psychiatry, 45,* 617–626.

Markus, H. R., & Kitayama, S. (1991). Culture and self: Implication for cognition, emotion, and motivation. *Psychological Review, 98,* 224–253.

Martin, J. N., & Nakayama, T. K. (1999). Thinking dialectically about culture and communication. *Communication Theory, 9,* 1–25.

Martin, J. N., Bradford, L. J., Drezewiecka, J. A., & Chitgopekar, A. S. (2003). Intercultural dating patterns among young white U.S. Americans: Have they changed in the past 20 years? *Howard Journal of Communications, 14,* 53–74.

Martin, J. N., Krizek, R. L., Nakayama, T. K., & Bradford, L. (1996). Exploring whiteness: A study of self-labels for white Americans. *Communication Quarterly, 44,* 125–144.

Martin, J. N., Moore, S., Hecht, M. L., & Larkey, L. K. (2001). An African American perspective on conversational improvement strategies. *The Howard Journal of Communications, 12,* 1–27.

Marwaha, S., & Livingston, G. (2002). Stigma, racism or choice: Why do depressed ethnic elders avoid psychiatrists? *Journal of Affective Disorders, 72,* 257–265.

Marwick, A. (1989). *The Nature of History* (3rd ed.). Chicago, IL: Lyceum Books.

Mastro, D. E. (2003). A social identity approach to understanding the impact of television messages. *Communication Monographs, 70,* 98–113.

Mastro, D. E., & Stern, S. R. (2003). Representation of race in television commercials: A content analysis of prime-time advertising. *Journal of Broadcasting & Electronic Media, 47,* 638–647.

Matsunaga, M. (2007). Shaping, masking, and unmasking of a stigmatized identity: The case of Japan-Residing Koreans. *Howard Journal of Communications, 18,* 221–238.

Matsunaga, M., & Torigoe, C. (in press). Looking at the Japan-Residing Korean identities through the eyes of the "outsiders within": Application and extension of co-cultural theory. *Western Journal of Communication.*

McCroskey, J. C., Fayer, J. M., Richmond, V. P., Sallinen, A., & Barraclough, R. A. (1996). A multi-cultural examination of the relationship between nonverbal immediacy and affective learning. *Communication Quarterly, 44,* 297–307.

McCurry, J. (2007, March 5). Japan rules out new apology to "comfort women." *The Guardian.* Retrieved August 2, 2007, from http://www.guardian.co.uk/international/story/0,,2026525,00.html

McEachern, D., Van Winkle, M., & Steiner, S. (1998). Domestic violence among the Navajo: A legacy of colonization. *Journal of Poverty, 2,* 31–46.

McIntosh, P. (2003). White privilege: Unpacking the invisible knapsack. In S. Plous (Ed.) *Understanding prejudice and discrimination* (pp. 191–196). New York: McGraw-Hill.

McKnight, A. N. (2004). Historical trauma, the persistence of memory and the pedagogical problems of forgiveness, justice, and peace. *Educational Studies: Journal of the American Educational Studies Association, 36,* 140–158.

McLeod, P. L., Lobel, S. A., & Cox, T. H. (1996). Ethnic diversity and creativity in small groups. *Small Group Research, 27,* 248–264.

McLeroy, K. R., Bibeau, D., Steckler, A., & Glanz, K. (1988). An ecological perspective on health promotion programs. *Health Education Quarterly, 15,* 351–377.

McMillan, D., & Chavis, D. (1986). Sense of community: A definition and theory. *Journal of Community Psychology, 14,* 6–23.

Meares, M. M., Oetzel, J. G., Torres, A. B., Ginossar, T., & Derkacs, D. (2004). Employee mistreatment and muted voices in the culturally diverse workplace. *Journal of Applied Communication Research, 32,* 4–27.

Media Report to Women (2004). Study: TV minority, women correspondents improve in visibility, but Blacks again not in top ranks. *Media Report to Women, 32(2),* 4.

Media Report to Women (2006). New study finds vast gender imbalance in top-grossing G-rated movies. *Media Report to Women, 34(1),* 1–2.

Mehrabian, A. (1969). Attitudes inferred from non-immediacy of verbal communications. *Journal of Verbal Learning & Verbal Behavior, 6,* 294–295.

Merskin, D. (2007). Three faces of Eva: Perpetuation of the Hot-Latina stereotype in *Desperate Housewives. Howard Journal of Communications, 18,* 133–151.

Miller, K. (2006). *Organizational communication: Approaches and processes* (4th ed.). Belmont, CA: Wadsworth Publishing.

Miller, W., & Rollnick, S. (2002). (Eds.), *Motivational interviewing: Preparing people for change* (2nd ed.). New York: Guilford Press.

Minkler, M. (2004). Ethical challenges for the "Outside" researcher in community-based participatory research. *Health Education and Behavior, 31,* 684–697.

Minkler, M., & Wallerstein, N. (2003). Introduction to community based participatory research. In M. Minkler & N. Wallerstein (Eds.), *Community-based participatory research for health* (pp. 3–26). San Francisco: Jossey-Bass.

Moon, D. G. (1996). Concepts of culture: Implications for intercultural communication research. *Communication Quarterly, 44,* 70–84.

Morris, R., & Stuckey, M. E. (1998). Destroying the past to save the present: Pastoral voice and Native identity. In Y. Kamalipour (Ed.) *Cultural diversity and the U.S. media* (pp. 137–147). Albany, NY: SUNY Press.

Morse, J. M., & Proctor, A. (1998). Maintaining patient endurance: The comfort work of trauma nurses. *Clinical Nursing Research, 7,* 250–274.

Mortenson, S. T. (2006). Cultural differences and similarities in seeking social support in response to an academic failure: A comparison of American and Chinese college students. *Communication Education, 55,* 127–146.

Moser, I. (2006). Disability and the promises of technology: Technology, subjectivity, and embodiment within an order of the normal. *Information, Communication & Society, 9,* 373–395.

Moussavi, C. (2006, June 11). The Iran I know. *Parade.* 20

Mulvaney, B. (1994). Gender differences in communication: An intercultural experience. *Computer Professionals for Social Responsibility.* Retrieved November 15, 2007, from http://www.cpsr.org/prevsite/cpsr/gender/mulvaney.txt/

Murguía, A., Zea, M. C., Reisen, C. A., & Peterson, R. A. (2000). The development of the Cultural Health Attributions Questionnaire (CHAQ). *Cultural Diversity and Ethnic Minority Psychology, 6,* 268–283.

Myers, S. A., Zhong, M., & Guan, S. (1998). Instructor immediacy in the Chinese college classroom. *Communication Studies, 49,* 240–254.

Nagata, D. K., & Tsuru, G. K. (2007). Psychosocial correlates of self-reported coping among Japanese Americans during World War II. *American Journal of Orthopsychiatry, 77,* 221–230.

Nance, T. A., & Foeman, A. K. (1998). On being biracial in the United States. In J. M. Martin, T. K. Nakayama, & L. A. Flores (Eds.), *Readings in cultural contexts* (pp. 53–62). Mountain View, CA: Mayfield.

National Center for Education Statistics (2004). *Digest of Education Statistics, 2004.* (Table 42). Washington, DC: U.S. Department of Education. Retrieved June 12, 2007, from http://nces.ed.gov/programs/digest/d04/tables/dt04_042.asp

National Center for Education Statistics (2005a). *Integrated Postsecondary Education Data System (IPEDS).* Washington, DC: U.S. Department of Education.

National Center for Education Statistics. (2005b). *Postsecondary Institutions in the United States: Fall 2003 and Degrees and Other Awards Conferred: 2002–03*

(NCES 2005–154). Washington, DC: U.S. Department of Education.

National Center for Education Statistics. (2006). *Digest of Education Statistics, 2005* (NCES 2006–030). Washington, DC: U.S. Department of Education.

National Coalition on Health Care (NCHC) (2006). *Health insurance coverage.* National Coalition on Health Care. Retrieved April 6, 2007, from http://www.nchc.org/facts/coverage.shtml

National Immigration Forum (n.d.) *Immigration reform.* Washington DC: National Immigration Forum. http://www.immigrationforum.org/DesktopDefault.aspx?tabid=808

National Institute of Mental Health (2008). *The numbers count: Mental disorders in America.* Washington DC: Author. Retrieved March 16, 2008, from http://www.nimh.nih.gov/health/publications/the-numbers-count-mental-disorders-in-america.shtml#Intro

Navarrette, R. (2006, June 22). Racism lurks beneath surface of immigration debate. *Albuquerque Journal,* A12.

Nemeth, C. J. (1992). Minority dissent as a stimulant to group performance. In S. Worchel, W. Wood, & J. A. Simpson (Eds.), *Group process and productivity* (pp. 95–111). Newbury Park, CA: Sage.

Neuliep, J. W. (1997). A cross-cultural comparison of teacher immediacy in American and Japanese college classrooms. *Communication Research, 24,* 431–451.

Ngom, F. (2004). Ethnic identity and linguistic hybridization in Senegal. *International Journal of Social Language, 170,* 95–111.

Novins, D. K., Duclos, C. W., Martin, C., Jewett, C. S., & Manson, S. M. (1999). Utilization of alcohol, drug, and mental health treatment services among American Indian adolescent detainees. *Journal of the American Academy of Child and Adolescent Psychiatry, 38,* 1102–1108.

Number of Japanese living abroad (1986–2004). (n.d.) Retrieved November 6, 2005, from http://web-japan.org/stat/stats/21MIG31.html

Numbers USA (n.d.). *Public opinion.* Arlington, VA: Numbers USA. Retrieved June 29, 2007, from http://www.numbersusa.com/interests/publicop.html

O'Kane, P., & Hargie, O. (2004). Technology travels: Can national culture impact upon attitudes toward communication technology? *Journal of Intercultural Communication Research, 33,* 49–62.

OASDI (2004). Projections of future financial status. *2004 OASDI Trustees Report.* Retrieved October 25, 2007, from http://www.ssa.gov/OACT/TR/TR04/II_project.html

Obama, B. (2004). *Dreams from my father: A story of race and inheritance.* New York: Three Rivers Press.

Oberg, K. (1960). Culture shock: Adjustment to new cultural environments. *Practical Anthropology, 7,* 177–182.

Oetzel, J. G. (2001). Self-construals, communication processes, and group outcomes in homogeneous and heterogeneous groups. *Small Group Research, 32,* 19–54.

Oetzel, J. G. (2005). Intercultural work group communication theory. In W. B. Gudykunst (Ed.), *Theorizing about intercultural communication* (pp. 351–371). Thousand Oaks, CA: Sage.

Oetzel, J. G., & Bolton-Oetzel, K. D. (1997). Exploring the relationship between self-construal and dimensions of group effectiveness. *Management Communication Quarterly, 10,* 289–315.

Oetzel, J. G., & Duran, B. (2004). Intimate partner violence in American Indian and/or Alaska Native communities: A social ecological framework of determinants and interventions. *The American Indian and Alaska Native Mental Health Research: A Journal of the National Center, 11, No. 3,* 49–68.

Oetzel, J. G., & Ting-Toomey, S. (Eds.) (2006). *The Sage handbook of conflict communication.* Thousand Oaks, CA: Sage.

Oetzel, J. G., Arcos, B., Mabizela, P., Weinman, M., & Zhang, Q. (2006). Historical, political, and spiritual factors for conflict: Understand conflict perspectives and communication in the Muslim world, China, Colombia, and South Africa. In J.G. Oetzel & S. Ting-Toomey (Eds.) *The Sage handbook of conflict communication* (pp. 549–574). Thousand Oaks, CA: Sage.

Oetzel, J. G., Burtis, T. E., Chew-Sanchez, M. I., & Perez, F. G. (2001). Investigating the role of communication in culturally diverse work groups: A review and synthesis. In W. B. Gudykunst (Ed.), *Communication Yearbook 25* (pp. 237–269). Mahwah, NJ: Lawrence Erlbaum.

Oetzel, J. G., Myers, K. K., Meares, M. M., & Lara, E. (2003). Interpersonal conflict in organizations: Explaining conflict styles via face-negotiation theory. *Communication Research Reports, 20,* 106–115.

Oetzel, J. G., Ting-Toomey, S., Masumoto, T., Yokochi, Y., Pan, X., Takai, J., & Wilcox, R. (2001). Face and face-work in conflict: A cross-cultural comparison of China, Germany, Japan, and the United States. *Communication Monographs, 68,* 235–258.

Oetzel, J. G., Torres, A. B., & Sanchez, C. (2004, November). *A multilevel analysis of process and performance in culturally diverse work groups.* Paper presented at the annual meeting of the National Communication Association, Chicago, IL.

Oetzel, J., & Ting-Toomey, S. (2003). Face concerns in interpersonal conflict: A cross-cultural empirical test of the face negotiation theory. *Communication Research, 30,* 599–624.

Oetzel, J., Duran, B., Lucero, J., Jiang, Y., Novins, D., Beals, J., Manson, S., & the AI-SUPERPFP team (2006). Rural Native Americans' perspectives of obstacles in the mental health treatment process in three treatment sectors. *Psychological Services, 3,* 117–128.

Office of Minority Health (n.d.). National standards on Culturally and Linguistically Appropriate Services (CLAS). U.S. Department of Health and Human Service. Retrieved April 10, 2007, from http://www.omhrc.gov/templates/browse. aspx?lvl=2&lvlID=15

Ogunyemi, O. (2007). The Black popular press. *Journalism Studies, 8,* 13–17.

Ohbuchi, K., Fukushima, O., & Tedeschi, J. T. (1999). Cultural values in conflict management: Goal orientation, goal attainment, and tactical decision. *Journal of Cross-Cultural Psychology, 30,* 51–71.

Oliver, M. L., Johnson, J. H., & Grant, D. M. (1993). Race, urban inequality, and the Los Angeles rebellion. In C. Calhoun & G. Ritzer (Eds.), *Introduction to Social Problems* (pp. 727–752). New York: McGraw-Hill.

`Ong, W. (1982). *Orality and literacy: The technologizing of the word.* New York: Methuen.

Orbe, M. (1998). An outsider within perspective to organizational communication: Explicating the communicative practices of co-cultural group members. *Management Communication Quarterly, 12,* 230–279.

Orbe, M. P., & Harris, T. M. (2001). *Interracial communication: Theory into practice.* Belmont, CA: Wadsworth.

Orbe, M., & Spellers, R. E. (2005). From the margins to the center: Utilizing co-cultural theory in diverse contexts. In W. B. Gudykunst (Ed.), *Theorizing about intercultural communication* (pp. 173–191). Thousand Oaks, CA: Sage.

Organisation for Economic Co-operation and Development (OECD) (2006). *OECD Health Data 2006.* OECD. Retrieved April 6, 2007, from http://www.oecd.org/health/healthdata

Osman, M. (2007, December 1). Death demanded for teacher. *Albuquerque Journal,* A1.

Ota, H., Giles, H., & Somera, L. P. (2007). Beliefs about intra- and intergenerational communication in Japan, the Philippines, and the United States: Implication for older adults' subjective well-being. *Communication Studies, 58,* 173–188.

Pabst, G. (2006, June 25). Building puentes. *Albuquerque Journal,* G1.

Padmanabhan, P. (2007). Technical communication outsourcing: The twelve driver framework. *IEEE Transactions on Professional Communication, 50,* 109–120.

Paris Riots in Perspective (2005, November 4). *ABC News.* Retrieved August 1, 2007, from http://abcnews.go.com/International/story?id=1280843

Park, C. C. (2001). Learning style preferences of Armenian, African, Hispanic, Hmong, Korean, Mexican, and Anglo students in American secondary schools. *Learning Environments Research, 4,* 175–191.

Parker E., Lichtenstein, R. L., Schulz A. J., Israel, B. A., Schork, M. A., Steinman, K. J., & James, S. A. (2001). Disentangling measures of individual perceptions of community social dynamics: Results of a community survey. *Health Education and Behavior, 28,* 462–486.

Pedersen, P. (1997). Do the right thing: A question of ethics. In K. Cushner & R. Brislin (Eds.), *Improving intercultural interactions: Modules for cross-cultural training programs* (Vol. 2, pp. 149–164). Thousand Oaks, CA: Sage.

Pescosolido, B., & Boyer, C. (1999). How do people come to use mental health services? Current knowledge and changing perspectives. In A. Horwitz & T. Sheid (Eds.), *A Handbook for the Study of Mental Health: Social Context, Theories and Systems* (pp. 392–411). Cambridge: Cambridge University Press.

Perreault, S., & Bourhis, R. (1999). Ethnocentrism, social identification, and discrimination. *Personality and Social Psychology Bulletin, 25,* 92–103.

Pettigrew, T. (1979). The ultimate attribution error. *Personality and Social Psychology Bulletin, 5,* 461–476.

Philipsen, G. (1987). The prospect for cultural communication. In D. L. Kincaid (Ed.), *Communication theory: Eastern and western perspectives* (pp. 245–254). San Diego, CA: Academic Press.

Philipsen, G. (1992). *Speaking culturally: Explorations in social communication.* Albany, NY: SUNY Press.

Philipsen, G., Coutu, L. M., & Covarrubias, P. (2005). Speech codes theory: Restatement, revisions, and response to criticism. In W. Gudykunst (Ed.), *Theorizing about intercultural communication* (pp. 55–68). Thousand Oaks, CA: Sage.

Phinney, J. (1991). Ethnic identity and self-esteem: A review and integration. *Hispanic Journal of Behavioral Sciences, 13,* 193–208.

Phinney, J. S. (1993). A three-stage model of ethnic identity development in adolescence. In M. E. Bernal & G. Knight (Eds.), *Ethnic identity* (pp. 61–79). Albany, NY: State University of New York Press.

Portes, A., Fernández-Kelly, P., & Haller, W. (2005). Segmented assimilation on the group: The new generation in early adulthood. *Ethnic and Racial Studies, 28,* 1000-1040.

Postman, N. (2004). The information age: A blessing or a curse? *Harvard International Journal of Press/Politics, 9(2),* 3–10.

Postmes, T. & Lea, M. (2000). Social processes and group decision making: Anonymity in group decision support systems. *Ergonomics, 43,* 1252–1274.

Putnam, R. (2000). *Bowling alone: The collapse and revival of American community.* New York: Simon and Schuster.

Putnam, R. D. (1995). Bowling alone: American's declining social capital. *Journal of Democracy, 6,* 65–78.

Ragusa, A. T. (2005). Social change and the corporate construction of gay markets in the *New York Times'* advertising business news. *Media, Culture & Society, 27,* 653–676.

Rahim, M. A. (2001). *Managing conflict in organizations* (3rd ed.). Westport, CT: Quorum Books.

Ramburuth, P., & McCormick, J. (2001). Learning diversity in higher education: A comparative study of Asian international and Australian students. *Higher Education, 42,* 333–350.

Rao, N., Singhal, A., Ren, L., & Zhang, J. (2001). Is the Chinese self-construal in transition? *Asian Journal of Communication, 11,* 68–95.

Reichert, T., LaTour, M. S., Lambiase, J. I., & Adkins, M. (2007). A test of media literacy effects and sexual objectification in advertising. *Journal of Current Issues & Research in Advertising, 29,* 81–92.

Reiter, M. D., Krause, J. M., & Stirlen, A. (2005). Intercouple dating on a college campus. *College Student Journal, 39,* 449–456.

Religious Tolerance.org (2006). Single U.S. public opinion polls: Same-sex marriages and civil unions. *Religious Tolerance.org.* Retrieved December 7, 2007, from http://www. religioustolerance.org/hom_marp.htm

Resnicow, K., Braithwaite, R. L., Dilorio, C., & Glanz, K. (2002). Applying theory to culturally diverse and unique populations. In K. Glanz, B. K., Rimer, & F. M. Lewis (Eds.), *Health behavior and health education: Theory, research, and practice* (3rd ed., pp. 485–509). San Francisco: Jossey-Bass.

Richardson, M., & Shiu-Thornton, S. (2002). Mental health services. In S. J. Williams & P. R. Torrens (Eds.). Introduction to health services (6th ed., pp. 280–307). Albany, NY: Delmar.

Rivenburgh, N. K. (2000). Social identity theory and news portrayals of citizens involved in international affairs. *Media Psychology, 2,* 303–329.

Roach, K. D., & Byrne, P. R. (2001). A cross-cultural comparison of instructor communication in American and German classrooms. *Communication Education, 50,* 1–14.

Roach, K. D., Cornett-DeVito, M. M., & DeVito, R. (2005). A cross-cultural comparison of instructor communication in American and French classrooms. *Communication Quarterly, 53,* 87–107.

Robberson, T. (2006, May 8). Immigration is hot button issue in Europe. *Albuquerque Journal,* C4.

Robert, S. A., & House, J. S. (2000). Socioeconomic inequalities in health: Integrating individual-, community-, and societal-level theory and research. In G. L. Albrecht, R. Fitzpatrick, & S. C. Scrimshaw (Eds.). *The handbook of social studies in health and medicine* (pp. 115–135). Thousand Oaks, CA: Sage.

Roberts, K. G. (2003). Emotivism and pseudocultural identities. *Howard Journal of Communications, 14,* 195–208.

Roberts, K. G. (2007). *Alterity and narrative: Stories and the negotiation of western identities.* Albany, NY: SUNY Press.

Robinson, E. (2006, August 2). Anti-Semitism deserves no slack. *Albuquerque Journal,* A7.

Rogers, E. M. (1999). Georg Simmel's concept of the stranger and intercultural communication research. *Communication Theory, 9,* 58–74.

Rogers, E. M., & Hart, W. B. (2002). The histories of intercultural, international, and development communication. In W. B. Gudykunst & B. Mody (Eds.), *Handbook of international and intercultural communication* (2nd ed., pp. 1–17). Thousand Oaks, CA: Sage.

Rogers, E. M., & Steinfatt, T. M. (1999). *Intercultural communication.* Prospect Heights, IL: Waveland Press.

Rosenthal, H. E. S., Crisp, R. J., & Suen, M-W. (2007). Improving performance expectancies in stereotypic domains: Task relevance and the reduction of stereotype threat. *European Journal of Social Psychology, 37,* 586–597.

Ross, L. D. (1977). The intuitive psychologist and his shortcomings: Distortions in the attribution process. In L. Berkowitz (Ed.), *Advances in experimental psychology* (Vol. 10). New York: Academic Press.

Rost, K., Smith, G. R., & Taylor, J. L. (1993). Rural-urban differences in stigma and the use of care for depressive disorders. *Journal of Rural Health, 9,* 57–62.

Rousseau, D. M., & House, R. J. (1994). Meso organizational behavior: Avoiding three fundamental biases. In C. L. Cooper & D. M. Rousseau (Eds) *Trends in organizational behavior* (Vol. 1, pp. 13–30). New York: John Wiley & Sons.

Rubin, J. Z., & Levinger, G. (1995). Levels of analysis: In search of generalizable knowledge. In B. Bunker, J. Rubin, & Associates (Eds.), *Conflict, cooperation, and justice* (pp. 13–38). San Francisco: Jossey-Bass.

Salacuse, J. W. (1993). Implications for practitioners. In G. Faure & J. Rubin (Eds.), *Culture and negotiation* (pp. 199–208). Newbury Park, CA: Sage.

Sampson R., Raudenbush, S. W., & Earls, F. (1997). Neighborhoods and violent crime: A multilevel study of collective efficacy. *Science, 277,* 918–924.

Sanchez Gibau, G. (2005). Contested identities: Narratives of race and ethnicity in the Cape Verdean diaspora. *Identities, 12,* 405–438.

Sanchez, M. I. C., Cramer, J. M., & Prieto, L. (2003). *Sábado Gigante* (Giant Saturday) and the cultural homogenization of Spanish-Speaking people. In L. Artz & Y. R. Kamalipour (Eds.), *The globalization of corporate media hegemony* (pp. 131–150). Albany, NY: State University of New York Press.

Santayana, G. (n.d.). *History quotes.* Retrieved July 18, 2007, from http://www.wisdomquotes. com/cat_history.html

Sayahi, L. (2005). Language and identity among speakers of Spanish in northern Morocco: Between ethnolinguistic vitality and acculturation. *Journal of Sociolinguistics, 9,* 95–107.

Schubert, F. (2003). *Voices of the buffalo soldier: Records, reports, and recollections of military life and service in the West.* Albuquerque, NM: University of New Mexico Press.

Shabbas, A. (1998). *The Arab world studies notebook.* Washington DC: The Arab World and Islamic Resources (AWAIR), and The Middle East Policy Council.

Shah, D. V., McLeod, J. M., & Yoon, S-H. (2001). Communication context, and community: An exploration of print, broadcast, and Internet influences. *Communication Research, 28,* 464–506.

Sharp, J. W. (n.d.) Desert trails: The Long Walk trail of the Navajos. *Desert USA.* Retrieved October 23, 2007, from http://www.desertusa.com/mag03/trails/trails09.html

Shaw, D. L., & McCombs, M. E. (1977). *The emergence of American political issues.* St. Paul, MN: West.

Shimoni, B., & Bergmann, H. (2006). Managing in a changing world: From multiculturalism to hybridization: The production of hybrid management cultures in Israel, Thailand, and Mexico. *Academy of Management Perspectives, August,* 76–89.

Shoemaker, P. J. (1996). Media gatekeeping. In M. B. Salwen & D. W. Stacks (Eds.), *An integrated approach to communication theory and research* (pp. 79–91). Mahwah, NJ: Erlbaum.

Shugart, H. A. (2003). Performing ambiguity: The passing of Ellen DeGeneres. *Text & Performance Quarterly, 23,* 30–54.

Shugart, H. A. (2003). Reinventing privilege: The new (gay) man in contemporary popular media. *Critical Studies in Media Communication, 20,* 67–91.

Simpson, J. S., Causey, A., & Williams, L. (2007). "I would want you to understand it": Students' perspectives on addressing race in the classroom. *Journal of Intercultural Communication Research, 36,* 33–50.

Singhal, A., & Rogers, E. M. (1999). *Entertainment education: A communication strategy for social change.* Mahwah, NJ: Lawrence Erlbaum.

Smith, A. (2007). Soul Wound: The legacy of Native American schools. *Amnesty Magazine.* Retrieved October 23, 2007, from http://www.amnestyusa.org/amnestynow/ soul-wound.html

Smith, E. (1994). Social identity and social emotions. In D. Mackie & D. Hamilton (Eds.), *Affect, cognition, and stereotyping.* New York: Academic Press.

Smith, J. L. (2006). The interplay among stereotypes, performance-avoidance goals, and women's math performance expectations. *Sex Roles, 54,* 287–296.

Smith, P. B., Dugan, S., Peterson, M. F., & Leung, K. (1998). Individualism, collectivism and the handling of disagreement: A 23 country study. *International Journal of Intercultural Relations, 22,* 351–367.

Sowell, T. (2005). *Affirmative action around the world: An empirical study.* New Haven, CT: Yale University Press.

Spellers, R. E. (1998). Happy to be nappy! Embracing an Afro-centric aesthetic for beauty. In J. M. Martin, T. K. Nakayama, & L. A. Flores (Eds.), *Readings in cultural contexts* (pp. 70–78). Mountain View, CA: Mayfield.

Stanford Encyclopedia of Philosophy (2005). *Affirmative action.* Palo Alto, CA: Stanford University. Retrieved March 20, 2007, from http://plato.stanford.edu/entries/ affirmative-action/

Steinberg, A. (1989). Holocaust survivors and their children: A review of the clinical literature. In P. Marcus & A. Rosenberg (Eds.), *Healing their wounds: Psychotherapy with Holocaust survivors and their families* (pp. 23–48). New York: Praeger.

Stephan, W. G., & Stephan, C. W. (1996). Predicting prejudice. *International Journal of Intercultural Relations, 20,* 409–426.

Stephan, W., & Stephan, C. (2001). *Improving intergroup relations.* Thousand Oaks, Sage.

Stephens, D. L. (1999). Battered women's views of their children. *Journal of Interpersonal Violence, 14,* 731–746.

Stohl, C. (2001). Globalizing organizational communication. In. F. M. Jablin & L. L. Putnam (Eds.), *The new handbook of organizational communication: Advances in theory, research, and methods* (pp. 323–375). Thousand Oaks, CA: Sage.

Stokols, D. (1996). Translating social ecological theory into guidelines for community health promotion. *American Journal of Health Promotion, 10,* 282–298.

Straus, S. G., & McGrath, J. E. (1994). Does the medium matter? The interaction of task type and technology on group performance and member reactions. *Journal of Applied Psychology, 79,* 87–97.

Suárez-Orozco, C., & Suárez-Orozco, M. M. (2001). *Children of immigration.* Boston, MA: Harvard University Press.

Tajfel, H. & Turner, J. C. (1986). The social identity theory of intergroup behavior. In S. Worchel & W. G. Austin (Eds.), *Psychology of intergroup relations* (2nd ed., pp. 7–24). Chicago: Nelson-Hall.

Tajfel, H. (1978). The achievement of group differentiation. In H. Tajfel (Ed.), *Differentiation between social groups: Studies in the social psychology of intergroup relations* (pp. 77–98). New York: Academic Press.

Tannen, D. (1994). *Gender and discourse.* New York: Oxford University Press.

Taylor, S. E., & Fiske, S. T. (1978). Salience, attention, and attribution. In L. Berkowitz (Ed.), *Advances in experimental psychology* (Vol. 11). New York: Academic Press.

Teng, L. Y-W. (2007). Collaborating and communicating online: A cross bordered intercultural project between Taiwan and the U.S. *Journal of Intercultural Communication, 13,* 8–15.

Ter Wal, J., d'Haenens, L., & Koeman, J. (2005). (Re)presentation of ethnicity in EU and Dutch domestic news: A quantitative analysis. *Media, Culture & Society, 27,* 937–950.

The Nation (2006). Life's hard and then you become a refugee. *The Nation,* September 10. Retrieved September 18, 2007, from South African Migration Project at http://www.queensu.ca/samp/migrationnews/article.php?Mig_News_ID=3805&Mig_News_Issue=21&Mig_News_Cat=8

Themba-Nixon, M. (2006). Co-opting consumers of color. *The Nation.* Retrieved July 5, 2007, from http://www.thenation.com/doc/20060703/thembanixon

Thompson, J., & Collier, M. J. (2006). Toward contingent understandings of intersecting identifications among selected U.S. interracial couples: Integrating interpretive and critical views. *Communication Quarterly, 54,* 487–506.

Thoreau, E. (2006). Ouch!: An examination of the self-representation of disabled people on the internet. *Journal of Computer-Mediated Communication, 11,* 442–468.

Ting-Toomey, S. (1994). Managing intercultural conflicts effectively. In L. Samovar, & Porter R. (Eds.), *Intercultural communication: A reader* (7th ed., pp. 360–372). Belmont, CA: Wadsworth.

Ting-Toomey, S. (1999). *Communicating across cultures.* New York: Guilford Press.

Ting-Toomey, S. (2005). Identity negotiation theory: Crossing cultural boundaries. In W. B. Gudykunst (Ed.), *Theorizing about intercultural communication* (pp. 211–234). Thousand Oaks, CA: Sage.

Ting-Toomey, S., & Kurogi, A. (1998). Facework competence in intercultural conflict: An updated face-negotiation theory. *International Journal of Intercultural Relations, 22,* 187–225.

Ting-Toomey, S., & Oetzel, J. (2001). *Managing intercultural conflict effectively.* Thousand Oaks, CA: Sage.

Ting-Toomey, S., & Takai, J. (2006). Explaining intercultural conflict: Promising approaches and future directions. In J. G. Oetzel & S. Ting-Toomey (Eds.), *The Sage handbook of conflict communication* (pp. 691–723). Thousand Oaks, CA: Sage.

Ting-Toomey, S., Yee-Jung, K. K., Shapiro, R. B., Garcia, W., Wright, T. J., & Oetzel, J. G. (2000). Ethnic/cultural identity salience and conflict styles in four U.S. ethnic groups. *International Journal of Intercultural Relations, 24,* 47–81.

Tomlinson, J. (1999). *Globalization and culture.* Cambridge: Polity Press.

Training and Development (1999, November). Training & development annual trend reports: Trends. *Training & Development, 53,* no. 1, pp. 22–43.

Treaty of Guadalupe Hidalgo (1848). Retrieved on July 17, 2007, from http://www.azteca.net/ aztec/guadhida.html

Triandis, H. C. (1972). *The analysis of subjective culture.* New York: John Wiley & Sons.

Triandis, H. C. (1995). *Individualism and collectivism.* Boulder, CO: Westview Press.

Trubisky, P., Ting-Toomey, S., & Lin, S. L. (1991). The influence of individualism-collectivism and self-monitoring on conflict styles. *International Journal of Intercultural Relations, 15,* 65–84.

Tsosie, L. (2006, June 9). English-only overlooks Indians. *Albuquerque Journal,* A13.

Turner, J. C. (1975). Social comparison and social identity: Some prospects for intergroup behaviour. *European Journal of Social Psychology, 5,* 5–34.

Tutu, D. (1999). *No future without forgiveness.* New York: Doubleday.

U.S. Bureau of Labor (2006). Current population survey. Washington: Author. Available: http://www.bls.gov/cps/cpsaat11.pdf

U.S. Census (2005a). *Global Population Profile: 2002.* Washington, DC: U.S. Census Bureau.

U.S. Census (2005b). *American Indian/Alaska Native Tables from the Statistical Abstracts of the United States 2004–2005.* Washington: Author. Available: http://www.census.gov/statab/www/sa04aian.pdf

U.S. Census (2006a). *American Community Survey.* Retrieved March 6, 2008, http://factfinder.census.gov/servlet/ACSSAFFFacts?_submenuId=factsheet_1&_sse=on

U.S. Census (2006b). *Annual estimates of the population by sex, race and Hispanic or Latino origin for the United States.* Retrieved April 4, 2006, from http://www.census.gov/popest/national/asrh/NC-EST2004/NC-EST2004–03.xls

U.S. Census (2008). *Population profile of the U.S.* Retrieved March 6, 2008, from http://www.census.gov/population/www/pop-profile/natproj.html

U.S. Commission on Civil Rights (UCCR) (2004). *Broken Promises: Evaluating the Native American Health Care System.* Washington DC: US Commission on Civil Rights: Office of the General Counsel.

U.S. Equal Employment Opportunity Commission (2007). Federal equal employment opportunity laws. Washington, DC: Author. Retrieved March 20, 2007, from http://www.eeoc.gov/abouteeo/overview_laws.html

(UNEP) United Nations Environment Programme (2007). *Economic impacts of tourism.* Retrieved January 18, 2007, from http://www.uneptie.org/pc/tourism/sust-tourism/economic.htm

USHHS (2007). *Office of human research protections*. U.S. Dept. of Health and Human Services. Retrieved June 21, 2007, from http://www.hhs.gov/ohrp/humansubjects/guidance/45cfr46.htm

van Dijk, T. A. (1993). *Elite discourse and racism*. Newbury Park, CA: Sage.

Van Ryn, M., & Fu, S. (2003). Paved with good intentions: Do public health and human service providers contribute to racial/ethnic disparites in health? *American Journal of Public Health, 93*, 248–253.

Varshney, A. (2003). *Ethnic conflict and civic life: Hindus and Muslims in India* (2nd ed.). New Haven, CT: Yale University Press.

Wakimoto, R. (2006). Mortality salience effects on modesty and relative self-effacement. *Asian Journal of Social Psychology, 9*, 176–183.

Walters, K. L. (1999). Urban American Indian identity attitudes and acculturation styles. *Journal of Human Behavior in the Social Environment, 2*, 163–178.

Ward, C., & Kennedy, A. (1996). Crossing cultures: The relationship between psychological and sociocultural dimensions for cross-cultural adjustment. In J. Pandey, D. Shinha and D. P. S. Bhawuk (Eds.), *Asian contributions to cross-cultural psychology* (pp. 289–306). New Delhi: Sage.

Ward, C., Bochner, S., & Furnham, A. (2001). *The psychology of culture shock*. Hove, England: Routledge.

Ward, C., Okura, Y., Kennedy, A., & Kojima, T. (1998). The U-curve on trial: A longitudinal study of psychological and sociocultural adjustment during cross-cultural transition. *International Journal of Intercultural Relations, 22*, 227–291.

Wareham, J., Mahnke, V., Peters, S., & Bjorn-Andersen, N. (2007). Communication metaphors in use: Technical communication and offshore systems development. *IEEE Transactions on Professional Communication, 50*, 93–108.

Warfield, W. (2006). Managing racial/ethnic conflict for community building. In J. G. Oetzel & S. Ting-Toomey (Eds.), *The Sage handbook of conflict communication* (pp. 479–500). Thousand Oaks, CA: Sage.

Waters, M. (1990). *Ethnic options: Choosing identities in America*. Berkeley, CA: University of California Press.

Watson, W. E., Kumar, K., & Michaelsen, L. K. (1993). Cultural diversity's impact on interaction process and performance: Comparing homogeneous and diverse task groups. *Academy of Management Journal, 36*, 590–602.

Williams, D. R., & Williams-Morris, R. (2000). Racism and mental health: The African American experience. *Ethnicity & Health, 5*, 243–268.

Watzlawick, P., Weakland, J. H., and Fisch, R. (1974). *Change: Principles of problem formation and problem resolution*. New York: Norton.Wenger, E., McDermott, R., &

Snyder, W. (2002) *Cultivating communities of practice: A guide to managing knowledge*. Boston, MA: Harvard Business School Press.

Whitbeck, L. B., Adams, G. W., Hoyt, D. R., & Chen, X. (2004). Conceptualizing and measuring historical trauma among American Indian people. *American Journal of Community Psychology, 33*, 119–129.

Wikipedia (2007). Universal health coverage. St. Petersburg, FL: Wikimedia Foundation. Retrieved April 10, 2007, from http://en.wikipedia.org/wiki/Image:Health.png.

Wikipedia (n.d.). *Long Walk of the Navajos*. St. Petersburg, FL: Wikimedia Foundation. Retrieved July 18, 2007, from http://en.wikipedia.org/wiki/Long_Walk_of_the_Navajo

Williams, D. R. (2001). Race and health: Trends and policy implications. In J. A. Aurebach & B. K. Krimgold (Eds.) Income, socioeconomic status, and health: Exploring the relationships (pp. 67–85). Washington, DC: National Policy Association.

Williams, D. R., & Williams-Morris, R. (2000). Racism and mental health: The African American experience. *Ethnicity & Health, 5*, 243–268.

Williams, S. J., & Torrens, P. R. (2002). *Introduction to health services* (6th ed). Stamford, CT: Thomson Delmar Publishing.

Wilmot, W., & Hocker, J. (2007). *Interpersonal conflict* (7th ed.). Boston: McGraw-Hill.

Wilson, C. C., & Gutierrez, F. (1995). *Race, multiculturalism, and the media: From mass to class communication* (2nd ed.). Thousand Oaks, CA: Sage.

Wilson, J. H. (2006). Predicting student attitudes and grades from perceptions of instructors' attitudes. *Teaching of Psychology, 33*, 91–95.

Witt, P. L., Wheeless, L. R., & Allen, M. (2006). The relationship between teacher immediacy and student learning: A meta-analysis. In B. M. Gayle, R. W. Preiss, N. Burrell, & M. Allen (Eds.), *Classroom communication and instructional processes: Advances through meta-analysis* (pp. 149–168). Mahwah, NJ: Lawrence Erlbaum & Associates.

Witte, K., & Morrison, K. (1995). Intercultural and cross-cultural health communication: Understanding people and motivating healthy behaviors. In R. L. Wiseman (Ed.), *Intercultural communication theory* (pp. 216–246). Thousand Oaks, CA: Sage.

Wood, J. (1995). The part is not the whole: Weaving diversity into the study of relationships. *Journal of Social and Personal Relationships, 12*, 563–567.

World Bank (2001). Life expectancy. The World Bank Group. Retrieved April 5, 2007, from http://www.worldbank.org/depweb/english/modules/social/life/datanot.html

World Health Organization (WHO) (1978). Declaration of Alma-Ata. International Conference on Primary Health